LORD AND PEASANT IN RUSSIA

FROM THE NINTH

TO THE NINETEENTH CENTURY

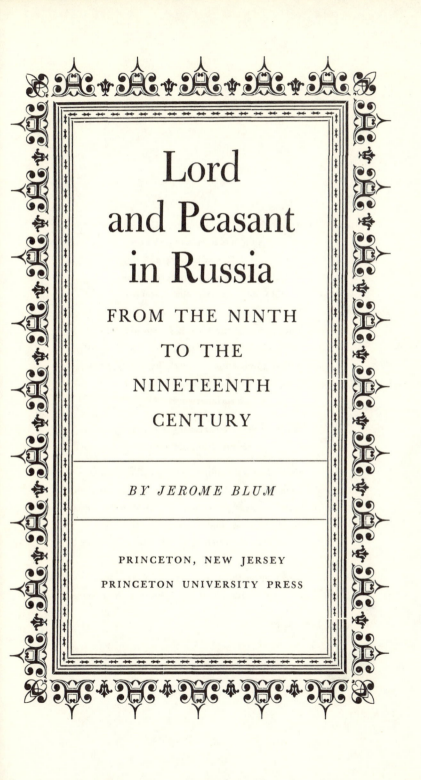

Lord and Peasant in Russia

FROM THE NINTH TO THE NINETEENTH CENTURY

BY JEROME BLUM

PRINCETON, NEW JERSEY
PRINCETON UNIVERSITY PRESS

Publication of the book has been aided by
the Ford Foundation program
to support publication, through university presses,
of works in the humanities and
social sciences.

❖

First PRINCETON PAPERBACK Edition, 1971

Second Printing, 1972

to Sis

FOREWORD

I OWE MANY LASTING DEBTS of gratitude for the counsel and support I have received at every stage in the writing of this book. Professors Hans Rosenberg of the University of California, Berkeley, Norman F. Cantor of Columbia, Cyril E. Black, Robert R. Palmer, and Joseph R. Strayer of Princeton, Evsey D. Domar of the Massachusetts Institute of Technology, and Albert Parry of Colgate University, were good enough to read parts or all of the manuscript. I have benefited much from their judgments and their suggestions. The late Dr. Vladimir Gsovski, Chief of the European Law Division of the Library of Congress, was always ready to place his encyclopedic legal knowledge at my disposal. Dr. Vladas Stanka of the Arctic Institute of America gave generous help in the analysis of old sources. Grants from the John Simon Guggenheim Memorial Foundation and from the Council of the Humanities of Princeton University freed me for three terms from teaching obligations, subsidies from the Princeton University Research Fund and the American Philosophical Society allowed me to work on the book during the summers, and a grant from the American Council of Learned Studies aided in its publication. Much of the research was done at the Library of Congress, where the unfailing kindness and cooperation extended me by the Library's staff made my task far easier than it might have been. I am particularly indebted to General Willard Webb and Mr. Gordon W. Patterson of the Stack and Reader Division, and to Dr. Sergius Yakobson, Dr. Paul L. Horecky, and Mr. John T. Dorosh of the Slavic and East European Division, for their friendship and their patience. I am indebted, also, to Mr. John B. Putnam of the Princeton University Press for his valued editorial assistance, and to Mr. Isser Woloch for making the index. Finally, special thanks are due to Thomas and Barbara Moriarty whose hospitality did so much to make my stays in Washington enjoyable.

A few words seem necessary about some of the technical features of the book. Short titles have been used in the footnotes;

full citations and place and date of publication are provided in the *List of Works Cited*. A glossary at the end of the book gives the meanings of the Russian terms and the American equivalents of the weights and measures that appear in the text. Most of these words are italicized, but certain ones that occur frequently and that have become familiar to readers of Russian history, such as mir, guberniia, obrok, barshchina, pomestye, pomeshchik, and a few others, are printed in roman type. Dates are all according to the Julian calendar, or the "old style," used in Russia until 1918.

JEROME BLUM

CONTENTS

[ix]

CONTENTS

THE LAST 150 YEARS
OF SERFDOM

MAPS

[x]

LORD AND PEASANT IN RUSSIA

FROM THE NINTH

TO THE NINETEENTH CENTURY

ABBREVIATIONS

AAE	Arkheograficheskaia Ekspeditsiia, *Akty sobrannye v bibliotekakh i arkhivakh Rossiiskoi Imperii.*
AI	Arkheograficheskaia Komissiia, *Akty istoricheskie.*
AIu	———, *Akty iuridicheskie.*
AIuB	———, *Akty otnosiashchiesia do iuridicheskago byta drevnei Rossii.*
ASEI	Akademiia Nauk, Institut Istorii, *Akty sotsial'no-ekonomicheskoi istorii severo-vostochnoi Rusi kontsa XIV-nachala XVI veka.*
DAI	Arkheograficheskaia komissiia, *Dopolneniia k aktam istoricheskim.*
DDG	*Dukhovnye i dogovornye gramoty velikikh i udel'nykh kniazei XIV-XVI vekov.*
MGI	Ministerstvo Gosudarstvennykh Imushchestv.
MKP	Akademiia Nauk, Institut Istorii, *Materialy po istorii krest'ianskoi promyshlennosti XVIII i pervoi poloviny XIX v.*
PSRL	*Polnoe sobranie russkikh letopisei.*
PSZ	*Polnoe sobranie zakonov Rossiiskoi Imperii.*
SGGD	*Sobranie gosudarstvennykh gramot i dogovorov.*
SIRO	*Sbornik Imperatorskago Russkago Istoricheskago Obshchestva.*
SZ	*Svod zakonov Rossiiskoi Imperii.*

INTRODUCTION

THE YEAR 1961 marks the hundredth anniversary of the emancipation of the Russian serfs. Of all the millions of Europeans who in centuries past had been held in bondage, they were almost last to be freed. Even then, the liberty they gained was not complete. They were not given full civil rights, they were still restricted in their ability to come and go as they pleased, and in most of the empire they did not become the individual owners of the land they tilled. Nor did the "peasant problem" vanish. On the contrary, in a different guise it became even more acute than it had been in the days of serfdom, and, indeed, still unsolved it remains to bedevil the rulers of the Russia of today. Nonetheless, the act of emancipation of 19 February 1861 is a crucial turning point in the history of the world's largest state, for in abolishing serfdom the tsar's decree not only ended the institution that had allowed one man to be the "baptized property" (to use Herzen's phrase) of another man: it also swept away the basis of the then existing social order, and thereby brought to a close an era of Russian history that had lasted for centuries.

The pages that follow trace the history of the lords and peasants, and of the relationships between them, from the time when large private landownership first established itself on Russian soil, to the abolition of serfdom a thousand years later. The reader will quickly discover, however, that this story, as it is related here, is not limited to agrarian matters alone. Much is said about political and economic affairs, too, for I have written the story of the lords and peasants against the background of Russian political and economic evolution.

The need for this method of presentation pressed itself upon me as my researches for this book proceeded. I came to this subject with no preconceived interpretations or hypotheses about Russian history. I soon learned that the problems in which I was interested could be comprehended only within the context of the political history of Russia, from Kievan times to the nineteenth century. The feuds of the Kievan rulers; the invasions and the princely rivalries of the Mongol era; the state-making ambitions of the Grand Dukes of Moscow; the savage resolution of the tsars of Muscovy to win absolute power for themselves; the conviction of the Romanov emperors that the private interests of their subjects must be subordinated to the imperial interests; each in its time was of critical importance in determining the roles of both lords and peasants, and the nature of the social and economic relationships between them. I have found it necessary, therefore, throughout the book to discuss these matters, sometimes at length, in order to provide the information needed for an understanding of what was happening out on the land.

It took me longer to realize that there was still another external factor that was also of great significance in the evolution of agrarian institutions. The economic aspects of these institutions and the interaction between agriculture and the other sectors of the economy made it essential to study the general economic development of Russia. As these investigations continued it became clear that Russian economic life (like that of other lands) had gone through long swings of growth and decline, and that these secular trends had been of major consequence in shaping the patterns of agrarian relationships. And so the long-term fluctuations in trade, manufacturing, market demand, prices, money values, and entrepreneurial activity, take their places alongside the history of political events as integral parts of the story.

The economic importance of agriculture throughout the centuries covered here, and the attention paid to general economic development, combine to make this book a study in the economic history of Russia from the ninth to the nineteenth century. But it is also meant to be a study in the history of human freedom. It attempts to explain how a few men were able to destroy the freedom of millions of their fellows, why this social injustice was allowed to endure for so long, and how men sought to lessen the injustice or to escape from it. Usually, books about freedom deal with politics, philosophies, and revolutions. They tell of the men of ideas who defined freedom in terms of concrete objectives, of the men of action who led in the struggle for these objectives, and of their triumphs and their defeats. These

works are, of course, important and instructive. But freedom
has an economic history, too, that is often overlooked, and that
is in some ways the most significant part of its history. I say
this not because I think that the modes of production always
and everywhere determine the course of events. This book is
not an exercise in the economic interpretation of history. But
to understand the system of values of a society it is necessary to
know its economic life. The following pages show that the history
of personal freedom in a society is intimately linked with the
arrangements that society makes in its efforts to satisfy its wants
from the resources at its command. F. C. Lane put it well when
he wrote:[1] "[T]he qualities expressed in economic activities
constitute the largest part of what life has been. Most men most
of the time have been occupied in making a living. The values
that existed for them, not merely as aspiration or as ideas to be
talked about, but in action and as qualities of personal character,
were those embodied in the daily activities by which they made
their living. If bullying and fawning, arrogant command and
servile obedience were the rule in economic life, that is the way
men were—that is what society was like. Other themes—religious
aspiration, artistic feeling, and creative intellectual vigor—reward endless historical investigation for their own sake, even
when they have no discernible connection with social organization, but historians interested in justice, freedom, or any other
qualities of social life have reason to give primary attention to the
human relations entered into during the processes of production
and distribution."

I have chosen to make a study of these relations in Russia
not only because of the importance of that country in the specu-
lations that go on in our time about the nature of freedom.
Inquiries into Russia's rural past reveal the inheritance of
modern Russia, and so cast light on the course that it is presently
following. I hope, in addition, that this book will contribute
ultimately to an understanding of the history of freedom in
the European world. The particulars of the Russian experience
differed, of course, from that of other European lands. But
studies similar to this one of these other societies should make

[1] In the *Journal of Economic History*, XVIII (1958), 417.

it possible to formulate generalizations about the history of freedom, in terms of aspirations, social patterns, and economic and political motives, that transcend national frontiers, and that are free from the methodological shortcomings that distort the Marxian synthesis.

I I

As I have just indicated, Russian history is viewed here as part of European, rather than of Oriental, history. There were many differences between Russian institutions and those of other lands of Europe, but as Marc Bloch once asked, "In what science has the presence of variations or varieties ever interfered with the recognition of a genus?" The structure of Russian rural society had the same fundamental features that characterized the agrarian societies of other European countries. Comparative study demonstrates the congruities between Russian and these other lands in such things as the nature of the legal and fiscal powers that lords had over their peasants, the forms of rural settlement, the agricultural techniques that were employed, and so on. The presence of these uniformities convinces me that Russia's agrarian institutions should be studied in a European frame of reference, and described with European terms, such as "serf" and "seignior" as synonyms for the dependent peasant and his lord. This, of course, is not to deny that non-European influences were felt in Russia, but their effect was only to modify what were fundamentally European institutions.

Most of these institutions need no detailed explanation. Such terms as the three field system, communal tillage, servile tenure, hamlet and village, seignioral jurisdiction, and the like, either are self-explanatory or can be quickly defined. But serfdom, the institution that occupies the central position in this book, defies easy explanation. The word "serf" or its equivalents were applied—on occasion in the same time and place—to a wide range of European peasants, from people whose condition could scarcely be distinguished from that of chattel slaves to men who were nearly free. The presence or absence of certain dues or fines that had to be paid the seignior has sometimes been proposed as a kind of litmus test of whether or not peasants were serfs, but these servile obligations were not infrequently demanded of men who are known to have been legally free. Often the serf is thought to have been a person who was bound to the soil, but this, too, is an inadequate and, for many times and places, even a mistaken concept. The deepest and most complete form of serfdom was precisely when the lord was able (as he often was) to move his peasants about as he wished, transferring them from one holding to another, converting them into landless field hands or into household servants, and even selling, giving, or gambling them away without land. On the other hand, there were periods in serfdom's history when the bondman had the right to leave his holding, after giving notice to his lord, whereupon he became a free man.

Nor is it any more accurate to define the serf as a person bound to the body of his lord, for this condition, too, was true only for certain times and places. In France, for example, the serf had once been attached to his lord by what has been described as an indissoluble, almost corporeal bond that had nothing to do with any land the serf might hold. Thus, if a free man took over a holding formerly occupied by a serf, he remained free. In short, there was a clear distinction between personal status and tenure. Then, beginning in the thirteenth century, the "blemish of serfdom" began to adhere to the land rather than to the man, so that a free peasant who took over a tenement recognized as servile was regarded as a serf so long as he remained on the holding. Now tenure determined status. In Russia the development took just the opposite course, at least so far as the serfs of the pomeshchiks (the seigniors holding on service tenure from the tsar) were concerned. In the sixteenth and seventeenth centuries these serfs were bound to their holdings (except under certain special circumstances), and not to the person of the pomeshchik. But this came to be disregarded by the pomeshchiks, who began to move their peasants about and even to sell them without land. In the eighteenth century the crown gave legal sanction to these practices so that these serfs of the pomeshchiks became bound to the person of their seigniors.

There was, however, one feature common to European serfdom wherever and whenever it existed: a peasant was recognized as unfree if he was bound to the will of his lord by ties that were degrading and socially incapacitating, and that were institutional rather than contractual. In practice, this meant that the lord had legal jurisdiction over his peasants to the complete, or nearly complete, exclusion of the state, so that to all intents and purposes the only rights the peasants had were those that the lord was willing to allow them. Concomitant circumstances of this condition were that the peasants were unable to come and go as they pleased without their lord's permission, and that the lord could demand whatever obligations he wanted. In actuality, it was a general, although far from universal, rule for these obligations to be fixed and even minutely defined by custom, but it was possible for the seignior to increase or decrease them, change their nature, or to command that they be performed in any order he wished. Yet the power of the lord over his serfs was not so great as to deprive them of their legal personality. Herein lay the difference between serf and slave. The serf, even when his status fell so low that he could be bought and sold without land, still had certain individual rights, albeit severely curtailed. The slave, no matter how well off he might be—and there were periods when at least some slaves seem to have enjoyed greater social and economic advantages than did serfs— was in the eyes of the law not a person but a chattel of his owner.

A sign of the waning of serfdom appeared when the central power began to intrude itself between lord and serf, chipping away at the lord's legal and administrative powers and establishing norms for the obligations he could demand of his peasants. Conversely, the withdrawal of the sovereign from interference in the lord-peasant relation doomed a free peasantry to serfdom.[2]

In our own day the word serfdom has become part of the vocabulary of polemicists who use it in describing societies of which they disapprove. In employing it in this fashion they subvert the historical meaning of the word. For though com-

[2] This discussion of the meaning of serfdom is from my article in the *American Historical Review*, LXII (1957), 807-809.

pulsion and subjugation have not disappeared from the world, the forms they take are very different from the forms of the institution that once bound millions of Europeans.

III

One further matter remains to be discussed before this history can begin: the physical setting in which it took place. As later pages will show, the topography, soil characteristics, and climate of the vast Russian land had much to do with the course of historical evolution there.

Nearly all of European Russia lies north of the 46th parallel.[3] In North America this line runs close to the border between the United States and Canada. Russia, then, is in both the cold and the moderate climatic zones. There are no neighboring great seas to temper the extremes of its weather, so that it has a continental climate—that is, sharp seasonal contrasts in temperatures. Winters are long and hard, and summers short, and in much of the country, hot. The growing season—the period free from killing frosts—is relatively short, even in the southern parts. In the Archangel district, in the far north, it averages 120 days a year, in the Moscow district 130 days, to the east in Kazan 146 days, in Kharkov in the Ukraine 151 days, and in Saratov, on the lower Volga, 161 days. In the United States the average growing season along our southern borders is more than 260 days, on the northern margin of the cotton belt, about 200 days, in the northern part of the corn belt, from 140 to 150 days, and in northern Maine and northern Minnesota, about 100 days.[4] The relative brevity of the frost-free season in Russia limits the choice and variety of crops that can be grown, and compels much work to be concentrated into a brief period.

The deficiency in moisture provides even greater handicaps to agriculture. The average annual precipitation ranges from 6 inches in the semi-arid dry steppe of the southeast, to 20-25 inches on the borders of Poland and the Baltic states. Again to use the United States for purposes of comparison, the line of

[3] This sketch is drawn from Berg, *Natural Regions, passim*; Timoshenko, *Agricultural Russia*, pp. 4-17; Volin, *A Survey*, pp. 1-9.
[4] U.S. Department of Agriculture, *Climate and Man*, p. 694.

20 inch rainfall here goes through the center of North and South Dakota and the western parts of Kansas and Oklahoma. In days gone by those parts of America were known as the Great American Desert, and, more recently, as the Dust Bowl. In the northern part of Russia, because of the low temperatures and consequent small amount of evaporation, the rainfall is usually enough for the crops that are raised there. In fact, that region, with its abundancy of marshes and lakes, suffers more often from an excess than from a deficiency of moisture. But in the southern and southeastern regions the light rainfall, high summer temperatures, and scorching dry winds hold down the moisture. To make matters worse, the amount of annual rainfall is irregular, and its seasonal distribution is often unfavorable. Dry spells not infrequently occur in May and June when the growing plants need water badly, and rains in July and August come too late to help many crops and sometimes interfere with the harvest. If a dry spring is preceded by a winter with little or no snow, and if the dry winds blow during the summer, crop failures, and often in the past, famine, overwhelm the countryside.

Topographically, European Russia is part of the Great Central Plain that reaches from northern France across Germany, Poland, and Russia, and on into Asia. The Russian part of this vast tableland is a low plain that is only occasionally hilly. Its average elevation is just 580 feet, and in its highest parts, the water divides between its rivers, it does not reach over 1,640 feet. Its northern limit is set by the Arctic Ocean. On the east it is bounded for 1,250 miles by the Ural Mountains. This long ridge, most of it too low and gradual to form a real barrier, is the conventional division between Europe and Asia. Between the southern end of the Urals and the Caspian Sea there stretches the broad lowland, called the Caspian Depression, that links the Russian plain with the steppes of Asia. On the south the plain is bordered by the mountains of the Caucasus and by the Black Sea, and on the southwest by the Carpathians.

Travelers journeying across this tableland are overwhelmed by its immensity and its sameness. Without visible boundaries, it seems to stretch on into infinity. But though there are few geographical features to lend variety to the landscape, the plain is actually divided into five great horizontal belts, each differing sharply from the others in its natural characteristics.

The first of these belts is the tundra zone. It lies above the Arctic Circle between the White Sea and the northern Urals. The frigid climate, poor soil, and insufficient precipitation severely restrict agriculture. In spring the lower courses of the rivers remain blocked with ice long after their headwaters have melted, so that there are many flooded areas and broad stretches of marshland. It is cloudier there than in any other part of Europe, and there are frequent fogs. Snow may fall in any month of the year, but the cover is negligible because of the small amount of precipitation, and because strong winds blow it away. As a result, there is not enough cover to protect the soil during the cold winters and much of the subsoil is permanently frozen. Along the region's northern borders there are no trees or even shrubs, but moving southward the vegetation gradually increases until, on its southernmost outskirts, the tundra merges into the next great belt, the forest zone.

This second region, by far the largest of the five major belts, stretches southward from the Arctic Circle to a line running from Kiev northeast to Kaluga, then east through Riazan, Nizhnii Novgorod (now called Gor'kii), Kazan, and on into Siberia. This boundary, roughly approximating the 55th parallel of latitude, is usually considered the dividing line between northern and southern Russia. The zone was once covered by coniferous and mixed deciduous forests. Many navigable rivers move slowly through it. It has many bogs, especially in its northern part where there also are numerous lakes. Its predominant soils are light gray earths known as podzols. Sandy, clayish, or stony in composition, they have a low humus content, and are deeply leached. They can be and are farmed, but without fertilizer they give relatively low crop yields.

South of the forest zone there is a comparatively narrow strip that combines the qualities of forest and steppe, and so is called the forest-steppe zone. Here woods alternate with prairies, or small stands of trees are scattered against a steppe background. The soils, like the topography, stand midway between the earths of the forest and the steppe. Dark gray in color, they are the result of the encroachment of the northern forests into the steppe, and are sometimes known as degraded podzols and degraded black soil, the process of degradation consisting of a gradual transition from the black soil to the podzolic type. Though these soils are not as fertile as the true black earth they are well suited for farming.

Proceeding southward the woods thin out until the traveler emerges into the treeless expanse of the steppe. This is the land of the chernozem, as the Russians call the black earth that makes this zone the most fertile region of European Russia. More than twice as large as France or Germany, the black earth belt covers about one fourth of European Russia. It goes from the Rumanian border across to the Urals, and reaches southward to the mountains of the Crimea and the Caucasus. Its broadest north-south width, in the valley of the Don River, is over 600 miles. The average depth of its soil is between 2½ and 3 feet, and in some places it is as much as 5 feet. The weather, though marked by the extremes typical of continental climates, is milder than it is in the forest zone, but precipitation is light.

On its southern border the chernozem belt gradually fades into the semi-arid region that is called the dry steppe. This zone, north of the Caspian Sea and in the basin of the lower Volga, forms the southeastern corner of European Russia. The chestnut and light brown soils that cover much of this region are usually included in the chernozem, though they are not as fertile. Because rainfall is so light, agriculture is unimportant in this region, but when artificial irrigation is employed the soils give high returns.

1

THE FIRST AGE OF
EXPANSION

IN THE FIRST MILLENNIUM after Christ the Eastern Slavic tribes who were the forebears of the Russian people settled in the valley of the Dnieper River. They chose well, for the region had fertile and easily worked soil. Open areas alternated with forests that served as shelter belts. A network of navigable streams laced the valley and connected it with the three great bordering seas, the Baltic, the Black, and the Caspian. As time went on the tribesmen spread along these streams until by the middle of the ninth century their settlements reached from Lake Ladoga south to the falls of the Dnieper, and from the Western Dvina to the banks of the Oka and Upper Volga.

Much of the history of this early period must remain conjecture for the sources are very few. Apparently the various tribes ultimately formed federations, each with a city as its center, and with a company of hired warriors as its defense force. Often these mercenaries were Vikings—or Varangians, as they are known in Russian history—who began to come down the Russian waterways from their native Scandinavia probably in the eighth century. Some of the chieftains of the Viking bands managed to establish themselves as the hereditary rulers of the towns they were hired to defend, and then extended their power over other cities. There was much conflict between these ambitious dynasts, but by the turn of the ninth century one of them had succeeded in getting all the Russian cities under his nominal sovereignty, with Kiev, chief city of the realm, as his capital. So began the Kievan era of Russian history.[1]

The union that was formed was an extremely loose federation of nearly autonomous city-states, each ruled presumably by a prince appointed by the prince of Kiev, who usually chose his

[1] Rybakov, "Obrazovanie," pp. 107-138; Rostovtzeff, "Les origines," pp. 5-18.

kinsmen for these thrones. The boundaries of the federation were uncertain, and its internal politics were riven by ceaseless discord. At first, no principle of succession to the thrones of Kiev and the other cities seems to have been established, and rival claimants to the thrones were a chief cause of domestic unrest and civil strife. Under Vladimir I (978-1015) and his son Iaroslav I (1019-1054) the realm attained the maximum stability it was destined to achieve. After Iaroslav's death the political organization of the federation, and especially the method of succession that was worked out, became remarkably involved, producing further dissension, while the natural increase in the ruling families led to successive partitions of territory in order to furnish principalities for the royal siblings. These divisive forces were aggravated by the military aggressions of the rulers against one another, and by periodic outbursts of popular unrest in which reigning princes were sometimes driven from their thrones and new ones invited in. To these factors that made for internal instability was added the ever present threat of barbarian invasion, for throughout its history the Kievan federation was threatened by waves of nomads rolling out of the Eurasian steppe.

The economic history of these first centuries is even more obscure and uncertain than their political history. Nonetheless, the available data make it clear that the Kievan era was an age of economic expansion that bore much resemblance to the experience of Western Europe in these same centuries. As in the West, there was an active growth of interregional trade. The Viking conquerors, after establishing their hegemony over the Dnieper valley, pushed on to Byzantium to sate their greed for the precious wares of the East. Though their relations with the Greeks were marred by armed conflicts, amicable trading connections were finally established. The "road from the Varangians to the Greeks"—as the chronicler called the great trade route that ran from the Black Sea up the Dnieper and Lovat Rivers, through Lake Ilmen past Novgorod, then down the Volkhov into Lake Ladoga and thence into the Baltic—became the chief artery of Russian commerce. In addition to the Byzantine trade the Russians had overland connections with the East, their merchants going to the shores of the Caspian and beyond. An active commerce with the countries of Central and Western Europe also grew up. Russia became well known and respected in the rest of Europe, as was evidenced by the marriages between the Kievan princely houses and the ruling families of Byzantium, Poland, Hungary, Sweden, Norway, Denmark, France, Germany, and England.

The extensive foreign trade gave a strong impetus to internal commerce. The merchants traveled through the land to buy goods for export and to sell the wares they had imported. The luxury items they offered for sale had only a limited market, but there was a mass demand for some of their merchandise, such as salt, metal articles, and cheap jewelry. The cities, especially Kiev, Novgorod, and Smolensk, were the centers of this commerce. Kiev, at the heart of the great river network that linked the Dnieper, Bug, Oka, Vistula, and Don valleys, and with the main overland routes running through it, was by far the most important.

Along with the growth of commerce and of a market economy, the use of money increased. In the pre-Kievan era cattle and furs had served as mediums of exchange and foreign coins had also been used. In the Kievan centuries metallic money came into general use. Coins were minted from the first half of the eleventh century on into the first quarter of the next century. Small silver bars were also used, and foreign coins had wide circulation.

Urban life quickened, too, just as it did in contemporary Western Europe. The old towns grew and many new ones were founded. Kiev became one of Europe's greatest cities. Thietmar of Merseburg (d. 1019) told of its 400 churches, its eight markets, and its "infinite multitude" of people. Adam of Bremen (d. 1076) wrote that it rivaled Constantinople, and a Russian chronicler reported that a great fire that raged through the city in 1124 destroyed 600 churches. The chroniclers of the era unintentionally provided a partial index to the increase in urban settlements, for though they had no interest in reporting on such mundane matters as the growth of towns, they frequently mentioned them by name in the course of their tales of heroism, treachery, and piety. In their annals for the ninth and tenth centuries they referred to 24, for the eleventh century 62 more, and for the twelfth century still another 120, for a total of 206 individual towns. In contrast, only 32 are mentioned by name for the first time in the sources of the thirteenth century when (as will be seen later) the secular trend in economic life swung downward.[2]

Presumably most of these towns were primarily centers for trade, but many of them also seemed to have been active in industrial production. Usually the markets for the wares turned out by their artisans were limited to the surrounding countryside, but some of their products were sold hundreds of miles away and even in foreign lands. As their markets expanded, the techniques of these workmen grew more complicated, and specialization increased. Rybakov, in his monumental work on the history of early Russian handicrafts, was able to identify as many as sixty special crafts in some of the cities of the twelfth and early thirteenth centuries.[3]

The colonization of new territory was further evidence that this period was one of economic growth—and bore further resemblance to what was happening in the West. In Western Europe settlers pushed out beyond the old frontiers, and a wave of German colonists swept eastward across the Elbe. In Russia, Slav colonists moved out of the old regions of settlement into the forested triangle formed by the Oka and Upper Volga. At first there was only a trickle of migrants, but in the eleventh century their numbers grew. Most of the newcomers in the first stage of settlement were from Novgorod, coming in search of furs and other forest products, or farmers looking for better soil than could be found in their infertile homeland. Then settlers began moving in from the Dnieper valley. In the latter twelfth and in the thirteenth centuries this stream grew rapidly, but these later migrants were seeking haven from new nomad invasions that were threatening the Dnieper region, and from internal political and economic troubles. Their movement, then, was not evidence of expansion, as the colonization up to this

[2] Grekov, *Feodal'nye otnosheniia*, p. 7; Tikhomirov, *Drevnerusskie goroda*, pp. 10, 21-24.

[3] Rybakov, *Remeslo*, pp. 501-522.

time had been; rather it was evidence of the opposite phenomenon—the economic decline of the old zone of settlement.[4]

All of these developments, and particularly the growth of cities and the colonizing movement up to the latter decades of the twelfth century, point toward the conclusion that there was a large increase in population during the Kievan period. In lands of Western Europe, during the long upward swing of economic life in these centuries, the spotty and inexact data indicate a doubling and even a tripling of the population. Unfortunately, the demographic information about Kievan Russia is so slight that not even the most imprecise generalizations about population size or growth can be made safely.[5]

Because the data are so scanty the nature of the basic occupation of the mass of the people in the Kievan and pre-Kievan eras was long a matter of debate among historians. One school insisted that most of the population earned their living in such forest occupations as fishing, hunting, and collecting honey, and that settled tillage was of minor importance in the economy. Trade in these forest commodities is assumed to have provided the foundation of economic development down to the disintegration of the Kievan federation. But the transfer of the center of

[4] Liubavskii, *Obrazovanie*, pp. 4-8.

[5] Abel, *Agrarkrisen*, pp. 20-21; Russell, *British Medieval Population*, p. 280, fig. 10.4.

Vernadsky, on what seem to me to be inadequate grounds, estimated the population of Kievan Russia in the twelfth century at between 7-8 millions, and without any presentation of evidence stated that it was much less than this in the tenth century, and still less in the eighth century. (Vernadsky, *Zven'ia*, I, 30.) Elsewhere Vernadsky estimated, again without providing the bases for his calculations, that urban population in the late twelfth-early thirteenth centuries was around one million, or about 13 per cent of the total estimated population. Not until the late nineteenth century did Russia again have so high a proportion of city dwellers. (Vernadsky, *Kievan Russia*, pp. 104-105.) Iakovlev arrived at the same estimate of total Kievan population by a somewhat startling procedure. He reasoned that since England and France's population are estimated to have increased seven times over between the eleventh and the beginning of the twentieth centuries the same should be true for Russian population growth. So he divided the early twentieth-century population of those areas of Russia that had been parts of the Kievan federation by seven. He "checked" this calculation by assuming that the population density per sq. km. in Kievan Russia was the same as that of North America at the end of the eighteenth century, or of Central Africa in the twentieth century, and then multiplied this density figure by the total area of the Kievan realm, and found that the product (ca. 7.5 millions) was very close to the figure he arrived at by his first calculation (7.9 millions). (Iakovlev, *Kholopstvo*, I, 298.)

RUSSIA IN THE 12TH AND EARLY 13TH CENTURIES

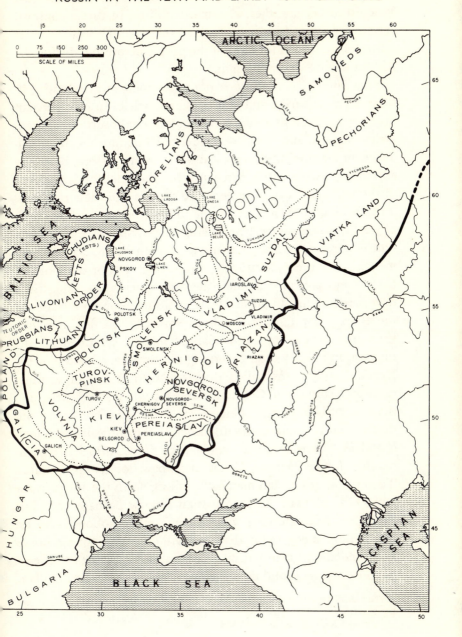

national life to the Northeast isolated the people from their old commercial connections and markets, and only then did settled agriculture become their dominant calling. In direct contrast, another group of historians asserted that farming was the chief source of livelihood for most of the people before and during the Kievan era, as well as after it.[6]

That both local and interregional commerce was extensive in these early centuries, and that the chief articles in it of Russian origin were forest products, has been well established by written, archaeological, and linguistic evidence.[7] The much scantier evidence on the trading class indicates that many persons, both Slav and foreign, were active merchants, but the chief foreign traders of the realm seem to have been the princes and their retainers. True Vikings, they had first come to the Russian land in search of wealth, to be gained by peaceful trade or by force as circumstances dictated—piracy has often been the first stage of commerce. After their elevation to the ruling class of the Dnieper basin they continued in their mercantile activities, using their new preeminence in government to insure profitable trade for themselves. Constantine Porphyrogenitus, who ruled in Byzantium from 945 to 959, in a manual that he compiled for the instruction of his son on governing the Empire, related how the Russian princes (he called them archons) and their retinues came each summer to Constantinople from Novgorod, Kiev, and the other river ports. Their vessels—made by hollowing out single great tree trunks—were loaded to the gunwales with merchandise. (Five hundred years after Constantine wrote his manual Josafa Barbaro, Venetian ambassador to the Crimean Tatars, told of Russian merchants sailing down the Volga in the same kind of craft. In the Russian forests, Barbaro recorded, "are great trees growing, which, being made hollow, serve for boats of one piece, so big that they will carry eight or ten horses at a time and as many men.") Constantine explained that each winter the princes and their men went through the Russian land

[6] For an historiographical discussion of this controversy see Grekov, *Krest'iane*, pp. 21-42.

[7] Hrushevsky, *Geschichte*, I, 278-308.

levying tribute on the Slavs over whom they ruled.[8] Doubtless this tribute made up a large part of the goods they brought to Constantinople. The articles in their cargoes mentioned most frequently in the sources were furs, honey, wax, and slaves. They exchanged these wares for luxury items such as silks, wines, fruits, and finely-made weapons.[9]

Despite the unquestioned prominence of commerce and the active trading role of the princes and their retinues, the available data, and particularly the archaeological evidence that has been unearthed in increasing quantities in recent decades, point clearly to farming as the predominant occupation for the mass of the people from the pre-Kievan centuries on. Even in frontier regions where forest industries could have been expected to have been of prime importance, the settlers practiced regular tillage from very early times. Trade may well have been the chief economic activity of the princes and nobles, but most people apparently made their livings by following the plow.[10] Forest products were major export articles because they were the Russian goods for which there was the largest foreign demand, and not because they were the chief products of the Russian economy. In internal trade farm goods were of much greater importance. The people of the cities, though they probably raised some truck in gardens, were dependent for much of their food upon the surrounding rural districts. There was also an active inter-regional trade in farm products. Novgorod, for example, drew grain supplies from the more southerly parts of Russia, and there is evidence that grain was perhaps sometimes shipped to Constantinople.[11]

Two major tillage systems had been used originally. In forested regions the slash-burn method was employed (*podseka*). Trees felled in spring were allowed to lie until fall when their branches were chopped off and the trunks hauled away on sledges. The following spring the brush and debris that covered the clearing was set on fire, and the ashes allowed to remain. The

8 *De administrando imperio*, pp. 47-62; Barbaro, "Travels," p. 31.

9 Vasiliev, "Economic Relations," pp. 324-325, 329.

10 Cf. Dovzhenok, "K istorii," pp. 116-131, 136-145; Hrushevsky, *Geschichte*, I, 245-256.

11 Vernadsky, *Kievan Russia*, pp. 116-117; Kliuchevskii, *History*, I, 80; Voronin, "K itogam i zadacham," p. 28.

area was then sown, often without plowing, the seed being broadcast and then covered by rakes or by dragging tree branches across the field. The clearing was used continuously for from two to eight years depending upon its fertility. When it was exhausted it was allowed to go back to forest, and other burned-out patches that had been prepared beforehand were sown. An estimated twenty-five to forty years were necessary for the field to recover its fertility and be ready to be used again to grow crops. Obviously, this was a wasteful system that was possible only where land was cheap and plentiful. It was equally wasteful in terms of labor. It has been estimated that seventy working days had to be expended annually to clear, prepare, and till one desiatin (2.7 acres) of arable land using this technique. A single family could not have been able to provide enough labor to work the land it needed to support itself, so that the use of the *podseka* system presupposed the existence of some form of communal organization.

In the forest-steppe and steppe zones field grass husbandry was employed. Here a field was cropped continuously for several years until its productivity fell. It was then allowed to go back to grass, while other fields were used. After an indeterminate number of years the field was once more tilled until it became exhausted again. There was no regular rotation of fields in this system. Like the slash-burn technique, this method was possible only where land was cheap and plentiful.[12]

As population increased and the man-land ratio rose, these wasteful tillage systems had to be abandoned. The practice of distributing fields on a permanent basis and working them continuously was gradually adopted. By the second half of the ninth century this stage had apparently been reached even in the North and Northeast, while in the Dnieper valley the old systems had long since been given up. Presumably the two- and three-field systems of husbandry became the dominant techniques, although it has been claimed they did not begin to displace the older methods until the first half of the fourteenth

[12] Savich, "Die Agrarwirtschaft," pp. 493-495; Dovzhenok, "K istorii," pp. 132, 156-157.

century.[13] Actually, indisputable evidence of the widespread use of the three-field system is found only beginning with the last part of the fifteenth century. Both field grass husbandry and *podseka* continued to be used in frontier regions and in the far north for many more centuries and were still being practiced in some places into the twentieth century.

In the first stages of agriculture the chief farm tools were the axe to clear the forests and a primitive hoe-plow to scratch the surface of the soil. As tillage advanced more efficient tools were adopted. Archaeological evidence shows that a true plow, with iron share, pulled by horses or oxen, was being used in the Dnieper valley at least as early as the seventh-eighth century. In the North the *sokha*, a forked wooden hoe, was devised. This light and mobile instrument, pulled by draught animals or by humans, proved well-suited for the shallow soil of the North, and continued in use there down into recent times. Besides these tools, a wide variety of other basic farm implements, such as sickles, scythes, mattocks, and so on, dating back to the Kievan and pre-Kievan eras, have been unearthed.[14]

The improvements in the techniques of farming, like the growth in the number of cities, the active internal and foreign trade, the increase in industrial production, the greater use of money, and the colonial movement, provide evidence that the Kievan era was a period of economic expansion. At the same time these improvements in tillage must themselves have been the results of economic growth, since it seems reasonable to assume they were adopted in response to a mounting demand for farm products. Nor were they the only innovations in agriculture. New forms of land tenure and new methods of farm management also appeared within the framework of the expanding economy and in response to the opportunities it offered. These changes in the rural economy are the subjects of the next two chapters.

[13] Grekov, *Krest'iane*, p. 48; Vernadsky, *Kievan Russia*, p. 109; Dovzhenok, "K istorii," pp. 157-158; P. Smirnov, "Obrazovanie," pp. 77-79; Smith, *The Origins*, pp. 66-70.
[14] Dovzhenok, "K istorii," pp. 125-134.

2

PEASANT COMMUNES AND PRIVATE
LANDOWNERS

IN KIEVAN RUSSIA, as in every society that was predominantly agrarian, the relationships between the members of the society must have depended primarily upon the ways in which land was held. But the scanty sources contain only small amounts of factual data about tenures and then only as information incidental to the main themes of the texts. So once again only dim outlines can be made out, and much has to be left to conjecture.

One of the most contested of the many debates that have marked—and enlivened—Russian historical writing concerns the origins and growth of the peasant commune and its role in Russian history. It should be pointed out that many of these controversies, during the Imperial regime as well as in the Soviet era, were not (and are not) carried on in academic isolation. They became affairs of much pertinence to the contemporary scene, with important political and philosophical implications, and excited wide interest. This was particularly true of the historiographical brouhaha about the commune. Because much of the sparring was about changes in this institution that took place after the fifteenth century, the issues in the controversy will be discussed in some detail in a later chapter. Here it will suffice to point out that nearly every assertion made about the commune has evoked at least a rebuttal, and often an extended debate. With time, however, a *communis opinio doctorum* has emerged on many of the controverted points.

It is generally agreed that the Eastern Slavs had left the tribal form of organization long before the Kievan era, save in some peripheral zones where it persisted into the eleventh century. The clans had broken down into free communes. These first communes are thought to have been large family units headed by a patriarch, with several generations living and working together as one household and sharing the fruits of their common labor. They are believed to have been much like the zadruga, the communal form found in the modern period among the South Slavs. This hypothesis is based upon comparative studies of Slavic social history, upon researches on peasant life in more recent times, and upon vestigial evidence provided by certain institutions that persisted in Great Russian village life until recent centuries.

The early Russian great family commune seems to have borne close resemblance to what is believed to have been the primitive form of social organization in the early centuries of the Germanic settlement of Central and Western Europe. This institution was described by Marc Bloch as follows:[1] *"Terra unius familiae*: Bede's words give us in all probability the key to the institution in its primitive form. But we are not to think of the little matrimonial family of our later ages. Ill informed as we are about the history of blood relationships in the dawn of our civilization, there is every reason to think that the group, whose original shell was the *manse*, was a patriarchal family of several generations and several collateral households living around a common hearth."

Some historians have insisted that the patriarchal commune was the dominant form of rural social organization into the Kievan era.[2] It seems more likely, however, that by the tenth-eleventh century the great family commune had changed, or was in the process of changing, into a territorial commune. The members of this new kind of organization were bound together not by blood, but by propinquity and by common social and economic interests. Each communer lived separately with his wife and children in his own dwelling, pursued his own individual economy, owned his own farm implements and animals, had private rights over the use and disposition of the land he tilled and of its produce, but shared with his fellows in the use of common pastures, forests, and streams, and in the meeting of communal obligations.

Because direct evidence about the history and internal struc-

[1] In *Cambridge Economic History*, I, 268.
[2] Cf. Grekov, *Krest'iane*, pp. 59-74.

ture of the patriarchal commune is lacking, only surmises are possible about the reasons for its decline. It was suggested in the preceding chapter that in the first stage of systematic agriculture many hands must have been needed for the heavy task of making clearings in the forests and preparing land for sowing. The single family unit—the conjugal family—lacked the labor resources for such operations, and so supposedly had grouped itself with kinsmen in a cooperative effort. When rural society had passed through the stage of slash-burn tillage the need for cooperative work no longer existed. Presumably the conjugal units then withdrew from the great family commune, each to run its own economy with its own labor resources. Mme. Efimenko was able to show that this transition from great family to individual family operation had occurred in more recent centuries in the far north of European Russia, when the peasants there had shifted to settled agriculture.[3] The natural increase within the patriarchal commune also may have been a factor in its disintegration. Possibly, this form of organization could not operate efficiently when it got beyond a certain size. When that point was reached it broke up and its land was divided among its constituent conjugal families. This presumed evolution in Russia is analogous to what is thought to have happened elsewhere in Europe, where the land occupied by the patriarchal family unit is believed to have been divided into smaller holdings worked by conjugal families.

The territorial commune that succeeded the patriarchal one was known as the *verv'* in the Dnieper basin and as the mir in the Novgorod region. These names had undoubtedly been used for the patriarchal communes, too. But it is clear from the context of the Kievan law codes that by the time these compilations were drawn up *verv'* and mir referred to geographical units with definite boundaries. For example, if a prince's man was slain "the *verv'* within whose boundaries the body lay" had to pay the wergild, or in the case of the recognition of stolen property, the owner could reclaim it immediately if the recognition was within the limits of his own mir.[4]

---

[3] Efimenko, *Izsledovaniia*, pp. 217-220.
[4] *Pravda Russkaia*, Short Version, sect. 13, 20; Expanded Version, sect. 3.

The free peasants who lived in the communes were known as *smerdy* (sing., *smerd*). Philologists have surmised that this word was derived from an ancient root meaning "man," and that once it may have been used to describe everyone. By the Kievan period, however, it was applied only to the lowest class of freemen and had become associated with the verb *smerdeti*, to stink.[5] The use of the name *smerd*, best translated, perhaps, as "stinker," is a telling indication of the very low esteem in which the peasant must have been held. It is difficult to imagine that people who were identified by so unpleasant a name could have been considered by their contemporaries to have been of much importance.

The hypothesis that is suggested by philology is borne out by the data found in the limited sources of the Kievan centuries. These point to the conclusion that the new social milieu created in this era by the emergence of princely retinues and bureaucracies, and especially by the growth of private landowning by men of the upper classes, produced a deterioration in the status of the free peasantry. Thus, the earliest known law code, the *Pravda* or Law of Iaroslav, set a wergild of forty grivnas for the unavenged murder of any free man, whether a member of the prince's retinue, one of his officials, a member of the group called the *izgoi*, or a Slav (*slovenin*).[6] This listing was apparently designed to cover all free men in the society, so it seems fair to assume that by *slovenin* was meant the categories of free men not specifically named. This would include the *smerdy*.[7] Iaroslav's *Pravda* dates from at least the early years of the eleventh century and many of its provisions are believed to be restatements of old customary laws. If these assumptions are correct, then in the first part of the eleventh century, and presumably during the preceding era, all free men were equal in the eyes of the law. In later Kievan codifications, however, this equality was supplanted by class distinctions. The *Pravda* of the Sons of Iaroslav, dating to the third quarter of the eleventh century, set a penalty of

---

[5] Grekov, *Krest'iane*, pp. 15-17.

In contemporary Polish and Lusatian documents the peasant was referred to as *smard* and *smurd*, respectively. Tymieniecki, "Le servage en Pologne," p. 12.

[6] Short Version, sect. 1.

[7] Grekov, *Kievskaia Rus*, pp. 69-70.

eighty grivnas for the murder of the chief officials of the prince. In the next codification, the so-called Expanded Version, believed to have been made in the early twelfth century, the wergild for the murder of "men of the prince," by which was meant his chief retainers and officials, was also raised to eighty grivnas. But the wergild of other freemen, including the *smerdy*, remained at forty grivnas.[8]

The *smerdy*, as might be expected, appear infrequently in the chronicles of the Kievan period, but some of the few references to them reveal their humble status. The Novgorod annalist in his entry for the year 1016 reported that Prince Iaroslav, after his victory over his brother Sviatopolk, paid each of the men from the city of Novgorod who fought for him ten silver grivnas, but gave only one grivna apiece to the *smerdy* in his army.[9] In 1100 a group of warring princes met for peace talks, and according to the chronicle's account, they instructed the brother princes Vasil'ko and Volodar to return the "slaves and *smerdy*" whom these two had taken captive. Vladimir Monomakh, Prince of Kiev, who died in 1125, in his testament told his sons that he had protected both the impoverished widow and the *smerd* from the abuses of more powerful people.[10]

---

[8] Short Version, sect. 19. The *Pravda* of Iaroslav and the *Pravda* of his sons are together known as the Short Version. Expanded Version, sect. 1, 3.

Section 3 of the Expanded Version of the *Pravda* referred to the classes for whom the wergild was forty grivna as *liudi*. By this term was meant the commonalty, both rural and urban. (Vladimirskii-Budanov, *Obzor*, pp. 35-37; Goetz, *Russische Recht*, II, 32.) Vernadsky, however, excludes the *smerdy* from the ranks of the *liudi*, claiming that by the latter term was meant those men who held enough land to guarantee them a comfortable living and a social position superior to that of the mass of the rural population whom he calls the *smerdy*. (Vernadsky, *Kievan Russia*, pp. 136, 141.) But the term *liudi* was used in the *Pravda* of the Sons of Iaroslav and in the Expanded Version as a designation for the members of the territorial commune. (Short Version, sect. 19; Expanded Version, sect. 7.) The *smerdy* were certainly members of these communes; e.g., one of the articles in the treaty made in 1270 between Novgorod and the Prince of Tver stated that "the merchant shall remain in his hundred, and the *smerd* shall remain in his commune" (*SGGD*, I, no. 3), and in charters and treaties of the succeeding centuries the mass of the peasantry were often referred to as *liudi*. (Sergeevich, *Drevnosti*, I, 232-233.)

[9] *Novgorodskaia pervaia letopis*, p. 175.

[10] *Letopis po lavr. spisku*, pp. 243, 264.

II

The peasant commune in one form or other was to persist throughout the centuries, and contributed much to giving Russian history a special and unique quality. But even while the *verv'* and the mir were growing out of the patriarchal commune another kind of landholding emerged that proved of greater significance in the evolution of Russian life. This new form was the private ownership of large tracts of land by members of the governing elite. The first appearance of this kind of tenure cannot with any certainty be dated earlier than the tenth century and its firm establishment took place in the eleventh. Its introduction marks the starting point of the central theme of Russia's subsequent—and tragic—history, the subjugation of the peasantry. For now the men who ruled the state added the role of seignior to their repertoire, and thereby reduced the peasants who lived on the lands they made their own into renters, at best, and thralls, at worst.

The most important single source for the story of the introduction of private landowning (as well as for all other parts of Russia's earliest history) is the *Primary Chronicle*, now often referred to as the *Tale of Bygone Years*.[11] Dating from the first part of the twelfth century, it was based upon earlier annals written in the preceding seventy or eighty years. The *Primary Chronicle*, then, contains eye-witness, or at least contemporary, accounts for the period from the last years of Prince Iaroslav of Kiev (d. 1054) through the reigns of his sons and grandsons. The entries for the earlier centuries (the chronicle begins with the year 852) were probably drawn largely from oral narratives, and to a lesser extent from Byzantine writings. Many of the happenings recorded for these first centuries were told by the chronicler in conventional epic forms that clearly were borrowed from other early folk literatures. Some of these tales contained the germs of historical truth but the majority of them were brought into Russia from other lands and linked by the story teller to Russian historical personages and happenings. But the chronicle

---

11 *Ibid.* English translation by Cross and Sherbowitz-Wetzor, *Russian Primary Chronicle*. Citations are made here from this translation except where references to the Russian text are necessary, e.g., for nomenclature.

also contains genuine annalistic entries for the early years, often imbedded in the legendary recital. These events were recorded in a matter-of-fact style that contrasts sharply with the poetic style of the literary accounts.[12] The annalistic entries, and the nomenclature used in both the historical and fictional reports, provide the largest part of the very slim data on landholding.

Other evidence of estate ownership is supplied by certain articles of the earliest law codes, the Short and Expanded Versions of the *Pravda Russkaia*, the *Russian Law*. These codes are believed by some to have been official enactments, but most authorities agree that the extant versions were private legal compilations drawn from a variety of sources. All agree that they are an authentic record of Russian law in the eleventh-thirteenth centuries. The data they provide about private landowning, then, are useful for the period in which the codes were compiled. But they provide meagre bases for the extrapolation of knowledge about earlier conditions of tenure.

In view of this paucity of information it is difficult to determine with any degree of precision when landownership by the ruling class first appeared on Russian soil. Kliuchevskii believed that there was no evidence of it before the eleventh century and that concrete indications of its existence date to the twelfth century. D'iakonov, Stählin, and Kulischer reached much the same conclusion. Eck, with less equivocation, placed the origins in the twelfth century, with churchmen as the first proprietors.[13]

The view that individual estate ownership began relatively late is based upon the opinion that into the twelfth century the ruling class, both Slavic and Scandinavian, had drawn its income from trade, tribute, and booty. Others, who have asserted that agricultural activity was the chief, or at least a very important, source of the economic power of the upper class, insist on an earlier origin. Khlebnikov claimed that in the ninth and tenth centuries wealth was in the form of landed property. Hötzsch wrote that by the ninth century members of the native Slav

[12] Stender-Petersen, *Die Varägersaga*, pp. 29-32, 36, 38-39; *Russian Primary Chronicle*, pp. 23-30.

[13] Kliuchevskii, *History*, I, 185; D'iakonov, *Ocherki obshchestvennago . . . stroia*, pp. 74-75; Stählin, *Geschichte*, I, 68-69; Kulischer, *Russische Wirtschaftsgeschichte*, I, 38-40; Eck, "Le grand domaine," p. 94.

aristocracy were owners of estates to which they had inalienable titles. According to Grekov and Iushkov, leading Soviet historians of early Russia, estate ownership began within Slavic society before the Scandinavian conquest, Grekov suggesting that its origins reached back to the sixth century and possibly even earlier.[14]

In normal circumstances, apparently, the political organization of the tribes into which the Eastern Slavs were originally divided was semi-anarchical. The individual tribe was broken down into a number of communes or groups, each with its own leader or leaders, with frequent armed conflicts marking inter-group relationships. The local leaders formed the tribal aristocracy, but when the entire tribe, or a large part of it, was united in a common effort—perhaps to resist invasion or to engage in aggressive warfare against another people—leadership of the combined groups was assumed by a "king." These "kings," who gained their posts through election or heredity, came from the ranks of the local notables.

Early sources reveal the existence of a ruling class of this sort among the Eastern Slavs from the beginning of their recorded history. Jordanes (sixth century) in his account of the war between the Ostrogoths and the Eastern Slavic tribe of the Antes around 375 A.D., told how the victorious Ostrogoths crucified the "king" of the Antes together with his sons and seventy "notables" (*primates*). Menander Protector (sixth century) wrote that after the Antes had been defeated by the Avars, a Turkish people, around 560, the Antic rulers (*archontes*) selected one Mezamerus to treat with the victors. He must have been of outstanding importance, for Cotragegus, an ally of the Avars, described him as having gained more power over his people than had any man up to that time. Because of his preeminence he was killed by the Avars, who then once more ravaged the land of the Antes.[15]

This primitive method of organization persisted on into the first centuries of the Kievan period. The Slavic aristocracy main-

[14] Khlebnikov, *Obshchestvo*, p. 102; Hötzsch, "Adel und Lehnswesen," pp. 544-545; Grekov, *Krest'iane*, pp. 93-94; Iushkov, *Ocherki*, pp. 143-144.
[15] Jordanes, *Romana et Gettica*, p. 121; Menander, *Fragmenta*, pp. 5-6.

tained a separate identity as an autochthonous elite, independent of the favor and bounty of the ruling princes. This is made clear by entries in the *Primary Chronicle* for the middle and latter parts of the tenth century. For example, in 945 Prince Igor of Kiev was killed on a campaign against the Drevlianians, a Slavic tribe living west of Kiev. The Drevlianians then sent twenty of their "best men" to Igor's widow, Olga, to ask her to marry their war chief, Mal. The vengeful Olga, according to the annalist's story, had these twenty emissaries buried alive. Then she sent word to the Drevlianians that she would come to their country if they would provide her with an escort of their "eminent men." The Drevlianians were reported to have sent "the best men who governed the Drevlianian Land." Olga arranged for these men to be burned alive, and then, after further adventures in guile and perfidy, she conquered and destroyed the chief Drevlianian city of Iskorosten, killing some of the "elders of the city" and enslaving others of them. In 987 Vladimir, Prince of Kiev, summoned his own chief followers, who were called boyars, and the "city elders," to aid him in deciding which of the major religions should be adopted by the state. The entry for 996 related that Vladimir invited the "eminent men" of the city, along with city militia officials and Vladimir's own boyars and court officers, to weekly banquets at his palace.[16]

There is no direct evidence that the members of this Slavic upper class were landed proprietors in pre-Kievan times. Grekov, however, using sources from the Kievan period deduced that these people did own estates in earlier centuries. He pointed out that the sources refer to large private holdings in the Kievan period without any indication that they represented an innovation. He took this to mean that landownership was such an accepted institution that the chroniclers did not feel that special comment about it was necessary.[17] Since there is ample evidence of the importance of settled agriculture among the Eastern Slavs before the coming of the Varangians, it seemed reasonable to him to assume that the native aristocrats must have been supported, at least in part, by land they owned. But the fact

[16] *Letopis po lavr. spisku*, pp. 54-58, 104, 123; cf. Odinetz, *Vozniknovenie*, pp. 14-17; Hrushevsky, *Geschichte*, I, 376-377, 384-386; Laehr, *Die Anfänge*, p. 11.
[17] Grekov, *Krest'iane*, p. 105.

that the chroniclers said nothing to indicate that private ownership of large tracts of land was something new can scarcely be
accepted as evidence for the long-time existence of this kind of
landholding. Nor does the predominance of agriculture as a way
of life necessarily support the assumption that the native aristocrats were large landowners. It is quite possible that they gained
their power and income entirely from their roles of political,
commercial and military leadership in the commune. The fact
of the matter seems to be that on the basis of the available information there is no reason to believe that there was private
landownership on a large scale in the pre-Kievan era.

Not until the tenth century are there any indications of
individual ownership of large land complexes, and then not by
the Slavic nobility but by princes of Varangian origin. When
the Scandinavians first came into the Russian land they contented themselves with the gains to be won from brigandage,
war, and trade. Then they began to shift the source of their
income to landed property. In the opening passages of the old
Novgorod Chronicle, written in the first half of the eleventh
century, the annalist commented bitterly upon this transfer in
economic interest. He wrote that in olden times the princes and
their retinues had gained their wealth from wars with other
peoples. Now, the exploitation of their holdings in Novgorod
Land had become the chief means of their enrichment. The
chronicler lamented the hardships this had produced among
the people.[18]

The first private landowner mentioned in the chronicles was
that formidable widow, Olga. After her defeat of the Drevlianians in 946 she established "residences and hunting preserves"
in the conquered territory. The next year she traveled north
into Novgorod Land where she collected tribute and appropriated land for her own uses. "Her hunting grounds, boundary
posts, towns, and trading posts still exist throughout the whole
region" wrote the annalist.[19] Most of the other infrequent references in the earliest sources to landed property of the princes

[18] *Novgorodskaia pervaia letopis*, p. 104.

[19] *Russian Primary Chronicle*, pp. 81-82.
The boundary posts were markers bearing Olga's device, setting off her property from the neighboring land. (Rybakov, "Znaki," p. 229.)

occur in connection with the accounts of gifts by rulers, usually to the church, of land or of the income from some of their estates. In 996 Vladimir, on entering the just-completed Cathedral of the Dormition of the Holy Virgin in Kiev is reported to have said "I bestow upon this church of the Holy Virgin a tithe of my property and of my cities." By his property Vladimir meant his personal holdings, which included among other things his landed estates.[20] Snorri Sturluson, in his history of St. Olav of Norway, related that Olav, after his deposition in 1028 went to live with his son-in-law Iaroslav, then Prince of Novgorod. Iaroslav greeted him warmly, and offered Olav as much land as he needed for the maintenance of the men he had brought with him. The monk Nestor, in his biography of Feodosi, abbot of the Monastery of the Caves, written about the end of the eleventh century, reported that Iziaslav Iaroslavich (d. 1078), prince of Kiev, gave villages to that monastery. Iziaslav's son and successor Iaropolk (d. 1086) gave this monastery estates he owned in three districts of his realm. In addition, he gave an annual tithe from his properties to the Church of the Holy Virgin in Kiev. The more plentiful sources of the twelfth century record a number of such gifts by princes to church foundations.[21]

Another indication of the existence and the expansion of private landowning by princes is provided by references in the *Primary Chronicle* to royal ownership of certain cities and villages. Vyshgorod is identified as Olga's city, and the annalist also mentioned "her towns" in Novgorod Land and "her village of Ol'zhichi." Vladimir, before his conversion to Christianity, was supposed to have kept a total of 800 concubines in his towns of Vyshgorod, Berestovo, and Belgorod. He founded the last named city and settled it with people from other towns. In order to protect his realm from the invasions of the Pechenegs he built a string of towns along the banks of rivers on the steppe frontier, peopling them with colonists drawn from the northern and northeastern parts of his realm. Iaroslav established towns along

[20] *Letopis po lavr. spisku*, p. 122; cf. Golubinskii, *Istoriia*, I, i, 509; art. 3 of Vladimir's Church Statute in Vernadsky, "The Status of the Russian Church," p. 306.

[21] *Heimskringla*, p. 423; Goetz, *Das Kiever Höhlenkloster*, p. 129; *Letopis po Ipat'evskomu spisku*, p. 338; *Russian Primary Chronicle*, p. 169; v. pp. 37, 45, for 12th century data.

the Ros River where he had settled prisoners captured during his campaign in Volynia in 1031.[22] These new towns are believed to have been fortified manorial seats, serving as military and governmental centers for the surrounding countryside. In addition, they were the administrative headquarters for the adjacent landed properties of the princes or of their most important servitors. As time went on merchants and artisans, as in many places in Western Europe, settled in and around these centers and they grew into true towns.

The available evidence, then, points to the princes of the Varangian dynasty as the first large-scale private landowners in Russia. They established and increased their holdings by conquest, frontier settlement, and by internal expropriation and colonization. Olga used the first method when she set up her residences and hunting preserves in the land of the Drevlianians. Vladimir and Iaroslav established settlements on the borders of their realms. Olga apparently expropriated the land of free peasant communes in her journey into Novgorod Land in 947. Finally, empty land was available, especially in the forested plain that lay between the Oka and Volga rivers. There the princes carved out large holdings for themselves. In Novgorod Land, however, royalty met with reverses in their efforts to acquire property. After a popular revolt in 1136 the assembly (*veche*) of Novgorod decreed that only Novgorodians could own land in the territories controlled by the city. The holdings of the prince were transferred to the patrimony of the Cathedral of St. Sophia, and the assembly laid a prohibition against the acquisition, whether by purchase or gift, of real property by the prince, by members of his family, or by his retainers.[23]

Since the Norsemen were acquainted with the institution of private property in their homeland,[24] there is the possibility that they carried it into Russia. It has even been suggested that Kievan Russia was brought under Norse rule directly from Hálogaland by men of the landowning class and "was ruled, not by kings, but by hereditary landowners, like parts of Háloga-

---

[22] *Russian Primary Chronicle*, pp. 81-82 (946, 947 A.D.), 94 (980 A.D.), 119 (988 A.D.), 136 (1031 A.D.).

[23] Grekov, *Feodal'nye otnosheniia*, p. 81; Iushkov, *Ocherki*, pp. 49-50.

[24] Cf. Wührer, *Beiträge*, pp. 46-47, 51, 61.

land, and other parts of central and southern Norway."[25] Snorri Sturluson's account of the offer of land made by Prince Iaroslav to the exiled Olav of Norway may be an illustration of this carry-over. The impoverished refugee was to be provided with the same form of wealth that he had owned in his native land. But the earliest evidences of the private ownership of large amounts of landed property in Russia cannot be dated before the tenth century, although the Scandinavians had come as conquerors long before. The explanation of this lag might be that the creation of landed estates had to wait until the Varangians had established their rule firmly. That happened in the last quarter of the ninth century. It was perhaps not until that time, not until they had confirmed their hegemony and gained a feeling of permanence in the land they had conquered, that they became landowners.

Landownership by the church began soon after Christianity became the official religion of Russia, although it probably did not take on large proportions until late in the eleventh century. Christianity had won converts in Russia during the ninth and tenth centuries but only became the religion of the land when Prince Vladimir accepted baptism in the Eastern Church (988 is the traditional date of his conversion). The clerical personnel who came to set up the new state church were of Byzantine origin. They brought with them the methods and traditions of church organization and of church-state relations that had been evolved in the Eastern Empire. Among these were the juridical autonomy of the church, its traditional role of providing asylum for persons who had lost their social status, and its right to own and exploit landed property.

Because the church had not been organized in Russia until Vladimir's conversion, it had not had the opportunity to build up resources with which to support itself. It had to rely at first upon the bounty of the prince for its maintenance. Probably, for the first few years after his baptism, Vladimir personally met the church's expenses as a sort of out-of-pocket expenditure. Then, as was pointed out earlier, he promised to give it a tithe of his "property and of his cities." The provision for the con-

[25] Chadwick, *Beginnings*, pp. 20-21, 24-25.

tinuance of this source of church revenue was included in the so-called Church Statute of Vladimir which laid down regulations for church organization and jurisdiction. The Prince of Novgorod supported the Cathedral of St. Sophia from the income of his properties until they were taken from him and turned over to the cathedral. And soon after its establishment the church began receiving gifts of land from princes.[26]

Besides gaining land through gifts, the holdings of the church were extended through the colonizing activities of monastic foundations. Monasteries had come to Russia with Christianity. The existence of twenty are known for the eleventh century, and approximately fifty new ones were organized in the next century. Most of them were located in or near large towns, but in the twelfth century a number were founded in the frontier lands of the Northeast. Many of these colonizing foundations had started as the hermitages of monks who wanted more solitude than they could find in their old monasteries. The reputation for sanctity of these eremites had drawn others to their retreats, and soon a new convent had come into being.

The total amount of land owned by the church, or by any individual church establishment, is unknown, but the existing sources make it clear that by the twelfth century the religious had extensive holdings. This is indicated by the accounts of the often lavish gifts by princes of villages, slaves, and land to the church, and by reference to the internal organization of what were obviously large complexes of church-owned land.[27]

The nobility formed the third element in the class of large landowners. As was the case with the church, these upper class proprietors owed their holdings, in largest part, to the bounty of the princes. A further similarity is that only a very few indications of noble landownership are found before the last part of the eleventh century.

[26] Gorchakov, *O zemelnykh vladeniiakh*, pp. 46-47; Goetz, *Staat und Kirche*, pp. 11-12, 133, 139; Golubinskii, *Istoriia*, I, i, 511, 513, 520, 621-627; Grekov, *Krest'iane*, p. 103.

[27] Cf. *Letopis po lavr. spisku*, p. 340; Golubinskii, *Istoriia*, I, i, 522n.; Grekov, *Feodal'nye otnosheniia*, p. 80; Goetz, *Staat und Kirche*, pp. 142, 146; *idem, Das Kiever Höhlenkloster*, pp. 132, 133.

When the Varangians established their domination of Russia a new elite had come into being that was distinct from the native Slavic aristocracy. It had its origins in the retinue (*druzhina*) or following of each Viking chieftain. These were the men who served him as aides and counsellors, and who, above all, fought for him. His fame, his power, even his life, depended upon their loyalty and bravery. In the *Tale of the Raid of Igor*, the great epic of the Kievan age, the bard sang the praises of these men, telling that they were:

. . . swaddled under trumpets, cradled among helmets, nursed at the spear's point.

To them the roads are known and the ravines are familiar; bent are their bows, open their quivers, sharpened their sabres.

Like grey wolves in the field they roam, seeking honor for themselves, and glory for their Prince.[28]

They served their leader by terms of mutual and voluntary agreement that could be terminated at any time at the wish of either the retainer or the principal. The retainer was free to leave his lord and enter the following of another, and the lord could dismiss a retainer whenever he wanted to.

In return for the services his retainers gave him, the prince supported and protected them. Originally, they lived with him as part of his household, and depended for their maintenance upon the booty won in the prince's wars and the tribute he exacted. The chronicler in his account for the year 945 told how the men of Prince Igor's *druzhina* said to their lord, "The servants of Sveinald are adorned with weapons and fine raiment, but we are naked. Go forth with us, O Prince, after tribute, that both you and we may profit thereby." In a later entry he wrote that Prince Vladimir's retinue complained because they had to eat with wooden spoons instead of with silver ones. Whereupon the prince hastened to order that silver spoons be provided "remarking that with silver and gold he could not secure a retinue, but that with a retinue he was in a position to win

[28] Cross translation in Gregoire, Jakobson, and Szeftel, *La geste du Prince Igor*, pp. 153-155.

these treasures, even as his grandfather and his father had sought riches with their followers."[29]

The increasing ramifications of the ruling families, the heightened internal strife, and the intensification of the fight against the nomads, led to a multiplication in the number of retinues. By the latter part of the twelfth century perhaps as many as 100 princes had their own *druzhiny*.[30] In addition, some of the most important of the princely servitors had their own followings. This happened as early as the tenth century. Sveinald, whose retainers were envied by Prince Igor's *druzhina*, was himself the most prominent member of that prince's retinue. In the saga of Olav Trygvason, later king of Norway, it was related that when he was a member of Prince Vladimir's retinue he "had himself a great company of warriors at his own costs with the means the king gave him."[31] By the latter part of the Kievan era, with the atomization of princely inheritances, it is probable that some of the greater nobles had retinues that were larger than those of the less important princes.

Early in its history the *druzhina* divided into a greater and a lesser, or senior and junior retinue. The senior group included those who had distinguished themselves in war or in the prince's councils, or who commanded sizable forces of their own which they could put at the disposal of the prince. These grandees filled the highest posts in the military and administrative organizations of the rulers. The retainers who held the lesser offices in their principal's service, either as men-at-arms or as administrative and manorial aides, were in the junior *druzhina*. Some of them were sons of senior retinue members, while others were of humble origin and even, like the *ministeriales* of medieval Germany, of unfree status. They could ascend to the senior *druzhina* when they grew older or when they became of greater military or administrative value to the prince. Wealth and family connections also aided in rising from the lower to the higher retinue.

29 *Russian Primary Chronicle*, pp. 78, 122.
30 Stählin, *Geschichte*, I, 68.
31 *Heimskringla*, p. 129.

A career in the *druzhina* of a great ruler or lord offered a road to fortune and prominence, no matter what the racial or social origins of the retainer. Until the end of the tenth century the princely retinues were composed mainly of Varangians. In the eleventh century members of the native Slavic aristocracy began to join them. This coalescence of the local nobility with the prince's servitors produced a new aristocracy that was known collectively as boyars, a term that had hitherto been applied only to the chief members of the princely retinues. The first indications of the creation of this new upper class appear in the *Primary Chronicle* at the end of the tenth century when the term boyars, retinue, elders, and prominent men, began to be used interchangeably.[32] From then on the chronicler no longer made any distinction between the native and the princely aristocracy, referring to all the leading men in Kievan social, political, and economic life as boyars. The fusion was completed by the twelfth century except for Novgorod. There the native nobility maintained its separate identity, with its own set of interests that clashed frequently with the ambitions of the princes and their followings.

A fundamental characteristic of the *druzhina* had been that its members had lived with their principal and had been entirely dependent upon him for their support. In the eleventh century this system began to be discarded in favor of grants of land made by the princes to their followers. This change is probably attributable to the greater size of the retinue, making it too expensive for a prince to maintain it out of his own income, and to the fact that the wealth of the princes was increasingly in land rather than in the more liquid form of war booty and tribute.

The prince, of course, expected the followers to whom he gave land to continue in his retinue, and to perform all the duties that had been demanded of them when they had been part of his household. But the Kievan man-at-arms, unlike his analogue in medieval Western Europe, did not receive this land as a fief to be held on condition of his continued service to his principal. Instead, he became the outright owner of the property. If he decided to leave the prince's service he kept the land, and owed

[32] Cf. *Letopis po lavr. spisku*, pp. 105-106, 123-124 (987 and 996 A.D.).

no obligation for it to the prince who had given it to him. Thus, it was possible for a man to be a member of the *druzhina* of one prince, and own land in the realms of one or more other rulers in whose retinues he had formerly served. On his death his property was divided according to the directions he gave in his will; if he died intestate it was divided equally among his heirs; and if he left no sons, daughters could inherit.[33]

Given these conditions, it was inevitable that the retainer who was granted land should assume a far more independent position than he had hitherto enjoyed. For now he was no longer dependent for his living upon the prince's continued bounty. His income, his power, and his social prestige became based increasingly upon the possession of real property. As could be expected, the first to break away from immediate dependence upon the prince were members of the senior *druzhina*. The lesser servitors found it more difficult to leave the court, so that their settlement on the land proceeded more slowly.[34]

References in the chronicles to boyar-owned land complexes are extremely infrequent before the late eleventh and early twelfth centuries. Then they begin to be mentioned more often, especially in connection with the destruction of boyars' villages in the wars between the princes. In addition, the Expanded Version of the *Russian Law* is informative with respect to noble landownership. In the earlier *Pravda* of the Sons of Iaroslav only the properties and manorial personnel of the princes are mentioned, but in the revised and enlarged edition, dating presumably from the early twelfth century, the boyar appears along with the prince as a great private landholder.[35]

There is no reason to believe that by the end of the Kievan era private ownership by princes, boyars, and the church had become so widespread that most of the land belonged to them. It seems much more likely that the largest part remained in the hands of the independent peasant communes. But it is certainly clear that well before the end of the Kievan period private

[33] *Medieval Russian Laws*, sect. 91-95, pp. 51-52; Hötzsch, "Adel und Lehns-wesen," p. 546; Grekov, *Krest'iane*, p. 267.

[34] Grekov, *Krest'iane*, p. 109; Vernadsky, *Kievan Russia*, pp. 139, 169; Iushkov, *Ocherki*, p. 145.

[35] *Medieval Russian Laws*, sect. 14, 46, 56-62, 64, 66, pp. 38 ff.; sect. 91-95, pp. 51-52.

ownership of large landed properties had become common among the topmost levels of Kievan society; that the land they owned either had been taken from the peasant communes or else had been newly colonized; and that the properties of some of these landowners must have been extensive rural economies. It is to a survey of the way in which these large complexes were run and of the labor force that worked them that we now turn.

3

ESTATE ORGANIZATION AND
LABOR FORCE

INFORMATION about the internal arrangements of the landed holdings of the great proprietors is sparse and indirect. But it is enough to indicate that they were carefully planned enterprises, staffed by an elaborate managerial hierarchy, and worked by large numbers of peasants, hired and indentured laborers, and slaves. In view of their complex organization it can be assumed that a large part of their output was for the lord's own account. The Kievan magnate apparently preferred to exploit much of his property by engaging in direct production, rather than turning it over to leaseholders and drawing his income from his land in the form of rents in cash and kind. Had he chosen the latter course he would not have needed the corps of managers and laborers that he did employ. The princes and the great lords had long been active in trade and, possibly, when they became landowners their commercial orientation persuaded them to take advantage of the expanding demand for rural goods by producing for the market themselves. It is, of course, probable that much of what they raised went to maintain their own large household establishments. But they could have gotten much of the goods they needed for this purpose by renting out their land in return for payments in kind. Since the scanty evidence points to the conclusion that they did engage in direct production, it seems justified to believe that at least some of what they raised, and perhaps a good deal of it, was intended for sale.

Already in the eleventh century the properties of the princes, the first great landowners, were well organized establishments. The headquarters of each land complex owned by the prince was the manor house where the *ognishchanin*, the major-domo, of the estate, lived, and where the prince stayed on his occasional visits. Surrounding the big house were the dwellings of other principal members of the staff, among them being the steward (*tiun*), and the chief groom or constable, who was known as the "master of the stable." The importance of these men (who apparently often were slaves) was shown by the wergild of 80 grivnas that was set in the later editions of the *Russian Law* for their murder—the highest amount levied by the *Pravda*. The complex was broken down into a number of semi-independent units, each called a *selo*, corresponding to the villa of contemporary Western Europe. Each *selo* presumably had its own fields, meadows, garden plots, barns, and so on. The *selo* was headed by an official called, in the *Russian Law*, the elder of the *selo*, who was the analogue of the *villicus* of the West. In addition, there were field supervisors who directed the work of the indentured peasants, the slaves, and the hired hands who tilled the lord's demesne in each *selo*.[1]

The earliest information suggestive of the actual size of individual princely latifundia is provided by an entry in the Hypatian Chronicle for 1146 describing the plundering of two properties belonging to two sons of Oleg, Prince of Chernigov. On one of the estates there were 700 slaves, and extensive cellars where 500 *berkovetsy* of mead and 80 tuns of wine were stored. The other had 900 grain stacks on its threshing floors, and warehouses and cellars with unspecified contents. The chronicler also reported that 4,000 horses owned by the two princes were taken by the looters.[2]

The early sources contain still less data about the properties of the church and the boyars. Their organization was apparently much the same as that of the manors of the prince, though undoubtedly not as elaborate since they must not have been as large. In the biography of Feodosi, abbot of the Kievan Monastery of the Caves, written not long after his death in 1074, there are references to a well-developed system of manorial exploitation on that monastery's lands, with mention of administrative officials, farm laborers, and slaves. Later records of the monastery frequently mentioned its villages and manors, and its hierarchy of estate managers and workers.[3]

---

[1] Grekov, *Krest'iane*, pp. 111-114; Iushkov, *Ocherki*, p. 130.

[2] *Letopis po Ipat'evskomu spisku*, pp. 235, 237.

[3] Goetz, *Staat und Kirche*, p. 146; *idem, Das Kiever Höhlenkloster*, p. 133.

A sampling of references to church holdings in the sources of the twelfth century indicate that they must have been extensive. When the eparchy of Smolensk was created in 1137 Rostislav Mstislavich, prince of that land, presented the new bishop with a large gift of property that included two villages, complete with renters and slaves, vegetable gardens, meadows, a stretch of untilled land, and lakes. Prince Iaropolk Iziaslavich of Kiev gave three districts of his realm to the Monastery of the Caves, and his daughter Anastasia, on her death in 1159, left this monastery five villages. When Prince Andrei Bogoliubskii built the Church of the Virgin in Vladimir-on-the-Kliazma (1158-1161), the annalist reported that he gave the church "many estates and the best villages and pieces of land."[4] These and other allusions to munificent gifts to churches and monasteries leave the impression that already in the twelfth century the religious owned much landed wealth.

The holdings of lay proprietors are mentioned much less frequently in the sources and without any information about their size. A number of articles in the Expanded Version of the *Russian Law*, however, dating from the early twelfth century, contain references to the managerial personnel, free and unfree laborers, livestock, and farm buildings and implements, of properties that belonged to boyars.[5] These articles make it clear that the holdings of some of the boyar landowners must have been of considerable proportions.

Despite the increase in the number of these large privately owned properties, it is likely that by the end of the Kievan era most of the land, as was pointed out earlier, was still in the hands of independent peasant communes. The *smerdy* who were members of these organizations continued to run their economies either as individuals or as collectives according to the nature of their commune. But when communal land was converted into the private property of a prince or boyar or of the church, the communers lost their economic autonomy together with their land. Those who were fortunate became renters. Others were apparently pushed off their holdings, possibly to

---

[4] Golubinskii, *Istoriia*, I, i, 522n.; *Letopis po Ipat'evskomu spisku*, p. 338.
[5] *Medieval Russian Laws*, sect. 14, 46, 56-62, 64, 66.

make room for the creation of seignioral demesne. They became the hired hands, or contract workers, or indentured laborers, of the proprietor. Still others must have been compelled to sell themselves into slavery in order to find livelihoods for themselves and their families.

The *smerdy* who became the tenants or hired laborers of the proprietors who had taken their land remained free men. But because they were now dependent for their living upon the proprietors, their legal as well as their economic status was more precarious than that of the *smerdy* who still lived in independent communes, and their social status was lower.[6] These conclusions emerge from an analysis of a series of articles in the two later codifications of the *Russian Law*, the *Pravda* of the Sons of Iaroslav and the Expanded Version. The former code was concerned, in largest part, with the protection of the private property of the princes, and with the people who managed and labored on their estates. In articles dealing with the damages to be paid the prince for offenses against his property and personnel, *smerdy* are listed along with the men who clearly were manorial employees of the ruler—his bailiffs, stewards, overseers, contract laborers, and his slaves (art. 19-28, 32-33). The rationale of these ordinances must have been that such offenses were contrary to the private economic interests of the prince, depriving him of the service of his employee or the use of his property, and therefore entitling him to an indemnity from the culprit. The damages that had to be paid the prince for the mistreatment of the *smerd* would indicate that the peasant was covered by this legislation only because he, like the bailiffs, stewards, and the others, worked directly for the prince, or because he was a tenant on one of the prince's properties.

---

[6] Not all the historians of this era are agreed that there was this division among the *smerdy*. Many, especially older authorities, maintained that the status of all *smerdy* was the same. For representative views see *Pravda Russkaia*, II, 171-176. Others, notably Iushkov and Vernadsky among modern writers, insist that the term *smerdy* was not a *nomen generale* for all the peasantry, but referred only to the "dependent" peasants, i.e., those who had come under the control of a private landlord (Iushkov, *Ocherki*, pp. 89ff.), or whose legal status was limited by the prince's authority (Vernadsky, *Kievan Russia*, pp. 143-146). The interpretation presented here is that suggested by a number or historians, among them Vladimirskii-Budanov, Pavlov-Sil'vanskii, and Grekov.

If this hypothesis is accurate, indemnity was not demanded by the prince for offenses against those *smerdy* who continued to live in their own independent communes, since they were neither his employees nor his tenants. Nor is there any reason to believe that the payment made to the prince replaced the wergild of forty grivnas that had to be paid for the murder of any *smerd*, whether a free communer, or employee or tenant of the prince. Apparently it was in addition to this.

These provisions for indemnities to be paid the prince not only indicate the dependent economic relation of the *smerd* tenants and hired workers to the prince, but also reveal their humble status. For the amount of damages levied for the murder or mistreatment of the prince's people varied with their importance. Eighty grivnas had to be paid for the murder of his bailiff, steward, or master of the stable; forty grivnas for the slaying of one of his pages or cooks; and twelve grivnas if the victim was one of his farm managers or overseers (art. 19-24). But only five grivnas were charged for the murder of a *smerd* (art. 26). That was the same amount that had to be paid for the murder of one of the prince's common slaves. The prince put the same value on his *smerd* renters and hired laborers that he did on the ordinary bondsmen who stood at the bottom of the Kievan social pyramid. If someone inflicted pain without the prince's orders on his bailiffs, stewards, or sheriffs, twelve grivnas had to be paid to him as damages. But only three grivnas were required if this happened to one of his *smerdy* (art. 33).

Evidence that the *smerdy* on private estates had fewer privileges than did those living in independent communes is afforded by an article of the Expanded Version, the twelfth century codification of the *Russian Law*. This ordered that if the *smerd* died without male heirs his holding reverted to the prince (art. 90). It seems to me necessary to agree with those historians who hold that this provision could have applied only to peasants who lived on the private property of the prince.[7] The ruler could not have asserted this prerogative of escheat on land held by the independent peasant communes. Although evidence for the Kievan centuries is lacking, the data from the succeeding

---

[7] E.g., Pavlov-Sil'vanskii, *Feodalizm*, pp. 56-59; Grekov, *Krest'iane*, p. 207.

period show that vacated holdings on such land reverted to the commune, and that the individual communer could bequeath his holding to whomever he chose including female heirs.

In the Expanded Version boyars appear along with princes as great landowners. A number of articles mention their employees, equipment, and livestock, but there is no direct reference to *smerdy* living or working on their holdings. Their presence seems to be implied, however, in the Expanded Version's reformulation of the series of articles dealing with the indemnity to be paid for the murder of manorial employees of the prince. One of these articles (14) reads, "and for a contract laborer (*riadovich*) five grivnas, and the same for a contract laborer of a boyar." It seems clear that this last clause was meant to be applied to the succeeding three (and possibly the preceding three) equally brief articles dealing with damages. Article 16 stated, "and for a *smerd* or a slave five grivnas; and for a female slave six grivnas." If the assumption made here is correct, the words "and the same for a *smerd* or a slave or a female slave of a boyar" were understood.[8] Other documents of the eleventh and twelfth centuries show that *smerdy* did live on the estates of secular lords and of the Church. In some cases they are specifically mentioned, as in the charter issued by Prince Iziaslav Mstislavich in 1148 in which he stated that he was turning over land and *smerdy* to the Panteleimon Monastery.[9]

The status of the *smerdy* who lived on the lands of non-royal seigniors must have been the same as that of their fellows on the personal holdings of the ruler. It seems probable that the provisions of the various codifications of the Pravda reflected the practices followed on the properties of lay and church lords, as well as those of the prince, even when the articles referred specifically only to the latter. One indication of this was noted in the preceding paragraph: the paying of damages to the boyar for the loss of the services of his employees. Other articles of the Expanded Version are capable of this same interpretation, that is, that they referred to the personnel and property of non-royal as well as royal landowners. The series of articles dealing

---

[8] Cf. Grekov, *Krest'iane*, p. 207.
[9] Cherepnin, *Russkie feodal'nye arkhivy*, II, 115.

with slaves and indentured laborers are examples of this, for these categories of workers were found on lay and clerical as well as royal manors. Another document of the era, the Statute on Church Courts of Iaroslav, dating presumably to the first half of the eleventh century, contains evidence indicating that the status of *smerdy* on properties of the church was the same as it was on those of the princes. One of its articles ordered that holdings of "church and monastery people" were to escheat to the bishop if the occupant died without a male heir.[10] This provision is obviously an analogue of that found in the Expanded Version of the *Russian Law* dealing with the reversion to the prince of the holdings of *smerdy* who died without male heirs.

II

Although their status was lower than that of their fellows who still lived in their own independent communes, there is no evidence that the *smerdy* who were the tenants and hired laborers of the private proprietors had lost their personal freedom. In the absence of any data to the contrary, and in view of the rights men in these categories are known to have enjoyed in the next era of Russian history, it seems safe to assume that they could come and go as they pleased providing they had not entered into some special arrangement with the proprietor. But there were two other groups in the rural labor force who did not have this freedom. These were the slaves and the peons.

Slavery was an ancient institution in the Russian land and bondsmen, as the earliest Greek and Arab accounts of Russia show, had long been one of the principal items of Russian export.[11] The princes, the greatest merchants of Kievan Russia, looked upon the sale of slaves as one of the prime sources of their wealth. When the dying Princess Olga urged her son Sviatoslav to take over the throne of Kiev he told her, "I do not care to remain in Kiev, but should prefer to live in Pereiaslavets on the Danube, since that is the center of my realm, where all riches are concentrated; gold, silks, wines, and various fruits from Greece, silver and horses from Hungary and Bohemia, and

---

10 Sect. 33, Vladimirskii-Budanov, *Khristomatiia*, I, p. 204.
11 Iakovlev, *Kholopstvo*, I, 9-10.

from Rus' furs, wax, honey, and slaves."[12] Sviatoslav's son, St. Vladimir, is said to have kept 800 concubines in three of his towns for his own pleasure before his conversion to Christianity. In view of this large number, and of the trading activities of the princes, these women might well have been Vladimir's stocks of human merchandise that he planned to sell[13] (although the chronicler did describe Vladimir in his heathen days as "insatiable in vice"). The Russians sold slaves to Byzantine and eastern buyers, and at least as early as the ninth century, Jewish merchants of Southern Germany were importing Russian bondsmen for resale in the lands of Western Europe.[14]

But slaves were not only valued as articles of export. The Russians themselves were slaveowners, and slaves were of major importance in the operations of the internal economy. More attention was devoted to them in the codifications of the *Russian Law* than to any other single subject. V. O. Kliuchevskii believed they were so prominent as a form of private wealth in these early times that the concept of private landownership grew directly out of slave ownership. "This land is mine because the people who work it are mine," he wrote, "such must have been the dialectical process by which the right to hold real property has come down to our day."[15] The law provided for substantial rewards to the captor of a runaway bondsman and imposed heavy fines on anyone who knowingly aided a fugitive.[16]

Information about the proportion of slaves in the labor force of the private proprietors of the Kievan era is lacking, but the scraps of data that are available seem to indicate that they formed a consequential (and to some historians the preponderant) part of it. There are a number of references in the codes of the *Russian Law* to slave workers on the lands of the great proprietors, ranging from stewards and other important officials down to field hands. According to a chronicle account there were, in 1146, 700 slaves on just one property owned by Prince Sviatoslav of Chernigov, and Nestor, in his life of Abbot Feodosi

---

[12] *Russian Primary Chronicle*, p. 86 (969 A.D.).
[13] Cf. Golubinskii, *Istoriia*, I, i, 146-147.
[14] Verlinden, *L'esclavage*, I, 218, 220.
[15] Kliuchevskii, *History*, I, 186.
[16] *Medieval Russian Laws*, Expanded Version, sect. 112-115, p. 55.

of the Monastery of the Caves, spoke of the slaves who worked on the lands of that monastery.[17]

A chief source of slaves must have been the prisoners taken in war, for the Russians, following a centuries-old custom, enslaved both captured soldiers and civilians. Many, perhaps most, of these captives were redeemed after the war ended, either by their families or friends, or by working out their ransom. Rulers also concerned themselves with recovering these people. The earliest Russian treaties, made with the Greeks in 912 and 945, contained provisions for the ransoming of prisoners of war.[18] Bondage for many war prisoners, then, must have been only temporary. Other sources of slaves were described in the Expanded Version of the *Pravda*. The children of slave parents were slaves, but the progeny of a union between a slave woman and her master were freed on the death of the father (art. 98).[19] Indentured peasants who tried to run away before the completion of their agreed term of service, or who stole, could be enslaved (art. 56, 64). It is possible, too, that bankrupt merchants whose insolvency was the result of their own misconduct or poor judgement could be sold into slavery to settle the claims of their creditors (art. 54, 55). The wording of the pertinent articles is ambiguous, however, so that perhaps the law's intent was that only the bankrupt's property, and not his person, should be sold.

Besides those who became slaves involuntarily there were others who entered bondage of their own free will. The *Pravda* (art. 110) explained they could do this by selling themselves into slavery, by marrying a female slave, or by accepting a post as a steward (*tiun*). Safeguards were set up by the law to prevent abuses of these provisions. A minimum price of one-half grivna was established for the man who sold himself, and the transaction had to be made in the presence of witnesses. The man who planned to marry a slave could escape enslavement for him-

---

[17] *Letopis po Ipat'evskomu spisku*, p. 235; Goetz, *Staat und Kirche*, p. 146.

[18] *Russian Primary Chronicle*, pp. 68, 75.

[19] In some of the extant copies of the *Pravda* the mother was also supposed to be freed. *Pravda Russkaia*, I, 446-447. Art. 98 ordered that these children had no rights in the estate of their father, but the statute of Prince Vsevolod of Novgorod (*ca.* 1135) provided that the son of such a union was to receive a horse, armor, and an appropriate amount of money on the division of his deceased father's property. Kulischer, *Russische Wirtschaftsgeschichte*, I, 61.

self if his future wife's owner gave his consent, and, similarly, a man who became a *tiun* did not become a bondsman if his employer was willing to let him keep his freedom.

The slave was the chattel of his owner and was completely without rights. A clause in the *Pravda* article on wardship ordered the guardian of the minor to account for all the property in his keeping, including "the progeny of both the slaves and the cattle" (art. 99). The procedure laid down for the recovery of a stolen slave was the same as that prescribed for getting back other stolen property, although the law explained that the slave "is not a beast," because he was able to talk and so could give information about his abductor (art. 38). But he was like a beast in that he was at the complete mercy of his owner, who could do anything he wanted with him, even to killing him. No penalty had to be paid for the murder of a slave unless the victim belonged to another master and was killed without provocation. That was considered a crime against property, and the male-factor had to compensate the dead man's owner for his loss and pay a fine of twelve grivnas to the prince in addition (art. 89). The master was legally responsible for all the actions of his slave (art. 46). Slaves could buy and sell, borrow, and own property, but always in the name of their owner (art. 116, 117).

Although all bondsmen were legally on the same footing, there were actually sharp distinctions among them. The thrall who managed his master's property, or who was allowed to engage in trade and acquire property of his own, or who served in the retinue of a prince or a boyar, was obviously far above the humble domestic or field slave. The difference was reflected in the penalties that had to be paid for the murder of a bonds-man belonging to the prince. If the victim was a *tiun* the levy was 80 grivnas, if a slave bailiff, tutor, or nurse, 12 grivnas, and if an ordinary slave, only 5 grivnas (art. 12, 13, 16, 17).

It was possible for a slave to buy his own freedom if his master agreed, but this road to freedom must have been available only to a few. More frequently, manumission was gained through the testament of the slave owner. This practice was encouraged by the church. Unlike the church in the West, the Russian church countenanced the enslavement of Christians. But it early sought to ameliorate the lot of the bondsmen, tried to raise the moral level of the master-slave relationship, and encouraged emancipation.[20]

On the basis of scattered references in the sources it has been estimated that the usual price of a slave during the tenth-twelfth centuries was around five grivnas. Other sources of the era show that a sheep or a goat sold for six *nogaty* (there were twenty *nogaty* in a grivna), a swine for ten *nogaty*, and a mare for sixty *nogaty*. In times of glut the price for humans broke sharply and great bargains could be had. That happened, for instance, in 1169 when Novgorod won a major battle against the forces of the Prince of Suzdal. The victors took so many prisoners that the market in Novgorod for slaves was flooded and they were forced to sell their captives for as little as two *nogaty*, or just one-fiftieth of the usual price.[21]

Indentured laborers made up the other large group of unfree men in early Russian society. These people had borrowed from a wealthier man who held them in compulsory servitude until they had paid him back. Actually, the work they performed for their creditor only paid the interest on their loans, so that it must have been well-nigh impossible for them to regain their freedom through their own efforts.

During the Kievan era these peons were known as *zakupy*. There seemed to have been a sizable number of them, since they were held partly responsible for an uprising of 1113 in Kiev. In the legislation issued after this revolt, and later incorporated in the Expanded Version of the *Russian Law*, considerable attention was given them. Not all the *zakupy* were necessarily rural laborers; merchants and artisans who were unable to meet their obligations could have been indentured to their creditors. But it seems clear from the contents of the pertinent articles of the *Pravda* that many, and perhaps most of them, were peasants.

The terms of *zakup* indenture were so harsh that only men in the direst need could have been willing to take loans under such conditions. The debtor had to perform whatever work his creditor (or lord, *gospodin*, as the creditor was called in the

20 Eck, "Les non-libres," pp. 30-31.
21 *Ibid.*, p. 23; Aristov, *Promyshlennost*, p. 281.

Pravda) ordered him to perform. If he tried to escape his obligation by fleeing, he became the permanent slave of his lord if he
was caught (art. 46). If he stole his lord had to reimburse the
injured party, but the peon thereupon became his slave, or, if the
lord chose, he could sell him into slavery, using the proceeds to
pay back the victim for his loss and pocketing any money left
over (art. 64). The *zakup* could not serve as a witness in court
actions except in minor disputes, and then only when it was
absolutely necessary to have his testimony (art. 66). On the other
hand, the law gave him a certain amount of protection against
wilful acts of his lord. He could come to the prince's court to
complain of injustices done him by his lord, and the court was
charged to give him relief (art. 56). If the lord tried to sell him
into slavery he was freed of his obligation to repay his loan, and
the lord had to pay a fine of twelve grivnas (art. 61). The lord
was also subject to a fine if he beat the debtor without cause
(art. 62), if he tried to sell the indenture on him to a third
person (art. 60), or if he possessed himself of the peon's personal
property (art. 59).

In addition to the *zakupy* the *Russian Law* mentioned two
other categories of farm workers who also were bound to the
performance of labor for the proprietors. One group, called the
vdachi, was made up of people who had received a subsidy
(*dacha*) from a landowner. Presumably they had been ruined by
some catastrophe, such as a famine or a war, and in their
distress had turned for help to a wealthy lord. The money or
grain he gave them was considered to be a gift from him and not
a loan. Nonetheless, the *vdachi* had to work for their benefactor
for a fixed period in return for his help.[22] The other group,
called the *riadovichi*, are believed to have been laborers who had
made a contract (*riad*) with the proprietor to work for him for a
specified term. They must have been used for ordinary field work
since the fine that had to be paid their employer (as compensation for the loss of their services) if one of them was slain was
only five grivnas, the same indemnity required if one of the
lord's *smerdy* or common slaves was murdered.[23]

[22] *Medieval Russian Laws*, Expanded Version, sect. 111; Vernadsky, *Kievan Russia*, p. 148.

[23] *Medieval Russian Laws*, Short Version, sect. 25.

Besides these people who had voluntarily bound themselves to work for a seignior there was still another group of free men who had fallen into a position of dependence. They were known as the *izgoi*. These were the *déclassés* of the Kievan civilization, men who had lost their roles and were unable to find new ones. Because one of the church's functions was to provide refuge for the casualties of society these people were put under its care. In return for the assistance and protection given them the *izgoi* were apparently required to work for the church or monastery to which they were attached.

The Statute on Church Courts, issued by Prince Vsevolod between 1125 and 1136, named three sources from which the *izgoi* came: the illiterate sons of priests, freed slaves, and insolvent merchants. Later "orphaned princes" were added to the list. This was a strange mixture, ranging from the lowly freedman to royalty. But each of these categories shared one common characteristic; they were all peculiarly liable to the danger of losing their social function. The clergy, few in number in these first years of Christianity in Russia, was an hereditary caste (the Eastern Church allowed its priests to marry). Sons were presumably trained to follow their fathers into the ministry; the boy who had not learned his letters was unable to enter the calling for which he was destined. Unless the freed slave who was without resources sold himself back into slavery, or found someone who was willing to make him a loan, he was unable to find a place in society for himself. The bankrupt merchant, if he was fortunate enough to have escaped being sold into slavery to satisfy the claims of his creditors, was without the capital he needed to continue in business, and so he also became declassed. The "orphaned prince" was that unlucky member of the ruling house who, because of the premature death of his father, had lost his position in the line of succession to the throne of Kiev. In the complicated and still obscure system of succession that developed after the death of Iaroslav in 1054, the Prince of Kiev apparently had a paternal rank with respect to his brothers who occupied the thrones of the lesser cities. When the Prince died his oldest surviving brother succeeded to the throne of Kiev, and all the other princes moved up one step. If one of the brothers of the

Prince of Kiev died before the Prince, the sons of the dead man were no longer in the line of succession, providing the Prince of Kiev or his surviving brothers had sons. Presumably, these were the "orphaned princes." Trained to be rulers and now deprived of the chance of following this career, they were without a social function and joined the ranks of the *izgoi*.[24]

[24] Szeftel, "La condition juridique," pp. 434-438.

4

THE TATAR YOKE: AGE
OF DECLINE

THE LIVELY ECONOMIC ACTIVITY of the Kievan era began to show signs of faltering in the twelfth century. The principal cause for this seems to have been the inability of the Russians of the Dnieper valley to defend themselves against the nomads of the steppe. The invasions were an old story in Kievan history. Up to the second quarter of the twelfth century the Russians had been able to check the successive waves of Patzinacs, Torks, and Cumans that rolled in. Then the outbreak of destructive civil wars after the death of Vladimir Monomakh in 1125, bringing internal unrest and anarchy, made it well-nigh impossible for the Kievans to maintain effective defenses against the invaders, and the raids came with unprecedented frequency and violence. The ever present threat and the all too frequent reality of these incursions, combined with the internal disorders, introduced a new and frightening insecurity into the life and commerce of the Dnieper valley. More and more of the people fled to the Northeast in the hope of finding safety in the forested land that lay between the Oka and Volga rivers. By the latter part of the twelfth century, Kiev's importance had declined so much that the chief prince of the Northeast was now recognized as the most powerful ruler in Russia.

The foreign trade that was so important in Kievan economic life suffered, too, from the conquests of the nomads. They established their control over the territory between the Don and the Danube, and made it increasingly difficult for Russian merchants to trade with Byzantium and the East. But the final collapse of this branch of Kievan commerce was brought about by the successes of the first crusades. The growth of direct trade between Western Europe and the East that followed the victories of the crusaders ended the need for the Kiev-Novgorod detour.

Still, these setbacks might well have been overcome and Kievan economic life could have at least held its own. Some of the losses in the eastern trade were cancelled out by an increase in the Baltic commerce of Novgorod and Pskov, and by the efforts made by the merchants of Smolensk to develop their overland trading connections with Central Europe. B. A. Rybakov, in his history of early Russian handicraft production, found that important branch of economic activity actually expanding in Kiev and elsewhere in the twelfth and early thirteenth centuries.[1]

In the thirteenth century, however, Russia received the hardest in a series of blows from which she was not to recover for well over two hundred years. This shock was the invasion in force of the Mongols, or Tatars. Their approach, heralded by raids of their horsemen, had long cast a premonitory shadow across the Russian land. Finally, late in 1237, under the leadership of Batu, grandson of the great Chingis-Khan, they burst into Russia. Sweeping through the Oka-Volga region they stopped short of Novgorod and turned southward into the Dnieper valley. In December, 1240, they wound up their Russian campaign by sacking Kiev, and then rode on into Poland and Central Europe. They left a trail of death and destruction behind them, for their standing operating procedure was to burn to the ground every city they took, to enslave as many of the vanquished as they wanted, and to put the rest to the sword. "Not an eye was left open to weep for those that were closed" was the way the chronicler described the fate of Riazan, first Russian city to fall to the Mongols. Six years after the taking of Kiev, Plano Carpini, papal envoy to the Mongols, passing through the Kievan territory, saw "countless skulls and bones of dead men lying about on the ground," and found that Kiev, itself, had scarcely two hundred houses left in it. City after city had met this fate. In just the month of February 1238 alone, the invaders destroyed fourteen towns, among them some of the most important cities of the realm.[2]

There is no data revealing the extent of the total Russian losses in people and goods from this first Mongol onslaught, but

---

[1] Rybakov, *Remeslo*, pp. 521-522.
[2] Hammer-Purgstall, *Geschichte*, pp. 101-104, 106-108; Plano-Carpini, *History*, pp. 29-30.

it must have been enormous. Besides the many thousands they slew and the property they destroyed, the Mongols' customary practice, according to Plano Carpini, was to take ten percent of all the people and all the goods that were left.[3] Nor did the losses end when the Mongols rode west out of Russia. They soon swung back and settled in the Eurasian steppes where the Mongol state called the Golden Horde came into being. From here they maintained an hegemony over the Russians that was to last for two and a half centuries. This was the era of the "Tatar yoke."

The Kievan federation, already greatly weakened by the earlier nomad invasions, by the internal feuds of the princes, by the dwindling in trade, and by the steadily declining prestige of Kiev itself, was unable to survive this last and greatest disaster. Many of the people who still lived in the once populous Dnieper princedoms fled westward into Galicia. Others migrated to the Northeast, into the princedoms that lay between the Oka and the upper Volga. This was the region destined to become the heartland of Russian national life. The Dnieper basin, the center of the Kievan era, was ultimately absorbed by the rulers of Lithuania and then became part of Poland. Thus came into being the tripartite division of the Russian people into the Great Russians, who lived in the Northeast and whose history now became that of Russia; the White Russians, who lived along the upper Dnieper; and the Little Russians, or Ukrainians, whose home was in the middle Dnieper valley.

The Mongols, ruling Russia from their headquarters in the steppe, collected heavy and continued tribute. Worse still, they made many more invasions in force into the Northeast in which the horrors of their first campaign were often repeated. Forty-five Tatar-Russian wars have been counted during the era of the Mongol domination, and in addition there were Tatar raids without number. Nor were the Mongols the only foreign enemies against whom the Russians had to fight in these centuries. There were at least forty-one wars with the Lithuanians, thirty with the German crusading orders, and forty-four more with Swedes, Bulgars, and others.[4]

[3] Plano-Carpini, *History*, pp. 38-39. [4] Eck, *Le moyen âge*, p. 59.

Invasion was just one of the ills that oppressed the land. Early in the 1350's the Black Death entered Russia. Pandemics were not new phenomena there, any more than they were in the rest of Europe. The first recorded outbreak was in the eleventh century. In an epidemic in Smolensk in 1230, 32,000, and in Kiev in two weeks in 1290, 7,000, were reported to have perished. But the epidemic in mid-fourteenth century Russia, as in the rest of Europe, was the most deadly of the plague's visitations. It raged through country and city—in two cities everyone is said to have died of it—and it kept returning. Twenty eruptions are mentioned in the chronicles between 1348 and 1448, and at least five of these engulfed all, or the largest part, of the land. After an outbreak in Smolensk in 1387 only five people were left alive, if a chronicler is to be believed, and a foreign writer claimed that 80,000 died of plague in Novgorod in the 1390's.[5]

Another affliction Russia suffered in these centuries was the almost ceaseless fighting between the principalities into which the land was divided. Ninety of these internal wars have been counted between 1228 and the accession of Ivan III to the throne of Moscow in 1462. Inevitably, they caused much death and destruction. Finally, famines, brought on by unfavorable weather, by locusts, by forest fires that swept across the tilled clearings, as well as by the destruction of wars and invasions, were frequent. Most of the time the crop failures were local phenomena, but on occasion they encompassed entire regions and sometimes all of Russia.[6]

The effect of all these calamities was to push Russia into a long period of economic, as well as political, decline. Because of the paucity of the data only the outlines of this downturn in economic life can be traced. But the available evidence, direct as well as indirect, indicates clearly that the depression was of long duration and considerable intensity, and that two of its outstanding characteristics were depopulation and a large number of empty peasant holdings. Remarkably enough, just as the Kievan prosperity had its European parallel, so, too, did this era

[5] Solov'ev, *Istoriia*, IV, 1210, 1221-1224; *Entsiklopedicheskii slovar*, XXXIX, 39.
[6] Solov'ev, *Istoriia*, IV, 1219-1221.

of decline from the thirteenth into the fifteenth centuries. The downturn in Russia began a century earlier than it did in the rest of Europe, which had escaped the Mongols save for their brief excursion into Central Europe. But once the long contraction began in other lands it was marked by the same features of depopulation and abandoned holdings that were so prominent in the Russian experience.

There are only occasional direct statements in the contemporary Russian materials relating to these phenomena. The most plentiful evidence is furnished by the frequent references in the sources to *pustoshi*, by which was meant abandoned lands. In document after document of the fourteenth and fifteenth centuries much land and many villages are described in this manner.[7] Equally significant, though indirect, indications of the sparseness of population are the many charters issued by princes giving landowners the right to offer peasants freedom from various governmental obligations so that they could attract them to settle on their lands; the care princes took to ensure that new settlers did not come from royal estates or from other manors in their realms, but were brought in from other princedoms; the willingness with which landlords advanced loans and subventions to prospective tenants; and the efforts that began to be made to restrict the peasant's freedom of movement.[8] The thinness of settlement impressed the Venetian, Josafa Barbaro, one of the very few Europeans to visit Russia during the Mongol era. In describing a journey from Moscow into Poland around the middle of the fifteenth century, he wrote that he travelled "through woods and little hills which be in manner desert." "It is true," he continued, "that travelling from place to place, whereas others have lodged before, you shall find where fire hath been made . . . and sometimes a little out of the way you shall find some small villages: but that is seldom."[9]

The depopulation was not limited to rural areas. The cities, so central in Kievan economic life, with only a few exceptions declined into unimportance. Their number was reduced to not

[7] See, for example, the entries listed under *pustoshi* in the indices of *DDG*, p. 521 and *ASEI*, I, 756.

[8] These matters are discussed in succeeding chapters.

[9] Barbaro, "Travels," p. 34.

much more than half of what it had been before the Mongols came. Only a few new urban settlements were established and these were of little significance. A listing of references to cities in the contemporary materials shows that a total of 79 cities were mentioned in the sources of the fourteenth century, of which number only four had been newly founded, and 78 in the fifteenth century, including nine new ones.[10]

With but few exceptions these cities of the Mongol era were little more than administrative and military centers. Their economic function did not go much beyond supplying some of the needs of the princes and their courts, and of the royal administrators. Since these men drew most of what they consumed from the output of their own lands, or, in the case of the administrators, in the form of payments in kind from the people they governed, the market they provided must have been a very limited one.[11]

Novgorod (which was never conquered by the Tatars) and Moscow were the two outstanding exceptions to this picture of general urban decline. Thanks in large part to the Hanseatic League trading station that had been set up there, Novgorod became one of the main commercial centers of the eastern Baltic. In its heyday, in the thirteenth to fifteenth centuries, its population has been estimated at from fifty to one hundred thousand people.[12] Moscow, at the beginning of the Mongol domination a place of little importance, grew steadily. In 1337 a fire levelled the town—like other Russian cities it was built almost entirely of wood—and according to the chronicle, eighteen churches were destroyed. In 1343 there was another great fire—the fourth in fifteen years—and this time twenty-eight churches were reported to have been consumed. In 1382, when the Mongols under Tokhtamysh sacked the city, 35,000 Muscovites are supposed to have lost their lives and another 25,000 to have been taken away as captives. But the city was already so large that it was able to recover speedily from this huge loss. Little more than a decade later it covered a larger area than it had before Tokhtamysh came. In 1446 the Mongols demanded

10 Smirnov, *Posadskie liudi*, I, 76, 77n.
11 Bakhrushin, "Predposylki," p. 38.
12 Vernadsky, *Zven'ia*, p. 126; Gitermann, *Geschichte*, I, 107.

2,000 rubles from the Muscovites, on the basis of two rubles per hundred residents, indicating that they reckoned the city's population at 100,000.[13]

If these estimates are accurate Moscow and Novgorod were among the greatest cities of all Europe. In the latter Middle Ages very few urban centers anywhere had more than 20,000 inhabitants. The only ones that rivalled the Russian metropolises in size were Milan and Venice, each with over 100,000 (mid-fourteenth century), Paris with an estimated 80,000 (1378), and Florence and Ghent with around 55,000 each (mid-fourteenth century).[14]

Apart from the physical destruction they suffered at the hands of the Mongols, the cities were unable to regain their erstwhile importance in the economy because the Tatars stripped them of their skilled craftsmen. These workmen were conscripted into the khan's service and were taken away to live in the Mongol world. The Tatars followed this practice not only because they wanted the goods these artisans knew how to make. They also had a military purpose in mind. They figured that by depriving the Russians of the services of the craftsmen who knew how to make weapons and armor and build fortresses they would weaken the Russian war potential. The result of this policy was the near-disappearance of urban handicraft production in the first century of the Mongol domination. This took away a major part of the economic function of the towns. Now, no longer able to get city-made goods, peasants had to depend upon their own skills and on village handicraft production, while landlords recruited or trained staffs of artisans to work in shops on the manor to meet their needs. Some of these workmen on princely and monastic properties were former city artisans who had managed to escape from their Mongol captors, or who had been ransomed from them by their seignior-employer.[15]

Another important reason for the deterioration in city life during these centuries was the decline in the importance of trade. The large amount of self-sufficiency that developed out

13 Nazarevskii, *Iz istorii Moskvy*, pp. 28, 52-53; Bazilevich, "Opyt periodizatsii," p. 79; Hammer-Purgstall, *Geschichte*, pp. 393-394.
14 Dollinger, "Le chiffre," pp. 34-35.
15 Rybakov, *Remeslo*, pp. 525-534, 591-592.

on the land bears witness to the low level of commerce. Internal trade was almost entirely on a local scale. The shipping of merchandise, always difficult and often perilous before the modern era of transport, now became even more hazardous because of Tatar and Russian brigands who preyed on travelling merchants. There was some regional exchange, though, and treaties between princes, and between the Republic of Novgorod and various princedoms, from the fourteenth century on contained such commercial clauses as tariff concessions and promises of unrestricted trading rights to one another's merchants. Novgorod was especially involved in interregional commerce, not only because of its preeminence as a commercial center, but also because the city was dependent for grain upon the Oka-Volga area.[16]

The Mongols were interested and active in foreign trade, and merchants, whether Mongol or foreign, enjoyed a special and high status among them. But they preferred to monopolize trade when they could, so that direct Russian exchange with the East all but disappeared in the first century after the Mongol conquest. In time Russian merchants began to penetrate into Mongol territory, but foreign merchants, except for Mongols, rarely came into the Oka-Volga region. The only place where commerce with Western Europe retained its importance was Novgorod. The chief exports of that city were furs, hides, leather, wax, hemp, flax, and fish oil. Some of these wares originated in the princedoms of the Oka-Volga region, but most of them came from Novgorod's own great colonial empire that stretched across the top of Russia from the Baltic to the Urals. In return for these raw and semi-processed goods, the Hanseatic Germans, who dominated Novgorod's foreign trade, brought in manufactured commodities, especially textiles.[17]

Russia still continued to be a supplier of slaves for foreign parts. In fact, the number of Russians in the human cargoes shipped by Italian merchants from the Black Sea to the western Mediterranean rose steadily from the thirteenth to the

[16] Eck, *Le moyen âge*, pp. 36, 334, 336-337; Kulischer, *Russische Wirtschaftsgeschichte*, I, 109-110.

[17] Spuler, *Die goldene Horde*, pp. 388-409; Vernadsky, *Mongols*, p. 343; Eck, *Le moyen âge*, pp. 338-341; Kulischer, *Russische Wirtschaftsgeschichte*, I, 118-155.

mid-fifteenth century (when the fall of Constantinople cut off Italian Black Sea commerce).[18] It seems probable that these were people who had been captured by Mongol raiders and sold to the Italians, though perhaps some of them may have been brought out of Russia by native merchants.

The overall unimportance of professional trade was reflected in the failure of a merchant class to develop in the towns of the interior. Even in the great trading center of Novgorod, the Russians who were most active in business and who held the highest offices in the city's government were, apparently, more landowners than merchants. Data on the holdings of about sixty of these oligarchs in 1478 when Novgorod was annexed by Ivan III of Moscow show that they, or members of their families, owned tracts of land in the Novgorodian hinterland. Most of them owned more than one, many owned more than ten, and two men, both of whom had served as mayors of the city, each owned twenty-nine. Presumably, the major part of their incomes came from the sale of the goods produced on their properties, particularly such products as furs, fish, salt, iron, and tar, rather than from their activities as commercial middlemen.[19]

The dwindling of foreign trade was also an important factor in isolating Russia from the rest of Europe. The wide commercial connections of the Kievan realm had made Russia well known in the west. Now the only direct contact with these lands was through Novgorod. The dread that filled Christian hearts at the thought of the Mongols kept all but a brave handful from venturing into the interior. Russia became a land of mystery to the rest of Europe.

I I

Yet, despite these sharp differences, and others discussed in later pages, between the conditions that prevailed in the two periods, there was still a continuous line of development from the Kievan centuries on into the era of the Tatar yoke. Many of the legal and social institutions and much of the culture that had evolved in the Dnieper valley lived on in the Northeast. The

---

[18] Verlinden, *L'esclavage*, I, 334-340.
[19] Artsikhovskii, "K istorii Novgoroda," pp. 112-117.

migrants who settled the Oka-Volga triangle even brought old place names with them, much as did the pioneers who colonized America, so that it is often possible to trace origins of colonizing groups by the names they gave the settlements and streams in their new home.[20]

Among the more unfortunate of the legacies from Kiev was the continuance of strife between the princes. The practice of splitting up princedoms to provide realms for the sons of each generation of the ruling houses was another unlucky inheritance. The fate of the Grand Duchy of Vladimir illustrates the effects of this custom. Two generations after the death of Prince Vsevolod in 1212 this principality had been split through inheritance into twelve parts, each with its own ruler. The process continued, so that by the fifteenth century there were scores of tiny princely seats in what had once been a single principality. A similar fate overtook other princedoms, the degree of their fragmentation varying directly with the fecundity of each successive generation of its ruling house.

These petty domains were called *udely*, portions, because they were their holder's alodial share in his family's patrimony. The individual *udel* was more the private manor of its possessor than a political unit, so that the *udel* prince was more seignior than sovereign. The people in his domain did not form a permanent political community. They were his subjects so long as they lived in his *udel*, but, with the exception of his slaves and indentured people, they were free, up to the latter fifteenth century, to leave whenever they wished, and, apparently, there was much movement between the *udely*. As a consequence of these developments, whatever community of princely interests that had existed in the loose Kievan federation disintegrated in the Mongol era.[21]

The only overall political supremacy that did exist was held by the Tatars. But they did not absorb the Northeast into their own political organization, the Golden Horde. The day-to-day rule of the Northeast was allowed to remain in the hands of the native princes. The khans of the Golden Horde gave patents to

[20] Liubavskii, *Obrazovanie*, pp. 4-16; Presniakov, *Obrazovanie*, pp. 34-36.
[21] Kliuchevskii, *History*, I, 256-263.

certain princes establishing them as the chief rulers of their principalities, or Grand Dukes as they were called, with the other princes who held *udely* in this principality being made subordinate to them. After the collapse of the Kievan federation, Vladimir had won general acceptance as the foremost Russian principality, so that the man who held the khan's patent recognizing him as Grand Duke of Vladimir was, at least nominally, first among the rulers of the Northeast. A struggle for the possession of this title, waged between the princely houses of Tver and Moscow, was finally won by the Muscovites, who thereby emerged as the dominant native rulers during the Tatar era, and ultimately became the unifiers and autocrats of the whole Russian land.

The story of the rise of the Muscovite dynasty from minor princelings to supreme rulers over a sub-continent began in 1263 when Daniel, youngest son of Alexander Nevskii, Grand Duke of Vladimir, was made prince of the provincial town of Moscow, thereby converting it into the capital of an independent, albeit small and unimportant, principality. Two centuries later, when his great-great-great-great-grandson Ivan III ascended the throne, the princedom, built up through purchase, conquest, inheritance, and diplomatic coups, covered about 226,000 square miles.[22]

The success of the Muscovite house seems best to be explained by a combination of the favorable geographical location of Moscow and lots of good luck. Their capital lay at the intersection of important overland routes, while the Moscow River, on whose banks the city rose, connected the two chief river systems of European Russia. But fortune played the major part in shaping Moscow's destiny. First and possibly of greatest importance, most of the twelve men of Daniel's line who sat on the throne of Moscow seemed to have possessed a greater amount of native ability and craftiness than is usual among princes. They were, on the whole, not particularly distinguished as war leaders, but they were astute politicians in their dealings with their fellow princes, and, above all, in their skill in keeping the favor of the Tatar suzerains as long as it was of benefit to them. And to a

22 Arsen'ev, *Statisticheskie ocherki*, pp. 53-54.

man they were ruthless. Only the last of the line, Fedor (1584-1598), was a simpleton, and by his time the great work had been done.

Still another piece of luck was that from the establishment of the dynasty to its extinction 335 years later, each prince, save one, had a reasonably lengthy reign, and the majority were on the throne for unusually long periods. Seven of them wore the crown for more than a quarter of a century and five of these seven had reigns of 36, 37, 42, 43 and 51 years respectively. These long tenures meant that the internal instability and the political disasters that so often attended a change of rulers in other places was greatly reduced at Moscow. And although the Muscovite princes followed the contemporary practice of dividing their realm among their surviving sons, fortune smiled again, for until the end of the fourteenth century their progeny were few. By the fifteenth century the family had multiplied and there was a danger of separatist tendencies that would have wrecked the growing power of the dynasty. But beginning with the heirs of Dmitrii Donskoi (d. 1389), the eldest son always inherited the largest portion of the princedom, and because of his greater wealth and power was able to assert control over the other members of the family. The success of the Muscovite house was also greatly promoted by the decision, in the first half of the fourteenth century, of the Metropolitan of the Russian church to make Moscow his official residence, thereby adding enormously to the prestige of that city.[23]

Deliverance from the Mongol hegemony was an essential element in the exaltation of the Moscow dynasty. This liberation actually was due more to the internal collapse of the Golden Horde than to Russian military prowess. During the fifteenth century the Horde had grown progressively weaker, and its control over the Northeast became ever more tenuous. Ivan III (1462-1505) made the final break, refusing to recognize the suzerainty of the khan, to pay tribute, or to make the customary visits to the Mongol court to render homage. Then the last khan of the Golden Horde was assassinated, his sons were slain in battle with the Crimean Tatars, and the Golden Horde disinte-

[23] Cf. Solov'ev, *Istoriia*, IV, 1119-1140.

grated. The hated Tatar yoke was at last gone. But the Mongol menace remained, for other hordes roamed the land along Russian frontiers. During the sixteenth century there were great Tatar raids, Moscow itself falling to the Crimean Tatars in 1571. Two years later the nomads came in force again, but this time they were stopped before they reached the capital. That was their last mass invasion, but Russia's fight against Tatar brigandage and razzias was to continue for the next three centuries.

Because the Tatars during the centuries of their domination did not occupy the forested plain of the Northeast, because of the considerable amount of autonomy they allowed the Russian princes, and because Muscovite scribes of the fifteenth and sixteenth centuries who wanted to elevate the importance of the native princes are believed to have altered the written sources, it is extremely difficult to ascertain to what extent Russian life and institutions were influenced by the Mongols. Scholarly opinion runs the full gamut, from those who argue that the effects of the Tatar yoke were negligible, to the opinion that the Russians were well-nigh asiaticized. It seems clear, however, that the Tatar impact was not great enough to break the continuity in the growth of the agrarian institutions with which this book is concerned. This is not to deny that it may well have been responsible for the accentuation of certain aspects of this evolution. For example, Russian princes may have decided that it would be easier to collect the tribute demanded of them by the Tatars if they limited the freedom of movement of the people who lived in their realms. But, as will be seen in later chapters, other motives seem to have been much more influential in persuading the rulers that such limitation was necessary. If the Tatar exactions did have an influence it was of a secondary and exogenous nature.

5

LANDLORDS OF THE MONGOL ERA

THE BOYARS OF KIEVAN RUSSIA had not been organized into a separate order or caste, nor had they been endowed with special individual or corporate privileges. In the eyes of the law they had no more rights than did any other free person. Nor was the boyardom a closed group. Anyone who distinguished himself in the service of a prince or of a city state, or who acquired great wealth, could become a member, regardless of his social origin, although it was undoubtedly easier for the son of a boyar to achieve boyarial rank than it was for a parvenu. Yet, despite this lack of any legal provisions guaranteeing them a superior status, the Kievan boyars occupied an exalted position in the social order because of their political, military, and economic importance.[1]

The social preeminence of the boyars continued after the breakup of the Kievan federation and the shift to the Northeast. But the character of the *druzhina*, the princely retinue in which the boyars had served during the Kievan period, underwent major alteration. Already by the second half of the twelfth century the chief boyars were beginning to withdraw from the princely retinues. The core of the royal *druzhiny* now was made up of the junior retainers, who came to be called, collectively, the prince's *dvor*—that is, his court. As time went on the boyars and the *dvor* became two distinct groups, and the term *druzhina* became obsolete. Boyars continued to serve the prince in peace and war, but the men of the court were the ruler's mainstay. They were of two types: those who, like the boyars, could leave the *dvor* at will, and were called "free servitors" (*slugi vol'nye*); and those called the "servitors under the major-domo" (*slugi pod dvorskim*), who were required to serve for a specified term. The free servitors included the category known as "boyar sons" (*deti boiarskie*). Originally, these "boyar sons" had probably been the scions of boyar families starting their careers, or, per-

---

[1] Vernadsky, *Kievan Russia*, pp. 140, 169.

haps, impoverished members of such families. But with time the name came to be applied to the mass of the free lesser servitors. Both the free men and slaves were among the "servitors under the major-domo." The free men upon entering the *dvor* could specify the term for which they wanted to serve, and could not leave before that period was over. The slave servitors, of course, remained in the court for as long as their owner, the prince, chose.[2]

Important boyars continued to have their own retainers, and great church lords, too, maintained corps of servitors. They used them for their own purposes but when the prince demanded military service of these grandees they, or their captains, were expected to lead their followings into battle for the prince. Grand Duke Vasilii I of Moscow, in a charter he gave to the Metropolitan around 1400, expressed this duty in picturesque language, declaring, "and should war come, when I, the Grand Duke himself, shall sit upon my charger, then also shall the boyars and servitors of the Metropolitan," explaining that they were to fight "under the banner of the Grand Duke" but "under the military commander of the Metropolitan."[3]

Meanwhile, the princely caste itself was undergoing a transformation. As early as the thirteenth century men of royal blood had become so numerous that the patrimony, and therefore the social and economic importance, of all save a few had shrunk to proportions that were equalled by the possessions of the greater boyars. In the fourteenth and the fifteenth centuries there were princes who owned just one village, and still others who were landless. This poverty-stricken royalty, along with other princelings who still had land but who wanted protection, entered the service of more powerful princes, especially of the Grand Dukes of Moscow. As a result, a new aristocratic class known as the "serving princes" came into being. Princes of foreign origin, too, took service with the Muscovite rulers and became members of this group. Their royal blood did not automatically win superior rank for these men in the prince's service, but it did give them social precedence over servitors of less distinguished birth.[4]

---

2 Vernadsky, *Mongols*, pp. 364, 371.
3 Pavlov-Sil'vanskii, *Feodalizm*, pp. 101-103.
4 Chicherin, *Opyty*, p. 284; Vernadsky, *Mongols*, pp. 367-368.

The servitors of the princes continued to receive land from their principals, but in the fourteenth and most of the fifteenth centuries, the chief form of their recompense was through appointment as governor of a district or city. The appointee was charged with the civil and military administration of the area to which he was assigned, and was also responsible for the management of any of the prince's properties that happened to be in the district. In return he received certain cash payments, such as court fees, and sometimes he was given the monopoly on the sale of spirits. His most important source of revenue, however, was in the form of produce paid him by the people he governed. This payment had to be made by everyone in the district or town, including, with only rare exceptions, upper-class property owners, though members of this group were sometimes given the right to meet the obligation in cash if they wished. The produce became the property of the administrator, who could sell it or use it himself. He also had the right to demand that the obligation be paid him either partially or entirely in cash.

This arrangement was known, appropriately enough, as a "feeding" (*kormlenie*), and the servitor holding such a post was called a *kormlenshchik*. It was scarcely a new technique of administration for, if the *Primary Chronicle* is to be believed, Riurik, the semi-legendary progenitor of the Kievan dynasty, had "assigned cities to his followers," and the practice of giving cities or districts to men of the ruling house for their support continued on after his day. In the post-Kievan era, however, it was used to provide for the servitors of the princes, regardless of whether they were of royal blood or not. The size of the *kormlenie* that was assigned varied with the importance of the servitor. The most prominent men were put in charge of major centers or wealthy districts, while lesser men were assigned to places where the revenues were smaller. The number of servitors who were supported by these appointments was increased by giving a "feeding" to an individual for only a short term of years, during which he was expected to build up a reserve that would carry him for the next few years when he was out of office. When his savings were exhausted he was given another *kormlenie*.[5]

[5] Veselovskii, *Feodal'noe zemlevladenie*, I, 76, 263-270, 279.

It seems very probable that the use of the *kormlenie* in the era of the Mongol domination was in largest part attributable to the disturbed economic conditions of that period. The income from land must have been low because of the many abandoned holdings and the decline in markets for rural products. A grant of land, therefore, would not have provided its recipient with enough means to satisfy his needs. Nor, presumably, was the prince able to pay his servitors in cash. The decline in economic activity was marked by a falling off in the use of money and in the amount that was available, so that the prince lacked the coin for monetary salaries. The only way, then, by which he could increase the revenues of his servitors was to arrange for them to receive payments in kind from the people in the districts they governed for him.

Land ownership, however, despite the low cash returns it apparently provided, assumed growing importance in social and economic life precisely because of the economic retrogression. The waning in the extent of market exchange compelled the individual consumer to become increasingly self-sufficient. He was forced to occupy himself in primary production, or depend upon rental income in the form of payments in goods, in order to satisfy his wants.

During the Mongol era, and on into the sixteenth century, there were no restrictions on the right to own land. Men of every class in society held real property in full alodial possession. Peasants, artisans, priests and their descendants, merchants, and even slaves, all appear in the sources as landowners, along with the great spiritual and temporal lords and the gentry. Slaves who owned land had to have the permission of their masters to become proprietors, but once this was given they bought, sold, and exchanged real property like free men and even gave land to monasteries. If their owners freed them they kept the land they had acquired as bondsmen. Other slaves upon emancipation were sometimes given full ownership of a piece of land by their master to provide them with the means to support themselves.[6]

The prevalence of full private landowners notwithstanding, the ruler of each princedom considered all the land in his

[6] *Ibid.,* pp. 205-208.

realm as his property in that it was part of his patrimony. He referred to his princedom as his *votchina* (from *otets*, father), the heritage that he as sovereign had received from his fore-bears. The fiscal revenue he drew from the land and people of his princedom was also called his *votchina*, for this, too, was part of his patrimony. He had to recognize the existence of pri-vately owned properties in his realm because during the era of the Tatar yoke no prince was strong enough to implement his claim to supreme ownership of all the land in the princedom. But he never relinquished that claim, and in his charters and treaties he referred to these privately owned properties as being "in my votchina." When a strong central power finally emerged in the Russian land this never-forgotten claim was to have momentous consequences.[7]

In addition to considering himself as the proprietor of all the land in his realm in his capacity as sovereign, the prince as a private individual was a landowner. The properties that he owned personally were described in the sources as his villages, his hamlets, or his purchases. The chief members of the most important ruling houses were the greatest individual private landowners of their time. Apparently their fiscal revenues as sovereigns were not big enough to meet their needs, for they seem to have depended heavily upon the income from their personal landed properties. They sought constantly to increase these holdings through purchase, marriage, conquest, confisca-tion, and colonization. As the power of a dynasty increased, so did the personal possessions of its members. Grand Duke Ivan I of Moscow (called *Kalita*, Moneybag), in the will he made in 1328 before going off to pay homage to the khan, arranged for the disposition of 54 properties that he owned. A century later his great-great-grandson, Vasilii II, in his will listed over 125 properties that belonged to him, and there were still others he did not mention by name. Vladimir Andreevich, Prince of Serpukhov (d. 1410), and grandson of Ivan I, left 38 separate properties; Iurii Vasil'evich, Prince of Dmitrov (d. 1472), son of Vasilii II, left 31; and Prince Ivan Borisovich of Volotsk (d. 1504), grandson of Vasilii II, left over 50.[8]

[7] El'iashevich, *Istoriia*, I, 159-170.
[8] Bakhrushin, "Kniazheskoe khoziaistvo," p. 14.

Church institutions, and especially certain monasteries, also owned huge complexes. In the Republic of Novgorod, for example, nearly 25 percent of the land belonged to the clergy in the latter fifteenth century. Most of the property of the religious came as donations from princes and lords. Often these men made their gifts in their old age and even on their death-beds to gain "eternal remembrance" for their souls through the prayers of the grateful monks. In addition, churchmen bought property, and sometimes acquired it by foreclosing on mortgage loans they had made to lay proprietors. Once in the possession of a religious body the land became inalienable, for church tenure was recognized as perpetual. As a result, there was a steady accretion in the total size and number of ecclesiastical holdings.

Remarkably enough, the church owed not a little of its worldly success to the religious policies of the Mongols. One of the few good things that can be said for the Mongols is that they practiced religious toleration. In fact, the khans gave the Russian clergy a specially privileged status, freeing them, their peasants, and all the non-clerical people connected with the church in various capacities, of all obligations and tribute. Mongol officials were ordered to keep out of church land, and were severely punished if they mistreated church personnel or appropriated or damaged church property. These privileges gave the church seigniors an advantage over other landlords in attracting men to enter their service and persuading peasants to rent land from them.[9] Religious institutions were also the most favored recipients of the charters of immunity given by Russian princes (pp. 85-89), so they were able to offer the further advantage of exemptions from many obligations due the prince.

During the Kievan period most monasteries had been established in or near cities. This practice continued in the succeeding era, but a much larger number were set up in frontier regions. One reason for this was that land there was easier to come by. Princes were glad to give it to the monks, or if it already belonged to someone, the proprietor was willing to sell it at a low price. A second and undoubtedly more basic explanation for this monastic pioneering was the outburst of religiosity that took place in Russia in the fourteenth and fifteenth cen-

9 Schultz, *Russische Rechtsgeschichte*, pp. 81-82.

turies. The sad state of the contemporary world seemed to make many people decide that living in it was futile and worthless, so they turned their backs on it and spent their lives in work and prayer under a monastic rule out at the edge of civilization. There were close connections, too, at this time, between Russian monasticism and the monks of Mt. Athos, in Greece. The asceticism and discipline practiced there inspired imitation on the part of the Russians.

The monks, with the devotion and industry often characteristic of their calling, brought much land under cultivation. Their pioneering role, however, has sometimes been exaggerated, for often new monasteries were established in regions that were already peopled, albeit scantily, by peasants who had been the original colonists. On occasion the monks tried to take over the lands of these settlers. Naturally, the settlers resisted, either legally by appealing to the courts of the prince, or with violence. There were instances when they burned down monasteries and destroyed their cattle, and in some places they actually succeeded in driving away the monks. The lives of saints of the Russian church who were founders of important monasteries tell of the "persecution" of these holy men by outraged peasants. Nor was it long before some of the communities forgot their original eremitic purpose, accumulated great wealth and lived in much comfort and even luxury.[10]

There were great landowners among lay seigniors, too. An incomplete listing of the properties confiscated from Fedor Andreevich Sviblo, once one of the chief boyars of Dmitrii Donskoi of Moscow (1359-1389), discloses that he owned not less than fifteen properties scattered over a wide area. Ivan Iur'evich Patrikeev, son of a former Grand Duke of Lithuania, grandson of Vasilii I of Moscow, and one of the chief serving princes of Ivan III, in his will of 1499 listed a total of fifty properties in fourteen districts, ranging from small holdings to large domains. The extensive holdings of the oligarchs of the Novgorod Republic at the time of its annexation by Ivan III were referred to earlier. The surviving fifteenth century land registers for

10 Liubavskii, *Obrazovanie*, pp. 17-30; Veselovskii, *Feodal'noe zemlevladenie*, I, 77-78; Miliukov, *Ocherki*, I, 52; Budovnits, *Russkaia publitsistika*, pp. 10-14; Danilova, *Ocherki*, pp. 146-181.

Novgorod show that before Ivan III's confiscations just 27 men had owned over one-third of all the land held by the 1,632 lay proprietors listed.

The great majority of private proprietors, however, owned small pieces of land. Thus, two-thirds (1,063) of the just mentioned 1,632 Novgorod landowners owned all together just about 10 percent of the total amount of land belonging to lay proprietors. These smallest landowners were known in Novgorod Land as the *zemtsi* or *svoezemtsi*. A few of them owned as much as 100 desiatins (270 acres) but the great majority had far less. In the princedoms the smallest proprietors were not distinguished by any special name. They were so unimportant that they were not given the immunities that customarily accompanied private landowning. Their holdings often were no larger than that of a peasant, and about the only thing that set them apart from the peasants was they were the owners of their land and not renters.[11]

The attitude of the great landowners toward their properties was in sharp contrast to what it had been in the Kievan era. The magnates of those centuries, as we have seen, had organized their holdings into latifundia, and market production had presumably been an important part of their economic activities. Now large proprietors, except for those in Novgorod, had little or no interest in raising goods for sale. Instead, they tended to be divorced from the market and to strive after as much self-sufficiency as possible. The small amount of trade in which they participated was primarily to get commodities that were not found on their lands, such as salt or metal products. They bought these wares with the income they received from the sale of wax, furs, honey, and other forest products, or by direct exchange. Everything else that was consumed in the peasant's hut, in the residences of the magnates, in the monasteries, and in the courts of the princes, was homegrown or homemade. Moreover, only a small part of the commodities that landlords consumed were produced by their own agricultural activity. On most properties there were only small demesnes, and on many

11 Veselovskii, *Feodal'noe zemlevladenie*, I, 146-148, 203-206, 287-288; Grekov, *Krest'iane*, p. 485; Brinkmann, "Die ältesten Grundbücher," p. 94; Danilova, *Ocherki*, pp. 99-146.

there were none. The proprietors turned over their land to peasants or to their slaves in return for rentals paid predominantly in kind, which the lord used to meet the needs of his household.[12]

This lack of interest on the part of proprietors in direct production and their preference for the role of rent receiver is readily understandable in view of the decline of markets and the drop in population. Even if a lord wanted to produce in quantity on his own account he had much difficulty in finding the necessary labor, unless he was fortunate enough to have a large number of slaves. For if he was successful in attracting peasants to settle on his land they preferred the status of tenant farmers to that of hired laborers, and rents in kind to labor rent. Since peasant-renters were much in demand, the lord had to give them what they wanted. Often, too, the properties of great landowners was broken up into relatively small sections by intervening forests and swamps. It was easier to lease out these holdings than to try to operate them as a unit.[13]

As could be expected, there were exceptions to this generalized picture. One of them was Medno, a medium-sized estate of about 435 desiatins. It lay on the main road between Novgorod and Tver, and on the banks of the Tvertsa River, a tributary of the Volga, chief water highway of the era. These good communications made markets easily available, providing the opportunity for Medno's owner to raise farm products for sale. A boyar named Mikhail Fominskii had purchased the estate around the year 1400 from a Novgorodian. Thirty-five years later Fominskii's son gave it to the Trinity-St. Serge Monastery. The deed conveying the gift listed as the donor's chattels forty-two horses, sixty-five head of horned cattle, 130 sheep and goats, and nearly 2,900 *korobei* (ca. 34,800 bushels) of grain in the barns, besides that standing in his fields. Obviously, intensive seignorial production must have been the practice at Medno. Much of the necessary labor was apparently provided by field slaves (*strad-*

---

[12] Sergeevich, *Drevnosti*, III, 92-93; Bakhrushin, "Kniazheskoe khoziaistvo," p. 41; Veselovskii, *Feodal'noe zemlevladenie*, I, 146-150, 155-156; Grekov, *Krest'iane*, pp. 500-506.

[13] Grekov, *Krest'iane*, p. 616; Liashchenko, *Istoriia*, I, 194-195.

niki), since twenty of Fominskii's horses are identified as being used by them. The deed also recorded that 54 rubles were owed him by peasants, so it is likely that additional labor was supplied by these debtors working out their loans. Hired labor, recruited from the families of peasant renters, may also have been employed.[14]

The usual proprietor, however, if he was interested at all in direct production, focused his attention on exploiting the natural resources of his property, such as fur, salt, honey, wax, and fish. These articles were not only useful in his own domestic consumption, but were in demand, were expensive in relation to their bulk, and could be shipped long distances over the existing poor means of communication without losing value. Lords sought estates where these resources had not yet been worked, or were still plentiful. Salt beds were especially valued. There were some good deposits in Novgorod Land, but in princely Russia they were few in number and low in productivity. Salt was therefore one of the most sought after commodities of the period. Furs, especially beaver, were also highly prized.[15]

In the charters of sale, gift, or exchange of land, conventional means of defining the boundaries of the property by references to topographical features were sometimes employed. But because land was so plentiful and population so scant, it was not unusual for the charter merely to state that the boundaries were to run "as far as the axe, the plow, and the scythe have gone." Beginning around the middle of the fifteenth century, this indefinite phrase was used much less frequently[16]—an indication, presumably, of a growing demand for land and an increasing population.

The organization of the economy of the landowner varied in complexity with the amount of property he owned. The smallest proprietors ran their holdings themselves. Medium-sized proprietors entrusted the general direction of their lands to a steward who was often a slave. The magnates needed more assistance to run the many individual properties they owned,

---

14 Veselovskii, *Feodal'noe zemlevladenie*, I, 157-158.
15 Veselovskii, *Feodal'noe zemlevladenie*, I, 154; Solov'ev, *Istoriia*, IV, 1164-1165.
16 Cherepnin, *Russkie feodal'nye arkhivy*, II, 68.

and to provide them with the large amount and variety of goods and services required for the maintenance of their households. Servitors, free and unfree, each with a staff of subordinates, were in charge of different branches of the magnate's economy, and often were allowed wide autonomy. Labor was supplied chiefly by slaves, supplemented by peasant-debtors working out their loans and by hired workers.[17] A glimpse into the manorial organization of a great proprietor at the end of the fifteenth century is provided by the will of Ivan Iur'evich Patrikeev. He mentioned over one hundred of his slaves by name, and for some of them included their occupation. Among those he listed were seven stewards who managed individual villages and their surrounding lands, two armorers, three tailors, two carpenters, four cooks, two bakers, three firemen, two archers, one clerk, six gardeners, two huntsmen, one fisherman, four millers, three falconers, one poultryman, one kitchen gardener, two stokers, and one master silversmith.[18] The wide range of occupations covered in this incomplete roster gives an idea of the extent of Patrikeev's operation and the degree of self-sufficiency he tried to attain.

II

Though the prince claimed ownership of all the land in his realm this meant little or nothing so far as the property rights of the private landowner were concerned. He was responsible neither for service nor allegiance to the ruler in whose realm his property was located. Just as in the Kievan era, the man who was in the service of a prince was free to leave when he wished and, even if he entered the service of another prince, he kept the land his former principal had given him. This remarkable independence continued on nearly undiminished until the sixteenth century, when the rulers of Moscow established their hegemony over the Russian land and there was but one prince left to serve. Already in the latter part of the fourteenth century, however, inroads began to be made by the Grand Dukes of Moscow upon the right of free departure of boyars

[17] Tarakanova-Belkina, *Boiarskoe i monastyrskoe zemlevladenie*, pp. 60-62; Bakhrushin, "Kniazheskoe khoziaistvo," pp. 15-16, 39-41.
[18] *SGGD*, I, no. 22.

and serving princes. In the reign of Vasilii I (1389-1425) the principle was established that the sovereign could confiscate the departing servitor's property if he decided that the boyar had committed treason. During the civil wars of the second quarter of the fifteenth century Vasilii II brought such charges against boyars who had left his service for that of his enemies. He confiscated the lands of some of these men, and allowed others to keep their properties on condition that they renounce their right of free departure.[19]

The landowner could dispose as he pleased of the land he had acquired through purchase, exchange, or gift. But before he could transfer ownership of inherited property to a stranger he had to have the consent of all members of his family (*rod*). Such property was considered part of the family patrimony (*rodovye votchiny*) rather than belonging alone to the person who had inherited it. The *rod* was a relatively small group of individuals claiming descent from a common ancestor, though it also included some who were related by marriage rather than blood. If the seller of inherited land failed to get the consent of any one of these kinsmen, that person, however distantly related, had the theoretical right to repurchase the property at the sale price. In practice this right was exercised only by near collateral relatives—brothers, uncles, and nephews. Direct offspring of the seller did not have this privilege, on the ground that being his children they were subject to his control and so were presumed to be of the same mind as their parent. At first there was apparently no time limit set on the kinsmen's right to repurchase, but by the fifteenth century the redemption had to be made within forty years of the alienation. (This time limit was retained until the 1830's when it was reduced to three years; thus modified the right of redemption continued until 1917.) If the property was not bought back by a member of the *rod* within this period the land was no longer considered part of the family patrimony. Land could also lose its special familial character and not be subject to redemption if the prince confiscated it because its owner had fallen under his ban; or if through court action the land was taken away from the owner because he was bankrupt

[19] Alef, *History*, pp. 397-405.

or had committed a felony; or if it passed by inheritance through the female line and thereby became the property of another *rod*.[20]

The landowner could bequeath his property in any manner that he chose (so long as he did not leave inherited property to strangers without the family's consent), but the usual procedure was to divide it between his male heirs. The successive splinterings of the patrimony that resulted from this practice could lead easily to the ultimate impoverishment of a family. Members of each successive generation inherited ever smaller and often scattered parcels. In Novgorod Land, the cadastral surveys made at the turn of the fifteenth century show that the ownership of a number of properties was split up unequally among as many as nine people, and at least one village was divided among sixteen people. Nearly all ranks were to be found among these owners of fractions of a property, from the humble farmer to the great clerical or lay magnate.[21]

The damaging effects of this mode of inheritance upon family fortunes were made all the worse by the uncertainties of contemporary political and economic life, and by such natural calamities as famine and plague. Thus, in 1332 a powerful noble named Rodion Nestorovich Kvashnin came to Moscow from Kiev with a following of 1,700 men to enter Muscovite service. Understandably, he was greeted with open arms by Grand Duke Ivan I, who made him a member of the Moscow boyardom and presented him with vast grants of land. After his death Rodion's properties began to be divided up among his heirs, the process continuing with each successive generation. In addition, pieces of the patrimony were given away as dowries for female mem-

[20] Veselovskii, *Feodal'noe zemlevladenie*, I, 18-32, 36-37.

A closely analogous system of repurchase by kinsmen, called *Aviticität* was established in Hungary in 1351 and persisted until 1848. Redemption by a kinsman of patrimonial land could be made at any time within 40 years of the sale. (Blum, *Noble Landowners*, pp. 64-66.) In Western France, redemption by kinsmen, called *retrait lignager*, was practiced from the 13th century to conserve patrimonial property, though the time limit for repurchase was far shorter (at the most just 40 days) than it was in Russia and Hungary. (Yver, "Les caractères originaux," pp. 342-343.)

[21] Sergeevich, *Drevnosti*, III, 68.

The splintering of a single rural property among a number of owners was not unique to Russia. For this practice in 13th century England see Kosminsky, "Services and Money Rents," p. 30.

bers of the family, some of it was sold, and other parts given to monasteries. Then, in the campaign against the boyars waged by Ivan the Terrible in the mid-sixteenth century, the family was threatened with the confiscation of all of its remaining property, and the execution of its members. To escape this fate the Kvash-nins turned over their holdings to monasteries, who then took the erstwhile landowners under their protection. By the 1580's all that was left to the family of the huge area that had belonged to their illustrious forbear, Rodion, was a farm of around 65 acres.

The disintegration of the patrimony of lesser clans often went much more quickly. Iakov Voronin, who lived in the second half of the fourteenth century, owned about 6,750 acres in Pereiaslav. He had five sons among whom his property was divided upon his death. Beset by the evils of plague, famine, and continued parcelling among heirs, Iakov's descendants were soon so impoverished they had to sell their patrimony, and by the second quarter of the fifteenth century were landless.[22]

Most of the land given away by princes in the era of the Mongol domination became the full, private possession of the grantee, and the prince had no further control over its disposition. But rulers also distributed land on condition of continued service. If the recipient failed to carry out his duties the prince could take the land back. Usually, these conditional grants were made to the lesser servitors, free and unfree, who made up the prince's *dvor*: his men-at-arms, some of his household servants, his artisans, stewards, huntsmen, and the like. The more important men in the royal service sometimes received conditional land grants, but they were more likely to be rewarded by an appointment to a lucrative "feeding," or by outright gifts of real property. The land the princes used for these benefices came from their own personal properties—the practice of distributing state lands on service tenure did not begin until the latter part of the fifteenth century. Wealthy boyars and monasteries also made land grants on condition of service to their free and unfree servitors. In addition, small and weak land-

---

22 Veselovskii, *Feodal'noe zemlevladenie*, I, 165-169, 192-202. For other examples v. *ibid.*, pp. 169-192.

owners sometimes put themselves and their property under the protection of some great church or lay magnate, voluntarily transforming themselves into servitors holding their land on condition of continued service.[23]

These conditional grants were made either because the princes, or the boyars, could not afford to maintain their courts out of their own revenues, or because they found that it was cheaper to provide for their lesser servitors by giving them benefices than it was to support them directly. This system, moreover, held definite economic advantages for the great landowners. Since their properties were often scattered over a wide area and split into many small pieces, it was difficult, and even impossible, to manage them efficiently and profitably. When the magnate handed out these units as benefices he not only provided a supervisor for the operation of the piece of land, in the person of the servitor, but also received income from the property in the form of the services furnished him by the man to whom he turned over the holding. Furthermore, the sparseness of the population and the sporadic distribution of peasant settlement meant that large parts of a great lord's properties must have been unworked. By giving out benefices to servitors the lord promoted the cultivation of unused land and the more efficient utilization of land already in cultivation, thereby adding to the overall value of his holdings.[24]

The earliest reference to the granting of a benefice is in one of the two extant wills written by Ivan I of Moscow, dating from 1328. Ivan explained that he had turned over a village in Rostov to Boris Volkov in return for Volkov's service to him and his descendants, and ordered that the land was to be taken from Volkov if he failed to live up to his obligation.[25] Later sources make it clear that the granting of land on conditional tenure became fairly common in the later fourteenth century and increasingly so in the fifteenth century. In the latter part

---

[23] Vladimirskii-Budanov, *Obzor*, pp. 582-585; Rozhdestvenskii, *Sluzhiloe zemlevladenie*, p. 43; Pavlov-Sil'vanskii, *Feodalizm*, pp. 104-107.

In Western Europe land grants on condition of service were also made to menials, such as cooks, carpenters, and grooms, as well as to men-at-arms (e.g., tenure by serjeantry in England, Pollack and Maitland, *History*, I, 282-390).

[24] Rozhdestvenskii, *Sluzhiloe zemlevladenie*, p. 42.

[25] *SGGD*, I, no. 22.

of the fifteenth century land held on condition of service began to be called a pomestye, and its holder a pomeshchik.

Service tenure did not become widespread, however, until the sixteenth century. The problem of its origins and early history has attracted much attention from Russian scholars because it ultimately became extremely important, and because of the historiographical debate on whether feudalism of the Western European type existed in medieval Russia. Although it has sometimes been claimed that service tenure was known in Kievan Russia it is generally believed that it originated during the era of the Mongol domination. The fact that it was apparently not used before that period has led to the suggestion that its introduction was the result of foreign, and especially Tatar, influence. It is, of course, entirely conceivable that the idea could have been borrowed from abroad, but it seems most probable that it was an indigenous phenomenon, rising out of the needs of the time. Given the problems of contemporary political and economic life, it seems a natural sort of solution for the princes and great landlords to adopt.

III

Another development of the era of the Tatar yoke that held much importance for the future was the acquisition by landlords of governmental powers over the people who lived on their lands. The princes gave them charters that allowed them such privileges as jurisdiction over their peasant renters, immunity from interference by royal officials in their relations with their renters, and exemptions from the payment of taxes and other obligations to the prince. The extent of the concessions made by the ruler varied; great proprietors were given wider powers than lesser men, and the prince always reserved certain rights for himself. But for most purposes the peasants living on privately owned land became more the subjects of their landlords than of the prince.

It is possible that this system of seignorial authority had already begun to emerge in the Kievan era, but if it did exist at that time it must have been quite limited, at least so far as nonroyal landowners were concerned. Apparently such a proprietor did not have the right to judge or to punish the free peasants who lived on his land. He did have this power over those peasants who had borrowed money from him and had bound themselves to work for him until they had repaid the loan. But even here his authority was limited, for, as was pointed out on an earlier page, the indentured peasant, or *zakup*, could appeal to the court of the prince if he felt that the lord had not given him fair treatment, and if the lord had the *zakup* beaten without cause he had to pay him damages. Moreover, whatever power the lord had over the *zakup* derived from the latter's status as a debtor and not from his residence on the lord's land. Once he paid off his debt he reverted to his prior condition of free peasant and was no longer subject to the lord's judicial powers.

The accident of residence on privately owned property, then, did not make the peasant a subject of the proprietor in the Kievan period. Nonetheless, there are indications that jurisdiction by seigniors over their renters was not unknown in that era. Peasants living on the personal properties of the prince must have been especially exposed to this possibility. These people had no one to whom they could appeal for protection against the actions of their lord. For all practical purposes they must have lived under a regime of seignioral authority because their landlord happened also to be their sovereign.[26] Surviving documents also show that on occasion public rights were transferred to private landowners. In a charter of 1130 giving land to the Novgorod Monastery of St. George the donors, Prince Mstislav Vladimirovich and his son Vsevolod, ordered that the monks were to collect taxes and levy fines on the people living on the land.[27] Similar privileges seem also to have been given in the charter granted in 1148 by Prince Iziaslav Mstislavich to the Pantaleimon Monastery of Novgorod.[28] Other data indicate that possibly by the end of the twelfth century private landowners, especially in the western part of the Kievan federation,

[26] Vernadsky, *Kievan Russia*, p. 204; Grekov, *Krest'iane*, pp. 114-115.
[27] Vladimirskii-Budanov, *Khristomatiia*, I, 112-113.
[28] Cherepnin, *Russkie feodal'nye arkhivy*, II, 115.

were exercising a large amount of governmental control over their peasants.[29]

During the period of the Mongol domination, however, seignioral immunities became a conventional institution. There are around 500 charters of immunities extant, most of them from the fifteenth and early sixteenth centuries, conferring privileges of various sorts upon their recipients. They were awarded not only to great church and secular lords but to lesser proprietors, too, and to holders of benefices. Sometimes even groups of peasants and artisans were allowed to have certain immunities for fixed periods to persuade them to settle in the realm of the prince offering the exemptions.

The charters that were granted down to the end of the fourteenth century were marked by the fulness of the privileges they allowed the grantee, and by their conciseness. In the fifteenth century the scope of the concessions began to be curtailed, the prince keeping more power for himself. Instead of an omnibus grant the rulers issued charters for specific privileges, such as exempting the renters of the recipients from certain taxes and obligations, keeping royal officials out of their properties, granting judicial authority, and so on.[30]

The awarding of judicial rights to a proprietor meant that the people living on his land were withdrawn from the jurisdiction of the royal courts entirely, or in cases explicitly mentioned in the charter. There was no indication in any of these grants of judicial immunities that the peasant could appeal to the royal courts against the decisions of the lord's courts, nor was any provision made to protect them against seignioral maltreatment. The extent of the fiscal exemptions also varied. Some grantees were allowed to excuse their peasant renters from all taxes and obligations for an indefinite period, others could offer them freedom from some of these burdens but not from all, and still others were allowed to offer exemptions only for a specified period.

---

[29] Cf. Odinetz, "Poteria," pp. 205-206.

[30] Cherepnin, *Russkie feodal'nye arkhivy*, II, 113, 135-136; El'iashevich, *Istoriia*, I, 303-304; Veselovskii, *Feodal'noe zemlevladenie*, I, 115; Odinetz, "Les origines," pp. 260-261.

A number of reasons explain this delegation by princes of their sovereignty to private landlords. The isolation and inaccessibility of many parts of their realms made it difficult if not impossible for rulers to govern their subjects directly. The transfer of some of their sovereignty to landlords was a solution to this problem. Moreover, the weakness of the rulers after the disintegration of the Kievan federation, and their dependence upon the support of the nobility and the clergy, must have been a powerful influence in persuading them to divest themselves of so much of their authority. They needed the nobles and this was an important way in which they could win and keep their allegiance. Economic motives, too, must have been influential. Immunity from royal taxation encouraged the bringing of empty land and other unused resources into productive use, drew peasants from other princedoms, and thereby enriched the realm. The lords, for their part, were understandably eager to gain as many concessions as they could from the prince that would aid them to attract and hold the peasant renters from whom they drew their incomes. It was a common practice in this era of underpopulation for landlords to offer prospective tenants exemptions from the payment of seignorial obligations for a stipulated period. Their offers became all the more attractive if they could also promise freedom from the prince's taxes.

This diminution in the power of the central authority and increase in the power of the nobles was not unique in these centuries to Russia. Throughout contemporary Eastern Europe rulers found themselves compelled to share their sovereignty with the landlords, for much the same reasons that made the Russian princes adopt this policy.[31]

With the increase in the power of the Grand Dukes of Moscow in the fifteenth century, and the expansion of the Muscovite hegemony at the expense of the other princely houses, the extent of the immunities granted landlords began to be cut down. For now the Muscovite rulers were not so dependent upon their nobles as once they had been. This became particularly evident after the end of the civil wars of the second half of the fifteenth century,

[31] Cf. Blum, "Rise," pp. 823-826.

when the triumphant Vasilii II set about making himself undisputed master of the Russian land.

In general, the most extensive immunities were granted to church seigniors, although there was much variation between the privileges given different religious establishments. Some of the greatest of the secular lords were awarded powers as extensive as those allowed church institutions, but lay proprietors, as a whole, received fewer privileges. Fiscal immunities, especially, were not awarded as often as they were to church lords, and apparently beginning with the reign of Vasilii III (1505-1533) were not given at all to lay seigniors.[32]

By the middle of the sixteenth century the lord-peasant relationship had reached the point where the subjection of the peasant to his seignior was so generally accepted that it was no longer necessary for the monarch to continue the practice of granting special charters of immunities. The throne had recognized that judicial and police powers of seigniors, great and small, over the peasants who lived on their lands were inseparable appurtenances of their tenurial rights. This recognition was a very important part of the mutually advantageous bargain the Grand Dukes of Muscovy made with the seigniors in the years when the unified Russian state was being formed. Since these powers were held by all landlords it would have been pointless for the monarch to issue special charters confirming these powers to each lord.

In the Kievan era the peasant had the right of appeal to the prince's court. During the centuries of semi-anarchy that followed he had been put under the jurisdiction of the lord on whose land he lived, and had been deprived of recourse to higher authority. Still, this subjugation to the will of the landlord had been the result of special acts by the prince, forced on him by the exigencies of the times. Besides, the peasants had often drawn gains, notably freedom from state obligations for often lengthy periods, at the same time that he lost the right of appeal. In the sixteenth century, however, with Russia at last free of the Tatar yoke and united under the supreme rule of a native princely house, the peasants remained under the author-

32 Veselovskii, *Feodal'noe zemlevladenie*, I, 138-142.

ity of their lords, and (as will be shown in a later chapter) in addition were burdened with increasing obligations to both the state and their seigniors.

The silence of the Law Code of 1649 on the juridical relation between the lord and the peasants who lived on his land bears meaningful witness to the complete acceptance by the central government of the principle of seignorial jurisdiction. In this long code, in which the laws and usages that had developed during the creation of the unified state were collected and arranged, only one article touched peripherally on this relation. It stated that the seignorial peasant, who by this time had been reduced to serfdom—in large part because of the jurisdictional powers his lord had over him—could go to the tsar's court if he wanted to report a treasonous act of his lord. If his complaint was unproved he was to be beaten with the knout and turned back to his master.[33]

I V

Similarities between Russian institutions of the thirteenth to fifteenth centuries and those of medieval Western Europe gave rise to a long, often heated, and still unended historiographical debate on whether Russian society should be called feudal. The argument started as a part of the Slavophil-Westernizer controversy that rocked the Russian intellectual world in the nineteenth century. The Slavophils, intent upon proving the uniqueness of the Russian experience, claimed that the Russian people passed directly from the patriarchal or communal stage of social development to political unity without an intervening stage of feudalism. The Westernizers, equally determined on showing that Russia shared in a common European experience, argued that their country had gone through a feudal epoch. The Slavophil-Westernizer controversy finally subsided, but the debate about feudalism continues on in modern Russia, albeit in a different form. Now all Soviet scholars are agreed that Russia did go through a feudal epoch, for the simple reason that Marx declared that feudalism is one of the stages through which societies go. They define feudalism as a form of social organization in which the landlord "appropriates" part of the peasant's out-

[33] *Ulozhenie*, Chapter II, art. 13.

put either in the form of labor services or of payments in cash and kind, and is able to do this because the peasant is under his seignorial jurisdiction. But the "classics of Marxism-Leninism" do not tell when this stage began and when it ended in Russia, and Soviet historians have engaged in long and tedious discussions to settle this problem.

In marshalling data for their arguments the controversialists of the past and present have turned up much useful information. But the debate itself has been in the main a war of words between defenders of ideal types that have often been quite different from one another, but which their builders all call "feudalism."

The Russians, of course, have not been alone in this model building. Historians of Western Europe have been doing it for a long time. In fact, the concept of feudalism itself is an invention of Western scholars, "an abstraction derived from some of the facts of early European history" as one writer has put it. The constructs that have been erected, though they may vary considerably from one another, share one or more of the following attributes. They all presuppose a predominantly agrarian society in an era of political or economic decline (or backwardness), in which the central power was unable to protect its subjects, and in which economic unity and the market economy had broken down (or not yet developed). To meet this challenge a mediatization of the supreme political authority took place. A hierarchy of lords and vassals, or greater and lesser men, came into being, in which each man was dependent upon the person immediately above him in the scale. This hierarchy had a monopoly or near-monopoly of military power. The members of the hierarchy were bound by oath to obey their superior and provide him with services that were primarily, though not exclusively, of a military nature. The superior, or lord, for his part was obliged not only to protect his vassals, but also to provide them with maintenance. To accomplish this he gave them fiefs which were usually, though not always, pieces of land. In order for the vassals to draw their livings from these fiefs without working themselves, they were given broad economic and governmental powers over the peasantry who lived on the land and did the actual working of it. A given society is deemed "feudal," or "quasi-feudal," or "para-feudal," or "proto-feudal," according to the presence or absence of those attributes of the model that the builder deems the essential element or elements of the model.[34]

Obviously some of the conditions of life and of social organization in Northeast Russia during the era of the Mongol domination meet various of these criteria. It was an agrarian society in a period of political and economic decline; military service was performed by lesser men for their principals; landholding was the chief source of the wealth and power of the ruling class; the lords had extensive authority over the people who lived on their lands; benefices were given out on condition of service to the grantor; and lesser men commended themselves and their property to powerful lords. On the other hand, the boyars and the lesser members of the ruling class were clearly not vassals of the princes. There was no contract of mutual fealty binding them, so that the lord could depart at will from the service of the prince. He held his land as personal or patrimonial property and not as a fief, and did not lose it when he decided to quit the ruler's service. Moreover, it was possible for a lord to own land without serving anyone. There were men who held land on condition of service, but this form of tenure was not dominant in the pre-Muscovite era.

To term Russian society of this era feudal or not feudal, then, becomes a matter of choice and of allegiance to one model or another. It seems worthwhile, though, to recall Frederick Maitland's opinion that "feudalism is an unfortunate word," and his warning that it is an impossible task to make this "single idea represent a very large piece of the world's history."[35] In the study of comparative history it seems more rewarding to investigate the reasons for the similarities and dissimilarities between the institutions of different societies, than it does to determine the congruities and incongruities between the institutions of one society and some ideal type.

[34] Cf. Bloch, *La societé féodale*, pp. 244-249; Hintze, "Wesen und Verbreitung," pp. 157-190; Ganshof, *Feudalism*, pp. xv-xviii; Holdsworth, *Introduction*, 1, 4; Coulbourn, *Feudalism*, pp. 4-8; Stephenson, *Mediaeval Feudalism*, pp. 10-14; Vernadsky, "Feudalism in Russia," pp. 300-323.

[35] Pollock and Maitland, *History*, 1, 66, 67.

6

BLACK PEOPLE AND LANDLORDS' PEASANTS

PRIVATE LANDOWNING by members of the upper classes, as preceding chapters have shown, had made great advances since its first introduction in the Kievan era. But down into the sixteenth century there continued to be a vast area, known as the "black land," where it had not yet been introduced. Though quantitative data are lacking, it seems probable that the total extent of the black land exceeded that of privately owned property.

The peasants who lived on this land were known from the twelfth century on (and possibly earlier) as the "black people," though sometimes they were also called "peasants of the Grand Duke," or "tax-bearing people," or "commune (*volost*) people." They acted as if the land belonged to them, buying and selling holdings to one another or passing them on to their heirs. But the ruler of each princedom considered the black land, like all real property in his realm, part of his patrimony. His claim was far more successful there than it was on privately owned property. The black people themselves accepted it by paying him a regular quitrent. A more significant recognition of his rights of ownership, however, was his ability to give black land at will to whomever he chose as alodial property or as a pomestye. When that happened the black peasants who lived on the land became renters of the new landlord.

The practice of turning over black land to private lords became increasingly frequent from the latter part of the fifteenth century on. So much of it was given away that by the end of the sixteenth century it had disappeared nearly everywhere save in frontier regions. As a consequence, the great majority of the peasantry in the sixteenth century were renters of land that belonged to private proprietors or that was held by pomeshchiks on service tenure.[1]

[1] El'iashevich, *Istoriia*, I, 34, 115; Grekov, *Glavneishie etapy*, p. 48; *idem*, *Krest'iane*, p. 484.

The conversion from black peasant to landlord's peasant, when it resulted from the grant of black land by the prince to a seignior, was made without any reference to the wishes of the peasant himself. But there were also black peasants who chose freely to become renters of private landowners. Individuals and sometimes entire communities, from the thirteenth century on and possibly earlier, decided on their own to leave the black land and settle on privately owned property. Some of them were drawn from the black land by the offers of exemptions from dues and taxes, and other inducements that were held out to them by seigniors. Even though the exemptions were for a limited period these people perhaps reasoned that in the long run they would be better off as landlords' peasants. It seems much more likely, however, that the voluntary adoption of renter status was less the product of this kind of rational calculus by the peasant than the result of the successive calamities that overwhelmed the countryside from the thirteenth century on. Invasions, civil wars, pestilence, famine, and fire—a special scourge in this land of forests where everything was made of wood—must have brought ruin to many black people. After being hit by one or more of these catastrophes they lacked sufficient means to continue as independent cultivators and meet the obligations that were demanded of them, and so were compelled to settle on a private estate in order to stay alive. Some of these people still had some capital, such as livestock and farm implements, and needed no assistance from the lord beyond the exemptions he offered them. Others were not so fortunate and had to borrow from the landlord in order to get started, thereby entering into a condition of dependence upon him.

II

The black peasants and landlords' peasants who colonized the Northeast were confronted with a land of dense forests, great marshes, and many rivers and streams. So they sought out the high, dry places or the narrow open stretches that sometimes lay between forest edge and river bank. From these places of vantage the pioneers worked out into the forests, clearing as much land as they wanted or needed. The terrain was more inviting further south where the forests thinned out and the marshes disappeared. But the advantages offered by nature were outweighed by the dangers presented by man, for the southern regions were much too exposed to Tatar raids to suit the colonists. They preferred the protection afforded by the natural fortress of forest and swamp, even though it meant a more frugal living for them and one harder to come by. They probably worked in groups for the initial and heaviest work of settlement, when many hands were needed to clear the land. Once this preliminary work was completed the cooperative effort ended, and each family settled on an individual homestead (*dvor*) along some stream, or in a forest enclave, with its own arable and meadows. The nearest neighbor often was far off, and sometimes could only be reached by water because of impassable forest and swamp. With time a second or third cabin might be raised in the clearing to house married children and their families, and a hamlet came into being.

The picture that emerges from the cadastral registers made at the end of the fifteenth century for Novgorod Land show that sometimes there were more than three homesteads, and very exceptionally as many as eight or nine, in one of these isolated settlements, but that most often there were only one or two *dvory* in each hamlet. The registers also reveal that these homesteads were the dwellings of conjugal families, for usually just one, and rarely more than two, adult male workers were recorded as living in each one. For example, in the Derevskaia district (one of the five parts into which Novgorod Land was divided), in 653 hamlets there was a total of 1,316 homesteads and 1,413 adult male workers, for an average of about two homesteads per settlement, and one worker per homestead. In 136 hamlets in the Votskaia district there were 475 homesteads and 684 workers, an average of 3.5 *dvory* per hamlet and 1.5 workers per *dvor*. In the Shelonskaia district data collected for 145 hamlets showed they contained 284 homesteads and 296 adult male workers.[2]

These individual homesteads and hamlets joined with their

[2] Sergeevich, *Drevnosti*, III, 42-44; cf. Danilova, *Ocherki*, tables 13, 15, pp. 362-363.

neighbors to form territorial communes. Sometimes as many as twenty of them were members of one of these organizations, but the number seems often to have been less. The commune was usually called a *volost*, though sometimes it was referred to as a *pogost* or *stan*. Each commune was semi-autonomous, and was run by officers chosen by the commune members from among their fellows. The *volost* managed all those parts of its territory that were not held by individual peasants, such as forests, common pasture, streams, and fisheries. It supervised the establishment of new homesteads within its boundaries, the distribution of unoccupied arable, and the resettling of vacated holdings. Newcomers were welcomed, sometimes being given several years of freedom from paying their share of the communal obligations. The prince levied his imposts upon the commune as a unit, and not upon the persons or lands or incomes of its individual members. The commune's own assessors had to apportion these royal taxes and obligations equitably among its members, gather the levies, and turn them over to the prince's officials. *Volost* officials were also responsible for the maintenance of public order and security within the commune's boundaries.[3]

On privately owned land the lord, or his agent, dealt directly with the elected officials of the commune. These functionaries assisted the lord's representatives in judging *volost* members, and were consulted by the lord in matters pertaining to the entire body of the commune. The seignioral dues were apportioned in the same manner as royal obligations, and were collected by *volost* officials who turned them over to the lord.

With the increase in privately held property resulting from royal distribution of black land to seigniors, the *volost* form of organization began to disintegrate. Often the princes paid no heed to *volost* boundaries in making their grants, so that the organic unity of the commune was destroyed by its land being distributed among several proprietors. The most debilitating development, however, was the penetration of the landlord into the *volost* organization. First, agents of the seignior began to bypass the commune's own officials. Then the lord forbad the

---

[3] Sergeevich, *Lektsii*, pp. 298-300; Kliuchevskii, *History*, II, 204, 268-269; El'iashevich, *Istoriia*, I, 52-53; Pushkarev, *Proiskhozhdenie*, pt. I, 111-113.

selection of these officials by the peasants. Instead he named them himself, often selecting them from among his own unfree servants. The final stage was reached when the lord took away all the remaining powers of self-government from the *volost*, and placed its entire administration in the hands of one of his employees or slaves. The gradual destruction of the power of the commune on privately-owned land, and the simultaneous disappearance of the black land in much of the state, ended the existence of the independent *volost* as a form of organization so far as most of the peasantry were concerned. A similar process took place in other parts of Eastern Europe where, in approximately the same time period, seigniors made progressive encroachments upon village autonomy and replaced elected officials with their own choices.[4]

Beyond the functions and activities sketched above, the *volost* had no control over the individual peasant communer nor over the land he tilled. Although the land held by the peasant actually belonged to a private proprietor, or to the prince if it was black land, the peasant had virtually all the rights of ownership over his holding, so long as he worked it, and so long as he paid the obligations demanded by its proprietor. He could rent or sell the use of all or part of it to anyone he chose, provided that the new occupant was a person capable of working the land and meeting the obligations attached to its possession, he could mortgage it, and he could dispose of it as he wished in his testament. He could stay on it as long as he wanted, and he was free to leave it at his own discretion (although, as will be seen in the next chapter, the time of his departure began to be regulated in the latter fifteenth century).[5] The extensive rights of the Russian peasants over their holdings were analogous to those enjoyed by peasants in other lands of Eastern and Central Europe, who lived under the provisions of the so-called "German law." These privileges had been restricted originally to the Germans who poured eastward in the great colonization movement that began

[4] Pushkarev, *Proiskhozhdenie*, pt. I, 141; Kulischer, *Russische Wirtschaftsgeschichte*, I, 255-256; Miller, *Essai*, p. 168; Stählin, *Geschichte Russlands*, I, 113; Blum, "Rise," pp. 824-826.

[5] El'iashevich, *Istoriia*, I, 35-46, 60-63, 66-69, 117-118, 127; Tarakanova-Belkina, *Boiarskoe i monastyrskoe zemlevladenie*, pp. 33-35.

in the twelfth century, in order to encourage them to leave their old homes west of the Elbe River. But they were soon extended to most of the indigenous population in the lands in which the Germans settled.

Obviously, these powers of the peasant over the use and disposition of the land he held represented a serious incursion upon the rights of the persons who were the owners of the land. Yet princes and seigniors in Russia, and elsewhere in Eastern and Central Europe, welcomed the opportunity to rent out their lands under these conditions. The probable explanation lay in the scantiness of the population, and the urgent need of the seigniors for peasants to put their properties into productive use. If the lords had offered less favorable terms they undoubtedly would not have been able to attract settlers. They apparently decided that a diminution in their prerogatives as owners was preferable to having their lands lying empty and yielding them no income.

The black peasants continued to enjoy their broad rights over their holdings so long as their land remained black land. On privately owned land, however, as time went on important distinctions rose, dividing the seignioral peasantry into separate categories with differing obligations and privileges. From early in the fifteenth century certain of these landlords' peasants were referred to as "old inhabitants" (*starozhil'tsy*) while others were known as "newcomers" (*novoprikhodtsy*). The old inhabitants had to meet all the obligations demanded of renters by landlord and by prince, while the newcomers were exempted from some or all of these burdens. Many of the old inhabitants were the black people who had lived on the land before it was converted into private property, or their descendants who had inherited their holdings. In fact, black people were sometimes identified as *starozhil'tsy*, for some of the charters giving black lands to private individuals referred to the people already living on it as "old inhabitants." Others of the *starozhil'tsy* were erstwhile newcomers who had remained on their holdings beyond a certain term of years. The length of this period was apparently set by agreement between the landlord and the new peasant on his arrival. It ran usually from five to fifteen years. During this time the peasant was excused from all or part of the obligations that his fellow renters had to pay. This was the lure the proprietor used to attract settlers to his land. After the expiration of the grace period the newcomer, if he chose to remain on his holding, became an old inhabitant and was responsible for all dues and services.[6]

The *starozhil'tsy* were, in all likelihood, by far the largest group among the seignorial peasantry.[7] They made up the backbone, as it were, of the rural community, and their payments and services formed the chief part of the revenues the lords drew from their lands. It is difficult to understand, however, why they remained on holdings where they had to pay full, and often heavy, obligations, when they could have freed themselves of these burdens by becoming "newcomers" on the property of some other lord who would have welcomed them with exemptions if they settled on his land. Possibly the *starozhil'tsy*, as a class, formed the most prosperous sector of the peasantry, were content with their lot, and had no reason to exchange their comfortable positions for an uncertain future as new settlers on some other lord's property. The sources provide no direct evidence to support this hypothesis, but it seems a warranted inference from the available information. The exemptions that were given other peasants were for the purpose of attracting settlers, but it is possible that they were also granted because the newcomers lacked the means to pay full dues and services if they had been demanded of them. Many of them were so impoverished that they had to get loans and subsidies from the landlord to get started on their new holdings. In contrast, the *starozhil'tsy* must have been relatively well off, for they could afford to remain on the same holding and pay full obligations year after year. There is evidence, however, that old inhabitants sometimes did leave indicating that not all of them were satisfied. It is quite possible, too, that landlords were able to exert effective, albeit illegal and unrecorded, pressures upon their *starozhil'tsy* to prevent their departure. Finally, the factor of human inertia must be considered. Perhaps the old inhabitant

6 Grekov, *Krest'iane*, pp. 627-641.
7 El'iashevich, *Istoriia*, I, 134; Grekov, *Glavneishie etapy*, p. 48.

was an old inhabitant because he lacked initiative enough to leave and thereby improve his position. Maybe, as one historian has suggested, the majority of the *starozhil'tsy* were of this type—people who accepted their existence, even though it was not a satisfactory one, because they were accustomed to it.[8]

The newcomers, the *novoprikhodtsy*, the other chief group of seignioral peasants, were the Russian analogues of the *hospites* of medieval Western Europe. The problem of attracting these newcomers was a matter of serious importance to the proprietors, who, as we have seen, depended for most of their income upon the payments they received from their peasants. The inducements they held out to prospective tenants were as attractive as they could make them. As already indicated, they included the promise of loans and subsidies, and exemptions from obligations, including taxes due the prince, the extent and the duration of the tax exemptions depending upon the fiscal provisions of the charter given the seignior by the prince.[9] Landlords also offered other inducements, such as the promise of their assistance in the event of famine or some other natural calamity, or a cheap price for salt if they happened to own a saltworks.[10]

There was sharp competition between landlords in this business of attracting new settlers. As might be expected, the greatest lords were the most successful in the contest. They could make better offers to prospective tenants because their wealth allowed them to grant more aids, their high position enabled them to get more extensive fiscal immunities from the prince, and their military strength and political importance attracted peasants who were seeking protection from the violence of the times.

Sharecroppers formed a third category of seignioral peasants. The sharecropper (*polovnik*) agreed to remain with the lord for an agreed upon number of years and to pay a fixed proportion of his crop to the lord as rental. The size of this share varied, ranging from one fifth to as much as one half.[11] On his arrival the

---

[8] Kulischer, *Russische Wirtschaftsgeschichte*, I, 214.

[9] Cf. *ASEI*, I, no. 52, 117, 128, 175, 278.

[10] Eck, "Le grand domaine," p. 111.

[11] Cf. Charter of Pskov in *Medieval Russian Laws*, sect. 42, p. 70; Odinetz, "Les origines," p. 245.

polovnik received a loan of cash or of grain from the landlord in order to get started on his farming, and to carry him over until he brought in his first crop. As a rule the sharecropper was either excused from paying the obligations due the prince, or else paid a lesser amount than did other peasant renters. The fact that the sharecroppers were given loans, that they were willing to work on shares, the most oppressive type of rental agreement, and that they paid little or no taxes to the government, are indications that they must have been in very reduced circumstances. Share-cropping was not limited to large holdings. The Novgorod land registers of the late fifteenth century show that sharecroppers sometimes worked land that belonged to *svoezemtsi*, the smallest proprietors, and even rented part of the holdings of seignioral peasants.[12]

Material on the nature and extent of the dues and services required of the peasants by landlords in these early centuries is fragmentary. It can be assumed, however, that since there were no generally accepted norms there must have been wide differences in the amounts demanded, not only among regions, but between neighboring properties. Evidence of this is provided by the lack of uniformity in the charters of exemption that were granted by the princes, allowing some landlords to make more extensive concessions to newcomers than others. The moving of peasants from one lord's property to another also seems to indicate that there was a variation in the amount of obligations demanded, since it seems natural to suppose that, other things being equal, they moved to the land of another lord because he asked a lesser amount of dues and services than did the lord from whom they were departing. Finally, the obligations of the peasants within a single property varied. That the old inhabitants were responsible for more payments than were newly settled peasants has already been pointed out. But the Novgorod land registers reveal that peasants of the same status on a given property often paid different amounts of dues and services.

The peasants' obligations were in the form of cash and kind (known collectively as *obrok*) and labor services (*barshchina*). Down into the sixteenth century the largest part of their dues

12 Grekov, *Krest'iane*, pp. 424-425, 684-685, 692-694.

were in kind, for reasons explained earlier. The Novgorod land registers show that the payments were usually fixed at a definite quantity, though in some places shares were required. The chief dues were in grain, notably rye and oats, and there were also a number of lesser payments of other products. For example, the hamlet of Vranikovo, consisting of two homesteads, paid its lord annually four *korobei* of rye, four *korobei* of oats, one-half *korob'ia* of barley, a ram, a half of a slaughtered animal, two cheeses, a certain amount (two *kovshy*) of butter, one *piatok* of flax, a sheepskin, and ten *den'gi*. Another two-homestead hamlet on this same property, with approximately the same amount of land, paid three and one-half *korobei* of rye, a like amount of oats, one-half *korob'ia* of barley, a ram, half an animal carcass, a cheese, two *kovshy* of butter, one *piatok* of flax, and ten *den'gi*.[13] On another property one homestead had to pay five *den'gi*, one and one-half *korobei* of rye, and the same amount of oats. Another homestead on this estate, with considerably more land, paid one and one-half *korobei* each of rye and oats, one half *korob'ia* of wheat and eleven *den'gi*.[14] A detailed analysis of the obligations of the peasants in a parish of the Obonezhskaia district of Novgorod Land showed that 129 of the 157 *obzhi* in this parish were worked on shares, the payment of 110 *obzhi* being one half the crop, on five one third, and on fourteen one quarter. In addition, these peasants made a number of lesser payments in kind, but none in cash.[15]

A description of all the obligations demanded of the peasants on one property has fortunately been preserved in a monastic charter of 1391. The events leading up to the issuance of this document are themselves of interest, for they provide additional information on the relation between lord and peasants. A priest named Ephraim had just been appointed abbot of St. Constantine's Monastery in Vladimir, replacing Abbot Tsarko who had become ill and had retired to Moscow. Ephraim, perhaps feeling that the new hand at the tiller had to make itself felt, tried to introduce some changes—which undoubtedly represented in-

13 *Novgorodskiia pistsovyia knigi*, I, 142.
14 *Ibid.*, pp. 413-414.
15 Perel'man, "Novgorodskaia derevnia," p. 140.

creases—in the labor obligations of the monastery's peasant renters. The peasants protested vigorously, on the grounds that these innovations represented a violation of the long-standing agreement between them and the monastery about the amount of their dues and services. Since St. Constantine's was part of the patrimony of the Metropolitan Cyprian in Moscow, they turned to that dignitary with their complaint. He decided to investigate, and sent an official to visit Tsarko, the retired abbot, to find out what dues the peasants had paid when he headed the monastery.

Tsarko told the emissary that the peasants of St. Constantine's were divided into two classes: the *bol'shie* (large) people and the *perekhodtsy* (pedestrians). The former group owned and used work animals, while the latter did not, doing all their work on foot—hence their name. The *bol'shie* were responsible for much heavier obligations than were the less prosperous "pedestrians." They had to put up fences around the monastery courtyard, erect buildings, keep the church in repair, plow, sow, and harvest the demesne and bring in the crops, cut hay and deliver it to the monastery, build fish weirs in spring and autumn and catch fish, hunt beaver, and dam ponds. The *perekhodtsy* were required to thresh and grind rye, bake bread, prepare malt, brew beer, spin yarn from the flax provided by the abbot, and make fishing nets. In addition to these labor services a number of payments in kind were enumerated. On Easter Sunday and St. Peter's Day the *bol'shie* came to the abbot and presented him with "what each had in his hand"—probably a reference to a cash payment whose amount was fixed by custom. All the peasants together had to give the abbot a barren cow, or three sheep. Finally, they were required to provide oats for the abbot's horses when he visited a peasant settlement.

Cyprian incorporated Tsarko's evidence in the regulatory charter, dated 21 October 1391, that he sent to St. Constantine's. He commanded that the old order of things be maintained without change, and concluded with the following charge: "And Cyprian, Metropolitan of all Russia, says this to the abbot and the peasants of the monastery: everything is to be done according to my charter; the abbot is to protect the peasants, and the peasants are to obey the abbot, and perform the monastery's work."[16]

The peasants had won. There are several possible explanations for Cyprian's decision in their favor. One might be that he accepted the custom of the manor as inviolable. It is possible, too, that he was content with the present yield from St. Constantine's, and saw no need for trying to increase it. The most probable explanation, however, was that he realized that if the discontent of the peasants was not allayed, they would leave the monastery's land to become renters of other lords who were willing to offer them more favorable terms.

In addition to the dues he paid his landlord the seignioral peasant had to pay a number of dues and services to the prince, unless he enjoyed exemptions from them. The peasants on the black land, too, bore these fiscal charges in addition to the quit-rent they paid the sovereign. During the era of the Mongol hegemony the word *tiaglo* came into use to designate both the total amount of the taxes levied upon the individual peasant, and also his capacity to meet his fiscal obligations.[17] The payments to the prince like those made to the seignior were in cash, kind, and labor. As was pointed out earlier, they were levied upon the commune as a whole rather than upon the peasant householder, and were divided among the individual taxpayers by the commune's own officials. The amount demanded varied widely between communes, and within the individual commune the tax burden of the members differed according to their tax-paying ability or to their status as "old inhabitant," "newcomer," or sharecropper. The unit of assessment bore differing regional names, among them being *vyt, sokha*, and *obzha*. Whatever it was called, it probably had corresponded originally, like the hide, the *hufe*, the *bol*, and similar units in Western and Central Europe, to the amount of land considered necessary to maintain a peasant family. But if this conception of the assessment unit as an area of land of specific size had indeed existed in Russia it had been abandoned. Now the amount and quality of the land held by a homestead was only one of the

[16] *AAE*, I, no. 11.
[17] Sergeevich, *Drevnosti*, III, 164-165.

elements considered in determining the tax-bearing capacity (the *tiaglo*) of the peasant household. Account was also taken of all the income-producing activities of the family, the number of workers in it, the number of animals it owned, the buildings and tools it had, and so on. The weights assigned each of these factors was determined according to local custom by the commune officials. This method of assessment explains why there was no uniformity in the relationship between the amount of land held and the tax that was paid.[18]

Other obligations required of both the black people and seignioral peasants included building and repairing fortifications, constabulary duty, carting and postal services, goods and cash for the maintenance of the *kormlenshchiki*—the prince's local administrative officials—and money for the ransom of prisoners. Although princely charters allowed landlords to excuse new settlers from most of these taxes for a specified period, exemptions were rarely given for the carting and postal services because the Mongols demanded that highway communications be maintained for the use of their officials. There was also a series of obligations that were quasi-governmental, such as providing forage for the prince's horses, or maintaining his huntsmen and dogs, serving as his beaters and stalkers when he hunted, and sometimes working on his properties. Finally, tribute had to be paid to the Tatar overlords. At first, the Mongols themselves collected the tribute. Then the Grand Dukes of Moscow succeeded in getting permission from the khans to do the collecting for them. Until the end of the fourteenth century they had dutifully turned over the money they gathered. In the next century, when the Tatar yoke began to slip, they continued to levy the tribute, but did not pay it regularly to the Mongol suzerain, and by the end of the century kept it all for their own uses.[19]

18 Miller, "Considérations sur les institutions financières," pp. 380-381.
19 *Ibid.*, 376; Veselovskii, *Feodal'noe zemlevladenie*, I, 134-137.

7

PEASANTS, SLAVES, AND PEONS

DURING the era of the Mongol domination a number of names were used for the peasantry, among them *sirota*, orphan; *liudi*, people; and, infrequently, the old Kievan name, *smerd*. But in the fourteenth century these and other terms began to be displaced by *krest'ianin*. The original meaning of that word had been Christian, *khristianin*. It had been employed from the twelfth century on into the Tatar epoch to distinguish the Russians from the non-Christian people with whom they were in contact. As time went on it was used just for the rural population and ultimately became the *nomen generale* of the Russian peasant.[1]

Whatever he was called, the peasant from the Kievan era on into the fifteenth century had the right to come and go as he pleased, so long as he had not indentured himself. He could choose where he wanted to live, and he could move from one place to another whenever he wanted. He was attached neither to the commune of which he might be a member, nor to the lord on whose land he was living, nor to the prince in whose realm he happened to reside. Moreover, such was the social fluidity of those centuries that he need remain a peasant only so long as he continued in some agricultural pursuit, and could leave the peasantry whenever he chose to abandon his rural calling. The concept of a formal peasant class into which a person was born, and in which he retained life-long membership regardless of place of residence or type of employment, was still unknown.[2]

But from the thirteenth century a paradoxical situation developed with reference to the peasants' freedom of movement. On one hand limitations began slowly to be imposed upon it, and on the other hand its continued existence was guaranteed. The explanation for this contradiction lay in the conflict of interests that beset the princes and seigniors of these centuries,

---

[1] Cherepnin, "Iz istorii formirovaniia . . . ," *passim*.
[2] Cf. Sergeevich, *Drevnosti*, I, 227-233, 246; El'iashevich, *Istoriia*, I, 150.

and that was attributable, in the last analysis, to the scantiness of the population. The peasants supplied the lion's share of the fiscal revenues of the prince; they formed an important part of his military force; and their payments in kind, cash, and labor were the chief source of seignorial income. They were much too important, then, to the strength and the economic well-being of the ruling class to be allowed to leave whenever they wanted. So from at least as early as the mid-thirteenth century, rulers began to agree in treaties they made with one another not to take peasants from one another's realm, nor to allow their subjects to do this.[3] These agreements were not directed against the peasant, nor were they intended to take away his right of free movement. They did not prevent him from moving from one princedom to another at his own volition. Rather, they were self-denying ordinances of the rulers—pledges not to entice peasants from one another's land by offering more attractive terms of tenure or subsidies, nor to take them by force, nor to give refuge to peasants who had fled to escape contractual obligations or who were fugitives from justice. Yet, they represented attempts on the part of the rulers to limit the opportunities offered the peasant to improve his condition by moving. In this light they can be viewed as restrictions upon the liberty of the free rural population.

In practice, however, these attempts proved unsuccessful. The need for their repetition in princely treaties over a period of two centuries is in itself an indication that peasants continued to pass from one realm to another. It could scarcely have been otherwise, in view of the small population, the existence of many independent realms and the prevailing atmosphere of rivalry between them, and the desire they all shared to increase their populations in order to get the taxes, goods, and services necessary for the maintenance of the ruling class. It seems highly likely that the will to carry out these agreements was conspicuous in its absence, but even if they had represented the sincere intentions of the contracting parties, the facts of contemporary political and economic life would have reduced them to dead letters.

[3] *SGGD*, I, nos. 1 (1265), 3 (1270), 9 (1305-1308), 27 (1362), 35 (1389), 45 (*ca.* 1433), 71 (*ca.* 1448); *AAE*, I, no. 57 (1456).

And during the same years that they were making these cov-
enants not to take one another's peasants, the rulers were affirm-
ing the peasant's right to freedom of movement. At least three
of the surviving treaties between princes included a provision
allowing peasants to go freely between their realms.[4] But the
most convincing evidence of royal sponsorship of the peasant's
ability to move were the charters of immunities given by the
princes to lay and church seigniors. These grants, permitting
lords to offer fiscal exemptions to prospective settlers to lure
them from their old homes, not only presupposed that the peasant could leave at will, but encouraged them to use this right.

At the same time the princes wanted to protect their own
interests. So even while they sponsored seignioral efforts to populate their holdings by giving these lords charters of immunities,
they sometimes tried to limit the places from which the lords
could draw their new renters. They were concerned particularly
with preventing a drain of peasants away from the black lands,
in order to avoid the loss of fiscal revenues. Because the princes
were so dependent upon the seignioral class they were unable to
lay down any general interdictions. Instead, they had to resort to
roundabout methods. One device they used was to include
certain restrictions in some of the charters they issued. These
curbs ranged from specific prohibitions to loose restraints. In the
charter Grand Duke Ivan I of Moscow gave to St. George's
Monastery around 1338-1340, he flatly declared that the monks
"shall not take tax-paying peasants of Volok and shall not take
peasants from the lands of the Grand Duke."[5] A less rigorous
limitation was imposed in a number of other charters which
allowed the grantee to offer fiscal exemptions only to peasants
who came from other realms, but laid no prohibition upon his
accepting local peasants as new settlers.[6] Still other princely charters allowed their recipients to offer exemptions to peasants living
within the princedom. The period of freedom from state obligations that these landlords could hold out to such prospective
tenants, however, was shorter than that which they could give to
peasants coming from other princedoms. Thus, a charter given

[4] *SGGD*, I, nos. 95 (1472), 127 (1496); *AAE*, I, no. 14 (1398).
[5] *AAE*, I, no. 4.   [6] *Ibid.*, no. 5.

by the ruler of Riazan in the mid-fifteenth century authorized the recipient to offer an exemption of two years from paying taxes to peasants of Riazan, and of three years to those who came from outside the princedom. In a charter issued by Vasilii I of Moscow in 1423 the grantee was permitted to offer freedom from taxes for three years to Muscovite peasants, and for ten years to peasants who came from other realms. In another charter awarded by Vasilii to Metropolitan Photius in 1425 the periods of exemption for Muscovite and non-Muscovite peasants were five and fifteen years, respectively.[7]

But in most of the charters that have survived no distinction was made between peasants who lived within the realm of the grantor and those who came from other princedoms. Their recipients could offer the same inducements to all prospective settlers regardless of their place of origin. Because of the relatively small number of charters still extant (most of them from religious institutions, since church records were more carefully preserved than private archives), it is impossible to state categorically that this was the usual type of grant. In view of the dependence of the rulers upon their nobles and the economic needs of the landowning class, however, it seems likely that the princes normally placed few, if any, barriers in the way of the efforts of landlords to attract renters.

When limitations were included in the charters they were restrictions imposed upon the landlord and not upon the peasant. Yet, like the treaties between the princes, and possibly with greater success, they curbed the peasant's freedom of movement by cutting down on the number of choices he had in selecting a new place of residence.

The era was not free, however, of restraints that bore directly upon the right of the free peasant to come and go as he pleased. The most common one was to prohibit him from moving except at certain specified times during the year, and then only after he had given his seignior due notice of his intention. Presumably the fixing of the departure time was set by mutual consent when the peasant made his rental agreement with the lord, or perhaps it was an accepted and traditional agreement. In any

[7] *AIu*, I, no. 36; *AAE*, I, nos. 21, 23.

event, this practice became converted into a legal norm in the course of the fifteenth century. The earliest known legislative effort at establishing uniformity in the time of departure was in the Charter of Pskov (between 1396 and 1467). In one of its articles the beginning of St. Philip's Fast (14 November) was set as the time for the termination of leases.[8] In the mid-fifteenth century the Ferpantov Monastery complained to Prince Michael Andreevich of Beloozero that peasants who were in debt to it were being lured away by other proprietors at times inconvenient to the monastery, and that they were allowed a two-year period after leaving to pay back their debts, without interest. Michael ordered that peasants could only leave the Ferpantov's lands two weeks before and one week after St. George's Day in autumn (25 November), and had to pay their debts before they could depart. In another charter Michael issued a general order establishing this period as the only legal time for peasant departure. Around the same time Vasilii II of Moscow gave the abbot of St. Cyril's the power to prevent the departure of peasants from that monastery's lands save at St. George's and a week thereafter.[9] In the 1460's and 1470's Prince Andrei Vasilievich of Beloozero, and Ivan III of Moscow, in charters to monasteries referred to St. George's as the time for peasant departure.[10]

Two other extant charters of the fifteenth century placed outright prohibitions upon peasant departure at any time. These were granted by Vasilii II of Moscow to the Trinity-St. Serge Monastery between 1455 and 1462. One of these charters gave the monks the right to bring back peasants who had moved from Trinity lands in the Uglich district to properties owned by Vasilii himself or by his boyars, and also ordered that none of the peasants living on the monastery's Uglits properties at the time of the charter's issue could leave. The other forbad the departure of "old inhabitants" living on Trinity's possessions in the Bezhetsk district.[11] These two documents were unique in their time because of these absolute bans on peasant movement. Possibly, as one historian has suggested, their unusual terms

[8] *Medieval Russian Laws*, sect. 42, p. 70.
[9] *AAE*, I, 48/I, II, III.
[10] *ASEI*, I, nos. 338 (1463-1468), 359 (1467-1474); *DAI*, I, 198/I, II (1462-1471).
[11] *ASEI*, I, nos. 264, 265.

were attributable to certain political ambitions of Vasilii. He had only recently established his hegemony over Bezhets and Uglits after long civil wars. To consolidate his rule over these regions, he sought to win for himself the support of the wealthy and influential Trinity Monastery by giving it complete control over the movements of its peasant renters in those districts.[12]

The final stage in the establishment of a fixed period as the only legal time at which all peasants everywhere could give up their holdings came at the end of the century. By then the Muscovite house had established its supremacy over the other princes and over the city states, and could legislate for the entire realm. In the Law Code (*Sudebnik*) of Ivan III, issued in 1497, the right of the free peasant to give notice and move away was confirmed, provided he had met all his obligations to the land-lord.[13] But the law ordered that he could leave only one week before and one week after St. George's in autumn. Moreover, to secure his release he had to pay his lord an exit fee as compensation for the use of the house he and his family had occupied during his tenancy. The amount of the payment depended upon the length of time he had been in the dwelling, and whether it was "in woods" or "in the field." "In woods" did not necessarily mean actually in a forest, but, like the terms "woodlands" and "bocage" in medieval England and France, meant that timber was nearby. "In the field," like the "champion" in England and the "champaign" in France, meant open or relatively treeless country. If the house was "in the field" the peasant had to pay one quarter of a ruble for each year of his occupancy up to four years, so that the maximum fee was one ruble. If the dwelling was in a wooded area the fee was half this amount. Apparently, the value of a peasant dwelling in open country was estimated to be one ruble, and half a ruble in wooded land where houses could be built more cheaply because of the availability of timber, while annual depreciation due to wear and tear by the occupant was set at 25 percent.

The exit fees must have been a formidable obstacle to peasant departure. They represented large sums of money for those

---

12 Cherepnin, *Russkie feodal'nye arkhivy*, II, 158.
13 *Sudebnik* 1497, art. 57, p. 355.

times. Price data from Novgorod for the beginning of the six-teenth century show that a ruble could buy 50 chetverts (300 bushels) of oats, 33 chetverts (200 bushels) of barley, 25 chetverts (150 bushels) of rye, and 20 chetverts (120 bushels) of wheat.[14] Data on crop yields later in the sixteenth century showing that the average peasant holding in the Novgorod region produced only 10 to 15 chetverts of rye and 14 to 21 chetverts of oats[15] affords further emphasis to the exorbitant size of the fee.

The many references, both direct and oblique, in the scanty sources of the era of the Tatar yoke to the movement of peas-ants from realm to realm and from manor to manor, gave rise to a widely accepted theory that the people of the Northeast lived an almost nomadic life in these centuries. This interpretation is usually associated with Kliuchevskii, though other historians before him had presented this same view. Kliuchevskii described the Great Russian peasant of the thirteenth-fifteenth centuries as a man who lived in one place for only a few years, and then moved on when the land in his clearing became exhausted. He believed that this constant migration was the "principal funda-mental factor" with which "all other factors have been more or less inseparably connected," not only in the history of this era but for all of Russian history.[16] The available evidence, however, indicates that this exaggerates the mobility of the population. Others have called attention to the many references in the sources to the "old inhabitants," who had gained this status by virtue of their long residence in the same place. These peasants were sometimes identified as persons who had lived for scores of years on one holding, and whose fathers had lived on it before them. The physical difficulties that would have been involved in the frequent reestablishment of homesteads by people whose main occupation was tilling the soil have also been pointed out.

Self-interest rather than a compulsive nomadism seems best to explain why some people did move. Many of the migrants must have been peasants who had been overwhelmed by some catastro-phe, such as a crop failure, or a Tatar raid, or civil war. These

[14] Man'kov, *Tseny,* table 1, p. 104.
[15] Rozhkov, *Sel'skoe khoziaistvo,* p. 260.
[16] Kliuchevskii, *History,* I, 2, 217.

men would have grasped the opportunity presented by their right of free departure, and by the inducements held out to new renters by landlords, to make a new start elsewhere. Others who were better off undoubtedly moved, too, but here also the exemptions offered by proprietors to new settlers seems a sufficient reason for their decision to leave their old homes.[17]

II

Not all of the rural population, however, were free men with the right to move at their own choice. Just as in the Kievan era there were people who were held by the bonds of slavery or debt servitude.

The legal position of the slave seems to have improved slightly over what it had been in the eleventh and twelfth centuries. Slave owners were apparently no longer allowed to commit premeditated murder of their bondsmen and go unpunished, and bondsmen could initiate court actions and bear witness. The sources of slaves remained the same as they had been in the Kievan centuries. War captives must have become of less importance, however, since treaties between rulers almost always contained provisions for the exchange without cost of prisoners and hostages.[18] Voluntary slavery, on the other hand, may well have increased, since the evils and uncertainties that plagued the land in those times must have convinced many people that the best way to find security was to sell or give themselves into bondage to a seignior. The three ways listed in the Expanded Version of the *Russian Law* by which a person could enter slavery voluntarily (by selling himself, marrying a slave, or accepting a job as a steward) were repeated in the *Sudebnik* of 1497.[19]

The church continued in its policy of urging humane treatment of slaves, and was particularly successful in its encouragement of emancipation by testament. By the fourteenth-fifteenth century this custom seems to have become well established. The princes of Moscow, beginning with Simeon I (1341-1352), and

<hr>

[17] Cf. Pavlov-Sil'vanskii, *Feodalizm*, pp. 63-65; El'iashevich, *Istoriia*, I, 36-37, 134; Grekov, *Krest'iane*, p. 805.

[18] Eck, "Les non-libres," pp. 24-25, 28-30, 36.

[19] Sect. 66, p. 373.

rulers of other princedoms, freed many of their slaves in their wills, and so did other slaveowners. In general, however, the non-royal seigniors emancipated their bondsmen subject to certain conditions, such as that the slave had to remain in the service of the testator's heirs for a specified number of years before being freed, or had to pay a sum of money to the heirs, or was set free only in the event his owner died without survivors.[20]

For many slaves emancipation turned out to be a gift of little value. Except for relatively isolated instances, the bondsman was given his freedom—and nothing else. A fortunate few were able to earn a living in the trade they had learned as slaves. Some were accepted as members of free peasant communes, and others threw themselves on the charity of the church. But many, knowing that freedom alone was not enough to keep body and soul together, sold themselves back into slavery. Freiherr von Herberstein, who visited Muscovy in the first half of the sixteenth century, was puzzled by this phenomenon. "This people," he wrote, "enjoy slavery more than freedom, for persons on the point of death very often manumit some of their slaves, but they immediately sell themselves for money to other families."[21] This practice aids in explaining why slaves remained numerous in sixteenth century Russia (if the frequent references to them in the sources of that period can serve as an index of their abundance) despite the widespread custom of testamentary manumission.

In contrast to their largely unchanged legal status, the economic functions of the slaves in the thirteenth-fifteenth centuries changed considerably from what they had been in the preceding period. With the diminution in direct seignorial production after the collapse of the Kievan economy, the need for a large slave labor force disappeared. Slaves were still used to till demesne that their masters retained to meet household needs, and they continued to serve as artisans, domestics, and administrative officials. But free hired labor and indentured peasants seemed to have been used at least as much, and possibly more, than were slaves, especially on the great church manors.[22] In-

---

[20] Eck, "Les non-libres," pp. 33-34.   [21] Herberstein, *Notes*, I, 95.
[22] Bakhrushin, "Kniazheskoe khoziaistvo," pp. 39-40; Eck, "Le grand domaine," pp. 99-100.

stead of using all their slaves as laborers the slaveowners began to settle some of them on the land, giving them holdings to till in return for payments of cash, kind, and labor. In short, these bondsmen began to play the economic role of free peasant renters. This was particularly true on monastic land where, by the fifteenth century, the use of slave labor seems to have ended completely. The bondsmen of the monasteries, including new slaves purchased by the monks, were settled on holdings, and in the course of time were fused with the other peasant renters.[23]

The slaveowners could have freed their bondsmen when they put them out on the land. On the other hand, the individual lord had nothing to gain (save, possibly, the psychic income derived from performing a "good work"), and much to lose, by emancipation. For so long as these people were slaves they remained part of his personal wealth, and he could sell or pawn them, or give them as dowry.

After the end of the Kievan period the *izgoi* no longer appear in the sources. Apparently, under the changed conditions of life that prevailed in the Northeast the danger of becoming declassed had all but disappeared. Commerce had become so reduced that the merchant class was now an unimportant category. Princes followed the patrimonial order of succession, and constant subdividing of patrimonies provided princedoms for the members of the ruling families, so that there were no more "orphaned princes." The priesthood was presumably educating its sons more carefully. Only the freed slave was still liable to the risks of being without a role.[24]

The use of the term *zakup* disappeared, too, but the institution of debt servitude lived on in the new centers of Russian life. Now the indentured person was known as a *serebrennik*, from *serebro*, silver—i.e., money. The earliest known use of the term was in a royal will of 1253.[25] In this and later wills of the fourteenth and, especially, the fifteenth centuries, the testators, in listing their assets, often included "money (*serebro*) in the villages," meaning debts owed them by peasants. Not all of these

---

[23] Tarakanova-Belkina, *Boiarskoe i monastyrskoe zemlevladenie*, pp. 58-59; Veselovskii, *Feodal'noe zemlevladenie*, I, 220.

[24] Szeftel, "La condition juridique," pp. 436-439.

[25] *AIuB*, I, 63/I.

debtors, however, were required by the terms of their loans to work for their creditor. Some had borrowed with the condition that they were to make their repayment in cash.[26]

Until the second half of the fifteenth century indebtedness seems not to have been a barrier to the peasant-debtor's freedom of movement, as it was during the Kievan period. The Charter of Pskov shows that if the debtor left without paying off his loan the landlord-creditor could sue to recover, but did not have the right to compel the debtor to remain on his land, nor bring him back if he had already left.[27] The complaints of the Ferpantov Monastery in the mid-fifteenth century to Prince Michael Andreevich of Beloozero about peasants who left the Monastery's lands without paying their debt to the monks were referred to earlier in this chapter. As was pointed out there, this freedom of the debtor began to be curbed by princely charters which prohibited the departure of *serebrenniki* save during the St. George's period, and then only if they had paid their debts to the seignior.[28]

In the second half of the fifteenth and particularly in the sixteenth centuries there was a remarkable increase in peasant borrowing. The causes of this growth of indebtedness, as well as its consequences, were of crucial importance in bringing about the ultimate enserfment of the mass of Russia's rural population. These developments were the result of the economic and political changes that took place in the next era of Russian history. To this new era we now turn.

[26] E.g., *ASEI*, nos. 108 (1431), 501 (1483), 562 (1491).
[27] Sect. 44, *Medieval Russian Laws*, p. 70.
[28] *AAE*, I, nos. 48/I, II; *DAI*, I, 198/I, II.

8

A NEW ERA OF ECONOMIC EXPANSION

DURING the course of the fifteenth century signs of recovery in economic life slowly evidenced themselves.
Indeed, already in the latter part of the fourteenth century Russian artisans began to use new techniques and resurrect
old ones, improve the quality and increase the quantity of their
output, and turn out new kinds of products. Among the innovations that were introduced in those years were water-powered
mills, casting of artillery pieces and other heavy objects such as
large bells that required complicated equipment, and a marked
increase in the use of stone in building.[1] A new, and at first
cautious and tentative, revival of interest in internal trade also
appeared. The leadership in this was taken not by the people of
the cities but by landowners, and especially by monasteries. The
commercial privileges the princes gave these proprietors allowed
them to set up business compounds in the towns and have
judicial powers over the people who lived and worked in these
establishments, guaranteed that royal officials would not interfere with their manufacturing and trading operations, and exempted them from various tolls. At first only a handful of
proprietors engaged in this kind of activity, but as the decades
went on an ever larger number were attracted to it. Of ninety
known charters of the fifteenth century granting commercial
privileges to monasteries, only fourteen were issued up to the
middle of the century, the rest being awarded after that time.[2]

The city establishment of the proprietor who was interested in
commerce served as administrative and economic headquarters
for the lord's business interests. It was managed by an official
who lived on the premises. His duties included supervising and
serving as judge over the other people who lived and worked
there, overseeing the operation of any of the lord's industrial
enterprises that might be located in or near the town, such as

[1] Rybakov, *Remeslo*, pp. 696-697.
[2] Cherepnin, *Russkie feodal'nye arkhivy*, II, 212-213.

saltworks, selling goods produced on the lord's rural properties or in his workshops, and buying what was needed for the operation of the seignioral economy that it could not produce itself. With the continued growth in trade and industry in the last years of the fifteenth and the opening decades of the sixteenth century, the activities of these city headquarters grew so much that it became necessary for a number of them to take over more land and buildings to house their expanding operations and staffs.[3]

Foreign trade, too, began to take on more importance. The decline of the Mongol power made it much easier for Russian merchants to travel and trade in the Black Sea and Caspian regions and in the Orient. Josafa Barbaro, who served as Venetian ambassador to the Mongols for much of the middle third of the fifteenth century, reported that Russian merchants sailed down the Volga each year to Astrakhan. Muscovite diplomatic missions with merchants in their entourages were sent out to Eastern potentates, and foreign diplomats and traders from the Orient and from Central Europe and Italy began once more to make their way into the Russian interior.[4]

The history of money provides another indication of the slow upturn in economic life.[5] Minting of new coins in Russia had ended in the reign of Prince Vladimir Monomakh of Kiev (1113-1125). The inflow of foreign coins dried up with the decline in the commerce with other lands, and furs and small silver bars had come into wide use as mediums of exchange, reflecting the low level of internal trade. Then, in the latter part of the fourteenth century, in the reign of Dmitrii Donskoi, Prince of Moscow, the minting of new coins was resumed. Foreign money began coming in again. In the first part of the fifteenth century silver coins were minted in other principalities, and in the republics of Novgorod and Pskov. Copper money also was turned out. The total quantity of currency minted was small until the latter part of the century, when Ivan III made the issuing of money a monopoly of the ruler of Moscow. Much

---

[3] *Ibid.*; Smirnov, *Posadskie liudi*, I, 21-27, 78-82.

[4] Barbaro, *Travels*, p. 31; Eck, *Le moyen âge*, pp. 349-352.

[5] For the history of money in this era see the works cited in Blum, "Prices," pp. 187-190.

larger amounts were now struck off, with the coins minted in Ivan's name used in all the Russian princedoms.

There was, however, a steady debasement of the coinage during the course of the fifteenth century. By the end of the century the silver content of the *den'ga*, the most commonly minted coin, was less than half of what it had been when minting had been resumed. A couple of possible explanations for this phenomenon suggest themselves. Thus, despite the signs of recovery the fifteenth century was still an era of hard times. The rulers were pressed for cash and were unable to resist tampering with the currency. This was especially evident in years of political crisis: coin weights dropped by over 40 percent between 1447 and 1453 when Vasilii II of Moscow was fighting for his throne against his kinsmen.[6] At the same time, the stirrings of economic revival must have set up a demand for more coins. Since there were no sources of new bullion in Russia this need was met by stamping out more coins from a given amount of silver. Parenthetically, the increase in the amount of money in circulation that resulted from debasement, whatever its cause, may well have served as a stimulant to further economic expansion.

Soviet scholars have claimed that evidences of revival are found in agriculture, too, from the middle of the fourteenth century.[7] They assert that improved farming techniques and better implements, notably the three-field system, manuring, iron plowshares, and water-powered mills, began to be employed on a much wider scale than hitherto on the lands of princes, nobles, and churchmen. These innovations are claimed to have led to an increase in tilled area and in productivity. The extant materials do not support these sweeping generalizations. Yet, in view of the other indications of a renewal in economic life, it seems entirely possible that some improvements leading to increased output were introduced into farming.

These signs of recovery that appeared in the fifteenth century proved the prelude to a remarkable upswing in the next century. Not all sectors of the economy were affected with the same

---

[6] Alef, *A history*, p. 379.

[7] Smirnov, "Obrazovanie," pp. 76-81; Danilova and Pashyto, "Tovarnoe proizvodstvo," p. 1270; Danilova, *Ocherki*, pp. 32-33.

intensity and, indeed, much of the "natural" economy that had been typical of the earlier period still persisted. But it is clear that Russia, in common with most of the rest of Europe, entered upon a new era of economic growth in the sixteenth century.

Among the most conspicuous evidences of this were the increases in the area and population of the realm. Russia, like the Atlantic states of Western Europe, embarked in the sixteenth century upon an ambitious program of colonial expansion. The collapse of the Mongol power, and the emergence of the united Russian state under the leadership of Moscow, offered the opportunity for seemingly limitless territorial acquisition in the vast Eurasian land mass that lay beyond Muscovy's borders. Beginning in 1552 the conquests of Ivan IV pushed the frontiers southward to the shores of the Caspian, and eastward into the Kama and Volga basins and the slopes of the Urals. Then the expansion into Siberia started, with deeper penetration in each successive decade until by the mid-seventeenth century Russian colonists had reached the Pacific. Ivan IV had inherited a realm of about 900,000 square miles. By the time Michael Romanov mounted the throne in 1613 it had grown to 3.3 million square miles, and when Peter I began his reign in 1682 the state covered 5.6 million square miles.[8]

Most of the new colonial empire had only a small native population and much of it was entirely empty of people. There is evidence, however, that indicates a large natural increase in the total population of Russia in the sixteenth century. The actual size of the population cannot be determined because of the scantiness of demographic information, and there are wide discrepancies among modern estimates that have been made.[9] But charters and other land records from the first half of the

[8] Arsen'ev, *Statisticheskie ocherki*, pp. 54-56.

[9] One estimate is that population in the late 15th century was 2.1 millions, and 4.3 millions in the late 16th century (V. Pokrovskii in Brockhaus and Efron, *Entsiklopedicheskii Slovar*, xxa, 631). Another is 9-10 millions at the end of the 15th, and 12 millions at the end of the 16th (Vernadsky, *Kievan Russia*, p. 104; *idem, Zven'ia*, p. 28). A third sets population at 3 millions in the mid-16th, and 4.5 millions at the end of the 16th century (P. Smirnov cited in Khromov, *Ekonomicheskoe razvitie*, pp. 77-78). A fourth estimate is 10-11.5 millions in the mid-16th, and 15 millions at the end of that century (Miliukov, *Ocherki*, I, 26-27). For other estimates v. Kopanev, "Naselenie," pp. 233-235.

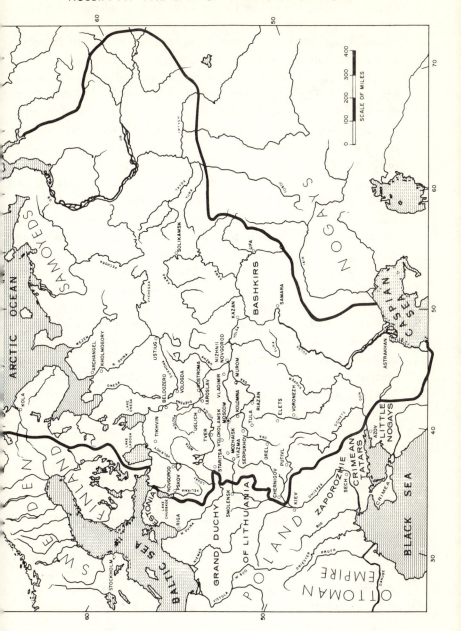

century for the Muscovite Center—the region between the Oka and the upper and middle courses of the Volga—and for Novgorod in the Northwest bear witness to this increase. In contrast to similar sources of the preceding era, they show that the number of abandoned holdings was small and that new clearings were being made. The cadastral survey for the Votskaia district in Novgorod Land reveal that in 1500 out of nearly 4,400 settlements 98 percent were occupied. Of forty-one properties described in documents from the *uezd* (county) of Moscow only six had empty holdings on them, and eight had new clearings. In forty-three charters from another county only four mentioned abandoned holdings and three referred to new clearings; in fifty-eight properties described in documents from Bezhetsk *uezd*, empty holdings are mentioned in seven and new clearings in nine, and so on. A cadastral survey of Tver *uezd* in 1548 showed that a little more than 5 percent of over 5,100 settlements were empty and nearly 13 percent were new clearings.[10] In 1553 Richard Chancellor, the English explorer, on his way to Moscow after landing on the shores of the White Sea, traveled through some of the central region and was struck by the thickness of settlement. "The countrey betwixt (Iaroslavl and Moscow)," he wrote, "is very wel replenished with smal Villages, which are so wel filled with people that it is a wonder to see them."[11] Chancellor's observations are borne out by the land registers of the era. These show that in the central part of the realm there was an average of seven to ten homesteads per settlement. Moving out toward the frontiers the average dropped to four to six homesteads, and in the northernmost parts of the state most of the settlements had just one *dvor* each.[12]

The territorial expansion and the growth in population were of major importance in contributing to economic development. Furs, salts, hides, and other wares streamed into the older regions from the colonies, creating new wealth and stimulating commercial and industrial activity. The increase in population provided a greater potential market for goods, and afforded further

[10] Rozhkov, *Sel'skoe khoziaistvo*, pp. 292-300, 314. For a discussion of the cadastral surveys v. pp. 230-232.

[11] In Hakluyt, *The Principal Navigations*, ii, 225, 262.

[12] Rozhkov, *Sel'skoe khoziaistvo*, pp. 347-358.

opportunity for profitable sale and for the spread of a market economy.

The new importance of exchange in economic life was signalized by the reemergence of the city as a center of industry and commerce and as a market for farm goods and other wares produced in Russia and in foreign lands. Old towns were revivified, new ones established, and some rural settlements (as Novgorod land registers show) began to abandon agriculture for trade and industry.

Moscow was by far the largest city of the realm. Baron von Herberstein reported that a census made six years before his arrival in the capital in 1517 showed there were over 41,500 dwellings there. Herberstein deemed this figure "scarcely credible."[13] But other foreign visitors to Moscow were overwhelmed by its size, a 1517 account claiming it was twice as large as Prague or Florence, while Chancellor in 1553 and his compatriot, Fletcher, in 1587 both said it was larger than London.[14] Novgorod and Pskov also continued as major centers until the second half of the sixteenth century. Lesser towns were strung along the great trade routes that laced the realm, from the mouth of the Northern Dvina south to Moscow, along the Volga from Iaroslavl east to Nizhni Novgorod and its competitor Kazan, and along the western marches on the roads leading into Europe. A very few of these towns may have had as many as 7,500 to 15,000 people in them, a larger number between three and five thousand, but most had not much over a thousand inhabitants.[15] The new importance of towns in economic life is shown, however, not so much by the size of the individual urban settlements as by the increase in their total number. New ones were established in both the old parts of the realm and in the annexed territories. In the first half of the century there were about 160 towns; by the century's end there were around 230.[16] Many of the new towns had originally been fortified border outposts. Then, when the swiftly moving frontiers were pushed out beyond them, and when merchants and artisans settled around

---

[13] Herberstein, *Notes*, II, 5. A population of over 200,000, assuming an average of 5 persons per dwelling (cf. Struve, *Sotsial'naia . . . istoriia*, p. 213).

[14] Bakhrushin, "Ruskii gorod," p. 152.

[15] Chechulin, *Goroda, passim*.   [16] Zimin, "Sostav," pp. 336-347.

their palisades, they grew into true towns. Still other places, old and new, became commercial or industrial centers thanks to their location on a trade route, or to some nearby supply of a natural resource such as salt or iron ore.

Despite their increased importance the towns contained a tiny part of the total population of the state. Moreover, towns large and small retained rural characteristics, raising much of their own food within their own limits or in the immediately surrounding countryside. Even in Moscow there were broad fields and meadows along the river and numerous house gardens, and the city was encircled by a wide belt of pasture land on which the Muscovites grazed their horses and cattle. Many smaller places—especially those that were primarily military establishments—were really large villages whose inhabitants supported themselves by working the fields that lay around their settlement.[17] But the great cities, and undoubtedly most of the lesser ones, were unable to raise enough food to meet their needs. The Venetian diplomat, Ambrogio Contarini, in Moscow in 1476, commented on the large amount of foodstuffs brought into the city for sale, and Chancellor, eighty years later, told of the great quantities of grain and fish shipped daily into the city.[18] Novgorod had long been dependent upon food imports from more fertile parts of the realm. The many weekly markets that grew up in other towns, large and small, in the sixteenth century, in which lords and peasants sold their produce to townsmen, are evidence of the dependence of the city dwellers upon rural producers for a good deal of their food supply.

Moscow was the preeminent economic center of the realm not only because of its geographical position and its political function, but also because of the favor shown it by the government. The tsars were determined to strengthen the importance of their hereditary capital at the expense of rival cities. They compelled merchants and artisans to move from these cities into Moscow, they spent much money in new construction and in maintaining their courts, and themselves engaged in extensive

[17] Bakhrushin, "Vozniknovenie," pp. 108-141; *idem*, "Moskva," p. 175; Platonov, *Smutnoe vremia*, pp. 54-58.

[18] Contarini, *Travels*, pp. 161-162; Hakluyt, *Principal Navigations*, p. 225; cf. Bakhrushin, "Moskva," pp. 175-177.

trading activities. Merchants came there from all parts of Russia and from abroad to buy and sell, and foreign visitors from the latter fifteenth century on were impressed by the amount of business activity they observed.

From Moscow merchandise was shipped in every direction, sometimes traveling hundreds of miles before reaching its destination. Other centers, such as Novgorod, Riazan, Vologda, Iaroslavl, Astrakhan, Nizhnii Novgorod, Kazan, and Putivl, also were staples from which both domestic and foreign wares were distributed to many parts of Russia. Smaller towns often had extensive trade connections. Ustiug, at the junction of trade routes that ran from the White Sea to Moscow, Siberia, and the Volga, did business with merchants from all parts of the realm. Viazma, between the headwaters of the Dnieper and Moscow Rivers, in the mid-seventeenth century had direct trading connections with over forty other towns scattered through Russia. Tikhvin, south of Lake Ladoga, did business with thirty or more towns stretching from the shores of the White Sea to the urban centers of the western frontier and to Kazan in the east. Besides participating in this interregional trade these lesser markets, like the major cities, were the chief suppliers of goods for the rural areas that surrounded them.[19]

The revival of urban handicraft was a significant indication of the expansion of the market economy, and of the part played by the city. As was pointed out in an earlier chapter, when the cities declined in the era of the Mongol domination, the demand for manufactured goods had been met primarily by peasant or slave artisans working on the manor, or in the commune, and producing for local needs. This practice, of course, persisted and, in fact, artisans remained an important part of rural society into the twentieth century. But in the sixteenth century village handicraft production no longer satisfied local demand and had to be supplemented by purchases from urban artisans, and the growing cities themselves provided an expanding market for manufactured goods. Industrial production began again to be concentrated in the towns, as it had been long before in the Kievan era. Unlike Western Europe, a craft gild system did not

---

[19] Tomsinskii, *Ocherki*, I, 29; Fekhner, *Torgovlia*, pp. 41-50.

develop (although there are a few indications of a rudimentary organization of smiths),[20] so that the division of labor between trades or within a trade was much less defined in Russia than in the West. Still, there was a considerable degree of specialization, one historian counting 210 different crafts in the towns and a later writer claiming that this listing was incomplete. Regional specialization also appeared, with individual urban areas becoming centers for the production of certain types of goods. Novgorod and Pskov, for instance, were centers for the making of wares of iron and of silver; Novgorod was also an important producer of leather goods, as were Kazan and Serpukhov; Mozhaisk specialized in wool cloth, and so on. Moscow had artisans of all sorts but if there was any specialty there it was the manufacture of arms.[21]

The recovery of trade was not limited to the towns. Markets, usually held once a week, were established in many villages in which locally produced wares were offered for sale. The customers were mainly the people of the village and its surrounding area, but sometimes traders and large consumers, such as monasteries, were among the buyers. There were probably twenty or so stalls in most of these markets, but a few of them had many more—at Mleva, a village on the Msta River in Novgorod Land, there were 332 in 1551. Fairs, meeting one or more times a year, also appeared. Often they were under the auspices of a monastery and were held on church holidays when many people made pilgrimages to monasteries. Merchants came to these periodic marts from many parts of Russia, and on occasion from abroad, to buy and sell.[22]

Agricultural products, and above all grain, were the most important articles in domestic commerce. Other chief market commodities included forest products, fish, and salt. The most active trade in farm goods, as in other wares, took place in the Center, the most heavily populated part of the realm. The farms of this region not only produced to meet the needs of the Center itself, but were the granary for the North and Northwest. Grain

[20] Rybakov, *Remeslo*, pp. 775-776.
[21] Bakhrushin, "O territorial'nom razdelenii," pp. 55-106.
[22] *Novgorodskiia pistsovyia knigi*, vi, 567-568; Bakhrushin, "Sel'skie torzhki," pp. 188-203; Danilova, *Ocherki*, pp. 38-41.

was also shipped from the Center into some of the newly annexed colonial areas, where agriculture lagged in the first stages of settlement.

The high costs of transport, particularly with such bulky commodities as grain, was a serious handicap to trade. Data from the end of the sixteenth century indicate that it cost 75 percent of the purchase price to ship a *bochka* (*ca.* 24 bushels) of grain from Moscow to Archangel, 650 miles away.[23] In 1596-1597 the agents of the Spaso-Prilutskii Monastery bought 4,100 chetverts (*ca.* 24,000 bushels) of grain in Vologda, shipped it north 600 miles to Kholmogory and sold it there for a gross profit of 228 rubles. But so much had to be laid out in transport that the monastery netted only between 125-150 rubles on the shipment. These excessive costs were due not only to the actual transport charges but also to the many tariffs and fees that had to be paid en route.[24]

In foreign commerce the revival that had gotten under way in the fifteenth century was greatly stimulated by the territorial expansion of the sixteenth. The annexations to the south and east gave the Russians control of the Don and the Volga and strengthened commercial connections with the East. The conquest of Smolensk in 1514 opened the doors to trade with Lithuania, Poland, and Germany, and the winning of the Baltic port of Narva in 1558 during the Livonian War, although it was retained only until 1581, aided in further development of commerce with the West. An all water route between Russia and the Atlantic states was opened in 1553 when English seamen, in search of a Northeast passage to the Indies, sailed above Scandinavia into the White Sea and reached the mouth of the Northern Dvina. A lively English-Russian exchange began and soon Dutch ships were also making the perilous journey. In 1584 the port city of Archangel was founded. Its harbor was open for only the three summer months and it was far from the chief Russian trading centers, but the advantage of the sea route outweighed these handicaps, for Russia's frequent political difficulties with her western neighbors impeded the flow of goods over more direct

23 Rozhkov, *Sel'skoe khoziaistvo*, pp. 287-288.
24 Man'kov, "Dvizhenie," pp. 147-148.

routes, and the tolls and other expenses that had to be paid in overland transport raised shipping costs. So Archangel became the focal point for Russia's trade with Western Europe. A great fair was held there each year, at first just in August, but in 1663, at the request of the foreign merchants, it was extended from the first of June to the first of September. Initially, the English were the most important foreigners in this trade, but in the early part of the seventeenth century the Dutch took over leadership.

In her trade with the West, Russia exchanged raw materials and semi-finished goods for manufactured wares. Her chief exports were vegetable and animal products, such as hemp cordage, flax, pitch, potash, furs, bristles, hides, salted meats, tallow, wax, and train oil. Grain, the principal export of contemporary Poland and East Germany, was of small importance in the Russian foreign trade. During the sixteenth century special permission was required of the tsar to ship it out of the country, and in the next century only limited amounts were allowed to be exported despite efforts of Western European governments to get leave for their merchants to buy more. Russian imports from the West were chiefly luxury wares but also included more prosaic goods—for example, base metals, munitions, and chemicals.[25]

The Eastern trade was probably of more importance to Russia than her commerce with the West. Certainly Russian foreign traders played a much more active role in it than they did in the exchange with Europe. The practice of allowing merchants to accompany diplomatic missions to Oriental potentates continued, and sometimes the merchants themselves served as the tsar's emissaries. A network of routes developed but the bulk of the trade moved on the Volga and Don Rivers. In contrast to the Western trade, manufactured goods formed a large part of Russian exports to the East. Of these the chief were metal wares, textile products, leather goods, weapons, and armor. Among raw material exports furs were the most important. Only a small amount of agricultural goods was shipped out. Russian merchants also reexported western products to the eastern markets,

25 Kulischer, *Russische Wirtschaftsgeschichte*, I, 321-322, 420-444; Willan, "Trade," p. 315; Muliukin, *Ocherki*, pp. 36-41; Amburger, *Die Familie Marselis*, pp. 71-73.

though this activity was apparently not of much significance in the sixteenth century. From the East, Russia imported luxury wares and also cheaper products such as cotton cloth. Large numbers of horses and sheep were brought in, chiefly by Tatars of the Nogay Horde, whose horses were highly valued by Russians for their speed and endurance.[26]

Unlike Western Europe where trade was predominantly a middle-class occupation, persons from all levels of Russian society engaged in commerce. The Austrian ambassador von Mayerberg, coming to Russia in 1661 from a world where aristocrats scorned business, was dismayed to find that noblemen there were active merchants. "All the people of quality," he wrote, "and even the ambassadors sent to foreign princes, trade publicly. They buy, they sell, and they exchange without a qualm, thereby making their elevated rank, venerable that it is, subservient to their avarice."[27] The tsar himself, like his ancient forebears, the princes of Kiev, was the single most important business man in the entire empire. Through his agents he carried on an extensive domestic and foreign trade, and a government bureau was charged with handling his commercial activities. The surplus produced on his personal properties was sold on the market and brought in, according to the English Dr. Giles Fletcher who visited Russia in 1588-1589, 60,000 rubles a year in Ivan IV's reign, and 230,000 rubles during the reign of Fedor (who, said Fletcher, lived less pretentiously than had his father). Nor did the tsars limit themselves to dealing in the products of their own holdings. They maintained monopolies on many articles, including at various times in the sixteenth and seventeenth centuries such wares as sables, grain for export, raw silks, caviar, potash, rhubarb (much esteemed as a purge), and walrus tusks (from which knife and whip handles were made). They also had the liquor monopoly. Sometimes the tsar, through his commercial agents and officials, engrossed the entire output of a commodity, raised its price, and then compelled merchants to buy. Or he would raise the price of a commodity and then not allow anyone else to sell it until he had disposed of his own stock of the item. All wares brought in by foreign merchants had first

---

[26] Fekhner, *Torgovlia, passim.* [27] Mayerberg, "Relation," I, 154.

to be offered to the tsar's representatives, and only after they had bought as much for their master as they wanted could the merchants sell to other persons.[28]

Engrossing was not limited to the tsar, although other traders did not have his unique power to corner a commodity and so had to resort to less spectacular devices. In a charter issued by Tsar Boris in 1601, reference was made to dealers who had agents everywhere buying up grain and holding it for higher prices. Forestalling, too, was practiced, the same charter reporting that peasants on their way to market were met on the road by merchants who bought their grain.[29]

Monasteries had early taken a leading role in commerce despite the Church's prohibition against trading for profit by its clergy. An account written in 1558 by one of the first English visitors to Russia reported that the monks of Trinity-St. Serge, the wealthiest monastery in the country, "are as great merchants as any in the land of Russia, and doe occupy buying and selling as much as any other men, and have boats which passe too and fro in the rivers with merchandize from place to place where any of their countrey do traffike."[30] The monasteries sold their own produce and also bought for resale on other markets.

The leading professional merchants were known as *gosti* (guests). Besides trading on their own account they were the tsar's business agents, being chosen for this function from among the most successful traders in the realm. They also were given responsibility for gathering certain taxes and were required to turn in a sum fixed by the government. In return for these duties they were accorded a special status akin to that of the serving nobility. Among these merchants the Stroganovs were the most famous. Of peasant origin, they began their rise in the latter part of the fourteenth century in the salt trade. As time went on they expanded their activities to other industrial and commercial enterprises. They became great landowners in the colonial north

---

[28] Fletcher, *Of the Russe Common Wealth*, pp. 49, 57-58; Kilburger, "Kurzer Unterricht," pp. 252 ff.; Herberstein, *Notes*, I, 111; Hakluyt, *Principal Navigations*, III, 94, 110; Konovalov, "Thomas Chamberlain's Description of Russia," p. 113.

[29] Grekov, *Glavneishie etapy*, p. 29.

[30] Hakluyt, *Principal Navigations*, II, 441.

and played the leading role in the commercial exploitation of the riches of Siberia.

Members of the peasantry were active in local trade. Doubtless the increased cash demands made upon them by their lords had much to do with bringing them into the market. But many of them apparently abandoned their rural occupations to become full-time operators of stalls and shops in the towns and the cities. In some of the smaller centers nearly all of the shop-keepers were from the peasant class. In addition, peasant artisans came to market and sold their products directly to the consumer or to traders, the putting-out system, so widely used in the West, being still unknown in Russia.[31]

The expansion in economic activity led to the increased use of money in every day life. Government officials who formerly had been paid in kind were now put on money salaries, more and more of the taxes were collected in cash, and, most important, many of the peasants' obligations to their seigniors were converted into money payments, especially in the regions where trade was most active. The heightened demand for coins from the people who had now become involved in the cash nexus could not be met completely by the government mints, and furs, long used as a medium of exchange, continued to be employed extensively in this role in the sixteenth and on into the seventeenth centuries.

Silver was the chief money metal, although copper was also minted. Copper money, according to John Hasse, one of the early English merchants in Russia, was used "only for the small purchases of the poor." Gold coins were struck on special occasions when they were given to persons whom the tsar wished to honor. The ruble—the earliest known use of the term is in a document of 1316—was not actually minted but was the money of account. It was considered to be equal to a *grivenka* of silver weighing 48 *zolotniki* (1 *zolotnik* = 4.26 grams). The coins that were issued were small silver ones called *den'gi*. Because of the debasement of the coinage in the fifteenth and first part of the sixteenth centuries the number of *den'gi* in a ruble and the silver equivalent of the ruble itself varied with time and place. In

31 Bakhrushin, "Predposylki," pp. 49-50.

Novgorod 216 *den'gi* had been minted from a *grivenka*, these 216 being equal to one ruble. The Novgorod *den'ga*, then, weighed .22 *zolotniki*. In Moscow in the latter fifteenth century 432 *den'gi* were coined from a *grivenka* so that the *den'ga* of Moscow weighed only .11 *zolotniki*, or half of the weight of the Novgorod *den'ga*. Furthermore, the ruble in Moscow was valued at just 200 of these Muscovite *den'gi* so that it was equal to only 22 *zolotniki*, or less than half of the Novgorod ruble. When Moscow annexed the Republic of Novgorod in 1478 the Novgorod coinage was maintained at a ratio of one Novgorod *den'ga* to two Moscow *den'gi*. The ruble of Moscow, valued at 200 Moscow *den'gi* or 100 Novgorod *den'gi* became the money of account. The Novgorod coinage continued in use, however, and proved so popular that by the end of the sixteenth century the Moscow system was suspended. Since then the Russian ruble has been valued at 100 kopecks (i.e. *den'gi*).

During the reigns of Ivan III and Vasilii III the coinage devaluation continued with up to 260 Novgorod *den'gi* or 520 Muscovite *den'gi* being coined from a *grivenka*. Finally, in 1535 the government during the regency of Elena Glinskaia, mother of the infant Ivan IV, used the debased condition of the currency as an excuse for the issue of a new coinage. Actually, the new money represented a still further devaluation, for now 300 Novgorod *den'gi* and 600 Moscow *den'gi* were minted from a *grivenka* of silver. The new Novgorod *den'ga* weighed only .16 *zolotniki* and the new Moscow *den'ga* .08 *zolotniki*, so that the ruble was equal to just 16 *zolotniki*, or one-third of its value at the beginning of the fifteenth century. Once this last debasement was carried through the money remained remarkably stable into the early seventeenth century, despite the troubles that plagued the country after 1550.

A study of sixteenth century prices in major Russian markets showed that they moved upward in the course of that century. Because of the paucity of data it is not possible to determine whether this rise was of the same proportions as the rise in the "Price Revolution" that was taking place in contemporary Western Europe. But it is clear that Russian grain prices were much higher in the second half of the century than they were before 1550. The price notations for other agricultural goods and for forest and industrial products are even scantier than those for grain, but the extant material points to an upward movement in the prices of these commodities also.[32]

The price increase can be attributed to a number of causes. Up to 1535 it seems likely that some (and perhaps much) of it was the result of currency debasement, but after the monetary reform of that year this factor was no longer operative. Crop failures, wars, and economic and social disturbances were of importance, especially in producing short-term price rises. Some of the long-term increase was undoubtedly caused by a growth in the quantity of money in circulation. Non-Russian coins, brought into the country through trade with foreigners, circulated freely as they always had, though sometimes they were melted down and recoined as Russian money. Usually, however, European merchants traded their own goods for Russian wares so that the contribution of this source to the money supply could not have been of major proportions. Money came in through the Eastern trade, but the scanty data do not indicate that the amounts involved were of major proportions.[33] There was undoubtedly some flow of money out of Russia, although in the second half of the sixteenth century measures were introduced that made it very difficult and sometimes impossible to export silver and gold in any form.[34] Bullion was imported, but most of it seems to have been used for non-monetary purposes. Visitors to the court of the tsars were overwhelmed by the vast amount of gold and silver plate, some of it encrusted with gems, that was used to feed hundreds of people at state banquets. Much bullion, too, was utilized for church decorations and sacred art. There is no evidence, then, of an influx of precious metals into Russia on a scale comparable to the stream of American treasure that poured into Western Europe in the sixteenth century. Still, the injection of small additional amounts of silver into a system where there was relatively little money in use could have exerted a decided inflationary effect. Finally, part of the price rise can be attributed to the growth of the market demand. The increase in the price of foodstuffs, especially of grain, indicates a pressure of population upon food supplies. To use the language of the

[32] Blum, "Prices," pp. 187-189.   [33] Cf. Fekhner, *Torgovlia*, pp. 84-85.
[34] Muliukin, *Ocherki*, pp. 27, 41-43.

economist, increase in demand and inelasticity of supply worked together to push up prices.

II

The fourteenth-fifteenth century was an era of contraction marked by depopulation and abandoned holdings, urban decline, and diminished trade. Yet, in the midst of this distress the stirrings of economic revival appeared. Only surmises can be offered to explain this paradox. Perhaps part of the answer lies in the activities of a few individuals who decided to try new tactics in their economic activities. These men may have figured that these innovations might enable them to better their own economic position despite the hard times. The landlord who began to engage in commerce, or who perhaps introduced more efficient agricultural methods on his lands, the artisan who improved his techniques and turned out new and better products, the trader who saw a chance to establish profitable commercial connections with a foreign land, may well have reasoned this way. Their successes could have inspired others to follow their examples, and whatever their motives may have been, the combined effect of the activities of these entrepreneurs introduced a kinetic force into a stagnant situation and must have served as a stimulus to revival. Possibly the dynamic they supplied might alone have been enough to bring about an upward movement in the secular trend. But as it happened, beginning in the latter part of the fifteenth century and continuing on into the sixteenth other developments occurred that provided a milieu offering far greater opportunities to the innovators and their imitators than had hitherto been available to them. The upswing of the sixteenth century was the result. Some of these new circumstances have been discussed in this chapter: the growth in population, the territorial expansion, and the probable increase in the supply of money. Another was the creation of a unified and centralized realm that afforded still more scope for the growth of trade and for the regional division of labor. The emergence of this new state and the establishment of autocratic rule over it by the princes of Moscow are the subjects of the next chapter.

9

ABSOLUTISM AND ARISTOCRACY

THE REIGN of Vasilii II of Moscow (1425-1462) proved to be a decisive turning point in the history of the Russian state. By virtue of his final victory in the civil wars that filled most of his reign, Vasilii was able to liquidate the old political system and to draw the powers of government into his own hands. In accomplishing this he laid the foundation for the establishment of autocratic rule by his successors. His son, Ivan III (1462-1505), and his grandson, Vasilii III (1505-1533), carried on the work he had begun. They did the job so well that Baron von Herberstein, who came to Russia twice as ambassador of the Holy Roman Emperor during Vasilii III's reign, reported that: "In the sway which he [Vasilii] holds over his people, he surpasses all the monarchs of the whole world. . . .He uses his authority as much over ecclesiastics as laymen, and holds unlimited control over the lives and property of all his subjects; not one of his counsellors has sufficient authority to dare to oppose him, or even differ from him, on any subject. They openly confess that the will of the prince is the will of God, and that whatever the prince does he does by the will of God. . . ."[1]

After Vasilii's death there was a short period of aristocratic reaction during the minority of Ivan IV, later called *Groznyi*, the Terrible.[2] But after Ivan took over personal rule in 1547 the absolutism reached its apogee. Ivan himself, in a letter in 1564 to Prince Kurbskii, once his favorite but now in exile, used the words of St. Paul to describe his conception of his own position: " 'Let every soul be subject unto the higher powers. For there is no power ordained that is not of God. . . . Whosoever, therefore, resisteth the power, resisteth the ordinance of God.' Think on this and reflect, [the tsar continued] that he who resists power,

---

1 Herberstein, *Notes*, I, 30, 32.

2 Though the most accurate rendering of the word *Groznyi* is "Awe-inspiring," Ivan is known best to English-speaking peoples as the Terrible which, although imprecise as a translation, seems a not unearned appellation.

resists God; and who resists God is called an apostate, which is the worst sin."[3]

The growth of absolutism was promoted by the ready subservience of leaders of the clergy. Important ecclesiastics, such as Zosima, the Metropolitan from 1490 to 1494, and Joseph Sanin (1440-1515) abbot of Volokolamsk, argued for imitation of Byzantine caesaropapism by the tsar because he was God's representative on earth, and taught that men must obey him in all things. Among churchmen, too, appeared the idea of Moscow as the "Third Rome," the successor to Rome and Constantinople as the center of true Christianity, with the tsar as the spiritual as well as the temporal heir of Byzantium.

The clerical enthusiasm for, and cooperation with, absolutism was in sharp contrast to the attitude and activities of the great landed nobility. The opposition of the men of this class to the ambitions of the tsars was so intense and enduring that it kept Russia in a condition of almost unceasing internal unrest for well over a century. The bitterest opponents of the Muscovite rulers' claims to autocratic power were found among the serving princes. The members of this group, known collectively as the *kniazhata,* could not forget that they were of the same royal blood as the Muscovite prince they now served, that they were descended of men who once had ruled, and that genealogically many of them were the equals, and some the superiors, of the descendants of Daniel of Moscow. They recognized—or had to accept—the political inevitability of the unification under the leadership of Moscow, but they wanted the new state to be established on oligarchic rather than on absolutist principles. And they felt that the least they deserved was precedence in the royal service over those servitors who came of less distinguished stock.

Understandably, the pretensions of the *kniazhata* were not appreciated by the servitors who were not of princely origin. Many of these boyars were of families that had long served the House of Moscow and had aided mightily in its rise. They had, of course, benefited from the successes of their sovereigns; indeed, that was the chief reason why they and their forebears had

[3] Fennell, ed., *Correspondence,* p. 19.

remained in Moscow's service. Some of them had become great landowners with their own servitors and their own military force.[4] Still, in the times when Moscow's fortunes had been at low ebb, their loyalty had been tried and not found wanting. Their faithfulness and their importance to their princes had not gone unmarked. Dmitrii Donskoi told his boyars, "I was born among you and grew up among you and reign with you. . . . I keep guard over my patrimony with you . . . and I have given you honor and love, and with you hold cities and great districts . . . and rejoice with you and share sorrows with you; to me you are not to be called boyars but princes of my land." And as he lay dying Donskoi is said to have advised his children to treat the boyars well. "Love them," he exhorted, "and undertake nothing without their consent."[5]

The rank of the boyars depended mainly upon the length of time their families had been in Moscow's service. About thirty-five clans, whose attachment dated back to the first century of the princedom's history, formed the élite of the fifteenth and sixteenth centuries. Those whose progenitors began their service with Donskoi were of considerably less eminence, while of the many who had enlisted under Moscow's banner in the reign of Donskoi's successors, Vasilii I and Vasilii II, only two established families that became of outstanding importance.[6]

After much friction between the rival groups a method based on genealogy was worked out for appointments in the tsar's service. This system was known as *mestnichestvo*, or "place order." The lineage of each candidate for a post and his place in the line of his descent (his *otechestvo*, as it was called) was compared. No one would take a position if in it he would be subordinate to a person of equal or inferior descent. If he found out after he had accepted the office that he was serving under such conditions, he petitioned the monarch to remedy this dishonor. The comparison of *otechestvo* was a remarkably complicated operation, for it was based upon the relative ranks occupied by the ancestors of the men doing the comparing, as well as upon the place of these men in the line of descent from these ancestors.

[4] Bakhrushin, *Ivan Groznyi*, p. 9.   [5] Platonov, *Boris Godunov*, p. 20.
[6] Veselovskii, *Feodal'noe zemlevladenie*, I, 84-85.

The fundamental principle of the system was that no one need serve under another person if he could show that one of his ancestors had held a higher position than had the ancestors of his proposed superior. Moreover, each servitor was responsible for the honor of all his living kinsmen and of all his descendants, for if he accepted a rank inferior to that warranted by his pedigree he set a precedent that would damage the careers of all his present and future relatives.

An example illustrates the intricacy and absurdity of this method of appointment. The post held by Prince D. M. Pozharskii was of a rank lower than that of Prince B. Saltykov. This was justified on the grounds that Pozharskii was the kinsmen and genealogical equal of Prince Romodanovskii, who had been the inferior in service to one M. Saltykov, who in turn was of a lower genealogical rank within the Saltykov family than was the above-mentioned B. Saltykov.[7]

The wrangles over lineage inevitably caused much trouble and interfered seriously with the functioning of the government. It became necessary both for the rulers and the serving families to take measures designed to regulate and authenticate opposing claims. The families compiled their own genealogical and service records to serve as documentary evidence in disputes over rank, and in the sixteenth century an official genealogical directory was compiled by the central government.

The *mestnichestvo* system acted as a limitation upon the power of the tsar since it compelled him to select his officials according to standards set up by his servitors, rather than by those he might have wished to establish himself. On the other hand, the system strengthened the sovereign's prestige and power. The eager competition for posts in his government was a recognition by the aristocracy that honor was to be found in his service, and the rivalry among aspirants for high office weakened the corporate strength of the nobility and so made easier the triumph of royal autocracy.[8]

The Boyar Duma (Council) was another aristocratic institution that conceivably could have served to limit the development

[7] Kliuchevskii, *History*, iii, 71.
[8] Hötzsch, "Adel und Lehnswesen," pp. 555, 556; Miliukov, *Ocherki*, i, 171.

of the monarch's power. This body dated back to the era of the independent princedoms, when rulers had stood in great need of the support and good will of their chief servitors. It had been of much importance in those times. But the Muscovite princes of the fifteenth and sixteenth centuries were able to reduce the Duma's function to that of an advisory body, whose members they selected, and whose counsel they sought at their own discretion.

Gaining the upper hand over their nobility was only one phase of the Muscovite rulers' campaign to unite Russia under their absolute rule. They knew that to reach their final goal they had to destroy the power of the princes and of the nobility in the lands they annexed. The most effective of the policies they adopted to accomplish this was to confiscate the land of the proprietors and force them to settle in other parts of Muscovy. The first large scale application of this technique was made by Ivan III after his annexation of Novgorod Land in 1478. Between 1483 and 1500 the tsar (as Ivan began to call himself) confiscated 80 percent or more of the properties there (including church possessions), containing an estimated total of one million desiatins of arable. The only proprietors whose holdings were not appropriated were some of the *svoezemtsi,* the smallest landowners. Ivan apparently felt that he had nothing to fear from these petty proprietors. But even they were shifted from alodial to pomestye tenure. The tsar retained about a quarter of the confiscated villages and hamlets with their attached fields for himself. The rest he distributed as pomestyes to around 2,000 of his followers. Many of the dispossessed Novgorodians were taken into the tsar's service but were moved from their homeland into Muscovite districts, often being settled as pomeshchiks on the eastern frontiers.[9]

When Pskov was annexed in 1510 by Vasilii III the policy of wholesale confiscations was again applied. In Riazan and Tver a large number of the servitors of the ousted rulers of these princedoms shifted their allegiance to Vasilii and were apparently allowed to continue, at least for a while, as alodial

[9] Bazilevich, "Novgorodskie pomeshchiki," p. 62; Veselovskii, *Feodal'noe zem-levladenie,* I, 287, 289; Kulischer, *Russische Wirtschaftsgeschichte,* I, 180.

proprietors of their holdings. In Chernigov-Seversk the proprietors were also permitted to remain on their lands, but were shifted from alodial to service tenure. In Smolensk the landowners retained complete ownership of their holdings for almost fifty years after Vasilii annexed that princedom in 1521. Then, during the reign of Ivan IV, mass confiscations were made there. Most of the Smolensk proprietors seemed to have been resettled in central Muscovy, and their lands distributed as pomestyes to Muscovite servitors.[10]

Neither Ivan nor Vasilii took members of the *kniazhata* into their innermost councils. Nor did they hesitate to banish a serving prince who had incurred their disfavor, or force him into a monastery, or even execute him. If a member of the *kniazhata* tried to leave their service for that of another ruler he was arrested and charged with treason and apostasy. When members of the *kniazhata* entered Moscow's service they were required to give a written promise that they would serve him and his children for the rest of their lives. But this pledge alone was in certain cases not enough to satisfy Ivan or Vasilii. In these instances they required the servitor to provide guarantors from among his fellows, who agreed to pay large cash forfeits in the event that he broke his word and left. In 1474 Prince Daniel Kholmskii signed a pledge of service to Ivan III that was backed by eight guarantors, who were to pay a total of 8,000 rubles if Kholmskii did not remain loyal. Vasilii III took this precaution with at least nine princes, and also with one untitled boyar. The guarantees for these men ran from 2,000 to 5,000 rubles.[11]

Such measures obviously were aimed at restricting or abolishing the traditional, albeit already limited, right of these servitors to choose their principal and to leave his service whenever he wished. But the right of free choice and free departure continued to be asserted by servitors on into the sixteenth century. In 1537, when Ivan IV was but seven years old his uncle, Prince Andrei of Staritsa, addressed a message to the minor servitors urging them to switch their allegiance from the child tsar to him-

[10] Veselovskii, *Feodal'noe zemlevladenie*, I, 86-88.
[11] Eck, *Le moyen âge*, p. 200.

self. A number must have answered his call, for the government ordered that those of higher rank who had entered Andrei's service were to be tortured and imprisoned, and the lesser men were hanged "along the road to Novgorod highway, at a goodly distance from one another." Thirty were strung up. Andrei himself was imprisoned and later executed.[12]

The melodramatic scene in 1553 at the sick bed of Ivan IV was another illustration of the conviction held by servitors that they were still free to choose whom they would serve. Ivan, believing himself dying, pleaded with his chief servitors to pledge their fealty to his infant son by kissing the cross—the Russian way of sealing an oath. A number, among them some of Ivan's closest friends and advisors, wanted to take the oath in favor of Prince Vladimir of Staritsa, son of the executed Andrei, even though Ivan, his voice weak with pain, asked them "Have you forgotten your oath to serve only me and my children?" Only after much suasion did they agree to do the tsar's bidding.[13]

The fact of the matter seemed to be that so long as the servitors felt that the prince was not strong enough to force his will upon them they tried to assert their traditional freedom of choice. But with the increasing power of the throne the opportunities to exercise their independence grew always fewer. Finally, in the seventeenth century the once important right of free choice of service was reduced to an empty formality in which the sovereign and the servitor went through a show of bargaining.

The policies followed by Ivan III and Vasilii III went into temporary eclipse during the minority of Ivan IV. That prince was only three when his father, Vasilii, died in 1533, and for the next thirteen years the government was in the control of great lords. Then, at sixteen, Ivan assumed personal rule and almost immediately embarked upon a program designed to strengthen the central power.

The most important innovation of this first period in his personal reign was the reorganization of the military obligation of the servitors. The state had to have at its disposal at all times an armed force strong enough to put down internal threats to its power, to protect itself from its foreign enemies, and to con-

12 Karamzin, *Istoriia*, VIII, 14-16.   13 *Ibid.*, pp. 201 ff.

tinue on its program of territorial expansion. That military force was supplied by the nobles, the servitors of the throne, from the great serving prince down to the insignificant pomeshchik. In return for their allegiance the princes had rewarded the servitors with property, or allowed those who already owned land to keep it. But there had been no relation between land-holding and the requirement to do military service, except for the pomeshchiks. Thus, out of 574 seigniors listed in a cadastral survey made in Tver sometime between 1539 and 1555, 150 were described as not serving anyone.[14] Ivan decided that all lay seigniors should be subject to military obligation. On 20 September 1556 he decreed that every landlord had to provide for the tsar's service a fully armed mounted warrior, with a second horse in case of a distant campaign, for every 300 chetverts (100 chetverts in each of three fields) of "good" land that he held. If he could not furnish the appropriate number of warriors his "surplus" land was to be taken from him. Those who could not perform military service themselves had to commute the obligation into a money payment. Nonfeasors were to have their land taken from them and given to men who were willing to render the service demanded by the tsar.[15]

Another major reform of these years was the abolition of the *kormlenie* system of administration. The official reason given for this action was that it was necessary to protect the people from the abuses of the *kormlenshchiki*. According to the contemporary account whole regions had been devastated by their exorbitant demands, and there had been many instances of rising of the people in outraged and violent protest.[16] Actually the powers of the *kormlenshchiki* had begun to be clipped in the latter part of the fifteenth century. The growth in the central power that started at that time apparently allowed a greater amount of direct government from Moscow. It seems likely, too, that the hobbling and then the abolition of the *kormlenie* system were reflections in governmental techniques of the upswing in economic life. The better times made it increasingly possible for the tsar to use means to provide for his servitor other than turn-

14 Sergeevich, *Drevnosti*, III, 17-18.
15 *PSRL*, XIII, pt. 1, 268-269.
16 *Ibid.*, p. 267.

ing over a "feeding" to them. Starting in the reign of Ivan III servitors were often given cash payments, but the most usual type of recompense was a grant of land, either on alodial or pomestye tenure, indicating that it had now become possible for a servitor to draw a satisfactory living from the operation of landed property.

These and other constructive measures of the first part of Ivan IV's reign, aimed at strengthening his realm and his own position in it, proved to be the prelude to a mighty—and insane —drive by the tsar to wipe out all resistance to his bid for absolute power. That his reign would turn out this way could scarcely have been suspected when he assumed power as a boy of sixteen. For though he had turned against some of the aristocrats who had run the state during his minority, he had chosen his intimate friends and advisors from among the greatest nobles. He got along well with these men until 1553. Then he apparently began to have suspicions that they were interested in relegating him to a subordinate position and taking over the reins of government. This idea had perhaps first entered his mind as early as 1547 when his high born councilors had opposed his marriage to Anastasia Romanova Iurieva because she was of non-royal boyar stock. In any event, the refusal of his closest associates to swear allegiance to his infant son when Ivan thought he was dying, made him realize how tenuous was his hold upon the loyalty of the great aristocrats. Still, after his recovery he remained on good terms with them, at least externally, until 1560. In that year Anastasia, with whom the young tsar had been very happy, died.

After her death—which he blamed upon his erstwhile intimates[17]—he turned completely against the high nobility, and particularly against the *kniazhata*, and launched a program designed to destroy its power. His first steps were of a restrictive and legal nature, for he knew he must go slowly. As Dr. Fletcher, in Russia soon after Ivan's death, put it: ". . . Ivan Vasilowich . . . being a man of high spirit, and subtill in his kind, meaning to reduce his government into a more strickt forme, beganne by

---

[17] Fennell, ed., *Correspondence*, pp. 191-192n.

degrees to clip of their greatnes, and to bring it downe to a lesser proportion."[18]

Following the precedent set by his father and grandfather he required a number of the serving princes, and also some non-royal boyars, to provide guarantors who agreed to pay large sums to the tsar if the servitor left his service. He also revived land policies of his predecessors, ordering the confiscation without compensation of all property that serving princes had bought or sold during his minority, on the ground that they had neglected to get the throne's permission for these transactions, and thereby broken laws issued by Ivan III and Vasilii III. In 1562 he decreed that if they did not have male heirs their land was to escheat to the sovereign, who would provide a life portion for the widow, dowries for the daughters, and prayers for the deceased. Ivan's purpose in these actions was the same as that which had inspired his father and grandfather; to surround the great lords with a fence of restrictions so that he could keep them and their lands under his surveillance, and thereby control the source of their wealth and power.[19]

These harassments were the initial steps. Then, in 1565, Ivan decided that the time had come for measures that would end forever the aristocratic threat to the absolutist claims of the throne. And here, too, he followed precedent. He adopted the same practice of wholesale confiscation and resettlement that Ivan III and Vasilii III had followed. But he placed the stamp of his own personality upon this inherited policy by adding extermination to it. The device he used to carry through his plan was the organization called the *Oprichnina*. To most of its contemporaries the purpose of this organization was unclear. Many, taken in by the trappings and by the mockeries of the established order with which the tsar embellished his strange creation, thought it was some gruesome pastime that Ivan had invented to amuse himself. Nor can there be much doubt that its savageries and obscenities were in largest part attributable to the twisted mind of the tsar. But Ivan knew very well what he was doing.

[18] Fletcher, *Of the Russe Common Wealth*, p. 32.
[19] Miliukov, *Ocherki*, I, 168; Pokrovskii, *Russkaia istoriia s drevneishikh vremen*, I, 242-243.

He prepared the way skillfully. Early in December, 1564, he suddenly left Moscow with a great retinue and threatened to abdicate because of what he said was the treasonous conduct of the boyars and clergy. He "allowed" himself to be persuaded to reconsider his decision, on his own terms. These turned out to be nothing less than a division of the realm into two parts. One part was called the *Zemshchina*, where the existing governmental machinery continued to operate and where landowners were undisturbed. The other part was called the *Oprichnina*. Private property in this zone was confiscated by Ivan who claimed he needed it for the support of his family and of the new court he had established.

The territory included in the *Oprichnina* was relatively small at the outset, but Ivan added more and more to it until it covered half the entire state. The tsar's purpose was revealed clearly in the land he chose to put into the *Oprichnina* zone. He took that part of his realm that contained the old princedoms annexed by Moscow in the first stages of its territorial expansion. This was where the estates of the *kniazhata*, the descendants of the former rulers of these princedoms, were concentrated. The *Zemshchina* was made up primarily of the territory that ringed these princedoms, and that had been conquered by Ivan III and Vasilii III. Here the great landowners had already been dispossessed or shifted to service tenure. Now Ivan IV was applying their policy to the older parts of the state. The proprietors in the *Oprichnina* region who had their lands taken from them, when they were not executed or banished, were given pomestyes on the frontiers, far from their old homes and from the people over whom they had any hereditary or traditional influence. Ivan kept about a quarter of this confiscated property for himself and distributed the rest as pomestyes to the *oprichniki*, as the men of the *Oprichnina* organization were known.[20]

These *oprichniki* were recruited chiefly from among the members of the lesser nobility. But the corps also included foreign adventurers who had been attracted by the opportunities for plunder it offered, and even some of the dispossessed proprietors were allowed to join. At the outset there were about a

---

[20] Platonov, *Boris Godunov*, pp. 31-36; *idem, La Russie*, pp. 113-117.

thousand of them, and at the peak, around five thousand.[21] Willing instruments of their master, they murdered, tortured, and pillaged at his command. Their organized terror was directed not only against the *kniazhata*. Non-princely boyars, and even the plain people of town and country, were also among their victims. If Ivan thought that the people of a town or of an entire region had become disaffected, or if the men-at-arms and peasants of a great noble were suspected of sympathizing with their lord, he loosed his bravoes to plunder, burn, and kill.

Ivan allowed his fantastic creation to live on until opposition to it which appeared in all levels of society, treachery among the *oprichniki*, and troubles with the Crimean Tatars, persuaded him that it was time to do away with it. It had accomplished its purpose. Contemporary estimates of the number of great lords who had been killed ran from 400 to as high as 10,000.[22] Whatever the true figure may have been, the *kniazhata* was so decimated that only a few of the old princely families remained. Now everyone in the realm had to accept the absolute power of Ivan, and to recognize the truth of the maxim that "the great and the small live by the favor of the sovereign." So, in 1572, Ivan declared that the *Oprichnina* no longer existed—and with characteristic brutality ordered the death penalty for anyone who even mentioned its name. Actually, a good deal of its program was continued for several more years under the name of the *Dvor* (Court), with the *oprichniki*, whose membership had been "purged," now called *Dvorovye liudi*, the Court people. The tsar still retained personal ownership and control over the vast area he had taken from its owners. But the terror had ended. Landlords were no longer evicted en masse, and soon some whose land had been taken from them were even permitted to reoccupy their old holdings.[23]

Absolutism had triumphed. But Ivan, to use Kliuchevskii's metaphor, was like the blinded Samson who in destroying his enemies had buried himself in the ruins of the temple. The shock of the *Oprichnina*, together with the steady drain of the

---

[21] Waliszewski, *Ivan*, p. 243.

[22] Schultz, *Russische Rechtsgeschichte*, p. 105.

[23] Platonov, *Boris Godunov*, pp. 36-37; Veselovskii, *Feodal'noe zemlevladenie*, I, 97.

long and unsuccessful Livonian War (1558-1583) upon the country's resources, deranged the social and economic structure of the realm. A major and prolonged economic crisis and a huge migration from the old regions of settlement in the last decades of the century were in large measure the results of Ivan's policies. The confiscation of the great landed complexes and their sub-division into pomestyes did violence to the agricultural system upon which the nation's economy was based, setting back tech-niques, cutting down on production, and creating new tensions between seigniors and peasants.[24] And although Ivan's repres-sions had greatly reduced the numbers and the power of the great aristocrats, he had not succeeded in erasing the potential threat they offered to absolutism. For soon after his death they began scheming to recover their old position, and took a leading part in the "Time of Troubles" of the first years of the seven-teenth century.

The tsar who had hoped to leave his heirs a united realm left instead a legacy of suffering, discontent, and disunity, that was not to be liquidated for many years to come. Giles Fletcher proved he had the gift of accurate prophecy when he wrote of the *Oprichnina*: "And this wicked pollicy and tyrannous prac-tise (though now it be ceassed) hath so troubled that countrey, and filled it so full of grudge and mortall hatred ever since, that it wil not to be quenched (as it seemeth now) till it burne againe into a civill flame."[25]

Fedor (1584-1598), Ivan's son and successor, and last of the line of Daniel, was totally incapable of handling the affairs of state. Weak in mind and body, his lips twisted into a perpetual smirk, whatever spirit he might once have possessed had been crushed by his life with his baleful father. He was only too glad to turn over the administration of his realm to his wife's brother, Boris Godunov, and so be free to devote himself to his beloved religion, constantly making pilgrimages, spending long hours each day in prayer, and reportedly taking a special delight in ringing church bells.[26] Boris, a vigorous and keen man, contin-

---

[24] These matters are discussed at length in succeeding chapters.
[25] Fletcher, *Of the Russe Common Wealth*, p. 34.
[26] *Ibid.*, p. 144; Margaret, *Estat*, p. 28.

ued Ivan's policies. He did not renew the terror, but he systematically removed men of great family who still held positions of power. He preferred such devices as banishment, or forcing male members of aristocratic clans into monasteries and their women into nunneries, by which bloodless expedient he hoped to extinguish their families, though he was not averse to resorting occasionally to murder. At the same time he sought to hold the loyalty of the gentry by gifts of land and money, by debt and tax moratoriums, and, most important, by greatly increasing their powers over the peasants who lived on their lands.

Boris was so successful in his program that when Fedor died childless in 1598 he easily gained the throne for himself, though he was not of royal blood. None of the surviving members of the princely families, who by virtue of their descent had a much better claim to the throne, were in a position to make an effective bid for it. Boris managed to keep control over his realm until the first years of the seventeenth century when a series of crop failures from 1601 to 1604 brought on famine, brigandage, and widespread popular unrest. This discontent was fed by the resentment of the peasantry against the increased powers and demands of their lords. Serious rural disturbances broke out in many parts of the land. Then in 1604 a pretender to the throne invaded Muscovy with the backing of the King of Poland. He claimed to be Dmitrii, son of Ivan IV and his seventh and last wife, and therefore the half brother and rightful successor to Fedor.[27] Actually Dmitrii had died in 1591 when he was nine years old. (He had given every promise of becoming a son worthy of his sire. Fletcher wrote that when he was just six he delighted "to see sheepe and other cattel killed, and to looke on their throtes while they are bleeding . . . and to beate geese and hennes with a staffe till he see them lie dead."[28]) An official com-

[27] After Anastasia's death in 1560 Ivan made several more marriages, besides having many mistresses. He apparently was wed to a total of seven women, five of whom were crowned as tsaritsas. Ivan claimed that three of the seven had been poisoned by his enemies, two others were forced to take the veil, and one was drowned at Ivan's order. The seventh and last was on her way to oblivion, too, when she was saved by Ivan's own death. For soon after her marriage to him the tsar had begun shopping for a new bride—this time offering his hand to Mary Hastings, an Englishwoman. (Florinsky, *Russia*, I, 188.)

[28] Fletcher, *Of the Russe Common Wealth*, p. 22.

mission of inquiry formed immediately after his death reported he had perished by accidentally stabbing himself during an epileptic seizure while playing a Russian variety of mumblety-peg.[29] But the belief became widespread that Boris had him murdered to clear his own way to the throne.

The pretender added a new, and completely false, dimension to the story by averring that Boris had planned to have him killed, that another boy had been slain in his stead, and that he had been spirited away. Now, grown to manhood, he was claiming his rightful inheritance. He quickly won a large following, and when Boris died suddenly in 1605 this First False Dmitrii (as he came to be known in Russian history) was able to depose Boris' son who had succeeded to the throne. But in short order he was murdered by a group of great nobles who saw in the unsettled state of affairs the opportunity to realize their long held ambition of taking over the realm. Prince Vasilii Shuiskii was chosen tsar and surrounded himself with the remnants of the high aristocracy who had survived the repressions of Ivan and Boris. To scotch the appearance of new pretenders after the assassination of the First False Dmitrii, Shuiskii's government brought the body of the real Dmitrii to Moscow, exhibited it as a sacred relic to the people (who were told that the boy had been slain at Boris' order), and had the little monster canonized by the church as a martyr. But the maneuver failed. Shuiskii's reign was marked by peasant and cossack risings, foreign invasions—and the appearance of a new False Dmitrii. Finally, in 1610 he was deposed and the Poles, who had occupied Moscow, became the strongest power in the land. Then a national army led by members of the gentry and by burghers came into being in the northeast. The foreigners were driven out, and in 1613 a national assembly, controlled by the gentry, elected a new tsar. Their choice was the sixteen-year-old Michael Romanov, member of an old non-princely family of Muscovite boyars, son of the Metropolitan Filaret, and grandnephew of Anastasia, first wife of Ivan IV.

The Time of Troubles was over. With the accession of the first Romanov the long struggle to create a unified and absolute

[29] Vernadsky, "The death of the Tsarevich Dimitry," pp. 13-19.

monarchy was brought to a successful conclusion. The rulers of Moscow from Vasilii II through Ivan IV had earned for themselves the highest rank among Europe's royal statemakers of the fifteenth and sixteenth centuries. The rulers of France, Spain, and England successfully established a new kind of monarchy, but none of them had been able to gain as much power for themselves as the Muscovite princes had. The state over which Michael was called to rule was a unique kind of political organization. It was a Service State and the tsar was its absolute ruler. The activities and the obligations of all subjects, from the greatest lord to the meanest peasant, were determined by the state in the pursuit of its own interests and policies. Every subject was bound to certain specific functions that were designed to preserve and to aggrandize the power and authority of the state. The seigniors were bound to service in the army and the bureaucracy, and the peasants were bound to the seigniors to provide them with the means to perform their state service. Whatever privileges or freedoms a subject might enjoy were his only because the state allowed them to him as a perquisite of the function he performed in its service.[30]

The great aristocratic clans who had been so important in the fifteenth and sixteenth centuries not only had failed in their ambitions to share the rule over the new state with their cousins of Moscow, but had been shattered by them. Only a few of these families still retained some of their prestige, and then only because they were kinsmen of the Romanovs, or else had proven their loyalty to the new dynasty.

The gentry, too, had suffered as individuals, especially during the Time of Troubles. Many had been killed and others had been pushed down into the peasantry by economic pressures. Data available on landholding in sections of the county of Moscow give an idea of the extent of their reverses. In the Surozh district only 6 out of 30 families listed in the land registers of the 1620's are listed in the cadastre made in the 1580's, in the Goretov district about 10 of the 115 families in the register of the

30 Leontovitsch, *Die Rechtsumwälzung*, pp. 116-120.

1620's are in the earlier one, and in the Bokhov district the ratio was 5 out of 46.[31]

But as a class the gentry shared in the victory of the absolutism. Loyal instruments of the tsars in the fight against the great nobility, leaders in the national revival of the Time of Troubles, and the electors of Michael, they were rewarded by being made the ruling class in place of the *kniazhata* and boyars. Those members of the old aristocracy who had managed to retain part of their power fought in vain against this conquest by the gentry of the highest posts in the state. They tried to prevent it by insisting upon the use of the now hopelessly antiquated *mestnichestvo* system, but the claims of genealogy could no longer withstand the will of the tsar. Appointments and promotions were made at the order of the throne, and were based on merit and probably more often on favoritism, but not on lineage.[32] Finally, in 1682, the long obsolescent *mestnichestvo* system was abolished.

The rise of the Russian gentry was part of a phenomenon of the fifteenth to seventeenth centuries that was nearly pan-European in scope. In all the lands of Eastern Europe and in some of those of the West, the lesser nobility won new power and prestige for itself at the expense of the old ruling elites. The extent of its gains varied from land to land but everywhere there was the same trend toward its corporate domination of political life. The Russian experience, though, differed in one important respect from that of the rest of Eastern Europe (and resembled that in the West). In the other Eastern lands the ascent of the lesser nobility was made possible by the decline in the powers of the sovereigns. In Russia the gentry owed its rise to the increase in the tsar's power. It was the tail on the kite of the new absolutism.

31 Got'e, *Zamoskovnyi krai*, pp. 307-308.
32 Kalachov, *Materialy*, III, 36-37.

10

DEPRESSION AND SLOW RECOVERY

THE UPSWING in economic life came to a halt in the last part of the sixteenth century when the Center and the Northwest, the most populous areas of the realm and the most important economically, were struck by catastrophic depression. The central phenomenon of the crisis was a mass flight from those regions. Actually, the migration began on a small scale around the middle of the century. In documents of the fifties and sixties deserted holdings were mentioned with greater frequency than in the records of the preceding decades. The flight was spotty, however, with empty holdings reported for one property while neighboring ones were unaffected. In the beginning the people who left were usually those in the lowest economic brackets—indigent or improvident peasants who decamped to escape their obligations, slaves who ran away to gain freedom, and some very petty serving people. Then more solid members of the rural community, such as village elders, joined the stream of migrants. The exodus continued to grow until by the seventies it had become a mass migration. By the early 1580's the old provinces were so depopulated that Ivan IV was unable to raise the soldiers and taxes he needed to prosecute the Livonian War and that long drawn out conflict came to its inglorious end.

The desolation in the old regions of settlement that was brought on by this great flight reached fantastic proportions. Whole districts were entirely or nearly emptied of their people: fields abandoned to fallow, without tillage; estates deserted and gone back to forest; villages stripped of their residents, their churches without song; wastes where there had been settlements—such were phrases used in the assessment rolls of the period.[1] In 1588 Giles Fletcher on his way to Moscow passed through the same countryside that his compatriot Richard Chancellor had described thirty-five years before as being so well

[1] Platonov, *Ivan*, p. 119.

inhabited (v. p. 122). Now Fletcher found the villages "vacant and desolate without any inhabitant." "The like," he continued, "is in all other places of the realm (as is said by those that have better travelled the countrie than my selfe had time or occasion to doo)." The Jesuit Possevino who came to Russia in 1581 as special ambassador of the pope, journeying overland from the west found that whole days passed without seeing a person, and reported that the untilled fields were covered with man-high grass and brush.[2]

The Northwest seems to have suffered the most. Out of a total of 34,000 settlements listed in land registers of the 1580's, 83 percent were described as empty. In the county of Pskov over 85 percent (7,900) of the homesteads in the rolls for 1585-1587 were vacant. The Derevskaia district of Novgorod Land was hit particularly hard. The cadastre of 1496-1497 had reported that out of 8,238 settlements 97 percent were inhabited. In, 1581-1582 out of 6,102 listed, 97 percent were unoccupied.

In the Center the depopulation, though apparently not as excessive as in the Northwest, was still catastrophic. Conditions were at their worst in the country surrounding Moscow. The cadastre drawn up in 1584-1586 showed that in eighteen divisions of the canton in which the capital lay, only 17 percent (23,974 desiatins) of the arable land was still under cultivation.

The depopulation was not limited to the countryside. In 1583 the population of the city of Novgorod was an estimated 80 percent less than it had been at mid-century. The number of people engaged in trade and industry there had dropped from nearly 3,000 to 545. In Kolomna, an important trading center at the juncture of the Moscow and Oka Rivers, 95 percent (622) of the houses were empty in 1578; in Mozhaisk not quite 90 percent (1,573) were deserted. In Murom, on the Oka, in 1566 (when migration had not yet reached its peak) there had been 587 occupied and 151 vacant dwellings; just eight years later 111 were occupied and 627 empty.

The most extreme depopulation was in the districts around Moscow, Novgorod, and Pskov. Other parts of the Center and Northwest were not affected as severely, and the peripheral areas

2 Fletcher, *Of the Russe Common Wealth*, p. 61; Possevino, *Muscovia*, p. 12.

least of all. Cadastral data from these border zones indicate a
large amount of population movement, with many empty holdings listed but new homesteads also recorded, showing migration
into these regions. The newcomers were undoubtedly fugitives
from the most depressed areas who, upon reaching the borders of
the Center and Northwest decided to go no farther.[3]

But most of the migrants went on into the great new colonial
regions that had been opened up to Russian settlement by
Ivan IV's conquests. There they hoped to find surcease from the
burdens and disasters that had oppressed them in the older parts
of the realm. The largest number went east into the Kama
River basin or south across the Oka. The soils in these new
territories were fertile and easily worked, the climate temperate,
and the rivers were broad highways leading into all parts of the
land. Settlers went everywhere and new forts and towns were set
up in many places, although, as could be expected, the migration
was heaviest into those areas that lay closest to the old regions.
Others went north into the basin of the Northern Dvina. Life
there was hard and rigorous for the climate was severe and the
soil infertile. Yet a steady stream came in, so that in the course
of a few decades there was a large increase in population. And
finally, the most adventurous who sought freedom from every
restraint went into the *dikoe pole*, the "untamed steppe," that
lay between the southern frontiers and the Crimean khanate, to
join the bands of cossacks who roamed this no-man's-land.

Inevitably, the depopulation of the Center and Northwest
had severe repercussions upon economic life. Agriculture, the
chief industry of the era, was affected by the withdrawal of so
much land from cultivation and by the migration of so large a
proportion of the farm labor force. Trade suffered from the
dropping off of supply and demand for agricultural and manufactured goods, and foreign merchants found it increasingly
difficult to buy and sell.[4] It is hard to decide, however, whether
the migration was the cause of the economic downturn, or
whether the worsening of economic conditions preceded and

---

[3] Rozhkov, *Sel'skoe khoziaistvo*, pp. 69, 310-313, 316; Smirnov, *Vosstanie*, pp.
47-48; Kulischer, *Russische Wirtschaftsgeschichte*, I, pp. 165-167.
[4] Cf. Willan, *Early History*, pp. 186-187; Fletcher, *Of the Russe Common
Wealth*, p. 62.

caused the mass flight. Clearly the two phenomena were functions of one another; the problem is to decide which was the independent variable. The solutions that have been suggested can be grouped around three major themes: the so-called "nomad theory" of Russian history; the impact upon the peasantry of the expansion of the pomestye system; and what, for want of a better name, can be called the "catastrophe theory." The first two interpretations point to the conclusion that the economic crisis was the result of the mass migration, while the third leads to the opposite conclusion.

The "nomad theory" holds that constant movement has been a characteristic of the Great Russian people throughout its history. Those who used this hypothesis to explain the migration of the second half of the sixteenth century claimed that the opening up of new regions to Russian colonization provided a powerful stimulus to this proclivity for nomadism, and the resulting depopulation of the old regions of settlement weakened the structure of the economy there to the point of collapse.

Some of the deficiencies of this theory have already been discussed (v. pp. 112-113). Moreover, the other two interpretations provide adequate reasons both for the depopulation and the hard times, and for the connection between them, so that it seems unnecessary to explain these phenomena by some supposed racial propensity of the Great Russians.

The view that the crisis was brought on by the growth in the use of pomestye tenure in the sixteenth century is based upon the fact that this form of landholding produced an increased exploitation of the peasant-renters. The pomeshchik was given a relatively small holding of land expropriated from a great proprietor or from a free peasant commune. Circumstances conspired to make him a harsher landlord than the wealthy proprietor or the communal authority he replaced. He suffered from a shortage of cash that became increasingly serious as the use of money expanded and as prices went up. He could not raise money by borrowing against his holding since he was not its owner. The income from his pomestye, plus irregular cash payments from the state, not only had to support his family but also had to pay for his armor, weapons, and mount, and his maintenance while on military service. If his holding was above a certain size he had to equip one or more additional warriors to go with him on campaigns. Much of the sixteenth century was taken up with wars, and in peacetime the ever-present threat of invasion required an unceasing guard of the frontiers, so that his military expenses must have been a never-ending burden. Since he held his land only so long as he continued to give service to the tsar he was disinclined to make any expensive improvements on it, for they would only benefit some stranger who would hold the land after him.

In view of all these conditions the pomeshchik was prone to consider his holding and the people on it as objects to be plundered, and tried to squeeze as much as he could out of them. This was particularly true of the *oprichniki* who often were soldiers of fortune out for all they could get. Thus, two Livonians, named Taube and Kruse, who served in that infamous corps, reported that some of their fellows who had been awarded pomestyes by Ivan IV "took away everything possessed by poor peasants who had been given to them; the poor peasant paid in one year as much as he used to pay in ten years."

Besides the increase in their obligations, the peasants who found themselves converted into tenants of pomeshchiks lost certain advantages they had enjoyed in their free commune or as renters of wealthy lords. During the sixteenth century the demands made by great proprietors of their tenants also increased. But because they had so many peasants they could afford to take less from each individual than could the pomeshchik. In addition, the benefits of communal organization went by the board when land was turned over to pomeshchiks. On the black land the free peasant commune had preserved much autonomy for its members. On privately owned lands the commune had been weakened through seignioral encroachments but it had still served as a buffer between the lord and his peasants, and commune officials had aided in running the lord's economy. The parcelling of these properties and of black land among pomeshchiks completely destroyed communal organization. Finally, the pomeshchik, lacking wealth and power, was unable to provide his peasants with the protection and the aids, such as loans and assistance in hard times, that had been extended by the great landlords.

The increase in the number of pomestyes after the middle of the sixteenth century meant that more and more peasants were subjected to the increased oppressions that were associated with this form of tenure. During these same years new colonial regions were opened up to Russian settlement. Although the pomestye system had taken root in these areas (except in the North and in Siberia), it was not yet widespread, nor had it existed long enough to develop the harmful attributes that characterized it in the Center and Northwest. So the peasants in the old regions of settlement fled to the colonies to escape the exploitation of the pomeshchiks. This caused a labor shortage, depopulation, and declining productivity in the Center and Northwest which in turn brought on the severe economic crisis there.[5]

It is entirely possible that the increase in the use of pomestye tenure was indeed responsible for the flight of many peasants. But this interpretation fails to explain why people who lived on alodial lands of great lords, and in the cities, also ran away. In 1593-94 (even though by then conditions had begun to improve) of the 40,000 desiatins of plowland owned by the Trinity Monastery in Moscow *uezd* only 30 percent was in cultivation. On land owned by Trinity in another county of the Center 95 percent of the arable had been tilled in 1562; in 1592-93 only 28 percent was being cultivated regularly. On land owned by the Kirzhats Monastery in this same *uezd* over 99 percent of the arable had been tilled in 1562; in 1592-93 68 percent was uncultivated and another 6 percent was worked only irregularly.[6] Obviously the depopulation of these monastic lands, and of many other alodial properties for which data are available, and of cities, cannot be attributed to the increase in the use of pomestye tenure.

The "catastrophe" theory, the third of the three suggested interpretations, finds the primary cause of both economic crisis and of depopulation in the series of disasters that overwhelmed

[5] Rozhkov, *Sel'skoe khoziaistvo*, pp. 456-458, 467; Platonov, *Ocherki*, pp. 140, 475; *idem, Boris Godunov*, 127; Ak. Nauk, *Istoriia*, I, 340-341.

[6] Rozhkov, *Sel'skoe khoziaistvo*, pp. 66-71. For other examples v. *ibid*; Eck, "Le grand domaine," p. 135; Grekov, *Krest'iane*, pp. 802-804.

the Center and Northwest after the middle of the sixteenth century. These calamities included the unsuccessful Livonian War that dragged on from 1557 to 1582, enemy invasions and raids, the heavy taxation occasioned by the military effort, the sack of Novgorod in 1570 and of Moscow in 1571, at least two plague epidemics, several years of crop failure and famine, and, finally, the violence of the *Oprichnina*. The cumulative impact of these afflictions is held responsible for bringing on an economic crisis, which in its turn was the cause of the mass flight from the old regions of settlement.

Some contemporary observers placed the full blame for Russia's troubles upon the inordinate demands and exactions of the state. Giles Fletcher wrote: ". . . the marchants and mousicks [peasants] are very much discouraged by many heavy and intollerable exactions, that of late have been imposed upon them: no man accounting that which he hath to be sure his own. And therefore regard not to lay up anything, or to have it before hand, for that causeth them many times to be fleesed and spoiled, not only of their goods, but also of their lives. . . . Besides the taxes, customes, seazures, and other publique exactions done upon them by the emperour, they are so racked and pulled by the nobles, officers, and messengers sent abroad by the emperour in his publique affaires . . . that you shall have many villages and townes of half a mile and a mile long, stande all uninhabited: the people being fled all into other places, by reason of the extreame usage and exactions done upon them. . . .

"The great oppression over the poore commons, maketh them to have no courage in following their trades. . . . And hereof it cometh that the commodities of Russia . . . grow and goe abroad in farre less plentie than they were woont to doo: because the people, being oppressed and spoiled of their gettings, are discouraged from their laboures."[7]

The exiled Prince Kurbskii also held the state responsible: "The merchant class and the peasantry are seen everywhere suffering, ruined by enormous taxes, oppressed by unpitying officials and by merciless tortures; one group of officials collect

[7] Fletcher, *Of the Russe Common Wealth*, pp. 12-13, 60-62.

the taxes, another sends them forward, and still another plans them."[8]

Ivan IV seems not to have been concerned about the effects of his excessive levies. He is said to have compared his subjects to sheep who must be sheared at least once a year to keep them from becoming overburdened with wool. This was scarcely an original trope, but Ivan added a Russian flavor when he further compared the taxpayers to his beard which "the oftener shaven, the thicker it would grow."[9]

Besides the fiscal oppressions of the government, economic life was seriously disrupted by crop failures, plagues, and especially by invasions. Between 1556 and 1576 the Crimean Tatars made five major raids and many small ones. Two great forays in the early seventies were especially severe setbacks. In 1571 the invaders swept into the Center and sacked Moscow. Contemporary accounts claimed that just in the capital and its vicinity alone they killed 800,000 and led another 150,000 away into captivity.[10] These figures are undoubtedly much inflated but clearly there was great loss of life and much destruction. An Englishman who arrived in Moscow that summer wrote home that: ". . . Mosco is burnt every sticke by the Crimme the 24. day of May last, and an innumerable number of people: . . . The Emperour fled out of the field, and many of his people were caried away by the Crimme Tartar: . . . and so with exceeding much spoile and infinite prisoners, they returned home againe. What with the Crimme on the one side, and with his [Ivan IV's] crueltie on the other, he hath but few people left."[11] The next year the Tatars came in force again, and though they did not reach Moscow this time, they ravaged the regions through which they passed, and it took a great military effort to repulse them.

But the greatest calamity seems to have been the creation of the *Oprichnina* by Ivan. The racking of the peasantry by members of that corps to whom land had been given by the tsar has already been referred to. In addition, the *oprichniki*, because of

8 Quoted in Bakhrushin, *Ivan*, p. 86.

9 Fletcher, *Of the Russe Common Wealth*, p. 54.

10 Pokrovskii, *Russkaia istoriia*, I, p. 218.

11 R. Uscombe to M. H. Lane, 5 August 1571, Hakluyt, *The Principal Navigations*, III, 169-170.

the favor they enjoyed with Ivan, freely looted the countryside. Heinrich von Staden, a Westphalian adventurer who was in the corps, told in his memoirs that he went out from Novgorod with one horse and came back with forty-nine horses and twenty-two sleds filled with loot.[12] The apogee of *Oprichnina* destructiveness was reached in 1570 when, at Ivan's order, the *oprichniki* harried the Northwest from Tver to Pskov. Thousands were slain and cities and villages plundered and burned. The tsar loosed his soldiers against his own subjects because he had some vague suspicions that they were plotting with his foreign enemies against him. The city of Novgorod and its surrounding countryside were the special targets of his vengeance, and the killing and looting there went on for five weeks. Novgorod was reduced to rubble, and though the town continued to live on, it never regained its former prosperity and prestige.

The "catastrophe" theory of the causes of the crisis seems to me to be the most cogent and comprehensive. But it is clear that regardless of whether the hard times were brought on by the increase in pomestyes or by a string of disasters, the chief responsibility for both economic crisis and depopulation lies with the government of Ivan the Terrible. Many of the calamities that overwhelmed Russia after the middle of the century were the direct consequences of his military, fiscal, and social policies. And the increase in the number of pomestyes, the central point in the argument that depopulation preceded economic crisis, was equally the result of Ivan's program.

In the late eighties signs of recovery began to evidence themselves. The Livonian War had ended, the *Oprichnina* had disappeared, the new tsar though incompetent was at least not thirsty for human blood, and Godunov, the power behind the throne, did not wish to renew the terror. The Center and Northwest began to fill up again. Many who had fled remained in their new homes in the colonial regions, but others—who perhaps had gone no further away than the forests and marshes that surrounded their homesteads or at most had fled to the borders of the Center and Northwest—came back and tilled their fields again. Data from the nineties show an increase in the amount of

---

[12] Staden, *Aufzeichnungen*, pp. 191, 194, 195.

arable under cultivation, grain prices fell as more was produced, and by the end of the decade agriculture had recovered so much that there were large surpluses stored in the granaries.[13]

But the period of recovery proved tragically short. In 1601 there was a great crop failure. The surpluses of the preceding years became objects of speculation and prices rose to prohibitive levels. Famine and pestilence were abroad in the land, and when the crops failed again for the next two years the situation became critical. Bands of peasants roamed the countryside, and contemporary reports told of people eating grass, tree bark, and even one another. In 1604 the First False Dmitrii invaded Russian soil and war was added to the miseries that beset the country. Once again people fled their homes and economic life came to a standstill. This time the depopulation and devastation affected a wider area than in the seventies and eighties, for armies and bandits went beyond the limits of the Center and Northwest into the colonial areas. Even the far North was not spared, invaders and robber bands burning and pillaging up to the shores of the White Sea.

The political difficulties of the Time of Troubles were ameliorated in 1613 with the election of Michael Romanov to the throne. But the economic dislocation continued. According to government land registers made between 1619 and 1630 depopulation in many areas was greater than it had been in the crisis of the preceding century. Actually, although much land was indeed abandoned, the number of empty holdings entered in these rolls was deliberately inflated by the registrars who drew them up. There had been great tax increases, and the assessors realized that if they entered the true amount of land being cultivated by the peasants the latter would be completely ruined by the fiscal levies they would have to pay. So they estimated on how much of his land the individual peasant could afford to pay taxes, entered this land as inhabited and taxable, and registered the rest of the land he was tilling as empty.

By the 1620's the bad times seemed to have ended and a very gradual and far from complete recovery got under way. Succes-

---

[13] Grekov, "Khoziaistvennyi krizis," pp. 18-19; *idem, Krest'iane,* pp. 802-803; I. Smirnov, "Klassovye protivorechiia," pp. 68-69; Got'e, *Zamoskovnyi krai,* pp. 234-235.

sive surveys show a recolonization of the Center, with wastelands cleared and restored, new settlements begun, and the total
amount of arable rising steadily. Population increased in the
Center from around 6-700,000 in the 1620's to more than two
millions by the last decades of the century. This rise was attributable to natural increase and also to the return of fugitives to
their old homes. Lords rented out untilled land on their holdings, and monasteries gave out portions of their properties as
pomestyes to their servitors who cleared and settled the land and
brought it back into production. Large proprietors transferred
peasants from their more populous villages to empty lands they
owned. The government offered exemptions from state obligations to those who undertook the resettlement of abandoned
holdings, or who cleared new land. It also went into the business
of selling land. A decree of 7 February 1628 ordered that
"boyars, government officials, serving and non-serving people
and powerful merchants" could buy empty land from the state
in order "to convert it from desolation to life," at three chetverts per ruble. This new legislation was applicable at first only
to the districts of the Center. In 1648 it was extended to the rest
of the realm. At that time, too, empty land belonging to the
Court was offered for sale at two chetverts per ruble. Complete
records of the use made of this legislation were not preserved,
but within a year of its promulgation in 1628 at least seventy-
five pieces of empty land in the county of Moscow were purchased under its provisions. The individual parcels were apparently not large, running around 100 to 150 desiatins each.[14]

Official sponsorship of the colonization of the new territories
had ceased during the anarchy of the Troubles. When order was
restored the government promoted the settlement of these
regions with renewed vigor. It resumed the practice, followed in
the sixteenth century, of building a line of fortified posts along
the frontiers, garrisoned by servitors who drew their livings
from pomestyes given them in the surrounding countryside, and
furthered the settlement of large parts of the new regions behind the frontiers by granting land to lesser servitors, great lords,
and to monasteries.

[14] Got'e, *Zamoskovnyi krai*, pp. 212-222, 244-245, 298-306, 317, 434-436, 438-443,
518-520.

The landlords in the colonial regions peopled their lands by transferring peasants and slaves from villages they owned elsewhere, by using the indigenous population, by pirating peasants from other landlords, and by receiving condemned felons and war prisoners transported to the frontiers by the government. But their chief source of settlers were the fugitives from the older parts of the state. Despite the stringent limitations imposed upon peasant freedom of movement from the latter sixteenth century on, there was a steady stream of runaways into the colonial areas throughout the seventeenth century (and, in fact, up to 1861). In years of crop failure, plague, or of economic and political disturbances, the number of migrants shot upward. At times there were mass flights from individual estates of the Center, not nearly as large as those of the late sixteenth and early seventeenth centuries, but still of surprising proportions.

Not all the fugitives were willing to become seignioral peasants again in their new homes. Many of those who fled into the Volga basin earned their livings in the fishing and shipping industries that grew up there, and some joined the robber bands that infested that region. Others went south into the Don River basin where much land was free for the taking. Many of those who fled into the steppe land joined the nomad cossacks, but in the course of the seventeenth century the government succeeded in establishing its hegemony over many of these bands, persuading them to enter military service and to settle down as farmers.[15]

A sizable number of people also migrated to Siberia. Although there was official sponsorship of this colonization most of the settlers came on their own. The government gave the newcomers land with exemptions from taxes for as long as was considered necessary. For a while they also received subsidies in money and grain, but this practice was discontinued. The chief obligation imposed upon the colonists was to till fields retained by the government on which foodstuffs for the soldiers and officials stationed in Siberia were grown. Often this labor obligation was converted into a grain payment. Private landholding by seigniors was not introduced into Siberia except for some monasteries.

15 Tomsinskii, *Ocherki*, pp. 70, 84; Stepanov, "Guliashchie-rabotnye liudi," pp. 142-143; Platonov, *Smutnoe vremia*, pp. 52-58.

The settlers, therefore, never became serfs save for those who lived on monastic land. At the end of the seventeenth century, these monastery peasants formed an estimated 14 percent of the Russian peasant population of Siberia. The rest were in the category known as black people, or later, as state peasants.[16]

During the course of the seventeenth century new difficulties constantly appeared to beset the economy. Some of these troubles were the consequence of the frequent, expensive, and rarely successful wars in which Russia became involved. There was also an almost continuous chain of outbreaks rising from the discontent of the peasantry and culminating in the great revolt led by Stenka Razin (1670-1671). The schism of the Old Believers created widespread religious discontent and disorders. In 1655 plague swept the country and according to Dr. Samuel Collins, an Englishman who served as Tsar Alexis' physician from 1659 to 1667, 7-800,000 people died in the epidemic.[17] The government, always in need of money, after increasing taxes as much as it could, turned to currency debasement. In 1656 it began to coin copper money with the same weight and names as the silver coins. The new money was used by the government to meet its obligations, but all payments to the government had to be made in silver. Prices rose precipitously. For example, in the Vologda market in the decade 1646-1656 the price of rye had fluctuated between 12 and 15 *altyny* per chetvert (one *altyn* was equal to six *den'gi*). After the issuance of the copper money the price started going up, so that by December, 1658 it was 26 *altyny* 4 *den'gi*, in 1662 it was as high as 8 rubles 13 *altyny* 2 *den'gi*, and in January, 1663 rye sold at 24 rubles per chetvert. Unrest became widespread and in 1662 there was a serious rising in Moscow, known as the Copper Riots. The next year the government decided to return to silver and agreed to redeem the copper coinage, but at a rate far below that at which the money had been issued so that the state made an enormous profit.[18]

The recovery of the Russian economy starting in the 1620's, slow and incomplete as it was, contrasted with the general trend

16 Nolde, *La formation*, I, 174-184.
17 Quoted in Adelung, *Kritisch-literärische Übersicht*, II, 344.
18 Bazilevich, *Denezhnaia reforma*, pp. 39-41; Kliuchevskii, *History*, III, 231-234.

in a number of other European lands in these same years. In those countries a long era of contraction seems to have started in the twenties, reaching its most acute phase between 1640 and 1670, and continuing on until the last part of the century. Population dropped in many places or remained at an unchanged or only slightly rising level, small and medium-sized cities frequently declined, and activity in important branches of international commerce fell off. England, the United Provinces, and Sweden, were the other major exceptions to what seems to have been a general pattern of retrogression.[19] But there was an important qualitative difference between the economic progress of these three lands and that of Russia. Their advances represented the continuation of earlier economic growth, while Russia was only making up some of the ground lost in the latter sixteenth and early seventeenth centuries.

II

Throughout the alternating eras of economic growth and contraction of the sixteenth and seventeenth centuries agriculture continued to be the primary occupation of by far the largest part of the population. Hunting, fishing, saltmaking, and other rural pursuits were also important rural callings, as they long had been, especially in the infertile regions of the North and in the new colonial areas. The Center remained the chief agricultural zone on into the seventeenth century. Farming was also widespread in most of the Northwest and in the North up to the banks of the Northern Dvina, despite the poor quality of the soil and the rigorous climate. In the seventeenth century, as the colonization of the steppe land south of the Oka proceeded, the center of farm production began to move out of the Oka-Volga triangle, where the soil was of medium to poor fertility, into this land of the chernozem—the black earth—that was destined to become the chief granary of Russia.

Rye and oats were the chief cereals that were produced. Much flax and hemp were also grown and in some areas hops were an important crop. Fruit and vegetables were widely raised—in the cities nearly every house had its own garden plot—with cab-

---

[19] Cf. Hobsbawm, "General Crisis," pp. 33-49.

bages, cucumbers, onions, and garlic the most popular plants. Animal husbandry furnished food and draught power for domestic consumption, and also provided some of the most important articles in Russia's export, such as tallow, meat, hides, and bristles. But in the overall agricultural economy it seems to have been subordinate to tillage just about everywhere.

The slash-burn and field grass techniques of cultivation were still frequently employed, notably in frontier regions. But in more heavily populated and long-settled districts the three-field system was used almost universally, although a regular rotation of the fields was apparently not always followed. This method of cultivation had become so usual by the end of the fifteenth century that the size of peasant holdings was described in cadastral surveys by the formula "*n* tills *x* chetverts of land in one field and the same in the other two," and in charters of the tsar granting land, the size of the grant was set as so much arable per field. Then, in the second half of the sixteenth century, because of the economic crisis and depopulation and the consequent labor shortage, the three-field system was abandoned in most of the Center and Northwest for more extensive systems. These methods continued to be predominant until well into the seventeenth century. As the country slowly recovered from the long decades of decline the three-field system began to be used more and more often—this in itself being an indication of revival. By the middle of the century it was being followed on an estimated half or more of the total arable of the Center, and its use continued to increase in the second half of the century. In some places the fallow field was planted in peas. In the colonial regions, though the three-field system was employed, more extensive methods of tillage were the rule during the seventeenth century.[20]

Winter grains were sown in the fields of the Center in August and September and reaped in late July and August. Spring cereals, planted in May, were harvested beginning at the end of August. The usual practice, apparently, was to sow about two

[20] Rozhkov, *Sel'skoe khoziaistvo*, pp. 104, 128, 473-474; Got'e, *Zamoskovnyi krai*, pp. 431, 443-444, 462; Kulischer, *Russische Wirtschaftsgeschichte*, I, 264-267, 269-271; Zaozerskii, *Tsarskaia votchina*, p. 101; Miliukov, *Ocherki*, I, 74; Tomsinskii, *Ocherki*, I, 66.

chetverts (*ca.* 12 bushels) of rye, or barley, or wheat, or four chetverts of oats per desiatin. Manuring seemed to have been common, the sources from the fifteenth century on referring frequently to it.[21]

The *sokha* continued to be the chief implement for tillage. Oxen and horses were both used for draught, but in the latter part of the sixteenth century the use of oxen began to diminish and in the seventeenth century, in the Center at least, horses seemed to have been employed almost exclusively. Land records of that region reflect this displacement when they described parts of a property with such phrases as "where the oxen formerly grazed," or "the oxen place where before were the master's oxen."[22]

Foreign visitors to Russia in the sixteenth and seventeenth centuries sometimes referred to the soil there as extraordinarily fertile. Data from contemporary sources do not support their claims. These show that for the most part the harvests of rye and oats, the two chief crops, were two or three to one, sometimes four to one, and rarely five or more to one.[23]

21 Paul of Aleppo, *Travels*, II, 304; Rozhkov, *Sel'skoe khoziaistvo*, pp. 117-118, 260; Got'e, *Zamoskovnyi krai*, pp. 455, 456; Shchepetov, "Sel'skoe khoziaistvo," p. 109.

22 Got'e, *Zamoskovnyi krai*, pp. 459-460; Shchepetov, "Sel'skoe khoziaistvo," p. 110.

23 Liashchenko, *Ocherki*, I, 87n.; Miliukov, *Ocherki*, I, 73-74n.; Shchepetov, "Sel'skoe khoziaistvo," pp. 107-108.

11

LANDLORDS IN AN AGE OF
REVOLUTION

FROM the Kievan era on, as earlier pages have shown, there was a close relationship between Russia's political and economic evolution and changes in her agrarian institutions. But in no period of her history before 1917 was this linkage as intimate and as direct as it was in the sixteenth and seventeenth centuries. Under the impetus and as part of the political and economic developments described in the preceding three chapters, a great revolution was carried through in the status of the landholding class, in the ways in which they held their land, and in the relationship between these lords and the peasants who lived on their land. And the changes out on the land, in their turn, gave form and direction to the conditions of political and economic life.

To begin with, there was a revolution in the property right itself. Into the sixteenth century men from all walks of life had been able to own, buy, sell, or exchange real property. Then, in the sixteenth century, and especially in its second half, the principle was established that, aside from churchmen, only persons able to perform state service could own landed property. Actually, this restriction was not rigorously enforced. For example, the law of 7 February 1628 allowed empty land to be purchased from the state by "non-serving people and powerful merchants." A decree issued later in the century restated the right of *gosti* (the wealthy merchants whose status resembled that of the serving nobility) to own land. But apparently few of these men took advantage of this privilege. Peasants and slaves continued to buy land but they made their purchases in the names of their masters, and in any event the number of these transactions seems to have been small. A special group of peasants known as the *iamshchiki*, who provided postal relay service, were allowed to own land in their own names but their total holdings amounted to a few thousand desiatins.[1]

---

[1] Got'e, *Zamoskovnyi krai*, pp. 422-425, 435.

For all practical purposes, then, the personal possession of landed property became a monopóly of a single class of Russian society—the servitors of the tsar. In no other European land was the sovereign able to make all non-clerical landholding conditional upon the performance of service for him. In medieval western and central Europe vassalage had been general, but there had been private individuals who owned real property without being subject to military duty at the call of a superior lord. In the states that emerged at the end of the Middle Ages all connections between landholding and required service were done away with, and landowning won universal recognition as a private right (though often members of certain classes were still excluded from owning land). The unique development in Russia was both an aspect and a result of the success enjoyed by the tsars in their establishment of autocratic power. As such it can be partially explained by the policies followed by the Muscovite rulers from the fifteenth century on, culminating in the reforms of Ivan IV. But only partially explained. For the tsars were able to carry through this part of their program because a foundation had been laid for it in the era of the independent princedoms. As was pointed out in an earlier chapter during these centuries the princes had considered their entire princedoms as their patrimony, their votchina. Even though private individuals had all the rights of proprietors over the land they held, the concept of the sovereign as the real owner of all the land was maintained. In the centuries of the Tatar domination the princes had been unable to exercise effectively their claim to supreme ownership, so that private persons occupied and bought and sold land without regard to these claims, and nobles had retained their property when they switched their allegiance from one prince to another. But as the power of the rulers of Moscow increased they were able to give more and more force to this concept, until finally, in the reign of Ivan IV, it received full expression in the requirement that all lay landholders had to perform state service as the condition for keeping their land.

In the sixteenth and seventeenth centuries, as in the preceding era, there were two forms of lay seignorial tenure: alodial ownership and the pomestye. Prior to the sixteenth century there had been no single word used for alodial land that belonged to a non-royal proprietor. His property was described as a hamlet, or a village, a clearing, forest, meadow, and so on. The word votchina (patrimony) was used only for land he had inherited, and *kuplia* (purchase) was used for property he had bought. But in the early part of the sixteenth century votchina began to be employed as the generic name for property owned by lay and clerical seigniors, its earliest known use in this sense being in a charter of 1516. In the decades that followed, when the number of pomestyes shot up, the necessity for distinguishing between the alod and the pomestye led to the increased use of the word votchina, so that by the second half of the century it had become the legal term for privately owned property. The landowning seigniors themselves come to be known as votchinniks.[2]

Ivan IV's introduction of the service requirement in 1556 was not designed ostensibly to alter the nature of alodial tenure. The votchinnik's right to own his property was still independent of his service. He served the state because all members of his class were now obliged to serve, and not because he held land. Nonetheless, Ivan's reform was a major step in restricting the independence of the votchinnik as a landowner and tended to reduce his status to that of the pomeshchik who held his land on condition of service. For, inevitably, the right to hold land did become identified with the obligation to do service and if service was not done the land was supposed to be forfeited.

Another revolutionary change was the decline in the sixteenth century in the importance of alodial possession as a form of seignioral tenure. Up to the latter part of the fifteenth century it had been by far the most common way by which members of the upper classes held their land. Then, starting in the reign of Ivan III it began to yield preeminence to the pomestye, hitherto a relatively exceptional form of tenure. The explanation for this shift lay in the state-making policies of the Muscovite tsars. Ivan and his successors were intent upon building up the military forces they needed to conquer their brother princes, to crush the oligarchic ambitions of their own boyars, to stave off foreign

2 El'iashevich, *Istoriia*, I, 170-171.

invasions, and to expand their realm. They needed an army that was as dependent as possible upon them, and upon whose loyalty, therefore, they could themselves depend. But they lacked the money to buy the men and the allegiance they required. So they decided to use land. Their conquests and their confiscations of alodial properties, beginning with Novgorod in Ivan III's reign and culminating in Ivan IV's *Oprichnina*, provided them with the necessary resources and brought about a decrease in the number of votchinas. For they distributed the land they seized as pomestyes, and not as votchinas. They figured that the pomeshchik, holding his land from the tsar on condition of his service and dependent for his continued welfare upon the favor of the tsar, could be expected to be more loyal than the votchinnik. Grants of votchinas were still made by the throne, but they fell far short of compensating for the decrease in the sixteenth century in the amount of land held by this kind of tenure.

Other factors that aid in explaining the attrition in the number of votchinas during the sixteenth century include the giving of land by proprietors to monasteries (a custom which increased greatly in the troubled second half of the century when votchinniks sought protection from the violence of the times by turning over their lands to the church); selling it, usually to monasteries, to raise money needed to meet the rising costs of living; and losing it through foreclosure. The end result was that by the latter decades of the sixteenth century about the only part of the realm where lay votchinas were still to be found in any quantity was in the Center, and there they were decidedly in the minority. In other regions they were all but unknown.

It seems probable, too, that there was a decrease during the century in the average size of the holdings of the remaining votchinniks. The largest complexes had been owned by the princes and great boyars who, as the chief targets of the throne's anti-aristocratic policy, had suffered the loss of all or most of their land. Then, too, the custom of dividing property among the heirs normally produced a diminution in the size of the individual holdings with each successive generation. The effects this practice could have over the period of just a few years were illustrated in cadastral surveys made in Tver. In 1540, 318 votchinas were listed as belonging to a total of 659 proprietors. Just eight years later the number of proprietors of these same votchinas had increased to 771. The average share owned by each individual diminished, of course, with the increase in owners. In one district it fell from 970 chetverts per votchinnik in 1540 to 176 chetverts in 1548.[3] Finally, giving away or selling pieces of property, or losing them through foreclosure, also must have resulted in reducing the size of individual holdings.

The histories of two great landowning families, the Monastyrs and the Golovkins, illustrate well the decline in the fortune of the votchinniks in the sixteenth century. Just about all the difficulties that beset this class—the effects of the government's policies, the ebb and flow in political and economic life, inheritance customs, and the towering importance of royal favor—can be seen in operation in their sagas.

Alexander Monastyr, owner in the fourteenth century of huge properties in the then independent princedom of Beloozero, was the founder of his family's fortune. He divided his lands among his three sons. These sons and their immediate descendants served the Prince of Beloozero, and one also served Dmitrii Donskoi of Moscow. Meanwhile the family continued to grow. In the third generation after Alexander there were twenty-eight male descendants, and by the fifth and sixth generations, in the fifteenth and sixteenth centuries, there were no less than fifty male and fifty female Monastyrs. The great holdings of Alexander were divided among all the heirs in each generation so that the individual property of each legatee grew smaller as time went on. Most of the family, however, continued in the service of Beloozero's prince and held important posts, so that these Monastyrs undoubtedly received new land grants and other favors that kept them prosperous. In any event, during the fifteenth century the family kept its patrimony. Then, in 1485, Beloozero was annexed by Ivan III. The Monastyrs, like the nobility of every princedom absorbed by Moscow, were faced with the difficult task of adjusting to the changed conditions and maintaining their high status. Unlike many others they were

[3] Eck, *Le moyen âge*, p. 227.

successful, and several of them became important personages in Moscow's service.

But they soon began to suffer the penalties of that service. For one thing it was expensive, and the reduced size of the properties of the individual Monastyrs did not provide them with enough income. They needed more land and Ivan III gave some of them large pomestyes from land he had confiscated in Novgorod. That meant leaving the "family nest" in Beloozero and forming new ties elsewhere. They started to dispose of their inherited land at the end of the fifteenth century, giving and selling large parts of it to religious organizations, and especially to St. Cyril's Monastery in Beloozero. Then, as time went on, they ran into political difficulties with the tsars. In 1542 Elizar Monastyr, who had been one of the most important servitors of his time, made a wrong political move and was dismissed from the tsar's service. Despite this, his son was able to rise in Ivan IV's entourage, reaching such a high position in court circles that his daughter married a prince. But during the *Oprichnina* he, too, fell into disfavor, was dismissed, and found refuge as a monk in St. Cyril's, to which he gave the property he still owned in Beloozero. Meanwhile, the Monastyrs who had settled in Novgorod had prospered there. Then in 1570 came Ivan's devastation of that land. They lost everything and had to flee. In this same year, in connection with his campaign against Novgorod, Ivan had incorporated into the *Oprichnina* that part of Beloozero in which the remaining land of the Monastyrs was located. Those members of the family who still had votchinas there lost them without any compensation. And so the once wealthy and powerful Monastyrs wound up a landless clan, victims of the ambitions and policies of the princes of Moscow.

The Golovkins, who probably were of Novgorodian origin, owned in the fifteenth century at least 10,000 chetverts of arable along the Mologa River in the Bezhetsk district of the county of Tver. In the early part of that century it was divided between two brothers. On their deaths the property was divided again among their heirs, one of the brothers having four sons and the other one. The shares of the members of this third generation and of their heirs in the next generation were still large enough to support their owners. But the multiplication of the family in the next century, the continued practice of subdividing among the heirs, and the consequent diminution in the size of the individual portions, prepared the way for the ultimate loss of all their property. Moreover, probably because of their wealth, none of the Golovkins of the fifteenth century had felt it necessary to enter the service of the princes of Moscow. Thus, their descendants could claim no family rank in the tsar's service nor hark back to any ancestral contribution to Moscow's successes. So no Golovkin of the sixteenth century was able to repair his family's fortunes through large grants of land from the throne, and when service became obligatory for all landlords they were entered into the lowest ranks. Meanwhile, the inadequacy of their individual votchinas was aggravated by the growing use of money and the price rise of the first half of the sixteenth century. To make ends meet some of them were compelled to sell all or part of their small properties. They found a ready purchaser in the Trinity-St. Serge Monastery which had long owned land adjacent to the family's holdings. In the second quarter of the century there were nine alienations of Golovkin land to that monastery, seven of them by sale and two by gift. In the next quarter century Ivan IV's drive against the votchinniks and the economic crisis of that period forced the Golovkins to sell the rest of their property. All of it went to Trinity, and several of the family members joined the monastery either as monks or as servitors. By 1580 the once great Golovkin complex had been completely absorbed by the monastery, save for two small plots that had gone through the female line to other families.[4]

II

The same decades that saw the waning of the votchina witnessed the rise of the pomestye as the dominant form of lay seignorial tenure. Princes had granted land on condition of service from at least the early fourteenth century. The land they had used for these benefices came from their own personal holdings, and the services they required were of a personal nature at the court of the donor, or in the management of his properties or

[4] Veselovskii, *Feodal'noe zemlevladenie*, I, 169-187.

his enterprises. Then, in the last part of the fifteenth century, the concept of the pomestye as a way by which the prince paid for personal services was radically transformed. The change was brought about by Ivan III's experiment of settling 2,000 military servitors as pomeshchiks on property confiscated in Novgorod Land, to act as the occupying force and hold the region for Moscow. The success of this venture made it a model for the land policies followed by the tsars of the sixteenth century. Now the pomeshchik served the state, and the holding that was turned over to him came from the state's lands and not from the personal properties of the tsar.

Anyone who was able to perform service for the state was eligible to hold a pomestye. Some of the new pomeshchiks had been landowners in the princedoms and city republics that had been absorbed by Moscow. Often their property had been taken away from them and they had been resettled as pomeshchiks in other parts of Muscovy, while in other instances they were allowed to keep their holdings but were shifted from votchina to pomestye tenure. Others were princes who had lost their patrimonies or were the descendants of such princes. Still others were members of once wealthy families whose lands had been fragmented by inheritance, or been dissipated through mismanagement, or lost in the vicissitudes of political and economic fortune. Soldiers who distinguished themselves on the field of battle were rewarded by their grateful sovereign with the grant of a pomestye. Household and manorial officials of the tsar, both slave and free, who had customarily received benefices, were now absorbed into the new pomeshchik class. Originally they had been exempted from the duty of military service, but this began to be required of them from the latter part of the fifteenth century. The core of the new pomeshchik class, however, from its first establishment by Ivan III, was formed from the minor servitors of the tsars, the *deti boiarskie*, who hailed from the regions that had long been part of the patrimony of the House of Moscow.[5]

The social origins of the 2,000 to whom Ivan III gave pomes-

---

[5] Kulischer, *Russische Wirtschaftsgeschichte*, I, 191-192; Adams, *The Newe Navigation*, p. 259; Kliuchevskii, *History*, II, 122-125.

tyes in Novgorod Land reveal this deliberate sponsorship by the throne of the lesser gentry. Only 61 were from the *kniazhata* and about 175 were from old Muscovite boyar families. The rest were from far more humble backgrounds. Around 150 had been slaves of boyars of Novgorod and Moscow. They had been given their freedom by Ivan because their masters had fallen into his bad graces and been banned. The remaining 1,500 or so were minor serving people from the old parts of Muscovy—Rostov, Suzdal, Vladimir, and so on.[6]

Ivan III's simultaneous allotment of pomestyes in one region, and his choice of lesser servitors for these grants, was imitated by his successors. The most remarkable instance of this was in 1550 when Ivan IV commanded that 1,000 of his "best servitors" who did not already hold land in the country around Moscow were to be given pomestyes in this zone, with none to be more than 60-70 versts from the capital. These men, who were known as the "Chosen Thousand" (actually there were 1,078 of them) received a total of somewhere between 175,000-225,000 desiatins of arable, most of it black land. Of these 1,078 "best servitors" 1,050 were *deti boiarskie*, and only twenty-eight were of higher stations, including eleven princes.[7]

The military activities of the state created an always increasing need for servitors. During the century from 1491 to 1595 Muscovy was at war with her western neighbors for at least a total of fifty years, fighting three wars with Sweden and seven with Poland and Livonia, while on her expanding eastern and

---

[6] Veselovskii, *Feodal'noe zemlevladenie*, I, 289-295.

[7] *AAE*, I, no. 255; *Tysiachnaia Kniga*, pp. 10, 103, and n. 35.

The settlement of the "Chosen Thousand" has sometimes been interpreted as one of Ivan IV's first moves in his campaign against the great aristocracy and as a sort of first draft of the *Oprichnina*. Cf. Platonov, *Ivan*, pp. 59-60; Leontovitsch, *Die Rechtsumwälzung*, pp. 102-103. Veselovskii, however, maintains that Ivan's purpose was simply to save money for servitors whom he needed in Moscow whose pomestyes were far away. They had either to bring supplies from their holdings at considerable expense or else buy them on the Moscow market where prices were rising. Veselovskii, *Feodal'noe zemlevladenie*, I, 315-316. It is, of course, possible that both hypotheses are correct. Use was indeed soon made by Ivan of his lesser servitors in his drive against the magnates. But the economic needs of these men could also have been his motive. A century later a provision for making supplementary land grants to men serving in the capital was included in the Law Code of 1649. (*Ulozhenie*, chapter XVI, art. 1.) This was probably done to make it easier for these men to support themselves.

southern frontiers she was engaged in an unceasing struggle with the nomads who roamed her borders. Since the tsars preferred to reward their followers with pomestyes rather than with votchinas, the demand for servitors produced an enormous and rapid growth in the number of benefices. Data assembled by Rozhkov, in his study of sixteenth century Russian agriculture, from extant cadastral surveys made during the century, show that everywhere save in the Center, where lay votchinas persisted, and in the North, where black land prevailed, pomestyes occupied by far the largest part of the arable. In Novgorod Land the registers made after Ivan III's confiscations revealed that the only land held on alodial tenure were the properties of the church and of the *svoezemtsi*. In later registers the *svoezemtsi* land had disappeared, having been converted into pomestyes, while church land increased slightly. Large stretches of black land had also been listed in the first cadastres—nearly a third of one of Novgorod's five chief divisions was so described—but all of it was distributed to pomeshchiks in the course of the sixteenth century. Before the middle of the century over 95 percent of the arable in some districts was held as pomestyes. Pskov was an exception to the general picture in the Northwest. In the 1580's church land took up slightly more than half of the arable there, and pomestyes a little less than half. Across the Oka River, in the steppeland, the cadastres made in the last part of the century show that immediately south of the river, where settlement predated the sixteenth century, there were still quite a few votchinas. In Riazan in 1594-1596, 17.3 percent of the arable was held by votchinniks and another 12.8 percent by monasteries. Beyond this area, in the regions colonized during the sixteenth century as Muscovy expanded southward, just about all the cultivated land was apparently held by pomeshchiks. Thus, in Dedilov *uezd* in 1587-1589, 98.6 percent, and in Orel *uezd* in 1594-1595, 99.3 percent of the arable listed in the existing cadastre was in pomestyes. The little that was not held as benefices belonged to the church or had been retained by the tsar. There were no lay votchinas. In other southern districts for which there are no cadastral data other sources point clearly to a similar monopoly of the pomestye form. To the east, in the Kama Basin, where

Russian colonization was just beginning, there are cadastral surveys for just two counties, Kazan and Sviiazhsk, in the 1560's. These show that the pomestye was the only form of lay seignioral tenure there, covering 65.7 percent of the arable in Kazan and 17.6 percent in Sviiazhsk. A large area was still held by the throne as palace land, and in Sviiazhsk 45 percent of the arable was registered as Tatar and Chuvasian holdings.

The extant cadastres for districts of the Center indicate that although the pomestye was widespread in this oldest part of the Muscovite state, the alodial form of seignioral tenure vied with it in importance. Available data for parts of Moscow county in 1584-1586 show that 34 percent of the arable was in pomestyes, 22.1 percent in votchinas, and 35.7 percent was owned by monasteries. In Kolomna *uezd* in 1576-1578 the proportions were 59.5 percent in pomestyes, 24.3 percent in votchinas, and 12.2 percent owned by monasteries. In Zvenigorod *uezd* in 1592-1593, 27 percent of the arable listed in the registers was in pomestyes, 27.7 percent in votchinas, and 41.5 percent in the hands of monasteries. The remaining land in each of these districts belonged to prelates and churches. The extreme North was all black land except for a small amount of monastic property. Further south, in the Vologda, Ustiug, and Beloozero districts, though black land remained abundant throughout the century, there were lay votchinas and pomestyes, personal properties of the throne, and especially monastic lands.[8]

The great increase in the number of the pomeshchiks, the favor shown them by the tsars, and the simultaneous derogation of the high nobility, gave the pomeshchik class ever greater influence in the political and economic life of sixteenth century Moscovy. But it also produced an enduring change in the nature of the relationship between the sovereign and the pomeshchiks. In the old days when benefice holders had been relatively few, and had served their principal in his court or on his properties, the bond between prince and subordinate had been of a close and personal nature. The former knew his servitors, could reward or penalize them according to his own judgement of them, and could himself see to it that they were active in his

---

[8] Rozhkov, *Sel'skoe khoziaistvo*, pp. 368-401, 433-435.

interests. The amount of service he required of them was usually determined by custom, rather than by fixed and impersonal norms. But when in the sixteenth century thousands of men were given benefices for which they served the state and not the tsar personally, it was impossible for the sovereign to have first-hand knowledge of the qualities and deserts of the servitors, or to exercise direct supervision of their activities. It became necessary to introduce standardization and bureaucratization into the serving relationship to ensure its proper functioning. Beginning in the last years of the fifteenth century periodic surveys were made to check on the general situation of the pomeshchiks, and to make such adjustments in the size of their holdings as were considered necessary. Registers compiled in the 1550's classified pomeshchiks according to the size of their holdings and the subsidies paid them by the state, and recorded the service required of them. A special government agency called the *Pomestnyi Prikaz* (Pomestye Bureau) was established to supervise the operations of the system. The decree of 1556, setting up the service norm for pomeshchiks and votchinniks alike of one mounted warrior for every 300 chetverts of arable, was an important part of this process of regularization.[9]

The movement toward uniformity was especially evident in the normalization of the size of the holdings turned over to the pomeshchiks. When the first mass distribution of pomestyes was made by Ivan III in Novgorod the grants ran from 200 to 600 chetverts of arable, plus pastures, forests, and meadows (called, collectively, *ugodia*).[10] The size of the individual grant depended upon the nature and the importance of the service required for it, and upon the rank and length of service of the man to whom it was given. The range of 200 to 600 chetverts of arable remained pretty much the standard until the seventeenth century. Ivan IV, for example, in his grants to the "Chosen Thousand" in 1550 ordered that each of the 28 boyars and high officials who were included in this group were to be given 600 chetverts of arable, the 40 *deti boiarskie* of the first rank were to receive 450

---

[9] Veselovskii, *Feodal'noe zemlevladenie,* I, 306; Kliuchevskii, *History,* II, 127; Eck, *Le moyen âge,* p. 223.

[10] Veselovskii, *Feodal'noe zemlevladenie,* I, 311.

to 600 chetverts, the 396 *deti boiarskie* of the second rank 300 to 450 chetverts, and the 614 of the third rank 300 chetverts. Each of these grants had an appropriate amount of *ugodia* attached to it.[11] By far the majority of the pomestyes in most of the districts for which information is available were somewhere in this range. Benefices larger than 600 chetverts were exceptional. They were mainly in the Center, and particularly around Moscow. On the other hand pomestyes smaller than 300 chetverts, or less than the minimum set by the law of 1556 for furnishing an armed warrior, were present in every district and were especially common on the southern steppes where many minor servitors had been set up as guardians of the frontier. In Orel the 1594-1595 cadastre showed that 32 percent of the arable was divided into pomestyes of between 150 and 300 chetverts, and 54 percent into pomestyes of less than 150 chetverts. In Dedilov in 1587-1589 31 percent of the arable was in pomestyes of between 150 and 300 chetverts, and 27 percent in pomestyes of less than 150 chetverts. Outside the steppes the only place where these small pomestyes predominated, according to the available data, was in the Obonezhskaia district in the northwest of Novgorod Land where in 1565-1566, 13 percent of the arable was in pomestyes of 150 to 300 chetverts and nearly 60 percent in pomestyes of less than 150 chetverts.[12]

In the seventeenth century the standards for the sizes of pomestyes were increased. In 1621 they were set at 900 chetverts of arable for servitors of the first class, 750 for those of the second class, 600 for the third, and 300 for the fifth. In addition, the Law Code of 1649 included provisions for supplementary grants. Everyone serving in Moscow was to have a piece of land in the district around the capital (where there was still plenty of empty land) ranging from 50 to 200 chetverts, depending upon the servitor's rank. Doubtless, as was mentioned earlier, this was done to save these men the expense of bringing supplies from their more distant holdings or buying them on the Moscow market. Supplementary grants were also to be given to persons holding benefices on the frontiers, the amount of land they were

11 *Tysiachnaia kniga*, pp. 55, 57, 61, 82, 83, 103.
12 Rozhkov, *Sel'skoe khoziaistvo*, pp. 438-441.

to receive being determined by the size of the pomestyes they already had. Finally, those whose pomestyes were on medium grade or poor soil were to be compensated by being allowed to have benefices 25 and 50 percent larger, respectively, than the norm for their rank. Sometimes, too, additional land was given to reward special services, as, for example, in 1649, when the servitors who sat in the National Assembly (*Zemskii Sobor*) held the year before were each given 300 chetverts.[13]

Besides granting land to its servitors the state also gave them cash subsidies. These payments, like the pomestyes, were scaled according to the rank of the servitor, the importance of his service, and the length of time he had served. The money was passed out at irregular intervals, or just before the beginning of a campaign. It was considered a necessary supplement to the pomeshchik's income, on the assumption that the revenues from his holding were not enough to cover the costs of his military obligations. If the servitor occupied a post that brought him additional income, or that kept him from doing military duty he did not receive a subsidy. According to G. K. Kotoshikhin, writing in the 1660's about the Russia of his day, there were seventeen pay grades, running from 200 rubles a year for the top ranks down to six rubles for the least important servitors. If the servitor's holding was larger than the norm for his rank a deduction of one ruble was made from his pay for every twenty chetverts he held above the norm. Extra payments were sometimes made to cover expenses incurred while on service and occasionally they were given out to celebrate a special event, as in 1668 on the announcement of the marriage of the heir to the throne, or in 1686 when peace was made with the Poles.[14]

Although the concept of the pomestye as a reward for service to the state rather than to a private individual became dominant in the sixteenth century, powerful private landowners still continued to give out pieces of their properties to persons who served them. In the cadastre drawn up for Tver between 1539 and 1555, 60 landholders of the 574 listed were described as

---

[13] *Ulozhenie*, ch. XVI, sect. 1, 40, 46, 48; Vladimirskii-Budanov, *Obzor*, pp. 583-584.

[14] Kotoshikhin, *O Rossii*, p. 108; Kalachov, *Materialy*, III, 39-43.

servitors of the Archbishop of Tver, one was in the Archbishop of Riazan's service, and 65 served lay seigniors (46 of these 65 were in the service of one princely family, the Mikulinskii's).[15] The theory still persisted that a servitor was free to choose the person he wished to serve, but from the first half of the six-teenth century it became increasingly difficult, and even im-possible, for magnates to take servitors of the tsar into their own service. Members of the *kniazhata*, including kinsmen of the tsar, were obliged to pledge they would not do this—a promise that at least one of their number, Andrei of Staritsa, tried to break with disastrous results for himself and for those who heeded his invitation. Great lay and clerical proprietors, how-ever, continued on into the seventeenth century to have their own servitors who held land from them on pomestye tenure, despite state legislation aimed at ending this practice.[16]

I I I

When the rulers of Moscow first began giving out pomestyes on a large scale, temporary occupancy and non-heritability were distinguishing characteristics of this form of tenure, since the pomeshchik held his benefice only so long as he performed his service. As a result, there was an extremely high turnover in the occupants of benefices over short periods of time. In one of the districts of Novgorod Land, out of 328 pomestyes listed both in the cadastre of 1500 and the one made in 1539, only half were occupied at the later date by the same person who held it in 1500, or by his kinsmen. The rest were held by persons not related to the former occupant. In the second half of the century the turnover rate was accelerated in the Center and Northwest by the disturbed conditions of those years. Thus, out of 118 pomestyes listed in the registers for another part of Novgorod Land for both 1575-1576 and 1584-1585, just 13 percent were occupied by the same man, 8 percent by his kinsmen, and 79 per-cent by strangers. In Kolomna *uezd* between 1560-1561 and 1576-1578 out of 361 pomestyes over half had gone to strangers, around one quarter were held by the same man, and the rest had

15 Sergeevich, *Drevnosti*, III, 17-18.
16 Got'e, *Zamoskovnyi krai*, pp. 424-426.

been taken over by kinsmen. In Pskov between 1556-1559 and 1585-1587, 333 of the 394 pomestyes had been transferred to strangers. In other districts for which there is information the turnover was not as high but was still sizable, running from 20 to 50 percent. The one exception was Kashira *uezd*, just south of the Oka River, where 544 pomestyes (83 percent) of 656 listed in both the cadastres of 1550-1551 and 1577-1579 were occupied by the same person or by his kinsmen.[17]

This insecurity of tenure was slowly overcome as time went on, and the pomestye gradually came to resemble the votchina. By the end of the seventeenth century the two forms were indistinguishable. The impetus for this change came from the pomeshchiks' natural desire to gain security for themselves and their families, and from the throne's willingness to permit the transformation of their tenure as part of the price it paid for the pomeshchiks' continuing support and loyalty. The first votchina-like right that developed was the passing of the pomestye to the male heirs of the occupant. As early as the first half of the sixteenth century it had become customary for sons or nephews to take over the pomeshchik's service when he died, or when illness or old age kept him from being able to do the service himself. The male heirs were considered old enough to serve at fifteen. This practice received its first official approval at the time of the grants to the "Chosen Thousand" when Ivan ordered that if one of these men died, a stranger was to take his place only if the decedent's sons were unable to perform their father's service.[18] The sons, or failing direct male heirs, the brother or nephew of the dead man, were obliged to provide for his widow until her death or remarriage and for his single daughters. If the son was under fifteen it had become customary by the middle of the century to allow all or part of the pomestye to be kept by the boy to support himself, his mother, and his siblings, with the understanding that he would enter the tsar's service when he came of age. If there were no male heirs the widow was permitted to retain a portion of her husband's holding to maintain herself until her death or remarriage, and her daughters until they mar-

17 Rozhkov, *Sel'skoe khoziaistvo*, pp. 446-451.
18 *AAE*, I, no. 225.

ried. This was regarded as a pension awarded for the dead pomeshchik's service, and was considered a special act of favor by the tsar.[19] In the next century, however, this provision for widows and unmarried daughters became automatic, with norms set by law for the size of the allotments. If the servitor was killed in action against the enemy his wife was to receive 20 chetverts of his pomestye for their maintenance. If he died on campaign the portions were 15 chetverts for the wife and 7½ chetverts for the daughters, and if he died when not on active service the shares were 10 and 5 chetverts, respectively. Nor were these portions considered pensions granted out of the sovereign's kindness, but rather dowers due the widow and daughters as rightful heirs to part of the dead man's estate. The remaining land was to be distributed among those collateral relatives of the decedent who had no pomestyes or only small ones. If there were no collateral heirs the residue reverted to the throne and was redistributed among other pomeshchiks of the district.[20]

Already in the sixteenth century there is evidence that pomeshchiks tried to pass on their benefices to their heirs by wills, and by the end of the next century this had become a common phenomenon. The practice of exchanging pomestyes also appeared in the sixteenth century and apparently became an ordinary occurrence in the next century. Up to the middle of the seventeenth century a pomestye could be exchanged only for another pomestye, but the Law Code of 1649 (chapter 16, art. 2-5) authorized the exchange of pomestye for votchina, in which case the pomestye became a votchina and the votchina a pomestye. Properties that were exchanged were required by the law to be of equal value, and permission from the government for the exchange was necessary. In the second half of the century, however, these hindrances were forgotten. Pomeshchiks also gave benefices to one another, often as dowries. This ability to transfer a pomestye freely to another servitor was probably used sometimes to camouflage the sale of the land. Sales were unlaw-

---

[19] Adams, *The Newe Navigation*, pp. 259-260; Rozhdestvenskii, *Sluzhiloe zemlevladenie*, pp. 366-371; El'iashevich, *Istoriia*, II, 51-52; Vladimirskii-Budanov, *Obzor*, p. 587.

[20] *Ulozhenie*, ch. XVI, sect. 13, 30-32.

ful, since the pomestye legally was the property of the state and not of the pomeshchik. For the same reason the pomeshchik could not mortgage his holding. But these limitations, too, came to be disregarded, so that in the last years of the century pomeshchiks and their heirs openly sold their holdings or pledged them for loans.[21]

By the latter part of the seventeenth century, then, there was no real difference between pomestye and votchina tenure. For all practical purposes the pomeshchik was as much the owner of his holding as the votchinnik was of his. Finally, in the early eighteenth century official recognition was accorded the *de facto* fusion of the two forms of landholding and the legal distinctions between them obliterated by a decree of 23 March 1714. Seventeen years later another imperial ukase ordered that henceforth the pomestye was to be known as a votchina.[22]

Yet, despite the great improvement in the conditions of pomestye tenure during the seventeenth century, the servitors of that era preferred by far to hold their lands as votchinas. Possibly, to their way of thinking the pomestye still retained the blemish of a temporary possession, while the votchina was viewed as durable and permanent—a true family possession. An even more important consideration may have been that the votchinnik had greater power over the movements of his peasants than did the pomeshchik. In any event, servitors importuned the throne for grants of votchinas. Their pressure, and the continued necessity to hold their loyalty in the long and trying period of adjustment that followed the Troubles, persuaded the government to abandon the anti-votchina policy it had pursued since the days of Ivan III.

The first departure from that policy came during the Troubles, in the brief reign of Vasilii Shuiskii (1606-1610). In 1610 Shuiskii ordered that those servitors who had aided in the defense of Moscow in 1608, when it had been besieged by the forces of the Second False Dmitrii were to be rewarded by being allowed to convert one fifth of the area of their pomestyes into

21 Vladimirskii-Budanov, *Obzor*, p. 588; Got'e, *Zamoskovnyi krai*, pp. 391-392; El'iashevich, *Istoriia*, ii, 149-150.
22 *PSZ*, v, no. 2789; viii, no. 5717.

votchinas. This ukase affected only the small number of servitors who had been loyal to Shuiskii. But it set a precedent that
was followed by his successors. A large number of votchinas
were handed out to men who took an active part in the national
rising that ended the Troubles, and who elected Michael
Romanov to the tsardom. In 1619-1620 Michael again gave land
on votchina tenure for special service, this time for aid in repul-
sing the Polish besiegers of Moscow in 1618. In later decades,
and especially during the reigns of Alexis Mikhailovich (1645-
1676) and Fedor II (1676-1682), small votchinas were handed
out liberally for participation in wars. In addition, in return for
a payment to the throne, pomeshchiks were allowed to convert
their benefices into votchinas. The government also sold vacant land, including abandoned pomestyes, as votchinas.[23]

As the result of this new policy, votchina tenure, seemingly
destined at the end of the sixteenth century for permanent
unimportance and possibly even extinction, underwent a renascence. By the end of the seventeenth century it had become
once again by far the predominant form of landholding, while
the importance of the pomestye dwindled steadily.

Successive land surveys reveal the proportions of the swing
back to the granting of votchinas. In Uglich, a district of the
Center, the total area occupied by votchinas before the Troubles
was scarcely 30 percent of that taken up by pomestyes. By 1620
votchina area there was 80 percent of pomestye area. For the
Center as a whole an estimated 30 percent of all non-clerical
landed property was held as votchinas in the 1620's; in the
second quarter of the century the votchina ratio had risen to
50 percent and in 1671 it was 60 percent. Other data show the
increase in the number of peasants who lived on votchinas,
reflecting the expansion in the use of this tenure. In Moscow
uezd, of the total number of peasant homesteads on privately
held property, 64.6 percent were on votchinas in 1624-1625, and
95.6 percent in 1646. In Kolomna *uezd* the proportions were
53.3 percent in 1627 and 71.6 percent in 1678; in Borovsk *uezd*
60 percent in 1629-1630 and 74.7 percent in 1678. By this last-

---

[23] Got'e, *Zamoskovnyi krai*, pp. 382-384; El'iashevich, *Istoriia*, II, 169-173.

named date, in seven of the most populous counties of the Center there were over 25,000 peasant and slave homesteads on votchinas owned by laymen, and less than 8,000 on pomestyes.[24]

Although the votchinniks of the seventeenth century were the proprietors of their land, their continued possession of it remained dependent upon their performance of state service. Nor could the votchinnik (or the pomeshchik) leave service. If he tried to run away the law ordered that he was "to be beaten mercilessly with the knout," imprisoned, and his property taken from him. Tsar Boris Godunov by a ukase of 12 June 1604 had lowered the service requirement by ordering that one armed and mounted warrior was to be supplied for every 600 chetverts of arable (200 chetverts in "each of three fields") instead of every 300 as Ivan IV had commanded. In 1617 Tsar Michael restored the old norm, but then in the 1620's a new system was instituted by which the size of the obligation was fixed not by the amount of land the servitor held but by the number of peasant homesteads on his holding. In 1633 servitors with less than fifteen adult male peasants were freed of the service requirement, but in 1642 the minimum was raised to fifty peasants. Seventeenth-century legislation also regulated and restricted the devising and alienating of votchina land, careful distinction being made between "family patrimony" (*rodovye votchiny*) which could not be sold or given away, and land the votchinnik had acquired by means other than through inheritance and which he could alienate as he chose.[25]

The transition from benefices held as grants from the sovereign to alienable, heritable properties was, of course, not unique to Russia. In Central and Western Europe the fief had gradually changed into an alodial property in the later centuries of the Middle Ages, when the system of vassalage declined and a centralized national power rose. In the Balkans the shift took place at approximately the same time that it occurred in Russia. When the Turks first gained their hegemony over southeastern

---

[24] Kulischer, *Russische Wirtschaftsgeschichte*, I, 195; Tomsinskii, *Ocherki*, table 14.

[25] Vladimirskii-Budanov. *Obzor*, p. 585; Leontovitsch, *Rechtsumwälzung*, p. 111; Gitermann, *Geschichte*, I, 269; *Ulozhenie*, ch. XVI, sect. 69, ch. XVII, sect. 1-3, 37, 42, 43.

Europe they gave benefices to their warriors in return for military service. By the end of the sixteenth century the Ottoman central power had weakened, so that these men were able to convert their holdings into heritable properties. What was unique to Russia was that the connection between landholding and service to the state continued during and after the period in which the central power was establishing its supremacy.

IV

There was, however, one important group of landowners who not only escaped the obligations that weighed upon the rest of the seignioral class, but gained in strength and wealth during the sixteenth and seventeenth centuries, battening on disasters that overwhelmed their fellow lords. These fortunate proprietors were church institutions and dioceses. Churches, and above all monasteries, had long been among the greatest landlords. In the sixteenth century they reached new heights in the extent of their holdings. Clement Adams, who was in Russia in 1553, claimed that one third of all the landed property there belonged to monasteries, and thirty years later another English visitor wrote caustically about this conventual affinity for real estate: "Of friers they have an infinit rabble, farre greater than in any other countrey where Popery is professed. Every city and good part of the countrey swarmeth ful of them. For they have wrought (as the Popish friers did by their superstition and hypocrisie) that if any part of the realme bee better or sweeter then other, there standeth a friery or a monastery dedicated to some saint."[26]

Actually, judging from the fragmentary data, these contemporary judgments seem to have been reasonably accurate only for some parts of the Center, where the oldest and wealthiest monasteries had most of their holdings. In Moscow *uezd* the cadastres of 1584-1586 showed that almost 36 percent of the arable was owned by monasteries, and in Zvenigorod *uezd* in 1592-1593 nearly 42 percent. But in Kolomna, another county

[26] Adams, *The Newe Navigation*, p. 267; Fletcher, *Of the Russe Common Wealth*, p. 114.

of the Center for which there is information, monasteries held only 12 percent of the arable. Data for other parts of the realm indicate that the monks owned far less property, the proportion of their land to the total arable generally being less than 5 percent and even less than 1 percent. Property owned by individual churches or by prelates comprised a very small percentage of the total arable land both in the Center and in the other parts of Muscovy.[27] The fact of the matter seems to have been that the holdings of the church were a much smaller proportion of the total arable in Russia than they were in England at the time of Henry VIII's dissolution of the monasteries.[28]

This is not to gainsay that there was a remarkable growth both in the number of monasteries and in the total amount of land they owned. At the beginning of the twelfth century there were perhaps twenty monasteries, at the end of the thirteenth century there were 100, and at the end of the seventeenth century over 350. The overwhelming majority of these establishments owned modest amounts of land, a few giants among them holding the greatest part of all monastic property. Trinity-St. Serge was the biggest of them all. According to incomplete data from the end of the sixteenth century it then owned over 200,000 desiatins of arable.[29] An Englishman who visited that monastery in 1558 was told that it had 700 members and that "the most part of the lands, towns, and villages which are within 40 miles of it, belong unto the same." Giles Fletcher reported that it had an annual income of 100,000 rubles.[30] St. Joseph's of Volokolamsk was another great landowner. It owned an estimated 26,070 desiatins of land in 1591, almost all of it in the Center. Epiphany Monastery owned land in ten counties of the Center, Trinity-St. Joachim's in seven, St. Simon's in eighteen, and the Monastery

27 Rozhkov, *Sel'skoe khoziaistvo*, pp. 368-369, 371-374, 399, 433-434.

28 Cf. Hill, *Economic Problems*, pp. 3-4. Kovalevskii, *Die ökonomische Entwicklung*, VI, 63-67, estimated that the monasteries owned over one-third of all the arable in England at the dissolution but the fanciful, albeit ingenious, method he used to arrive at this figure does not inspire confidence in its accuracy.

29 El'iashevich, *Istoriia*, I, 270; Rozhkov, *Sel'skoe khoziaistvo*, p. 402.

30 Hakluyt, *Voyages*, II, 440. This account is believed to have been written by Robert Best (Hakluyt, *Works*, LXXIII, 355n.); Fletcher, *Of the Russe Common Wealth*, p. 115.

of the Miracle in ten.[31] Data from the second half of the seventeenth century show that just 34 monasteries were the proprietors of two-thirds of all monastic land. In 1678 Trinity-St. Serge had 16,813 peasant homesteads on its properties, St. Cyril's of Beloozero had 5,430, St. Saviour's of Iaroslav had 3,879, St. Hypatius, of Kostroma 3,657, and St. Saviour-St. Joachim's 2,886.[32]

The monks acquired a huge proportion of their total holdings during the sixteenth century and especially after 1550 (for reasons to be discussed shortly). St. Cyril's of Beloozero, for instance, founded around 1400, owned 3 villages, 133 hamlets, and 16 abandoned settlements in 1482; 3 villages, 4 small villages, 241 hamlets, and 145 new settlements in 1544; and 11 villages, 5 small villages, 607 hamlets, and 320 abandoned settlements in 1601. Trinity-St. Serge was founded in the first half of the fourteenth century. Seventeen percent of the land it owned at the end of the sixteenth century had been acquired before 1500 and the dates of the acquisition of another 16 percent are unknown. So at least 67 percent of its vast property was gained in the sixteenth century. The Volokolamsk Monastery, another of the giants, was only established in 1479. Nearly all of its land came to it after 1500; before that date it owned just two properties.[33]

Monasteries increased their holdings through gifts and legacies, purchases, and foreclosures on mortgages they gave. The first two were by far the most important sources of their wealth. Thus, of the 153 separate land transfers by which the Volokolamsk Monastery accumulated the huge complex it owned at the end of the sixteenth century, 98 were gifts, 14 were legacies, 23 were purchases, 12 were exchanges, and 6 were by other means.[34] The primary motive that inspired the donations was the familiar mixture of piety and insurance. Laymen were convinced that masses and prayers of the monks for the dead were the best

[31] Shchepetov, "Sel'skoe khoziaistvo," p. 93; Rozhkov, *Sel'skoe khoziaistvo*, p. 428.

[32] Tomsinskii, *Ocherki*, I, 62; Veselovskii, "Iz istorii," pp. 69-70.

[33] Kopanev, *Istoriia*, p. 140; Rozhkov, *Sel'skoe khoziaistvo*, pp. 405-407; Shchepetov, "Sel'skoe khoziaistvo," table 1, pp. 118-121; v. Rozhkov, *Sel'skoe khoziaistvo*, pp. 421-431 for the growth of other monasteries in the 16th century.

[34] Shchepetov, "Sel'skoe khoziaistvo," p. 94.

guarantees of a contented after-life. To win these good offices for themselves they made liberal gifts of land, as well as of cash, jewels, and goods of all sorts. In fact, this practice was so customary that if a man died without making a bequest to a religious body it was assumed that he had forgotten to do so, and the oversight was remedied by his heirs who turned over a portion of their legacies to the church for masses and prayers. In time a fixed scale was worked out so that the testator could know how much clerical assistance for his soul his bequest would purchase. The more he gave, of course, the more splendorous the services of remembrance and the more frequent their repetition. Unfortunately, the monks sometimes were remiss in fulfilling their obligations to the souls of their departed benefactors. Ivan IV pointed this out in one of the thirty-seven queries he addressed to the Church Council of 1551. "Who will be responsible," the tsar wanted to know, "for these abuses on the Day of the Last Judgement?" The Council modestly chose not to answer this question directly, and instead explained that masses were said in all monasteries for the repose of the souls of all Orthodox Christians to the end of the world.[35]

Rich donations were also made by proprietors who forsook the world for the cloisters. Among these initiates were men of high position, even ruling princes. Some of them were inspired by an inner call. Others joined in their last illness, and even with their last breath, in the hope of gaining credit for this holy act in the next world which they expected momentarily to enter. Still others took the vows to gain sanctuary from enemies or threatened punishments, for, as Fletcher noted, the fugitive "if hee gette a monastery over his head, and there put on a coole [cowl] before hee be attached, it is a protection to him for ever against any law, for what crime soever; except it be for treason."[36] Admission into a convent, whatever its motive, usually had to be purchased, and the fees were high.

Land acquisitions by the monasteries reached their zenith during the political and economic crises of the latter part of the sixteenth century. Many votchinniks, to preclude the loss of

---

[35] *Stoglav*, pp. xxviii, 35-36, 129; Kliuchevskii, *History*, II, 173-175.
[36] Fletcher, *Of the Russe Common Wealth*, p. 115.

their land through economic disaster or royal confiscation, gave their property to monasteries in return for life tenancies of all or part of the land they donated, or of some other land owned by the monastery. Thereby the erstwhile proprietor was able to live out his life peacefully under the protection of the monastery, enjoy the income from his property, and escape the perils that beset the votchinnik class during Ivan the Terrible's reign. The practice of turning over property to a monastery in return for a life tenancy was not a new phenomenon. It is known to have happened at least as early as the first part of the fifteenth century[37] and it continued on into the seventeenth. But it reached its peak during Ivan's reign. Other proprietors were compelled by the reverses they suffered to sell all or part of their properties. Monasteries, well supplied with cash from gifts and from their own economic activities, eager to increase their holdings, and free from molestation by the throne, were about the only buyers in the market. Still others mortgaged their lands with the monks and then lost it to them when they were unable to pay back the money they had borrowed. Finally, the flow of legacies was swollen by the bequests of proprietors who, bereft of their heirs by some calamity—a not infrequent occurrence in those disturbed times—left their lands to the monks.

Available data on gifts to monasteries in the second half of the sixteenth century reveal clearly the correlation between political and economic conditions and the frequency of transfers of votchinas to the religious. Between 1552 and 1557, when the first signs of economic disorder evidenced themselves, the known number of gifts of votchinas to monasteries rose from seven to thirteen. Beginning in 1558, when the Livonian War started, the number continued upward, and then when the *Oprichnina* was established it mounted rapidly. Between 1569 and 1578, the worst decade economically and politically of the entire half-century, 346 votchinas are known to have been turned over to monasteries by their proprietors. In 1570 and 1571 when the bad times were at their height—with widespread famine, pogroms in Novgorod and Pskov, mass executions at the order of the tsar,

[37] *ASEI,* I, nos. 163, 164.

and destructive Tatar raids—44 and 55 votchinas, respectively, were donated. In the eighties, after the ending of the Livonian War and the relaxation of Ivan's bloodthirsty program, the number of gifts dropped sharply, so that between 1582 and 1590 only 25 votchinas were presented to the religious.[38]

In addition to land the faithful poured a large and steady stream of gold into the monastic coffers. In the seventy-five years between 1550 and 1625 the cash donations received by St. Cyril's of Beloozero totalled 80,000 rubles (estimated to have been equal to eight million pre-1914 gold rubles). The total income of this monastery during these years from its ordinary operations—agriculture, fisheries, saltworks, rentals, and the like—was about 75,000 rubles, so that the donations more than doubled its revenues. During the sixteenth century St. Joseph's of Volokolamsk was given a total of 30,861 rubles, 10,031 of this amount coming from the tsars, 4,389 rubles from princes, 7,095 from prelates, and 9,346 from lay lords. These offerings in some years formed as much as half to three-quarters of this monastery's cash income.[39]

The greatest individual donor to the monasteries during the sixteenth century was Tsar Ivan IV, this despite his attempts (described later in this chapter) to limit monastic wealth. His gifts to the religious were so huge that they have been suggested as a chief cause for the financial difficulties of his reign. His cash contributions just to the largest monasteries were estimated at not less than 25,000 rubles, of which almost half went to Trinity-St. Serge. Ivan seemed to be trying to atone for his crimes through this munificence, even going so far as to set up liberal endowments for prayers for the souls of men whose death he had ordered. Great noble clans also gave freely and often. Sometimes there was a long-standing connection between one family and a monastery, each successive generation making gifts to the favored cloister. The Monastyrs were benefactors of St. Cyril's, the Golovins favored St. Simon's, the Godunov's St. Hypatius', and so on..

[38] Veselovskii, *Feodal'noe zemlevladenie*, I, 94-97.
[39] Kulischer, *Russische Wirtschaftsgeschichte*, I, 382; Shchepetov, "Sel'skoe khoziaistvo," pp. 94-96.

Church landlords, like the great lay seigniors, had their own servitors (*slugi*) who held land from them. Some of these *slugi* aided in the commercial operations in which monasteries often engaged, and others were responsible for the management of rural property belonging to the monks. In the sixteenth century monasteries formed detachments of military servitors, and several of the biggest monasteries built fortifications and maintained permanent garrisons. An Englishman who visited Trinity-St. Serge in 1558 reported that it was "walled about with bricke very strongly like a castle, and much ordinance of brasse upon the walles of the same."[40] Servitors of the metropolitan and of the bishops were expected to perform military duty for the state, but those of monasteries were exempt from this obligation.[41]

The number of monastic servitors seems to have been small until the 1570's when it rose abruptly. Most of these new *slugi* were undoubtedly former votchinniks who had turned over their properties to monasteries in return for life tenures, or who had lost title to their lands through foreclosure. Sometimes life tenancies were also guaranteed to the sons of the donor who then succeeded their father as monastic servitors. Land was also given out by the monks on service tenure to men who had not themselves given any property to the monastery, or who were not the prior owners of the land they received. These servitors were expected to support themselves from their own agricultural operations. Others who were charged with various duties in the administration, economy, or defenses of the monastery were not given land, but drew their livings from the monastery treasury.[42]

The increasing wealth of the monasteries inevitably produced a good deal of uneasiness among some members of the clergy, as well as at court and among lay seigniors. The churchmen feared that the acquisition of material goods would subvert the ascetic ideals of monastic life. The question was debated often and at length at clerical conclaves during the fourteenth and fifteenth centuries, with the decision always going to those who main-

---

[40] Hakluyt, *Voyages*, II, 440. Cf. also Fletcher *Of the Russe Common Wealth*, p. 115.

[41] El'iashevich, *Istoriia*, II, 175-176, 182-183.

[42] Veselovskii, *Feodal'noe zemlevladenie*, I, 231-233, 254.

tained that monasticism and wealth were not necessarily incompatible. The climax in this long argument came at the Church Council held in Moscow in 1503 when two great protagonists appeared to represent the opposing views. One was Joseph Sanin (1440-1515) and the other was Nil Sorskii (1433-1508).

Joseph, who was the abbot of the Volokolamsk Monastery, was the leader of those who supported the monastic accumulation of wealth. His role as the defender of this position was so preeminent that his party came to be known in Russian church history as the Josephians. Of upper class origins himself, Joseph believed that monasteries should seek wealth not only so that they could use their riches for good works, but also to make monastic life sufficiently attractive to draw high-born persons to it. For, as he argued at the Council of 1503, "If a monastery does not own villages how can an honorable and well-born man become a monk, and if there are no monks of noble origin where will men be gotten who are worthy of becoming metropolitans, archbishops, bishops, or of filling other high church offices? Therefore, if there will be no honorable and well-born monks the faith will be weakened."[43]

Nil, born into a peasant family named Maikov, was the founder of a monastery not far from Lake Beloozero on the Sora River, and so was called Sorskii. He was the leader of those who believed the monk's life should be one of poverty, prayer, and solitude, and who pursued their ascetic ideal in the inhospitable land that lay north of the River Volga. They were known as "the brethren from beyond the Volga," or the Transvolgans, or more pointedly, as the *Nestiazhatelnyi*, the "Not Greedy." In the rule Nil drew up for his disciples at his monastery he explained that monks should earn their bread by manual labor, and although they could accept alms they must not take an excessive amount. He warned them to "resist and avoid like deadly poison the desire to possess earthly goods," and instructed them that their lodgings should be of the cheapest materials and should be undecorated, and that they should never have anything beyond their simplest needs.[44]

43 Kliuchevskii, *Kurs*, II, 359-360.
44 Fedotov, ed., *Treasury*, pp. 91-94.

At the Council Nil denounced monastic landowning as contrary to the spiritual ideals of monasticism. At his request Ivan III submitted to the Council a proposal that monastic land be secularized and that all monks be required to live in poverty and by their own labor. But the majority decided in favor of the Josephian view and a statement was drawn up supporting church ownership of land.

The tsars themselves followed a wavering policy on the question of monastic landownership. Ivan III seemed to side with the Transvolgans at the Council in 1503, though given the man it is likely that his partisanship stemmed more from his craving to get the monastic land for himself than from theological conviction. In Novgorod he confiscated much church property, but in the other parts of his realm he neither took land away from the religious nor did he make any attempt to limit their further acquisitions. His son and grandson did make some efforts at restriction but these met with scant success. Vasilii III ordered that in certain of his subject princedoms his permission had to be secured before votchinas could be given to monasteries. Ivan IV in 1551 had this requirement extended to the entire state, made it applicable to land acquired by all church establishments and not just monasteries alone, and included purchases as well as gifts. If his permission was not first asked for and granted, the land, and in the case of purchased land the money paid for it by the monastery, was to be confiscated. A special government bureau was set up to supervise the carrying out of this legislation, and for a few years it seems to have been enforced. Then it fell into disuse and gifts and sales of land were once again made freely without asking for the throne's approval.[45]

The attempts by the state to limit church landholding were made at least partly in response to pressure upon the tsar from his lay servitors. These men saw in the monasteries, with their wealth, their exemptions, and their resulting ability to buy valuable land and attract peasant settlers, the enemies of their own interests. But determined measures to control monastic acquisition of land were not taken until the 1570's. In 1573 a

[45] *AAE*, I, no. 227; Veselovskii, *Feodal'noe zemlevladenie*, I, 90, 93; Vernadsky, *Russia at the Dawn of the Modern Age*, p. 119.

Church Council decreed that property could be given only to monasteries that had little land and then only with the tsar's approval. Gifts to wealthy establishments had to be in the form of cash. In 1580 another Church Council reaffirmed this decree and, with the tsar pressing for further action, ordered that no church dignitary nor institution could buy land nor give mortgages on real property.[46]

Another infringement upon the privileges of the monasteries came in June, 1584 when their special exemptions from government taxation were taken from them. These exemptions made monastic land more attractive to peasant-renters than the property of lay seigniors, for on the latter they had to pay taxes besides their other obligations. The depopulation of the Center, where most monastic land was concentrated, had produced a labor shortage of vast proportions. The exemptions enjoyed by the monasteries enabled them to outbid other landlords for the labor that was available and so made the scarcity of peasants all the more serious to lay seigniors. The government, faced with the dangerous possibility of the economic collapse of its main support, the serving class, and disturbed by the loss in tax revenues it suffered from the monastic exemptions, took a series of measures to stabilize the labor market. One of these measures was to do away with the monastic exemptions.[47]

Yet, in the face of these restrictions, the holdings of monasteries continued to grow. Long established traditions were hard to curb, particularly when the leaders of Russian society, including the tsars themselves, chose to disregard the provisions of the law. Ivan IV, for example, gave land and villages to the monks in 1583. His son Tsar Fedor made donations of property to a number of monasteries. Fedor's wife and her brother, Boris Godunov, made large gifts of land to St. Hypatius' Monastery, the long-time beneficiary of Godunov generosity. In the next century Tsar Michael and his successors gave land to monasteries. These royal examples were followed by a number of other people. In addition, monasteries in direct contravention of the

46 *AI*, I, no. 154/XIX; *AAE*, I, no. 308.
47 *SGGD*, I, no. 202.

laws added to their holdings through purchases and through foreclosures on mortgages they had given.[48]

The rate of growth of monastic land, however, slowed down in the seventeenth century. Perhaps one reason for this may have been that the legislation had some effect. Then, too, most of the great families who had owned vast stretches of land and had been the chief donors had succumbed to the throne's campaign against the magnates. The new nobility was not as plentifully supplied with property and so could not afford to be as generous. Possibly, too, the growth of the exchange economy and the increased use of money provided new opportunities for monasteries to enrich themselves through trade and money lending, so that they were no longer as interested in nor as dependent upon the acquisition of land as they once had been.[49]

[48] *Stoglav*, p. xxxii; Veselovskii, "Iz istorii," pp. 77-78; El'iashevich, *Istoriia*, II, 184-185; Kulischer, *Russische Wirtschaftsgeschichte*, I, 187-188.
[49] Kulischer, *Russische Wirtschaftsgeschichte*, I, 188.

12

CHANGES IN THE SEIGNIORAL
ECONOMY

DURING the long era of economic stagnation that lasted from the thirteenth into the fifteenth centuries the income most proprietors drew from their lands had been in the form of rents in kind, and to a much lesser extent, in cash. The usual Russian landowner had no interest in direct production and had little contact with the market. His needs were satisfied in greatest part by the goods he received from his renters and by the services of his household staff. Then, beginning in the second half of the fifteenth century the growth of a market economy and the increased use of money, the prolonged political unrest that was the birth pang of the unified and absolutist state, the demands made by the tsar's service upon the time and income of nobles and gentry, and the economic crisis and depopulation of the last part of the sixteenth and early seventeenth centuries, produced a new economic milieu to which the landlords of Russia had to adjust themselves. For many of them the task proved insuperable.

Information about seignioral wealth during this era is extremely scanty. A possible guide to the pattern of income distribution among votchinniks around the middle of the sixteenth century is afforded by the size of the pledges Ivan IV demanded as guarantees for the loyalty of some of his servitors. If it is assumed that the size of the pledge corresponded to the annual income of the guarantor, then three of the men whose names appear as guarantors had around 7,000 rubles a year, twelve from 2,000 to 4,000, seventy from 300 to 500 rubles, 250 from 200 to 250 rubles, 150 from 130 to 160 rubles, 600 from 75 to 120 rubles, and 200 from 50 to 70 rubles.[1] Some idea of the real value of these sums can be gained from prices then current

[1] Khlebnikov, *O vliianii*, pp. 22-23.

in the Center. A chetvert of rye cost between one-eighth and one-quarter of a ruble, a chetvert of oats sold for about half that amount, geldings sold for from 4 to 7 rubles, and chargers brought from 5 to 15 rubles.[2] Most of these votchinniks, then, appear to have been men of moderate means—provided that the size of the guarantee required of them did indeed correspond to their incomes.

There were proprietors, of course, who owned much wealth. The fifteen guarantors who pledged more than 2,000 rubles must have had large means. Some men inherited fortunes, others became rich through royal grants of land or of offices, and some managed to accumulate enough capital to build up large complexes for themselves. For example, D. D. Kholmskii, a member of the royal house of Tver, was a servitor of Ivan III who favored him with a number of lucrative "feedings" but gave him no land. Prince Kholmskii used the revenues he received from his posts to buy a large amount of property. P. M. Pleshcheev was a scion of one of the old Muscovite boyar families. When he began his career he had one village and several hamlets in Pereiaslavl that he had inherited from his father. He became one of the most important servitors of Ivan III and then of Vasili III. The only grants he received were two small villages from a minor prince for whom he had done a favor. But he was able to accumulate money that he used to buy land, so that at his death he left large holdings in four counties to his heirs.[3] In the last part of the sixteenth century Boris Godunov was reputed to be the richest man of his day. Giles Fletcher set his annual income in the 1580's at nearly 100,000 rubles, and Jerome Horsey, another English traveler, claimed it was 180,000 rubles. Other evidence indicates that although Godunov was indeed very wealthy these estimates were much inflated.[4]

But even the least affluent among the votchinniks must have seemed a Croesus to the great mass of the lesser servitors. The only regular income these men had came from their pomestyes. It has been estimated that the income from a pomestye of 300

2 Man'kov, *Tseny*, pp. 104-105, 122-125.

3 Veselovskii, *Feodal'noe zemlevladenie*, I, 81-84.

4 Cf. Seredonin, *Sochinenie*, pp. 190-191.

chetverts was between 5 and 8 rubles in the early sixteenth century and 10 to 20 rubles at the end of the century. And many pomestyes were much less than 300 chetverts in size. The money subsidies the government paid the pomeshchik were small and came irregularly. He not only had to provide for his family out of his income but had also to furnish his own armor, weapons, mount, and keep when on service. In the second half of the sixteenth century the cost of his equipment is said to have been 5 to 7½ rubles, and his expenses for his horse and himself on campaign ran around 7 rubles.[5]

Some of the lesser servitors gave up the unequal struggle to make ends meet. Abandoning their pomestyes and their obligations, they ran off to the frontiers where they settled as peasants, or threw in with the cossack nomads of the steppe. Others voluntarily became slaves of wealthy lords to escape the duties of state service. This latter practice became frequent enough for the government to take steps from the mid-sixteenth century on, first to limit it and ultimately to forbid it.

The great mass of the nobility and gentry, however, resorted to a traditional expedient of the seignioral class in every European land in a time of transition. They borrowed. Indebtedness was so general that it became a normal part of the economic life of these men, from the greatest lord down to the small servitor. They borrowed goods as well as cash. They borrowed large sums, they made a continuing series of small loans to meet incidental household expenses for such things as food and clothing, and they borrowed money and equipment to provide for themselves and their retinues when they went on the tsar's service. Prince Ivan Vasil'evich Gundorov, for example, borrowed three chargers, five geldings, four sets of armor, and velvet clothes, valued all together at 54 rubles, and 74 rubles in cash, from the St. Saviour-St. Joachim Monastery. Fedor Ivanovich Khabarov borrowed from this same monastery seven chargers and nine geldings, worth 64 rubles, nine sets of armor valued at 30 rubles, and 150 rubles in cash.[6] They borrowed on anything the money-lenders would accept as security. Sometimes this led to embar-

5 Khlebnikov, *O vliianii*, pp. 30-32; Eck, *Le moyen âge*, pp. 232-233.
6 Rozhdestvenskii, *Sluzhiloe zemlevladenie*, p. 82.

rassing situations. The wife of Prince Alexander Gorbatyi, for instance, must have been much put out when Tsar Ivan IV learned of the plight to which she had been reduced by the indebtedness of her spouse. The tsar had arranged a marriage between the Gorbatyi's daughter and Prince Ivan Fedorovich Mstislavskii. Prince Alexander, who was an important military commander, was away on service. Ivan wanted the girl's mother to come to court but learned that a barrier insurmountable to a woman prevented her from obeying her sovereign's command. She had nothing to wear. Her husband, needing money for his campaign, had pawned all her clothes. The tsar, who was still in his teens, was touched by her predicament and wrote her these lines: "Your brother Foma told us that Prince Alexander, going on service, pawned all your clothes. We would have ordered that your clothes be redeemed, but your brother Foma does not know with whom Prince Alexander pawned them. We have ordered that clothes be sent you from ourselves in which you should come. God grant that you come to Moscow and tell us with whom your clothes have been pawned and we will order them to be redeemed."[7]

The wills of great aristocrats of the latter fifteenth and early sixteenth centuries show the debts some of them had piled up. Prince Iurii, brother of Ivan III, owed 717 rubles at his death in 1472. Prince Andrei, another brother of Ivan, in 1481 owed the enormous sum of 31,050 rubles. Prince Mikhail Andreevich's debts in 1486 amounted to 267 rubles, and Prince Ivan Borisovich of Volok, nephew of Ivan, owed 600 rubles in 1504. Obligations of this size were, of course, exceptional but men of lesser rank were, in proportion to their wealth and income, far more weighed down by their burden of debt. Surviving wills of votchinniks of the sixteenth century show that debt was a nearly universal phenomenon among them. The pomeshchiks were probably in even worse condition, for, as pointed out earlier, their incomes must have fallen far short of covering their needs. In such circumstances, it is not surprising to find lesser servitors owing as much as 50 to 100 rubles.[8]

[7] *AI*, I, no. 146 (1547).
[8] Bakhrushin, "Kniazheskoe khoziaistvo," p. 44; Rozhdestvenskii, *Sluzhiloe zemlevladenie*, pp. 78-83; *DAI*, I, no. 52/xvi, xvii, xx (1556).

The people who lent the money came from many levels of society. Sometimes they were merchants and artisans, sometimes they were priests, and most frequently they were monasteries, this despite the Russian Church's long-held position against its clergy lending money at interest. Boyars, too, who were themselves in debt lent money, weapons, horses, clothes, and other goods to fellow servitors. In fact, everyone who was able to spare the money was apparently ready to lend. Or so it seemed to Freiherr von Herberstein who wrote that "usury is prevalent; and although they acknowledge it to be a great sin, yet scarcely anyone refrains from it."[9] The fact that some of the lenders were able to advance big sums points to their possession of large accumulations of capital, in itself a sign of economic revival and growth. A merchant named Vepr appeared as a creditor in the wills of two princes. His loans to these two men totalled 460 rubles. An archpriest named Vasilii Kuzmich in his will of 1531-32 listed debts totalling 737 rubles that were owed him by nine princes. Prince Mikhail Andreevich of Vereia in his will of 1486 mentioned a debt of 150 rubles to St. Cyril's Monastery, Prince Fedor Borisovich of Volots owed 100 rubles in 1523 to the Volokolamsk Monastery, and so on.[10]

The usual rate of interest that was charged on loans was as much as 156 percent a year, and even got up as high as 1 percent per day. Such rates made full repayment extraordinarily expensive. To relieve his servitors of some of this burden Ivan IV issued a decree in 1558 ordering that they were not to pay any interest on their loans after five years.[11]

Another way in which seigniors tried to accommodate themselves to the new economic conditions was to introduce money dues into the obligations of their peasants, or to increase them if they were already being paid. In this way they hoped to get more of the cash they now needed to meet their own heightened cost of living. The shift to money dues began to be made in the latter fifteenth century. The cadastral surveys for Novgorod Land in the last decade of that century recorded the frequent

9 Herberstein, *Notes*, I, 116.
10 Rozhdestvenskii, *Sluzhiloe zemlevladenie*, p. 81; Bakhrushin, "Kniazheskoe khoziaistvo," p. 42.
11 *AI*, I, no. 154/VII; Kulischer, *Russische Wirtschaftsgeschichte*, I, 386-387.

substitution of money for various dues hitherto paid in kind by the peasant renters. Normally, some payments in kind continued to be demanded, but sometimes, as on the properties of the Archbishop of Novgorod in the Bezhets district, all the obligations of the peasants were commuted into cash.[12] Sources from the last part of the fifteenth century for other parts of Muscovy also reveal this transition from kind to money rentals. During the sixteenth century dues in money became increasingly common. This shift was most pronounced in those regions of the state where market activity was most vigorous, evidencing the connection between the development of a money economy and the conversion of peasant dues into cash. In the Center the commutation of a number of obligations, especially of the many lesser ones, was nearly universal by the end of the sixteenth century, and apparently in many villages and hamlets all dues had been changed into money. In Novgorod Land, though the proportion of money dues in the total payments of the peasants grew steadily, they did not become as general as they were in the Center. In the colonial regions, where market exchange was least developed, cash dues were far less frequent and in some places were entirely unknown. Toward the end of the century they began to become more common in the Kama basin, the peasants there getting the money now demanded of them from the development of such rural industries as trapping, saltmaking, and collecting of wild honey, rather than from the sale of farm products.[13]

The most effective way in which the landlords could have met the challenge of economic change would have been to direct their energies toward a more efficient operation of their own economies. This would have involved a rationalization of their agricultural operations, including unification of their holdings, and close personal management. Such practices, however, presuppose a frame of mind and interests that were conspicuously absent from most of these men. Great princes and boyars,

[12] Grekov, *Krest'iane*, p. 500; Danilova, *Ocherki*, pp. 34-35, 138, 144-145, 157, 160-161.

[13] Rozhkov, *Sel'skoe khoziaistvo*, pp. 234-241, 271, 275-276, 280; Struve, *Krepostnoe khoziaistvo*, p. 6.

haughty, long used to the possession of wealth, and supremely confident that they would always have it, could not be bothered with such matters. The circumstances in which minor servitors found themselves made it hard for them to devote their energies to the improvement of their holdings. The usual pomeshchik was away on service so frequently and for such long periods that it was impossible for him to give much attention to running his land. Often, too, the amount of arable he received from the tsar was less than that to which his rank and service entitled him. In such cases he was sometimes given additional arable elsewhere until the total amount he had added up to what was due him. That meant that these servitors had their land broken up into parcels scattered through one or more districts, thereby increasing the difficulties of management and making operations less efficient and more costly. The practice of turning over part of the pomestye on the death of the occupant to his widow and dependent children for their support aggravated this tendency toward parcelling.

Yet, despite these barriers to innovation, there is striking and widespread evidence that many landlords made changes in their agricultural operations. This evidence was the great increase in the amount of land that seigniors set aside for farm production on their own account, and the accompanying increase in the labor obligation they demanded of their peasants. The principal explanations for this phenomenon were the expansion of the market and the increased cost of living. Many Russian landlords, like their analogues in other parts of Eastern Europe, decided that the best way to get the money they needed was to take advantage of the growing demand for farm goods by producing for sale. In the other Eastern lands the stimulus for market production came mainly from the West where a large, new demand for Eastern grain developed. In Russia seigniors produced for the expanding domestic market. In the latter part of the sixteenth century, during the years of economic crisis, other considerations undoubtedly played a prominent part in promoting the growth of demesne. The flight of the peasants from the old regions of settlement confronted landlords there with a severe drop in their revenues. To compensate for this loss many of them decided to raise produce on their own account, using the labor of slaves and of those peasants who had remained. Still others were given pomestyes that were partly or entirely abandoned. To get any revenue at all from such a holding the pomeshchik had to devote his personal attention to it. Given the serious shortage in peasant renters, he must often have decided to farm the land on his own, using whatever labor he was able to get.

Though demesne was present in every part of the state the scattered data make it clear that it was much more prevalent in some regions than it was in others. The cadastral surveys of Novgorod Land at the end of the fifteenth century show that before the confiscations of Ivan III many properties there had no demesne and those that did had small ones. Some of the pomeshchiks to whom the confiscated land was given created demesnes but these, too, were small. They were most common on pomestyes located near the city of Novgorod or on those on which the pomeshchik made his home. But most of the men who were settled by Ivan III in Novgorod Land followed the agricultural pattern they found, satisfied to turn over all their land to peasant renters. The largest demesnes at the end of the fifteenth century relative to the total size of the individual holdings were on the farms of the *svoezemtsi*, the smallest landowners of the region. On the average they worked between 25 percent and 35 percent of the arable on their properties on their own account. This was not because they produced for markets but rather because like peasants, to whom they bore many resemblances, the *svoezemtsi* did their own farm work to raise what they needed for their own consumption.

In the first half of the sixteenth century the picture in Novgorod Land began to change. In the Votskaia district in 1500 only 5 percent of the arable on the pomestyes listed in the cadastral survey of that year had been described as demesne. In the survey made in 1539 this figure had risen to 15 percent. In the Shelon-skaia district the incomplete data show that demesne increased from 8 percent to 18 percent of the arable in these same years. Data available for other districts show comparable increases. The expansion in the demesne of pomeshchiks was paralleled on monastic and archepiscopal property. In the registers of the fifteenth century no demesne was listed for any monastic property in two of the districts for which data are available, and there were just five desiatins of it in a third district. Similarly, there was no demesne on the lands belonging to Novgorod's St. Sophia's Cathedral. In the first half of the sixteenth century demesnes, albeit of relatively small size, appeared on monastic properties, and in the 1540's on the holdings of the cathedral. The decision of the wealthy Novgorod archbishop to raise farm goods on his account is particularly interesting documentation of the new interest of landlords in direct production.[14]

The available information for the Center indicates that demesne production there reached considerably larger proportions than it did in Novgorod Land. Material studied by Rozhkov in his careful analyses of agriculture in sixteenth century Russia, led him to the conclusion that by the second half of that century demesne was a general characteristic of the holdings of lay seigniors in the Center. He found only one case in which there clearly was none. The more plentiful sources on the internal organization of properties of the hierarchy and of monasteries show that, in general, demesnes were less usual on church lands until the last years of the century.[15] Data from the end of the fifties to the beginning of the nineties on twenty-three land complexes belonging to monasteries in fourteen districts of the Center show there was demesne on just four of the complexes. The total arable of all twenty-three amounted to nearly 130,000 chetverts, while the total amount of demesne was only 1,725 chetverts, or not much more than 1 percent. In the last decade of the century, however, there are many indications that a radical change took place. In the spring of 1590 Trinity-St. Serge replaced the dues in cash and kind paid by the peasants in some of its villages with the single obligation to till ten chetverts of demesne for every *vyt* of land they held from the monastery.[16] On others of its properties the requirement to work on the

[14] Rozhkov, *Sel'skoe khoziaistvo*, pp. 186-189; Perel'man, "Novgorodskaia derevnia," p. 138; Grekov, "Khoziaistvo," p. 249.
[15] Cf., e.g., *Akty feodal'nogo zemlevladeniia*, II, nos. 3, 434, 435.
[16] *AAE*, I, no. 348/II.

demesne was also introduced, but the obligation there was not as heavy nor did it replace all other dues. This new policy enabled the monastery to carry through a program of demesne expansion. Data from the nineties for 182,000 chetverts of arable held by Trinity-St. Serge in twenty counties of the Center show that over 11 percent was worked for the monastery. In eight counties the demesne on Trinity's property was between 2 percent and 10 percent of the total arable, in nine it was between 11 percent and 20 percent, and in two it was between 20 percent and 30 percent. In only one *uezd*—the one in which the monastery had the least amount of land—was there no demesne. In Zvenigorod in 1592-1593 of the 26,230 chetverts of arable of monasteries other than Trinity-St. Serge almost 6 percent was in demesne, in Pereiaslavl-Zalesskii about 42 percent of the 2,900 chetverts owned by Trinity of Kirzhach, and in Kostroma nearly 5 percent of the 15,000 chetverts belonging to the St. Hypatius Monastery were in demesne. Demesnes also became extensive in the last part of the century on properties of the patriarch and other church dignitaries.[17]

Because of the great size of the properties owned by church institutions the demesnes on these lands were usually much larger than on the holdings of laymen. On one of the complexes belonging to Trinity-St. Serge demesne amounted to nearly 2,500 chetverts, or more than the total area held by all save a few of the greatest lay proprietors. In view of this very considerable amount of land given over to seigniorial production on these church estates, it seems justifiable to conclude that the religious carried on what was for those times large-scale farming operations on their own account.

The other great landowner of the Center was the tsar. Demesne was conspicuously absent from his personal holdings in the sixteenth century with one exception. This was in Volokolamsk where in the 1540's 1,020 chetverts were listed as his demesne land.[18]

Demesnes were most common, surprisingly enough, in the colonial regions that lay south of the Oka River. Nearly all of the

[17] Rozhkov, *Sel'skoe khoziaistvo*, pp. 131-132, 134-137.
[18] *Ibid.*, pp. 130-131.

cultivated land there was held by pomeshchiks (v. p. 177), and on many of their holdings all of the arable was worked on the pomeshchik's own account. This was true of 161 pomestyes in Kashira in 1578-1579, on 204 in Tula and 40 in Dedilov in 1587-1589, and 692 pomestyes in Orel in 1594-1595. The explanation for this high incidence of demesne was not that these pomeshchiks were producers for the market, but that many of their benefices were so small that they, like the *svoezemtsi* of Novgorod, were not much different from peasants in their economic status. Like peasants they worked their fields themselves, aided sometimes by a slave or two, living off what they raised and sending little if anything to the market. In Orel for example (where 54 percent of the pomeshchiks had less than 150 chetverts of arable) in 1594-1595 there were almost as many pomeshchik homesteads (1,304) as there were homesteads of peasant renters (1,335). Many of the small pomeshchiks there had no peasant renters and tilled all their plowland for themselves.

Monasteries owned only a small amount of the steppe land. The area of demesne relative to the total arable of the individual monastic properties was about the same that it was on monastic holdings of the Center. On the tsar's land, in contrast to his properties in the Center, there was a considerable amount of demesne.[19]

In the Kama basin, the other major region of colonization in the sixteenth century, there was also much demesne. At the end of the 1570's the Stroganovs were using 42 percent of 1,650 chetverts of arable they owned in the Sol-Kamskaia district for their own production. On several monastic properties in other parts of the basin demesnes were even larger in proportion to total arable. On the votchinas of the archbishop of Kazan in 1566-1567, 13 percent of nearly 1,800 chetverts of arable, and on the tsar's lands in Kazan in 1599, 15 percent of 5,300 chetverts, was in demesne. In the North the very scanty data indicate that demesne was usual on both lay and monastic land. In the larger monastic properties the amount apparently increased toward

---

[19] *Ibid.*, pp. 176-177, 180; Platonov, *Boris*, pp. 266-267.

the end of the century, but, on the whole, demesne in the North was smaller in proportion to total arable than it was in other and more fertile parts of the realm.[20]

In the seventeenth century the demesne remained a normal part of seignioral operations and, in general, increased in importance as time went by. The continued expansion of commerce and in the use of money, combined with the enserfment of the peasantry (v. Chapter 14) which gave the seigniors well-nigh limitless powers of exploitation of his labor, promoted an increase in the lords' interest in direct agricultural production. Another stimulus to greater participation by the seignior in farming was the lessening of the service obligation, particularly for those who lived far from the frontiers. Around the middle of the century the military burdens of these men became perceptibly lighter, giving them more time to devote to the management of their lands. It seems probable, too, that the increase in votchinas at the expense of pomestyes in the seventeenth century furthered direct seignioral production. Got'e, in his study of the economic life in the Center during that century, found that in all save one district the ratio of demesne to total arable was higher on votchinas than it was on pomestyes. The seignior felt more secure on land of which he was the legal proprietor, was more interested in it, and worked it more efficiently, despite the fact that by this time the pomestye was for all practical purposes the property of its holder. This preference for the votchina over the pomestye was so strong that in those instances where a seignior had a votchina and a pomestye that were contiguous he almost always had his demesne on the votchina part of his land and made his residence there.[21]

In the 1620's, when the land was just beginning its painful recovery from the bad times, cadastral records of the Center show that the area of demesne in some districts ran as high as 90 percent and more of the total arable. The flight of so many peasants from that region and the impoverishment of those peasants who remained explain this development. Because of the

---

[20] Rozhkov, Sel'skoe khoziaistvo, pp. 156-160, 168-169, 174.
[21] Got'e, Zamoskovnyi krai, pp. 422, 492-493, 521-525; Petrikeev, "Zemel'nye vladeniia," pp. 52-53.

large amount of land that was abandoned, the absolute size of demesne need not have increased significantly, or even at all, for it to comprise a much greater proportionate share of the land still under cultivation. In addition, the poverty of those peasants who continued to live in the Center forced many of them to give up their holdings and become cotters or landless laborers, thereby reducing the total arable still more and pushing up the ratio of demesne. In later decades the less detailed information that is available indicates a decrease in the proportion of demesne to total arable in the Center, and a rise in the amount held by peasants. This was a reflection of the better times and of the recolonization of the Center, and not of a decline in the agricultural production of the seigniors.

The biggest votchinas often had hundreds of chetverts of demesne. Monasteries continued to have the largest demesnes in absolute size, but in general, monastic demesnes did not increase in area. Possibly this may have been because of the slackening off in monastic farming activity that seemed to have accompanied the retardation in the seventeenth century in the rate of growth of monastic land. On the other hand, demesne on the tsar's personal properties in the Center was no longer the rarity it had been in the preceding century. It was found most frequently on the palace lands that were closest to Moscow. The personal interest of the sovereigns in direct agricultural production on their own properties reached its peak in Alexis Mikhailovich's reign. After his death in 1676 demesne on palace land began to decrease, and early in the next century it was cut back still more when Peter I ordered a simplification of the economic organization of the Court.[22]

II

The many landlords who failed to adjust successfully to the economic and political changes of the sixteenth century disappeared from the seignioral class, but their places were quickly filled by new men. Even the great proprietors, who had been the special targets of Ivan IV's wrath, were replaced in the seventeenth century by other magnates. For when the Time of

[22] Got'e, *Zamoskovnyi krai*, pp. 463-500.

Troubles ended the government of the new tsar decided that the restoration of the economic power of the landlord class was its most urgent problem. So between 1612 and 1625 a great amount of land was given to servitors. Most of it came from the palace lands, the personal properties of the throne, since the greatest part of the black lands had been distributed in earlier reigns. The palace lands had apparently suffered less devastation than had the properties of many private landlords, and besides, the superior economic resources of the tsar made possible a more rapid recovery of his lands. Many grants went to the gentry to whom Michael owed so much, but great amounts were turned over to a few families who were close to him. Michael handed out so much that he began to have second thoughts about his generosity and in a ukase of 26 February 1627 announced that he was not going to give away any more. But, characteristically, Michael, and his successors after him, disregarded the decree, and palace lands continued to be distributed. The amount given away, however, did taper off until the last two decades of the century when grants were made with renewed liberality. This time the gifts were primarily to relatives and favorites of the tsars. From the death of Tsar Fedor II in 1682 to 1711, 506,000 desiatins of arable and 43,500 peasant homesteads were presented to these people. Sporadic efforts to restrain this practice were unsuccessful, and during the eighteenth century the amount of land given by the tsars to kinsmen and favorites reached fantastic heights.[23]

The magnates of the seventeenth century were predominantly new men. Just nine of the twenty-three wealthiest men in the tsar's service at the middle of the century were descendants of old princely families. The rest were non-royal kinsmen of the tsar (whose family was of Moscow boyar origin) and other members of the untitled serving class, including men who came from the lesser gentry.[24] The greatest proprietor among these twenty-three was I. N. Romanov, the tsar's uncle. He had 7,012 peasant homesteads (the unit for state taxes was now the peasant home-

---

[23] *Ibid.*, pp. 325-327, 426-427; Voznesenskii, *Ekonomika Rossii*, p. 17. For the 18th century v. pp. 355-359.

[24] Rozhkov, *Russkaia istoriia*, IV, ii, 39.

stead, or *dvor*, instead of a given area of land, so that the size of holdings was usually measured by the number of *dvory* on it). Two others had over 6,000 and 5,000 homesteads, respectively, one had nearly 3,000, and eight others had from 1,000 to 2,500. A half century later another roster of magnates named eighteen who had over 1,000 homesteads.[25] The Naryshkins, another family related to the tsar, were the greatest proprietors on this later list. They owned 12,000 homesteads. They had become kinsmen of the crown through Natalia Naryshkin, second wife of Tsar Alexis and mother of Peter I. In the latter part of the century they were the single greatest beneficiaries of the tsars' gifts; for example, in 1683 they received 14,000 desiatins of land with 2,500 homesteads, and in 1691, 34,180 desiatins and 2,563 *dvory*.[26]

There was, of course, a wide disparity between the wealth of the magnates and that of lesser proprietors. This was true even of the top levels of the nobility. A list prepared in 1646-1647 of the property of 53 of the tsar's chief servitors showed that all together they owned 49,438 peasant homesteads. The twelve who each had over 1,000 *dvory* owned 33,695 or 68 percent of the total, nine who had from 500 to 1,000 homesteads owned nearly 13 percent of the total, 29 with 100 to 500 homesteads had 19 percent, and three who owned less than 100 *dvory* had among them 213 homesteads, or less than .5 percent of the total number.[27]

III

Studies made of seignioral economies of the seventeenth century make it possible to gain an insight into and to compare the operations of several landlords, ranging from Tsar Alexis to a landowner of relatively modest means. Alexis (1645-1676) was the greatest private proprietor of his day. The vast lands that belonged to the state were divided into two categories, black land and court land. As was pointed out on an earlier page, the former was under the territorial sovereignty of the tsar as ruler

[25] Miliukov, "Zur Geschichte," p. 98.
[26] Tomsinskii, *Ocherki*, I, 61; Pokrovskii, *History*, p. 240.
[27] Tomsinskii, *Ocherki*, I, 58.

of the state, while the latter was the personal property of the crown. But since there was no distinction between tsar and state, and since the income from both black and court land belonged to the tsar, he could take as much of the former as he wanted for holdings of the crown. The court lands had been put under the administration of a special bureau called the *Bol'shoi Dvorets*, the Great Court, in the sixteenth century. Tsar Alexis separated certain properties from the rest of the court lands and put them into a special personal category. At the time of his death there were 17,342 homesteads on these holdings. Being tsar he decided to use a government agency to run these personal possessions for him. The choice he made was an odd one—he turned over the job to the Bureau for Privy Affairs (*Prikaz Tainykh Del*) which was primarily a police agency. Alexis, however, took a close interest in the management of his properties, was kept informed of what was being done on them, and on occasion intervened in their operation.

The tsar and his bureau were enterprising managers. They imported cattle, horses, and poultry from abroad to improve the quality of the livestock. They tried to grow mulberry trees and cotton on Alexis' properties in the Moscow area, but found the climate unsuitable. By far the largest part of the goods produced was consumed by the court. But the tsar—or rather the Bureau— was very much in the market. Surpluses of some commodities were produced regularly and were sold. Distilling was an especially important activity with large amounts of grain used for this purpose. Most of the output was consumed at court or was given away (liquor was a favorite gift of Alexis), but a good deal was put on the market and brought in thousands of rubles. Much potash was also sold—in 1670 the income from sales of this commodity was 34,190 rubles. Flax was another cash crop, the tsar himself giving the order that it be raised for sale.

In addition to these agricultural activities the Bureau also handled some of Alexis' commercial operations. For instance, it bought as much as 200,000 *pudy* of salt a year, going as far as Astrakhan to get it in order to save money since it was much cheaper there than in the Moscow area. Most of this salt was used by the Court but a large amount was resold. In 1663 the Bureau sent an expedition to Persia to buy silks, providing the caravan with goods worth nearly 77,000 rubles and with 17,200 rubles in cash.[28]

B. I. Morozov (1590-1661) was another great proprietor. He had inherited 2,500 desiatins and 151 homesteads. Beginning in 1616 he started to receive land grants from Tsar Michael and within a decade the size of his holdings had more than doubled. But his rise to great riches dated from 1633 when he was appointed tutor to Alexis, the tsarevich. The next year he was elevated to the rank of boyar and took a leading role in the inner councils of the government. In addition to getting more grants from the throne he purchased land from other proprietors and also bought uninhabited land from the state. On Alexis' accession in 1645 Morozov became his chief advisor. He used this new eminence to gain still more land for himself. By 1647 he had property in ten counties with over 6,000 homesteads and was second only to the tsar's uncle, I. N. Romanov, as the biggest lay proprietor of that day. His holdings continued to grow, until by the time of his death they were exceeded only by those of the tsar himself. He is estimated to have owned about 80,000 desiatins scattered through 19 counties, with over 9,000 homesteads and a total population of about 55,000 people. He died childless in 1661, and left his empire to his wife. After her death in 1667 it quickly began to fall apart, some of it being bequeathed to various persons and some of it being taken back by the government and redistributed. The chief heir was I. G. Morozov, a nephew, who got the patrimonial votchinas Morozov himself had inherited, and also some of his uncle's other properties.[29]

The records of Morozov's operations[30] show that he paid close attention to the running of his properties and kept the reins in his own hands. He issued a constant stream of instructions from his headquarters in Moscow to the regiment of managers who were in charge of his individual properties, and who, in turn, sent frequent reports to him. When a new manager was ap-

28 Zaozerskii, *Tsarskaia votchina*, pp. 8-9, 18-19, 85-96, 216-226.
29 Petrikeev, "Zemel'nye vladeniia," pp. 51-83.
30 Akademiia Nauk, *Khoziaistvo krupnogo feodala-krepostnika XVII v.*; Iakovlev, *Akty khoziaistva boiarina B. I. Morozova*.

pointed it was standard procedure for Morozov to send him a memorandum telling him what was expected of him on his new job. If the property itself was newly acquired Morozov's instructions were to make a complete survey of the population, resources, and boundaries of the votchina immediately, with a full report to be sent to the central office in Moscow.

The amount of demesne on his properties varied with local conditions, but in general the practice was to require every six to eight peasant homesteads to till three desiatins for Morozov. Like Tsar Alexis—and every other seignior—Morozov tried to be as self-sufficient as possible. He was his own best customer, for he lived in grand style, but his lands produced surpluses which he sold. His money crops, like those of Alexis, were liquor and potash. He sold the liquor through the taverns he operated on his properties and also sold some to the state for sale in government-owned taverns. He turned out a great deal of potash, his shipment from Nizhnii Novgorod to Archangel for export running as high as 55,900 *pudy* (in 1653). He was also interested in the manufacture of iron wares and hired German and Polish artisans to work in his shops. He apparently did not produce enough ore to meet his needs since he made purchases of both domestic and foreign iron.[31]

A. I. Bezobrazov was a medium-sized proprietor. His family had been in Moscow's service since the fifteenth century. Bezobrazov himself held fairly high rank, being a *stolnik*, the fifth in the eleven service ranks of his time. In 1670 he inherited his father's property. Most of it lay in the Center. Bezobrazov, in common with many landlords of the Center, hungered after the more fertile land south of the Oka. So he set about an active program of buying, selling, and exchanging land, with the aim of disposing of as much of his property in the Moscow area as he could, and building up his holdings in the steppe. A few of his transactions were with large proprietors, but most of them were with lesser gentry. When he bought land he generally paid a low price, for much of what he purchased was uncultivated. He picked up some pomestye land this way, disguising his purchases as exchanges to evade the prohibition against the sale of pomes-

---

[31] Zabelin, "Bol'shoi boiarin," *passim*; Bakanov, "Tovarnoe proizvodstvo," p. 95.

tyes. His largest single acquisition was 78 chetverts and his smallest one was just two chetverts. He received only two pieces of land as grants from the throne.

His efforts to get steppe land were in large measure successful. By 1689 his property was scattered from Vologda *uezd*, in the northern part of the Center, to Kromy on the southwestern frontier. Of his total holdings 1,345 chetverts were pomestye and 1,107 votchina. But like other seigniors he was far more interested in his votchinas than in his pomestyes. He had all together 239 homesteads, with about 1,100-1,200 people in them. All save 33 of these homesteads were on his votchinas, and much of his pomestye land lay untilled.

Bezobrazov kept full control of his lands in his own hands, directing everything down to the smallest details, and constantly on guard against waste and inefficiency. Like Morozov he was a careful and autocratic manager, but was able to do a more thorough job because he did not have to spend time on the many other activities that occupied Morozov's attention. His scattered properties were supervised by fifteen slave-stewards who had long belonged to the Bezobrazov family. He also sent out special agents to his properties to carry out his orders.

His holdings in the relatively infertile Center had only a small amount of demesne. Most of the revenue he drew from these lands came from the dues in cash and kind paid him by his peasants, and from hay, timber, and fish. His chief economic activities and interests focussed on his southern holdings from which he drew the greatest part of his income. He carried on a detailed and extensive correspondence with the stewards who managed these steppe holdings for him. His operations were directed primarily at meeting his own needs. His connection with the market was irregular and sporadic, and was unimportant in the overall structure of his economy.[32]

As things turned out Bezobrazov's careful management and his deep interest in his land went for naught. In 1689 in the last days of the regency of Sophie, elder sister of Ivan V and Peter I, Bezobrazov was ordered to go on service to a far distant post. Just when he was ready to set out Sophie was removed from her

[32] Novosel'skii, *Votchinnik*, *passim*.

office. His absence from Moscow meant he would not be able to look out for his own interests during this critical period when power was changing hands. So he consulted a sorcerer and paid him to cast a spell over the new administration that would make it look upon him with favor. Sometime later there was a police round-up of the wizards of Moscow and the authorities learned about Bezobrazov's séance. He was brought back to the capital, questioned, tortured, and found guilty of treason. He was sentenced to death and his properties were confiscated by the throne.[33]

The Spaso-Prilutskii Monastery was a much larger proprietor than Bezobrazov, but ran a small operation in comparison to Tsar Alexis or Morozov. In relation to its size, however, it was much more involved in the market than they were. In 1635 it owned 6 large villages, 7 small ones, and 72 hamlets, with a total of 496 homesteads. It also owned two saltworks on the White Sea, each run by a resident manager. A large proportion of its arable was demesne tilled by its peasants as part of their obligations to the monastery. Additional labor was hired when more hands were needed, as at haying or harvesting. The large surpluses of grain and other farm goods that it produced were sent to market. It did most of its buying and selling in the nearby city of Vologda and in the distant river port of Kholmogory, near Archangel. The monks had their own business offices in both these towns, and in Vologda they also had a grain warehouse. Prices of farm goods were usually higher in Kholmogory (which lay in the infertile soil of the far North) than they were in Vologda, and so the monastery preferred to sell on that market. Nearly every year it sent representatives down the river network to Kholmogory with a cargo of its own products and of wares bought in the Vologda market for resale in the North. After they disposed of their goods the monk-merchants loaded their boats with salt from the monastery's own saltworks and with additional salt purchased in Kholmogory, where salt prices were lower than in the Center, returned to Vologda, and sold the salt there.[34]

---

[33] *Russkii biograficheskii slovar*, II, 647-648.
[34] Savich, "Agrarwirtschaft," VI, 23-24, 30-31.

13

THE PLIGHT OF THE
PEASANTRY

ALL THE CHANGES that have been traced out in the five preceding chapters—the rise of absolutism and the demands it made upon the seigniors, the decline of the old aristocracy and the ascendancy of the pomeshchiks, the growth of the market and in the use of money, the great crises of the latter sixteenth and early seventeenth centuries, the efforts of the seigniors to adapt to the new conditions—all these things combined to bring about sweeping rearrangements in the relationship between the landlords and the peasants who rented their land. The final outcome was serfdom for the mass of Russia's rural population. The origins of this transformation of a free peasantry into serfs bound to the will of their masters can be traced back to conditions and practices that had appeared in earlier times. But the course of Russian history during the sixteenth and early seventeenth centuries channeled and intensified the already existing tendencies toward the binding of the peasant.

Like any great historical movement the story of the enserfment is an interlacing tangle of events and motives that can be unravelled only at the risk of oversimplification of what actually happened. The approach used in this and the next chapter is to study the impact of the ambitions, policies, and needs of the landlords and of the state upon the peasantry as evidenced in the changes in the composition of, and the over-all increase in, the dues and taxes of the peasants, their heavy indebtedness and impoverishment, the increase in the limitations upon their right to move about freely, and the growth of the seigniors' powers over them.

Sources dealing with the direct relations between lords and peasants—particularly with the obligations required of the latter —though still inadequate, are much more plentiful for the sixteenth and seventeenth centuries than for the preceding era. As could be expected, these show a broad variety in the amounts and types of dues and services that were demanded. But they also show a common pattern of evolution in these obligations. Many dues in kind were commuted into cash, labor services (barshchina) increased, more had to be paid to the government, and the total amount of obligations required of the individual peasant household rose.

The dues and services demanded by the Solovetskii Monastery in 1561 from the peasants who lived in the village of Pozyrevo, by Prince Simeon Bekbulatovich in 1580-81 from his village of Mar'ino, and by Trinity-St. Serge Monastery from the peasants of Sobolevo in the 1580's, can serve as illustrations of the kinds of obligations now paid by peasants to their seigniors. For every *vyt* (the amount of land considered necessary to support a peasant household) held by the peasants of Pozyrevo the village had to pay the Solovetskii Monastery annually 4 chetverts of wheat, 4 chetverts of oats, a cheese or 2 *den'gi*, 50 eggs, a loaf of rye bread and a loaf of white bread, 2 wagonloads of firewood, 1 wagonload of pine wood cut to size, 10 pieces of wood suitable for preparing kindling, and long sticks used for lighting. In addition to these payments in kind the peasants had to farm two chetverts of demesne for every *vyt* they held, and had to repair and rebuild monastery buildings. Peasants doing labor services had to start work at sunrise. Absentees were fined 4 *den'gi*. The peasants also had to make an annual cash payment of 10 *den'gi* per *vyt* and 2 *den'gi* per homestead. Cash fines were levied when a peasant moved or married. Finally, for every *vyt* one horse had to be furnished once a year to carry monastery produce to the market and to bring back salt. This service could be commuted by paying 80 muscovite *den'gi*.[1]

The peasants of the village of Mar'ino, for every *vyt* they held, paid Prince Simeon Bekbulatovich one-half ruble in cash, 4½ chetverts of rye, 7½ chetverts of oats, a series of lesser dues in kind, such as eggs, cheese, poultry, and the like, which could be commuted into a cash payment of 1 ruble 56 *den'gi*, and 40

[1] *AAE*, I, no. 258.

den'gi for the steward who managed the property for Bekbulatovich. Payments of wool, hay, and wood were commuted into a
cash sum.[2] The peasants of Sobolevo made a payment of 3 rubles
a year to Trinity-St. Serge. In addition, four times a year, at
Easter, St. Peter's day in June and in November, and at Christmas, they had to pay 6 *den'gi* for each *vyt* they held, plus one
ruble for the entire village. They also paid fees when they married, transferred holdings, bought and sold produce, and came
into the lord's court. They were required to deliver 20 chetverts
of rye and 20 of oats annually to the monastery and to mow
60 ricks of hay each year.[3]

The practice of collecting a set share of the crop as rental
(*polovnichestvo*) continued to be used. It was particularly common in the first half of the sixteenth century in Novgorod Land,
and was also widespread in the North where it was much employed by monastic landlords in the seventeenth century. It was
used only infrequently in the Center. The shares ranged from
one-fifth to one-half of the harvest, with one-third apparently
most favored.[4]

The data are much too scanty to allow exact comparisons
between the total amount of the obligations paid by the peasants
to their seigniors at different times during the sixteenth and
seventeenth centuries. But there are many indications that these
payments grew markedly during these years. This is not surprising in view of the new pressures upon the seigniors, and of their
growing power over their peasants. The rise in the obligations
apparently began in the sixteenth century. In the immediately
preceding period they seemed to have remained largely unchanged. For example, in Novgorod Land the cadastral surveys
made at the turn of the fifteenth century show that there was no
increase in dues and services between 1478, when Ivan III
annexed Novgorod and began to replace the old landlords with
his pomeshchiks, and the end of the fifteenth century. Apparently, the new landlords were content with the amount that
had been paid their predecessors. But in the sixteenth century
they jacked up their demands.

2 Seredonin, *Sochinenie*, pp. 194-195.   3 *AAE*, I, no. 307.
4 Rozhkov, *Sel'skoe khoziaistvo*, pp. 162, 175, 191, 238.

The rise in the amount of money dues was a particularly striking phenomenon. In the Votskaia district of Novgorod Land the cash payments per *obzha* (a full-sized peasant holding) at the end of the fifteenth century had been between .25 and .45 rubles. By the 1560's they were up to 1 to 1½ rubles and in the 1580's they were as much as 2 rubles—an increase of four to eight times over in less than a century. Similar increases took place in other districts of Novgorod Land and in the rest of the Muscovite realm.[5] A detailed study of four parishes in the Obonezhskaia district showed that peasants' payments increased by five to six times per *obzha*, and six to ten times per person, between the 1490's and the 1560's. In 1496 the average obrok in the four parishes had been from 27 to 40 muscovite *den'gi* per *obzha*, and from 8 to 20 *den'gi* per person. In the 1560's the averages were 169 to 203 *den'gi* per *obzha*, and 70 to 109 *den'gi* per person. In addition, many of the peasants now had to make a grain payment that amounted to four to five chetverts per *obzha*, or about 1.8 to 1.9 chetverts per person.[6]

The largest part of this rise, however, and in some instances all of it, must have been only nominal because of the decline in the value of money during the sixteenth century. Changes in the buying power of the ruble cannot be determined with any degree of precision because of the exiguity of price notations. It is possible, though, to arrive at a very rough approximation on the basis of the price indices constructed by Man'kov from the scanty data that are available. The index for rye, the most important commodity of the era, shows that for most of the 1560's rye prices were from three to six times as high as they had been in 1500, and for most of the 1580's and 1590's they were from six to eight times as high.[7] If these figures are valid guides to the changes in the value of money, then the increase in the cash obrok during the sixteenth century just about kept pace with the fall in the purchasing power of the currency.

In the seventeenth century the amount of money dues the peasants had to pay continued to mount. Payments of 15 rubles

[5] *Ibid.*, pp. 242-244, 252-258.
[6] Perel'man, "Novgorodskaia derevnia," pp. 157-159, 173-174.
[7] Man'kov, *Tseny*, table 2, pp. 114-115.

per *vyt* were not unusual and often much more was demanded. In addition, many lords demanded more dues in kind and added new obligations. The peasants on the properties of B. I. Morozov paid in the mid-seventeenth century an annual money obrok of from 6 to 24 rubles per *vyt*. The payment was as little as 6 rubles when the peasants had to do much barshchina, while those who paid 24 rubles had few other burdens. The money obrok for all of Morozov's villages averaged out at around 15 rubles per *vyt*, amounting to .75 to 1.25 rubles per peasant homestead. Data on the holdings of other landlords of this time show that this was the general level of money dues on their lands also. Besides the cash payments Morozov levied a number of other dues in kind either per homestead, per *vyt*, or per village. On his properties in Nizhnii Novgorod, for example, each village in addition to a cash obrok of 15 rubles was also required to give Morozov 2 *pudy* (*ca.* 72 lbs.) of swine's flesh, 1 goose, one suckling pig, 30 *arshiny* (*ca.* 23 yards) of cloth or 10 *funty* (*ca.* 9 lbs.) of wool.[8]

Since the value of money continued to fall in the seventeenth century much of the increase in cash obrok was accounted for by this decline. But the depreciation apparently did not cancel out all of the rise, so that there was probably a sizable real increase in the amount of cash dues the peasants had to pay.[9]

The more frequent demand for money payments that resulted from the growing need of the lords for cash was pointed out in the preceding chapter. Usually, only part of the obrok was converted into coin. By still receiving the rest in the form of kind the lord could maintain some measure of self-sufficiency, and could sell whatever he did not use for his own consumption. Another reason why seigniors did not demand all dues in cash must have been because they realized it was impossible for their renters to raise enough money to meet the bill. That the peasants were able to pay an increasing proportion of their dues in currency is evidence for the growth of the market and money economy, since they got the cash they needed by selling part of their product. But this development had not yet progressed far

---

8 Zabelin, "Bol'shoi boiarin," pp. 25-26.
9 Got'e, *Zamoskovnyi krai*, pp. 518, 542; Rozhkov, *Russkaia istoriia*, IV, ii, 46.

enough to allow complete conversion to cash dues. The difficulties they had in getting together the money they did have to
pay must have been considerable. The monk Ermolai-Erazm,
writing in the mid-sixteenth century, reported that of all the
peasant's obligations the money dues were the hardest for him
to meet, and urged that they be converted into payments
in kind.[10]

When money obrok was demanded, an effort was made to
equalize the overall obligation of those peasants who had to pay
more of their dues in cash than did their fellows. For example,
in two parishes of Novgorod Land at the end of the fifteenth
century the usual obrok per *obzha* was one *korob'ia* (*ca.* 12 bushels) of rye, two of oats, and 1 to 3 *den'gi*. Some of the peasants,
however, had to pay an additional 5 *den'gi* in cash, but as compensation their grain obrok was reduced by one *korob'ia* of
oats.[11] Those peasants of the Volokolamsk Monastery whose
dues were in both cash and kind in the 1570's paid one eighth of
a ruble for every *vyt* of land they held. Others of the Volokolamsk peasants whose entire obrok was in cash paid .9 to 1 ruble
per *vyt*.[12] The wide disparity that sometimes existed between
districts in the amount of money demanded from those peasants
whose obrok was all in cash seems also to have been the result of
an effort at equalization. Thus, at the end of the fifteenth century the *obzha* in the Derevskaia district of Novgorod Land was
smaller than it was in the Shelonskaia and Votskaia districts. So
the all-cash obrok in the first-named district ran from .1 to .3
rubles per *obzha*, while in the latter two it was .25 to .45 rubles
per *obzha*. It was also low in the Bezhetskaia district, but the
reason there seems to have been the infertility of the soil.[13] The
highest known cash obrok in the sixteenth century was that paid
by the peasants of Sobolevo, who were charged 3 rubles per *vyt*
by the Trinity-St. Serge Monastery.[14]

The second major change in peasant obligations was the increase in the use of barshchina, and in the amount that

10 Budovnits, *Russkaia publitsistika*, pp. 225-226.
11 Perel'man, "Novgorodskaia derevnia," p. 155.
12 Shchepetov, "Sel'skoe khoziaistvo," p. 99.
13 Rozhkov, *Sel'skoe khoziaistvo*, pp. 247-248, 252-253.
14 *AAE*, I, no. 307.

was demanded of the individual peasant. In the era of the Mongol domination, when seignioral production in any significant amount had been exceptional, barshchina was uncommon. When there was demesne it was usually tilled by slaves, although labor services by peasant renters had not been unknown. The growth of demesne in the next period produced a heightened seignioral demand for labor, and so barshchina was required much more frequently than it had been before.

To some Marxist historians the greater demand for labor services in the sixteenth century is a "second edition" of the practices of the Kievan era. This view gives a misleading impression of the importance of barshchina by implying that it became the chief form of peasant obligation.[15] The economic and political changes of the sixteenth century certainly made it expedient for many seigniors to engage in production on their own account. Their ability to take as much land as they wanted from their peasants for demesne, and their power to alter the form of the obligations the peasants paid them, facilitated the spread of barshchina. But the fact of the matter is that throughout the sixteenth and seventeenth centuries obrok in cash and kind remained the predominant type of peasant obligation. In large parts of Russia, and especially in the North where most of the land was held by black peasants, barshchina was either entirely unknown or else little used. In Novgorod Land it was demanded more frequently than hitherto, but in many places there it still was not required. In the steppe, where small pomestyes prevailed, there was much demesne, but often it was worked by slaves or by the pomeshchiks themselves. Only in the Center and in the Kama basin, where there were large holdings and extensive demesnes, did it become a major peasant obligation.[16]

At the end of the fifteenth century, when barshchina was demanded it seems to have been for just one day a week. In the next century the obligation not only became much more common but was often increased to two and three days a week. (An increase of much the same proportions in labor dues took place in other lands of Eastern Europe in this same period.) Freiherr

[15] Cf. Grekov, *Krest'iane*, pp. 8-9, 375, 413.
[16] Rozhkov, *Sel'skoe khoziaistvo*, pp. 160, 174-175, 180-181, 190-191, 200.

von Herberstein, in Russia in the first part of the sixteenth century, claimed the peasants (he called them *coloni*) worked six days a week for their lord. "The seventh day was allowed them for their own work," he wrote, "on fields and meadows turned over to them by their lords from which they got their livings."[17] In the light of what is known about the organization of agriculture at that time Herberstein's statement cannot be accepted as an accurate report of typical labor obligations. He must have confused peasant renters with slaves, who did spend all their time working for their owners, and who tilled small pieces of land turned over to them by their masters for their own use in whatever spare time they could find.

Usually, neither the amount nor the exact nature of the labor service were stipulated in the agreements lords made with peasant renters. Instead, such phrases as the peasant having to perform barshchina "like the (lord's) other peasants" or that he had "to do work" for the lord were employed.[18] In a series of over 1,300 agreements made by two monasteries with their peasants in the seventeenth century in which there were about 1,100 references to barshchina, the extent of the obligation in nearly every case was baldly stated to be "according to the order of the monks."[19] Data for a number of properties in the Center and in the Kazan district between the 1540's and the 1590's show that peasants who had to do barshchina usually tilled 3 to 4½, and in several instances 6 desiatins of demesne for every *vyt* of land they held.[20] This meant that from one third to one half of the time they spent working in the fields, or two to three days a week, was used in farming the demesne. They were also responsible for payments in cash and kind which meant the expenditure of still more time to meet the demands of their seigniors. On the other hand, when in 1590 the Trinity-St. Serge Monastery introduced the requirement on a number of its properties of tilling 5 desiatins of demesne for every *vyt* held

---

[17] Herberstein, *Rerum muscovitarum*, p. 55.

[18] *Svodnyi tekst*, p. 35.

[19] Kulischer, *Russische Wirtschaftsgeschichte*, I, 203.

[20] Rozhkov, *Sel'skoe khoziaistvo*, p. 258.

by the peasants—amounting to a barshchina of three days a week —it excused the peasants from all other payments.[21]

A particularly interesting illustration of the introduction of barshchina (as well as of the new interest of seigniors in increasing their production) concerns St. Constantine's Monastery in Vladimir. At the end of the fourteenth century the attempt by the abbot, Efrem, to increase peasant dues had been thwarted by Metropolitan Cyprian (v. pp. 102-104). Around 1499-1500 Abbot Matvei decided, as Efrem had a hundred years before, that the monastery's peasants were not charged enough rent. He complained to the Metropolitan, whose name was Simon, that the peasants "tilled many fields for themselves and tilled few fields for the monastery." He asked for remedial action, and Simon, unlike Cyprian, acceded to the abbot's request. Times had changed. Simon ordered that the monastery's lands should be remeasured and redistributed to the peasant-renters. The standard holding was to be 15 desiatins (5 desiatins in each field), although peasants who wanted more or less than this were to be accommodated. Each renter was to till for the monastery an area equal to one fifth of his holding.[22] This was the equivalent of one sixth of the peasant's working time during the farming season, or one day a week. In addition, the renter had to pay other dues. That meant further expenditure of his working time to produce the various kinds of goods he had to give the monks, to raise the money he had to pay them, and to perform the lesser services required of him.

In the seventeenth century the barshchina, when required, continued to be between one and three days a week. On B. I. Morozov's properties the usual obligation for the peasant homestead responsible for labor services was to till an area one half the size of its holding. Thus, the family spent one third of its field labor time, or two days a week, working for Morozov. Peasants who did barshchina on Tsar Alexis' votchinas apparently were required to spend two to three days a week on this obligation. On the lands of A. I. Bezobrazov a barshchina

[21] *AAE*, I, no. 348/II.
[22] Charter in Miliukov, *Spornye voprosy*, p. 32n.

of three days a week was the rule in the 1680's for nearly all his peasants. Most of the peasants in the villages of the Novgorod Cathedral of St. Sophia did not have to do labor services, but those who did were held usually to less than three days a week.[23] In all these cases the peasants who had to do barshchina also paid other dues in cash and kind and performed minor labor services, such as mowing the lord's meadows, carting for him, repairing his buildings, and so on.

The introduction of the barshchina, even when it replaced some other obligation, could result in an overall increase in the peasant's payments, as the experience of the Volokolamsk Monastery showed. In 1590 that monastery had received a total of 71 rubles from a group of peasants whose obligations were all in cash. In terms of grain prices current in their region at this time, their payment was equal of 157 chetverts of rye and 55 chetverts of oats. In 1591 these peasants were shifted by the monastery from money payments to barshchina. In 1592 their labors on the monastery's demesne produced 680 chetverts of rye and 231 chetverts of oats. This was worth over 306 rubles. By switching these peasants to barshchina the monastery had more than quadrupled the revenue it got from them. This great increase was entirely at the expense of the peasants, who paid for it in additional labor time. In 1590 they had to work long enough to earn the 71 rubles they owed the monastery as obrok. In 1592 they worked long enough to produce the equivalent of four times more than they had paid in 1590.[24]

II

Besides the mounting burden of his obligations to his lord, the taxes the peasant had to pay rose steadily through the sixteenth and seventeenth centuries. In fact, the degree of their increase was greater than that of the seignioral obligations. The emergence of the unified state, its ambitious program of expansion, and the greater use of money in the economy, made it

---

[23] Zabelin, "Bol'shoi boiarin," p. 27; Zaozerskii, *Tsarskaia votchina*, p. 162; Novosel'skii, *Votchinnik*, p. 135; Grekov, "Khoziaistvo," p. 253.

[24] Shchepetov, "Sel'skoe khoziaistvo," pp. 100-102.

impossible for the government to meet its cash requirements through the forms and levels of taxation of the preceding era. In the latter fifteenth century a start was made in shifting taxes hitherto paid in labor and kind into cash levies, and in the sixteenth century the changeover was completed. At the local level the payments in kind to the *kormlenshchiki* also began to be converted into coin. Towards the end of the fifteenth century the government started to supply *kormlenshchiki* with lists giving the money equivalents of the payments in kind the people of their districts were supposed to pay them. Instead of the customary amount of meat the official was to be paid 12 *den'gi*, in lieu of the grain payment 120 *den'gi*, and so on.[25] This process of commutation continued until the abolition of the *kormlenie* system in 1555.

Not only were taxes changed into money but there was an enormous increase in the amount demanded. In the first two decades of the sixteenth century the money tax rate is estimated to have been about 5 rubles per *sokha*, from the twenties to the forties 8 rubles, from the fifties to the eighties 42 rubles, and at the end of the eighties and beginning of the nineties 151 rubles. Actually, the growth of the tax burden was not as large as these figures seem to indicate. Some of it was accounted for by the commutation of taxes in kind into cash. And some of it was explained by the drop in the value of money during these decades. Nonetheless, there was a very considerable real increase in the amount that had to be paid. Much of the rise was attributable to the long and costly wars of the tsars. But, as the above figures show, the greatest boost came in the latter decades of the century, when the devastation of so much of the realm reduced state revenues drastically and compelled the government to tax even more heavily the people who still remained on the land.[26]

Great as the fiscal demands of the state were in the sixteenth century, they were dwarfed by those it made in the first half of the next century. The Time of Troubles had emptied the

25 Cf. Vladimirskii-Budanov, *Khristomatiia*, II, 73-81 (1488); *AAE*, I, nos. 44 (1506), 150 (1509), 181 (1536).
26 Rozhkov, *Sel'skoe khoziaistvo*, pp. 233-234.

treasury, and the great devastation and depopulation that followed in its wake reduced the tax base. To this was added the costs of the wars fought by the first Romanovs. Higher tax rates were inevitable. In the second decade of the seventeenth century the rate is estimated to have been 1,200-1,600 rubles per *sokha*. In the twenties and thirties it fell back to 500-560 rubles and then in the forties went up to 1,700 rubles per *sokha*. Once again the nominal rise was greater than the real one because of the continued fall in the ruble's value. But even if it is assumed that the ruble of the mid-seventeenth century was worth but half of its value at the end of the sixteenth century, the absolute increase was of enormous proportions.[27]

The effects of the tax increases in the seventeenth century were made all the worse by a retrogression in the methods of assessment. In 1550 Ivan IV had introduced more efficiency and equality in tax assessments by establishing a new tax unit.[28] The old name of *sokha* was retained but the ambiguity that had surrounded the old *sokha* and other tax units was cleared up. On the lands of pomeshchiks and votchinniks the new *sokha*, or great Muscovite *sokha* as it was sometimes referred to, was declared to be 800 chetverts of good land, 1,000 of medium, and 1,200 chetverts of poor land. On monastic properties it was 600 chetverts of good, 800 of medium, and 1,000 of poor land. The special favor shown the lay seigniors was in all likelihood connected with the introduction of the service requirement. The taxes were paid by the servitor's peasants, but by reducing the amount they had to pay the state, more was available for the lord to take for himself. Thereby he received some compensation for the services the state demanded of him but not of monasteries.

The assessments were made by periodic cadastral surveys. The first of these registers, or *pistsovye knigi* as they were called, had been drawn up in the thirteenth century to serve as the basis for

[27] *Ibid.*; Got'e, *Zamoskovnyi krai*, pp. 540-542; Rozhkov, *Russkaia istoriia*, iv, ii, 46.

[28] The following discussion of assessment methods is from the summary of Veselovskii, *Soshnoe pis'mo* in Miller, "Considérations sur les institutions financiéres."

the collection of the Tatar tribute. In the next two centuries they were made irregularly at the order of the native princes. The oldest surviving *pistsovye knigi* are those made for Novgorod Land at the end of the fifteenth century at the order of Ivan III. In the sixteenth and seventeenth centuries three cadastres were carried through for the entire realm, the last one being completed in 1630. Only parts of these records are still extant.

The officials who were sent out to make the cadastres used rough methods of measurement. They surveyed only the fallow fields of a settlement and assumed that these represented one third of the total arable. In places where the fields were worked irregularly under field grass or slash-burn husbandry even rougher methods were employed to estimate the tilled area. The surveyors, however, corrected the gross errors that resulted from these procedures by checking with data supplied them by the peasants. The latter, despite their illiteracy and primitive measuring techniques, were justly famed for their ability to figure out exactly how much land they held. The usual practice was for each commune to select a jury from among its oldest and most respected members to provide information and assistance to the official surveyors. The surveyors also consulted other villagers when necessary. As a further aid the officials carried with them copies of the last cadastre made for the district. One source of error, however, proved unconquerable. This rose out of the surveyors' imperfect knowledge of arithmetic. Since the *sokha* was a large unit fractions were a constant problem for them. Their mathematical learning did not go beyond simple fractions, and in fact the only ones they seemed to know were $\frac{1}{2}$, $\frac{1}{4}$, $\frac{1}{8}$, $\frac{1}{16}$, $\frac{1}{32}$, and $\frac{1}{3}$, $\frac{1}{6}$, $\frac{1}{12}$, and $\frac{1}{24}$. Nor did they know how to add and subtract fractions with different divisors. This led them to some remarkable arithmetic circumlocutions. If, say, they wanted to express 80 chetverts in terms of a *sokha*, they did not enter it as $\frac{1}{10}$ of a *sokha*, but instead recorded it as "one half of one half of one quarter, and one half of one half of one half of one quarter of a *sokha*, and 5 chetverts more." Long practice made them extraordinarily skillful in these mathematical acrobatics, but there were times when they became hopelessly lost in their forests of fractions. On occasion they escaped from their dilemmas by rounding off unfamiliar ones into old friends they knew, so that, for example, $\frac{1}{15}$ was considered as $\frac{1}{16}$.

The surveyors did not limit themselves to determining the size and quality of the arable. Their mission included assembling complete data on all the actual and potential income-producing elements in every settlement. So they collected information on the number of homesteads, and on pastures, meadows, untilled land, forests, vegetable gardens, fisheries, flour mills, and everything else of economic value in each place they visited. This raw data then underwent a subjective analysis by the assessors to determine the ability of each settlement, and of each peasant in it, to meet tax levies. Their object was to tax the peasant to the maximum of his capacity to pay but not to overburden him. If they decided that the peasants of a certain community were too poor to meet the full load of taxes on all the land they held, the number of chetverts of arable declared taxable and recorded in the assessment registers was less than the amount actually tilled. The holdings of peasants who were judged unable to pay any taxes, such as widows or those who had been ruined by some natural catastrophe, were omitted entirely from the rolls.

This remarkably equitable system broke down during the first half of the seventeenth century and ultimately had to be abandoned. In the years of the Troubles many of the old tax registers had been destroyed, and those that had survived were of little use for assessments because of the many changes in landholding that had taken place since they were drawn up. When civil order was restored in 1613 new registers were ordered for many local areas. But these were made hurriedly and haphazardly. Because there had been so many changes the old records, if they were available, were of little or no aid to the surveyors, nor were they able to get assistance from the peasants as they had in the past. The flight from the old regions of settlement and the devastations of the Troubles had broken the chain of continuity in most places, so that the collective memories of the peasant communities were no longer available to provide data for them. Finally, the great increases in the tax rate contributed to making these registers inaccurate. For the assessors realized that if they entered the amount of land really under cultivation, the peasants, already impoverished by the economic setbacks of the preceding decades, would be completely ruined by the taxes they would have to pay. So they deliberately falsified their returns by reporting much land actually under cultivation as empty. Thus, in a settlement where say 100 chetverts were being farmed, the assessors, after evaluating the tax capacity of the villagers, might report 80 chetverts as empty and only 20 as "living chetverts"—the phrase used to describe revenue-producing land. But since the assessors had neither the old records nor peasant advisors to guide them, nor any norms established by the government, their estimates were often arbitrary and unjust. Still another evil resulting from their procedure was that it made necessary further increases in the tax rate on land still listed as taxable, leading in turn to further removals of arable from the rolls.

The inadequacies of these surveys quickly evidenced themselves. The government thereupon decided that another method of assessment had to be employed. It ordered that the "living chetvert" was to be equated with a certain number of peasant and cotter homesteads instead of with tilled land. The principle of capacity to pay was preserved by assigning different numbers of homesteads to the chetvert according to the wealth of the peasants. The range was from two peasant and two cotter homesteads to a "living chetvert" in the most prosperous districts, to twelve peasant and eight cotter homesteads in the poorest ones. New registers according to this method were made between 1619 and 1631 (except in the North where the old type of assessment was retained).

It soon became apparent, however, that the new system was not going to work either. For the surveyors in the field continued to use their own judgment of the peasants' capacity to pay. If they believed the official norms would work undue hardship on a settlement they did not register all the homesteads in it, thereby reducing the tax burden of that community. The only way out of this predicament seemed to be to disregard capacity to pay. In 1645 a census was taken of all homesteads and their inhabitants, and two years later all special taxes began to be levied as a flat sum per homestead. The land tax, however, continued to be based upon the *pistsovye knigi* of 1619-1631. By the 1670's these registers were recognized as being completely out of date, and in 1676 a new general cadastral survey was begun. The next year another census of homesteads and their inhabitants was made, and in 1679 the government decided that, until the completion of the new cadastre, this census was to be used for the basis of all taxes and that all taxes were to be levied per homestead. Work on the land survey dragged, and taxes continued to be assessed upon each homestead. Finally, in the reign of Peter I, both the *pistsovye knigi* and the homestead system of assessment were abandoned, and taxes were ordered levied on each individual male. This was the famous "soul tax" reform.

The sixteenth century system of assessment, though it had many imperfections, represented a genuine effort to adjust taxes to the peasant's ability to meet them. The substitution of the homestead as the tax unit, and then of the individual, was a complete abandonment of this principle.

Taxes had long been levied upon the commune of which the peasant was a member rather than upon the individual himself. As was pointed out on an earlier page, the group was charged with the responsibility of dividing the taxes among its members, collecting them, and turning them over to the government. If any member of the commune failed to meet his share his fellows had to make it up. When taxable land fell vacant it was the commune's task to find an occupant for it or else pay the taxes on it. But this tradition of communal responsibility broke down in the sixteenth and seventeenth centuries with the disintegration of the peasant commune on privately held land. The state could not expect the peasants of one lord to pay taxes for a delinquent who lived on the land of some other lord, or to assume responsibility for finding renters for empty holdings on another lord's property, or pay the taxes on it. So now taxes were levied upon each individual votchina or pomestye, and the seignior was made responsible for the payment of the taxes of his peasants. If they did not meet the levies he had to pay them. This inevitably promoted the extension of seigniorial power over the people who lived on his land, for it gave legal sanction to force-ful measures he might adopt to collect the tax money. It also strengthened his position over his peasants in that when he paid their taxes for them they became his debtors, and thereby much more under his control. On the other hand, it had an adverse effect upon the lords, too, for the added financial burden of this tax responsibility made their economic position all the more precarious, and when they were forced to make good for de-linquent peasants they were pushed still further into debt themselves.

Up to the last part of the sixteenth century arable tilled for the lord had been taxed on the same basis as the land held by his peasants. In the 1580's and 1590's demesne on the property on which a military servitor lived was exempted from taxes, but they were still levied on the demesne on other pomestyes or votchinas he might have. Then, in the seventeenth century, upon the introduction of assessments upon the homestead of the peasant and cotter, all seignioral demesne was freed from taxes.[29]

III

The augmentation in the obligations of the peasants to their seigniors and to the state was not offset by any major improve-ments in the techniques of production. On the contrary, as we have seen, there was a regression in the latter sixteenth and early seventeenth centuries. As a result, the economic position of the peasantry steadily worsened. This deterioration was evidenced by a drop in peasant income, a decrease in the size of their hold-ings, an increase in the numbers of cotters, and a great rise in peasant indebtedness.

Estimates of peasant income are available only for the second half of the sixteenth century, and then only for their revenues from tillage. They were calculated by N. I. Rozhkov from data in the cadastral records. Rozhkov figured that after deducting obrok, taxes, the value of the grain consumed by the peasant household and of that set aside for seed, the net income for the average peasant holding in four of the five chief zones of the

---

[29] Kulischer, *Russische Wirtschaftsgeschichte*, I, 205; Kliuchevskii, "Podushnaia podat," pp. 349-350; Rozhkov, *Sel'skoe khoziaistvo*, pp. 266-268.

realm in the 1550's to 1580's and in the late 1580's and 1590's was as follows:[30]

	1550's-1580's	Late 1580's-1590's
	(in rubles)	
Center	.3 to 1.4	.03 to .95
Kama Basin	.3 to 1.4	.03 to .95
Northwest	−.2 to .9	−.47 to .24
Steppe	3.6 to 4.2	2.9 to 3.9

These estimates indicate that the peasant of the steppe was much better off than his fellows in the other parts of Muscovy—which helps explain why so many people fled from the old regions of settlement into the steppe. In the Center, the Kama basin, and the Northwest, the peasant's position worsened to the point where many of them must have barely covered costs or fallen short of doing this. These peasants had to find additional sources of revenue to make ends meet, and the cadastres reveal that many of them engaged in transport, small trade, house industry, fishing, beekeeping, salt-making, and so on. Their incomes from these activities are not included in the above figures.

Actually, Rozhkov's estimates are somewhat inflated. He did not include the value of the barshchina among the costs of those peasants who had to pay this obligation. The grain yields he used to calculate peasant income (5 and 6 to 1 for rye and 3½ and 4 to 1 for oats) are much higher than seems warranted (v. p. 167). Yet, even with this upward bias his estimates show how very small the average peasant's revenue was from tillage, and how this tiny income decreased in the last years of the century. Moreover, this income was possible only in years unmarred by reverses. A crop failure or an illness, let alone such a major disaster as an invasion or a Tatar raid, meant complete ruin for the peasant entirely dependent on farming, since he was unable to build up a reserve to cushion himself from such blows. In the event of such a catastrophe his only recourses were either to borrow from his seignior and thereby imperil or even give up entirely his personal freedom, or to run away without paying his obligations and start all over again in some other place. This

---

[30] Rozhkov, *Sel'skoe khoziaistvo*, pp. 259-265.

second alternative was really no escape, unless the runaway chose to join the cossacks or made his way to Siberia, for in beginning afresh he had to borrow enough from his new landlord to get started, and to support himself and his family, until he brought in his first crop.

The decrease in the average size of their holdings in the latter part of the sixteenth century was further evidence of the retrogression in the economic fortunes of the peasantry. Data for nearly 88,600 peasant homesteads in Novgorod Land listed in the cadastres of the end of the fifteenth century, and in those of the 1520's and 1540's, show that for nearly 57 percent the average holding was between 12 and 18 chetverts of arable, for 15 percent between 18 and 24 chetverts, for over 24 percent between 24 and 30 chetverts, and for 3 percent between 30 and 36 chetverts. Only one half of one percent had an average of less than 12 chetverts of arable. In the Center the holding considered necessary to support a peasant homestead was known as a *vyt*. In the sixteenth and seventeenth centuries this was equal to 30 chetverts of good arable, 36 of medium quality, 45 to 48 chetverts of poor soil, plus 3 chetverts of meadow or 30 hayricks. Many of the holdings described in the slim sources on peasant tenements in this region during the first half of the sixteenth century were close to or equal to a *vyt* in size. In the North the amount of arable in holdings was on the average much smaller than it was in other parts of the realm. Farming there was an unequal struggle with poor soil and harsh climate and the peasant drew much of his income from other occupations. Though there were a few exceptional instances where the average arable per *dvor* was 30 chetverts the usual average, as seen in data from the fifties and sixties for over 8,500 homesteads, was between 3½ and 4½ chetverts, and in one commune the average for 231 homesteads was only 1.5 chetverts.[31]

Beginning in the 1570's the average for the amount of arable in individual peasant holdings began to decline in the Center and Northwest. Of more than 9,000 homesteads listed in surviving Novgorod cadastres for the 1580's the average amount of

[31] *Ibid.*, pp. 144-149, 152, 168, 170-172, 196-198; Miliukov, *Spornye voprosy*, p. 32n.

arable for 17 percent was just 4.5 chetverts; for 68 percent it was between 6 and 12 chetverts; for 14 percent between 12 and 18 chetverts, and for less than 1 percent it was over 18 chetverts. Information for 9,313 homesteads in the Center reveals the same order of drastic reduction in the amount of arable per holding. The *vyt* was still retained as a unit but very few peasants now held that much land. For example, of the 919 homesteads on the properties of Trinity-St. Serge in Dmitrov *uezd* in 1592-1593 only two had arable equal to a *vyt*. The rest had from one-half down to one-eighth of a *vyt*. Out of a group of 141 peasants who were in arrears in their payments to the Volokolamsk Monastery in 1591, 22 had one-third of a *vyt*, 86 had one-quarter, 17 had one-sixth, 14 had one-eighth, and two just one-twelfth. That these were considered normal holdings, and were not the result of parcelling among the peasants themselves, is shown by the fact that peasants newly settling on Volokolamsk property in 1579-1580 were given holdings of one-half to one-sixth of a *vyt*.[32]

In the North the already small average amount of plowland per holding apparently remained unchanged. Information for the new colonial areas that were just being opened up is scanty, but indicates there may have been some shrinkage in the size of holdings there also between the 1560's and the eighties and nineties. The average for peasant holdings in the steppe zone in the last years of the century was from 15 to 18 chetverts per homestead. This was larger than the averages in other parts of the realm, yet even in this frontierland the average per *dvor* was less than for the Center up to the 1570's.[33]

A sizable decline in the average amount of arable per *dvor* could be expected during the first half of the sixteenth century because of the population increase. In the Shelonskaia district of Novgorod Land according to the 1497-1498 cadastre 2,087 peasant homesteads had 68,544 chetverts of arable, for an average of nearly 33 chetverts per *dvor*. In the 1539 cadastre 3,443 homesteads had 69,054 chetverts, giving an average of only 20 chet-

[32] Rozhkov, *Sel'skoe khoziaistvo*, pp. 147-153, 198-199; Got'e, *Zamoskovnyi krai*, p. 502; Shchepetov, "Sel'skoe khoziaistvo," pp. 98, 100.
[33] Rozhkov, *Sel'skoe khoziaistvo*, pp. 168, 170-173, 178-179, 181-182.

verts per *dvor*. In four Novgorod parishes in another district there were 933 homesteads in 1496 and 1,347 in 1563, with a consequent decrease in arable per *dvor* at the later date.[34] If comparable data were available for the Center it seems certain in view of the evidences of population increase there, that they would reveal a similar increase in the number of homesteads and decrease in arable per *dvor*.

But the sharpest decline occurred in the last three decades of the century when crises engulfed the realm and when population fell off drastically in the old regions of settlement. The usual peasant who, at best, had been able barely to meet his obligations and stay free of debt, was ruined economically. Those who did not seek escape in flight had no incentive to till as much land as they formerly had, because the mounting burden of taxes and seignioral obligations meant they would only be working for lord and state. So they reduced their holdings to the point of barest subsistence. Theirs was the reaction of a defeated and hopeless people. Giles Fletcher, living among them at this time, was struck by their despair and their helplessness and realized that inactivity was the only defense they had— other than flight. He wrote: ". . . concerning the landes, goods, and other possessions of the commons, they assume the name and lie common indeed without any fence against the rapine and spoile, not onely of the highest [the tsar] but of his nobilities, officers and souldiers. . . . This maketh the people (though otherwise hardened to beare any toile) to give themselves much to idleness and drinking."[35]

Even in their dissipations they contributed to the tsar's coffers for taverns were a state monopoly. And, if Fletcher is to be believed, the neglected wife or child could not come to the saloon in the time-honored manner to plead with the sot to come home because, wrote Fletcher, "none may call them foorth whatsoever cause there be, because he hindereth the emperours revenue."[36].

Peasant holdings continued to be of reduced size on into the

[34] *Ibid.*, pp. 196-197; Perel'man, "Novgorodskaia derevnia," pp. 163-166.
[35] Fletcher, *Of the Russe Common Wealth*, p. 62.
[36] *Ibid.*, p. 58.

THE PLIGHT OF THE PEASANTRY

seventeenth century until some measure of recovery began to evidence itself. Then more and more land was taken under the plow, so that the average amount of arable farmed by each homestead grew larger during the course of the century. On the other hand, two other contemporary developments served as retardative factors in the growth of the individual peasant's arable. These developments were the increase in population, and the new government policy of assessing taxes upon the *dvor* rather than on the arable. In preceding centuries grown sons customarily had gone off on their own, so that there had been just one or two adult males in each peasant homestead. But during the seventeenth century this practice began to be abandoned. Though new homesteads were established, many of the adult sons now preferred to stay on in their father's *dvor* rather than start a new one and thereby take on the heavy burden of seignioral obligations and state taxes. In 9,042 homesteads in nine districts of the Center listed in the cadastres of the 1620's there were 16,241 males, an average of 1.8 per *dvor*. In the census of 1678 the number of homesteads had risen 2.8 times over to 25,336, but the number of males had increased over six times to 100,903, or four per *dvor*. It has been estimated that while the average amount of arable per homestead in the Center rose from about 12 chetverts in the first half of the century to from 14 to 18.6 chetverts in the second half, the amount of arable per male fell on an average of from 20 to 25 percent.[37]

The growth in the number of cotters, or *bobyli* as they were called, was another significant indication of the economic decline of the peasantry. The earliest known reference to these landless, or nearly landless, rustics is in a document from the year 1500, indicating that this status was probably of recent origin. During the sixteenth century, and particularly in its second half, references to the *bobyli* became more frequent, though it is clear they still formed an unimportant part of the total peasant population. Some of them were skilled craftsmen and others were engaged in trade and transport, but most were

[37] Got'e, *Zamoskovnyi krai*, pp. 263, 513-514.

impoverished peasants who eked out a precarious living from the land. Then, as a result of the economic regression of the late sixteenth and early seventeenth centuries, their numbers rose to record heights in all parts of the realm. Surviving cadastral data from the 1620's show that in the Center *bobyl* homesteads made up over 40 percent of all peasant homesteads, in districts along the Volga 20 percent, and in some parts of the steppe 40 percent to 58 percent. For example, on properties owned by Trinity-St. Serge Monastery in Dmitrov *uezd* in the Center there had been 917 peasant and 40 *bobyl* homesteads in the 1590's. In the 1620's there were 220 peasant and 207 *bobyl* homesteads. In land belonging to Trinity in the Uglits district there were 477 peasant and 13 *bobyl* homesteads in the 1590's, and 111 peasant and 145 *bobyl* homesteads in the 1630's.[38] Moreover, the *bobyl* of the seventeenth century was worse off than his predecessor of the sixteenth. Originally the *bobyl*, since he held no arable, had not been responsible for taxes. In fact, he came by his name because of this freedom from state levies, for the word *bobyl* meant a "single man," not in the sense of a bachelor (though often the *bobyl* was unmarried), but in the sense of a man standing by himself apart from the compulsory fiscal group. But in the seventeenth century, when the tax base was shifted from the peasant's arable to his *dvor*, the cotter's hut was included in the tax unit. He now had to bear part of the fiscal burden of the village, though normally his share was less than that of his fellow peasants who had holdings.[39]

With the gradual recovery in economic life during the seventeenth century the proportion of *bobyli* in the peasant population declined in nearly every part of the empire. They were able to pull themselves up out of their landless status and take over a peasant holding. In 115 properties in the Center for which data are available for the 1620's and the 1680's, there were at the earlier data 126 homesteads of slaves, 802 *bobyl* homesteads with 1,073 males in them, and 1,189 peasant homesteads with 2,620

38 D'iakonov, *Ocherki iz istorii*, pp. 224-225; Rozhkov, *Russkaia istoriia*, IV, ii, 41, 44.

39 Struve in *Cambridge Economic History*, I, 435; Grekov, *Krest'iane*, pp. 755, 757-758.

males. In the 1680's the number of slave homesteads was virtually unchanged, there now being 131. But the number of peasant homesteads had grown nearly four times over to 4,648, and
the number of peasant males had increased by more than six
times to 16,525. The number of *bobyl* homesteads, however, had
decreased by nearly 50 percent to 407, while the number of
bobyl souls remained almost exactly the same (1,072) as it had
been in the 1620's.[40]

The next lower level in the rural social structure after the
bobyli was that of the free hired laborers. Their number was
small, since the work performed by peasants on barshchina, by
slaves, and by peasant debtors, usually met the lord's need for
labor. When workers were hired they were paid in cash or in
kind, and apparently were sometimes provided with their board.
Some of them were permanent residents of the manors where
they were employed, while others lived elsewhere, hiring themselves out as seasonal workers. Their number rose somewhat at
the end of the sixteenth century, especially on monastic properties (where the hired laborers were known as *detenyshi*). In the
seventeenth century they continued to be used, chiefly by
monasteries in the North and in Kazan, but also by lay lords and
sometimes by well-to-do peasants.

The fall in incomes, the dwindling in the size of holdings, and
the increase in the number of cotters all bear witness to the
deterioration in the economic condition of the peasantry. But
perhaps the most striking evidence of this decline was the great
rise in the incidence of peasant indebtedness to the seigniors.
As earlier pages have shown, this was an old phenomenon in
Russia, but from the latter part of the fifteenth century it became
far more common than it had ever been before. Hit hard by the
increase in his obligations and then by the bad times of the
latter sixteenth and early seventeenth centuries, it was extremely
difficult for the peasant to avoid debt. If he remained on his old
holding he could not meet his obligations without recourse to
loans in cash or kind from his landlord. If he left to settle elsewhere he had little or nothing to begin farming with, or to

[40] Got'e, *Zamoskovnyi krai*, pp. 136, 259-260; Tomsinskii, *Ocherki*, 1, 79.

carry him over until he harvested his first crop, so that he had to
borrow from his new seignior. Some of these new renters were
described in the sources as arriving with only "a cap and a
caftan," others were reported to have "brought of his own
nothing," and some were described as having brought with them
only "body and soul."[41]

The loan contracts made by the peasant borrowers specified
various means of paying back the principal and interest. But
from the latter fifteenth century on the practice became increasingly frequent for the borrowers to agree to meet the
interest payments by working for the seigniors from whom they
borrowed. The loan agreements had apparently been made
orally, depending for their fulfillment upon the good faith of
the contracting parties, until the turn of the fifteenth century.
Then they began to be written down. The document by which
the peasant acknowledged his indebtedness and agreed to the
terms set for repayment was known as a *kabala* and the peasant
borrower was called a *kabal'nyi chelovek*, a *kabala* person. The
word *kabala* and its use in the sense of an acknowledgement of
debt had been brought into Russia by the Mongols, but the
custom of working out a loan had long been known.

The increase in the use of the *kabala* arrangement was an
indication of the growing need of the seigniors for labor as they
turned more and more to production on their own account, and
of the worsening condition of the peasantry, since this was an
extremely unfavorable contract for the borrower. The usual
loan was between 3 and 5 rubles. Sometimes the agreement
stipulated that the borrower was to repay the principal at the
end of a stated period, usually given as one year, and was to pay
the interest by working for the lender during this period. If at
the end of the specified term the peasant did not pay back the
principal, the contract required that he continue working for
his creditor every day until the loan was repaid. The creditor
was to feed and clothe him, and he was excused from paying the
obligations to lord and state demanded of the other peasants. In
other cases no date of repayment was named, the borrower agree-

---

[41] D'iakonov, *Ocherki . . . stroia*, pp. 345-346; Kliuchevskii, "Proiskhozhdenie,"
p. 227.

ing to work every day for his creditor in payment of interest on his loan until such time as he paid back the principal.[42]

The establishment of a fixed time by which the loan was to be repaid must have been little more than a convention. For it could hardly have been expected that a borrower who agreed to work every day for his creditor just to pay the interest on his loan could ever have amassed enough money to pay back the principal. In actuality these debtors became life-long peons of their creditors, paying interest by their labor on a debt they could never hope to wipe out by their own efforts. Their status was not much different from that of slaves and, indeed, they came to be known as *kabala* slaves. Seigniors tended to lump them together with their bondsmen, and in their wills they sometimes freed their *kabala* peasants from their debts in the same sentence in which they emancipated their slaves.[43]

Cancellation of his debt by the testament of his creditor was just about the only way the *kabala* peasant could hope to be freed legally of what he owed. It was possible for him to change creditors by borrowing from another lord to pay off his debt, but this did not change his position for now he was obliged to work for his new creditor. The chances are that this transfer of indebtedness from one lord to another was sometimes used by the seigniors themselves as a cover for buying and selling *kabala* people, who were nominally free men and so were not supposed to be sold. It was also a way by which a seignior in need of labor could lure peasants away from other lords. He lent money to another lord's *kabala* peasants on slightly more favorable terms than their existing loans. The peasants used their new loans to pay off their old ones, and then worked for their new creditor.

The *kabala* contract was entered into not only by the heads of peasant households, but also by husbands and wives jointly, and sometimes by the parents and their children. In cases where the family was the borrower each member had to work in payment of the interest, and the loan remained a charge against all members of the family for the rest of their lives. Such an agree-

---

[42] Lappo-Danilevskii, *Zapisnaia kniga krepostnym aktam*, pp. xv-xvi; Vernadsky, "A propos," pp. 360-361, 362; Grekov, *Krest'iane*, pp. 668-672.
[43] Cf. *SGGD*, I, no. 12.

ment made the debt servitude last for two generations. A similar result was arrived at when the peasant borrowed from a father and son, in which case he had to work for two generations of his creditors.[44]

There was a close resemblance between the *kabala* peasant of the sixteenth century and the *zakup* of the Kievan era. That debt servitude should have become important in these two eras was not coincidental. Both were periods in which trade and the use of money were of much more consequence than in the centuries that separated them, and in both periods, too, there was a seignioral demand for labor and a decline in the economic condition of the peasantry.

Though the *kabala* was known in the fifteenth century it apparently had not yet become of sufficient importance to warrant legislative attention. In any event, the Law Code of Ivan III, put out in 1497, contained no reference to it. But a half century later the *Sudebnik* of Ivan IV dealt with peasant borrowing at some length. This code ordered that only free men could enter into *kabala* contracts, loans made to slaves being declared forfeit. Doubtless this provision was designed to prevent runaway slaves from finding a haven, as well as to discourage seigniors from luring slaves away from their owners. The law also provided that debtors who had agreed to pay back in cash could not be made to work out their loans, that is, they could not be converted into *kabala* peasants.[45]

Several decades later two decrees, in 1586 and 1597 (of which only the latter has been preserved), radically altered the legal nature of debt servitude so that it approximated full slavery. This was done as part of the government's effort to protect seigniors from the economic disaster of losing their peasants to other lords who paid off their debt for them. Each *kabala* contract now had to be reported to a special government bureau where it was recorded in special registers. The entry served as official evidence of the peasant's obligation. The right of the peasant debtor—who was bluntly referred to in the new legisla-

[44] Lappo-Danilevskii, *Zapisnaia kniga krepostnym aktam*, pp. xviii-xix.
[45] Akademiia Nauk, *Sudebnik* of 1550, arts. 78, 82, pp. 169, 170, and commentaries, pp. 284-290, 293-296.

tion as a *kabala* slave—to pay off his debt, or to have some one pay it for him, was abolished. Now he had to remain the peon of his creditor until the latter's death, and only then did he become free. Thus, the seignior was protected from the loss of his *kabala* peasants to another lord. The law also provided some measure of protection to the peasant in that the creditor was forbidden to sell or give away his *kabala* people, he was not to transfer them and their debt by testament, and above all, they had to be freed at his death.[46]

46 Vladimirskii-Budanov, *Khristomatiia*, III, 75-81.

<h1 style="text-align:center">14</h1>

THE END OF THE ROAD

THE INCREASE in the obligations of the seignioral peasants, their indebtedness, and their impoverishment, though they worked great hardships, were by themselves not enough to bring about the enserfment of these peasants. One further component was necessary. That was provided by the series of restrictions that were placed by state and lord upon the individual peasant's ability to come and go as he pleased. Each of these restraints, more severe in its provisions than its immediate predecessor, marked successive stages in the history of the peasant's loss of his freedom. The process was long and drawn out, reaching from the fifteenth to the middle of the seventeenth century. But slow though it was, there was never any turning back once it got under way. And each step in it led further down the road to serfdom.

By the end of the fifteenth century the right of the peasant to free movement had already been curtailed. The Code of 1497 had fixed the two weeks at St. George's Day in autumn (25 November) as the only legal time at which the peasant renter could leave his landlord, and had fixed heavy fees that he had to pay before he could depart. These regulations were a major gain for the landlords, providing them with the legal sanction to refuse their renters permission to leave save in the prescribed period. But they were also official recognition of the peasant's time-honored right of departure, protecting him against seignioral attempts to take that privilege from him. If the landlord tried to hold him against his will the peasant could turn to governmental authority to enforce recognition of his freedom to leave at the appointed time.

Though the law specified St. George's, other holidays were sometimes used as the time when moving was permitted. In a series of rental agreements of the 1540's St. George's was named in only two instances, Lent was specified in eighteen, Shrovetide in seventeen, Easter in six, Christmas in five, Epiphany in three, St. Peter's Day in two, St. Nicholas' Day in winter in one, St. Phillip's Day in one, and just simply "in winter" in one.[1] But St. George's seems to have been the most generally used, and in any event continued to be specified in the law as the time for departure. By late November the harvests were in and the farming year had drawn to a close. This was obviously the most convenient time for both landlord and peasant to settle up, and either renew or end their contract. One Soviet historian, though, has suggested that St. George's was purposely selected by the seigniors as a device to hold their renters. He claimed the landlords reasoned that with the long, hard, Russian winter already upon them by St. George's Day, the peasants would be much less inclined to leave than they might be in a more clement season.[2]

The Code of 1550 reaffirmed with some additions the provisions of the Sudebnik of 1497 on peasant departure. The exit fee was raised by 2 *altyny*. The peasant also now had to pay another 2 *altyny* as compensation for the carting service he would have rendered his lord during the winter had he remained. If he had planted winter grain he was given the right to return the following spring and harvest it. He had to pay his former landlord 2 *altyny* if he did this, but was freed from paying obligations due at that season to the seignior whose land he now was renting. The 1550 Code also defined a homestead "in the woods" (where the exit fee was half that charged for a *dvor* "in the fields") as one that was within "10 versts to timber suitable for construction." This clarification was probably made to put an end to what must have been a frequent cause of dispute between landlord and departing renter, with the former claiming the *dvor* was "in the fields" and so demanding the full exit fee, and the peasant asserting it was "in the woods" and willing to pay only the lesser fee.[3] A decree issued a few years later ordered that peasants working as hired hands could leave their employers whenever they wanted.[4]

---

[1] Eck, "Le grand domaine," pp. 109-110.

[2] Iushkov, *Istoriia*, p. 169.

[3] Akademiia Nauk, *Sudebnik* of 1550, sect. 88, and commentary, p. 320.

[4] Vladimirskii-Budanov, *Khristomatiia*, III, 4 (11 October 1556).

In the light of these guarantees it would seem plausible to assume that the peasant-renter had complete freedom of movement providing he met the not unreasonable conditions set by the laws. From this juristic point of view B. N. Chicherin, one of the first historians of the Russian peasantry, was right when he wrote in 1858 that "the free movement of the peasantry was a universal phenomenon of old Russia until the end of the sixteenth century."[5] But he, and others who agreed with him, confused legislative fiat with historical fact. Despite the laws the peasant-renter found it increasingly difficult to leave his landlord when he wanted, for the seignior was able to employ a number of devices, both legal and illegal, to keep him from going.

To start with, the peasant who planned to leave was required to give the landlord or his agent formal notice, or *otkaz* as it was called, of his intention to move. If he left without doing this he was considered a fugitive and could be made to return. If the lord or his representative chose to make themselves unavailable as St. George's drew near there was no one to whom the peasant could give his notice. He then had no choice but to remain for another year until the next St. George's, unless he was willing to become a runaway.[6]

This shabby device was only one of the weapons the lord had in his arsenal. Another one was provided him by the law's requirement that the departing peasant pay an exit fee. If he left without paying it, he and his family could be made to return and work it out. As was pointed out earlier, this charge must have served as a deterrent to people whose annual net income from their tillage was not much more (and often was less) than the amount they had to pay to leave. Moreover, some lords made certain that their peasants would not be able to pay the fee by pushing it up to illegal heights. In 1555 there were complaints about seigniors who set the fee at five and even ten rubles. These same landlords were also accused of beating, torturing, and chaining peasants to prevent them from leaving.[7]

[5] Chicherin, *Opyty*, p. 174.
[6] Odinetz, "Les origines," pp. 268-270.
[7] *DAI*, I, no. 56.

The debts peasants owed their lords, or their long residence in one place, also acted as barriers to peasant departure, although neither were legal grounds for refusal of permission to leave. But landlords reasoned that the peasant who had borrowed from them and had agreed to pay back his debt in cash or kind was more likely to meet his obligation if he was forced to remain on the lord's property, than if he moved elsewhere. As for the *starozhil'tsy*, the "old inhabitants," they were in a sense the backbone of the rural community, and were probably better off than newly-arrived renters. They were the kind of peasants the seignior wanted particularly to keep, and so he made it especially difficult for them to leave.[8]

The responsibility of the seignior for the taxes of his renters was another factor that operated against the peasant's freedom of movement. The lord felt he had the right to refuse permission to leave to peasants who were in arrears in their taxes, since he himself would then be liable for them. It seems entirely possible, in view of the increase in taxes in the sixteenth century, that this may have been among the most important reasons for seignioral restraints upon peasant departure.

The peasant was powerless to resist illegal actions by his lord to prevent his departure, unless he himself resorted to the illegal act of running away. For he was under the jurisdiction of the seignior. That meant that the seignior sat as judge in disputes between himself and his renters. In such a court the peasant-plaintiff had small chance of finding protection against the injustices visited on him by his seignior.

For many peasants, then, the laws that were supposed to guarantee them freedom of movement had become meaningless. In actuality they were bound to the lord on whose land they lived. Still there were people who were able to leave legally at their own choice. Records of the Volokolamsk Monastery show that in 1573-1574 24 peasants left monastery land and 24 came in as new renters, in 1575-1576 a total of 25 peasants left or came in, and in 1579-1580 76 left and 20 came in. Of those who departed in the last-named year 30 paid the full exit fee, show-

[8] D'iakonov, *Ocherki iz istorii*, pp. 24-31; Kliuchevskii, *History*, II, 227-228, 240-241.

ing they had rented from the monastery for at least four years. Nearly all who left had borrowed from the monks, and these debts were paid off before they departed.[9] But the only way by far the majority of peasant-renters could leave by their own will was to run away, chancing the perils of severe punishments and even slavery if they were recovered. Many were willing to take these risks, and, as we have seen, in the latter decades of the sixteenth century the number of runaways reached seemingly incredible heights. Some found the freedom they sought among the cossacks or in Siberia or in the White Sea littoral. But for most of the runaways flight was only a palliative, and a temporary one at that, since the lands on which they settled belonged to seigniors who exercised the same powers over them that their old landlords had. And in the end their flight served to worsen their status. For it stimulated the government to do away with the guarantees of the peasant's right of free movement and give the sanction of law to his enserfment.

There was, however, another and entirely legal way by which peasants could move from one place to another, albeit not by their own unaided action. This was by having their exit fees, debts, and tax arrears paid for them by another lord on whose property they then settled and in whose debt they now were. This was known as *vyvoz*, or "exportation." Actually, it was a form of labor pirating. The peasants often gained by it since the labor-hungry seignior offered them inducements, such as freedom from taxes for a number of years, to persuade them to accept his offer.

Seigniors used this device more and more as the century wore on, and as the problem of getting enough peasant-renters became more acute. The "exported" peasant's landlord still had to give his permission before the former could leave, but it was much more difficult for him to withhold it when another landlord had entered the picture. If he did refuse, his action was subject to review by a court on which sat representatives of the government.

Luring away peasants by promises of easier rental terms was not a new development. Landlords in the mid-fifteenth century

[9] Grekov, *Krest'iane*, p. 843.

had petitioned their rulers for protection against it. But no remedial action had been taken by the sovereigns other than naming the St. George's period as the only legal time for moving. In effect, rulers gave their tacit approval to "exportations." They continued in this attitude until the last decades of the sixteenth century.

By that time the difficulties that stood in the way of the peasant leaving by his own unaided action must have made *vyvoz* the principal lawful way by which renters transferred from one lord to another. Meanwhile the competition for peasants had grown keener, at first because of the growth of demesnes, and then because of the depopulation. "Exportations" not only increased, but desperate landlords resorted to illegal means to get peasants. In this struggle for renters victory went usually to the richest seigniors. Their greater wealth enabled them to lure peasants from the lands of the lesser gentry by paying off their obligations, and by offering terms that were more attractive than the usual pomeshchik could afford to give. If the latter tried to keep his peasants illegally the magnate quickly became the defender of peasant freedom and brought the matter into court where he won easily. These rich lords were equally prepared, if the occasion demanded it, to use guile or force to get peasants for their lands. They took renters from other seigniors without notice being given of their impending departure, without settling the obligations of the peasant, and, above all, often without consulting the peasant. In short, they kidnapped labor. They preyed especially upon properties whose lords were absent or that were masterless through death or banishment, and upon seigniors who were too weak to resist them.[10] Even stewards of the tsar's own properties were guilty of these illegal practices. In 1580 Ivan IV ordered one of his estate managers to stop taking away peasants from monasteries at other than the legal time for departure "and without giving notice and without paying the obligations, and without the free consent of the peasants."[11]

[10] Samokvasov, *Arkhivnyi material*, II, pt. i, 45.
[11] Quoted in Eck, *Le moyen âge*, p. 301.

The lawlessness and confusion of the years of the *Oprichnina* encouraged illegal *vyvoz*, especially by the *oprichniki*. Enjoying the special favor and protection of the tsar, and counting many unscrupulous and violent men among them, they did not hesitate to use force to get peasants for the pomestyes Ivan gave them in the *Oprichnina* part of the realm. Heinrich von Staden, the German freebooter who served as a member of the corps, noted in his memoirs that those peasants who "were not willing to be taken from the *Zemshchina* into the *Oprichnina*, these were taken by force outside the regular period [for leaving]."[12] In 1570 a servitor named Neledinskii became an *oprichnik*. His pomestye, located in the *Zemshchina* territory, reverted to the crown. In the few months that elapsed between Neledinskii's transfer to the *Oprichnina* and the occupation of his old pomestye by representatives of the government, 31 of the 64 peasants who had homesteads on the property had been taken away by other seigniors. Because this had been done without the permission of the peasants' seignior, who now was the tsar himself, the abductors were ordered to return the peasants. In deference to the power of the tsar 26 of the peasants were recovered. Of the five who were not returned four had been taken into the *Oprichnina* half of the realm. They had been brought back when the order for the return of the peasants was issued, but then *oprichniki* had raided the pomestye and abducted these four peasants and their belongings once more.[13]

As was pointed out above, the right to "export" peasants favored the wealthier lords. In the great political and economic crises of the second half of the sixteenth century, when great numbers of peasants fled the old regions of settlement, the superior ability of the great lords to attract and hold the peasants who still remained seemed to endanger the existence of the state itself. For now the pomeshchiks, who had become the chief support of the regime, were threatened with economic ruin and consequent inability to meet their service obligations, because they lost so many of their peasants through flight and exportation. Ivan could not help them financially, for his wasteful wars

12 Staden, *Aufzeichnungen*, p. 47.
13 Samokvasov, *Arkhivnyi material*, I, pt. ii, nos. 22-27.

had emptied the treasury. At the same time the magnates, who benefited most from the right of the peasant to move, lost favor with the tsar, and he had decided to destroy their power. The government was also faced with the necessity of protecting itself against further losses in tax revenues resulting from the desolation of so much pomestye land. The problems rising out of the continued right of free movement for the peasant, then, had come to have serious effects upon the power and well-being of the state.

The solution that presented itself to the government was to put an end to this freedom. Thereby peasant-renters would be available to the pomeshchiks and the government's political and fiscal interests would be served. The initial move on this new course was directed against the wealthy monasteries (v. p. 197). The first direct attack upon the peasant's right of free departure came in 1580. In that year Ivan IV issued a decree that has not been preserved but whose contents have been made clear by other contemporary materials. It forbad the departure of all peasants either by their own efforts or by "exportation" from their present place of residence, whether on seignioral, church, palace, or black lands, until such time as the tsar ordered that free departure was once more permissible. The period of interdiction was known as the *zapovednye gody*, the forbidden years. During its duration the provisions of the Code of 1550 guaranteeing peasants the right to move were suspended. The first nationwide "forbidden year" seems to have started in 1581. The experience of the Volokolamsk Monastery illustrates the effectiveness of this 1580 decree. In 1579-1580, as was mentioned earlier, 76 peasants left Volokolamsk land and 20 arrived as new renters. In 1581 not a single peasant either departed or came to settle.[14]

Years in which peasant departure was forbidden soon became the rule. At least half, and probably more, of the decades of the eighties and nineties seemed to have been "forbidden years," and from 1603 on every year was declared to be a "forbidden year." Yet these periods continued to be viewed by contempo-

[14] Grekov, *Glavneishie etapy*, p. 64. Polosin, "Le Servage," p. 617, found mention in a document of 1570 of a prohibition on peasant departure for the Shelonskaia district of Novgorod Land.

raries as temporary expedients, and on into the seventeenth century rental agreements between lords and peasants contained the stipulation that the peasant would remain "until the years of departure," or "until the tsar's ukase," by which was meant the decree that would end the "forbidden years." It was to be over 250 years before that ukase was issued.[15]

On the face of it, the government's ban on peasant departure save in certain years should have been enough to solve the problems that had called forth the measure. But the necessary condition for its successful operation was that both landlords and peasants would abide by the terms of the legislation. Instead, peasants continued to run off to other seigniors, and lords continued to lure them with better offers, or to abduct them. The machinery of government was not yet sufficiently developed to be able to enforce laws that were being evaded on so large a scale. The injured landlords were unable to protect themselves, either because they were away from their pomestyes on service, or because they lacked the power and the means to organize defenses against the flight and kidnapping of their peasants.

The government realized that it would have to take stronger measures. It so happened that in 1581 Ivan IV had ordered a new cadastre of his realm to find out the extent of the desolation that had been brought on by the bad times, and to collect accurate information for tax purposes. The registers that were drawn up contained the name of each adult male peasant and the place of his residence. The survey was completed in 1592. Five years later, on 24 November 1597, the throne issued a ukase whose purpose, according to the wording of the decree, was "to give justice" to landlords against their peasants who had run away, and against the seigniors who had received them. The new law ordered that peasants who had left within the period of five years before the promulgation of the ukase were to be sought out and returned, along with their families and their personal property, to their former residence. Those who had left more than five years before could not be made to come back if no complaint had been made to the authorities about their depar-

<hr/>

[15] Grekov, *Glavneishie etapy*, p. 64; Odinetz, "Les origines," p. 286.

ture, nor could the seigniors who had received them be prose-cuted.[16] The five year period must have been chosen because the cadastre had been completed just five years before. Hitherto, the absence of accurate official data had made it difficult, and often impossible, for the courts to determine whether a peasant was residing legally on a seignior's land, or whether he was a fugitive or had been abducted from another lord. Now the land registers provided irrefutable evidence of his residence at a given date, and so gave complaining lords the proof they needed to recover the peasant who had left illegally.

This decree of 24 November 1597 contained nothing that was startlingly new. The principle that a peasant renter became a fugitive if he left without his seignior's permission had been accepted since the fifteenth century. The establishment of the five year period for recovery was actually a compromise with the existing state of affairs. By setting this limit the government was legalizing flight or illegal "exportation" that had taken place before 1592, if the injured seignior had not gone to law to gain recovery before the publication of the 1597 decree. The govern-ment thus accepted violations of the "forbidden years" for departure that had occurred before 1592. Possibly, the reason for this compromise was that the courts had become so cluttered and entangled with suits for the return of peasants that it be-came necessary to wipe the slate and make a fresh start.[17] None-theless, the decree was a major step in the enserfment of the peasantry. Though it sanctioned illegal departures that had taken place before 1592 it gave all landlords protection against future departures, and, in effect, bound the peasant to the lord on whose land he was living as of 1592. Those who had left illegally before 1592 had been entered in the cadastre as renters of the lord who had received them, and so were subject to the provisions of the 1597 law if they left their new seignior. Thus, the use of the land registers as the documentary evidence of the peasant's residence provided the legal basis for his permanent attachment to the seignior on whose land he lived.

Besides this law, decrees put out in 1586 and 1597 made important changes in the status of the *kabala* peasants (v. p. 245).

---

[16] *AI*, I, 221/III.   [17] M. M. Speranskii quoted in Grekov, *Krest'iane*, p. 872.

These ukases were part of the government's attempt to stabilize the labor force for the benefit of the pomeshchiks.

The continued concern of the throne with the plight of the lesser nobility was vividly evidenced in two decrees issued by Tsar Boris in 1601 and 1602. Apparently the existing laws were still not enough to protect the gentry and, in any event, their economic position must have been seriously affected by the great famines of the first years of the new century. On 28 November 1601 Boris ordered that all lesser servitors except those of Moscow *uezd* were to be allowed that year to "export" not more than two peasants from any one estate at the St. George's period. All persons of higher rank, lay and clerical, were specifically excluded from this privilege. A year later the decree was repeated.[18] For two years, then, the tsar partly lifted the restrictions on departures—the last time that happened. It is likely, however, that this special favor proved of little value to the small seigniors, for in 1604 the Time of Troubles began in earnest, great stretches of land were laid waste, and many of the pomeshchiks were ruined.

In 1607, in the midst of the Troubles, the then tsar, Vasili Shuiskii, issued a ukase extending the period of recovery from five to fifteen years—that is, back to 1592. This law stated that all peasants registered in the cadastres completed in that year ought still to be residents of the same places in which they then lived. If they were not, and if complaints had been entered with the authorities that they had left illegally, they were to be returned to the seigniors on whose land they had lived in 1592. An effort was made to put teeth in the law by ordering that fines had to be paid by the lord who had received, or taken, these peasants. He had to pay 10 rubles to the tsar for each one found on his land, and 3 rubles to the peasant's rightful seignior for each year he had been there.[19] Like most of Shuiskii's legislation this decree had little or no effect. It was an attempt to tie the peasant closer to his lord at a time when society was near anarchy, and when peasants were openly evading their obligations and disregarding the restrictions placed by law upon their free movement.[20]

18 *AAE*, II, nos. 20, 23.   19 Samokvasov, *Arkhivnyi material*, II, pt. i, 51-56.
20 Kliuchevskii, *History*, II, 238.

The illegal actions of the peasantry during the Troubles were not a new phenomenon. They had not accepted the steady deterioration since the fifteenth century in their economic condition and in their personal freedom without resistance. The most common form of their protest was flight, but as was mentioned earlier, this was not a remedy for most of them, since it usually meant exchanging their old seignior for a new one. On occasion they voiced their discontent by resorting to violence. Only a few instances of such activities are known about, though it is entirely possible that there were many more. Peasants rebelled in Pskov in 1483 and disorders there continued until 1486, ending only after the government intervened. In 1578 Ivan IV gave a number of black peasant hamlets to St. Anthony's Monastery. The monks demanded much heavier obligations than the peasants had been paying. They rose in protest, force had to be used against them, and many of them ran away. In the fall of 1593 disturbances broke out on lands of the Volokolamsk Monastery and lasted until the following February when rigorous measures finally succeeded in restoring order.[21]

During the Time of Troubles many peasants, and especially those who had fled to the frontiers, saw an opportunity to bring about a social revolution that would end the system that had put them under the rule of the seigniors. In 1606 there were serious outbreaks in every part of the realm, and a major revolt got under way in the south. It was led by a sanguinary ex-slave named Ivan Bolotnikov who once had belonged to Prince Teliatevskii, then had been captured by Tatars and sold by them in Turkey. He managed to escape and, after travels in other lands, returned to Russia. Here he preached the abolition of restrictions on peasant freedom, the extermination of the boyars who supported Tsar Vasili Shuiskii in particular and of all rich people in general, and the distribution of their lands, their wealth, and their wives and daughters, among the peasants. He gained wide support among the rural masses. But his following lost its homogeneous character when he was joined by gentry who hated the boyar-dominated government of Shuiskii. He

---

[21] Grekov, "Dvizhenie," pp. 3ff; Smirnov, *Vosstanie*, pp. 57-61.

won a number of victories and got as far as Moscow when some of his upper class adherents deserted him and he was defeated. He fell back on Tula to regroup his forces, was besieged there, and in the fall of 1607 was completely routed. Many of his supporters were enslaved and Bolotnikov himself was probably executed. After the collapse of this rising, many slaves and fugitive peasants, still seeking reform, turned to the support of the Second False Dmitrii who appeared on the scene in June, 1607. This movement failed, too, its only positive result being to weaken the state even more and so make easier the victory of the invading Poles.[22]

The efforts of the peasants to regain their lost freedom had come to naught. When Michael Romanov ascended the throne in 1613 their legal status was the same as it had been at the beginning of the Troubles. Their right of free departure was gone, albeit in theory it was just in suspense during the "forbidden years." The law had bound the once free peasant and made him subservient to the will of his seignior. Still, he was clearly distinguished from a slave, for in so far as persons other than his lord were concerned he had many of the rights of a free man. He was recognized as a legal individual by the law which protected his life and in certain circumstances his property, he was a taxpayer, he could appear in government courts in cases not directly concerning his seignior, he could make contracts, buy and sell, and so on.[23] In short, the Russian peasant renter had become what in the West was called a villein or a serf and in Russia a *krepostnoi chelovek*, a "bound" person.

But not all the peasants who lived on seignioral land became serfs at the same time. The restrictions that were imposed in the sixteenth and first half of the seventeenth centuries applied only to the peasant who was entered in the registers as the legal occupant of a homestead, the head of a household. The others who lived with him could leave the *dvor* when they wished. If they decided to establish their own homestead they entered into an agreement with the seignior of the land on which they decided to settle. The contracts they made were like

22 Platonov, *La Russie*, pp. 150-151, 174-175.
23 Cf. *Ulozhenie*, ch. X, sect. 124, ch. XI, sect. 32, ch. XIX, sect. 15, 16.

those made between lords and new renters in the sixteenth century save in one significant respect. Now the peasant agreed either that he would never leave his landlord, or that he had the right to depart only at the death of the seignior, or that he would pay a large fine if he should decide to leave.[24]

The existing state of affairs, favorable as it might seem for the seigniors, still did not satisfy them. Peasants continued to run away, and there still were illegal "exportations." I. N. Romanov, uncle of the tsar and greatest private proprietor of his day, actually organized armed bands that raided the villages of other lords and carried away their peasants.[25] So the seigniors, and particularly those of lesser means, pressed for stronger legislation and for a definitive statement by the government of the attachment of the peasantry. They were especially eager to extend the period for the recovery of peasants who had left illegally. Shuiskii's act lengthening the period of recovery to fifteen years had been ineffective, and at the end of the Troubles the five year term had been restored. The landlords felt that this was not long enough. Even so rich and powerful a proprietor as Trinity-St. Serge Monastery complained that it was unable to search out and recover its fugitives within the prescribed period. It asked the throne for an extension, and in 1614 it was empowered to reclaim peasants who had departed from its lands within the preceding nine years.

If Trinity-St. Serge and other important proprietors had serious troubles in operating within the terms of the existing legislation, the difficulties that beset ordinary pomeshchiks must have been insuperable. In petitions to the throne these lesser lords reported that not only was it impossible for them to get back their own peasants, but that powerful lords took back peasants who had been living on the lands of the lesser lords for longer than the prescribed period for recovery. According to the law such peasants could not be made to return, but the magnates forced them to come back anyway. Interestingly enough, Trinity Monastery was one of the proprietors about whom the gentry complained. They accused Trinity of compelling them to return

24 Sergeevich, *Drevnosti*, I, 282-284.
25 Stashevskii, *Narodnyia volneniia*, pp. 11-12.

peasants who had left the monastery's lands twenty or more years before.[26]

In response to such complaints the government increased the period for recovery for all landlords. It was first extended to nine years, and then in 1642 to ten years for peasants who had run away, and fifteen for those who had been taken away illegally by other lords. But the gentry still complained that they were unable to prevent the pirating of their peasants by more powerful seigniors, and pointed out that the extension of the recovery period meant little to them, because they lacked the means or the power to get back their peasants. Finally, the government announced that it was going to abolish the recovery period as soon as it had completed the new land register it planned to make. From then on the fugitive or "exported" peasant was to be returned to the lord on whose land he was living when the registers were made, no matter how long it had been since he had left.[27]

Before this promise could be kept Tsar Michael died (in 1645) and was succeeded by his son Alexis. The new sovereign, only sixteen and still unsure of himself, entrusted the direction of his government to his tutor, B. I. Morozov. Morozov was one of that group of magnates about whom the gentry had been complaining for so long. Now, as acting head of the state he took advantage of his position to gain more wealth for himself, his kinsmen, and his friends, and surrounded himself with coadjutors who were as grasping as he was. The abuses of this regime awakened widespread resentment, and in June of 1648 there were riots in Moscow and unrest in other cities of the realm. The tsar decided to replace Morozov with another of his favorites, Prince N.I. Odoevskii. The new administration recognized that reforms were needed to restore order. A chief source of discontent was the chaos into which legislation and court procedures had fallen. It was decided that one of the first steps that must be taken was to codify the laws so that (to quote the preamble of the code that resulted from this decision) "to all the classes of the Muscovite state from the greatest to the least law

---

[26] D'iakonov, *Ocherki iz istorii*, pp. 49-51; Grekov, *Glavneishie etapy*, pp. 70-71.
[27] Sergeevich, *Drevnosti*, I, 281; Grekov, *Glavneishie etapy*, pp. 71, 73-76.

and justice shall be equal in all things." Odoevskii himself became chairman of the five man committee charged to carry out this task. In a little over six months the conferees turned over their results to the *Zemskii Sobor*, the National Assembly that had meanwhile been convened. The *Sobor*, which was dominated by the lesser gentry, after amendments and additions, gave its approval, and the new code was issued in 1649.[28] It was called the *Sobornoe Ulozhenie*, the Assembly Code.[29] It was to remain the legal code of Russia until the second quarter of the nineteenth century.

The object of this codification was not to introduce innovations nor to remodel the legal structure, but rather to present an orderly arrangement of existing legislation and custom. But even though the *Ulozhenie* contained little that was new, it marked the end of one epoch in the history of the lord-peasant relation and the beginning of a new one that lasted until the emancipation of 1861. It sealed the fate of the seignioral peasantry, once free renters of land belonging to members of the upper classes, and now converted into the serfs of their erstwhile landlords. It marked, too, the victory of the servitors with middle-sized and small holdings over both the magnates and the peasantry, for nearly all their wishes were met in the code.

Chapter 11 of the code dealt with the peasants. Its chief concern was the recovery of peasants and *bobyli* who had left their seigniors illegally; all but four of the 34 sections of the chapter deal with this problem. This preoccupation with fugitive peasants can be taken as evidence of how common illegal departures were, and how seriously they affected landlords. The chapter opened with the abolition of the time limit for the recovery of these peasants. The peasant, with his wife and family and all his property, including the grain that he had raised, was to be returned if the lord from whom he had departed demanded it, regardless of how long it had been since he had left (sect. 1, 2, 3). The spouses of those of his children who were married and their children were also to be returned (sect. 17, 18). The complaining seignior proved his claim to the peasant

---

[28] Platonov, *La Russie*, pp. 195-220.
[29] For text of the *Ulozhenie* see *Pamiatniki Russkogo Prava*, VI.

by referring to the entry in the tax rolls showing that the fugitive or his father was listed as residing on his land (sect. 2).

The abolition of the time limit for recovery was one of the two major innovations contained in Chapter 11. The other was the ending of freedom of movement for all the members of the peasant family. In 1646 the government had announced that the registers to be drawn up that year were to be used to bind not only the head of the household, but also his sons, brothers and nephews who lived with him.[30] This decision was incorporated into the *Ulozhenie* (sect. 9).

The peasant not only lost his right to leave his seignior, but his lord gained the power to move him about under certain circumstances as if he were a piece of movable property. The purchaser of a votchina who had not been informed by the seller that some of the peasants on the property were there illegally, and who then had these people taken away by their legal seignior, could demand that the seller give him peasants from other votchinas owned by the seller to make up for the peasants he had lost (sect. 7). A peasant who married a fugitive, or the child of a fugitive, was transferred with his spouse when the latter was reclaimed by the fugitive's rightful lord. If the peasant had children by a previous marriage these children did not accompany him, so that families could be torn apart (sect. 12, 13, 17, 18). If a seignior, or his son, nephew, or steward, without premeditation murdered the peasant of another lord, he had to replace the slain peasant with the best of his own peasant families. A peasant who killed another lord's peasant without premeditation was to be beaten with the knout, and then was to be transferred with his family to the lord whose peasant he had slain. If that seignior did not want the murderer, he could demand by name another peasant and his family from the murderer's lord (Chapter 21, sect. 71, 72, 73). Premeditated murder of a peasant, whether by a lord or by a peasant, was punishable by death.

The legal ability of the lord to move his peasants about, however, was not unlimited. The man who owned more than one votchina could transfer his people from one to another of his

[30] Sergeevich, *Drevnosti*, I, 281-282.

properties. If he held more than one pomestye he could shift his peasants among them. But he could not move them from his pomestye to his votchina. The reason for this limitation was that the pomestye was the property of the throne, and, theoretically at least, was only in the temporary possession of the pomeshchik. The state feared that pomeshchiks would depopulate their benefices by transferring pomestye peasants to votchinas they might own (Chapter 11, sect. 30). Following this line of reasoning, the law allowed a votchinnik to give his peasants freedom to depart, but denied this right to pomeshchiks (Chapter 15, sect. 3). The pomestye peasant, then, was bound to the pomestye, while the votchina peasant was bound to the person of the votchinnik.

Besides the loss of their ability to move save at the will of their seignior, the peasants were also deprived of their right of full ownership of personal property. The law considered all their goods as belonging ultimately to their lords. The fugitive peasant had to be returned with everything that belonged to him, including his crops (Chapter 11, sect. 3). The debtors of a bankrupt seignior could collect from the seignior's peasants and slaves (Chapter 10, sect. 262). The peasant who married a fugitive or a fugitive's child was returned with his spouse, but his property remained with his own seignior (Chapter 11, sect. 12). The lord's property right also extended to the labor power of his peasants. When a fugitive was returned, the seignior who had received him was supposed to pay 10 rubles to the rightful seignior for every year he had kept the peasant (Chapter 11, sect. 10), as compensation and damages for the loss of the peasant's services suffered by his rightful seignior.

Finally, the peasant was stripped of most of his legal competence. He had long been under the jurisdiction of his lord in all save the most serious cases rising within the boundaries of the lord's property. The *Ulozhenie* provided that in disputes with persons outside the votchina or pomestye the peasant was to be represented before the court by his lord, except in cases of murder, theft, highway robbery, and the possession of stolen goods (Chapter 13, sect. 7). The reasoning here seems to have been that the welfare of the seignior was affected when his peasant stood trial, and so to protect his interests he appeared for the accused man. The latter was of course personally responsible for the crimes he committed. But at least in the case of unpremeditated murder by a peasant of the peasant of another lord, the culprit's lord shared some of the punishment since, as already mentioned, the murderer and his family, or another peasant family, had to be given to the seignior of the victim.

The state's intent in depriving the peasants of their freedom was to ensure a labor force for its servitors and not to reduce the peasants to thralldom. But neither in the *Ulozhenie*, nor in any other legislation of the seventeenth century, was any precise legal definition given of the position of the peasant or of his relation to his seignior. Consequently, there were no legal norms to protect the peasant against the will of his lord. The inevitable result was a quick deterioration in the former's status. Seigniors took peasants off the land and put them into their own households to serve as domestics. Lords extended their jurisdiction over their peasants to include sitting in judgment in criminal cases that were supposed to be tried in government courts, and inflicted cruel punishments and even death sentences. The law that forbad pomeshchiks to move peasants from their pomestyes to their votchinas was apparently disregarded, for the prohibition had to be repeated on at least six occasions in the second half of the seventeenth century.[31]

Actually, the publication of the *Ulozhenie* did not put an end to the illegal departures of peasants. They still continued to be lured away or kidnapped from their legal place of residence. The stewards of B. I. Morozov, for example, were ordered by their master not to receive peasants from other seigniors. But these instructions were given only for the sake of appearing to conform to the laws. Morozov constantly enjoined them to settle people on all empty land in the votchinas they managed. The meaning of this order was clear—get new peasants no matter how. That this is precisely what they did is shown by the complaints Morozov received from small lords demanding that their peasants, now living on Morozov properties, be returned to

---

31 Kliuchevskii, *History*, IV, 102; Khlebnikov, *O vliianii*, p. 273; Paul of Aleppo, *Travels*, I, 314; Zabelin, "Bol'shoi boiarin," pp. 17-19; El'iashevich, *Istoriia*, II, 172.

them. A. I. Bezobrazov, too, urged his stewards to get peasants for the land he acquired in the south. "I don't need land, I need peasants," he wrote in 1681 to one of his managers who had informed him about a recent land purchase. He lured peasants away from other lords by giving them advances, or promising them exemptions from obligations for the first few years. He also took them by force. In 1677 some of his men raided a village that belonged to a minor servitor and carried off three peasant families consisting of eight men and seven women, and also took some live stock. These abducted peasants were settled on one of his properties and then were moved to another one. Like acts were reported of other seigniors. Sometimes they received indirect support from the government itself in these illegal activities. Thus, there were instances when the government refused to allow a pomeshchik to recover his peasants from an influential boyar because he had waited too long to petition for their return, although the *Ulozhenie* had abolished the time limit for recovery.[32]

There were also a few peasants who somehow managed throughout the century to preserve their right to leave a seignior freely, and apparently entirely legally. They moved from one place to another, making agreements with their landlords that guaranteed them the right to depart.[33] Perhaps the best explanation for this phenomenon was that given by M. N. Pokrovskii, when he described the legislation of this era as "crude and summary, registering facts in the mass," and so inevitably having many lacunae.[34]

Finally, peasants still continued to run away. Many fled from the old regions of settlement to the frontiers. But others chose to go shorter distances, settling with some seignior who asked no questions and who demanded lighter obligations than did the master whom they had left. It was an easy matter to run away, for the land was huge and communications were poor, so that it must have been difficult to trace the fugitives. Yet they were sometimes captured. In 1664-1665, 2,994 of them were picked up

[32] Zabelin, "Bol'shoi boiarin," p. 21; Novosel'skii, *Votchinnik*, pp. 45-46, 48, 109; D'iakonov, *Ocherkii iz istorii*, pp. 339-341.

[33] D'iakonov, *Ocherki iz istorii*, pp. 105-109.

[34] Pokrovskii, *History*, p. 231.

in Kozlov *uezd* on the border of the "untamed steppe" and returned to their masters. A record made of the disposition of 341
of these peasants indicates that sometimes there were mass flights
from individual estates. Two seigniors each owned 40 of these
341, two owned 21 to 30, 14 owned 11 to 20, 36 owned 6 to 10, and
61 owned 1 to 5 of the runaways. In 1675, out of 664 homesteads
on one of the personal properties of Tsar Alexis, the occupants of
481 had run away, and the rest were reported to be about to flee.
On another of his estates 219 families had run away.[35]

The government deplored the departures and tried to prevent
them by ordering heavy penalties for those who received the
runaways. A law of 1661 ordered that stewards who accepted
these peasants were to be beaten with the knout. If the steward
had received them with the knowledge of his seignior the latter
not only had to return the fugitive, but also had to give one of
his own peasant families with all its belongings to the runaway's
lord. In 1664 the number of peasant families that had to be
given to the runaway's lord was increased to four. The fine the
seignior who received a runaway had to pay the fugitive's lord
was increased from 10 to 20 rubles for each year the peasant had
lived on his land. But the flights still continued. The state itself
was partly responsible for the failure of its program. By a decree
of 17 December 1684 it ordered that peasants and *bobyli* who
had run away to the cities since 1649 could not be made to
return to their seigniors, although the *Ulozhenie* had specifically
directed that peasants could be recovered from urban settlements (Chapter 11, art. 2).[36]

Flight remained by far the most common form of the peasant's
protest against the treatment accorded them by their lords and by
the state. But there still continued to be times when they turned
to violence. According to a ukase of 1658, before running off they
sometimes "laid waste the holdings of their lords, stole their
animals, burned their houses, and massacred them and their
wives and children."[37] Sporadic outbreaks such as these offered
no threat to the established order. In 1670, however, there was a
mass rising of the peasantry in the Volga basin that did prove

---

[35] Tomsinskii, *Ocherki*, p. 70; Zaozerskii, *Tsarskaia votchina*, p. 170.
[36] D'iakonov, *Ocherki obshchestvennago . . . stroia*, pp. 341-342.
[37] *Ibid.*, p. 341.

dangerous. It was led by Stepan (Stenka) Razin, a cossack of the Don who had won notoriety for his filibustering along the shores of the Caspian. In the spring of 1670 he and his gang of free-booters attacked the Volga town of Tsaritsyn (modern Stalin-grad), sacked it, and then marched along the Volga, burning, looting, and killing as they moved northward. As he moved up-stream he issued proclamations that urged the peasants to turn against their masters and promised them freedom. Thousands heeded his call and there was much destruction throughout the region. Within a few months he had control of 800 miles along the Volga from its mouth up to Simbirsk. Then, in August 1670 he was defeated in a pitched battle with the tsar's troops and his movement collapsed. Razin himself was turned over to the government by some of his fellow cossacks, and after excruciat-ing tortures was executed in 1671.

I I

The peasants who lived on the land belonging to boyars, the gentry, the church, or the Court formed the vast majority of the population of seventeenth century Russia. In the 1680's they occupied 90 percent of the estimated 880,000 homesteads of the realm. These were the people who had been enserfed. About 3 percent of the homesteads were of city people. The rest were those of the black peasants.[38] Two centuries before they had formed the largest part of the peasantry. Now they were an insignificant fraction of it.

The dwindling in their number started in the latter part of the fifteenth century with the practice of giving black land to private landlords. By the end of the sixteenth century most of the black land had disappeared in the Center and the Northwest. The little that remained there after 1600 was given to servitors by Tsar Michael soon after his accession. The only places in the realm where it still persisted were in the far north on the shores of the White Sea, in the region of the Northern Dvina River, in the northeastern part of the Kama basin, and in Siberia. In eleven counties of the White Sea littoral in the 1620's, 75 per-

[38] Ak. Nauk, *Istoriia*, I, 421; Lebedev, *Krest'ianskaia voina*, p. 26.

cent to 100 percent, and in other northern districts as much as
two thirds of the land, was held by black peasants. The infertility of the soil and the harsh climate acted as barriers to the
expansion of seignioral landowning in these regions. But it was
not entirely absent, for monks, drawn to the region by its very
inhospitability, established monasteries there and received grants
of black land and peasants by the tsars.[39]

The peasants who lived on the black land given to seigniors
not only suffered the loss of freedom, but also had their obligations increased. When they were black peasants they had paid
dues and services only to the state. Now, as seignioral peasants,
they still had state obligations, albeit less than they had previously paid, and in addition had to meet the demands of their
new landlords. Thus, in 1578 St. Anthony's Monastery was given
61 black peasant homesteads in the Emets district. These peasants had been paying a total cash obrok of 2 rubles, 26 *altyny*,
4 *den'gi*. The monastery raised this by 4 rubles, and also required the peasants to do barshchina. To give another example,
on some land Tsar Alexis gave Morozov soon after his accession
the peasants had been paying 7½ rubles per *vyt*. Morozov
pushed this up to 15 and 20 rubles per *vyt*. He informed the
peasants they would have no other obligations, but despite his
promise demanded additional dues and services from them.[40]

The black people who escaped the seignioral yoke, however,
also experienced some loss in their personal freedom. The fees
their communes (*volost*) paid were an important source of state
revenue. To make sure that the individual black peasant would
not leave, and so escape his share of the communal obligation,
the state proceeded to bind him to his *volost*. This was accomplished without any legislation that specifically deprived the
peasant of his right to depart. Instead, by a gradual process the
tax-bearing black peasant who left his commune without providing a substitute to take over his share of the fiscal burden came
to be regarded as a runaway who could be made to return to his
volost. If he found some one to take his place he could leave

[39] Got'e, *Zamoskovnyi krai*, p. 427; Kulischer, *Russische Wirtschaftsgeschichte*,
I, 181-182.
[40] Smirnov, *Vosstanie*, pp. 59-60; Zabelin, "Bol'shoi boiarin," pp. 28-29.

freely. Those of the black people who did not have holdings, and therefore were not liable to the tax, continued to be able to move about as they pleased.

The city people who were liable to taxes, or the *posadskie liudi* as they were called, were also gradually deprived of their freedom of movement. Ivan IV's decree of 1580 establishing the "forbidden years" had applied to the *posadskie liudi* as well as to the seignorial peasantry. A ukase of 1613 ordered all urban tax-payers who had fled Moscow during the Troubles to return, and in 1619 this law was extended to the residents of all other towns who had left their homes. This command was repeated in later decrees and severe punishments ordered for those who disregarded it. Then, in 1649 the *Ulozhenie* (Chapter 19) definitively bound the *posadskie liudi* to their urban communes. They were forbidden to move from their towns without the tsar's permission, and were threatened with a beating with the knout and exile to Siberia if they disobeyed. In 1658 the death penalty was ordered for townspeople who left illegally.[41]

In medieval Western Europe the city had been an oasis of freedom in a servile society. The burghers enjoyed the protection of special laws that guaranteed them their rights and privileges as free men, and serfs who ran away to the city became free men if they lived there for a year and a day. "City air makes free" was the way it was sometimes put. In Russia there was no such legal distinction between town and country. City people, though not serfs, had lost their freedom to move, and the peasant who came to the city legally to live and work remained a peasant, and was always subject to being called back to his village by his lord or by his commune.

III

The fact that barshchina became a far more common peasant obligation in the sixteenth century than it had been before, points to the conclusion that the slave labor force was inadequate to meet the new seignorial demand for farm hands. Moreover, the widely followed custom of testamentary manumission should have produced a steady diminution in the number of

[41] Vladimirskii-Budanov, *Obzor*, p. 142.

bondsmen. And if Soviet scholars are to be believed, slave labor had become an anachronism in the sixteenth century, because Russian economic development had gone beyond the stage of slave production into the "more progressive means of feudal production" in which labor was furnished by peasants who were in the process of falling into "feudal dependence" upon their seigniors.[42] The available data, however, show that slaves remained an integral part of the rural scene throughout the sixteenth and seventeenth centuries. Of 5,615 homesteads listed in the cadastre for Tver for 1539-1540, 9 percent were those of slaves. In the registers made in the late fifteenth and first part of the sixteenth centuries for the Northwest, the proportion of slave homesteads ran from 4 to 10 percent of all *dvory* on the pomestyes listed in the rolls. During the depopulation of the later sixteenth century the ratio of slave *dvory* there had a tendency to rise, going up to as much as 15-17 percent in some districts, although the absolute number of slave homesteads dropped sharply—for the bondsmen ran away, too.

Slave labor was particularly important in the steppe. On many of the small pomestyes of that zone there were no peasants at all, but only slave workers. In one of the districts there the proportion of slave homesteads in 1578-1579 was 23.4 percent, in another in 1587-1589 it was 35 percent, and in a third there were as many slave homesteads as there were those of peasants. In the Kama region, too, slaves were widely used. Many of the votchinas in the North had slaves, although apparently in a smaller proportion than existed in other parts of the realm.

A comparison between the distribution of slave homesteads and the incidence of demesne shows that, as could be expected, there was a close correlation between the two. In the regions where demesne was widespread, as in the steppe, the proportion of slave homesteads to those of peasant renters was much higher than it was in those areas where the lord's own fields were not so common. On properties belonging to the crown and to the hierarchy demesne was unusual in the sixteenth century, and there were only a few slave *dvory* on these lands, or none at all.

---

[42] Cf. Grekov, *Krest'iane*, pp. 580-587; Ak. Nauk, *Istoriia*, I, 280; Liashchenko, *Istoriia*, I, 234-235.

On the other hand, on palace land in the steppe district of Venev where 23 percent of the arable was worked for the tsar, about 8 percent of the homesteads were those of slaves.[43]

The cadastres only recorded those slaves who had homesteads and pieces of land that had been turned over to them by their masters. These bondsmen, who came to be known in the seventeenth century as *zadvornye liudi*, "people who lived away from the master's *dvor*," performed barshchina and other obligations for their owner. Other slaves who lived in and around the master's homestead and worked for him as field hands, artisans, and domestics, were not included in the registers. Scattered information about the economies of individual lords, large and small, show that there were a large number of these people, who were sometimes called *delovye liudi*, "men of all work."

Finally, if the *kabala* peasants are included among the bondsmen the number of slaves used in agriculture undoubtedly rose in the sixteenth and seventeenth centuries, in view of the increase in peonage. Though the legal status of the *kabala* peasant differed from that of the "full" slave, for all practical purposes they were slaves of their creditors. Contemporaries certainly regarded them as bondsmen, referring to them as *kabala* slaves, and including them among the *zadvornye liudi* in the land registers.

In the seventeenth century slave labor continued to be used and, in fact, the scanty data indicate that it grew in importance in the second half of that century. The surviving cadastres for the 1620's for districts of the Center list a number of seignorial holdings on which there were only homesteads of *zadvornye liudi*, and many others in which they formed the major proportion of the total number of *dvory*. In Dmitrov the number of slave homesteads on almost every property equalled or exceeded the number of peasant *dvory*. In the latter quarter of the century the practice of using only slave labor on the demesne seems to have increased, and the data of the seventies and eighties indicate a rise in the number of bondsmen. In the cadastre made in the 1630's for the steppe *uezd* of Belev, about 9 percent of the homesteads were those of slaves; in 1678 this

43 Rozhkov, *Sel'skoe khoziaistvo*, pp. 140, 156-160, 169-180, 186-190.

proportion was 12 percent. Data from 1677-1688 for ten other districts in various parts of the realm indicate that nearly one out of every ten peasant homesteads was occupied by the *zadvornye liudi*, and in Moscow *uezd* over 14 percent of the rural homesteads were in this category.[44]

The presence of slaves in the realm, and their increase, presented a serious dilemma to the government. The pomeshchiks, the throne's chief supporters, needed labor, and slaves were an important part of the labor force, so the government was interested in assuring them an adequate supply of bondsmen. But slaves did not pay taxes, and the state sorely needed every possible taxpayer. To make things worse, the increase in slaves meant a decrease in the numbers of those who did pay taxes. This was because the chief outside source of slaves—prisoners of war—had dried up. A few still came in; Metropolitan Macarius of Aleppo, travelling through Russia in 1653, told of Russians on the steppe frontiers who ambushed Tatar bands and sold them into slavery.[45] But now virtually all the additions to the slave force were recruited from the ranks of the taxpaying subjects of the tsar.

In choosing the course to follow the state gave most weight to its own interests. But it moved slowly. Legislation designed to limit entry into slavery by free Russians was included in the Codes of 1497 (sect. 66) and 1550 (sect. 76, 81). Additions and amendments to these enactments were issued in the second half of the sixteenth and first half of the seventeenth centuries, and the legislation was restated in detail and further amended in Chapter 20 of the Law Code of 1649. But those who were slaves still were not liable for taxes. This may well have been a chief reason for the apparent increase in *zadvornye liudi* in the seventeenth century, for it seems likely that seigniors would have preferred people who owed obligations only to them and for whom they had no tax responsibility, while peasants, who had lost their liberty anyway through the enserfment, would have welcomed a situation in which they did not have to pay taxes.

[44] Got'e, *Zamoskovnyi krai*, pp. 316, 496; Rozhkov, *Russkaia istoriia*, IV, ii, 42-43; D'iakonov, *Ocherki iz istorii*, pp. 267-269; Kliuchevskii, *Kurs*, III, 218; Tomsinskii, *Ocherki*, I, table facing p. 80.
[45] Paul of Aleppo, *Travels*, I, 285-286.

The government finally found the solution to its problem when it shifted the tax base from the arable to the *dvor*. A law of 1680 ordered that all slaves who lived in their own homesteads had to pay the same tax as did peasants. Now only those who lived in the homesteads of their masters were exempt from taxation. And when Peter I introduced the soul tax in 1724 to replace the hearth tax these slaves, too, had to pay the government's levy. Thus fell the last distinction between slave and peasant-serf. The long process of fusion that had begun in the days of the independent princedoms was completed. Slavery as a separate legal institution disappeared and the slaves became serfs.[46]

Before leaving the subject of slavery one further—and peculiar—group of bondsmen should be mentioned. This was the category known as "free" slaves (*volnye kholopy*), or voluntary servants (*dobrovolnye posluzhiltsy*). Despite their name these people were not true slaves. They voluntarily adopted the status of bondsmen without selling themselves, or borrowing money, or making a formal agreement in which they declared themselves the slaves of their master. They merely recommended themselves to a seignior who provided for them and used them as his slaves without actually owning them. They were free to leave their servitude whenever they wanted. Usually they were men who were unable to make a living for themselves, or who needed protection. Newly freed slaves, peasants impoverished by some disaster, vagabonds, and the like were frequently found among these people (who were reminiscent of the *vdachi* of the Kievan era). But sometimes men of the servitor class, among them men of high origin, found security by becoming the voluntary slaves of some powerful seignior.[47]

So long as these people remained voluntary slaves they, like other bondsmen, were not responsible for state taxes, nor, if they were men of the serving class, did they have to perform service

[46] Slavery persisted in Siberia (where there was only a small number of serfs) into the nineteenth century. The steppe nomads sold their children to Russians or abandoned them at frontier posts in times of famine. The government tried to limit Siberian slavery from the eighteenth century on, and finally succeeded in ending it in 1825. Raeff, *Siberia*, pp. 13, 62-63.

[47] Eck, "Les non-libres," pp. 44-45.

for the state. The government became concerned about this evasion of responsibility and took measures against it. Article 81 in Ivan IV's law code of 1550 forbad *deti boiarskie*, the lesser servitors, and their children from becoming slaves unless they had been released by the tsar from his service. A decree of 1597 ordered that any person who served more than six months as a free slave automatically became a *kabala* slave even though he had not borrowed any money, and therefore had to remain in his master's service until the latter's death. Later this period was reduced to just three months.[48] These and other steps taken by the government, however, were not entirely effective in dissuading people—particularly servitors—from becoming "free" slaves. In 1642 members of the nobility complained to the throne about the many persons eligible for service who had evaded their obligation by becoming the slaves of important lords. In response to this petition Tsar Michael issued a decree ordering that all servitors now slaves were to leave their masters and resume their state service, and forbad servitors from entering slavery in the future.[49] The Code of 1649 allowed slaves who were of the serving class, but had not yet entered service and did not have pomestyes, to remain slaves, but commanded that in the future men of this class could not become bondsmen (Chapter 20, sect. 1, 2). Apparently this legislation was effective, for voluntary servitude became far less frequent, although it still persisted in the courts of some great boyars, and as late as the 1680's had not yet entirely disappeared.[50]

IV

By the second half of the seventeenth century the long process of enserfment had been completed. The progressive diminution in the freedom of the peasant-renter that had started in the days of the Tatar yoke had finally reduced the great mass of Russia's rural population into serfs bound to the person of their seignior and subject to his will. In the words of the *Svod Zakonov*, the law code of the nineteenth century, the peasant had been

[48] *AI*, I, 221; *Ulozhenie*, ch. xx, sect. 16.
[49] Vladimirskii-Budanov, *Khristomatiia*, III, 162.
[50] Got'e, *Zamoskovnyi krai*, p. 314.

delivered "into the private power and dominion" of his master. To all intents and purposes, the only rights that had been left to him were those that his lord was willing to allow him; the only recourse he had against the exactions and oppressions of his seignior were the illegal expedients of flight or violence.

As the preceding chapters have shown, this annihilation of the peasant's freedom was intimately linked to the course of Russia's economic and political evolution. Serfdom rose out of the adjustments of Russian society to alternating periods of economic decline and expansion, to the establishment of absolutism, and to the demands the central power was able to make upon the seignioral class. It is the task of the chapters that follow to deal with the subsequent history of the now mature institution, within the context of the nation's continuing economic and political development.

15

TRADE AND INDUSTRY

THE REFORMS and innovations of Peter I (1689-1725) laid the foundations for the transformation of the tsardom of Muscovy into a modern empire. Russia became one of the great powers of Europe, her area and population grew mightily, domestic and foreign trade increased many times over, factory industry spread, and Russian culture and learning entered into the mainstream of European thought. Yet Russia remained a "medieval" society. For the reforms and the progress did not extend to the peasantry. Peter and the rulers who followed him on the throne for the rest of the eighteenth century intensified the bonds of serfdom, forced it upon millions who had been free men, and transformed other millions into the less onerous but still unfree category of state peasants. A servile peasantry became, more than it had ever been before, the basis of the empire's social and economic structure. During the first half of the nineteenth century slight ameliorations that aided some of the peasantry were introduced. But not until the 1860's, in the reign of Alexander II, did Russia free her peasants. Only then did the old order disappear.

When Peter's reign began the economy had not yet fully recovered from the disasters of the late sixteenth and early seventeenth centuries. A census of homesteads made in 1710 for tax purposes had indicated the startlingly large drop of nearly 20 percent in population since the last count made in 1678. A large part of this shrinkage, however, is believed to have been fictitious. Many peasant settlements in the still unsettled frontiers had not been included in the census, and in the older regions peasants, seeking to reduce their tax liability, combined homesteads or conspired to report several *dvory* as one.[1] None-

[1] Pavlenko, "O nekotorykh storonakh," p. 398.

theless, total population probably did decline. A drop during this period was apparently not unique to Russia; the scanty data indicate that population fell in other European lands, too.[2]

Starting in the second quarter of the eighteenth century the empire's population began a spectacular climb. In the early 1720's the first census of males, or revision as it came to be called,[3] indicated a total population of around 14 million. By the time of the Tenth Revision in 1858 population had more than quintupled. Estimates of total population at each revision are:[4]

REVISION	DATE	ESTIMATED POPULATION (IN MILLIONS)
I	1724	14
II	1743-45	16
III	1762-64	19
IV	1782-83	28
V	1796	36
VI	1811	41
VII	1817	45
VIII	1835	60
IX	1851	68
X	1858	74

Part of this enormous increase was explained by the annexation of new territories. When Peter I began his rule his state covered 5.7 million square miles. By the time Alexander II became tsar in 1855 the realm had grown to 7.8 million square miles. The European part of this vast domain—Great Russia, White Russia, the Baltic lands, New Russia, the Kingdom of Poland, Little Russia, and the Grand Duchy of Finland—formed less than one quarter of the total area over which Alexander ruled.[5] Large parts of the newly annexed lands, however, were only scantily peopled, so that most of the rise in population was attributable to a great natural increase in the old parts of the

[2] Cf. Abel, *Agrarkrisen*, pp. 99-101.

[3] The returns from the first census were deemed unsatisfactory, and so a verification or supplementary census, called a *reviziia*, revision, was ordered. This term became the official name for all subsequent censuses up to 1858. Florinsky, *Russia*, I, 363.

[4] Voznesenskii, *Ekonomika Rossii*, p. 17. For a discussion of these estimates through the Ninth Revision v. Schnitzler, *L'empire*, II, 60-63.

[5] Arsen'ev, *Statisticheskie ocherki*, pp. 56-57; Tsentral'nyi statisticheskii komitet, *Statisticheskiia tablitsy . . . za 1858 god*, p. 58.

realm. In 1724 the provinces that made up Petrine Russia had 14 million people in them. In 1858 these same provinces had a total population of 45 million.[6] Moreover, the natural increase in these guberniias was far greater than even these figures show, for there was a steady and huge drain of migrants out of the older zones of settlement to the southern and eastern frontiers. The new regions were colonized almost exclusively by people from the Center. Foreign settlers began to come in under government sponsorship during Elizabeth's reign (1741-1762), but their numbers remained small in comparison with the never-ceasing flood of Russian colonists. The New World, as a French writer of the mid-nineteenth century observed, had been colonized by the men and money of the Old World; Russia colonized herself without outside aid.[7] The rich, black soil of the empty eastern and southern borderlands acted as a magnet that drew millions from the more populous parts of the empire. Some of the newcomers were seigniors who brought their serfs with them, like the grandfather of Sergei Aksakov, the nineteenth century writer. The elder Aksakov had to share his ancestral *votchina* with four kinsmen, so he decided to sell out and move with his peasants across the Volga to establish a new manor that would belong only to him.[8] Other proprietors remained behind themselves but sent out some of their serfs to work new lands they had acquired through gift, purchase, or exchange. Many state peasants who had trouble earning a living in the crowded and infertile provinces north of the Oka came out under government auspices. And finally, countless thousands fled to the frontiers to escape the serfdom that oppressed them in their old homes.

As a result of this internal migration, and of natural increase, the population of the frontier regions soared. When Catherine II annexed New Russia in 1787 there were around 808,000 people in what became Ekaterinoslav, Tauride, and Kherson guberniias. By 1862 this number had risen to 3.1 million. In those sections of the Ukraine that were part of Peter I's empire the

[6] Liashchenko, *History*, p. 273.
[7] Leroy-Beaulieu, *L'empire*, I, 45.
[8] Aksakov, *Semeinaia khronika*, pp. 3-6.

population went up from half a million in 1724 to 1.9 million in 1858. In the southern steppes the increase was from an estimated 400,000 in 1724 to 1.7 million in 1858, and in the land along the Volga from 1.1 million to 3.9 million.[9]

The growth in the population of the colonial areas made possible in turn the continued growth of population in the older parts of the realm. For the new, fertile lands provided food-stuffs and raw materials needed to support the expanding population of central and northern Russia. A regional division of labor began to emerge, with factory and handicraft industry concentrated in the non-black earth provinces north of the Oka, while the people of the chernozem engaged almost exclusively in agriculture.

The upswing in Russia's population was paralleled in the rest of the Western world. Between 1750 and 1860 Europe's population doubled, from an estimated 140 million to 283 million.[10] The rate of population increase in Russia, however, was un-equalled by any other European nation, so that the empire became by far the most populous country in Europe. Between 1750 and 1860 her population almost quadrupled, Great Britain's tripled, in Germany population doubled, and in France it went up by two-thirds.[11]

The pattern of Russian population increase, however, differed strikingly from that of other great nations of Europe in one important respect. This was the degree of urbanization. Statistics on the size of Russian towns are especially unreliable because the census takers did not always count peasants who lived in the towns, nor did reports include the artisans and traders in the suburbs that surrounded important cities. The data, therefore, has a strong downward bias. The estimates often given for urban population are:[12]

[9] Voznesenskii, *Ekonomika Rossii*, pp. 18-20.

[10] Kuczynskii, "Population," pp. 241, 243.

[11] Russia's population: 1762, 19 mill.; 1858, 74 mill. (Voznesenskii, *Ekonomika Rossii*, p. 17.) Great Britain's population, 1750, 7.9 mill., 1860, 23.2 mill.; France, 1750, 23 mill., 1861, 37.4 mill.; Germany, 1750, 16-18 mill., 1858, 34.6 mill. (Kirsten et al., *Raum*, II, 60, 144, 149, 160.)

[12] These estimates are from Miliukov, *Ocherki*, I, 79. According to Rashin, *Formirovanie*, pp. 82-83, these figures are too low. Rashin's estimates are: 1794, 2,279,000; 1811, 2,851,000; 1825, 3,521,000; 1840, 4,906,000; 1856, 5,684,000.

DATE	URBAN POPULATION	PERCENT OF TOTAL POPULATION
1724	328,000	3.0
1782	802,000	3.1
1796	1,301,000	4.1
1812	1,653,000	4.4
1835	3,025,000	5.8
1851	3,482,000	7.8

Comparable data show that in England and Wales the cities held 32 percent of the population in 1801 and 50 percent in 1850; in France the ratios were 20.5 percent in 1801 and 25.5 percent in 1851.[13] A Westerner travelling in Russia in the 1850's scarcely exaggerated when he wrote that the empire of the tsars "taken as a whole is just one vast village."[14]

Most of the cities were small, and many of them were villages in everything but name and the tax status of their inhabitants. Even in larger towns the burghers continued their centuries-old practice of raising much of their own food in fields and gardens in and around the settlement, and some of them produced surpluses that they offered for sale.[15] When Catherine II introduced her reform of provincial government in 1775, around 250 villages had to be raised to city rank to serve as centers for the new administrative districts created by the law. In later years scores of these "cities" were allowed to revert back to villages and their residents became peasants once again.[16] Data on the population of 678 cities in 1856 show that 119 of them had less than 2,000 inhabitants, 236 had 2,000 to 5,000, 256 had 5,000 to 15,000, 57 had 15,000 to 50,000, 7 had 50,000 to 100,000, and 3 had over 100,000.[17]

II

The increase in population produced a greatly expanded potential market for goods, and the settlement of the colonial

---

13 *Bol'shaia Sovetskaia Entsiklopediia*, 2nd ed., XII, 189.

14 Jourdier, *Des forces*, p. 118.

15 Kulischer, "Die kapitalistischen Unternehmer," pp. 328-329, 329n.

16 Miliukov, *Ocherki*, I, 179-180.

17 Tsentral'nyi statisticheskii komitet, *Statisticheskiia tablitsy . . . za 1856 god*, pp. 222-223.

The three largest cities were St. Petersburg (490,808), Moscow (368,765), and Odessa (101,320).

areas, as already noted, facilitated the emergence of a regional division of labor. But the fantastic inadequacy of the empire's system of communications was a massive barrier to the growth of trade. The shortcomings of transport made it expensive and sometimes impossible to send goods to the markets. This difficulty was compounded by the sheer size of Russia, for great distances often had to be traversed to bring wares from producer to consumer. Roads were few and were usually unsurfaced and undrained. In summer their low-lying sections often became impassable bogs, and in rainy weather entire roadbeds became seas of mud. D. Mackenzie Wallace, who journeyed through most of European Russia in the early 1870's, described the highways over which he travelled with these words:[18] "Now, in Russia, roads are nearly all of the unmade, natural kind, and are so conservative in their nature that they have at the present day precisely the same appearance as they had many centuries ago. They have thus for imaginative minds something of what is called 'the charm of historical association.' The only perceptible change that takes place in them during a series of generations is that the ruts shift their position. When these become so deep that fore-wheels can no longer fathom them, it becomes necessary to begin making a new pair of ruts to the right or left of the old ones; and as the roads are commonly of gigantic breadth, there is no difficulty in finding a place for the operation. How the old ones get filled up I cannot explain; but as I have never seen in any part of the country a human being engaged in road-repairing, I assume that beneficent Nature somehow accomplishes the task without human assistance, either by means of alluvial deposits, or by some cosmical action best known to physical geographers."

The carriage of most goods, and especially of heavy wares, had to wait upon the coming of winter when the snow cover allowed transport by sled. Then the roads came alive with literally millions of peasants carting all manner of merchandise and foodstuffs. But winter travel had its perils, too, and each year many succumbed to cold and storms, or lost their way in unmarked and endless snowfields and perished. If by unlucky chance the winter brought only light snowfall, as happened for instance

18 Wallace, *Russia*, pp. 13-14.

in 1789-1790, transport by sled became difficult, and gluts piled up out in the land while townspeople suffered shortages and high prices.[19]

The government made remarkably little effort to improve the roads of the empire. Perhaps, if one is inclined to seek an excuse for this inactivity, the immensity of the task discouraged the bureaucrats. In 1816 the state did embark upon a program of laying down metalled highways, or *chaussées* as the Russians called them. But construction seemed barely to inch ahead. The *chaussée* between Moscow and St. Petersburg, the first to be built, was not completed until 1830. Thirty years later there were in all Russia only about 5,300 miles (8,000 versts) of these highways; 4,700 miles of the 5,300 were accounted for by just two roads from St. Petersburg, one going through Moscow to Irkutsk in Eastern Siberia, and the other through Warsaw to the Austrian frontier. Progress was even slower in the succeeding three decades; by 1893 only 2,300 miles had been added to the *chaussée* system making a total of 7,700 miles (11,500 versts). This was just one third of the length of the trunk highways of contemporary England and less than one twentieth of those of contemporary France.[20]

The rivers of Russia had always been of prime importance in the transport network, and, in fact, often were the decisive factors in determining the direction and nature of Russian growth. The usefulness of the river system was much enhanced in the eighteenth and nineteenth centuries by state-built canals that connected major streams and eliminated costly and time-consuming portages. Hundreds of thousands of workers were employed in shipping, most of them serving as human draught animals to pull the barges and boats upstream against the current. In 1815 an estimated 400,000 of these boatmen, or *burlaki* as they were called, worked on the Volga, the empire's busiest river. The hardships and brutality of their occupation were so great that of these 400,000 an average of 7,000 were said to have perished on the job each year, and thousands more returned to their villages ruined in health. In succeeding years as shipping

[19] Portal, "Manufactures," p. 169; Tooke, *View*, I, 27-28.
[20] Miliukov, *Ocherki*, I, 90; Gille, *Histoire*, pp. 152-153.

increased the numbers of the *burlaki* must have gone up proportionately, for only little use was made of steam navigation until the 1850's.[21]

But there were serious barriers to the utilization of rivers presented by what Soviet leaders, whose impatience with non-cooperation extends even to geography, refer to as "defects of nature." Many of the streams could not be navigated for a large part of the year because of ice in winter, floods in spring, and low water in the dry summer months. Several of the important ones flowed into landlocked seas, or into remote Arctic waters. Their most important failing, though, was that most of them ran north and south and so were of little or no use in the east-west flow of trade. In addition, they sometimes presented obstacles so formidable to the passage of overland traffic that one observer compared them to the mountains of Western Europe. For bridges were few, and often so poorly constructed that travelers hesitated to use them, and floods easily carried them away. "To cross a river by a bridge," Mackenzie Wallace wrote, "is often what is termed in popular phrase 'a tempting of Providence.' The cautious driver will generally prefer to take to the water, if there is a ford within a reasonable distance. . . ."[22]

The shortcomings of river transport could have been (and ultimately were) largely overcome by railroads. One might suppose that this would have stimulated railroad construction but, instead, Russia lagged far behind the West in developing a rail network. The first steam line began operations in 1838 with 27 kilometers of track. Built by private capital, it went from St. Petersburg to Pavlovsk, the summer residence of the imperial family. To attract passengers the promoters built a resort hotel and amusement park, called Vauxhall after the famed London pleasure resort, at the end of the line. So Russia's first railroad, as Finance Minister Kankrin (who had opposed its construction) observed, "ran from the capital to the cabaret."[23] The venture

---

[21] Virginskii, *Nachalo*, p. 7; Portal, "La Russie," p. 155.

Between 1825 and 1844 the number of freight-carrying boats on rivers and canals rose from 23,749 to 59,069. In 1861 there were 200 steamships on the Volga and its tributaries. Portal, "La Russie," p. 155.

[22] Wallace, *Russia*, p. 14.   [23] Portal, "La Russie," p. 153.

Vauxhall (*Vokzal* in Russian), the empire's first railway terminal, became the

did not make money, and possibly its lack of success discouraged further private investment in railroads. In 1843 the government started to build two trunk lines, one from St. Petersburg to Moscow and the other from Warsaw to the Austrian frontier. Their construction was undertaken with misgivings in high places. Kankrin opposed railroads because he believed they would increase vagabondage.[24] Tsar Nicholas himself, revealing a clouded vision of truly imperial proportions, stated that railroads were useful only in exceptional cases, could not carry heavy freight, absorbed enormous amounts of capital unproductively, and "as for the speed of communication for the passengers, this is an acquisition that seems rather a luxury and favors the spirit of inconstancy which characterizes our century."[25] (At that Nicholas was more radical than his fellow autocrat, Francis I of Austria. Despite his low opinion of the value of railroads Nicholas allowed them to be built. Francis to his death in 1835 would not allow steam railroads in his empire because he feared they might bring in political revolution.)[26]

The Polish line was completed in the latter forties and the St. Petersburg-Moscow road in 1851. But elsewhere construction lagged, so that in 1855 Russia with 1,044 kilometers of railroad was far behind other European lands. Of the major countries only Italy and Spain had less trackage. Then the defeat in the Crimean War, brought on in no small measure by the difficulties of shipping men and matériel to the war theater, forced home the need for more railroads. The government turned over further construction to a private company, financed mainly by French capital, guaranteeing the investors a return of 5 percent. By 1865 Russia had nearly four times as much track (3,926 km.) as it had ten years before. But other nations had also been making much progress during this decade, so that Russia was

---

common noun for railway station in the Russian language. For a delightful account of the chain of circumstance by which one Falkes, or Faukes, an unpleasant Norman adventurer in the service of King John of England, had his name preserved in Russian speech (and in other languages too), v. Tesnière, "Les antécédents," pp. 255-266.

24 Virginskii, *Nachalo*, p. 7.
25 Quoted in Gille, *Histoire*, p. 153.
26 Blum, "Transportation," p. 26.

still far behind. In fact, now even Italy and Spain had more mileage.[27]

Because of these many deficiencies in transportation, quantities of goods never reached the market, and high shipping costs inflated the prices of the wares that did get there. In the middle of the nineteenth century a *pud* of iron that cost 80 to 90 kopecks at the plant in the Urals sold for 2 rubles or more in the western provinces; a *sazhen* of wood for which the forest owner got 20 to 30 kopecks brought 3 rubles in St. Petersburg; a beef carcass that sold for 15 to 20 rubles in the southern steppes cost 50 to 60 rubles in St. Petersburg. Grain rose sharply in price as it moved from the producing regions to the markets of the Center and Northwest. In 1835 the price of a sack of rye flour ranged from 6 to 8 rubles in the fertile provinces of Orenburg, Penza, and Poltava to 30 rubles in Pskov guberniia; in 1836 the range was from 1.60 rubles in Poltava to 22 rubles in Lifland; and in 1837 from 1.80 rubles in Tomsk to 22 rubles in Lifland.[28]

Under such conditions the odds seemed against the expansion of trade. But the opportunities presented by the always growing market presented so strong a stimulus to Russia's merchants that, despite the handicaps, commerce surged forward. Its growth became especially pronounced after the government in the second half of the eighteenth century abolished internal tariffs, ended monopolistic privileges, and established freedom of enterprise by wiping out most of the barriers to entrance into any branch of trade and industry.

The cities of the empire continued as before to be active trading centers. The special feature of Russian trade in the eighteenth and nineteenth centuries, however, was the central role of fairs. Incomplete data from 1818-1820 show that over 4,000 of these periodic markets were held in those years, and by the early 1860's the number had grown to almost 6,000. They maintained their importance until the railroad network had expanded enough to allow the regular flow of goods between all parts of the empire. Most of these fairs were small operations that served as markets for local products, or, at most, as regional

27 "Statistische Übersicht," p. 230; Tschuprow, "Eisenbahnen," pp. 496-497.
28 Tegoborskii, *Etudes*, III, 277; Kulischer, "Die Leibeigenschaft," p. 60.

markets. But a few score of the largest ones had national and even international connections. The greatest of them all was held each summer at Nizhnii Novgorod from 10 July to 15 August. It had been moved there in 1817 from the nearby town of Makar'ev. Lying at the junction of the Oka and Volga rivers, and near the border of Europe and Asia, Nizhnii Novgorod was ideally located to become a great emporium. Sales at the 1817 fair totalled 19.8 million rubles, by 1841 they had reached 41.7 million, in 1851 52.9 million, and in 1861 83.6 million. The growth of the fair at Irbits in the Eurasian province of Perm was even more spectacular. Sales there in 1817 amounted to 2.9 million rubles, 9.5 million in 1841, 28.7 million in 1851, and 45.9 million in 1861.[29]

Statistics on foreign trade in the eighteenth century are very unsatisfactory, but estimates indicate a large increase in both imports and exports. In 1726 exports amounted to an estimated 4.2 million rubles and imports to 2.1 million; estimates for 1762 are 12.8 million for exports and 8.2 million for imports. By 1812-1815 the average annual value of exports was 62 million rubles and of imports 39.1 million, and by 1856-1860 the annual average had gone up to 225.6 million for exports and 205.9 million for imports.[30]

In the eighteenth century and on into the 1840's flax and hemp were Russia's most important exports. The governmental restrictions on grain exports remained in force until the second half of the eighteenth century, so that only small amounts were sent abroad. Shipments rose when the restrictions were lifted, but cereals remained of secondary importance in the export trade until the acquisition during Catherine II's reign of New Russia and of ports on the Black Sea. Then cereal exports began to mount. In 1778-1790 they totalled around 400,000 chetverts a year, and by the end of the nineties they were around one million chetverts annually. In succeeding decades the quantities

---

[29] Rozhkova, "K voprosy," pp. 299-300, 307; Khromov, *Ekonomicheskoe razvitie*, p. 92.

[30] Voznesenskii, *Ekonomika Rossii*, p. 151.

Russia almost always had a favorable trade balance. Between 1800 and 1860 the value of exports exceeded that of imports in all but seven years. (Khromov, *Ekonomicheskoe razvitie*, p. 94.)

sold abroad continued to rise (after a low period from 1806 to 1816), a particularly notable leap forward coming after the repeal of the British corn laws in 1846. In 1801-1805 the value of the average annual grain exports amounted to 16 percent of the total value of Russia's exports; in 1856-1860 they represented 35 percent of the value of all exports. Wheat led other cereals in foreign sales, making up between 55 and 80 percent of total grain exports. Nearly all of this wheat grew in southern Russia and was shipped from southern ports, above all from Odessa. Total grain exports, however, even after the mid-century boom, accounted for only a small part of Russia's total cereal production. At the beginning of the century exports were equal to just 1 to 1.5 percent, and in the late fifties and early sixties, around 3.5 to 5 percent, of the estimated grain crop of the empire.[31]

Industrial wares, and especially pig iron, had been major export items in the eighteenth century; in 1778-1780, for example, they made up 20 percent of the value of all exports. In the nineteenth century their relative importance steadily declined, so that by 1856-1860 manufactured goods comprised just 2.9 percent, and base metals 1.5 percent, of the total value of exports.[32]

In Western Europe both foreign and domestic commerce were the special preserves of the bourgeoisie. In Russia, however, there were only a relatively small number of people in the merchant class, they were distributed unevenly through the empire, and many of them were commercially inactive. A government study made in 1764 estimated that 1.9 percent of the urban population (excluding members of the nobility, clergymen, bureaucrats, and peasants living in the towns) engaged in interregional or foreign trade, and 40.7 percent traded only within the limits of their home towns. The rest were artisans, laborers, or unemployed.[33] A number of delegates to the Legislative Commission called by Catherine II in 1767 to draw up a new law code for the empire, commented upon the shortage of members of the merchant class in their localities and their com-

---

[31] Voznesenskii, *Ekonomika Rossii*, pp. 75-76, 79; Khromov, *Ekonomicheskoe razvitie*, pp. 95, 97; Popov, "Khlebnofurazhnyi balans," p. 151.

[32] Voznesenskii, *Ekonomika Rossii*, p. 155; Khromov, *Ekonomicheskoe razvitie*, p. 97.

[33] *MKP*, I, 248-249.

mercial unimportance. In many places the persons registered as merchants earned their livings in other fields, and there were towns where there were no merchants at all.[34]

Enterprising peasants seized the opportunity to fill the gap between producers and consumers. In doing this they broke laws that restricted trading to duly registered members of the merchant class. This legislation dated back to the late sixteenth and early seventeenth centuries. Suburbs (*slobody*) of traders and artisans who were mainly of peasant origin had grown up on privately owned land around the towns. These people did not pay city taxes, but they competed with the commercial and industrial activities of those who lived within the town limits and who bore the fiscal burdens of urbanites. The town dwellers complained about the injustice of this situation, and the state issued a series of decrees aimed at abolishing the fiscal advantage enjoyed by the people of the *slobody*. Now they had to pay the same taxes as city residents and the *slobody* themselves were converted into state property. Peasants were forbidden to have shops or warehouses in the towns, and were allowed only to sell their wares at the town market, and then only from wagons or barges.[35]

The peasants were able to disregard these restraints because they had the protection of their seigniors, and because of the need for their services. The serfowners, especially those in the less fertile parts of Russia, had a deep personal interest in protecting and promoting the growth of peasant business activity, for it increased peasant incomes and thereby enabled seigniors to demand more obrok. Also, the serfs who grew wealthy from these non-agricultural pursuits served as guarantors for the obligations owed the seignior from the less prosperous members of the village commune. An urban delegate to the Legislative Commission complained that city officials were afraid to confiscate the wares of serfs in trade as the law provided, lest the peasant's master regard the action as robbery and enter suit for recovery (legally the master owned all the property of his serf). "Every merchant," said this speaker, "will prefer to suffer some

---

[34] Kulischer, *Ocherk istorii russkoi torgovli*, pp. 250-253.
[35] *Ulozhenie*, ch. XIX, sect. 4, 5, 11, 12, 15, 16, 17; *MKP*, I, 267-268.

damage rather than get involved in a law suit with a nobleman."
In answer to complaints of this sort Count Münnich, speaking
for the government, pointed out that "many merchants either
from lack of capital or lack of the necessary skill or bad conduct
devote themselves but little to commerce," while peasants "for
the last hundred years, despite all the prohibitions laid against
it, have been occupied constantly in trade and have invested
quite considerable sums in it." Münnich attributed the growth
of Russian commerce, and what he termed "its present flourishing condition," to the competence, hard work, and investments
of these peasant traders.[36]

The government continued to promulgate decrees aimed at
restricting peasant commerce,[37] but finally decided around the
middle of the eighteenth century to adjust its legislation to
reality. Beginning in 1745 the new laws became increasingly
permissive, until by the early nineteenth century there was no
substantive difference between the right of peasants to engage in
trade and that of members of the merchant class.[38]

Most peasants entered trade to supplement the income they
drew from agriculture. This was particularly true in the
provinces of the Center and Northwest, where the farmers had
to face the competition from the fertile chernozem regions that
were brought under the plow during this era. Some became part-
time peddlers or small merchants, while others abandoned the
soil entirely for commerce. Most of them sold goods they raised,
caught, or made themselves. The more enterprising among
them bought up the output of their fellow villagers for resale,
often carrying their wares to distant markets. Nor did they limit
themselves to rural or itinerant trading. Delegates to the Legislative Commission complained that peasants had moved into cities
with their families and had opened shops selling all manner of
goods, including luxury wares and imported products, and were
active, too, in wholesale trade.[39]

[36] *MKP*, I, lxxix; Tugan-Baranovskii, *Russkaia fabrika*, I, 39-40; Kulischer,
Ocherk istorii russkoi torgovli, pp. 251, 253.
[37] Cf. Pavlenko, "O nekotorykh storonakh," p. 386.
[38] Druzhinin, *Gosudarstvennye krest'iane*, I, 78-83.
[39] *Ibid.*, pp. 70-71, 381-382, 384-393; *MKP*, I, 251-256.

Quantitative data are lacking on the total number of serfs and state peasants engaged in commerce but clearly it was large. In 1857 an estimated 100,000 travel passes were issued to peasant peddlers in just two provinces, Vladimir and Nizhnii Novgorod.[40] In some villages all the inhabitants were traders who paid their dues in cash and whose owners allowed them to travel freely and even to live elsewhere. In Moscow and St. Petersburg, where each house had a plaque telling who owned it, every building in some streets of the merchants' quarter was said to have borne the name of Sheremetev or Orlov. Actually they were the homes and shops of serfs who belonged to these two great seigniors, and who had purchased the dwellings in the names of their masters, for the law did not allow serfs to own real property in their own name.[41]

By far the greatest number of the peasant traders carried on small operations, but a significant minority built up large enterprises. These men had started out like their fellows on a very small scale, usually as peddlers of articles they made themselves. Then they branched out into dealing in wares made by other peasants, or in addition to their own goods they took the output of their neighbors, on consignment, to the market. The next step for some of these men was to give up their own primary production entirely and buy all their wares from fellow peasants, sometimes supplying them with raw materials to be worked up into finished goods. Others spent all of their time on the road, journeying from place to place to buy and sell. Some among these travelling merchants owned as many as fifty freight wagons and hired many employees and agents.

The success of these men in building up business of large size and complexity gives impressive testimony to their entrepreneurial skills. For they had to overcome formidable obstacles. The story of one of them, Nicholas Shipov by name, reveals the kind of trials they had to undergo and illustrates their daring and initiative. Shipov belonged to Count Saltykov. His father, also a Saltykov serf, had accumulated a large fortune in trade,

---

[40] Jourdier, *Des forces*, p. 190.
[41] Turgenev, *La Russie*, ii, 124-125, 125n.
For the extensive trading activities of Sheremetev serfs, v. Shchepetov, *Krepostnoe pravo*, pp. 96-98, 192-196.

and Nicholas himself built up a business that was so prosperous that his master charged him the enormous obrok of 5,000 rubles a year. The first of his many troubles came in 1828 when his father, who managed one of the Saltykov properties, was accused of misusing funds that had been put in his charge. It cost the family 18,000 rubles to clear the elder Shipov. Later Nicholas was jailed by Count Saltykov on charges that turned out to be false. He was soon released, but these difficulties combined with some business reverses had seriously weakened his financial position. Yet Saltykov refused to reduce his obrok. Unable to recoup his losses and burdened with this great liability to his master, Shipov saw no way out save flight. In 1832 he became a fugitive. Using false names he was always on the move, and lived in constant fear of informers. He occupied himself in trade and quickly managed to build up a prosperous business. Then he was caught, imprisoned as a runaway, and in 1841 was returned to Count Saltykov. His business, of course, evaporated. After living for a while in his home village he persuaded the estate steward to give him a travel pass that was good for half a year. He again went into business and in a short time had a thriving enterprise. But at the end of six months his pass was not renewed and he had to come back to his village. He hired a manager to run the enterprise but the man proved incompetent and the business failed. Meanwhile an uncle with whom he had left some money before his flight in 1832 refused to return it. Shipov sued for recovery. The court refused to hear his plea because a serf could not bring legal action himself, but had to be represented by his master or his master's agent. Shipov was cleaned out. Yet Count Saltykov demanded that he pay an obrok of 400 rubles. Desperate, frustrated at every turn, Shipov hit upon a fantastic scheme. He knew that the law permitted a serf who had been captured in war and escaped to demand emancipation for himself and his family. He managed to get another six-month travel pass and hurried southward where Russian troops were fighting with the mountain people of the Caucasus. He became a sutler, allowed himself to be captured, then escaped. In 1845 he was rewarded with his freedom.[42]

[42] Kulischer, "Die kapitalistischen Unternehmer," pp. 338-341.

The growth of commerce was paralleled by a rapid expansion in both factory and handicraft production. The factory, in the sense of a centralized workshop where a large number of people using simple and almost entirely manual techniques were employed, made its debut in Russia in the seventeenth century.[43] Strictly speaking, then, Peter I did not introduce this mode of production, as is sometimes supposed. But Peter's forceful guidance was responsible for making it an integral part of the national economy. His industrial policy was prompted by the same considerations of state power and public welfare that moved other European rulers of the seventeenth and eighteenth centuries to foster the development of manufacturing and the introduction of new branches of production. He wanted Russia to be able to take care of its own war needs, and he hoped that by promoting industry he would increase the prosperity—and thereby the tax-paying ability—of his subjects. He ordered the establishment by the state of mines, foundries, arsenals, cloth factories, and other enterprises to produce goods for his army and navy. He brought in skilled foreigners to run these plants and to train native workmen. Above all, he encouraged private entrepreneurs by offering them subsidies, loans, exemptions from taxes and military service, and free importation of material and equipment; he compelled peasants to work as forced laborers in their factories; he set up high tariffs to protect them from foreign competition; he gave some of them monopolies; and he turned over a number of state-owned enterprises to them.

The inadequacy of the sources make it difficult to measure the increase in the number of factories from Peter's time on to the end of the eighteenth century. For many years the estimates that had been worked up in 1833 from archival and other contemporary sources and materials were accepted, especially after they were used by Tugan-Baranovskii in 1898 in what was for long the standard history of Russian industry. According to these figures there were 233 factories when Peter died in 1725, 984 when Catherine II came to the throne in 1762, and 3,161 (not

43 Kulischer, *Russische Wirtschaftsgeschichte*, 1, 389-403.

including mining and metallurgical plants) when she died in 1796. Work by Soviet scholars indicate that these figures are much inflated. Their estimates run from 80 to 200 at the end of Peter's reign, between 650 and 700 in the sixties, and around 2,000 at the end of the century.[44] The reason for the discrepancies lay in the failure of the industrial census takers of the eighteenth century to discriminate between a true factory, in which a number of laborers are brought together in one location to work with equipment and materials belonging to their employer, and other forms of industrial organization. They lumped together all types of manufacturing establishments under the rubric of "factory" or "plant." Thus, household enterprises in which all the work was done by members of the family unit, or shops of artisans with perhaps a couple of employees, or manorial workshops that produced only for the estate's consumption and had as few as three workers, were sometimes counted as factories.[45]

Despite these imprecisions, the data show that factory industry made much progress in eighteenth-century Russia. Its growth was most pronounced in the century's second half, for which the government's new policy of industrial freedom deserves the lion's share of the credit.

Nearly all of the empire's factory production, except for mining and metallurgy, was in the Center, and much of it was concentrated in and around Moscow. The other chief manufacturing zone was in the Urals, where a great iron and copper industry had grown up on foundations laid by Peter I. In 1716 there had been just four enterprises there, by 1745 the number had grown to around fifty, and by 1762 there were over a hundred. The Urals metal industry became the single most important sector of Russian factory production. In fact, by the mid-eighteenth century the Urals had become a great industrial region not just on the Russian, but on a world scale. Over half the empire's iron production was exported, most of it to England. In 1800 the empire held top rank in world pig-iron

---

[44] Portal, "Manufactures," pt. 1, pp. 174-177.
[45] *MKP*, I, 247; Meshalin, *Tekstil'naia promyshlennost*, p. 93; Zlotnikov, "K voprosu," pp. 42-44.

production with an output of 162,427 tons. England was second with 156,000 tons. But already the industry had begun to decline, and by 1860 Russia had fallen far behind. By that time England produced 3,982,000 tons while Russia turned out 335,500 tons. One of the chief reasons for the decline stemmed from the failure of the Russian manufacturers to adopt technical improvements. This was due partly to their inertia, and partly to the rising costs, especially in transport.[46]

The stagnation in the first half of the nineteenth century in metallurgical production was unique in the Russian industrial picture. The rest of factory industry continued to advance, although the data for the nineteenth century are hardly any more adequate than those for the eighteenth century, so that only estimates of growth can be made. The figures that are usually cited are around 2,400 factories with 95,200 workers in 1804, 5,261 factories with 210,600 workers in 1825, and 14,000 to 15,000 in 1861 with between 522,000 and 565,000 workers. These figures did not include mining and metallurgical plants, distilleries, flour mills, and breweries, nor factories in the Kingdom of Poland and in the Grand Duchy of Finland.[47] Of the branches of production included in the estimates for 1804, the manufacture of woolens was the most important in terms of the number of workers employed. Linen was in second place. By 1825 cotton textiles had displaced linen as runner-up to woolens, and by 1860 cotton goods were in first place, woolens second, and beet sugar third. In that year there were 1,200 cotton textile plants with 152,236 workers, 706 factories making woolens with 120,025 workers, and 467 beet sugar mills with 64,763 workers. Linen production, loser in the competition with cottons, was far down on the list with only 117 establishments and 17,284 workers.[48]

The Soviet historian, Zlotnikov, arguing that establishments with fewer than sixteen workers should not be counted as

[46] Portal, *L'Oural*, pp. 52, 131, 372-377; Crisp in *Slavonic Review*, pp. 310-311; Khromov, *Ekonomicheskoe razvitie*, p. 62; Strumilin, *Istoriia chernoi metallurgii*, I, 204, 227-229.
[47] Liashchenko, *History*, p. 337; Voznesenskii, *Ekonomika Rossii*, p. 99.
[48] Rashin, *Formirovanie*, pp. 26-27, 30-31.

factories, estimated that in 1804 there were only 1,200 true factories, 1,800 in 1825-1828, and in the latter 1850's, 2,818. His estimates included mining and metallurgical plants. Estimates by Zlotnikov of the number of workers employed in these plants, however, are much larger than those usually given, because he included mining and metallurgy. He claimed that there were 225,000 factory workers in 1804, 340,600 in 1825, and 860,000 in 1860.[49]

The expansion in cotton textile production and its increasing mechanization was the outstanding industrial phenomenon of the period in Russia, as it was in other lands. The rise in the imports of raw cotton provides a gauge of the growth of the industry: in 1812-1815 the average annual import amounted to 1.8 million pounds, for 1831-1835 it was 5.4 million pounds, in 1846-1850, 40.4 million pounds, and in 1856-1860, 94.6 million pounds.[50] Spinning machines were introduced in 1793,[51] but were not widely employed until the 1840's. Then their use spread rapidly, largely through the efforts of a remarkable businessman, the German-born and English-trained Ludwig Knoop.[52] By the early 1850's Russia was said to have had the fifth largest number of spindles in the world, coming after England, France, the United States, and the Habsburg Monarchy. Machine looms came in more slowly; in 1860 there were about 16,000 of them in operation.[53]

In general, however, factory owners were slow to adopt machinery and mechanical power. In 1831 the steam engines then employed in the empire developed an estimated total of only 2,200 horsepower, and in the 1850's, 15,423 horsepower. Most of the engines and other machines in Russia were imported, so that once again import data furnish a guide to growth. In the mid-twenties the average annual value of these imports

[49] Zlotnikov, "Ot manufaktury," pp. 36-39.

In choosing sixteen workers as the minimum for a factory Zlotnikov was doubtless influenced by the practice followed in Soviet statistics by which a plant with over sixteen workers and using mechanical power was classified as a large scale operation. Cf. Bergson, *The Structure of Soviet Wages*, p. 215.

[50] Tugan-Baranovskii, *Russkaia fabrika*, I, 60.

[51] Meshalin, *Tekstil'naia promyshlennost*, p. 96.

[52] Schulze-Gaevernitz, *Volkswirtschaftlichen Studien*, pp. 89-97.

[53] Tegoborskii, *Etudes*, III, 46-47; Iakovlev, *Ekonomicheskie krizisy*, p. 22.

amounted to around 42,500 rubles, two decades later it was nearly 1.2 million rubles, and by the last years of the fifties it was over 3 million rubles. Domestic manufacture of machines lagged badly until the decades of the fifties. Partial data for the early twenties show only four shops. In 1851 the number had risen to 19, with 1,349 workers, and total production valued at 478,000 rubles. By 1860 there were 99 shops with 11,600 workers, turning out a product worth nearly 8 million rubles. In most of these shops, however, skills were at a low level and the equipment was primitive.[54]

Industry other than mining and metallurgy continued to be concentrated in the Center and Northwest. In 1860 40 percent (227,500) of all factory workers included in the official data worked in the three provinces of Moscow, Vladimir, and St. Petersburg. The city of Moscow and its environs remained the chief manufacturing region, though starting in the forties the relative importance of the St. Petersburg area increased. This was promoted by St. Petersburg's new position as principal terminus of the empire's railroad system.[55]

Men of the merchant class played the preeminent role in the growth of Russia's large-scale factory industry. But nobles, and remarkably enough, a small number of peasants, made significant contributions. As could be expected, nobles took over the leadership in the processing of agricultural products, but they also interested themselves on many other lines of manufacture. During Peter's reign a number of magnates, doubtless inspired in part by a desire to win the tsar's approbation, set up factories. Some of them quickly tired of their new enthusiasm and sold out to merchants, but others held on to their plants. In Peter's reign these seignioral factories made up only an estimated 8 percent of all manufacturing establishments. Participation by nobles in industry continued during the succeeding decades, but did not constitute an important part of the empire's industry until the 1760's. Then an increasing number of landowners began to establish factories on their properties. By 1813-1814 an official report on manufactures showed that 64 percent of the mining

[54] Zlotnikov, "Ot manufaktury," pp. 43-47.
[55] Voznesenskii, *Ekonomika Rossii*, p. 102.

enterprises, 78 percent of the woolen cloth factories, 60 percent of the paper mills, 66 percent of the crystal and glass works, and 80 percent of the potash works belonged to nobles.[56]

The social and economic privileges enjoyed by the proprietors afforded them important advantages in the organization and operation of factories. They could require their serfs to work in these establishments, as part of the peasants' barshchina obligation. They were free of governmental restrictions or regulations on the use of labor, other than the very general and largely disregarded rules against the mistreatment of serfs. They could regulate the production of their factories to demand, and could lay off workers without fear of losing them to another employer. They could mesh their manufacturing and agricultural operations, and apportion the working time of their serf laborers between factory and field. They had a ready and cheap supply of raw materials for many of their enterprises, produced on their demesnes by the unpaid barshchina of their peasants, or delivered to them as obrok payments. Transportation services, too, were provided by their serfs as part of the peasant's seignorial obligation. Finally, because of all these advantages the noble needed a minimum of capital to establish a factory, especially since little machinery was as yet in use in industry.

These favorable conditions for enterprises owned by nobles had, of course, existed for a long time. Yet very few proprietors made use of them until the latter part of the eighteenth and first half of the nineteenth centuries. It has been suggested that the intensification during Catherine II's reign of governmental policies that favored the nobility stimulated the interest of the serfowners in factory enterprise.[57] It seems more likely that these nobles awakened to the opportunities offered by the expansion of the market to increase their incomes. The declining importance of farming in the provinces north of the Oka, and the successful operations of factory owners of other social classes, could well have served to persuade landowners that it was to their advantage to manufacture for market. In any event, only a very small proportion of the many thousands of nobles were

---

[56] Zaozerskaia, "K voprosu," pp. 58-60, 68.
[57] Liashchenko, *History*, pp. 300-302.

involved in factory production even in the heyday of seignioral industrial activity. The mass of the serfowners stood completely outside this development. Moreover, a number of factory owners among the nobility, particularly those who owned plants in the Urals, had only recently been raised into that class as a recognition of their business success. Such men can scarcely be considered as evidence for the appearance of a new interest in manufacturing among the nobility. Finally, a number of establishments that belonged to nobles were leased to men of the merchant class, and still other plants, supposedly owned by nobles, actually belonged to serfs who used their masters' names in their business operations.

The peasant who owned a factory usually started his manufacturing career as an artisan working in his home or shop. Possessed of more initiative and daring than his fellows, he began to put out materials to other peasants for them to work up. If things went well he opened a small factory, hiring his neighbors as his workers, and continuing to put out work. The number who reached this stage is unknown, but scattered information makes it clear that it was large. Finally, a few went on still further to become owners of great enterprises, with hundreds and even thousands of employees.[58]

Paradoxes abound in things Russian, at least to Western ways of thinking, but surely few have been stranger than this phenomenon of the peasant industrialist—above all when the peasant was a serf owned by another man. Serf factory owners not only hired other serfs to work for them but also employed free men, sometimes to do menial tasks, and a few among them actually owned serfs themselves. Some of them were even millionaires.[59]

Despite their economic success these men often retained their peasant outlook and way of life. Nikita Demidov (1656-1725), founder of the great Demidov industries in the Urals, offered a striking illustration of this pattern of behavior. He was a state peasant of Tula who followed the trade of gunsmith—a specialty of the people of his region. He won the attention of Peter when

[58] Kulischer, "Die kapitalistischen Unternehmer," pp. 335-338, 345-352.
[59] Turgenev, La Russie, II, 125; cf. Shchepetov, Krepostnoe pravo, pp. 102-107.

in 1700 he presented six guns he had made to the tsar. Peter took a liking to him and showered him with favors. Soon he was the owner of a vast industrial complex. In 1725 his annual income was said to have been 100,000 rubles. He was a skillful manager, a shrewd and ruthless business man, and the employer of thousands. He was fully aware of his own great power and was knowledgeable in the ways of holding his sovereign's favor. Yet Nikita lived near his forges in a small wooden house (a stone house was a sign of affluence in Russia), never learned to read or write, wore a beard, never drank—in this he was spectacularly unlike the usual peasant—and refused to take the honors and decorations offered him by the tsar until five years before his death, when he finally accepted a patent of nobility.[60]

An exceptional number of large peasant-owned factories were concentrated in the villages of Ivanovo in Vladimir guberniia, and in Pavlovo and Vorsma in Nizhnii Novgorod. These settlements and just about everyone in them belonged to the Sheremetevs. Ivanovo, the most important of the three, became the cotton textile center of Russia—a foreign visitor in the 1840's called it the Russian Manchester—while Pavlovo and Vorsma specialized in the manufacture of hardware, such as locks, scissors, axes, and so on. Already in the sixteenth century most of the people of Ivanovo had earned their livings in trade and industry. But the village's emergence as a major industrial center began in the early eighteenth century, when several factories were established in and near it to weave and print linen. The peasants employed in these plants learned the techniques, and since little mechanical equipment was needed, some of them set themselves up as artisans. A few quickly prospered and opened factories of their own. Then, in the latter part of the century, a peasant of Ivanovo named Sokov returned home from a job in a plant that printed cotton cloth. He opened a shop of his own, other peasants learned the trade from him, and soon cotton-printing became the village's main occupation. By 1803 there were 49 of these plants in and around Ivanovo, with a total output valued at 426,300 rubles. In 1812 the burning of Moscow destroyed the chief competitors of Ivanovo's cotton printers, and

[60] Portal, *L'Oural*, pp. 55-59.

their business boomed. The village's historian, himself the son of a wealthy serf factory owner, called these years "the golden age for the cloth printers; only the lazy and the profligate could not accumulate capital for themselves. . . ." According to some accounts, the profit margins of the factory owners went up as high as 500 percent. In 1817 the value of Ivanovo's output was estimated to have been 1.75 million gold rubles. By the 1840's there were 130 cotton printing plants there, 63 of them belonging to serfs, and nearly all the rest owned by former serfs who had purchased their freedom after they succeeded in business. Total production in 1844 was valued at nearly 8 million rubles, and the industry employed an estimated 50,000 people.[61]

Interestingly enough, Ivanovo was a center of the schismatic sect of the Old Believers, illustrating the often noted connection between religious dissent and entrepreneurial leadership. It was told of the first generation of factory owners that even the wealthiest among them would forsake business duties for long-winded, hairsplitting arguments with members of the orthodox church over matters of ritual. Their sons, who were more sophisticated than their fathers had been, were not interested in such matters, and the heresy gradually died out among them.[62]

Despite the importance of Ivanovo and other centers of peasant-owned factory enterprise, the plants that belonged to peasants formed only a small portion of the total number of Russia's large-scale manufacturing establishments. But when all manufacturing is considered, and not just factory production alone, then the importance of peasants far outweighs that of men from the merchant class and the nobility. For peasants dominated handicraft production, and though comparative data are lacking it is clear that the largest part of the domestic market demand for manufactured goods was met not by factory production, but by the output of peasant artisans working in their own homes or in their shops.

Peasant handicraft production for sale, or *kustar* industry as it was called, had a long history in Russia. Usually peasants en-

---

[61] Tugan-Baranovskii, *Russkaia fabrika*, I, 97-98; Shchepetov, *Krepostnoe pravo*, pp. 99, 185-189.

[62] Schulze-Gaevernitz, "Die Moskauer-Wladimirsche Baumwollindustrie," pp. 767-768.

gaged in it as a supplementary occupation. But already in the sixteenth century in some places they had made it their chief source of income, and had relegated agricultural work to a secondary position or abandoned it entirely. It grew in importance in the seventeenth and first half of the eighteenth centuries, but its greatest development came between 1750 and 1850, and particularly in the last twenty-five years of that period. It tended to be concentrated in the non-black earth provinces and was most common among those peasants who paid only obrok. Some of the craftsmen lived in towns, but most of them stayed on the land and engaged in some agricultural activity.

The absence of restrictive gilds, the repeal by the government of the barriers to free entry into trade and industry, and the lagging of handicraft production in the cities, had much to to with the burgeoning of *kustar* production. Craft gild organizations that regulated the quality and character of the products made by their members, and set up standards for entrance into a trade, never established themselves in Russia. Peter I tried to introduce them among urban artisans but his efforts had small results. In the early 1730's there were only 15,000 gild members in the entire empire. In the last years of the eighteenth century the government sought to build up the gild system by publishing regulations for craftsmen in 1785, and by issuing a Code of Gilds in 1799. These attempts proved no more successful than the ones made by Peter. Handicraft gilds remained largely paper organizations with practically no influence or control over craftsmen and their production.[63]

The effects of the abolition of monopolies and the adoption of a liberal industrial policy quickly manifested themselves. Thousands of peasants took advantage of the new legislation to manufacture for market. By the end of the century they were turning out a wide range of goods, from the coarse, cheap wares bought by peasants at village market days, to expensive luxury articles such as silks and objects made of gold and silver. The success they enjoyed brought relative economic wellbeing and even prosperity to many of the peasants engaged in it, and to those

[63] Meshalin, *Tekstil'naia promyshlennost*, p. 40; Liashchenko, *History*, pp. 208-209, 297-298, 302.

regions where it was especially widespread. The *kustar* was likely to live in a better-built home than the peasant who depended entirely upon agriculture, to wear leather boots instead of bast shoes, and to buy the things he needed instead of making them himself.[64]

Peasant artisans retained their importance in manufacturing so long as factory production did not become mechanized. Using family labor and burdened with light fixed charges, they could produce more cheaply than the factories, and could adapt their products more readily to market demands. As a result, though the number of people engaged in cottage industry is unknown, it is certain that it was far larger than the factory labor force. It seems equally certain that the total value of *kustar* production was considerably greater than the value of the output of the empire's factories.[65]

IV

The expansion of commerce and industry was accompanied by a steadily increasing use of money. Some groups in the population had closer connections with the market than did others, so that the demand for money varied. But the growth of the exchange economy drew more and more people into relationships that involved the use of currency.

The capital needed in the development of trade and industry came from the savings of the entrepreneurs and from the government. In Peter's day, as was pointed out earlier, the state had established a large number of enterprises; it had set up nearly half of the estimated 200 or so factories that existed in the mid-1720's.[66] Many of these plants were later sold at bargain prices to private operators. Peter and his successors also aided private enterprise by direct subsidies, loans, tax exemptions, and by giving entrepreneurs vast grants of land containing timber and ore and compelling hundreds of thousands of state peasants to work

---

[64] Tooke, *View*, II, 348-349, 597; Tugan-Baranovskii, *Russkaia fabrika*, I, 258-259; Druzhinin, *Gosudarstvennye krest'iane*, I, 73-74.

[65] Peasant handicraft production for sale continued to loom large in Russia's industrial production on into the Soviet era. Cf. *Statesman's Handbook for Russia*, II, 2-4; *Bol'shaia Sovetskaia Entsiklopediia*, 1st ed., XXXV, 574-575.

[66] Zaozerskaia, *Manufaktura*, pp. 9-10, 37-39.

for them. In the later decades of the eighteenth century and the first half of the nineteenth century, however, the chronic deficits in the state's fiscal operations made it much more difficult for the state to continue as a source of capital for private enterprise.[67]

Organized credit facilities for the use of businessmen were virtually non-existent. The state had established so-called commercial banks on several occasions, but these had served more as banks of deposit, mortgage banks, and state fiscal agents, than as institutions making loans to industry and commerce. There were no private banks until the middle of the nineteenth century. Money lenders remained almost the only source of credit. The joint stock method of raising capital was not used until 1799, when the Russian-American Company was established. The next joint stock company, the First Russian Fire Insurance Company was founded in 1827, and by 1835 four more had been organized. Then flotation of new companies became more frequent. Between 1835 and 1860 190 were established. Of this number 108, with a total capital of 317 million rubles, were organized just between 1856 and 1860. Nobles were among the largest investors in some of these corporate enterprises.[68]

The value of money went through many changes during the era. Peter I had coined a lighter silver ruble and had also minted copper money. His successors continued to strike off copper coins. Though this inferior money tended to drive silver out of circulation, the ruble's value remained stable until the last quarter of the century. In 1769 Catherine II's government began to print paper money. At first, because of governmental restraint and public preference for notes over the heavy copper coins, the paper ruble, or assignat—as it was called in Catherine's legislation[69]—remained at par. But the empress's ambitious foreign policy demanded ever greater state expenditures and the tempta-

[67] At the end of Catherine II's reign the government's cumulative deficit amounted to 200,000,000 rubles. To cover this the government had issued 157.7 million paper rubles and had borrowed heavily. In 1796 the state owed 15,570,000 rubles to Russian lenders and 33,173,000 rubles to foreigners. Sixty years later, on the eve of the emancipation, the state's total debt amounted to 1,978,800,000 rubles. Voznesenskii, *Ekonomika Rossii*, pp. 177-178.

[68] *Ibid.*, p. 145; cf. Kusheva, "Proekt," pp. 50-51; "Count A. A. Bobrinskii" in *Russkii Biograficheskii Slovar*, p. 113.

[69] Cf. *PSZ*, XVIII, No. 13,219, 29 Dec. 1768, pp. 787-792.

tion to turn the presses loose could not be resisted. By 1796, when Catherine died, a total of 157.7 million paper rubles had been issued and the assignat ruble exchanged at 79 silver kopecks. Her successors, who needed cash even more than she did, continued to print money. By 1817 the total had reached 836 million assignat rubles, with each ruble worth only one fourth of a silver ruble (25 kopecks). In that year the government, using money raised by foreign and domestic loans, began to call in the assignats. By 1823 596 million paper rubles remained in circulation. This level was maintained until 1839-1843. The value of the assignat during these years fluctuated between 25 and 28 silver kopecks. In 1839 the government announced that from 1 January 1840 the silver ruble was to be the basic monetary unit, but that assignats would circulate as legal tender at the rate of 3½ assignat rubles to one silver ruble. Then, in 1843 the government ordered that assignats were to be exchanged for a new paper money called credit rubles. This currency was partially backed by bullion. For a number of years care was taken to keep the amount issued in close correspondence with the guarantee fund, and the credit rubles stayed close to par. In the latter half of the fifties, however, the government, hard pressed by the cost of the Crimean War, began to run off large amounts of the new money, so that by 1861 the credit ruble's value had dropped to 88.7 silver kopecks.[70]

The long currency inflation, the many wars, the growth of the market, and the expansion in trade, industry, and the use of money, all had deep effects upon the price structure. The inadequacy of the price data, the wide fluctuations between markets, and the absence of special studies, makes it impossible, however, to trace price movements with any precision. Grain prices, the chief market commodity and the best barometer of price changes, apparently rose in the latter years of Peter's reign. Then they remained fairly stable until around the middle of the century, when they started going up again. The increase, at first, was apparently small, until the government started issuing

[70] *Ibid.*, 2nd series, XIV, No. 12,867, 9 Nov. 1839, pp. 839-840; Miliukov, *Ocherki,* I, 105-107; Khromov, *Ekonomicheskoe razvitie*, pp. 120-126; Florinsky, *Russia*, II, 708-709, 787-788.

assignats. Then prices began to race upward. The estimated price of a chetvert of rye in the non-black earth region in the sixties was around 1 ruble, in the seventies and first half of the eighties it went up to 2 rubles, and in the first half of the nineties it was something over 4 rubles.[71] According to a contemporary, prices in Moscow guberniia rose from 86 kopecks per chetvert in 1760 to 7 rubles in 1790.[72] The price rise may not have been as great in the chernozem if prices in Tula were typical. In 1760 a chetvert of rye sold there for 1.09 rubles, in 1770 for 1.18 rubles, in 1780 for 2.40 rubles, and in 1790 for 2.84 rubles.[73]

The price inflation was reflected in the amount the government-owned Bank of the Nobility advanced to seigniors who mortgaged their serfs with it. In 1766 the Bank increased its loan per serf from 10 to 20 rubles, in 1786 to 40 rubles, and in 1804 to 60 rubles.[74] The rise in the selling prices of serfs and recruit substitutes, and in the obrok and taxes of the peasant (v. Chapter 22), provide other evidence of mounting prices.

The high price level continued on into the beginning of the 1820's—in 1821 rye prices at Moscow were higher than they had been for nearly twenty years. Then grain prices turned downward, and stayed low until around 1832, when they moved to a somewhat higher level where they remained until the mid-forties. In the second half of that decade, and continuing on in the 1850's, they rose briskly.[75] These generalizations, however, conceal extreme fluctuations in price between markets, and on individual markets, from year to year. The source of most of this unsteadiness lay in the inadequacies of the empire's transportation system. Because it was so difficult and so expensive to ship bulky farm goods from one place to another markets were often virtually non-competitive. To give just two illustrations of this: in 1843 in St. Petersburg grain cost five times as much as it did in the Central Agricultural province of Kursk, and in the spring of

[71] Portal, *I.'Oural*, pp. 255-256; Semevskii, *Krest'iane*, I, 55.

[72] Prince Shcherbatov quoted in Liashchenko, *Ocherki*, I, 100.

[73] Shchepetov, *Krepostnoe pravo*, p. 46.

[74] Borovoi, "K voprosu," p. 74.

[75] Struve, *Krepostnoe khoziaistvo*, pp. 112-116, 118-119; Tsentral'nyi Statisticheskii Komitet, *Statistika Rossiiskoi Imperii*, x, 131; Khromov, *Ekonomicheskoe razvitie*, p. 15.

1845 a *kul* (*ca.* 360 lbs.) of rye sold for 1.50 rubles in Kursk and for 14 to 15 rubles in Pskov.[76]

The difficulties of transportation bore primary responsibility also for the fluctuations in price over time in a single market. If a district had a bumper crop it had trouble in shipping its surplus to a less favored area, and if it suffered a crop failure it was expensive to bring in grain. This oscillation between feast and famine was reflected in a roller coaster movement of prices. A study in 1842 of the ratio between mean highest price and mean lowest price for the years 1833-1841, showed that in the grain importing provinces of the non-chernozem the ratio ran from 4.2 to 1 in Moscow to 2.2 to 1 in St. Petersburg. That is, the mean highest price for these years in Moscow guberniia was 4.2 times greater than the mean lowest price, and in St. Petersburg guberniia it was 2.2 times greater. In the grain exporting provinces of the chernozem the range was much more extreme, going from 4.8 to 1 in Simbirsk to 11.1 to 1 in Stavropol.[77]

[76] Struve, *Krepostnoe khoziaistvo*, pp. 123-124, 127-128; Liashchenko, *Ocherki*, I, 122-124. For other examples v. Liashchenko, *Ocherki*, I, 100, 123; Kulischer, "Die Leibeigenschaft," p. 60; Tegoborskii, *Etudes*, I, 352 ff.

[77] Struve, *Krepostnoe khoziaistvo*, pp. 127-128.

16

THE FACTORY LABOR FORCE

WHEN LARGE-SCALE FACTORY INDUSTRY took firm root in Russia in the early part of the eighteenth century the entrepreneurs faced the problem of recruiting a labor force in a land that was almost entirely agricultural. The speed with which factory organization was first undertaken, the large size of many of the establishments, and the sparseness of the population in regions where some of the new plants were established, provided additional complications. But the peculiar nature of the Russian social structure allowed these seemingly formidable obstacles to be vanquished with relative ease; the plant owners turned to the peasants and compelled them to take jobs in the new enterprises. In government-owned factories the needed workers were drawn from the state peasantry. The government attached these people to a specific enterprise, and so they were known as "assigned (*pripisnye*) peasants." They either worked in the plant itself, or had to supply it with raw materials, fuel, and transportation. Some of them were required to spend full time on these tasks, while others were called upon periodically.[1] The government also put soldiers, vagabonds, and criminals to work in its factories. In plants owned by nobles the necessary labor was furnished by serfs who belonged to the factory's proprietor.

Men of the merchant class who owned factories did not enjoy the privilege of having peasants they could order about as they pleased. In the first years of industrialization they had to rely entirely upon hired labor. The shortage of available free workers placed these middle class manufacturers at a disadvantage. The government, or more precisely, Tsar Peter I, quickly recognized their handicap and took measures to overcome it. At Peter's

---

[1] In the seventeenth century there had been a few instances in which the government had assigned a relatively small number of peasants as forced industrial laborers. Semevskii, *Krest'iane*, II, 295-297; Amburger, *Die Familie Marselis*, p. 123.

command thousands of state peasants were assigned to enterprises owned by merchants; paupers, vagabonds, criminals, and others were bound to these factories; metallurgical plants in the Urals and Siberia were allowed to keep skilled runaway serfs as assigned peasants instead of having to return them to their rightful owners; merchants were given the right to buy serfs to work in their factories; and when state-owned establishments were transferred to private ownership the assigned state peasants went along as integral parts of the plant.

The government assigned peasants to a wide range of privately-owned industries, but by far the largest number were attached to mining and metallurgical plants in the Urals. Hosts of workers were needed in these enterprises, many of them just for short periods. The wages the factory owners were willing to pay were too low, and the work too hard and disagreeable, for the local population to take jobs in the plants voluntarily. So the expedient of forced labor was adopted. At first state peasants were assigned to each plant by a special act, the number of households assigned being determined by an evalutation of the needs of each individual plant. Then a decree of 23 March 1734 established a general policy. Now anyone starting an iron mill could get 100 to 150 families of state peasants assigned to his plant for each blast furnace he operated, and 30 households for each forge, while copper smelters could get 50 households, or 200 male peasants, for every thousand *pudy* of refined copper they produced.[2]

As might be expected, this new system did not sit well with the people who lived in the Urals. Up to the time of the introduction of industry that thinly-populated region had been almost entirely state domain, and the peasants had been as nearly free as was possible for peasants to be in the Russia of that day. Now they were confronted with the prospect of servitude at hard and unpleasant work. Thousands of them decided they would have none of it, and fled eastward into Siberia or into the southern Urals, where industry had not yet made its appearance.

[2] Portal, *L'Oural*, pp. 92-93.

At the same time, however, a steady stream of newcomers poured into the Central Urals where the plants were located. This inflow was made up of serfs purchased by factory owners for use as industrial laborers, of Old Believers, and above all, of runaway peasants.[3]

The Old Believers came to find surcease from the persecutions they suffered in their native provinces. In 1727, according to an official report, no Old Believers lived in the Urals; by 1735 an estimated 3,000 of them had already made their homes there. These people were distinguished by their industry, reliability, and self-discipline. They took jobs in the plants, and many of them rose to important positions in management and in the economy of the area. Doubtless this explains why the government's repressive measures against Old Believers were carried out only half-heartedly by the local authorities in the Urals.[4]

By far the largest part of the new labor supply, however, was provided by the never-ending stream of runaway serfs and state peasants. Some of these fugitives hoped to find unsettled land in the Urals and start their lives over again. Others passed through on their way to the empty and free soil of Siberia. Many of these people never achieved their goals, for the wages offered free hired labor in the Urals plants acted as irresistible lures, and thousands of runaways took jobs as factory workers. By the early 1720's an estimated 5,000 of them were employed in the mills and mines of the region, and in 1732 government officials counted 2,604 fugitives working in the plants owned by the Demidovs alone.

The law of the land required that those who received runaway serfs had to return them if they were claimed by their legal owners. The industrialists of the Urals were willing to give up fugitives who did common labor for them. But they felt differently about their skilled workers, no matter what the law said. Such workers were far too valuable to let go. So the government, anxious to promote industrial development in the Urals, issued a series of decrees in 1722, 1725, and 1736 that permitted plant owners to keep skilled runaways if they paid indemnities to the owners of the serfs. The runaway, however, lost his status as a

---

[3] *Ibid.*, pp. 43-46, 76-78, 380-381.   [4] *Ibid.*, pp. 94-96.

free hired worker. He and his family became attached to the plant in perpetuity, and his children had to follow his trade. Fugitive serfs whose owners were unknown, and state peasants who had run away to the Urals, were also ordered to be assigned in perpetuity to the plants in which they were employed. And so the peasants who had sought to find liberty through flight had only exchanged one form of servitude for another, and often harsher, form.[5]

By the second half of the eighteenth century the Urals mining and metallurgy industry, the largest and most important branch of Russian large scale manufacturing, was manned almost entirely by assigned workers. The total number employed in this sector of production rose from 31,383 male workers in 1719 to 312,218 in 1796.[6] Legislation in the first half of the nineteenth century freed many of these peasants from their assignments, so that on the eve of the emancipation there were about 201,000 males assigned to mining and metallurgy. These official figures, however, are much larger than the number actively employed in the factories and mines. For the entrepreneurs did not use all of the peasants assigned to their plants, and many of those they did employ worked for only limited periods during the year. In the eighteenth century as few as 25 percent of the assigned peasants, and in the mid-nineteenth century about 50 percent, are estimated to have worked either full or part time in the enterprises to which they were attached.[7]

In the plants of the Urals the usual work day for those employed full-time ran for eleven hours in winter and thirteen hours in summer. Night work was exceptional except in the smelters, where two shifts were used to keep the furnaces in continuous operation. Most full-time workers put in around 200 to 260 days a year, although in a few plants they were permitted to take off as much as one to two months during the summer to work in the fields. Women and children were widely employed. The full-time workers lived on small pieces of land

[5] Ibid., pp. 44-45, 81-82, 93-94.
[6] Semevskii, Krest'iane, II, 304-305.
[7] Portal, "Manufactures," p. 181; Pazhitnov, "K voprosu," pp. 238, 243. Another 24,000 were assigned to other branches of manufacturing.

near the plant, or rented lodgings for themselves, and sometimes they were housed in barracks at the factory. Others who were not required to spend all their time working in the plants were called upon periodically to work in extracting and transporting ore, limestone, and timber, and in transporting finished goods. The larger plants of the eighteenth century needed as many as one to three thousand carters alone, and still larger numbers for employment as timber cutters and charcoal burners. These tasks were often performed at certain fixed periods each year, so that the peasant usually knew when he was going to be needed by the plant owner and for how long.[8]

When assigned peasants first began to be used extensively their pay was set by agreements between their employers and themselves. Then in a ukase of 1724 Tsar Peter established uniform wage scales. At the outset these rates corresponded to the wages paid free hired labor for the same work, but soon a gap appeared. In 1743 peasants assigned to a plant in Olonets complained that their wages were less than half—in some instances just one third—of the pay received by hired workers, and according to official data of the 1760's the pay of assigned workers was sometimes one fifth to one tenth that of free employees. Yet the pay scale remained unchanged until 1769 when the government finally ordered it raised. The effects of these increases, however, were quickly cancelled out by the price rise that began in the seventies and that apparently was especially severe in the Urals.[9]

The natural resentment of the peasants who were compelled to perform forced labor was aggravated by the excessive demands of the factory owners. The enterprises that belonged to the state were run with military severity, and with little or no thought for the health and welfare of the workers. Conditions in privately-owned establishments were far worse. Contemporary accounts told of the extremes of exploitation and of the cruelties practiced in some of these plants. The Demidovs, greatest of the industrialists of the Urals, won an especially sinister reputation for themselves. On several occasions in the eighteenth century

[8] Tugan-Baranovskii, *Russkaia fabrika*, I, 113, 116-118; Portal, *L'Oural*, pp. 238-241; Semevskii, *Krest'iane*, II, 305-307.

[9] Portal, *L'Oural*, pp. 273-277, 322-323; Pavlenko, "O nekotorykh storonakh," pp. 388-389.

the news that they were going to take over a plant was enough to spark riots among the workers. Attempts by some of their employees in the early nineteenth century to present petitions to the tsar were punished by shooting the would-be petitioners, or by throwing them alive into a blast furnace.[10]

One of the most onerous of the demands made upon peasants assigned to plants in the Urals was to require them to journey many miles to perform their work obligation. The thin settlement of the region compelled the manufacturers to draw the large contingents they needed for short-term employment from distant places, and with their lack of concern about the peasants' welfare they made little or no effort to minimize the inconveniences. Instances in which the assigned workers had to travel several hundred versts were apparently not uncommon, and in at least one case the peasants lived nearly 800 versts from their work site. Sometimes these trips had to be made several times a year, and since travel was slow that meant the peasants spent much time, and until 1769 all of it at their own expense, just in going to and coming back from their jobs. A report made to Catherine II in 1762 by a specially appointed investigator told of peasants who three times each year had to come to plants that lay 400 versts from their homes to work for a total of 120 days. Those who travelled on foot for want of horses averaged 25 versts a day and so spent 96 days a year on these journeys.[11]

The exactions made of the assigned peasants, and the callous and often brutal treatment accorded them by their employers, provoked answers in kind from the workers. Unrest and violence became nearly endemic. By the middle decades of the eighteenth century outbreaks and refusals to work became so serious that the employers had to call in armed forces to restore order. Fierce reprisals were taken against the rioters and strikers, but no effort was made to improve conditions, and the disorders continued. When Emilian Pugachev raised the banner of revolt in 1773 the industrial peasants of the Urals rushed to serve under it. The bloody lesson taught by this great *jacquerie* awakened the

[10] Portal, *L'Oural*, pp. 58, 73-74; Kulischer, "Die kapitalistischen Unternehmer," p. 371.

[11] Semevskii, *Krest'iane*, II, xix, xxi-xxii; Portal *L'Oural*, p. 271. The new pay scale introduced in 1769 provided for the peasant to be paid 3 kopecks for each day he spent in traveling between his home village and the work site.

central government to the need for reform in the plants. Between 1779 and 1781 it ordered improvements in working conditions, placed limitations on the factory owners' power to punish their workers, and ordered wages to be increased so that they were double what they had been before 1769. An increase of two rubles in the annual payment the peasants had to make to the state wiped out much of the benefit of the pay raises, but the condition of the assigned workers seemed to have been considerably better than it had been before the Pugachev rising. The workers appeared contented. It seemed as if labor peace had come at last to the Urals.[12]

The calm lasted twenty years. Then at the century's very end new troubles flared up and lasted for a decade. The government finally recognized that strife was inevitable under the existing system. Possibly, too, the fact that the industry's expansion had begun to slow down, so that it no longer needed big labor drafts to meet its needs, aided in persuading the authorities that changes had to be made. In any event, a decree of 15 March 1807 freed all but 8 percent of the peasants who had been subject to call for seasonal or part-time work in the plants of the Urals from this obligation. Those who remained assigned, totalling 17,850 workers, were considered necessary for the continued operations of the industry. They were in addition to the 100,000 or so who in earlier years had been permanently attached to the plants as full-time workers.[13]

Early in the nineteenth century plants owned by merchants to which peasants had been assigned, along with all other manufacturing establishments that received aids and subsidies from the government, were given the name of "possessional" factories, and the peasants assigned to them were now called "possessional" peasants. The legal position of these people was defined in the law as being a "special type of limited serf status."[14] The factory owner could not move them from the plant to which the government had assigned them; he had to pay them wages; he could not furlough or dismiss them; widows and girls among them could marry without first getting his permission and did not have to pay him a fee; and the peasants had the right to complain to

[12] Portal, *L'Oural*, pp. 348-349, 368; Semevskii, *Krest'iane*, II, xxviii-xxix.
[13] Portal, *L'Oural*, p. 391.   [14] *SZ*, 1857, IX, sect. 996, par. 1.

governmental authorities if they felt their employer treated them unfairly. On the other hand, the law gave the factory owner the right to use corporal punishment to maintain order and discipline, and allowed him to exile assigned peasants to Siberia, though he had to get governmental approval for this. The state reserved for itself a general supervisory function over all possessional factories, could intervene at any time in a plant and if conditions warranted take it over, and could release the peasants from their assignment if they were unduly exploited or were used for work not connected with the plant's operations. In practice, however, officialdom made little effort to defend the rights of the possessional peasants, or to restrict the demands of the factory owners.[15]

Industries other than plants in the Urals that used assigned peasants also experienced periodic labor upheavals. Data on these disturbances in 23 possessional textile plants during the first half of the nineteenth century show that low wages were the most frequent cause of discontent. In many cases free hired hands received twice as much as assigned workers. The latter's wages were further reduced by deductions made on one pretext or other by their employers, and by required patronage of the company store. Other causes of discontent included cruel treatment, long hours—in one mill ten year old children worked fourteen to seventeen hours a day, compulsory work in the home and fields of the factory owner, and the practice followed by some employers of turning over possessional peasants to the army as substitutes for their own serfs.[16]

The labor problem was just one of the disadvantages of the possessional factory system. Another handicap was that the state, in return for the assistance it gave these enterprises, demanded the right to supervise all their operations, including the decision of what and how much the factory should produce. Nor, as already mentioned, would the state allow the plant owners to lay off full-time workers in slack seasons or to discharge them. These controls made it difficult for the factory management to adjust

[15] Tugan-Baranovskii, *Russkaia fabrika*, I, 114-115; Semevskii, *Krest'ianskii vopros*, I, ii-iii.
[16] Tugan-Baranovskii, *Geschichte*, I, 159-161. This material was not published in the original Russian edition of Tugan-Baranovskii's book; doubtless it had been deleted by the censors.

output to market conditions, to turn out new or improved products, or to introduce money-saving innovations. The owners of other factories, unhampered by this kind of bureaucratic interference, could outproduce and undersell competing possessional factories.

By the early nineteenth century these inefficiencies had become widely recognized, and beginning in 1816 the government issued a series of decrees that abolished some of the more stringent controls. Finally, a law of 18 June 1840 allowed the owners of possessional factories to release their assigned peasants and take over full, unregulated control of their plants. Half or more of these manufacturers are believed to have taken advantage of this legislation and turned to the use of nothing but hired workers. Only the plant owners of the Urals preferred to retain the old system.[17]

The widespread and persistent discontent of the assigned laborers make it evident that they were unhappy with their employment. Yet studies made by Frédéric Le Play, the French mining engineer and sociologist, of two families of assigned peasants in the Urals, indicate that some of these people were not at all badly off in comparison with free workers in other European lands. Le Play, who pioneered in family budget studies, collected his data firsthand and claimed that he chose representative families. It should be pointed out, though, that Le Play believed that an industrial system in which the workers lived on the land and drew part of their incomes from their own independent enterprise was preferable to the Western mode of industrialization, in which the workers became urban proletarians entirely dependent upon their factory wages. He analyzed the family budget in 1844 of an ironsmith with a wife and five children, and a carpenter with a wife and four children who ran a small grain business on the side. Both men were assigned to plants in the Urals. The cash value of the annual incomes of the two families, including revenues in kind, computed in francs, were 1,165.77 francs and 815.62 francs, respectively. The cash value of the annual income of free workers in other lands engaged in similar occupations were, with one exception, higher.

[17] Tugan-Baranovskii, *Russkaia fabrika*, I, 104-162; Strumilin, "Promyshlennyi perevorot," p. 47.

The annual family income of a Swedish ironsmith with a wife and four children was 1,624.21 francs in 1845; of an English ironworker, also with a wife and four children, 2,008.85 francs in 1850; and of a Parisian carpenter with a wife and two children, 2,103.88 francs in 1856. The annual family income of a Slovak gold smelter with a wife and two children was 975.80 francs in 1846, more than the Urals carpenter but less than the ironsmith.[18] But the data on food consumption of these families showed that, despite their smaller money incomes, the two Russian households ate better than any of the others save the Swedish one, while the families of the English and French workers, though they had the highest incomes, were the worst fed.

Annual Per Capita Food Consumption of Worker
Households (in kgs)[19]

HOUSEHOLD OF

	Urals Ironsmith (1844)	Urals Carpenter (1844)	Swedish Ironsmith (1845)	English Iron Smelter (1850)	Slovak Gold Smelter (1846)	French Carpenter (1856)
reals	289.6	212.7	282.9	107.6	183.9	117.6
ts	3.14	4.6	14.6	8.4	8.0	3.6
lk	314.3	263.6	257.1	89.1	165.0	40.0
eese	–	–	–	3.4	1.4	1.8
gs	6.14	2.9	4.3	.7	2.9	1.4
at & Fish	40.7	37.3	60.0	34.3	27.3	27.6
getables d Fruits	109.1	136.4	105.3	53.3	138.6	59.7
eetening & ndiments	8.0	8.3	32.1	24.4	5.0	6.5
mented verages	2.3	141.4	166.8	150.6	18.9	13.0

[18] Le Play, *Les ouvriers européens*, II, 101, 116-119, 144, 156-159; III, 4, 14-17, 401, 414-417; IV, 4, 16-19; V, 425, 444-447. Cf. Baster, "Some Early Family Budget Studies," pp. 468-480.

[19] Le Play, *Les ouvriers européens*, II, 120-121, 160-161; III, 18-19, 416-417; IV, 20-21; V, 448-449.
Le Play gave figures only for family consumption. I computed the per capita consumption by dividing Le Play's figure by the number of persons in each household.

The assigned state peasants made up only part of the empire's compulsory factory labor force. Serfs, too, were compelled by their owners to work in industry. This use of bondsmen was not new, but it did not become important until the second half of the eighteenth century when members of the nobility began to participate more actively in manufacturing. By 1825 government data on the size of the labor force in seven branches of factory production showed that plants owned by nobles and manned by serfs, had 31.7 percent (66,275) of all the workers in these particular industries.[20]

The government reports, however, covered only a part of the manufacturing establishments operated by members of the nobility, and so gave an incomplete picture of the extent to which serfs were employed in seignioral factories. Distilleries, beet sugar mills, potash and saltpetre works, and other "agricultural industries" were almost entirely owned by members of the nobility and were staffed predominantly by serfs doing compulsory labor. In the mid-nineteenth century an estimated 170,000 bondsmen worked in these enterprises. Though most of the plants were seasonal operations, the value of their total output made agricultural industry one of the most important sectors of the empire's factory production.[21]

In some of the seignioral factories the work of the serfs counted as their barshchina, and so was unpaid. In others they received wages in cash, or in a combination of cash and kind. As could be expected, their pay was considerably lower than that received by hired workers. The serfs sometimes used the so-called "brother-for-brother" system by which the obligation to work in the lord's factory was rotated among members of the village. In a number of places seigniors converted field or domestic serfs into full-time factory workers entirely divorced from the land, though on occasions they were allotted small pieces of land near the plant, and some seigniors allowed their

[20] Rashin, *Formirovanie*, pp. 63-64. The seven branches of factory production were woolens, iron and steel, glass and crystal, writing paper, linen, potash, and silk.

[21] Pazhitnov, "K voprosu," pp. 239-243.

full-time serf employees to take off two months a year for haying and harvesting. Hired laborers were used in a number of plants in supervisory capacities, or during rush seasons when the seignior did not have enough serfs available to meet his labor needs of the moment.[22]

The work day in these factories was long, and the laborers were sometimes badly treated. The serfs dreaded having to work in them. According to a writer of the 1840's, they said, " 'There is a factory in that village' in such a way as if they really meant, 'The plague has broken out in that village.' "[23] The government followed its traditional policy of minimal intervention between master and serf and did nothing to improve working conditions. In 1843 the throne did instruct the marshals of the nobility of each province to see to it that the serfowners of their guberniias should exercise restraint in converting agricultural serfs into factory hands; that the general rule of not demanding more than three days of barshchina a week and not requiring work on Sundays and holidays should be observed in seignioral factories, or the factory serfs should be split into two shifts, each of which would work for two full weeks of the month; that workers who did not farm should be paid wages; and that seigniors should be mindful of the welfare of their serf factory hands. These were only recommendations, however, and not commands of the tsar. The marshals were to bring them to the attention of the serf-owners of their provinces, but were not to enforce them.[24]

Some lords who did not own factories, or had more serfs than they could use profitably in their own operations, rented out their peasants to manufacturers or to labor contractors. This seems to have been a particularly common practice in the populous and infertile western provinces of White Russia. Contractors there leased serfs from their masters and then drove them under close guard, like herds of cattle, to the Central Industrial zone where they rented them out to factory owners. Sometimes the leasing of serfs cloaked their sale to persons of classes not allowed by law to own bondsmen. To stop this decep-

[22] Tugan-Baranovskii, *Russkaia fabrika*, I, 107-110; Rashin, *Formirovanie*, p. 68; Pazhitnov, "K voprosu," pp. 239-240; Haxthausen, *Studien*, II, 528.

[23] Turgenev, *La Russie*, II, 143-144.

[24] Tugan-Baranovskii, *Russkaia fabrika*, I, 112.

tion the government in the mid-1820's forbad the practice, but the legislation was so worded that it proved easy to evade it.[25]

In light of the way in which they were recruited, the reported demoralization and inefficiency of the leased peasants seem entirely understandable. Yet manufacturers continued to rent them because they needed workers, and because these peasants cost them so little. But they were scarcely getting a bargain, at least according to an economist who wrote in the forties as follows:[26] "The worst kind of workers are the peasants who are rented out by seigniors to the factories and plants of others. . . . It is useless to expect any diligence or order from them; the factory owner is menaced at every instant by workers running away, cheating, playing knavish tricks. We have heard of these workers, upon whom neither warnings nor threats have any effect, often fleeing the plant in a body, abandoning their work at the most costly moment."

The right to own serfs had, for all intent and purposes, become an exclusive privilege of the nobility in the seventeenth century, and during the eighteenth century the general direction of government policy was toward strengthening this monopoly. But the state's desire to promote industrial development came into conflict with this policy when, as mentioned earlier, Peter in the decree of 18 January 1721 gave merchant industrialists the right to buy serfs to work in their plants. The law ordered that these industrial serfs could not be separated from the plant nor used for any other work. The tsar's intent, of course, was to provide the new factories with a cheap and plentiful labor supply. In a subsequent chapter the fate of this legislation is discussed in some detail, so that it suffices here to mention that in later years the merchants' right to buy serfs was limited, and then abolished. During the decades in which bourgeois factory owners could purchase people for their factories, however, they made very limited use of the privilege.[27] They found

25 *Ibid.*, p. 95; Schulze-Gaevernitz, *Volkswirtschaftlichen Studien*, p. 22.

26 A. Butovskii quoted in Tugan-Baranovskii, *Russkaia fabrika*, I, 105-106.

27 Cf. Zlotnikov, "K voprosu," pp. 60-62 and studies of other Soviet scholars summarized in Portal, "Manufactures," pt. 2, pp. 31-38. These findings controvert the opinion of Tugan-Baranovskii (*Russkaia fabrika*, I, 21-22) that thanks to the decree of 18 January 1721 the factory labor force shifted rapidly from predominantly hired labor to predominantly forced labor.

that they could recruit hired labor, and apparently they preferred it to forced labor. They discovered that it was uneconomical to buy a serf village, for it might not always include workers with the skills they needed for their plants, and more important, the village always had unemployables among its members—the young, the old, the sick, and the infirm. A report of 1767 showed that out of 21,286 serfs belonging to 127 factories only 8,332 (39 percent) actually worked in the plants.[28] Finally, much of the purchase price of a village went for land and buildings, none of which contributed to the output of the factory. It was obviously more advantageous for the manufacturer to employ wage workers than to tie up his capital in this manner.

III

Hired workers made up the third group in the factory labor force. At the outset most of them had been city dwellers, runaway serfs, and people who had not yet been attached to any class. But as the demand for labor grew, the factory owners turned increasingly to the peasantry to find workers. They were able to hire the hands they needed because more and more serfs were able to get permission from their seigniors, or from government officials if they were state peasants, to leave their villages to take employment. Many of these rustics, as was pointed out in the preceding chapter, found work in trade and transportation, but a number of them took factory jobs. They worked for wages, they took employment when and where they wished, and they quit or changed jobs at their own initiative. So appeared one of the most curious of the anomalies of Russian history; people who were at one and the same time serfs or state peasants, and free industrial workers.

The greatest number of these workers came from the Center and Northwest, where agriculture could not meet the competition of the black earth. Seigniors there gave ready consent to their serfs to go off and work elsewhere because it increased the serfs' incomes, and thereby enabled the seigniors to charge higher obroks than they could if their serfs depended upon agri-

---

[28] Rashin, *Formirovanie*, p. 19.

culture alone. It also saved owners of overcrowded properties the expense of buying more land to provide their serfs with holdings large enough to support themselves. Similarly, the government recognized the advantages of non-agricultural work for state peasants in the less fertile and more crowded provinces, and was also generous in granting permission to these people to leave their villages for work.

The search for jobs carried peasants into every kind of employment and to the fartherest corners of the empire—in 1849 over 2,000 of them, mostly from Nizhnii Novgorod guberniia, were working in gold mines in Eastern Siberia.[29] They were welcomed by employers, not only because they provided the additional labor needed for expansion, but also because they were better workers than were the peasants who were assigned to the factories, or the rabble who floated from job to job.[30]

The supply of these hired workers was restricted, however, by the extent to which their masters were willing to give them permission to leave their villages; by the degree to which the peasants preferred (or were compelled by their lords or their communes) to till their holdings during the growing season; and by the increase in the number of peasants who engaged in *kustar* production. As a result of these limitations peasants who sought jobs in the factories offered their services on a "seller's market" and commanded correspondingly high wages. Baron Haxthausen, travelling in Russia in the 1840's, was astonished by the factory pay scale. He was certain that it was much higher than in his native Germany, and in fact he believed that "there is no country where workers' wages are relatively and on the average as high as they are in Russia." Employers told him they had to pay particularly high wages in summer to keep their workers from returning to their villages. The average increase was about one-third above the winter scale, and some claimed they had to double winter wages to hold their employees.[31]

Because of the fragmentary and imprecise nature of the official statistical data, the size of the total factory labor force,

[29] *Ibid.*, pp. 80-81.
[30] Tugan-Baranovskii, *Russkaia fabrika*, I, 92; Haxthausen, *Studien*, I, 116.
[31] Tugan-Baranovskii, *Russkaia fabrika*, I, 180-204; Haxthausen, *Studien*, I, 13, 170, 199.

and the proportions in it of forced and free hired labor, can only be estimated. The information is especially scanty for the first decades of the eighteenth century, though the available evidence makes it reasonably certain that forced labor, chiefly assigned peasants, became more numerous than hired workers.[32] The more plentiful material for the second half of the eighteenth and first half of the nineteenth centuries show that the proportion of hired workers increased steadily. Confusion has arisen, however, about the size of the total labor force and the amount of increase in hired workers. Earlier historians, relying entirely upon government reports, arrived at the following estimates.[33]

YEAR	NO. OF WORKERS	HIRED WORKERS	FORCED WORKERS
1770	55,300	17,700 (32 percent)	37,600 (68 percent)
1804	95,202	45,625 (48 percent)	49,577 (52 percent)
1825	210,568	114,515 (54 percent)	96,053 (46 percent)
1860	565,100	491,637 (87 percent)	73,463 (13 percent)

These estimates led to the long-maintained conclusion that forced workers had become an unimportant part of the factory labor force well before the emancipation.[34]

The official reports on which these calculations were based, however, omitted most or all of the mining, metallurgical, and agricultural industries, and even left out some state enterprises. These were precisely the branches of production in which forced labor remained predominant down to 1861. The earlier estimates were therefore strongly weighted in favor of hired labor. More recent studies have tried to eliminate this bias by using available information for all factory industry. Estimates resulting from their findings are:[35]

[32] Cf. Bak, "K voprosu," pp. 71-72.

[33] Estimates for 1770 and 1860 from Liashchenko, *History*, p. 337; for 1804 and 1825 from Tugan-Baranovskii, *Russkaia fabrika*, I, 85, 89.

[34] This interpretation was first developed by Tugan-Baranovskii, *Russkaia fabrika*, I, 90-91, 110-111, 125-126.

[35] Estimates for 1767 from Meshalin, *Tekstil'naia promyshlennost*, p. 45; for 1804 and 1825 from Zlotnikov, "Ot manufaktury," p. 39; for 1860 from Pazhitnov, "K voprosu," pp. 243-244.

YEAR	NO. OF WORKERS	HIRED WORKERS	FORCED WORKERS
1767	199,300	18,700 (9 percent)	180,600 (91 percent)
1804	224,882	61,600 (27 percent)	163,282 (73 percent)
1825	340,568	114,515 (34 percent)	226,053 (66 percent)
1860	862,000	479,000 (56 percent)	383,000 (44 percent)

These estimates, based as they are on a more complete analysis of the source materials, not only show that the factory labor force was much larger than hitherto supposed. They also demand serious qualifications of the older view about the progressive decline in the importance of forced labor. The proportion of forced labor in the total factory labor force did indeed fall off. Even in those branches of production where it remained predominant until 1861 the trend toward hired labor evidenced itself. In mining and metallurgy, for example, less than 1 percent of the labor force in the 1760's were hired workers; just before the emancipation estimates of the proportion of hired workers range from 19 to 30 percent.[36] In some industries hired labor came to be used almost exclusively, as in cotton factories where by 1825 95 percent of the employees were hired workers.[37] Similarly, forced labor just about disappeared in plants in and around large cities; in 1814 an estimated 98 percent of the workers in factories in Moscow and its environs were free hired employees.[38] Nonetheless, in 1860 forced laborers still made up 44 percent of the industrial labor force. Their absolute number had grown throughout the preceding decades; between 1825 and 1860 it went up by 70 percent (226,100 to 383,000). This rise is overshadowed by the more than four-fold increase (320 percent) in free hired workers in these same years. But the fact of the sizable expansion in the use of forced labor in industry belies the opinion that it was on the way out. Actually the employment of forced labor was growing, but at a much slower rate than that of free hired labor.

[36] Meshalin, *Tekstil'naia promyshlennost*, p. 45; Pazhitnov, "K voprosu," p. 238; Rashin, *Formirovanie*, p. 92.

[37] Tugan-Baranovskii, *Russkaia fabrika*, I, 89.

[38] Rozhkova, "Promyshlennost," pp. 89-90.

The reputed decline in the use of forced labor was attributed by earlier writers to the inefficiency of the forced workers in comparison with hired hands, and the difficulties in training them in new techniques. Since forced labor made up the greatest part of the work force in factories owned by nobles, the belief that it was on the way out led to the opinion that the importance of the nobility in industrial enterprise also declined in the last decades of serfdom.[39] This view not only fails to take into account the increase in the number of forced workers, but also disregards the remarkable development of agricultural industry in the years before the emancipation. Nobles, using serf labor, were the innovating entrepreneurs in beet sugar manufacture and in distilling, and were responsible for the introduction of technical improvements in these industries, both of which were among the most important branches of Russian factory production.

[39] Tugan-Baranovskii, *Russkaia fabrika*, I, 90-91; Kornilov, "Gubernskie komitety," pp. 125-126; Schulze-Gaevernitz, "Die Moskau-Wladimirische Baum-wollindustrie," p. 765; Kulischer, "Die kapitalistischen Unternehmer," p. 316.

17

AGRICULTURE

THOUGH TRADE and industry made many advances in the era from Peter I to Alexander II, as the two preceding chapters have shown, they presented no challenge as yet to the predominance of agriculture. On the eve of the emancipation less than 8 percent of the empire's population of 74 millions lived in cities, and considerably less than a million worked in factory industry. Nearly all the rest drew their living from the land. Agriculture was by far the chief industry of the country. Russia's economy was almost entirely dependent upon it.

Yet, during the century and a half when so many innovations were introduced into other sectors of economic life, farming remained all but unchanged from what it had been for centuries. Its backward state was recognized and freely commented upon by many observers among the landowners and bureaucrats of the era. In the instruction manuals drawn up by the great proprietors of the first half of the eighteenth century for the guidance of their estate managers, concern was often expressed about small yields, soil exhaustion, and the inefficient methods of cultivation used by the peasants.[1] Around the middle of the century a number of writers, including some of the most knowledgeable men of that time, discussed the shortcomings of Russian agriculture.[2] At meetings of the Free Economic Society, established in 1765 by a group of important aristocrats, in the pages of the Society's journal that began to appear in 1766, and in the essays submitted in the prize competitions that it conducted, frequent expression was given to the dissatisfaction of landlords and government officials with the existing conditions of agricultural production. Other journals, too, that began to appear around this time, published articles on this theme.[3] In the nineteenth century the chorus swelled, with men like

[1] Alefirenko, "Russkaia obshchestvennaia mysl," pp. 528-529.
[2] Bak, "Vozniknovenie," pp. 53-62.
[3] Sivkov, "Voprosy sel'skogo khoziaistva," pp. 553-560.

A. A. Shakhmatov, one of Russia's leading agriculturists, pointing out to his fellow landlords that the welfare of the empire depended upon the condition of its agriculture, and Count P. D. Kiselev, chief of the Ministry of State Domain, in reports to the tsar calling the sovereign's attention to the lagging economic development out on the land.[4]

There were a number of reasons, many if not all of them mentioned by contemporary observers and critics, that explained this backwardness. Surely one of the most important was the niggardliness of nature herself. The soils of the forest zone north of the River Oka, where until the nineteenth century most of Russia's people lived, were relatively infertile and much of the region was covered by great bogs. In the open steppes that lay to the south the soil was far more fertile, for this was the land of the chernozem—the black earth. But the rigors of Russia's continental climate reduced the growing season in even these more favored zones, and inadequate rainfall nearly everywhere held back crop yields.

These disadvantages of soil and climate were aggravated by the attitude of the people who owned the land and the techniques of those who worked it. Most Russians, whether lords or peasants, seemed content with the traditional pattern of agricultural exploitation. The only interest most landowners had in their properties was in the revenues in cash and kind they drew from them. Many of them spent most of their lives in government service and so did not have the time to look after their properties even if they had been so inclined. Others preferred city life to their country seats, and those who did live on the land usually made no effort to introduce improvements. Their neglect of their properties led to their own impoverishment, to misery and low morale among their peasants, and to the retardation of agriculture. The inefficiency of their operations and their own improvidence brought them into serious economic difficulties. The government tried to come to their aid by establishing special banks for them, but instead of using the money they borrowed to improve their properties and so increase their incomes, they spent it on consumption goods. The net result of

4 Cf. Kusheva, "Proekt," p. 60; *SIRO*, xcviii (1896), 489-490.

the attempts made by the state to aid them was to increase their indebtedness to incredible proportions (v. pp. 379-385) without advancing agriculture.

The techniques of tillage employed by the peasants, whether serfs on privately owned land or the half-free peasants who lived on state land, were virtually unchanged from what they had been in the middle ages. Inadequate fertilizing or none at all, primitive tools, work animals of poor quality, and all the other accoutrements of obsolescent farming, combined to hold back productivity. The methods of field management that were used offered especially serious obstacles to agricultural improvement. In the three-field system, the most commonly used technique, the plowland of each peasant household (and usually the demesne land of the lord) was divided into strips scattered through the fields allotted to the village. Sometimes these strips lay at a considerable distance from the settlement so that the peasants lost much time in going to and from their work. The strips themselves were generally about ten to fourteen feet in width, so that cross plowing was not possible. Furthermore, a sizable amount of arable was lost to cultivation because it had to be used for boundaries between the strips and for the access roads and paths to the many individual parcels. Communal tillage was the rule, everyone being compelled to grow the same crops and perform the same farming operations at the same time, so that any individual initiative that might have led to innovations and improvements was stifled.[5]

The handicaps of the open-field system, and particularly its effects upon individual initiative, were found in all countries where this method of tillage was used. But in Russia its disadvantages were intensified by the practice of periodic redistribution of holdings that became widespread in the eighteenth and especially in the nineteenth centuries. The peasant was converted into the temporary occupant of the strips allotted him by his commune. He had little or no interest in increasing their fertility, because they might well be assigned to some other

[5] Baranovich, *Materialy*, pp. 237-239; Haxthausen, *Studien*, I, 157; II, 10; Buschen, "Die Freibauern," pp. 232-233 and note; Shchepetov, *Krepostnoe pravo*, p. 57; Druzhinin, *Gosudarstvennye krest'iane*, I, 325.

household at the next repartition. Land that needed improvement before it could be planted, and fields that gave only mediocre yields, often were left empty because no one was willing to expend the effort involved in reclaiming or improving them when the rewards of his labor would possibly go to some one else. Meadows frequently were divided anew each year just before haying, so no one bothered to drain or clear them. Consequently their productivity was much less than it might have been.[6]

Finally, the development of Russian agriculture was immeasurably retarded by the incredibly bad condition of the empire's communications system. Farm goods often could get to market only with much difficulty and expense and sometimes were unable to get there at all. The problems of reaching the market and the risk of surpluses piling up in the villages acted as a brake to any interest in improvements or in increasing output. Russian observers and foreign visitors alike stressed the need for more and better means of communication as the indispensable condition for agricultural progress.[7]

II

Low yields and frequent crop failures were the not unexpected results of these many shortcomings. Incomplete data show there were at least 34 partial or general crop failures in the eighteenth century, and contemporary statisticians of the early part of the nineteenth century estimated that there was one total crop failure and two partial ones out of every ten years. Information on yields collected between 1759 and 1786, though imprecise, indicated that the chief cereals (rye, oats, barley, wheat) gave three to five times the seed. Data collected for 1802 showed that the average yields in the black earth for winter grains was around 4.4 times the seed, and for spring cereals 3.3 to 1, while in the forest zone the comparable figures were 3.0

6 Köppen, *Statistische Reise*, pp. 122-123; Baranovich, *Materialy*, pp. 178, 239.
7 Haxthausen, *Die ländliche Verfassung*, p. 4; *idem*, *Studien*, II, 104; Count Kiselev to Tsar Nicholas I, *SIRO*, xcVIII (1896), 490; Jourdier, *Des forces*, pp. 36-37; Hommaire de Hell, *Les steppes*, I, 46-47; Kulischer, "Die Leibeigenschaft," 61.

and 2.4.[8] These averages, however, conceal wide fluctuations both within each of these two regions and between them. Farmers in the richest parts of the chernozem in some years got eightfold returns on winter grains and sixfold on spring cereals. In unusually good years rye and wheat were reported to have returned as much as fourteen and sixteen times the seed, and millet yields were even higher.[9]

Estimates made for the first half of the nineteenth century show that yields were just about the same as they had been in the preceding century, and indeed as far back as the sixteenth century and probably even earlier. The yields for European Russia averaged out at about 3½ to 1 for both winter and spring cereals.[10] Comparative data collected around the middle of the century revealed that Russian yields were lower than those of any other European nation. The average in Belgium and Holland was 14 hectolitres per hectare, in Saxony, Great Britain, Württemberg, and Baden it was 13.2 hectolitres, in Austria 10.3, France 9.3, Sweden 9.3, Prussia 9.1, Italy 9.0, Norway 7.6, Spain 6.2, Greece 6.1, and in Russia 6 hectolitres per hectare.[11]

Despite the fact that yield per unit remained the same, the total output of Russian agriculture climbed steadily during the eighteenth and nineteenth centuries. This, of course, was because of the great increase in the amount of land under cultivation. In the older regions of settlement north of the Oka just about all the land suitable for crops had been put into use by 1800. After that date the area of plowland there remained relatively stable. But the population kept on going up. As a result, the peasantry could no longer support itself from the land alone. Data for 1783-1784 for the province of Tver, directly northwest of Moscow, showed that the cash income from agriculture of the peasants covered only 40-50 percent of the money they needed to meet expenses.[12] A government survey made in Pskov in the 1830's revealed that over 70 percent of the peasant

[8] Liashchenko, "Krepostnoe sel'skoe khoziaistvo," pp. 116-117; *idem, Ocherki,* I, 120.

[9] Domontovich, *Materialy,* p. 183; Tegoborskii, *Etudes,* I, 39; Druzhinin, *Gosudarstvennye krest'iane,* I, 401, 409, 417.

[10] Storch, "Der Bauernstand," 1849, p. 86; Jourdier, *Des forces,* p. 145; Liashchenko, *History,* p. 324.

[11] *Ob'iasneniia,* p. 115.   [12] Bak, "K voprosy," p. 74.

families on state-owned land in that province did not have enough arable and cattle to meet their minimum requirements.[13] The only way these people and most of the other peasants who lived in the non-black earth provinces could make ends meet was to engage in cottage handicraft production, or to leave their villages to find work elsewhere in trade and industry.

In the black earth zone, however, where the land was fertile and in many places sparsely settled, there was a large expansion in the area of plowland. During the eighteenth century the center of agricultural production had completed the shift that had started in the previous century from the Muscovite center into the steppelands. By the turn of the century more than half of European Russia's sowed area lay in the black earth provinces, although the total area of these guberniias was only three-fifths that of the non-black earth provinces. During the nineteenth century production in the chernozem continued to grow. The spread of settled tillage into New Russia and along the middle and lower Volga accounted for most of this increase. At the end of the eighteenth century those frontier regions had been very thinly populated, and had been used primarily for cattle raising. During the next half-century a great wave of colonists moved into them from the center, so that by 1860 several of the provinces there had a population density as heavy as that of some guberniias in the older parts of the realm, and in a couple of provinces (Simbirsk and Saratov) it was considerably heavier.[14] At the outset of the nineteenth century the sowed area in New Russia was estimated to have been 800,000 desiatins, and in four Volga provinces 1,000,000 desiatins. In the 1860's these figures had risen to 6 million and 4.6 million desiatins, respectively.[15]

An estimated 96 percent of the arable in chernozem and non-chernozem alike was planted in cereals. In the eighteenth century rye was by far the single most important crop. Wheat was paramount in only a few regions, and in many places it trailed

[13] Druzhinin, *Gosudarstvennye krest'iane*, I, 385-387.
[14] Cf. Tsentral'nyi statisticheskii komitet, *Stat. tabl . . . za 1858 god*, pp. 158-174.
[15] Liashchenko, *Istoriia*, I, 519; *idem*, "Krepostnoe sel'skoe khoziaistvo," pp. 99, 106-107.

behind barley and oats in order of importance after rye. By the middle of the nineteenth century, however, rye remained the dominant crop only in the north and center down to 50-52 degrees of latitude. South of this line, wheat, and particularly spring wheat, had become the principal crop. In the rye-growing zone oats were the chief spring grain, taking up as much as three-fourths of all the arable devoted to spring cereals. Much less oats were grown in the southern provinces. Buckwheat and millet were other important spring grains, the latter being particularly popular in the black earth. In the southwest, and chiefly in Bessarabia (annexed by Russia in 1812), Indian corn was a major crop.[16]

Precise figures on the size of the grain harvests in the pre-1861 era are not available. In 1873, however, an official commission published the following estimates for European Russia:[17]

AVERAGE ANNUAL HARVEST
(millions of chetverts)

1800-1813	155.0
1834-1840	179.0
1840-1847	209.7
1857-1863	220.0

Because of the vast area devoted to cereals, Russia produced more grain per capita than did any other European land, even though the yield per unit of arable was the lowest in Europe. A mid-century estimate placed the empire's output at 9 hecto-litres per capita, Sweden next with 6.6 hectolitres per capita,

---

[16] Liashchenko, *History*, p. 324; *idem*, "Krepostnoe sel'skoe khoziaistvo," pp. 114-115; *Ob'iasneniia*, pp. 116-120.

[17] Khromov, *Ekonomicheskoe razvitie*, p. 19.

These figures are lower than other estimates made at various times during the preceding half century. Thus, Androssov in 1813 estimated the annual crop at 189 million chetverts; Arsen'ev in 1818 set it at 200 million chetverts (*ibid.*, pp. 18-19); Köppen, on the basis of admittedly incomplete data estimated it at 186 million chetverts in the mid-thirties (Köppen "Über den Kornbedarf," pp. 526-527). Tegoborskii's estimate was 260 million chetverts in the latter 1840's (Tegoborskii, *Etudes*, I, 205); and Vil'son of the Ministry of State Domain estimated 265 million chetverts for the early sixties (*Ob'iasneniia*, p. 112).

then France with 6.3, Prussia with 6.2, Austria 5.7, Great Britain 4.9, Belgium 4.7, and Italy 4.[18]

Both contemporary and later observers sometimes claimed that despite the low level of productivity Russia suffered from a chronic overproduction of grain during the first half of the nineteenth century. The inadequacy of the data made it impossible for these writers to calculate the amount of the surplus, but their estimates ran as high as 10 percent of the harvest. They claimed that this constant surplus was unmarketable and was extremely damaging to the economy, depressing prices, acting as a deterrent to the introduction of better farming methods, and contributing significantly in the creation of a "general crisis in serf agriculture" in the mid-nineteenth century. This widely-held view has been brought into serious question by a statistical analysis of the available information made by P. I. Popov in the 1920's. Popov argued that, far from suffering from chronic overproduction in the period from 1840 to 1860, Russia did not produce enough grain to meet the needs of her people. He pointed out that the estimates of grain production in these (and earlier) decades were based upon theoretical appraisals of the size of the average annual harvest. Actually, sharp fluctuations in output and partial crop failures, rather than a uniform output, were the rule. The surpluses produced in the good years did not represent over-production but were needed to meet the deficiencies of the bad years, and were carefully stored away for that purpose. These reserves, when they could be accumulated, were vitally important, for the shortcomings of the transportation system often made it prohibitively expensive to bring in foodstuffs.[19]

After cereals, flax and hemp were the most important crops. Flax was grown everywhere in Russia save in the extreme north, but by the mid-nineteenth century the chief regions of production were the Baltic, White Russian, and Central Industrial provinces, and along the shores of the Black and Azov Seas. Hemp culture centered in the provinces of Smolensk, Mogilev,

---

[18] *Ob'iasneniia*, p. 116. According to another computation, however, in 1851-1860 Denmark was first in per capita output with 43 bushels, Rumania second with 23, and Russia third with 20 bushels. Mulhall, *Dictionary of Statistics*, p. 7.

[19] Kritzman, Popov, Iakovlev, *Sel'skoe khoziaistvo*, pp. 1-3, 5-15.

Chernigov, and in the Central Agricultural zone. These plants had been among the chief products of Russian agriculture for centuries, their fiber and their oil-yielding seeds being of prime importance in meeting the domestic demand for textiles and fats. They had also long been major items in Russia's export list; up to the mid-1840's the value of hemp and flax exports exceeded that of grain.[20]

Little attention was paid to the commercial production of vegetables save around large cities, where the peasants raised truck for sale in the nearby urban market. Peas, beans, and lentils were sometimes planted in the spring field in lieu of a grain, and peasants grew large quantities of cucumbers and cabbages in garden plots. An Englishman who traveled in northern Russia around 1790 wrote that in summer nearly every peasant he saw had "a bit of black bread in one hand, and a cucumber in the other." Cucumbers and cabbages had the advantage of being able to be preserved in palatable form as pickles and sauerkraut, for which delicacies the Russians had a well-developed taste.[21]

Potatoes were an unimportant crop until the middle of the nineteenth century. In the eighteenth century they had been all but unknown except among the German colonists in the steppe, who had brought the plant with them when they migrated from their homeland in the latter half of the century.[22] When Baron von Haxthausen visited some of these colonies in 1843 he thought he was back home in his native Germany. "The design of the villages and all of the buildings," he enthused, "the gardens, their layout, the plants, the vegetables, and above everything else the potatoes, all is German."[23] The plant was also reported to have been grown in the latter eighteenth century in the far north in the province of Archangel, where not much else could be raised with any success. The chief barrier that stood in the way of its spread in Russia, as in other lands, was the prejudice of the peasants. With an obstinacy and unreason-

[20] *Ob'iasneniia*, pp. 222-228, 261-263; Khromov, *Ekonomicheskoe razvitie*, p. 97.
[21] Swinton, *Travels*, pp. 442-445; Tegoborskii, *Etudes*, II, 98; *Ob'iasneniia*, p. 120.
[22] Pallas, *Voyages*, VII, 304.
[23] Haxthausen, *Studien*, II, 172.

ableness that are supposedly traditional characteristics of their station, they resisted efforts of the government and of improving landlords to introduce potatoes, even when there was famine and the peasants were actually starving.[24] The government had evinced an interest in promoting potato culture as early as 1765,[25] but did not engage in a sustained effort until the serious crop failures of 1839 and 1840. Then the Ministry of State Domain, only recently established to administer the vast lands owned by the government, initiated a "crash program" that combined compulsion and encouragement. The Ministry ordered potatoes planted on the common lands of all state-owned properties with the seed provided by the state. It published instruction manuals on the culture, storage, and uses of the plant for such products as starch and syrup, and offered medals and cash awards to outstanding producers. In 1843 the Ministry announced that commons did not have to be planted with potatoes in those villages where the peasants produced one-eight of a chetvert per adult male on their own holdings, and in 1844 the award of prizes was discontinued save in certain southern and eastern provinces where little progress had thus far been made in potato cultivation.[26]

These efforts apparently had a remarkable effect not only among the peasants on state land, but also among the serfs who lived on privately-owned estates. A report of the Ministry of State Domain to the tsar in 1850 estimated that in 1837 a million chetverts of potatoes had been sowed with over a third of this amount planted by state peasants; in 1850 5.8 million chetverts were sowed, of which only 1.6 million had been planted by state peasants.[27] Other contemporary reports confirm the introduction and large increase in potato production during the forties and fifties.[28] By the early 1860's an estimated 6.4 million chetverts were sowed. The chief producing areas were the Baltic

---

[24] Tooke, *View*, III, 274-275; Tegoborskii, *Etudes*, II, 104.

[25] Cf. *PSZ*, XVIII, no. 12406, 31 May 1765.

[26] Tegoborskii, *Etudes*, II, 105; *Mittheilungen*, 1844, 261-263.

[27] *SIRO*, XCVIII (1896), 492.

[28] Mikhalevich, *Materialy*, p. 199; Poprotskii, *Materialy*, pp. 459-460; Krzhivo-blotskii, *Materialy*, pp. 286, 303; Haxthausen, *Studien*, I, 159; cf. Druzhinin, *Gosu-darstvennye krest'iane*, I, 381; Sivkov, *Ocherki*, pp. 24-25.

and Western provinces. Only small amounts were grown in the eastern half of European Russia and in New Russia.[29]

The empire did not escape the potato disease of the latter 1840's, but it seems to have been much less virulent there than in the lands of Central and Western Europe. The blight first appeared in the Baltic provinces and in the succeeding two years spread north and east into Russia proper. Yields and total production did not fall off seriously, however.[30]

Sugar beets were another innovation of the first half of the nineteenth century, but the area given over to them was small.[31] Forage crops were of very little importance, although some efforts began to be made in the nineteenth century by enterprising landlords to introduce these grasses.[32]

III

Everywhere in Russia the crops grew in open, unfenced fields that sprawled across the vast plains as far as the eye could see, overwhelming the observer with the monotony of their sameness. A French visitor in the 1870's wrote:[33] "The fields here have none of the life and variety that they often have in other lands. . . . There is hardly any of the juxtaposition of different crops that give so much animation to our Western countryside. It's as if everything is the same field stretching out to infinity, broken only now and then by vast fallows. Not a hamlet, not a house, not an isolated homestead. On the steppe as in the forest the Russian seems afraid to find himself alone in the immensity of his environment. Communal property . . . augments the default of nature; it deprives the Russian of those enclosures, of those capriciously shaped hedges, which are much of the charm of the villages of England and Normandy. Instead there is the mournful flatness, the dull boredom of the impersonal and collectivized countryside where the fields lie undivided in long, equal, and symmetrical strips."

The three-field system remained the dominant method of cultivation in the old regions of settlement as it had been for

[29] *Ob'iasneniia*, pp. 112, 124.
[30] *Mittheilungen*, 1847, 397-406; Tegoborskii, *Etudes*, II, 108.
[31] Tegoborskii, *Etudes*, I, 215; *Ob'iasneniia*, pp. 293ff.
[32] Tegoborskii, *Etudes*, II, 1-2.   [33] Leroy-Beaulieu, *L'empire*, I, 160.

centuries. But in the great steppes that reached to the south and east, field grass husbandry was in general use until the end of the eighteenth century. This wasteful technique, in which a field was cropped continuously for several harvests and then left untilled for as much as seven years or more before being worked again, was possible so long as these regions were thinly populated. As they filled up, field grass husbandry gave way steadily to the less wasteful—albeit still inefficient—three-field system. Often during the period of transition the two methods would be in simultaneous use on a single property. By the 1860's field grass husbandry remained predominant only in some of the steppe frontiers where population was still sparse and land still plentiful. Elsewhere the three-field system prevailed.[34]

In the forested, thinly populated, and infertile northern provinces of Archangel, Olonets, and Vologda, and to a lesser extent in the neighboring provinces of Novgorod, Kostroma, Viatka, and Perm, primitive slash-burn tillage was frequently employed. The peasants in these regions drew their livings primarily from such pursuits as lumbering, fishing, and hunting and trapping, but they often took advantage of the short growing season to raise a crop in a forest clearing. They grew cereals and flax mainly, and the ash-enriched soil reportedly gave good and sometimes spectacular yields. The field was used continuously for from two to eight years, depending upon its fertility. When it was exhausted it was allowed to go back to forest and other burned-out patches that had been prepared beforehand were sown.[35]

Besides these three chief methods of cultivation, a number of other tillage systems, usually variations of the three field system, were employed locally and on a relatively small scale. Rotations designed to restore fertility by planting a crop rather than by fallowing were scarcely used at all. The technique had been introduced into the empire in the late eighteenth century, and a few progressive landlords tried it out on their estates.

[34] *Ob'iasneniia*, pp. 52-53, 56; Red. Kom., *Pervoe izdanie*, xiv, 9-10; Liashchenko, "Krepostnoe sel'skoe khoziaistvo," p. 109, Bak, "K voprosu," p. 73; Haxthausen, *Studien*, ii, 15, 164.

[35] Tooke, *View*, iii, 248-249; *Ob'iasneniia*, p. 49; Wallace, *Russia*, pp. 114-115.

But the apathy of most proprietors to agricultural improvement, and the resistance to change of the tradition-bound peasantry, operated against its general adoption. It caught on only in the Baltic provinces, where from the 1830's it came into wide use. By the middle of the century it had begun to spread from these provinces into the neighboring Lithuanian provinces of Kovno, Vilna, and Grodno.[36]

Manuring had long been a standard practice in the non-black earth center. But with the existing level of cultivation, an insufficient amount of dung was available because not enough forage was raised to support the necessary amount of cattle. Contemporary agriculturists held that ideally one third of the arable should be manured each year, and that one desiatin of meadow for each desiatin of plowland was required to produce appropriate amounts of fertilizer. Data from the mid-nineteenth century show that in the central non-black earth provinces the ratio was less than one fourth of a desiatin of meadow to one desiatin of arable. The peasants tried to stretch out the available manure by mixing it with straw. Other restorative materials such as marl, chalk, and pond mud seem to have been applied only rarely. An additional barrier to proper fertilizing, apart from the inadequacy of the supply, was the already mentioned disinclination of the peasant to expend time and effort in improving land that would go to someone else at the next communal repartition.

In the black earth, the fields, with rare exception, were never manured. In fact, many there seem to have believed that fertilizing was harmful to the soil. The dung in these treeless regions, when it was not thrown away, was dried into bricks and used for fuel. When it was put on the fields, it was applied sparingly and infrequently.[37]

The agricultural implements used by the peasants, like the tillage systems, changed little if at all from what they had been for centuries, and there was remarkably little interest shown

---

[36] Haxthausen, *Studien*, I, 273; II, 76, 85; *Ob'iasneniia*, pp. 65-68.

[37] *Ob'iasneniia*, pp. 44-45, 48, 69; Tooke, *View*, III, 256, 259, 264; Haxthausen, *Studien*, II, 15; Köppen, *Statistische Reise*, pp. 47, 61, 122-123; Ministerstvo Gosudarstvennykh Imushchestv, *Statisticheskii obzor*, p. 4; Domontovich, *Materialy*, p. 182.

during the eighteenth and for most of the nineteenth centuries in adopting more efficient tools. The most important implement in all of the non-black earth, and in most of the chernozem, too, was the ancient hook-plow, the *sokha*. This light tool, made of wood save for its iron shares, could be drawn by a single small horse. Because of its weight and inefficient design, it could only cut a shallow furrow, and could not turn over large clods nor thoroughly tear up weed roots. It was a poor tool at best, and it was particularly unsuited for working the heavy chernozem. Yet it continued to be used because it was cheap and easy to make and, most important, because the usual peasant lacked the animals needed to pull a heavier and more efficient plow. A somewhat better implement called the *kosulia*, midway in design between *sokha* and true plow, was employed to a limited extent in the north and non-black earth center. Heavier than the *sokha*, but still able to be drawn by one horse, it cut deeper and was more effective in turning sod and breaking new land. In Little Russia (Kharkov, Poltava, Chernigov) the peasants used a heavy wheeled plow, called the *saban*, drawn by two or four horses, or four, six, and even eight oxen. In light soils, however, the Little Russians used the *sokha*, including a two-wheeled version of that implement. Heavier plows were also used in districts bordering Little Russia, and in New Russia and along the Middle Volga, where, probably, they had been introduced by the German colonists.[38]

The harrow used in the forested zones of the center and north was often simply branches lashed together and dragged across the sown field. In some parts of the center, and in the steppe, it was a wooden frame into which wooden pegs had been driven. Rollers were hardly ever used. The sickle was the favored tool for harvesting cereals in most of European Russia, though the scythe was used for mowing hay and in some areas for grain, too. In Little Russia and in the Baltic littoral, the scythe was in general use for all harvesting. Threshing was done with flails,

[38] Pallas, *Voyages*, I, 3-4; Tooke, *View*, III, 240-243, 263; *Mittheilungen*, 1846, 109, 110; 1849, 65, 146; 1852, 15, 461; Haxthausen, *Studien*, II, 15, 23, 154; Domontovich, *Materialy*, p. 179; Druzhinin, *Gosudarstvennye krest'iane*, pp. 401, 417; Liashchenko, "Krepostnoe sel'skoe khoziaistvo," p. 110.

though sometimes horses or people were used to tread out the grain.[39]

Improved implements and farm machinery were only beginning to be used by the middle of the nineteenth century. Sources of the forties and fifties contain references to new implements, and especially threshing machines, in use on properties that belonged to wealthy landowners.[40] The establishment in 1831, under the aegis of the Moscow Agricultural Society, of the firm of Butenop Brothers was a landmark in this development. Between 1833 and 1846 the value of this company's output of tools and machinery amounted to one million rubles, and included 1,100 threshers, 6,060 winnowing machines, 1,600 plows, and 1,200 harrows. Butenop Brothers had been the first farm tool factory in Russia. By 1850, according to a government report, there were nineteen firms in this line of manufacture. This figure, of course, did not include the many small village shops engaged in this line of production.[41]

IV

Animal husbandry occupied a secondary role in agriculture in most of European Russia. It was generally conducted in an inefficient manner, partly because of the forage shortage that resulted from the prevailing modes of cultivation, and partly because of the lack of interest of both proprietors and peasants. No attention was paid to selective breeding, the animals were underfed, and they were given little care. As soon as weather permitted, they were turned out to fend for themselves in the common pastures and in the stubble fields. In winter they were cooped up in ill-kept barns and fed meager rations that often were just straw. The results of these practices were weak and scrawny beasts who were easy victims to the frequent animal epidemics that swept through the land. An English traveler in

---

[39] Pallas, *Voyages*, I, 4, 17; Haxthausen, *Studien*, I, 231, 247, 274, 282, 484; II, 6, 25, 155; Tooke, *View*, III, 244-245, 256; Georgi, *Geographisch-physikalische* . . . *Beschreibung*, II, pt. 1, 187; Weber, *Das veränderte Russland*, III, 120; Baranovich, *Materialy*, p. 183; Alefirenko, "Russkaia obshchestvennaia mysl," p. 531.

[40] Domontovich, *Materialy*, p. 181; Baranovich, *Materialy*, p. 183; Haxthausen, *Studien*, I, 107; Sivkov, *Ocherki*, pp. 93-94.

[41] *SIRO*, XCVIII (1896), 491-492; Struve, *Krepostnoe khoziaistvo*, pp. 75-76.

the latter eighteenth century wrote that at the end of winter the cattle sometimes were too weak to rise without aid, and a hundred years later another British visitor made the same observation. There were a few areas in the Don steppes, in Little Russia, and in Archangel, where more attention was paid to stock raising and good animals were produced. The kholmogor cattle, developed in Archangel, were the best native stock. The breed originated when Peter I brought in Dutch bulls to cross with native cows, and had been maintained by subsequent importations of Dutch animals. In other parts of the empire a corporal's guard of improving landlords brought in blooded animals from abroad to build up their herds.[42]

Sheep raising was the great exception to the general disinterest in animal husbandry. The native animals, of which there were a large number, were small creatures and bore coarse wool. Efforts made by the government in the eighteenth century to improve the breed by importing blooded stock from England and Silesia had little effect. Then at the beginning of the nineteenth century the government succeeded in establishing merino sheep herding as a major industry by offering vast stretches of empty land in New Russia, and sometimes loans, to persons raising these animals. The land became the property of the grantee if he met certain conditions. A number of those who took advantage of these offers were foreigners who had gained experience in merino breeding in their homelands and were attracted to Russia by the lures held out by the government. A Spaniard named Rouvier was given 30,000 desiatins of land in the Crimea and a loan of 100,000 paper rubles to build up a herd of 100,000 merinos and train 100 students in sheep farming. A German named Müller received 130,000 desiatins on condition that in three years he was to have a flock of 30,000 sheep, a third of them pure merinos and the rest of mixed blood. These men, and other foreigners with whom similar arrangements were made, became the pioneers in merino production in the empire. They did their work well, for by 1846 over 7.5 million of the estimated 41.6 million sheep in Euro-

[42] Tooke, *View*, III, 181-188; Wallace, *Russia*, p. 96; *Ob'iasneniia*, pp. 387, 388, 392, 393-394.

[341]

pean Russia were merinos. Despite a falling price for fine wool, the merino flocks continued to grow, so that by the early 1860's the number of merinos had risen by over 50 percent to 11.6 million. At that time 61 percent of the merinos were in the four provinces of New Russia where the industry had centered from the beginning; 20 percent were in the provinces of Little Russia and the southwest; 13 percent were in the Great Russian provinces, chiefly in those of the southeast; and 6 percent were in the western and Baltic provinces. They belonged almost exclusively to members of the landowning class, some of whom owned huge numbers of these animals. In the Crimea flocks of 25,000 were not unusual, and one owner had 400,000 head.[43]

V

The picture that emerges from the pages of this and the two preceding chapters does not support the claim sometimes made that the Russian economy was disentegrating on the eve of the emancipation because of the existence of serfdom. It is equally clear, however, that in relative terms the empire's economic evolution was much behind that of many Western lands. It is impossible to make precise quantitative comparisons between the economic growth of Russia and of other nations because of the absence of detailed information, both for Russia and other countries, about the total amounts of goods and services that they produced. But other materials show that Russia was much less advanced. Though there was a large expansion in commerce, it was organized along lines that had been abandoned long before in the West. Russian commerce was still in the stage of the "traveling merchants" who journeyed from fair to fair carrying their merchandise with them. Commercial banking was still conducted at the level of the private money-lender. Industry, even though it had made much progress, lagged far behind parallel developments in other lands. Some Soviet historians, in what seems to me to be an over-enthusiastic evaluation of the industrial advances made in the last century of

[43] *Ob'iasneniia*, pp. 399-406; Tooke, *View*, III, 194-200; Tegoborskii, *Etudes*, I, 485.

serfdom, have asserted that their native land went through an "industrial revolution" during that era. One dates the revolution to the years 1790-1825, another puts it in the 1830's to 1850's, a third gives the dates as roughly 1830 to 1860, and still another sets it in the 1850's and 1860's.[44] Unfortunately, the term "industrial revolution" has been employed in so many contexts and so loosely that its meaning has become uncertain. But to use it to describe Russian industrial change in any of the time periods just mentioned is to stretch this rubbery term beyond the limits even of its elasticity. In 1860 scarcely more than 1 percent of the empire's population was engaged in factory production, and many of these people were part-time workers. The use of machinery and of mechanical power in industry and transportation was still exceptional. The factory was far from being the typical unit of manufacturing production. Urbanization, sometimes posited as an indicator of industrial revolution, had made little progress; in 1860 less than 8 percent of the population lived in cities.

The relative retardation in Russian economic growth has often been blamed on serfdom, on the grounds that the serf was an inefficient worker who could not—or would not—adapt himself to new techniques of production, while the limitations on his freedom of movement are supposed to have produced a shortage of industrial labor.[45] But this explanation understates the very considerable freedom of movement allowed peasants who were seeking work, and it neglects the technical and commercial skills developed by serfs and by state peasants who were engaged in *kustar* production and in trade.

It seems to me that there are more cogent explanations for Russian retardation. Among these the low quality or poor distribution of her natural resources, and the inadequacies of her transportation system, hold high priorities. The infertile soil and the rigorous climate of a large part of European Russia meant that the Russian farmer in these parts of the empire had

[44] 1790-1825, Iakovlev, "Vozniknovenie," pp. 102-104; 1830's-1850's, Zlotnikov, "Ot manufaktury," p. 41; 1830-1860, Strumilin, *Promyshlennyi pereverot*, p. 21; 1850's-1860's, Iatsunskii, "Promyshlennyi perevorot," pp. 67-69.

[45] Cf. e.g. Brutzkus, "Die historischen Eigentumlichkeiten," p. 91; Liashchenko, *History*, pp. 327-328, 337; Zlotnikov, "Ot manufaktury," pp. 41-43.

to overcome more handicaps than did his counterpart in Western Europe. The difficulties of transport made the carriage of raw materials and finished products expensive, and there were periods during the year when goods often could not be moved at all. The effects of this handicap upon economic growth are obvious, particularly when the Russian conditions are compared with the relative ease with which goods could be moved all year around in the geographically more fortunate lands of the West. Similarly, Russia was less favored than were these lands in the location of her mineral resources. To get the iron they needed the Russians had to go to the thinly settled Ural borderlands, far distant from the centers of population, trade, and industry. Despite this Russia was able to become a leading iron producer until the ironmakers of other lands, and above all of England, began to smelt with coke instead of charcoal. When that happened Russia could no longer compete, for unlike England her deposits of coal suitable for coking lay far from the iron mines, and the costs of bringing fuel and ore together would have been prohibitive.[46]

[46] Cf. Baykov, "The Economic Development," pp. 137-143.

18

THE DVORIANSTVO ASCENDANCY

DURING the eighteenth century an upsurge of the nobility, sometimes labelled by historians as a "feudal reaction," seems to have been nearly a pan-European phenomenon. In country after country a new class cohesiveness appeared among members of the ruling class. They revived old and well-nigh forgotten corporate privileges, they demanded new ones, and they made a bid for greater power for their caste in government.

The nobility of Russia shared in this movement. But the Russian experience was unique in at least two respects. First, in other lands the renascence of aristocratic pretensions came to an early end—victim of revolution, or centralization, or bureau-cratization, or parliamentary reform. In Russia the story turned out differently. The Russian nobles won their freedom from the galling obligation of state service; they were granted a charter that guaranteed their rights as members of a privileged class; they gained a monopoly on the ownership of land and serfs; they were able to reduce their peasants to the condition of chattels; they made and unmade tsars; and they ruled in the provinces.

The second unique feature of the Russian experience was that until the reign of Peter I there had not even been a noble caste in the Western European sense of a distinct corps, all of whose members were equally endowed with special class privi-leges that raised them above other subjects. The honor and precedence that a Russian lord enjoyed came from his ancestry, and not from his membership in a special caste, nor from serving the tsar. The scions of old families scorned their fellow servitors who sprang from less distinguished lines, and saw no reason to identify themselves or their interests with them.[1]

The consciousness of belonging to a single class only appeared during Peter's reign. As with so much else that was new in that

[1] Romanovich-Slavatinskii, *Dvorianstvo*, pp. 2-3.

era, primary responsibility for this development lay with the tsar himself. Peter established and enforced the principle that social distinction rose from state service and not from ancestry. To his way of thinking the demands of the state outweighed all other considerations, including the claims of lineage. He needed officers and administrators for his mushrooming army and bureaucracy, and he decided that the rights of nobility would go only to those who filled these posts. He took decisive and sometimes severe measures to compel landowners to serve. He ordered the compilation of a register of all eligibles, kept records of their service, confiscated the property of those who evaded service, and ordered that evaders could be assaulted, robbed, and even murdered with impunity because their evasion had put them outside the law.[2] All those eligible for service had to enter upon it at the age of fifteen and remain in it until disability, senility, or death ended their usefulness. They were expected to begin training for service in special schools when they were ten, but this requirement was nullified by a combination of evasions and of inadequate educational facilities. To ensure a steady flow of noble sprigs into the armed forces Peter charged the director of the government's genealogical bureau with the task of seeing to it that not more than one third of the members of a family were in civil service. The rest had to be in the military. On entering active duty with the troops the young noble was required to serve in the ranks before he could be commissioned. Sons of wealthy and important families were posted to one of the three Guards regiments, while others went to a line outfit where they lived the lives of ordinary recruits.[3]

The decree of 24 January 1722 by which Peter created a Table of Ranks in imperial service represented the culmination of his plans for the nobility. Service grades had of course existed for a long time, and by the end of the sixteenth century twenty-two separate ranks had been established.[4] During the seventeenth century the elaborate system of genealogical precedence known as *mestnichestvo* which had regulated the distribution of these offices had deteriorated. By the time of its formal abolition

---

[2] Florinsky, *Russia*, I, 417-418.   [3] Kliuchevskii, *History*, IV, 77-80.
[4] Khlebnikov, *O vliianii*, pp. 10-11.

on 12 January 1682 the principle that promotions depended upon merit or the tsar's favor, rather than upon ancestry, had become generally accepted. Now Peter gave precise formulation to what had become the established pattern. His Table of Ranks set up fourteen parallel grades in the military, civil, and imperial court bureaucracies. Every servitor, no matter what his pedigree, had to begin his career in the lowest rank, or *chin*, and promotions were supposed to depend upon merit and length of service. The man of common birth who entered military service won hereditary nobility when he was commissioned a second lieutenant or ensign, lowest of the fourteen military ranks. If he chose a career in the civil bureaucracy he gained nobility only if he rose to the eighth *chin*, that of collegiate assessor. Peter's law remained in force with only minor modifications made in it until 1917. In 1845 Nicholas I, in response to long-expressed desires of the high aristocracy, made it more difficult to become a member of the nobility by ordering that, henceforth, hereditary nobility came only with the eighth *chin* (staff officer rank) in the military, and fifth rank in the civil service.[5]

By making the acquisition of noble status dependent upon government service Peter welded the servitor-nobles into a single class that was held together by common interests, and that shared common corporate privileges. In fact, Peter not only called this corps of the nobility into being but also gave it its first corporate name. Indulging his weakness for foreign words he chose the name the Poles used for their nobility, russifying it into *shliachetstvo*. In the second half of the century, however, Peter's selection was replaced by an old Russian word, *dvorianstvo*. Centuries before that name had been used for the *dvoriane liudi*, the lesser servitors of the prince who lived in his *dvor*, his court. Now it was applied to all nobles, great and small—a fitting name for a noblesse that owed its preeminence to service to the tsar.[6]

Peter was responsible, too, for the adoption of both honorific and hereditary titles for the nobility. Prior to his reign the title

---

[5] *PSZ*, VI, no. 3890, 24 Jan. 1722, pp. 486-493; *ibid.*, 2nd series, XX, no. 19086, 11 June 1845, pp. 450-451.
[6] Romanovich-Slavatinskii, *Dvorianstvo*, pp. 3-4.

of honor of *blagorodnyi*, well-born, was restricted to members of the tsar's family. Everyone else was formally addressed as a "slave" of the tsar. In 1721 Peter changed the titles of the ruling family and substituted *blagovernyi*, true believer, as the proper form of address for the tsar's kinsmen. *Blagorodny*, well-born, now began to be used for nobles. By the middle of the eighteenth century it had become the accepted form, so that both as individuals and as a class they were identified as "*blagorodnyi*."[7]

The only hereditary Russian title in the pre-Petrine era had been that of *kniaz*, prince. It was borne by those who claimed descent from Riurik, from Gedimin, Prince of Lithuania (1316-1341), or from Tatar and Georgian princes. (In Russia, as in other continental lands, all the children of a titled father had the same title he had even while he was still alive.) In 1707 Peter honored his favorite, Alexander Menshikov, son of a stable hand, with the title of *kniaz*. This was not Menshikov's first princely title; two years before the Holy Roman Emperor had made him a prince of that empire. No more Russian princes were created until the reign of Paul, at the end of the century, though several Russians, among them Catherine II's favorites, Potemkin, Orlov, and Zubov, were named princes of the Holy Roman Empire. Paul, and his sons Alexander I and Nicholas I, awarded the title to a number of people, so that by the second half of the nineteenth century sixteen families had been elevated to princely rank. Peter introduced the title of Count (*Graf*) in 1706 when he raised B. P. Sheremetev to that rank. By the reign of Alexander II 63 counts had been created by the tsars. There were also a number of counts whose titles came from the Holy Roman Emperor. Peter introduced the title of baron, too. In 1710 he gave it to Peter Shafirov, who had risen from an humble Jewish origin to high rank in the tsar's service. The title in succeeding years was awarded to successful business men, and so came to be held in low regard by the old aristocracy.[8]

Data on the size of the dvorianstvo are lacking until the mid-nineteenth century. But its numbers grew steadily, for the Table of Ranks offered a door through which men of the most hetero-

---

[7] *Ibid.*, pp. 71-72; *Entsiklopedicheskii slovar*, x, 205.
[8] Romanovich-Slavatinskii, *Dvorianstvo*, pp. 38-41.

geneous backgrounds and origins could pass to become members of the ruling class. Its ranks were swollen by the nobles of the annexed Baltic and Polish provinces who were allowed to keep their privileged status and their titles. At the end of the seventeenth century there had been an estimated 2,985 noble families.[9] Estimates made during the eighteenth century are too much inflated to be of use, so that stages in the growth of the dvorianstvo cannot be marked out. But by the time of the Tenth Revision in 1858 there were 886,782 nobles in European Russia, and another 30,000 in Siberia and the Caucasus, or one noble for about every 80 inhabitants of the empire.[10]

In theory, all these hundreds of thousands of people were equally noble and all had the same privileges. The daughter of a prince could marry an ordinary noble without blemishing her family's honor. No noble had legal precedence over his fellows. But snobbery could not be legislated out of existence. There were bound to be social gradations in a class that extended, as a minister of Nicholas I put it, "all the way from the steps of the throne almost to the peasantry."[11] The strata were formalized in registers called Books of the Nobility that were kept by the central government until 1785, when they were turned over to the noble assemblies of each province. The dvorianstvo was divided into six classes: nobles by patent, nobles by military service, nobles by civil service, foreign nobles, titled nobles, and, finally, the old aristocratic families. The members of the last-named group, the *noblesse de race*, considered themselves superior to all the others. They reserved a special scorn for the first three classes, whom they regarded as an upstart nobility—descendants of burghers, priests, and peasants. They were more tolerant of the foreign nobles, and were willing to accept the holders of Russian titles (except barons) as equals. Men in the top brackets of the military and civil service were also acceptable in the highest social circles, even though they were entered in classes two and three of the dvorianstvo registers.[12]

9 Kliuchevskii, *History*, IV, 82.
10 Romanovich-Slavatinskii, *Dvorianstvo*, pp. 508-509.
11 Prince K. A. Liven quoted in Florinsky, *Russia*, II, 802n.
12 Romanovich-Slavatinskii, *Dvorianstvo*, pp. 43-46, 66.

The uppermost levels thought of themselves as the aristocracy. To distinguish themselves from the rest of the nobility they adopted Western manners and dress, and above all aped the French noblesse of the *ancien régime*. To insure the perpetuation of their distinctiveness they set up special schools that admitted only children of the "best" noble families. There the students, as one writer (who disapproved) put it, "were soaked in the finest Parisian French accent, in the *angelic* Parisian dialect, in the elegant manners of the aristocrats of the old regime. . . . and emerged as genuine marquises of good old France."[13] An Englishwoman in Russia in the first years of the nineteenth century commented—with feminine illogic, be it noted—that it seemed "childishly silly" for the Russians to oppose Napoleon "when they can't eat their dinners without a French cook to dress it, when they can't educate their children without unprincipled adventurers from Paris to act as tutors and governesses, when every house of consequence. . . . has an outcast Frenchman to instruct the heir apparent—in a word when every association of fashion, luxury, elegance, and fascination is drawn from France. . . ."[14]

Yet, despite the internal stratification, a sense of unity and cohesiveness grew among all the levels of the nobility from the reign of Peter on. By the time of the convening of the Legislative Commission of 1767, nobles forthrightly identified themselves as belonging to a corporate body all of whose members shared the same interests and ambitions. The dvorianstvo of Moscow in its instructions to its delegates to the Commission, spoke of the "corps of the nobility which includes within itself its own prerogatives and invulnerability," and called attention to the general needs of the entire noble class; the nobility of Volokolamsk demanded that rights and preeminence be accorded the corps of the nobility; the *cahiers* of the Kostroma dvorianstvo lamented the fate of impoverished nobles who could not afford to educate their children properly, so that these youths grew up in ignorance and stagnation and lacked the

[13] *Ibid.*, pp. 66-67. Cf. Haumont, *La culture française*, pp. 184-222.
[14] Catherine Wilmot quoted in Putnam, *Seven Britons*, p. 130n.

cachet of nobility. Like sentiments were voiced in the *cahiers* of other groups of nobles and in the statements of their deputies.[15]

The series of concessions the dvorianstvo gained as a class from the throne provides the clearest evidence of the growth of this new corporate feeling. Peter I had kept the nobles subservient to the crown. After his death the absence of a stable principle of succession to the throne, and the character of the monarchs who reigned after him, gave the new noble class the opportunity to win great power and wide privileges for itself. The bizarre creatures who wore the crown after Peter—a lewd child, lascivious women, and a deranged German prince—depended upon the support of the dvorianstvo to get and keep the throne. The predominantly noble Guards regiments, above all, made and broke sovereigns. As the price of their support, the dvorianstvo demanded concessions from rulers and would-be rulers.

The abolition of the service requirement was their most spectacular gain. To most nobles compulsory service was an extremely distasteful duty. They used every possible pretext to dodge it, giving bribes, pleading illness, and even feigning insanity. They pressed constantly for its repeal. Already in Anna's reign concessions began to be made. In 1731 a military academy for noble youths of 13 to 18 opened in St. Petersburg. Its graduates received commissions and thereby avoided the detested obligation of beginning their military careers in the ranks. In 1736 Anna reduced the service period from life to 25 years, and excused one male member of each family with two or more men in it, on the condition that the exempted son manage the family property. Finally, Peter III, on 18 February 1762, abolished all compulsory service, allowed the individual to decide for himself whether he wanted to serve the tsar, and permitted nobles to travel abroad freely, and to enter the service of a foreign ruler.[16]

Catherine II, even more than her predecessors, acquiesced to the demands of the dvorianstvo. Her policy of concession has sometimes been interpreted as a clever maneuver on her part to

[15] Romanovich-Slavatinskii, *Dvorianstvo*, pp. 58-62.
[16] *Ibid.*, pp. 181-194; Florinsky, *Russia*, I, 482-483.

keep the nobility satisfied, so that it would not protest against control by the government and "merchant capitalists" over matters of national import.[17] Be that as it may, Catherine identified herself with the nobility—"je suis aristocrate," said she, "c'est mon métier"—and her long reign turned out to be the Golden Age of the dvorianstvo.

The gains they made at the expense of the throne and of other classes in society reached their apogee in the Charter of the Nobility that Catherine granted on 21 April 1785.[18] The first section of the charter confirmed and codified the privileges that had already been won. The noble's freedom from compulsory service was restated. His right to enter the service of a foreign ruler who was friendly to Russia was confirmed, although he had always to come to the tsar's defense when needed. If he was the first of a family to hold a property he could dispose of it however he wished, but the alienation of inherited land was limited. He was declared the owner of the timber and the sub-soil wealth on his property, and he could do as he pleased with these resources. He could buy villages, establish factories and mills in them, and could sell the agricultural and manufactured goods he produced at wholesale to both foreign and domestic buyers. He could not be deprived of his privileged status unless he committed deeds unworthy of the honor of his caste, such as treason, banditry, or breaking his oath. He could be imprisoned or exiled, but could not be given corporal punishment. He was free of all personal taxes, and soldiers could not be quartered on him.

The next section of the charter granted new and extensive powers to the nobility in provincial administration. Catherine, in the interests of more efficient administration, had increased the number of guberniias to fifty by splitting the existing provinces into new units, each of which was supposed to contain

---

[17] Cf. Sacke, "Adel und Burgertum," *passim.* Sacke, on the basis of what seems to me to be an entirely incorrect analysis, arrived at the conclusion that Catherine's policy, despite its external appearance, was actually anti-noble and pro-bourgeois. Sacke was a German follower of M. N. Pokrovskii, once the dictator of official Communist historiography. Pokrovskii claimed that the period between the reigns of Peter I and Catherine II had been an era of reaction of the gentry against the domination of merchant capitalism, and that during Catherine's reign the preeminence of the capitalists had been reestablished.

[18] "Zhalovannaia Gramota Dvorianstvu," in *Akty tsarstvovaniia Ekateriny*, pp. 104-123.

300,000-400,000 inhabitants. The dvorianstvo had been clamoring for a greater voice in local affairs, and Catherine, in the charter, ordered that the nobility of each guberniia should organize itself into a provincial estate. These bodies were given control over nearly all the local governmental functions of the province, either directly or through officers they chose from among themselves. They named the majority of the administrative and judicial officials in their guberniia, and directed recruiting, tax collecting, police work, and the many other activities of local government. The charter instructed that they were to meet triennially. All nobles of the province had the right to attend, but only those who were over 25, owned property, and had reached the rank of company grade officer (subaltern through captain), or its civilian equivalent in the imperial service could vote or hold elective office.[19] Thus, even though the obligation to do service had been abolished, active participation in local affairs depended upon its performance. Moreover, the central government maintained firm control over the assemblies, and any independent expression or action by one of these provincial estates was viewed as dangerous resistance to the will of the tsar.[20] Despite these restrictions, the fact remains that on the very eve of the revolutionary movement that was destined to sweep away or greatly reduce the authority of long-existing noble provincial estates in Western lands, the Russian nobility for the first time won the right to form privileged assemblies entrusted with powers of local government.

In 1831 Nicholas I restricted the right to a direct vote in the provincial assemblies to nobles who owned a minimum of 100 male serfs, or had at least 3,000 desiatins of arable land. This new law produced a drastic reduction in the electorate, since only about 16 percent of the serfowners had more than 100 males.[21]

In 1836 another decree lowered the property qualification for those who had reached the grade of colonel in the army, or the

---

19 Provincial assemblies were not established in provinces of northern and northeastern Russia nor in Siberia because of the small number of nobles in those regions. (Florinsky, *Russia*, I, 571.)

20 Engelmann, *Die Leibeigenschaft*, pp. 283-284.

21 Troinitskii, *Krepostnoe naselenie*, p. 67.

fifth rank in the civil hierarchy. These men needed only five serfs or 150 desiatins to vote. Even with this liberalization only a small proportion of the nobility were able to qualify. For example, in 1858 in Riazan just 635 of the 3,926 male hereditary nobles, in Chernigov 476 out of 6,268, and in Kaluga 463 out of 3,406 could cast individual votes.[22] Nobles who owned at least five peasants or 100 desiatins of arable could pool their holdings to obtain the necessary amount of serfs or of land, and be represented by a delegate who voted for them.[23]

The predominance of the nobility received a temporary setback during the brief reign of Catherine's son, Paul I (1796-1801). Obsessed apparently by a pathological hatred of his mother—who for her part had treated him shamefully—Paul seemed determined to wipe out her accomplishments. (A curious story tries to explain the wretched relationship between mother and son by claiming that Paul was not Catherine's child. According to this tale he had been substituted in the cradle, against Catherine's wishes, for a girl born to Catherine. The then empress, Elizabeth, is said to have ordered this substitution because she wanted Catherine and her husband to have a male heir.)[24] On the day of his coronation Paul issued a series of decrees aimed at curtailing the power of the nobility, and for the rest of his tenure on the throne he continued in an anti-dvorianstvo policy. He recognized that the absence of a fundamental law of succession to the throne had enabled the dvorianstvo to aggrandize its position through palace revolutions, and so he established a fixed order of succession through primogeniture; he amended the Charter of the Nobility to weaken the dvorianstvo control over local government; he restored corporal punishment for nobles; he imposed a tax on them; and so on.

[22] Baranovich, *Materialy*, p. 139; Domontovich, *Materialy*, p. 150; Poprotskii, *Materialy*, I, 292.

Besides hereditary nobles, i.e., those nobles who passed on their noble status to their children, there were "personal" nobles. The rank of personal nobility went with the grade in the civil service just beneath the grade that carried hereditary nobility with it. Personal nobility extended only to the official and his wife and was not hereditary. The personal noble had most of the privileges of the hereditary noble, but was not allowed to participate in the corporate activities of the nobility. (Schultz, *Russische Rechtsgeschichte*, p. 180 and note.)

[23] Miliukov, *Histoire*, II, 760.　　[24] Kukiel, *Czartoryski*, pp. 17-18.

Disaffection spread among the dvorianstvo and plans to overthrow the tsar were quickly spun. His brutal murder by a small band of nobles ended the threat to their caste. One of the first acts of his son and successor, Alexander I (who was privy to the plans for his father's deposition) was to restore all the privileges of the nobility that Paul had taken away. To the dvorianstvo he was "Catherine's grandson" and they hailed his accession with joy. The throne in his day, and in the reigns of his brother Nicholas I and his nephew Alexander II, identified itself with the nobility as it had done in Catherine's time. Nicholas publicly echoed his grandmother when, in an address in 1848, he told the dvorianstvo of St. Petersburg guberniia that he and his wife, as landowners in that province, considered themselves members of its nobility.[25] But though they cherished the dvorianstvo, the sovereigns of the nineteenth century did not shower it with concessions as their predecessors had done, and as later chapters will show, they sought for ways and means to limit the control of the nobles over their serfs.

II

The enormous gifts of land and serfs lavished by the tsars of the eighteenth century upon members of the dvorianstvo provides striking evidence of the great favor these people enjoyed. Land had always been plentiful in Russia, and princes had long followed the practice of giving it out in generous portions to their followers. In the seventeenth century the Romanov dynasty gave a new twist to the practice by making excessively large gifts to kinsmen and favorites. The vast expansion in territory and population in the eighteenth century provided the tsars with resources in land and peasants that went beyond the wildest dreams of earlier rulers. At the same time, the eighteenth century was the age of the favorite in Russian history. Never before had favorites wielded so much power and influence, and never before had their sovereigns showered so much wealth upon them. Men of lowly origins and bearers of great names shared alike in the imperial bounty. Alexander

25 *Russkaia starina*, Sept. 1883, p. 596.

Menshikov, the groom's son, Alexis and Cyril Razumovskii, sons of a Little Russian peasant, Alexis Dolgorukii, descendant of Riurik, and Boris Sheremetev, scion of an ancient boyar house, and others like them, had thousands of peasants and great stretches of land bestowed upon them.

Peter I, in comparison with those who ruled before him, was overwhelmingly generous in his gifts, but his successors seemed determined to outdo him in prodigality. Between 1740 and 1801 they gave away over 1,304,000 adult male peasants with their wives and children.[26] Catherine II alone turned over 800,000 peasants of both sexes to private proprietors. Remarkably enough, Paul nearly outdid his mother in his gifts to nobles despite his animus against their class. In his brief reign, and mainly in the first ten months of his rule, he managed to give away 600,000 peasants of both sexes. But Paul's motives were not quite the same as those of his predecessors. While heir to the throne he somehow conceived the strange notion that privately-owned serfs were better off than the peasants who lived on the estates that belonged to the tsar and his family—a theory that was certainly contradicted by the facts (v. pp. 485-491). When he ascended the throne he was able to implement his conviction, and half of the 600,000 people he gave away came from imperial properties. The ensuing serious decline in his income compelled him to slow down on his program, and finally to abandon it.[27]

Alexander I vowed that he would not indulge in this form of imperial extravagance.[28] But both he and his successor Nicholas continued to give away land and people, though not on so grand a scale as their forbears. Between 1804 and 1836 they distributed over a million desiatins of state land to a total of 368 persons. Most of their grants lay in sparsely peopled regions of the south and east.[29]

By far the greatest part of the largesse of the eighteenth century rulers went to the handful of men who enjoyed their

---

[26] Schiemann, *Geschichte*, I, 391-392.
[27] Semevskii, *Krest'ianskii vopros*, I, xiv, 16-17.
[28] Schnitzler, *Histoire intime*, I, 49-50.
[29] Druzhinin, *Gosudarstvennye krest'iane*, I, 87-88.

special favor. In the reigns of Catherine II and Paul, 111 lucky courtiers received a total of 385,700 male peasants. These serfs were distributed among the 111 as follows:[30]

	CATHERINE II		PAUL		TOTAL	
	Lords	Peasants (in 1000's)	Lords	Peasants (in 1000's)	Lords	Peasants (in 1000's)
10,000 souls	5	97.5	3	56.7	8	154.2
5-10,000 souls	5	37.0	1	6.0	6	43.0
3- 5,000 souls	11	41.8	7	26.3	18	68.1
1- 3,000 souls	21	42.0	58	78.4	79	120.4
Total	42	218.3	69	167.4	111	385.7

A host of much smaller grants were frequently made. Special events such as a christening in the tsar's family, the cutting of the first tooth by an imperial infant, or a military victory, were marked by the distribution of land and peasants. Palace revolutions were accompanied by awards to the supporters of the new ruler. Elizabeth gave 29 to 45 male souls to each of the guardsmen who aided in her elevation to the throne, and similar bequests were made by other rulers.[31] Lesser services were sometimes rewarded with breathtaking generosity. Alexander Vasilchikov, a Guards lieutenant, who was Catherine II's fancy man for twenty-two months, received from his pleased Empress 7,000 peasants, 100,000 rubles in cash, a furnished palace worth 100,000 rubles, jewelry valued at 50,000 rubles, porcelains worth another 50,000 rubles, and a pension of 20,000 rubles. Others of her passing loves were treated with equal consideration, while those who had more lasting holds on her affection, such as Gregory Orlov and Gregory Potemkin, had astronomical amounts heaped upon them. Potemkin, for instance, on his fortieth birthday received a gift of 900,000 rubles, partly in cash and partly in land.[32] Tsar Paul was said to have given 2,000 souls to a man who dedicated a poem to him. At the request of Prince Bezborodko he gave a property with 850 souls to the Prince's mistress, who reputedly was by profession a strumpet.

---

[30] Voznesenskii, *Ekonomika Rossii*, p. 47.
[31] Kliuchevskii, *History*, IV, 62; Akademiia Nauk, *Istoriia SSSR*, I, 604.
[32] English diplomatic reports quoted in Gitermann, *Geschichte*, III, 461-462.

At a review an officer gave Paul a witty retort that so pleased the tsar that he presented him with 1,000 souls.[33]

Such were the whims of the Emperors and Autocrats of All the Russias.

III

The success of the nobles in the eighteenth century in establishing their sole right to own land and serfs provides further evidence of the appearance among them of class cohesiveness, and of the willingness of the sovereigns to accede to their demands. Their monopoly on land and serfs had come into being in the preceding century but had not been complete, for men of various non-serving groups had been able to continue to own land and peasants. Then, in a series of decrees and instructions issued between 1730 and 1758 the throne deprived one after another of these groups of this privilege, and ordered that if they did not dispose of their property within a set period it was to be confiscated by the state.[34]

The fact that the government had to repeat its injunctions against the ownership of land and serfs by non-nobles bears witness to evasions in the law, and to vacillations in the policy of the government. The want of a settled purpose was evidenced most clearly in the backing and filling that went on about the right of merchants to own serfs. As mentioned in an earlier chapter, Peter I had allowed merchants to buy serfs for their factories, and other laws of the 1720's and 1730's permitted industrialists in the Urals to keep skilled runaway peasants by paying indemnities to the owners of the fugitives. A decree of 7 January 1736 declared that factory owners could only purchase serfs without land, but as a result of complaints this limitation was removed. In 1752 the Senate fixed the maximum number of serf workers a merchant factory owner could have, the quota being adjusted to the size and nature of his enterprise. Finally, on 29 March 1762 Peter III forbad merchant manufacturers to buy peasants, and a few months later Catherine, now on the throne, confirmed the prohibition. (In the following year an

---

[33] Simkhovitch, *Die Feldgemeinschaft*, p. 189n.; Kliuchevskii, *History*, v, 126.
[34] *PSZ*, VIII, no. 5633, 25 Oct. 1730, p. 331; Semevskii, *Krest'iane*, I, 2-3, 3-4; Kliuchevskii, *Kurs*, IV, 426-427.

exception was made for foreigners who established factories in Russia.)

The conflict over the right to buy serfs has sometimes been viewed as important evidence of a class struggle between the factory-owning bourgeoisie and the serf-owning nobility, and the law of 29 March 1762 is seen as heralding the triumph of the "feudal reaction." It was pointed out on an earlier page that merchants had made comparatively small use of their legal right to buy serfs, so that this interpretation seems over-drawn. But the dvorianstvo had indeed become alarmed at this encroachment upon its monopoly. The cahiers of the nobility of the Lukh district to its delegate at the Legislative Commission— where class antagonisms were openly expressed—complained that bourgeois factory owners had purchased villages (before the decree of 1762) and "like genuine nobility enjoyed privileges that did not belong to them." Nobles of other districts voiced similar complaints, among them the dvorianstvo of Krapivna who with unconscious irony pointed out that "the factory owners of the merchant class, owning many serfs . . . live off the fat of the land in pleasurable luxury and idleness." Some feared, too, that if merchants were permitted to buy peasants there would be fewer left for the nobles, and since serfs were the lords' chief source of income their revenues would therefore decline. Merchants, for their part, instructed their delegates to demand that they not only be allowed to buy serfs once again for their factories, but also for use as domestics.[35]

The merchants were not alone in wanting the right to buy serfs. Delegates from every one of the social groups that were represented at the Legislative Commission asked for it, and those who did not have their own representatives, such as priests and government clerks, were spoken for by representatives of other groups.[36]

The dvorianstvo resolutely and successfully opposed these and later demands by commoners, and retained its monopoly on serf ownership until the emancipation. There were, however, a few groups outside the dvorianstvo who by special favor of

[35] Tugan-Baranovskii, *Russkaia fabrika*, I, 28-31, 48.
[36] Semevskii, *Krest'ianskii vopros*, I, 96-98.

the throne shared this privilege. The small pomeshchiks known as the *odnodvortsy* who had been reduced to the status of state peasants in the eighteenth century, had been allowed to keep their right to own serfs. Only a small and diminishing minority of them, however, exercised this privilege, so that by the 1850's there were not many more than a thousand serfs owned by these people. The law permitted the "military residents" and the "tax-free proprietors" of Olonets guberniia, and the Mirzas who descended reputedly from Tatar nobles, to own serfs, too. The total number in their possession was extremely small, probably not being more than a couple of hundred.[37]

Citizens of certain towns in the western provinces, charitable foundations, peasants on personal estates of the imperial family, and the state peasantry, also were allowed to own serfs and land. The right of cities went back to the period when they had been under Polish rule. After their annexation by Russia they were permitted to keep the privilege until the 1830's. Charitable foundations had received their serfs as gifts.[38] A decree of 31 October 1766 empowered the peasants on estates of the imperial family to buy land and serfs from neighboring landowners. They could not pay more than 30 rubles for each male soul, and had to pay the state an annual obrok of 1 ruble 25 kopecks for each desiatin of land they purchased. In 1788 another decree extended this privilege to the state peasantry.[39] These measures were undoubtedly inspired by the state's desire to give its peasants the same opportunity to evade personal military service that seignioral peasants had. The seignioral peasants could buy serfs in their master's name to serve as substitutes for themselves when recruit calls were made. Now the peasants of the imperial family, and the state peasants, could meet their recruit obligation in the same manner.

Actually, men of all classes continued to disregard the restrictions against their ownership of serfs. Some of them used ruses, such as registering their people in the name of a cooperative nobleman, but others made no effort at concealment. During

[37] Köppen, "Über die Vertheilung," p. 410. For the composition of these groups v. pp. 478-479, 483-484.

[38] Troinitskii, *Krepostnoe naselenie*, pp. 14-16.

[39] *PSZ*, XVII, no. 12772, p. 1031; XXII, no. 16619, 29 Jan. 1788, p. 1025.

Catherine's reign there were priests who owned sizable properties, merchants who bought villages for themselves, and government clerks and other *roturiers*, who owned serfs. Even serfs had their own serfs, though they always bought them in the name of their masters. In 1777, for instance, a serf who belonged to Count Sheremetev bought a property with 429 male souls on it for 29,560 rubles. In 1794 the wealthy serf manufacturers of Ivanovo owned a total of 528 male and 659 female serfs. In the 1840's some Sheremetev serfs were said to have owned as many as six to seven hundred bondsmen.[40]

Tsar Paul gave further evidence of his spite against the dvorianstvo when in 1798 he restored the right of merchants to buy serfs for their factories. The number they could purchase for each plant was to be fixed according to the Senate decree of 1752. But this revival was short-lived. Alexander I on 3 July 1802 placed serious limitations on the privilege, and finally in a ukase of 6 November 1806 definitively abolished it.[41] Decrees of 1804 and 1814 ordered that henceforth "personal" nobles could no longer own serfs. The personal noble who had serfs at the time of the issue of these laws could keep them until his death, after which his heirs had to dispose of them. In 1841, the government, as part of a program to reduce the number of landless peasants, commanded nobles who owned no landed property to divest themselves of their serfs.[42]

In contrast to its preservation of the exclusive right to own serfs, the dvorianstvo's monopoly on landownership crumbled in the nineteenth century. Despite Alexander's pro-noble orientation he felt he should "do something" about the agrarian problem. His efforts at genuine reform proved futile, chiefly because the failings of his own character made it impossible for him to face the difficulties and dangers of radical revisions. Still, some changes emerged from the long deliberations he held with his counselors on these matters. One of these was the ending of the sole right of the dvorianstvo to own land. The

[40] Semevskii, *Krest'ianskii vopros*, I, 5-9, 296; Shchepetov, *Krepostnoe pravo*, pp. 103-104, Table 7, p. 355; Semevskii, *Krest'iane*, I, 298.
[41] Tugan-Baranovskii, *Russkaia fabrika*, p. 88.
[42] SZ, 1857, IX, sect. 208, 228-231. For personal nobles v. note 22, above.

government argued that this monopoly had been justified only so long as nobles had to do compulsory service, and needed land to support themselves while they performed their obligations for the state. When that duty passed into limbo the justification went with it. So late in 1801 Alexander decreed that any of his subjects, except serfs, could own uninhabited land. The tsar set great store by this law, emphasizing his high opinion of it by having it published on his birthday. In 1817 another decree permitted these non-noble landowners to mortgage or alienate their property.[43]

Members of the merchant class took advantage of this legislation to buy land. Some of them engaged in sizable farming operations; in the 1840's merchants owned holdings of 500 to 1,000 desiatins or more in Voronezh, Tambov, and Saratov. They worked their farms with hired laborers or sharecroppers, and also rented serfs from nobles.[44]

Serfs had always been able to buy land by using the name of their master, and some of them apparently purchased considerable amounts. Between 1770 and 1830 serfs who belonged to the Sheremetevs bought 32,710 desiatins in this manner.[45] Since the seignior held title to the property he could—and sometimes did—sell it or take it for his own use without compensating the serfs who had laid out the money to buy the land. In 1848, however, the law was amended to allow serfs to buy uninhabited property in their own names, although they had to have their master's consent for the transaction. The new decree was not retroactive, so that land bought by serfs prior to its publication remained in the name of the seignior.[46]

IV

The ascendancy of the dvorianstvo in the eighteenth century provided a sharp contrast to the fate of the other great group of Russian proprietors—the churchmen. For the same monarchs

[43] *PSZ*, XXVII, no. 20075, 12 Dec. 1801, pp. 862-863; Druzhinin, *Gosudarstvennye krest'iane*, I, 81.
[44] Semevskii, "Po povodu," p. 135; Haxthausen, *Studien*, I, 286-287; II, 92, 128.
[45] Shchepetov, *Krepostnoe pravo*, p. 355.
[46] *SZ*, 1857, IX, sect. 1138; *PSZ*, 2nd series, XXIII, no. 22042, 3 Mar. 1848, pp. 157-158.

who welded the nobility into a caste and elevated it to the highest levels in the state, crushed the independence of the church, and ultimately took away its land and peasants.

When the century opened, the church, despite efforts to curb its wealth that dated back to the sixteenth century, remained in possession of vast holdings. In the Second Revision in 1747 over 900,000 male peasants in Great Russia and Siberia belonged to religious institutions, and the census made two decades later showed that the church now owned 991,761. As in the past, the monasteries were by far the greatest proprietors among the church seigniors. In 1747 they owned 728,736 males, prelates owned 116,376, the Holy Synod had 37,426, and cathedrals and parish churches owned 23,767. Trinity-St. Serge Monastery continued as the single greatest private serfowner in the empire. It had about 106,000 male peasants on the properties it owned in five provinces of Great Russia. Trinity-St. Alexander Nevskii had 25,464, the Convent of the Assumption had close to 24,000, St. Cyril's in Beloozersk had 21,590, and at least nine others had between ten and twenty thousand. These, of course, were the Croesuses of cloistered society. Out of close to a thousand monasteries in the mid-eighteenth century, well over half owned no serfs. But of the 457 who did, 70 percent had over 100 males, and 5.7 percent had over 5,000. In comparison with lay serfowners these monasteries were great proprietors, for scarcely more than 16 percent of the lay seigniors of that time had more than 100 serfs. Prelates also owned many peasants. In 1744 the bishops in twenty-four dioceses had an average of 7,500 male serfs, and some had well over 10,000. Churches were much less wealthy. Only 566 of them—50 cathedrals and 516 parish churches, representing not much over 3 percent of the total number of churches—owned peasants, and most of them had fewer than twenty.[47]

Tsars had long had their troubles with the wealth and power of the church, but it took a man of Peter's will to settle matters. That monarch decided that it was high time to put an end to the church's pretensions. In 1701 he announced that the newly-

[47] Semevskii, *Krest'iane*, II, 194-199. There were 966 monasteries in 1762. El'iashevich, *Istoriia*, I, 270n.

revived Monastery Bureau, originally established by Tsar Alexis but abolished in 1667, would manage the properties of prelates and monasteries. The Bureau gave part of the revenues from these lands to their clerical owners, and the rest went to the treasury. In 1721 Peter abolished the office of Patriarch, the head of the Russian church, and replaced it with a government bureau called the Most Holy Synod. The church's properties were transferred back to the direct control of the religious until 1726, when they were turned over to a new body made up of laymen, known as the Economic College. (Peter had introduced the foreign word *kollegia* for new administrative agencies that operated on the collegiate or council principle, rather than being directed by individual ministers.)

After Peter's death the Economic College fell under the authority of the Synod, but in 1738 Empress Anna transferred it to the control of the Senate. Then, when Elizabeth, who had a reputation for piety, came to the throne she abolished the College and gave the Synod complete control over all ecclesiastical property. In 1757, not much more than a decade later, she reversed that decision and returned the administration of church lands to lay officials. She used the widespread unrest among church peasants as the excuse for her action. But the real reason was her need for more revenues. The Seven Years' War had just begun, and Russia needed money to carry on its share of the battle against Frederick of Prussia.

It was an easy step from the arrangement set up in 1757 to secularization, especially for Elizabeth's successor, Peter III, who was openly scornful of the Orthodox Church and its ritual. On 21 March 1762 he reestablished the Economic College and placed all church property under its administration. The church peasants were to be allotted the land they tilled, and the myriad of dues and services they paid their clerical masters was to be replaced by a single payment of one ruble per peasant per year to the Economic College. The College was to use part of this revenue to support the clergy, and the rest was to go into the state's treasury for general purposes.[48]

[48] Semevskii, *Krest'iane*, II, X, 199-201; Miliukov, *Histoire*, II, 498-501.

The new law raised a storm of protest among the churchmen and their supporters. In fact, the British envoy at St. Petersburg reported that this action of Peter's, combined with his general neglect of the clergy, provided the principal motive for the revolution that overthrew him just three months later.[49] Catherine II, to win the church's support, repealed Peter's reforms, and gave back the land and serfs to the clergy. This reversal enraged the peasants who had hoped to escape from their heavy-handed clerical masters, and thousands of them turned to violence to express their displeasure. Meanwhile, Catherine, who in the ukase returning the church land had solemnly declared that she had neither the desire nor the intention to appropriate it, had made up her mind to do exactly that when she felt she could do it safely. The church peasants' rising, in which over 100,000 people were involved, gave her the chance. In May 1763 she revived the Economic College, and the following February ordered the confiscation of all ecclesiastical property, turning over its administration to the Economic College, and converting the church peasants into state peasants. 252 monasteries were shut down, 161 others were allowed to remain open on condition that they be supported by donations of the faithful, and the rest, along with all other church institutions, were to be supported by government subventions.[50]

Some nobles proposed to the empress that the state lease or sell the secularized properties to members of the dvorianstvo. Catherine, however, had announced that the income from these lands was going to be used for public education and welfare, and rejected these suggestions. Actually, the state used the income for many other purposes. And even though Catherine did not distribute church lands to nobles, her conversion of them into state property enabled her to make her generous gifts of other state lands to her favorites.

[49] Robert Keith to George Grenville, 1 July 1762, *SIRO*, XII (1873), 9.
[50] Miliukov, *Histoire*, II, 548-550; Semevskii, *Krest'iane*, II, xi.
Returns of the Tenth Revision in 1858 showed 1,927 male souls owned by churches and monasteries. These institutions, however, belonged to sects other than the Russian Orthodox, and were in provinces annexed from Poland. Troinitskii, *Krepostnoe naselenie*, p. 46.

In her correspondence with Western men of letters the empress preened herself on the secularization, as evidence of her sympathy with the ideals and philosophy of the Enlightenment. The truth, of course, was that she had carried out the program initiated by her predecessors, none of whom (as one historian tartly observed) has ever been considered a disciple of Voltaire and the Encyclopedists.[51]

Naturally enough, the clergy bitterly opposed the secularization, but many private landowners also criticized it severely. They feared that it might well establish a precedent that would lead to limitations or even abolition of their own powers over their serfs. Some found flaws in the results of the reform, claiming that the secularized properties were going to ruin, that the condition of the peasants on them had worsened, and that these developments damaged the economy of the empire. Their charges found important supporters, and in the last years of her life Catherine seemed ready to yield. The proposal was made to rent out all secularized properties, and also all Court estates, to private landlords. The empress died before the scheme was implemented and it was not renewed in the following reigns. Paul, however, gave away 50,000 secularized peasant souls to commanders of Russian knightly orders, and Alexander I in 1816-1818 transferred some of them into the status of military colonists.[52] With these exceptions the former peasants of the church and their descendants remained state peasants.

[51] Miliukov, *Histoire*, II, 550-551.
[52] Semevskii, *Krest'iane*, II, xlii-xliii, 278-286.

19

RICH NOBLE, POOR NOBLE

THE RUSSIAN NOBLE measured his wealth not by the amount of land he owned, as did his peers in other countries, but by the number of male serfs (or revision souls as they were called because they were entered in the census, or revision, lists) that belonged to him. In the first half of the eighteenth century a proprietor who had over 1,000 revision souls was held to be of vast wealth, if he had 500 to 1,000 he was a great proprietor, if he had 100 to 500 he was well off, if he had 25 to 100 he was a petty noble, and if he had less than 25 he was poor. Then, starting in the second half of the century standards soared as a result of the increase in population, and the lavish gifts of peasants made by the tsars. The great magnates now counted their serfs in many thousands, while the lord who had 500 or so was considered to be just well-to-do.[1]

But the magnates and even the men of moderate wealth made up a very small minority of the nobility. The usual landlord owned less than 100 serfs, and a large number of them owned less than 10. Partial information collected in 1777 showed that 32 percent of the serfowners for whom data were available had fewer than 10 male serfs, 30.7 percent had 10 to 30, 13.4 percent had 30 to 60, 7.7 percent had 60 to 100, and only 16.2 percent owned over 100.[2] The much fuller (though still incomplete) data collected in 1834 and 1858 for the eighth and tenth revisions, covering all the provinces of European Russia, reveal the continued predominance of the small serfowner, and the unevenness of the distribution of serfs among proprietors.[3]

In 1834, as the table shows, 84 percent of the serfowners owned less than 101 males, and 16 percent owned over 100 (the same proportions as those for 1777). The 84 percent who

[1] Miliukov, *Histoire*, II, 502, 633; Leroy-Beaulieu, *L'Empire*, I, 411-412n.
[2] Semevskii, *Krest'iane*, I, 30; Voznesenskii, *Ekonomika Rossii*, p. 35.
[3] 1834 data from Köppen, "Uber die Vertheilung," pp. 420-422; 1858 data from Troinitskii, *Krepostnoe naselenie*, p. 67.

	NO. OF SERF-OWNERS	PERCENT OF ALL SERF-OWNERS	NO. OF REVISION SOULS OWNED	PERCENT OF ALL REVISION SOULS	AVERAGE NO OF REVISION SOULS PER SERFOWNER
Serfowners without land	17,763	14	62,183	1	3
Landlords with:					
1 to 20 souls	58,457	46	450,037	4	8
21 to 100 souls	30,417	24	1,500,357	14	49
101 to 500 souls	16,740	13	3,634,194	34	217
500 to 1,000 souls	2,273	2	1,562,831	14	687
over 1,000 souls	1,453	1	3,556,959	33	2,448
	127,103		10,766,561		

had less than 101 souls owned altogether just 19 percent of the total male serf population. The 16 percent who owned over 100 had 81 percent of all male serfs. By 1858 the proportion of serfowners with less than 101 had decreased. Now only 78 percent of the serfowners were in this category, and 22 percent owned more than 100. The division of serfs between the two groups, however, remained unchanged. The men with less than 101 male serfs had 19 percent of all male serfs, and those with 100 or more owned 81 percent.

The inequality in the distribution of serf ownership becomes even more striking when only the smallest and the largest proprietors are compared. In 1834 60 percent of the serfowners owned fewer than 21 souls. Altogether they owned just 5 percent of all male serfs. One percent of the serfowners had more than 1,000 souls each. Their total serf ownership accounted for 33 percent of all male serfs. In 1858 44 percent of the serfowners had less than 21 males, and together owned 3.1 percent of all males. One percent owned 1,000 souls or more, and together owned 29 percent of the male serf population.[4]

[4] The Russian serfowner had on the average many more serfs than the contemporary American slaveowner had slaves. In 1850 19.8 percent of the 347,525 American slaveowning families had just 1 slave, 30.4 percent had 2 to 5, 23.2 percent had 5 to 9, 15.7 percent had 10 to 19, 8.6 percent had 20 to 49, and 1.8

	NO. OF SERF-OWNERS	PERCENT OF ALL SERF-OWNERS	NO. OF REVISION SOULS OWNED	PERCENT OF ALL REVISION SOULS	AVERAGE NO. OF REVISION SOULS PER SERFOWNER
			1858		
Serfowners without land	3,633	4	12,045	.1	3
Landlords with:					
1 to 20 souls	41,016	40	327,534	3	8
21 to 100 souls	35,498	34	1,666,073	16	47
101 to 500 souls	19,930	19	3,925,102	37	197
500 to 1,000 souls	2,421	2	1,569,888	15	648
over 1,000 souls	1,382	1	3,050,540	29	2,207
	103,880		10,551,182		

The revision returns showed a drop of 23,223 (over 18 percent) in the number of serfowners between 1834 and 1858. The sharp decrease in the number of serfowners who had no land accounted for over three-fifths (14,130) of the decline. The 1841 law that forbad landless nobles to own serfs brought about the decrease in the size of this category. Shifts occurred in other groups, too. The number of landlords with less than 21 male serfs fell by 30 percent (17,441), and the total number of souls they owned declined by 27 percent (122,503). The number of proprietors with over 1,000 males decreased by 5 percent (71), and they owned 14 percent (506,419) fewer serfs. The middle groups increased in size. In the 21 to 100 rubric the number of serfowners went up by 17 percent (5,081), and the number of their serfs rose 11 percent (165,716). In the 101-500 category, the number of serfowners increased by 19 percent (3,190), and the number of their serfs went up 8 percent (290,908).

Assuming equal accuracy for the data from the two revisions,

percent had 50 to 99. Thus, 99.5 percent owned less than 100 Negro men, women, and children. (The Russian figures are for males only.) Of the .5 percent (1,733) who owned more than 100 slaves, 1,479 owned 100 to 200, 187 owned 200 to 299, 56 owned 300 to 499, 9 owned 500 to 1,000 and 2 owned over 1,000. In 1850 there were 3,204,313 slaves in the United States. DeBow. *Statistical View*, pp. 87, 95.

the decline in the number of proprietors with over 1,000 souls must have resulted from the partition through inheritance of the great holdings that favored nobles had received from the tsars and empresses of the eighteenth century. As for the decline in the numbers of the smallest serfowners, perhaps many of these men decided that their holdings were too small to support both themselves and their serfs, and so they sold their peasants to wealthier seigniors.[5] The effects of these developments at the top and bottom would be to increase the proportion of serfowners in the middle categories.

Of the proprietors who owned over 1,000 males, a handful counted their serfs in the tens of thousands. The Sheremetevs headed the roster of these fabulously wealthy people. Count N. P. Sheremetev owned 185,610 male and female serfs and 990,793 desiatins of land in the last part of the eighteenth century. A half century later his son, Count D. N. Sheremetev, owned almost 300,000 serfs of both sexes, though his land holdings had decreased to 714,000 desiatins.[6] The Vorontsovs, Iusupovs, Stroganovs, Orlovs, and Golitsins were other great proprietors, though they owned far fewer people than the Sheremetevs. Count Vorontsov owned 54,703 serfs of both sexes and 271,363 desiatins of land at the end of the eighteenth century, and in 1851 his successor owned 37,702 male souls alone. In the 1840's Prince Iusupov had 33,000 male souls and 300,000 desiatins.[7]

Every province had a large number of serfowners who had less than 21 male serfs. These petty proprietors were most common, however, in the Little Russian provinces of Chernigov and Poltava, where 65 percent of the seigniors were in this category. Other provinces with unusually high concentrations of these smallest serfowners were Kursk with 60 percent, Kharkov with 50 percent, and Smolensk, Novgorod, and Voronezh, all with 48 percent.[8]

Since the wealth of seigniors was measured by the number of male peasants they owned, the cost of serfs provides an index

[5] Troinitskii, *Krepostnoe naselenie*, p. 68.
[6] Shchepetov, *Krepostnoe pravo*, pp. 20-21, 26.
[7] Indova, *Krepostnoe khoziaistvo*, pp. 39-47; Sivkov, *Ocherki*, p. 14.
[8] Computed from data in Troinitskii, *Krepostnoe naselenie*, p. 45.

to their gross worth. Only scattered price data are available, however, up to the middle of the nineteenth century.[9] Then, in 1859, the Ministry of Interior collected data on 18,000 sales of populated and unpopulated land made between 1 January 1854 and 1 January 1859. This material provides a mass of information on the prices paid for serfs and land in the last decade of serfdom.[10] In the following table the 37 provinces of European Russia for which this information is most complete are grouped according to geographical regions. The Ministry's data for each province included the number of sales of populated land, the number of male serfs and of desiatins of land involved in the sales, the total amount of money that changed hands in the transactions, the number of sales of unpopulated land, the amount of unpopulated land that was involved, and the total amount of money paid for the unpopulated land. The Ministry's figures do not include the cost of serfs without land. Since the higher prices paid for populated land was due to the presence of serfs on that land, the value of the individual male serf can be computed from the data given.[11]

Using the computed average price of a male serf with land as a guide, it is possible to gain an idea of the average cash value of seignioral holdings in the 1850's. For example, the holding of a landowner in New Russia who had 21 male serfs on his property was worth on the average 7,936 rubles (377.9 rubles x 21). A property in the Southwest with 21 souls was worth 4,511 rubles (214.8 rubles x 21); in Lithuania such a

9 Cf. Hupel, "Ueber den Nationalkarakter," p. 218; Drakokhrust, "Rassloenie," pp. 115-118; Tooke, *View*, III, 318n.; Kusheva, "Khoziaistvo," pp. 598-599, 676-677; Semevskii, *Krest'iane*, I, 153-154, 155-156; Miliukov, "Zur Geschichte," p. 104.

10 The Ministry's data are condensed in tabular form in Rikhter, "Zabytyi," pp. 16-21.

11 This was done by multiplying the number of desiatins of populated land by the average price of a desiatin of unpopulated land, subtracting the product from the total sales in rubles of populated land, considering the remainder to be the value added to the land by the presence on it of serfs, then dividing this figure by the number of serfs on the populated land: the quotient is the computed average price of the male serf soul without land.

Maslov, *Agrarnyi vopros*, I, 376-377, using the same data, computed the average value of populated and unpopulated land and of the individual male serf without land for two regions (Central Industrial and Central Agricultural). He arrived at incorrect results, however, because he made the arithmetical error of averaging the averages he found in his source.

property was worth 4,177 rubles (198.9 rubles x 21); and so on down to 3,108 rubles for a property in White Russia (148 rubles x 21).

Land Transfers, 1854-1859

Region	A. POPULATED LAND		B. UNPOPULATED LAND		Percent difference in price, A and B	Av. price male serf with land (rubles)	Av. price male serf without land (rubles)
	No. of sales	Av. price per desiatin (rubles)	No. of sales	Av. price per desiatin (rubles)			
Central Industrial	1026	19.6	1849	14.9	32	169.8	40.9
Central Agricultural	845	32.7	2647	26.4	24	193.8	37.5
Lake	378	10.7	1257	8.1	32	191.9	46.9
Lithuania	585	20.3	1497	19.8	3	198.9	5.1
White Russia	222	11.0	778	10.3	7	148.0	9.4
Little Russia	605	22.2	2796	17.8	25	182.0	35.8
Southwest	570	30.8	140	12.8	141	214.8	125.7
New Russia	247	18.1	416	15.0	21	377.9	64.3
Volga	331	17.4	748	10.4	67	169.2	68.2

The provinces included in this tabulation are:
CENTRAL INDUSTRIALS Tver, Iaroslav, Kostroma, Nizhnii Novgorod, Vladimir, Moscow, Smolensk, Kaluga
CENTRAL AGRICULTURAL: Orel, Tula, Riazan, Tambov, Voronezh, Kursk
LAKE: Novgorod, Pskov, St. Petersburg
LITHUANIA: Kovno, Vilna, Grodno
WHITE RUSSIA: Vitebsk, Mogilev, Minsk
LITTLE RUSSIA: Chernigov, Poltava, Kharkov
SOUTHWEST: Kiev, Volynia, Podolia
NEW RUSSIA: Kherson, Ekaterinoslav
VOLGA: Kazan, Simbirsk, Penza, Saratov, Samara, Orenburg

The most remarkable finding, however, that emerges from the table is the relatively small difference in much of the empire between the prices of populated and unpopulated land. The presence or absence of serfs made startlingly little difference in many places in the amount of money people were willing to pay for a property. In six of the 37 provinces included in the table land with serfs on it cost only 1 to 9 percent more than unpopulated land; in eight it cost 11 to 20 percent more; in ten it cost 21 to 29 percent more; in five it cost 31 to 39 percent more; and in eight it cost between 43 and 74 percent more.[12]

Nearly half the sales analyzed in the table took place in the Central Agricultural, Central Industrial, and Lake zones. Over 46 percent of the empire's serfs lived in these three regions in the 1850's.[13] As the table shows, land cost much more in the Central Agricultural than it did in the other two zones (and, in fact, more than it did in any other region). This higher price was undoubtedly attributable to the fertility of the soil in the Central Agricultural, and to its proximity to major markets in the Central Industrial provinces. But the average price of a serf without land in the Central Agricultural was less than it was in the Central Industrial and Lake regions. In other words, serfs were valued more highly in these latter two regions than they were in the Central Agricultural, and so added more to the value of the land.

The explanation of this regional difference in the price of serfs seems to me to lie in the use serfowners made of their peasants. By the last part of the eighteenth century a regional barshchina-obrok pattern had worked itself out. Labor services predominated in the obligations demanded by the seigniors of the Central Agricultural provinces, while obrok predominated in the obligations demanded by the lords of the Central Industrial and Lake regions. The fact that these latter proprietors valued their serfs more highly than did their peers of the Central Agricultural indicates that serfowners received a higher net re-

[12] 1 to 9% more: Grodno 1%, Chernigov 3%, Podolia 4%, Kursk 5%, Voronezh 6%, Minsk 9%. 11 to 20 % more: Tula 11%, Orel 12%, Riazan 12%, Mogilev 15%, Novgorod 15%, Simbirsk 18%, Penza 19%, Tambov 20%. 21 to 29% more: Poltava 21%, Kherson 22%, Kovno 22%, Vilna 23%, Saratov 24%, Kazan 27%, Vitebsk 28%, Moscow 29%, Tver 29%, Smolensk 29%. 31 to 39% more: Ekaterinoslav 31%, Nizhnii Novgorod 35%, Kaluga 38%, St. Petersburg 38%, Pskov 39%. 43 to 74% more: Vladimir 43%, Iaroslav 48%, Kostroma 52%, Kiev 54%, Kharkov 56%, Orenburg 63%, Volynia 71%, Samara 74%.
Maslov, *Agrarnyi vopros*, I, 431, made these calculations for each province, but managed to make the astonishingly high score of 21 errors out of a possible 37 in computing the percentages.
[13] Troinitskii, *Krepostnoe naselenie*, pp. 49-50.

turn from serfs on obrok than they did from serfs on barshchina. Therefore, serf prices were higher in the regions where obrok predominated. This, in turn, points to the conclusion that a premium attached itself to seignorial non-participation in market production, for the obrok was the form of serf exploitation used by those proprietors who eschewed commercial activity and drew their incomes from quitrents.

This explanation is at variance with the one advanced by the Russian Marxist economist, Peter Maslov, early in this century.[14] Maslov's interpretation has been one of the most influential expressions of the view that there was a close and direct link between developing capitalism and the abolition of serfdom in Russia. He argued that the development of the market economy, and seignorial participation in this development, accounted for the small price differentials between populated and unpopulated land. The greater demand of the expanding market for farm goods made agricultural land more valuable. This stimulated proprietors to increase their arable, and thereby produced an increase in the demand for unoccupied land. For these reasons the difference in price between populated and unpopulated land was less in the Central Agricultural, a fertile farming area, than it was in the Central Industrial and Lake regions, where the soil was less fertile and farming was of much less importance. Part of the landowner's income, according to Maslov, now assumed the nature of land rent. This was separate from the income he received from the labor of his serfs, which Maslov called profit. By the 1850's the price of populated land was determined by the capitalized value of the rent and profit it yielded. The price of unpopulated land was determined by the capitalized value of the rent alone. The price of the serf was determined by the capitalized value of the profit his owner could draw from his labor. Land in the Central Agricultural cost more than it did in the Central Industrial and Lake provinces because the landowners there realized more rent from their land than did the landowners in the other two regions. Serfs cost less in the Central Agricultural because a larger proportion of the seignior's income came from the rent yielded by his land,

14 Maslov, *Agrarnyi vopros*, I, 376-380.

than from the profit he made on the labor of his serfs. Land, from the viewpoint of the seignior in the Central Agricultural provinces, began to become more valuable than the serfs who lived on it. Maslov saw this as a sure sign of the decline of serfdom. For, said he, when lords reckoned their incomes according to the amount of land they owned, and not according to the number of their serfs, when land rose in price of and by itself, "then serfdom lost its importance for the landowner, since the expansion of his land increased the value of his property to a greater degree than did increasing the number of his serfs."

Maslov's attribution of a rational capitalistic attitude to the landlords of the Central Agricultural region, and his argument that they were losing their interest in serfdom as a result of this new attitude, has been repeated by others after him. Later pages will show that there is little evidence to support these views. It suffices here to observe that much of the production of the barshchina peasants in the Central Agricultural zone was consumed by the households of the proprietors, and did not go to market; the available data indicate that direct seignorial production did not increase during the first half of the nineteenth century, and indeed, on larger estates seems to have decreased; and the serfowners of the Central Agricultural provinces, like their fellows in most other parts of the empire, were nearly unanimous in their disapprobation of the government's decision to emancipate the serfs.

II

The unequal distribution of serfs among the proprietors, and the low cash value of land and serfs, meant that a large sector of the Russian seignorial class was made up of men of very limited means. The thousands of serfowners who owned less than twenty-one males, and particularly those who had less than ten, were in especially straitened circumstances. Engaged in a constant struggle to make ends meet, they had neither the time nor the means to care about the amenities appropriate to their social status. They rarely had the opportunity to leave their petty rural world, and when the chance came they often could not afford it. A representative of a group of provincial nobles told the Senate in 1771 that over 200 young nobles among the people he represented had informed him that they wanted to enter imperial service, but did not have the clothes and boots they needed to report for duty. Many among these least of the seigniors adopted peasant ways and peasant manners, tilled their land themselves, and gradually sank into the mass of the peasantry.[15] A representative of the nobility of Riazan reported in 1857 that 1,700 noble families, or one-fourth of all the noble households of that province, were so poor that "together with their peasants they form one family, eat at one table and live in one hut."[16] Tsar Nicholas' government embarked on a program of direct relief that helped a few of these pauperized nobles. The state moved them from crowded regions to less populous parts of the empire, and gave them land and money subsidies. In the forties and fifties several hundred families benefited from this policy.[17]

Much of the responsibility for the existence of this large number of poverty-stricken noble families lay with the nobles themselves. Their stubborn maintenance of the centuries-old custom of dividing their real and personal possessions among their heirs had the inevitable result of splintering patrimonies with each successive generation. As in earlier centuries, once wealthy families were reduced to poverty in as few as three generations. Sometimes one branch of a family was able to hold on to its share of the patrimony, while another more prolific line became impoverished through the operations of equal inheritance. When a member, say, of the Golitsin clan was mentioned in a conversation, it was not uncommon to ask, "Who is this Golitsin? A rich one or a poor one?" Many small villages were divided up among ten to fifteen proprietors, and larger settlements with 400 to 500 souls in them were split up among as many as thirty to forty separate owners. Baron Haxthausen heard about one village that was parcelled among 83 proprietors.[18]

15 Romanovich-Slavatinskii, *Dvorianstvo*, p. 64; Tooke, *View*, II, 306; Baranovich, *Materialy*, p. 140.

16 Solov'ev, "Zapiski," xxx, 746-747.

17 Romanovich-Slavatinskii, *Dvorianstvo*, pp. 65-66.

18 *Ibid.*, p. 25; Haxthausen, *Studien*, II, 81, 126-127; III, 59.

Only the vast reservoirs of empty land in the colonial regions kept all estates from being reduced to petty holdings in a few generations. Sometimes heirs, discontent with their small portion, sold out to their coheirs and with the proceeds bought property on the frontiers where land was cheap. In the fertile Volga provinces, for example, a desiatin of unpopulated land cost 60 percent less in the 1850's than it did in the Central Agricultural zone (v. table p. 372). A man who inherited land and serfs in the latter region could sell the land, use the money to buy more than twice as much land across the Volga, and settle there with his serfs.

An effort to supplant the system of equal inheritance was made by Peter I as part of his reform program. In a ukase of 23 March 1714[19] he ordered that henceforth the owner of real property had to pass it on to a single heir, whom the owner had the power to designate. The heir did not have to be the eldest son unless the owner died intestate, in which case the first-born son inherited, or failing sons the eldest daughter. If the decedent had no surviving direct heirs he could bequeath his property to a kinsman, and if he died intestate the nearest kinsman inherited.

In the text of the decree Peter explained that equal inheritance led to the impoverishment and eventual disappearance of once eminent families, and that it reduced the general welfare and tax-paying ability of the peasantry. The heirs tried to live on the same scale as their father, but owning fewer serfs had to exploit them more harshly than their parent. He also pointed out that when all sons shared in the patrimony each was likely to try to live on the income he drew from his inheritance, instead of engaging in productive enterprise. For Peter, in trying to establish the principle of sole succession, was not only concerned with protecting the landowning class from impoverishment. He also wanted to encourage scions of the nobility to go into trade, industry, government service, and the arts. He reasoned that by allowing only one son to inherit the remaining sons would have to seek their fortunes elsewhere. He hoped that these landless cadets would become—as they had in England—

19 *PSZ*, v, no. 2789, 91-94.

an adventurous and energetic breed of men whose poverty and ambition would goad them into the fields that Peter wanted them to enter.

But Peter's effort at reform failed. It ran too strongly against old tradition. Landowners used dodges of one sort or other to get around the new legislation so that they could provide for all their children. Jealousies and feuds disturbed family relationships when the decree was obeyed. Finally, in 1731 Empress Anna repealed the unpopular law and the old order was restored.[20] The method of distribution of real and personal property, as worked out over the centuries in custom and legislation, was later systematized in the *Svod Zakonov*, the codification made in the nineteenth century of the laws of the empire. The chief heirs were the sons of the decedent. They received equal shares of the estate. Each daughter was supposed to receive one fourteenth of the real property and one eighth of the movable property of her parent. Failing male descendants daughters inherited everything, and if there were no direct heirs the property went to collateral relatives. Wives received one seventh of their late spouse's real property and one fourth of his personal property, regardless of whether there were any children.[21] Although primogeniture was recognized neither in law nor custom, the eldest son generally took his father's place as head of the family. It was not unknown, however, for the father to designate another of his sons to succeed him in this position.[22]

Some of the wealthiest proprietors, however, awakened to the dangers of equal inheritance, and tried to protect their patrimonies by entailing them and passing them on by primogeniture. They had to get permission from the throne to do this. Until the reign of Nicholas I only two men, General-Field Marshal Count Chernyshev in 1774 and Count Stroganov in 1814, had succeeded in gaining the necessary imperial assent. Nicholas I allowed the creation of entails in fourteen individual instances, and in 1845 issued a decree that permitted any noble to entail his property if it met certain specified qualifications.

[20] *Ibid.*, VIII, no. 5717, 396-398; Kliuchevskii, *History*, IV, 89-90, 331-332.
[21] *SZ* (1832), x, sect. 700, 701, 703, 704, 706, 717.
[22] Haxthausen, *Studien*, I, 153n.

These qualifications, however, were so high that only the wealthiest could meet them. To be eligible for entail the property had to have at least 10,000 and not more than 100,000 desiatins of improved land, or have at least 400 and not more than 4,000 peasant homesteads on it, and produce an annual income of not less than 12,000 rubles and not more than 200,000 rubles. Apparently just a few proprietors among those rich enough to qualify took advantage of the law; between 1845 and 1861 only twelve entails were created.[23]

III

Because so many of the empire's serfowners had such limited means it is not surprising to discover that most of them had to borrow constantly to make ends meet. But the greatest proprietors, too, lived out their lives under the ever-present shadow of debt. Some of these magnates owed fantastic sums of money. Count N. P. Sheremetev, who had more serfs and more land than anyone else in the empire, owed 2,018,839 rubles in 1800. He piled up this enormous debt by the simple procedure of spending more than his income. In 1798, for example, his revenues amounted to 632,200 rubles, but he spent 692,000 rubles. He used 29 percent of this expenditure to service his debts, nearly 35 percent went for personal expenses, and he spent the rest on the maintenance of his household and on charity. N. P. was overshadowed by his heir, D. N. Sheremetev. In 1822 D. N. spent 2,100,000 rubles, or 600,000 rubles more than his income for that year. In 1838 he spent 3,442,500 rubles. This exceeded his income for that year by 1,200,000 rubles. The result of this scale of living was that by 1859 he owed 6,000,000 rubles.[24] Prince I. B. Iusupov, another of the greatest serfowners, owed 100,000 rubles in 1798 to government lending agencies. By 1818 his indebtedness to these agencies had gone up to 693,630 rubles, and at the time of his death in 1831 he owed three times as much as he had owed in 1818.[25] B. A. Kurakin, who owned over 7,000 serfs and had an income of around

---

[23] Romanovich-Slavatinskii, *Dvorianstvo*, pp. 254-255, 528-529.
[24] Shchepetov, *Krepostnoe pravo*, pp. 85, 235; Sivkov, "Biudzhet," pp. 149-150.
[25] Sivkov, "Biudzhet," pp. 140-141.

7,500 rubles a year, left debts totalling 207,032 rubles when he died in 1764. The interest charges alone on his indebtedness amounted to 12,422 rubles, or one and two thirds times as much as his income.[26]

The debts piled up by the grandees suited their eminence. Lesser men involved themselves in proportion. The consequence was that Russian serfowners became burdened with an unbelievable amount of debt that increased from decade to decade. They borrowed most of the money they craved by mortgaging their serfs with special governmental credit bureaus that had been established for their convenience. Records of these institutions showed the size and growth of their indebtedness in the last decades of serfdom.[27]

YEAR	NO. OF REVISION SOULS MORTGAGED (IN MILLIONS)	PERCENT OF ALL SERF REVISION SOULS	AMOUNT OWED STATE CREDIT INSTIT. (MILL. OF RUBLES)
1820	1.8	20	110 (assignat)
1833	4.5	37	950 (assignat)
1842	5.6	50	
1855	6.6	61	398 (credit rubles)
1859	7.1	66	425 (credit rubles)

Data on the number of serfs mortgaged by the lords of each province and region in 1856 reveal marked regional differences in the extent to which the serfowners had borrowed.[28]

With 71.3 percent of their revision souls mortgaged, the seigniors of the Central Agricultural region, chief granary of the empire, were the most heavily indebted landowners. They were followed closely by the lords of the Lower Volga, another fertile agricultural zone. In contrast, the proprietors in the guberniias of the Southwest, and especially in the provinces of New Russia, stood far below the national average in the degree of their indebtedness. The landowners in these provinces were taking the lead in new agricultural developments, and in finding new markets for their products.

26 Kogan, "Volneniia," p. 105.
27 1820 and 1833 data from Voznesenskii, *Ekonomika Rossii*, p. 185; 1842 data from Haxthausen, *Studien*, III, 49; 1855 and 1859 data from Skrebitskii, *Krest'ianskoe delo*, IV, 1245-1249.
28 "Bankovye dolgi," pp. 229-231.

REGION	MORTGAGED SERFS AS PERCENT OF TOTAL MALE SERF POPULATION
Central Agricultural	71.3
Lower Volga	68.5
Far North	68.3
White Russia	65.7
Central Industrial	63.2
Lake	61.6
Little Russia	55.6
Urals	52.5
Southwest	52.4
New Russia	49.4
Lithuania	39.3
All regions	61.7

The dvorianstvo's borrowings were not limited to the state's lending institutions. These banks, despite their liberality, could not meet the apparently insatiable demand of the seigniors for cash. The serfowners borrowed from agencies set up by the provincial governments, and they borrowed from private moneylenders. The global amount of their private loans is unknown, but it must have been considerable: information collected in Voronezh in the late 1850's (nearly 70 percent of the serfs there were mortgaged with the state banks at this time) indicated that almost 17 percent of the total debt of the seigniors was owed to private individuals.[29]

Until well into the eighteenth century private moneylenders had, in fact, been the only sources of credit in Russia. The monks, merchants, and nobles who engaged in this trade charged from 12 percent to 20 percent, and sometimes as much as 40 percent, for their loans. The government, evincing its new interest and solicitude for the nobility, decided that it must save the seigniors from the clutches of the usurers. In 1729 an imperial ukase authorized a government bureau, the *Monetnaia Kontora*, to aid insolvent nobles in redeeming valuables pawned with the moneylenders. In 1733 another ukase declared that the high rates charged by the private lenders could not be

[29] Mikhalevich, *Materialy*, pp. 146-147.

tolerated, and ordered the *Monetnaia Kontora* to make loans at 8 percent to landowners against jewelry and gold and silver articles. The *Kontora* carried on these operations until 1736, but lent money only to a narrow circle of courtiers.[30]

These and other disorganized efforts to provide credit fell far short of meeting the needs of the seigniors. The rise in their scale of living and the increase in prices involved them all the more deeply with moneylenders. Thoughtful members of the dvorianstvo began to discuss ways of establishing other sources of credit sources, for as one of them warned, "the luxurious tastes and the excessive prodigality of a large part of our nobility will lead soon to most of our villages winding up in the hands of manufacturers, merchants, clerks, secretaries, doctors and surgeons, and they, not we, will be the masters and the proprietors."[31]

The ascendancy of the nobility made it almost inevitable that the state would come to its aid. In 1754 the government established the Noble Bank with branches in Moscow and St. Petersburg; in 1772 it ordered the Foundling Homes it operated in these two cities to make loans from their funds to nobles; in 1786 it set up a new bank called the Government Loan Bank with which the Noble Bank was merged; and in 1797 it established the Auxiliary Bank of the Nobility which in 1802 was also merged with the Government Loan Bank. In addition, in 1775 the state authorized the charity boards of the provincial governments to make loans to local proprietors, and the Charter of the Nobility in 1785 gave permission to the noble assemblies of each guberniia to form provincial Noble Banks. The Assignat Bank, established by the government in 1769 to issue the new paper money, was also allowed to make loans by special arrangements to important aristocrats.

The sovereigns candidly stated that their aim was to rescue the landlords from the private moneylenders. Empress Elizabeth in her ukase that created the Noble Bank in 1754 declared that "many of our subjects, mostly from the nobility, having need of

[30] Borovoi, "K voprosu," pp. 72-73; Alefirenko, "Russkaia obshchestvennaia mysl," pp. 526-527.
[31] A. Bolotov quoted in Borovoi, "K voprosu," p. 72.

money, have been compelled to borrow from others at a high rate of interest and with big collateral." Similar expressions were included in the later decrees that expanded the state's credit services to the seigniors. For example, in the manifesto of 1797 that established the Auxiliary Bank for the Nobility, Tsar Paul allowed that "with extreme grief we see that many noble families are groaning under the burden of debt . . . having fallen into the hands of greedy misers and usurers. . . ."[32]

When the government organized the Noble Bank in 1754 it provided it with a capital of 750,000 rubles. By the mid-eighties it had increased the bank's capital to 6 million rubles, most of this sum being supplied by the Assignat Bank. The new Government Loan Bank, established in 1786, had even greater resources furnished it—by 1796 it had 11 million rubles available for loan. But this institution was dwarfed by the Auxiliary Bank of the Nobility which lent a total of 50 million assignat rubles between 1798 and 1802, when it merged with the Government Loan Bank. Lesser but still sizable sums were available for loan to serfowners from imperial and provincial charitable foundations and credit organizations. Most of these funds came from the government, but some came from depositors, and in the case of the charitable foundations, from gifts made by private persons for philanthropic purposes. By the turn of the century the amount of the government's loans to seigniors actually exceeded its expenditures for all other purposes. The throne was determined to have an abundance of credit available for the dvorianstvo, even though this meant cutting back on other governmental functions, and putting a great strain on the state's finances.

The government's credit agencies made their loans against the real property of the borrower. But since the value of the property was determined by the number of serf souls on it, the loans were actually made on the serfs. At first the government set a maximum loan of 10 rubles per soul, but in 1766 raised the limit to 20 rubles, in 1786 to 40 rubles, and in 1804 to 60 rubles. The loans were made at 6 percent. Initially they were for three years, but that limit was lengthened, too, so that by

[32] *Ibid.*, pp. 73-74.

the beginning of the nineteenth century the borrower could have up to 37 years for repayment.[33]

The usual landlord, whether he borrowed from a government institution or from a moneylender, rarely employed his loan for capital improvements on his property. Instead he used it for consumption. The improvidence and profligacy of the Russian nobility is familiar to every reader of the great Russian novels of the nineteenth century. There is no question that in these faults lay much of the explanation for their ever-increasing indebtedness. Moreover, the lenient policy of the governmental lending agencies encouraged excessive borrowing and extravagant spending. These institutions granted extensions and postponements freely, and they rarely foreclosed, since their *raison d'être* was to save properties for the dvorianstvo, and not to take them away. Delinquents were allowed to remain in possession, so that loans often amounted to outright gifts from the state.[34] Private moneylenders and creditors had to go through long and expensive legal proceedings to force payment, and had to overcome the venality and prejudices of the officials, themselves nobles, with whom they had to deal. Some of them resorted to unusual tactics to get their money, if a story told by a Frenchman who lived in Russia in the early years of the nineteenth century can be believed. According to his tale a certain noble who never paid his debts made it a practice to distribute alms to beggars, who waited for his appearance on the steps of his home. One day, to his astonishment, he saw one of his most persistent creditors in the crowd who had gathered for his largesse. The man held out his palm and cried, "Give, for this is perhaps all I will get from you to relieve the misery to which you have reduced me."[35]

Already in the 1790's an English visitor had marvelled at the ability of bankrupt nobles to "live in a sort of affluence and at a greater expense than would be reasonably imagined."[36] A few years later John Quincy Adams, then serving as American

---

[33] *Ibid.*, pp. 74-77; Schnitzler, *Les institutions*, II, 201-202.
[34] Borovoi, "K voprosu," p. 76.
[35] Passenans, *La Russie*, II, 112-114; cf. Tegoborskii, *Etudes*, I, 346.
[36] Tooke, *View*, II, 600-601n.

Minister to St. Petersburg, wrote in a letter to his mother:[37] "The tone of society among us is almost universally marked by an excess of expenses over income. The public officers all live far beyond their salaries, many of them are notorious for never paying their debts, and still more for preserving the balance by means which in our country would be deemed dishonorable, but which are here much less disreputable than economy."

But high living was not the only cause for the heavy indebtedness of nobles. There were other reasons, too. One was the low salaries paid government officials and army officers. The only way many of these men could live at a scale befitting their social position was to borrow or peculate, or both.[38] Another and far more basic reason for their insolvency was the low return most of them received from their properties. Part of the responsibility for this lay in the inadequate transportation system that made it so difficult to send goods to market. But the landowners themselves were chiefly responsible for the failure of their lands to produce more revenues for them. As the next chapter shows, most of them had no interest in improving their agricultural operations, and thereby failed to take advantage of the opportunity that was available to them to better their own economic position. The attitude they did have toward their properties, the uses they made of them, and the ways they went about operating them, are the subjects of the next chapter.

[37] 8 Feb. 1810 in Ford, ed., *Writings*, III, 396.
[38] Passenans, *La Russie*, II, 109-112.

20

THE SEIGNIORAL ECONOMY

IN THE FIRST QUARTER of the eighteenth century most landowners had been, perforce, absentee proprietors, for the demands of state service kept them away from their lands. The decrease in the post-Petrine era in the length of the term of service, and a reduction in the size of the army, gave many of them a chance to do other things, and the final abolition of the service requirement in 1762 freed all of the dvorianstvo from the obligation to serve. Some returned to their rural seats—or nests as they were called—and immersed themselves in rusticity, a few even going so far as to grow beards and wear old-fashioned costumes. But many, and especially the wealthier among them, were attracted to St. Petersburg and Moscow by the gay social life, and to government service by the opportunities for personal advancement that it offered.

Years sometimes passed between the visits of these men to their lands. They preferred the pleasures of one another's company to the monotony and obscurity of country life and the boorishness of their less cultivated neighbors. It seems very possible, too, that the vivid memories of the great peasant revolt of 1773-1774, and the unceasing series of local disturbances, persuaded many a serfowner that it was healthier for him to be an absentee proprietor. Those of the upper strata of the nobility who did live on their lands not infrequently had some special reason, which, as one observer put it, was apt to be not the most honorable one.[1] Rustication as expiation for a moral or political offense was often imposed upon a noble by social pressure or by direct command of the tsar.

In the latter part of the eighteenth century, however, life in the provinces began to take on a lustre of its own, and a provincial society began to take form. Part of the stimulus came from the reforms of provincial administration in 1775.

[1] Haxthausen, *Studien*, III, 50-51.

This legislation created a number of new local offices, and men of the dvorianstvo found status and self-gratification in occupying these not unimportant posts. The provincial noble assemblies, called into being by the Charter of the Nobility in 1785, lent further prestige and importance to provincial life, and apparently an increasing number of landowners spent a greater amount of their time on their properties or in the provincial capitals.[2] According to Baron Haxthausen, the burning of Moscow in 1812 also served to promote this return to the provinces. Many of the nobles who lived in Moscow lost their houses and much of their wealth in the great blaze, and had to seek haven in their hitherto shunned country homes.

Haxthausen recognized the dangers to aristocratic supremacy offered by absentee ownership, and as a firm supporter of the prerogatives of the nobility he applauded the movement back to the land. "A great revolution in social conditions is taking place," he wrote in the early 1840's. "The noble now lives more in the country than he did previously, although still not for long enough periods to be called a provincial noble, but he visits his properties [and] concerns himself with their management. . . ." Other contemporary observers, too, commented upon the tendency of seigniors to spend more time on their lands.[3] Other evidence indicates that the proportions of this return to the land was not anywhere near as large as Haxthausen's enthusiastic estimate. In Saratov guberniia, for example, at mid-century only six of the 62 proprietors of that province who owned more than 1,000 male serfs lived on their properties.[4] A. A. Shakhmatov was undoubtedly closer to the truth, at least so far as wealthy landowners were concerned, when, in a memorandum written around 1836, he said that "Russian nobles, particularly the owners of large properties, spend the best part of their lives in government service . . . (and) have neither the time nor the means to take care of making necessary improvements to their lands."[5]

---

[2] Kusheva, "Khoziaistvo," p. 585; Semevskii, *Krest'iane*, I, 212-213; Akademiia Nauk, *Istoriia*, I, 603.

[3] Haxthausen, *Studien*, II, 118-119, III, 56-57; Struve, *Krepostnoe khoziaistvo*, pp. 56-58.

[4] Köppen, *Statistische Reise*, p. 30n.   [5] Quoted in Kusheva, "Proekt," p. 62.

Absentee ownership, however, did not necessarily mean that the proprietor paid no attention to the operation of his lands. Some owners of great complexes had an elaborate managerial organization, directed from a central office, to supervise and direct their holdings and serfs. These managers kept careful records and made periodic reports to the proprietor.[6] Landowners of lesser magnitude, who were unwilling or unable to live on their lands, turned over its administration to trusted employees, who often were serfs of superior abilities. Master and manager kept in touch by letter, the stream of mail between them being greater or smaller according to the lord's interest in his property, or his confidence in his steward. A few proprietors, including some of the greatest magnates, wrote lengthy and detailed instruction manuals for their managers, to ensure that their holdings would be run in the manner that the owner deemed best.[7]

The landowner who lived on his property—and the mass of the lesser seigniors were in this category—often managed it himself. Usually he had the sketchiest kind of administrative organization. The only records he was likely to keep were a list of his serfs for taxation and recruiting purposes, the documents that proved his ownership of his land and peasants, and skimpy notations of his income and expenditures. Some of these proprietors did not even bother to do this much, and instead allowed their properties to be run by a steward, or by the serfs themselves under the direction of the village elder.[8] Still others spent time and energy on their holdings and were careful and efficient managers.

A gallery of portraits of these resident proprietors, and a description of their methods of operation, has been preserved in the tales of Nicholas Gogol, who spent his youth among such people and knew them well. They are, of course, fictional char-

[6] Cf. Sivkov, *Ocherki*, pp. 27-53; Shchepetov, *Krepostnoe pravo, passim*; Indova, *Krepostnoe khoziaistvo*, pp. 47-66; Semevskii, *Krest'iane*, I, 215; Liashchenko, *Ocherki*, I, 126n.

[7] Cf. Ustiugov, "Instruktsiia," pp. 157-183; Volkov, "Instruktsiia," pp. 156-198; Andreev, "Nakaz," pp. 269-277; Petrovskaia, "Nakazy," pp. 221-268; Grekov, "Tambovskoe imenie," *passim*; Kusheva, "Khoziaistvo," *passim*.

[8] Haxthausen, *Studien*, I, 126; Sivkov, *Ocherki*, p. 4.

acters. But Gogol's genius gave them a living dimension, so that it is easy to believe that they really existed, and that the way Gogol describes them was the way they really were. He told about Ivan Fedorovich Shpon'ka, owner of a small property and 18 serf souls. While he was serving as an army officer Shpon'ka's spinster aunt ran his farm for him and did it so well that when Ivan retired at 40 from the army he found a thriving enterprise waiting for him. Gogol recounted how the aunt "stood over the reapers while they worked; knew exactly how many melons there were in the melon patch; collected a toll of 5 kopecks for every wagon that passed over her road; climbed the trees and shook down the pears; slapped lazy peasants with her terrible hand, and the same awesome hand bestowed a glass of vodka on the deserving. At almost one and the same time she scolded, dyed yarn, raced to the kitchen, brewed kvass, cooked honey jam, and busied herself all day and had her nose into everything." Then there was the elderly Afanasi Ivanovich Tovstogub, owner of a somewhat larger place. He lived a contented existence with his beloved wife, knew nothing about what went on in his property and cared less, and was mercilessly robbed by his steward and bailiff and by his house serfs. Manilov, who was a man of some means and also a sentimental fool, never rode out to look at his fields, gave immediate assent to anything his steward suggested, and did not even know how many serfs he owned. In contrast, Korobochka, a miserly crone, knew every detail about her property, including the names and even most of the nicknames of her seventy-odd serfs, although she kept no records. Shrivelled, senile Plushkin, master of 1,000 souls, who once had run his large estate efficiently and profitably, had allowed it to decay. Konstantin Fedorovich Skudronzhoglo, bustling with energy and ideas, managed his holding with a firm and knowing hand, and in ten years had increased his income from it ten times over.

II

As things turned out, it rarely made any difference so far as agricultural progress was concerned, whether the proprietor lived on his land or whether he was an absentee owner. In either case nearly all seigniors, particularly in the older parts of the empire, continued to operate their economies in the traditional way, making no attempt to raise the level of technical efficiency, or to increase the quantity and quality of the goods they produced. The few among them who introduced innovations designed to increase the yields of their lands were leaders with only a few followers.

Above all, most proprietors did not change their concept of the primary purpose of their holdings: to provide them and their households with foodstuffs and other products. This was true especially of the men who owned less than 100 revision souls, the rubric that included nearly three-quarters of all serfowners. The properties of many, and perhaps most, of these men seemed to have little or no connection with the market. But the lands owned by many medium-sized and great proprietors were also oriented toward production for consumption rather than for sale. Trains of carts and sleds, driven by serfs and drawn by serf-owned horses, came regularly from the provinces to the town houses and country villas of these proprietors, bringing supplies from their estates to maintain their households. Men of means kept large establishments with many domestic serfs, and lived on so lavish a scale that they needed vast amounts of foodstuffs and other rural products. The greatest houses in Moscow were said to have had a thousand or more domestics, all of them serfs, and all of them fed and clothed by their masters.[9] Those of lesser means lived proportionately. It would have been a strain, if not ruinous financially, for these lords to buy all the things they needed to support their small armies of retainers. So each winter they sent lists of their requirements to their stewards, and soon the courtyards of their homes in St. Petersburg and Moscow were filled with peasants' sleds loaded with the ordered provisions.[10]

But during the eighteenth and nineteenth centuries the disposition of the nobility to hanker after goods that their serfs

[9] Schulze-Gaevernitz, "Die Moskau-Wladimirsche Baumwollindustrie," p. 750.
[10] Cf. Kropotkin, *Memoirs*, pp. 36-37; Sivkov, *Ocherki*, pp. 54, 71, 73, 114-116; Bibikov, "Rassloenie," p. 80.

could not produce, and their fondness for extravagant living, already marked in earlier centuries, became more pronounced as Western tastes penetrated into the Russian world. They needed cash to get what they wanted. They tried to raise it by borrowing excessively and constantly, so that, as the preceding chapter showed, overwhelming indebtedness became a characteristic of their class. They also tried to get more money for themselves by turning the screws on their serfs. A third recourse that was open to them was to increase their own production of goods for sale on the market.

Seignioral production for sale was, of course, an old affair in Russia, and the available information for the eighteenth and first half of the nineteenth centuries shows that they were by far the chief suppliers of the market. Peasant agricultural production for sale was limited in the main to serfs on obrok and to state peasants. The man on barshchina, spending as much as half the week working for his master, usually had time to grow only enough on his own holding to meet his own needs for food and seed and for payments in kind to the seignior. At most he produced just a small surplus for market. The serfs on obrok and the state peasants had all their working time at their own disposal and so could produce a larger surplus. In certain areas and in some crops the peasant was an important commercial supplier. Internal customs data from the 1720's and 1730's show that a sizable portion of the grain brought into Moscow was grown by peasants of the surrounding countryside and of neighboring provinces. In 1723 nearly a quarter of the city's supply came from this source.[11] Peasant output of flax, hemp, and potatoes by the middle of the nineteenth century began to displace seignioral production in meeting the demands of the domestic and foreign markets. These crops were grown primarily in the non-black earth belt, where the trend in agriculture was away from grain and toward products that required more intensive cultivation. This kind of tillage was more successful on small peasant holdings than on demesne land

---

[11] Kafengauz, "Khlebnyi rynok," pp. 462-465, 483-485.

worked by serfs performing their compulsory labor obligation. In areas near large urban markets peasants raised vegetables for sale.[12]

Landowners, however, dominated the market as a whole for they could produce far in excess of their needs. Contemporary statisticians estimated that in the mid-nineteenth century they provided 90 percent of the grain sold on both the domestic and foreign markets. Peasants supplied just 10 percent.[13]

Despite the undisputed importance of seignioral production for sale, the available evidence points clearly to the conclusion that in the Central Agricultural and Central Industrial provinces, where nearly 50 percent of the empire's serfs lived in the 1850's, most proprietors did not increase their output of goods for the market. This was true not only for small lords, but for larger ones, too. In fact, in the first half of the nineteenth century some of the greatest proprietors drastically reduced their own direct production on land they owned in these regions, or gave it up entirely, and drew their revenues from these properties in the form of cash obrok from their serfs. Because it has sometimes been assumed that during the first half of the nineteenth century serfowners everywhere in the empire increased their production of agricultural goods for sale, it is necessary to go into some detail here.

Some of the goods that seigniors sent to market came undoubtedly from the payments in kind of their serfs. But most of what they sold came from their own demesnes. The best way, then, to find out whether seignioral production for market increased or decreased in the last century or so of serfdom would be to compare data for successive periods on the total amount of land the proprietors tilled on their own account. Unfortunately, the only information available on the extent of seignioral demesne is for the latter 1850's[14] (and then only for 28

[12] Liashchenko, *History*, p. 366; Tegoborskii, *Etudes*, II, 98; Druzhinin, *Gosudarstvennye krest'iane*, I, 73, 396-397, 401-403.

[13] Cited in Liashchenko, *Ocherki*, I, 124-125; Struve, *Krepostnoe khoziaistvo*, pp. 183-184n.

[14] Cf. Voznesenskii, *Ekonomika Rossii*, p. 51.

EUROPEAN RUSSIA IN THE 1850'S

REGIONS

1. **FAR NORTH:** Archangel, Vologda
2. **LAKE:** Olonets, St. Petersburg, Novgorod, Pskov
3. **BALTIC:** Estland, Lifland, Courland
4. **CENTRAL INDUSTRIAL:** Moscow, Tver, Iaroslav, Kostroma, Nizhnii Novgorod, Vladimir
5. **CENTRAL AGRICULTURAL:** Riazan, Tula, Kaluga, Orel, Kursk, Voronezh, Tambov, Penza
6. **URAL:** Viatka, Perm, Orenburg
7. **LOWER VOLGA:** Kazan, Simbirsk, Samara, Saratov, Astrakhan
8. **LITTLE RUSSIA:** Kharkov, Poltava, Chernigov
9. **NEW RUSSIA:** Ekaterinoslav, Tauride, Kherson, Bessarabia
10. **SOUTHWEST:** Kiev, Volynia, Podolia
11. **WHITE RUSSIA:** Smolensk, Vitebsk, Mogilev, Minsk
12. **LITHUANIA:** Kovno, Vilna, Grodno

provinces), so that a comparison over time of the amount of land used for direct seignioral production is not possible.

In the absence of this comparative material, indirect evidence has to be utilized to determine changes in the extent of seignioral market production. Information that is available on the use of barshchina and obrok in various provinces in the latter part of the eighteenth and the mid-nineteenth century provides such evidence. The prevalence of barshchina in some of these guberniias points to the conclusion that demesne, and therefore seignioral production, played a more important part in the seignioral economy than it did in other provinces where obrok was the chief obligation demanded of the serfs. In earlier centuries the region around Moscow had been the center of agricultural production, and barshchina and demesne had been widespread there. In the later seventeenth and in the eighteenth century the center of agricultural production had moved southward across the Oka into the Central Agricultural zone. As a result, obrok grew and barshchina waned in the regions north and northeast of Moscow, while in the Central Agricultural provinces barshchina emerged as the chief peasant obligation.

Data collected in the last third of the eighteenth century in a cadastral survey of twenty Great Russian provinces show how far this regional differentiation had progressed by that time.[15] Nearly 85 percent of the empire's serf population now lived in these provinces. In thirteen non-black earth guberniias[16] 55 percent (1,228,133) of the serfs were on obrok, and 45 percent (1,009,226) had to do barshchina. In seven chernozem provinces,[17] all in the Central Agricultural region, only 26 percent (274,723) were on obrok, and 74 percent (769,022) on barshchina. For all twenty provinces together, the ratios were 44 percent (1,502,856) on obrok, and 56 percent (1,778,248) on barshchina.

The predominance of obrok in the northern provinces and of barshchina in the Central Agricultural district, reflected the

[15] Semevskii, Krest'iane, I, 492.

[16] Olonets, St. Petersburg, Pskov, Novgorod, Smolensk, Tver, Iaroslav, Kostroma, Vologda, Vladimir, Moscow, Kaluga, Nizhnii Novgorod.

[17] Orel, Tula, Riazan, Penza, Tambov, Kursk, Voronezh.

development of the increase in regional economic specialization brought about by the economic expansion of the eighteenth century. The growth of trade and industry enabled more people to earn all or part of their livings in non-agricultural pursuits. Serfs, now receiving money incomes from their labors in commerce and manufacturing, were better able to pay cash obrok than when they were entirely dependent upon agricultural occupations. The serfowners, always hungry for cash, recognized the advantages to be drawn from the changed circumstances, and shifted their peasants from barshchina to obrok, or from obrok in kind to obrok in cash. Simultaneously, the peasants in the Central Agricultural zone could devote more of their time to farming, for now they could get manufactured goods from the non-black earth provinces in return for the foodstuffs they raised. Barshchina, demesne, and seignioral production for market therefore increased in the Central Agricultural provinces.

If the development of regional specialization had continued in the nineteenth century along the lines just indicated, the ratio of peasants on barshchina should have increased in the Central Agricultural zone, indicating an increase in direct seignioral production, and the ratio should have decreased in the northern provinces. But a comparison of data collected by the government at the end of the 1850's on the use of barshchina and obrok with the material from the latter eighteenth century reveals that this did not happen. V. I. Semevskii, writing in 1881, made this comparison for thirteen provinces, eight of them in the non-black earth and five in the chernozem,[18] and a few years later Mme. I. I. Ignatovich made it for twenty provinces, thirteen of them in the non-chernozem and seven in the chernozem. Mme. Ignatovich also presented data collected by the commissions charged with drafting the emancipation legislation, on the use of barshchina and obrok in the 1850's on properties with over 100 souls. Her findings are summarized in the following table:[19]

[18] Semevskii, *Krest'iane*, I, 492-493.
[19] Ignatovich, "Pomeshchich'i krest'iane," IX, 46-48; cf. Skrebitskii, *Krest'ianskoe dielo*, III, 1227-1273.

Percentage of Serfs on Obrok and Barshchina

	LATTER 18TH CENTURY		MID-19TH CENTURY			
			on all estates		on estate with over 10(	
NON-BLACK EARTH PROVINCES	obrok	barshchina	obrok	barshchina	obrok	barsh
Olonets	66	34	72	28	88.64	11
St. Petersburg	51	49	–	–	63.14	36
Pskov	21	79	23	77	32.81	67
Novgorod	49	51	45.5	54.4	65.14	34
Smolensk	30	70	27	73	33.89	66
Tver	46	54	40	59	68.25	31
Iaroslav	78	22	87.4	12.6	90.87	9
Kostroma	85	15	87.5	12.5	89.13	10.
Vologda	83	17	84	16	80.04	19.
Vladimir	50	50	70	30	92.53	8.
Moscow	36	64	68	32	80.27	19.
Kaluga	58	42	55	45	58.79	41.
Nizhnii Novgorod	82	18	68	32	74.38	25.
BLACK EARTH						
Orel	34	66	28	72	25.88	74.
Tula	8	92	25	75	27.23	72.
Riazan	19	81	38	62	47.98	52.
Penza	52	48	25	75	18.52	81.
Tambov	22	78	22	78	21.60	78.
Kursk	8	92	24.5	75.5	16.67	83.
Voronezh	64	36	45	55	58.76	41.

As the table shows, the proportion of serfs on obrok in twelve of the thirteen non-black earth provinces increased in seven guberniias by the following amounts:

	percent
Moscow	32
Vladimir	20
Iaroslav	9.4
Olonets	6
Kostroma	2.5
Pskov	2
Vologda	1

In five other provinces it declined by the following amounts:

	percent
Nizhnii Novgorod	14
Tver	6
Novgorod	3.5
Kaluga	3
Smolensk	3

Data for the thirteenth province, St. Petersburg, in the middle of the nineteenth century, are lacking.

The increase in the use of obrok, and the decline in the use of barshchina, in these non-black earth provinces was marked only in Moscow and Vladimir. On the other hand, there was a sizable decrease in the use of obrok, and an increase in barshchina, in Nizhnii Novgorod. For the thirteen provinces as a whole there was at most a relatively small increase in the use of obrok.[20]

In the seven chernozem provinces the proportion of serfs on obrok increased in three provinces:

	percent
Riazan	19
Tula	17
Kursk	16.5

In three others it decreased:

	percent
Penza	27
Voronezh	19
Orel	6

In the seventh province, Tambov, the proportion remained the same. In other words, in the last half-century or so of serfdom the use of barshchina declined sharply in three of these seven chernozem provinces, and increased by an important amount in two of them. For the seven provinces as a whole the proportion of serfs on obrok and barshchina remained pretty much the same between the latter part of the eighteenth century and the 1850's.[21]

20 Cf. Semevskii, *Krest'iane*, I, 48.   21 Cf. *ibid.*, pp. 48-49.

As a matter of fact, the strong probability exists that the proportion of serfs on obrok was actually higher, and the proportion on barshchina lower, in black earth and non-black earth guberniias alike, than these figures indicate. Mme. Ignatovich pointed out that her calculations (like those of Semevskii) contained a bias against obrok, because of the increase in the nineteenth century in the practice of demanding both obrok and barshchina from the same peasants. In her analysis she counted these serfs only as barshchina peasants. In addition, she based her calculations on the number of serf assessment units (*tiagla*) that were composed of several persons, rather than upon the number of individual male peasants. She, therefore, had to omit those properties for which her sources did not give the number of assessment units on barshchina and obrok. It so happened that the *tiaglo* assessment system was used less frequently by landowners whose serfs were on obrok than it was by those who demanded barshchina.[22] Thus, Mme. Ignatovich left out an unknown, but certainly sizable, number of obrok peasants from her calculations.

These comparisons in the use of obrok and barshchina lead to the conclusion that in these twenty provinces (in which nearly 50 percent of the empire's serfs lived in the 1850's), most seigniors did not increase the amount of their own direct production, and that therefore they did not increase their production of goods for sale on the market.[23]

The table also lists the percentages of serfs on obrok and barshchina in the 1850's on properties that had more than 100 male peasants. The men to whom these estates belonged made up only 22 percent of the total number of serfowners, but they owned 81 percent of all serf revision souls (v. p. 369). Presumably they were the chief producers for market, since they were in a position to turn out larger surpluses than were

[22] Ignatovich, "Pomeshchich'i krest'iane," IX, 47-48n. For the *tiaglo* system v. pp. 512-514.

[23] Semevskii, after making a comparison of barshchina-obrok ratios in thirteen provinces, realized that his findings refuted his own personal conviction that there was an important increase in seigniorial market production. So he figuratively threw up his hands, declared he was "leaving a more exact explanation of this question to future historians of serfdom in the nineteenth century," and turned his attention to other problems. Semevskii, *Krest'ian*, I, 47-49.

lesser landowners, who had to use much of what they raised for their own needs. If this assumption is correct, then it could be expected that the barshchina ratio on these properties would be higher than it was on all properties. The table shows, however, that in three of the Central Agricultural provinces the proportion of serfs on barshchina on properties with over 100 souls was less than it was on all properties in these guberniias (14 percent less in Voronezh, 10 percent less in Riazan, 2 percent less in Tula). In one (Tambov) it was just about the same. In the remaining three it was larger, but not by much (2 percent more in Orel, 6 percent more in Penza, 8 percent more in Kursk). In twelve of the thirteen non-black earth provinces listed in the table, the percentage of serfs on barshchina on properties with over 100 revision souls was less than it was on all properties in these provinces. Vologda was the only province where the percentage was greater, and the relatively small number of serfs in this infertile and agriculturally unimportant northern guberniia made it a minor exception.

In sixteen of these twenty provinces, then, direct seignioral production on large properties was of less importance, relatively, in the 1850's, than it was on the holdings of men who owned less than 100 adult male serfs. Furthermore, the use of barshchina apparently decreased on the large properties in these guberniias between the latter eighteenth century and the 1850's. That is, the importance of direct seignioral production on these properties seems to have declined during the first half of the nineteenth century. Information on the barshchina-obrok ratio for properties with over 100 revision souls in the latter eighteenth century is not available. But a comparison of the percentage of serfs on obrok on all properties in the last third of the eighteenth century, with the barshchina ratio on the large ones in the 1850's, points to this conclusion. As the table shows, in thirteen of the twenty provinces the percentage on barshchina on the large properties was less in the 1850's than it was on all properties in the late eighteenth century, in five provinces it was higher, and in two it was about the same. Monographic studies of the holdings of three of the empire's greatest landowners, the Sheremetevs, Iusupovs, and Vorontsovs, provide direct evidence for the existence of this trend on the part of large proprietors toward decreased production on their own account.[24]

It has been suggested that owners of large complexes withdrew from direct production because they were loathe to spend the time and money needed to operate their holdings on barshchina, especially on those of their properties that lay far from their central managerial headquarters. Obrok was a much simpler obligation to collect, and required a minimal operating outlay on the part of the proprietor.[25] This rationale, however, disregards the fact that in the eighteenth century the difficulties of supervision of an estate on barshchina could have been no less troublesome and expensive, yet barshchina had apparently been more frequently demanded then by great proprietors than it was later. It seems to me that the growth of the exchange-money economy provides a more convincing explanation. It became progressively easier for serfs to accumulate cash. As a result, lords who owned many serfs decided that it was easier to increase their own money incomes by putting their peasants on cash obrok, than by engaging in production for the market.

III

The conclusions presented in the preceding section are drawn from information for nineteen provinces of the Central Industrial, Central Agricultural, and Lake districts and one province of the North. Because of the lack of data for the eighteenth century a similar comparison over time in the barshchina-obrok ratios for other parts of the empire cannot be made. But evidence that is available shows that in certain of these regions production for market by landowners did grow during the first half of the nineteenth century. Thus, in New Russia commercial farming boomed in these decades, and in Little Russia and the Southwest there also seems to have been a major increase in production for the market by many landowners.

[24] Sivkov, *Ocherki*, pp. 132-135; Shchepetov, *Krepostnoe pravo*, pp. 9, 49-50, 132-133, 165, 286-287; Indova, *Krepostnoe khoziaistvo*, pp. 29-30.
[25] Ignatovich, "Pomeshchich'i krest'iane," IX, 50.

The seignioral demand for farm labor provides evidence of this regional difference in the importance of seignioral production for market. In the Central Industrial, Lake, and Central Agricultural districts the barshchina of the serfs met all the farm labor needs of the proprietors. In fact, they had more labor available than they needed. In the 1850's the lords of the Central Industrial and Lake districts demanded barshchina of only 41.1 percent of their adult male serfs, and the seigniors of the Central Agricultural zone required it of 71.2 percent. The rest of the serfs in these provinces were on obrok. In contrast, 99.9 percent of the adult male serfs in New Russia, 99.3 percent in Little Russia, and 97.4 percent in the Southwestern guberniias had to perform the barshchina obligation.[26] But even though barshchina was virtually universal in these regions it fell far short of meeting the labor needs of the seigniors. Each year they hired thousands of serfs and state peasants who came from the Central Industrial and Central Agricultural provinces in search of seasonal employment. By the mid-nineteenth century there were an estimated 300,000 of these migratory workers. Many of them came just for haying and harvesting, but a large number arrived in early spring and worked through the entire summer. They were paid relatively high wages and received good food and lodging. A worker could earn enough in a few weeks to meet all his cash obligations to his own lord and to the state, and have a fair amount left over, and those who worked all summer made (in the 1830's) from 40 to 100 rubles.[27]

The expansion in the raising and processing of sugar beets is another indication of the increasing participation by the landowners in these regions in market production. Proprietors in many parts of the empire established refineries—in 1860-61 there were beet sugar mills in 22 provinces. But the industry centered in Little Russia and in the Southwest, and above all in Kiev guberniia, where soil and climate were most favorable for sugar beet culture. In 1860-61 the refineries in that province accounted for nearly half of the empire's beet sugar production

[26] Liashchenko, History, p. 310.
[27] Druzhinin, Gosudarstvennye krest'iane, I, 407-411, 417; Voznesenskii, Razlozhenie, pp. 190-191; Kulischer, "Die Leibeigenschaft," p. 48; Haxthausen, Studien, II, 128.

(without the Kingdom of Poland), and those in Podolia, Chernigov, and Kharkov turned out another 25 percent of the total.[28]

Nearly all of the mills were owned and operated by serf-owners. A few merchants established plants, or leased them from nobles, or entered into partnership with nobles, but they played a minor role in the industry. For beet sugar production was particularly well suited to the seignioral economy. It provided work for the serfs at a period when there was no field work to be done, the beets gave a relatively high yield per desiatin so that they could be raised in sufficient quantity on the lord's own fields, and there was a ready sale for the finished product.

The first beet sugar mill in Russia (and according to Soviet claims, the first in the world) was established in 1802 by Major General E. I. Blankennagel, a landowner of Tula. It was a small operation—in 1803 it produced only 300 *pudy* of sugar—but it excited official interest. The government decided to offer inducements that included credit and land to encourage others to build plants, and it raised the tariff on imported sugar to protect the new industry. Despite these efforts production lagged; in 1825 there were only seven beet sugar mills in the entire empire. Then the introduction of improved techniques developed in the West, and the steady increase in tariff protection, served to arouse a new interest among the seigniors. By 1830 there were 20 plants, and by 1840 the number had gone up to 140. In 1841 the tariff was raised again, and though the government abandoned its program of direct assistance to new plants, more and more refineries were built. By 1848 there were 340 of them, and by 1861 the number had increased to 448. A large proportion of these mills used machinery, including steam engines, so that by 1860 steam power was employed in the production of 85 percent of Russia's beet sugar output. Most of the mills, however, were less efficient than those of Western Europe. Normal yields of German and French refineries in the 1840's ran between five and six pounds of sugar

[28] *Ob'iasneniia*, pp. 294, 302; cf. Tegoborskii, *Etudes*, I, 213-215.

for every 100 pounds of beets. Russian mills got only three to four pounds per 100.[29]

Sugar beet processing was a seasonal industry. Production began immediately after the beets were harvested and was carried on as rapidly as possible for the next two or three months, since the sugar content of the beets decreased the longer they remained out of the ground. Around 40,000 hands worked in the mills in 1849, and by 1860 estimates of the number employed ran from 64,000 to 74,000. Between 40,000 and 50,000 of these workers at the later date were serfs doing barshchina in plants owned by their masters. The rest were hired laborers. These wage workers had to be employed because the speed required in sugar manufacture demanded more labor than the serfs who belonged to the millowner could provide.[30]

The landowners of Little Russia, New Russia, and the Southwest also took a leading part in distilling, though they did not dominate in this branch of production. The manufacture of spirits had attracted the interest of proprietors in many parts of the empire. It provided them with a way of using grain surpluses to make a readily marketable commodity that was easy to ship to market. As one contemporary put it, "One horse can carry as much brandy to town as six horses can carry grain."[31] Even more important, the throne in the eighteenth century had given the proprietors in the largest part of the empire a monopoly in the manufacture of spirits.

At the end of the eighteenth century there were 23,300 distilleries in Russia. Most of them were small, so that the average annual output per plant had been only 800 vedros (2,600 gallons). During the succeeding decades many proprietors closed down their operations. By 1860 there were only 6,080 distilleries. These plants, however, were much larger and much more efficient; average annual production per unit now amounted to around 15,000 vedros (48,750 gallons). From 70,000 to 100,000 people, 90 to 95 percent of them serfs, are

[29] *Ob'iasneniia*, pp. 295-296, 299; Tegoborskii, *Etudes*, II, 226n., 234-235; Portal, "Das Problem," p. 208.

[30] Pazhitnov, "K voprosu," pp. 239-241.

[31] Quoted in Voznesenskii, *Ekonomika Rossii*, p. 84.

estimated to have been employed in these distilleries. Nearly one fifth of all the plants were located in Ekaterinoslav and Kherson in New Russia, and in Chernigov and Kiev.[32]

IV

Among the seigniors who participated in direct production for market, both in the older parts of the empire and in the southern and southwestern provinces, there were some who through their activities and interests revealed themselves as representatives of that pan-European phenomenon of the eighteenth and nineteenth centuries, the "improving landlord." In country after country, from England to the Urals, nobles of this turn of mind took the lead in agricultural innovations. Their aim was not only to increase their revenues from their own lands. They also hoped that their success would prompt their less enterprising fellows to imitate them, and thereby raise the level of productivity of their nation's agriculture. Their activities have been aptly described as "the last great flowering of the landed aristocracy, functioning as a pioneering economic elite."[33]

In Russia, from the time of Peter I on, the ruling class had turned westward for guidance and example. The introduction of improved agriculture was part of the Europeanization of Russia. The early innovators took for their models the improving landlords of the West, they read and translated writings of the Western agriculturists, and they copied Western techniques.[34] Some of the greatest aristocrats were among these pioneers, and the tsars gave their strong approval and support to their efforts.

Beginning in the second half of the eighteenth century newly-founded journals began to publish hundreds of articles on agricultural subjects. The authors of these pieces made it evident that their primary aim was to suggest to proprietors ways of increasing their production for market. An analysis of 450 articles published just in the last third of the century showed

[32] Pazhitnov, "K voprosu," pp. 240-242; Tegoborskii, *Etudes*, II, 209-210.
[33] Hans Rosenberg in *Journal of Economic History*, X (1950) 79.
[34] Cf. Bak, "Vozniknovenie," pp. 55-56, 58-61.

that crop rotations, fertilizers, problems of estate management, the relative merits of barshchina and óbrok as ways of exploiting a property, and the raising of industrial crops, such as flax, hemp, tobacco, hops, and silk, were among the most frequently discussed subjects. Some interest was shown in sheep raising, and in increasing and improving meat and dairy production for the proprietor's own household consumption. Hardly any attention was given to draught animals and to farm implements. Serfs had to provide their own horses and oxen and tools when they performed their barshchina, so that seigniors were uninterested in these subjects.[35]

In every country in which they appeared, improving landlords established societies for the promotion of agriculture. In Russia the first, and for three decades the only association of this kind was organized in St. Petersburg in 1765. Its founders were a group of lords, many of whom held high government posts and were close to the throne. Empress Catherine readily gave the new organization a charter and, under the imposing name of The Free Economic Society for the Encouragement in Russia of Agriculture and Household Management, it entered upon a long and distinguished career that lasted until 1917. In 1796 landowners in Lifland, and in 1808 in Estland, formed provincial agricultural societies. In 1818 the Imperial Agricultural Society at Moscow was founded as the outgrowth of conversations of a group of nobles meeting in the home of Prince S. I. Gagarin. The new society held its first official session in 1820. It began with 45 members and grew rapidly, with many important and wealthy proprietors on its rolls. After this there was a rash of new societies, so that by mid-century there were 29 of them in the empire. Most were provincial or regional societies, such as the Iaroslav Agricultural Society, or the Southeastern Russian Agricultural Society, while the others were devoted to the promotion of a particular branch of agriculture, such as sheep raising or gardening.[36]

These organizations, like their counterparts in other lands, undertook a wide range of activities. The Free Economic Society

35 Sivkov, "K voprosy," pp. 567-611.
36 Tegoborskii, *Etudes*, II, 184-185; Semevskii, *Krest'ianskii vopros*, I, 45; Sivkov, *Ocherki*, pp. 56-57; Storch, "Der Bauernstand," 1850, 419-420.

maintained an agricultural school, a model farm, a seed depot, an herbarium, a library that had in 1849 over 9,000 volumes, and a museum for models of new and improved farm implements and machines. It put out three serial publications, one of them in German for Balt proprietors; subsidized two other journals; collected data on the Russian economy; and held essay contests on a wide range of economic and social subjects. The Imperial Agricultural Society of Moscow carried on nearly as broad a program. Among its accomplishments its part in establishing the firm of Butenop, Russia's chief producer of farm equipment, and its leadership in promoting the beet sugar industry, held high place. The other societies did not engage in as many undertakings as did these two leading organizations, but all of them sought to promote agricultural improvements through such projects as publications, exchange of information, contests, prizes, and the like.[37]

Some of the improving landlords were not content to limit their joint action to these non-profit organizations. They resorted to the capitalistic device of forming stock companies to raise money for large-scale agricultural enterprises. A glance at some of these undertakings reveals their diversity. The Company for the Raising of Fine-Wooled Sheep in the Baltic Provinces was established in 1826. Besides an undetermined sum raised by sale of its stock, the company received a loan of 109,000 rubles from the government. It owned five sheep farms, each with 700 to 1,000 electoral sheep and goats. Each farm had a school attached to it to train men in raising sheep. In 1831 the Company for the Improvement and Spread of Sericulture in Russia was set up with a capital of 570,000 rubles. This enterprise, organized to advance the manufacture and dying of silk, owned several factories. The Kamchatka Agricultural Company was established in 1833 with a capital of 11,500 rubles to promote agriculture and forestry in Kamchatka, where it owned large tracts of land. The Company for the Promotion of Sericulture, Trade and Industry in Transcaucasia, organized in 1836, had for its purpose the planting of mulberry trees on land owned or leased by the company, had a model garden, and ran

37 Storch, "Der Bauernstand," 1849, 418-426.

a school to train workers in silkworm culture. The Company for Growing Dye Plants, created in 1837, had a capital of 1,285,000 rubles, and owned 12,000 desiatins of land and a factory. The Kharkov Stock Company for the Wool Trade was organized in 1838 to protect raisers of fine wool from price fluctuations. It had a capital of 96,000 rubles, owned warehouses, and did business in neighboring provinces as well as in Kharkov. It bought the wool from the producers, or took it for sale at a 2 percent commission, or made advances to the raiser of up to 60 percent of the value of his clip. An enterprise for the manufacture of flax and hemp products was created in 1839 in White Russia where these two fibres were major crops. Its purpose was to increase the demand for flaxen and hempen wares by improving their quality. Its capital amounted to 137,126 rubles. It owned a factory in Vitebsk. The Company for Cutting and Supplying Peat to Moscow, founded in 1841 with a capital of 250,000 rubles produced (in the late 1840's) 30 to 50 million peat bricks a year.[38]

A number of other efforts by seigniors to form stock companies proved unsuccessful. The St. Petersburg Company for the Introduction and Establishment of Crop Rotation, organized in 1829, was one of these failures. Its promoters were less interested in profit than they were in improving the empire's tillage systems by starting a model farm near the capital to demonstrate better methods of cultivation. In 1831 N. S. Mordernov, an important government official, proposed the creation of a company to buy properties and operate them with improved methods, but his suggestion was not acted upon. In 1838 a company was organized for the manufacture and sale of artificial fertilizers, but the sum total of its activities seems to have been the publication of a small brochure. In the early 1830's a group of wealthy nobles carried on discussions about a particularly ambitious scheme that never got beyond the talking stage. Their idea was to set up a business called the Company for the Improvement of Private Agriculture, with a capital of 10 million assignat rubles (*ca.* 2.7 million silver rubles), to lease and operate private estates with a total serf

38 *Ibid.*, pp. 426-430.

population of half a million souls. The leases would run for periods ranging from four to twenty-four years during which the owner would receive a guaranteed annual income. The planners had a dual purpose in mind; to make money for themselves, and to improve Russian agriculture. They figured that by using modern techniques they could increase the revenues from the properties and so operate at a profit. At the expiration of the lease the owner would get back a much improved property. In 1858, by which time emancipation was being widely discussed, a like proposal was made in the *Landowner's Journal*, except that the leased properties were to be worked by hired labor rather than by serfs.[39]

The efforts of seigniors to promote agriculture had the strong support of the government, and the throne itself took the lead in several important innovations. The tsars, for fiscal and welfare reasons, had an understandable interest in building up the national economy, and besides they themselves owned great tracts of cultivated land. Peter I charged one of his new bureaus with the responsibility of concerning itself with improvements in tillage and animal husbandry. He ordered the planting of staples such as flax, hemp, and wheat in regions suitable for their culture but where they had not been grown, and sponsored the introduction of such new crops as tobacco and cotton, and the importation of blooded livestock to improve the native herds. Russians were sent abroad to study techniques and foreign experts were brought into the empire. Peter even tried to supplant the sickle with the scythe as the standard harvesting tool. In 1721 he sent peasants from the Baltic regions, where the scythe was in general use, to other parts of his realm to introduce the scythe, and instructed local officials to send him reports on the progress of his scheme. By 1726, 92 peasant instructors had visited ten provinces. Information available for just four of these provinces shows that over 13,000 peasants received training. Peter's efforts, however, proved unsuccessful, for the Russian peasantry continued to prefer the sickle.[40]

[39] Kusheva, "Proekt," pp. 46-47, 55-56, 58-59.
[40] Alefirenko, "Russkaia obshchestvennaia mysl," pp. 520-526; Spiridonova, *Ekonomicheskaia politika*, pp. 183-189.

After Peter's death the government made periodic attempts to raise the level of agriculture and to introduce new crops. For example, in 1763 the English ambassador at Moscow reported that "Every method is taken in the Ukraine to advance, and improve the cultivation of [tobacco]. Books of instruction are printed and distributed, a bounty promised to those who produce such a quantity, and plants are sent from England."[41] The government did not engage in a sustained effort, however, until the nineteenth century, especially after the establishment of the Ministry of State Domain in 1839. At that time a continuing program designed to encourage the adoption of improved techniques and new products, particularly by state peasants, was instituted. The government distributed plants and seeds free or at low cost, held exhibitions, set up model farms and experimental stations, opened training schools, published and distributed manuals and periodicals, translated foreign works on agriculture, awarded prizes, sometimes offered tax deductions and subsidies, and in certain instances exempted peasants who engaged in improved farming from military service.[42]

In contrast to the government's efforts to help the peasants, the interest of landowners in improved agriculture seems to have been limited almost exclusively to the operations they conducted on their own account. Apparently the selfishness and unconcern for peasant welfare that characterized the seignioral class as a whole was typical even of its most progressive members. Still, these men had some justification for their attitude, for they had to overcome the tradition, superstition, ignorance, and suspicion of the serfs before they could persuade them to change their old ways. The seigniors who tried to do this must have found the experience formidable and disheartening. Leo Tolstoi in his story, "Morning of a Landed Proprietor," based upon his own experiences, recounted how difficult a task this was. In 1847, when he was 19, Tolstoi settled on his estate to become an improving landlord, and to work for the welfare of his serfs. His

<hr/>

[41] Earl of Buckingham to Earl of Halifax, Moscow, 14 Mar. 1703, *SIRO*, XII (1873), 86.

[42] Tegoborskii, *Etudes*, II, 2, 4-5, 47-48, 54-56, 89-91, 120-121, 130-131, 180-187; Storch, "Der Bauernstand," 1849, 432-437.

story tells how his good intentions foundered on the distrust of the peasants, who suspected everything he tried to do for them.

Sketches of a few improving landlords of the first half of the nineteenth century can give an idea of the kind of men who took part in the movement, and the nature of their activities. D. M. Poltoratskii (1761-1818), after study in Germany and travel in Western Europe, returned home to enter state service. He had been inspired by what he had seen and read of agricultural progress in the West. In 1792 he purchased Avchurino, a property of 2,700 desiatins in Kaluga, on the banks of the Oka, and immediately set about making it a progressive agricultural enterprise. Six years later he resigned from his government post so that he could devote all of his time and energies to this work. He used Western, and above all, English methods of tillage and improved farm implements. He was among the first, if not the very first, Russian proprietor to replace the traditional three field system with crop rotations, he used marl to fertilize his fields, planted forage crops and potatoes, engaged in scientific cattle breeding, using imported animals as well as domestic kholmogors to improve his herds, and maintained a stud, managed by an English expert, with Arab and English stallions that produced fine animals (including race horses, for Poltoratskii had acquired a taste for this pastime of Western aristocrats). He was a zealous propagandist, and persuaded a number of his neighbors to adopt innovations they had originally mistrusted. He invited other seigniors to send serfs to Avchurino for free training in improved farming. A number of proprietors are reported to have taken advantage of his offer. In the last years of his life he aided in the organization of the Moscow Imperial Agricultural Society, served as an officer, and at one of its first meetings urged the society to set up a model farm for the conduct of experiments, and to award prizes to encourage the introduction and spread of new techniques and crops.[43]

Count A. A. Bobrinskii (1800-1868), Master of the Horse in the Imperial Court, high official in the Ministry of Finance, and grandson of Catherine II and her favorite Gregory Orlov, was one of Russia's greatest landlords. He early became interested in

[43] D. M. Poltoratskii in *Russkii biograficheskii slovar.*

many aspects of progressive farming, including crop rotations, scientific fertilizing, forage crops, forestry, more efficient implements (he himself devised an improved plow), and better farm buildings. But his main interest and greatest contribution was in the development of the beet sugar industry in Russia. Early in the 1830's he set up a beet sugar mill on his property in Tula where he owned 12,000 peasants and 40,000 desiatins of land. He spent thousands of rubles in improving this plant and in importing machinery for it. In the latter thirties he built several more mills on his properties in Kiev guberniia. This started the industry in the Ukraine which, as was pointed out earlier, soon became the center of Russian beet sugar production. At Bobrinskii's urgings a French manufacturer of refinery machinery opened a branch in Kiev, and built up a lively business supplying the plants of the region. Bobrinskii also supported scientific research in beet raising and refining, and invited young men to work in his plants to gain practical experience, so that they could get jobs as refinery managers.[44]

E. S. Karnovich (1793-1855), after study at the University of Moscow, entered government service. While working in Moscow he came into close touch with members of the Agricultural Society there, and aided in the translation sponsored by the Society of works by Albrecht Thaer, the famed German agronomist. At an early age, and while still in low rank, he retired from his government post and spent the rest of his life running his estate in Iaroslav guberniia. Here he became the first proprietor to sow fields in clover, introduced crop rotations, planted potatoes, devoted special attention to flax, one of Iaroslav's chief crops, was one of the very few seigniors anywhere in the empire who tried to improve the practices the serfs used on their own holdings, and wrote a number of articles on agricultural topics. His achievements won him the reputation of one of Russia's outstanding agriculturists, and the government sent him on special missions to many parts of Russia and to Western Europe. He brought back new ideas from his foreign journeys that he applied on his own property and tried to convince other landowners to adopt. He was one of the founders of the Iaroslav

---

[44] A. A. Bobrinskii in *ibid.*; Dolgorukii, *Notice*, p. 74.

Agricultural Society, established in 1843, and served as its secretary for the first six years.[45] Baron Haxthausen made a special point of visiting Karnovich, and found him a man fired with patriotic zeal to improve the agriculture of his homeland. Haxthausen, who was a very knowledgeable agriculturist himself, was much impressed by what Karnovich had accomplished.

"He has tried much on his estate [Haxthausen wrote], many things failing, and many succeeding; he has had to struggle with the obstinancy and folly of the peasants, with blind adherence to the traditional, the old, with hatred of every innovation, and singlehanded has won out, and has achieved an agricultural success on his estate that I, at least, have not found excelled in Russia, and that certainly is not frequently encountered there. The innovations and the science in his operations were not new to me, but I found it interesting to discover it here in Russia!"[46]

Haxthausen later visited another progressive landowner, named Bunin, who lived in Tambov. He found himself charmed by the old-fashioned patriarchal atmosphere of the manor house and of the family's life—apparently it was an ideal "nobleman's nest." But Bunin abandoned tradition in running his property. He used a nine year crop rotation cycle, planted red clover and timothy, used improved implements including a threshing machine, and kept a small but excellent stud. He had enclosed a number of his fields with hedges, something that Haxthausen did not see anywhere else in his wide travels through Russia.[47]

N. A. Zherebtsov owned property in Moscow guberniia and had a total of 600 serfs. He held important offices in government, and from 1839 to 1844 was vice-director of a bureau of the Ministry of State Domain charged with planning ways to improve the farming practices of state peasants. He belonged to the Moscow Agricultural Society, headed the school run by the society, was a member of a number of other agricultural societies, and wrote articles about scientific farming and new agricultural machines. In one of these articles, published in 1856, Zherebtsov described one of his properties. It was a relatively small one near Moscow, with 400 desiatins and 105 revision souls who

[45] E. S. Karnovich in *Russkii biograficheskii slovar.*
[46] Haxthausen, *Studien,* I, 106. [47] *Ibid.,* II, 83-86.

were divided into 42 assessment units. These serfs had been on obrok until 1849 when Zherebtsov put 17 assessment units on barshchina, converted one third of the land held by the peasants into demesne, and cleared and plowed some woodland and meadow. He introduced a seven field system of rotation, grew truck for sale in Moscow, and raised dairy cattle to produce milk and butter for city consumption.[48]

A. E. Zhadovskii, holder of high office in the Ministry of Finance, owned more than 800 male souls and over 12,000 desiatins of land in 1860. Most of his land and nearly half of his serfs were in the fertile Volga province of Orenburg. He was a member of the Free Economic Society and contributed articles to its publications, was one of the founders of a stock company organized in 1836 to promote industry and commerce in the Caucasus, and with other proprietors tried unsuccessfully to start the Company for the Improvement of Private Agriculture referred to on an earlier page. His annual income in 1860 from his Orenburg property alone was estimated at 100,000 to 200,000 rubles. He operated a distillery, a sawmill, boat building shops, and a stud, and ran large sheep flocks that included 2,000 head of blooded animals. All of his serfs were on obrok, but he required them to work in his industrial enterprises at low wages. He apparently was a harsh master, for in the fifties the government took official cognizance of complaints from his peasants about his abusive treatment and the excessive punishments he meted out to them.[49]

Admirer of the West, great aristocrat, country squire, old style patriarch, government expert and agronomist, and hard driving businessman, these six proprietors illustrate the heterogeneity of the seignioral class. Yet all six of them were joined in a common interest; to increase the yields of their own properties, and to spread improved agricultural practices throughout the empire. They, and the others like them, succeeded in the improvement of their own operations. But they failed in their efforts to raise the general level of Russian agriculture, for they were unable to persuade the mass of their fellow proprietors to adopt the innovations they urged upon them.

[48] Kusheva, "Proekt," pp. 53-55.   [49] *Ibid.*, pp. 51-52.

21

MASTERS AND SERFS

AS THE PRECEDING CHAPTERS have shown, the economic and social position of the nobles rested upon their ownership of serfs. Their incomes came from the payments in cash, kind, and labor of their serfs, and their right to own peasants distinguished them from the other ranks of society. They realized this, of course, and they tried with every means at their command to maintain and strengthen that privilege. Their success in establishing their monopoly on serf ownership, and the aid given them by the tsars in the acquisition of this exclusive right, have already been described. They also knew that they would gain in prestige and in economic benefits if they could increase the number, and win greater control over the lives, of the men and women who belonged to them. Here, too, they succeeded, and here, too, they had the throne as their coadjutor. The tsars forced millions of free peasants to become the serfs of private seigniors, and allowed the seigniors to reduce these people, and the other millions already enserfed, to the condition of human chattels.

In giving their cooperation to the serfowners the tsars were moved by their own interests, as well as the interests of the dvorianstvo. The sovereigns of Russia had long maintained that all of their subjects, noble, townsmen, and peasant alike, existed to serve the state. To achieve their goal of universal service they assigned each class in society a specific role, charged it with specific obligations, and demanded that each of their subjects be a member of one of these classes. But up to the eighteenth century they had been hampered by an inefficient governmental organization, and so had not been completely successful in carrying out their designs. Some of their subjects still remained outside the recognized social categories. Among these were emancipated or runaway serfs and slaves, vagabonds, illegitimate and abandoned children, sons of priests and of soldiers, hangers-on at churches and monasteries, and unruly and criminal elements. These people occupied, as it were, the interstices of the social order. Sheltered by the anonymity of their classlessness, they were able to avoid contributing either taxes or services to the state. They lived as free men, coming and going as they pleased, and earning their livings however they could.

The modernization of the central administration that began in Peter I's reign remedied many of the organizational shortcomings that had handicapped the earlier tsars. Now the monarchs had the machinery needed to register each of their subjects as a member of an established social category, and to hedge him with restraints that prevented him from escaping the obligations of his class.

The process began when Peter I, in a decree of 31 March 1700, ordered that all serfs and slaves freed by their masters had to report to army recruiting officers immediately upon their emancipation. If fit they were drafted; if rejected for military service they had to return to bondage, though they could choose their new master.[1] Thus Peter abolished the centuries-old right of the emancipated thrall to live as a free man. But not until the introduction of the soul tax in 1724 did the state have a really efficient mechanism by which it could sweep all the unorganized elements of society into recognized classes. A series of decrees arranged for these people to be entered on the tax rolls. To make sure they would pay their obligations they were compelled to become serfs or state peasants or soldiers. Their registration and assignment were carried through in the successive revisions.

Other legislation gave landlords and factory owners powers that enabled them to make serfs out of free men. In 1747, for example, the government announced that to expedite the taking of censuses it would accept lists submitted by proprietors of their serfs without verifying the entries. Since inclusion on the revision rolls was legal proof of serfdom, an unscrupulous proprietor had only to put the names of free persons on the list he turned in to make them his serfs. A decree of 1759 permitted factory owners to convert a free laborer in their plant into a

---

[1] Engelmann, *Die Leibeigenschaft*, pp. 81-82.

serf by sending a substitute for him when he was called to military service. The factory owner could do this without the worker's consent.[2] Besides these and similar laws that allowed proprietors to reduce free men to serfdom, the tsars themselves created hundreds of thousands of new serfs by giving away state peasants to members of the dvorianstvo.

The greatest part of the increase in the number of serfs, however, came about through the expansion of the empire. In many of the territories the tsars acquired at the expense of the decaying Swedish, Polish and Turkish realms they either introduced serfdom, or gave it official sanction where it already existed.

Much of the land gained in the west and southwest had long before been part of the Kievan federation. In the centuries after the federation collapsed, various parts had been under the real or nominal sovereignty of Tatars, Lithuanians, Poles or Turks. In some of this region a harsh form of serfdom had developed, particularly in the Lithuanian and White Russian sections after the union of Poland and Lithuania in 1569. To escape this oppression peasants had fled in large numbers down the Dnieper and Bug rivers into the Ukrainian steppes.[3] There they lived the free life of cossacks, some as small farmers and others as nomads, under their own autonomous semi-military organization, and acting always as a constant thorn in the sides of both Poland and Russia.

After years of war with Poland and involved territorial exchanges, Russia gradually absorbed these western borderlands. By the Treaty of Andrusovo in 1667 Tsar Alexis annexed Smolensk, the city of Kiev and its environs west of the Dnieper, and the region east of the Dnieper that later formed Chernigov and Poltava guberniias. Chernigov and Poltava, together with Kharkov, were known collectively as Little Russia. In the next century Catherine II, through the successive partitions of Poland,

---

[2] *Ibid.*, pp. 110-111; Miliukov, *Histoire*, II, 504-505.

[3] *Ukraina* means frontier in Russian. The word became the generally accepted (though not official) name for the southwestern quarter of the black earth belt that was for so long a no-man's land between Slav, Turk and Tatar. At the end of the seventeenth century the name was applied to the region which later became the southeastern part of Podolia guberniia, much of Kiev guberniia, the southwestern part of Chernigov, all of Poltava, and most of Ekaterinoslav and Kherson. *Entsiklopedicheskii slovar*, XXXIVa, 633.

gained all of White Russia (Vitebsk, Mogilev, and Minsk guberniias), Lithuania (Vilna, Grodno, and Kovno guberniias), and the northern part of western or right bank Ukraine (Kiev, Volynia, Podolia). The portion of right bank Ukraine that lay between the Dnieper and the Southern Bug was won from Turkey by the Treaty of Kuchuk Kainarji in 1774, and nine years later the Crimea was annexed. These territories became the provinces of Ekaterinoslav, Kherson, and Tauride, known collectively as New Russia. In 1812 Bessarabia, ceded by the Turks, was included in New Russia.

The tsarist government left undisturbed the system of serfdom it found entrenched in White Russia, in Lithuania, and in some parts of the Ukraine. In Little Russia, however, most of the land was held by peasant communes who had homesteaded the empty steppe. Their rights to their holdings had been recognized by the Polish government when it was sovereign, and by Moscow after the Russian annexation. But the cossack chieftains who were the indigenous ruling class, and Great Russian landlords who began to come in, pressed for legal sanction to take the peasants' land from them, and to limit their right to come and go as they pleased. The government held out against these demands for a long time. In 1739 a ukase abolishing peasant freedom of movement was issued, but three years later it was repealed, and a series of subsequent decrees declared that the Little Russian peasants were to remain free landholders. These laws were evaded on a wholesale scale, particularly by the cossack chieftains. By 1765 only 1,717 homesteads still belonged to free peasants. All the rest of the land was owned by men of the seignioral class.

Confronted with this *fait accompli*, the government of Catherine II began to retreat from the position taken in previous reigns, and decided to regularize the seignioral expropriations. A law of 1763 limited freedom of movement by requiring the peasant to get a permit from his lord before he could leave the property. In 1764 Catherine ended the local autonomy of Little Russia by abolishing the office of hetman, and appointed a governor-general to administer the region for her. She gave her first appointee to this new post a secret directive in which, among other things, she indicated that she planned to abolish peasant freedom of movement in Little Russia because, said she, it was bad for lord, for state, and for peasant. But she waited until after the next revision (the fourth, in 1782) before she acted. Then, on 3 May 1783 she decreed that the peasants in Little Russia were to be bound to the lords on whose land they lived when the census was made. The revision lists were to serve as the legal proof of their bondage.

Nowhere in this decree did the words serf or serfdom appear. The text of the law stated that the need to maintain order, and to insure payment of taxes, made it necessary to take away freedom from the peasants. Once again the throne enserfed its subjects in the name of fiscal expediency and public order, and once again it showed its disinclination to call serfdom by its true name.[4]

According to one account, insiders who knew that Catherine had made up her mind to introduce serfdom into Little Russia, used this knowledge to their own advantage. They enticed peasants to settle on land they owned there, by offering terms that seemed highly advantageous to the tenants. When the decree of 1783 was issued, these renters were trapped as serfs to the landowners who had lured them by now worthless inducements.[5]

A few years later Emperor Paul, by a ukase of 12 December 1796, extended serfdom to New Russia and the Caucasus. Paul explained in the decree that the continued existence of peasant freedom in these regions menaced the welfare of serfowners in neighboring provinces, for their peasants fled to New Russia and the Caucasus, or were attracted there by the offers of "greedy, disloyal" proprietors.[6]

Russian expansion in the eighteenth century also included the annexation of the Baltic provinces of Courland, Lifland, and Estland. The latter two had been ceded by Sweden at the end of the Great Northern War in 1721. Courland became a Russian protectorate, but remained autonomous in name until 1795, when it was made a province of the empire. Most of the

[4] Engelmann, *Die Leibeigenschaft*, pp. 36-37, 146-150; Semevskii, *Krest'ianskii vopros*, I, 148-152.
[5] Turgenev, *La Russie*, II, 112-113.
[6] *PSZ*, XXIV, no. 17638, pp. 233-234.

soil in these lands belonged to German seigniors who had long before managed to enserf their peasants. The Swedish government in the last decades of its sovereignty had taken steps to improve the status of the serfs, and had tried to persuade the proprietors to emancipate them. When the Russians took over they scrapped this program, and abandoned the peasants to the oppressive rule of their Balt masters.[7]

As things turned out, Paul's ukase of 1796, establishing serfdom in New Russia and the Caucasus, marked the end of an era. In the next century, and under new rulers, the Russian government forbad the spread of the institution into newly-won lands, and abolished or restricted it in other parts of the empire. Finland, annexed in 1808, had never known serfdom, and the government took steps to insure that it would not be introduced there. In Bessarabia, gained in 1812, the only serfs were gypsies (in 1838 out of nearly 9,500 male gypsies about 7,000 were serfs).[8] The Russians maintained the existing agrarian order and issued laws designed to prevent the growth of serfdom. In 1804 Alexander approved reforms in the status of the Baltic peasants, and then in a series of decrees emancipated them without land. In western Poland Napoleon had freed the serfs in 1807 when he created the Duchy of Warsaw. Actually, this much-heralded reform had benefited the Polish proprietors, for the freed peasants were not provided with holdings, so that the landowners now had a cheap and plentiful labor supply. At the Congress of Vienna the Powers turned the Duchy over to Alexander, under the name of the Kingdom of Poland. The Russian rulers did not try to reestablish serfdom, and in 1836 ordered that serfs from other parts of the empire could not be settled there. Serfdom had never established itself in Siberia, and in 1839 the possibility of that ever happening vanished when Tsar Nicholas forbad proprietors to bring serfs from other parts of the empire. In Transcaucasia, annexed in the course of the eighteenth and nineteenth centuries, the indigenous landowners held much of the peasantry in serfdom, or near it, and slavery was not unknown. These arrangements had

[7] Bilmanis, *History*, pp. 175-178, 216; Semevskii, *Krest'ianskii vopros*, I, 13.
[8] Haxthausen, *Studien*, II, 466.

been accepted by the Russian conquerors. In 1839, however, an imperial decree ordered that the proprietors there could not import serfs from Russia, nor sell the bondsmen they already owned.[9]

The enserfment of millions of free people, and natural increase, combined to produce an enormous growth in the number of serfs, as the following table shows.[10]

REVISION		MALE SERFS (IN MILLIONS)	TOTAL MALE POP. (IN MILLIONS)	MALE SERFS AS PERCENT OF TOTAL MALE POP.
I	(1724)	3.2	5.8	55
II	(1743-5)	3.4	6.6	51.5
III	(1762-4)	–	7.4	–
IV	(1782-3)	6.7	12.8	52
V	(1796)	8.7	17.8	49
VI	(1811)	10.4	17.9	58
VII	(1817)	9.8	17.0	57.5
VIII	(1835)	11.4	21.8	52
IX	(1851)	10.7	22.3	48
X	(1858)	10.7	24.0	44.5

Despite the great increase in the number of serfs, the table shows that the rate of growth in the male serf population during the eighteenth century was slightly less than that of the total male population. In 1724 the ratio of male serfs to the total male population had been 55 percent; in 1796 it was 49 percent. During the nineteenth century the rate of growth of the serf population fell still further behind that of the total population. In the Tenth Revision in 1858 the male serf population equalled just 44.5 percent of the total male population.

The reasons for the failure of the serf population to maintain

[9] Semevskii, *Krest'ianskii vopros*, II, 543-547.

[10] Male serf population: 1st Revision, Mavor, *Economic History*, I, 418, 590; 2nd Revision, Semevskii, *Krest'iane*, I, 16; 4th-9th Revisions, Schnitzler, *L'empire*, II, 60-100, 107; 10th Revision, Semevskii, *Krest'ianskii vopros*, II, 570. Total male population, 1st to 10th Revisions, Voznesenskii, *Ekonomika Rossii*, p. 17.

Because of the imprecisions and deficiencies of the census data, there is considerable diversity in estimates of the size of the serf population. Thus, according to Liashchenko, *History*, p. 273, who presents estimates of the total male and female population, the proportion of serfs dropped from 55.5 percent in the 5th Revision to 30.7 percent in the 10th.

the same rate of growth as the rest of the population are not readily apparent. The relative decline cannot be explained away by blaming it on the incomplete and inaccurate statistical reporting of the census takers. The data certainly have many deficiencies, but if these shortcomings were responsible, the ratios of serfs to total population could be expected to show inconsistencies in their secular trend, instead of the pattern they do follow. Nor can the decline be explained by emancipations, or by urban growth. There were no wholesale emancipations during these years, save in the Baltic provinces, yet the ratio of serfs to the total population fell in every part of the empire except the North, where the serf population had always been very small, and where the increase in its size was unimportant.[11] Urban population did grow, but the serfs who lived in the cities retained their servile status and were counted as part of the serf population.

Part of the decline can be attributed to a drift from serfdom into the state peasantry. The serfs who migrated—or fled—to Siberia and to other frontiers became state peasants. The increase in the size of the army from around 200,000 for most of the eighteenth century to well over a million in the 1850's,[12] also produced some diminution in the serf population. The serf recruits were freed from their bondage as a reward for their military service. Finally, serfs who lived on properties that escheated to or were bought by the crown, or that were confiscated because of illegal activities of their owners, became state peasants instead of being given to other seigniors, as had usually happened in the eighteenth century.

The total number who left the serf class for these reasons cannot be determined. But the partial information that is available makes it obvious that it was far from large enough to account for the relative decline in the serf population. One authority suggested that the net rate of natural increase of serfs was lower than that of the rest of the population, because of the less favorable conditions under which they lived.[13] Unfortunately, the absence of information on net reproduction

11 Voznesenskii, *Ekonomika Rossii*, p. 22.   12 *Ibid.*, p. 179.
13 Miliukov in *Entsiklopedicheskii slovar*, xviA, 684.

rates of serfs and other groups makes it impossible to test this hypothesis. It finds support, however, in the work of Popov, who argued that in the decades before the emancipation the serfs were exploited so much that they were unable to raise enough grain to support an increase in their numbers.[14]

The accidents of history and geography had distributed the serf population unevenly among the regions of the empire. The number of serfs in the fertile colonial lands in the south and east rose steadily, for in addition to the enserfment of the indigenous peasantry, landowners moved serfs into these regions from properties they owned in older parts of the realm. Despite this outward movement, however, the older provinces retained a heavy concentration of serfs. At the end of the 1850's only 30 percent of the empire's total population lived in the eighteen provinces of the Central Industrial, Central Agricultural, and Lake districts. But these guberniias had over 46 percent of all of Russia's serfs. In seven of these provinces (Pskov, Tver, Iaroslav, Kostroma, Nizhnii Novgorod, Vladimir, Riazan) serfs made up between 50 and 60 percent of the population, and in two others (Kaluga and Tula) between 60 and 70 percent. The western tier of provinces, the thirteen guberniias of White Russia, Lithuania, Little Russia, and the Southwest, also had a high serf population density. Together these four regions had about 22 percent of the population of the empire, but nearly 36 percent of its serfs. In contrast, the ten provinces of the Lower Volga, New Russia, and the Urals had 20 percent of the population and only 14 percent of the serfs.[15]

II

During the years in which millions of free peasants were forced to become serfs the nature of serfdom grew ever more oppressive. By the last part of the eighteenth century the Russian serf was scarcely distinguishable from a chattel slave. That was able to happen because the state withdrew almost entirely from supervision and interference in the relationship between lord and peasant, and thereby allowed the serfowners to gain nearly unlimited powers over the people they owned.

[14] Popov, "Khlebnofurazhnyi balans," p. 15.

The deterioration in the status of the seignioral peasantry had been going on since the fifteenth century. But the concessions to the dvorianstvo made by Peter I and his successors up to the accession of Paul in 1796, gave a great new impetus to the decline in the position of the peasants. Peter, who needed a large and steady supply of men and money to carry out his grandiose schemes, introduced more efficient systems of taxation and conscription, and made the serfowners responsible for their successful operation. To make it easier for them to perform these duties he allowed them to have new rights over their serfs, and gave legal sanction to powers they had preempted. The rulers after Peter followed his precedent, so that seignioral authority continued to grow. In the last part of the century the increase in prices and the rise in the standard of living of the nobles, made it harder for them to make ends meet. Inevitably, they took advantage of their favored position in the state to demand still greater controls over their peasants, in order to be able to extract greater quantities of goods and services from them.

The *Ulozhenie* of 1649 had confirmed the serfowner in his possession of broad, though not unlimited, powers over the peasants who were bound to him. But, as was pointed out on an earlier page, the code provided no effective machinery to

---

15 Troinitskii, *Krepostnoe naselenie*, pp. 49-50.

Region	Serfs (percent)	Percent of empire's total population	Percent of empire's serf population
Lake	36	4	4.8
Central Ind.	53	10.2	17.4
Central Agric.	46	16	24
White Russia	63.5	5	10
Lithuania	41	3.7	5
Little Russia	38	6.5	7.8
Southwest	59	7	13
Lower Volga	26.5	7.9	6.7
New Russia	25	3.7	3
Urals	14.8	8	4.2
Total		72.0	95.9

The remaining 4 percent of the serf population was scattered through other parts of the empire. The remaining 28 percent of the empire's total population lived in the Baltic provinces, Siberia, the Kingdom of Poland, the Grand Duchy of Finland, and Transcaucasia. In these regions there were very few serfs or none at all.

protect these people against the arbitrary acts of their masters, so that the lords did pretty much as they pleased. Nonetheless, the government had not countenanced the excesses in seignorial behavior, though it did nothing to stop them. In the eighteenth century, however, these hitherto illegal practices were given the sanction of law. Thus, the *Ulozhenie* had forbidden the sale of peasants without land, but this prohibition had been widely disregarded.[16] In a ukase of 15 April 1721 Peter stated that it had been, and still was, customary in Russia for peasants and domestics to be sold "like cattle," and for families to be split up in these transactions. With obvious censure (but complete inaccuracy) Peter stated that there was nothing like this in the whole world, and commanded the practice to cease.[17] Yet in earlier decrees he had not only given recognition to the sale of human beings, but had encouraged it by allowing persons subject to military draft to buy substitutes.[18] In fact, in the very ukase in which he condemned the trade in serfs, he went on to say that if it was impossible to stop it the serfs should be sold only in cases of need, and then by family rather than by individual. He repeated these pious sentiments three years later in another decree. But the sales went on, and families continued to be broken up, without reproof from the government.

The trade in peasants reached its peak—as did so many of the cruelest aspects of Russian serfdom—during the reign of Catherine II. To give that self-proclaimed disciple of Voltaire her due, she did try to do something about this. In 1771 she decided that the spectacle of human beings on the block should be banned, and ordered that the serfs of bankrupt seigniors could not be sold at public auction. Her prohibition was disregarded, and so in 1792 she amended the law to allow these sales—but forbad the use of the hammer by the auctioneer! She also took measures to cut down on the commerce in recruit substitutes. This traffic always boomed whenever the army issued its draft calls. In 1766 Catherine decreed that men suit-

[16] *Ulozhenie*, Chapter xx, sect. 97; Vernadsky, "Serfdom in Russia," p. 266. The Ulozhenie did allow the sale of non-Christian serfs without land.

[17] *PSZ*, VI, no. 3770, p. 377.

[18] Engelmann, *Die Leibeigenschaft*, p. 104.

able for military service could not be sold during the recruiting period, or for the three months that preceded it. This law, too, was generally evaded.[19]

The sale of peasants without land had been illegal in the White Russian provinces when they had been part of Poland. After their annexation by Russia the landlords there began to follow the example of their peers in the rest of the empire, and a lively business in humans grew up. The terms of the annexation, however, had guaranteed the maintenance of the existing laws, so the legality of the trade was brought into question. The Senate, after deliberating on the problem, solemnly informed Catherine in 1775 that "the proprietors of White Russia as subjects of Your Majesty must enjoy the same rights that the Russian nobility enjoy, and therefore they cannot be deprived of the right to sell their peasants without land."[20] In Lifland the provincial diet in 1765 ordered the imposition of heavy fines on serfowners who sold peasants without land. This measure, inspired apparently not by humanitarianism but by the desire to keep peasants within Lifland, proved unsuccessful, and in 1804 new legislation was adopted to end the practice.[21] In 1798 Paul, overruling a recommendation of the Senate, declared the sale of serfs without land in Little Russia illegal and ordered it to cease. Yet fifty years later the seigniors there were reported to be evading the law, and selling recruit substitutes to buyers in the Central Industrial region.[22]

The purchasers of serfs included peasants as well as nobles. Communes of serfs and state peasants made cash levies on their members, and wealthy peasants used their own money to buy men whom they could send into the army in their stead. Because of this demand, the substitutes sold for high prices. In 1766 the government fixed their price at 120 rubles, in 1786 it raised it to 360 rubles, and in 1793 to 400 rubles, but these ceilings were frequently disregarded.[23] Count N. P. Sheremetev,

---

[19] Semevskii, *Krest'iane,* I, 148-149, 151.

[20] Engelmann, *Die Leibeigenschaft,* pp. 143-144.

[21] Semevskii, *Krest'iane,* I, 158.

[22] *PSZ,* xxv, no. 18706, 16 October 1798, pp. 419-420; Samarin, *Sochineniia,* II, 409.

[23] Semevskii, *Krest'iane,* I, 155-156, 306-307.

who sold substitutes from among his peasants to others of his serfs who could afford to buy them, asked 400 rubles per substitute in the late 1780's, a decade later 600, and in 1808 he was getting 800 rubles. He made the wealthiest of his serfs pay even more, scaling the price to the purchaser's capital. The man worth over 10,000 rubles had to lay out 2,000 rubles for a substitute, if he had 5,000 to 10,000 the price was 1,500, and those who were worth 3,000 paid 1,000 rubles.[24]

Nobles who bought peasants without land, for use as field and domestic workers, paid much less for them. In the middle decades of the eighteenth century male serfs without land could be bought for around 30 rubles, and sometimes they sold for as little as 3 to 5 rubles.[25] In the eighties the price went up to 70 to 100 rubles, and in the nineties contemporaries reported that ordinary serfs never sold for less than 100 rubles, and sometimes cost 200 rubles or more.[26]

Serfs who had some special skill commanded the highest prices of all. Prince Potemkin paid 40,000 rubles to Field Marshal Razumovskii for a fifty piece serf orchestra. A talented serf actress was sold for a reported 5,000 rubles in the early nineteenth century.[27] Pretty young serf girls also brought good prices. Around the turn of the century men-about-town in Moscow paid as much as 500 rubles at the serf market for girls who caught their fancy.[28] Even as implacable an enemy of serfdom as Ivan Turgenev was not above this practice. When the tsar exiled him to his estate in 1852 because of his stories about the injustices and immorality of serfdom, he fought boredom by entertaining himself with an attractive young chambermaid. He reportedly bought the girl from his cousin, paying 700 rubles for her. Ordinary housemaids sold at most for 50 rubles.[29] Serfs indulged themselves, too, buying the girls in the name of

[24] Shchepetov, *Krepostnoe pravo*, pp. 143-144; cf. Sivkov, *Ocherki*, p. 203; *MKP*, I, 352; Tooke, *View*, III, 318n.

[25] Semevskii, *Krest'iane*, I, 153-154; Kusheva, "Khoziaistvo," pp. 598-599.

[26] Tooke, *View*, 318n.; Semevskii, *Krest'iane*, I, 156.

[27] Semevskii, *Krest'iane*, I, 156.

[28] Gitermann, *Geschichte*, II, 490.

[29] Yarmolinsky, *Turgenev*, pp. 122, 125. The official reason for his confinement (which included a month in jail) was his publication of an obituary of Gogol after the St. Petersburg censors had refused to approve it.

their masters. Ivanovo, the textile center owned by the She-remetevs, had a widely know girl market. Serfowners in other parts of Russia shipped girls there for sale. Buyers came, too, from other places, but many of the customers were drawn from among the wealthy serf industrialists of Ivanovo. In 1793 and again in 1804, Count Sheremetev forbad them to make these purchases, but apparently those who could afford it somehow managed to continue.[30]

In the nineteenth century the government made a few feeble attempts to curb some of the excesses that attended the traffic in human beings. Alexander I, soon after his coronation, or-dered newspapers to discontinue advertisements for the sale of serfs.[31] Sellers easily evaded the ban by placing notices in the press that the services of a serf were available. Everyone under-stood this meant the serf was being offered for sale.[32] To restrict the trade in recruit substitutes a law in 1804 decreed that serfs sold without land could not be sent into the army for three years after their sale; if purchased by state peasants they could not be drafted before the next general revision. These provisions were repeated in later decrees, but with the time limit on in-duction reduced to one year.[33] This legislation doubtless served to reduce the traffic in recruit substitutes, though it did not end it. A law of 1808 forbad the sale of serfs without land at fairs and auctions, but these public sales continued to be held.[34]

Alexander seemed to believe that his measures had put an end to the trade in humans. In 1820 Count V. P. Kochubei, then Minister of Interior, told N. I. Turgenev that the tsar had recently declared that serfs had not been sold at retail for the last twenty years. Yet peasants of bankrupt nobles were sold by court order at public auctions that were held close by the tsar's own residence in St. Petersburg.[35] That same year Alexander received a petition from some unhappy peasants who had been sold without land. He forwarded the document

[30] Shchepetov, *Krepostnoe pravo*, p. 104.
[31] *PSZ*, XXVI, no. 19892, 28 May 1801, p. 662.
[32] Mazour, *First Russian Revolution*, p. 3.
[33] *PSZ*, XXVIII, no. 21442, 7 Sept. 1804, sect. 1, 3; *SZ*, 1857, IX, sect. 1086.
[34] Cf. Turgenev, *La Russie*, II, 110.
[35] Semevskii, *Krest'ianskii vopros*, II, 473.

to the Council of State with an endorsement that said "I am quite sure that the sale of serfs without land has been forbidden by law for a long time," but nonetheless he ordered the Council to check the pertinent legislation. The only prohibition it could locate was Paul's ban on the sale of serfs without land in Little Russia. The Council then searched for laws that specifically permitted the practice. The only legal sanction it could find was in the instructions given to tax collectors during the reign of Empress Anna (1730-1740). The list of taxes that had to be paid on the receipts from the sale of a property included an impost on the income from the sale of serfs without land. This provision had been repeated in tax instructions issued in 1807 during Alexander's own reign. The Council decided that this incidental fiscal regulation provided the necessary authorization for the trade in serfs.[36]

Nicholas I in 1833, and again in 1841, ordered that parents and their unmarried children could not be separated by sale or gift, whether they were transferred with land or without it.[37] Families could still be sold as units and, of course, individuals who were not members of a family group could be sold singly. In the last decades of serfdom, however, a mistaken belief that the sale of serfs without land was illegal spread widely among serfowners. To evade this imagined prohibition they customarily included a small piece of land when they sold peasants, and after the transaction was completed bought back the land from the purchaser of the serfs.[38]

Besides acquiescing in the reduction of the seignioral peasantry to human chattels to be bought and sold, the government sanctioned a wide expansion in the judicial and police powers of the serfowners. The lords held jurisdictional powers over their peasants, but the laws of the land had set limits beyond which they were not supposed to go. Certain criminal offenses, for example, lay outside the seignioral competence. If a lord tried his peasants for such offenses he exposed himself to severe penalties. He could also be held to account if he handed out

[36] Turgenev, *La Russie*, II, 100-101, 102-104.
[37] *SZ*, 1857, XII, sect. 1081.
[38] Haxthausen, *Die ländliche Verfassung*, pp. 109-110; Turgenev, *La Russie*, II, 101.

excessive or illegal punishments. Though much of this legislation lacked in precise definition, it marked off the general limits of the lord's judicial powers. In the eighteenth century, however, these boundaries were well-nigh obliterated by loosely phrased imperial legislation and unimpeded seignorial arrogation. The government did make some attempts, notably in the 1830's and 1840's, to place curbs on punitive powers of the serfowners. It ordered that the master could not sentence his serf to more than 40 blows with the rod, or 15 with the cudgel, nor could he imprison the serf for more than two months in the seignorial jail. If the serfowner felt that more severe punishment was justified, he could sentence the culprit to imprisonment for a maximum of three months in a government house of correction, or have him assigned to hard labor on a government work gang. If he wanted to inflict heavier punishment he was supposed to turn the serf over to government authorities who would decide upon the appropriate sentence. Or he could turn the culprit over to the army as a recruit and get credit, or a "recruit quittance" as it was called, for him at the next regular conscription.[39]

The enforcement of these limitations, however, depended almost entirely upon the seigniors themselves. If a serfowner did exceed his legal powers it was highly unlikely that the authorities would find out about it. The serfs did not have the right to enter complaints against their masters—the law demanded their "silent obedience" to their seigniors. Only the most extreme and flagrant violations could possibly have come to official attention, and even then investigation was difficult. The serfs would be afraid to testify, the accused lord could use influence and bribes to have the affair hushed up, the local officials were strongly biased in favor of the seigniors, and finally and most important, the government was really not very interested since it depended upon the dvorianstvo to police itself.

The most extreme punishment the seignior could hand out legally was to banish his serf to Siberia. Empress Elizabeth had given this power to serfowners in 1760 to stimulate the settlement of Siberia. The peasant was supposed to be exiled only

---

[39] *SZ*, 1857, IX, sect. 1052, 1053, 1055.

for major offenses, but the government left it to the seignior to decide whether the offense was serious enough to warrant this action. The serfowner received a recruit quittance for the man he exiled, so that he did not suffer a permanent loss in his labor force. The law required the exiled peasant to be under 45 and able to work, and if married his wife was to accompany him. His children joined him or remained at home, depending upon the proprietor's wishes. If he did allow them to go with their parents, the government paid him an indemnity of 10 rubles for boys up to five, 20 rubles for boys of five to fifteen, half as much for girls, and gave him a recruit quittance for boys over fifteen.

These rules were often disregarded by the serfowners. When P. S. Pallas toured Siberia in the 1770's he met men over 45, and married men without their wives, among the exiles. Count J. E. Sievers, who stood high in the counsels of Catherine, in memoranda to the empress in 1768 and in 1773 claimed that some landlords, to save good workers from the army draft, banished inefficient and infirm serfs whose only offense was their ineptitude or incapacity. The lords received recruit quittances for these exiles and used them at the next conscription to meet the recruit obligation, thus avoiding the loss of any of their good workers to the army. Sievers estimated in 1773 that this ruse had cost the army seven to eight thousand conscripts at the last recruitment. He might also have pointed out that seven to eight thousand innocent people had been condemned to Siberian exile.[40]

The seignior was supposed to provide the serf he banished with clothes and footwear, 20 rubles if he was a bachelor, 30 if his wife went with him, and 10 rubles for each child who accompanied him. The money was to pay for the expenses of the journey. The trip was long and hard and made mainly on foot. Many perished along the way—estimates of mortality run as high as 75 percent. Once he reached Siberia the exile, if he had not been sentenced to hard labor, was given land by the government and became a state peasant. The sole restriction placed on him was that he could not leave the area in which he had

[40] Semevskii, *Krest'iane*, I, 159-162.

been settled. The government exempted him from taxes for his first three years, lent him a horse, plow, and axe, and during his first year gave him a regular soldier's ration plus 2 kopecks a day. His wife and children received half rations and 1 kopeck each. In his second year of settlement his subsidy was reduced by half, and in the third year it was ended.[41]

Early in Alexander I's reign the government suspended the serfowners' right to deport their peasants, but soon restored it with undiminished vigor, so that once again the master could banish his serf for "impudent conduct" or "intolerable behavior."[42] In 1827 a few minor changes were made, including the provision that the exile could not be over 50, and that he had to be accompanied by his wife, and by sons under 6 and daughters under 11 years of age.[43]

In 1765 Catherine gave lords the right to sentence a serf "who deserved it" to hard labor with the Admiralty. The serfowner himself set the length of the sentence. In 1809 this power was taken away. An incident in 1807 in which a serfowner sent peasants to the Admiralty with the order that they be kept at hard labor for twenty years "in order to moderate the impudence of their behavior," is supposed to have persuaded the government to rescind this particular privilege.[44]

The serfs had already been stripped of most of their legal personality by the Code of 1649, and later legislation imposed still further restrictions. A series of decrees in the second half of the eighteenth century made it illegal for serfs to contract a loan or other liability, enter into a lease, or work for someone else, without the permission of their master. If they had his authorization to borrow, they had to have him or some other free person as a guarantor. Serfs whose owners had given them the right to engage in regular business activity could act as guarantors, and a special exception allowed all Little Russian serfs to give surety for loans up to 9 rubles.[45] The serfowners continued to represent their peasants in civil actions, and to be

---

41 *Ibid.*, I, 159, 161, 164-165; Schkaff, *La question*, p. 59.
42 *SZ*, 1857, IX, sect. 1056.
43 *PSZ*, 2nd series, no. 1339, 30 Aug. 1827, sect. 1, p. 478.
44 Semevskii, *Krest'ianskii vopros*, I, 495.
45 *SZ*, 1857, IX, sect. 1144, 1145, 1146.

responsible for damages done by them. In the event of the un-premeditated murder by a serf of a peasant who belonged to another seignior, the culprit's owner had to pay 600 rubles damages to the victim's owner. This replaced the old law that had required the owner of the murderer to give a serf to the dead man's owner as indemnity.

A glimpse of seignorial justice in action in the villages of a great serfowner is provided by records from the Sheremetev archives. The Sheremetevs had a special code drawn up for the managers of their many individual properties so that there would be uniformity among all their peasants in the imposition of punishments. The penalties specified were sometimes harsh, but the code protected the serf against the arbitrary behavior of his overseers. He knew what to expect if he did something wrong. For instance, if he failed to meet his barshchina obliga-tion he would be sentenced to a week of digging ditches or laboring in a quarry. If he repeated the offense he received the same penalty, plus a flogging with a rod. If he did it a third time, the labor sentence was increased to a month, and he was beaten with a cudgel.[46]

In the Sheremetev's industrial village of Ivanovo, where the population in 1800 was 9,204, only 109 people received seign-iorial punishment in the twenty years from 1790 to 1809. Most of the wrongdoers were habitual offenders. Seventy-eight of them were punished from one to ten times during this period, and thirty-one of them more than ten times. Intoxication was by far the most common misdemeanor with 552 cases—Ivanovo obviously had its share of topers. The other offenses were disorderly conduct, 107 cases; suspected of stealing, 51 cases; disobeying officials, 45 cases; going out at night, 39 cases; dis-obeying parents, 25 cases; malingering, 20 cases; flight and absenteeism, 7 cases; and not paying seignorial obligations, 5 cases. The punishments handed out for these transgressions were: 407 beatings of which 263 were with the stick and 140 with the lash, two put in the stocks, two put in spiked collars, 277 given oral reprimands, 49 jailed for not more than three days, 29 put on labor details, 4 fined, and 20 dismissed.

[46] Shchepetov, *Krepostnoe pravo*, p. 52.

Ivanovo seems to have been a peaceful town, and the punishments meted out to those who had brushes with the law are mild in the context of that era. A somewhat harsher picture emerges from the data for Iukhotsk, another Sheremetev property, for the years 1821 to 1854. Iukhotsk lay not far from St. Petersburg, and a number of its peasants went there or to other large towns to earn their livings. Judging from the village police records the "Iukhotskers" did not have as good work habits as did the people of Ivanovo, but on the other hand they held their liquor better. Their most frequent offense was vagrancy and idleness with 126 cases. Stealing or suspicion of stealing was in second place with 108 cases, then drunkenness with 65 cases, 51 cases of not paying obrok, 46 cases of bad conduct, 22 cases not paying for purchases, and 54 cases divided between fifteen other offenses that included such things as insolence, lewdness, and aiding escaped prisoners. The most frequent penalty was to order the culprit to give up his job in the city and return to Iukhotsk, where it was much harder for him to earn his living. This sentence was handed out in 164 cases. Eighty-eight serfs were flogged with the cane, 58 sent off as recruits, 31 forbidden to leave the area, 28 sent to work for a merchant in Kronstadt, 15 whipped with a lash, 5 condemned to penal servitude, 3 sent to the workhouse, 2 to the house of correction, 2 beaten with the cudgel, and 4 banished, two of them to Siberia. Seventeen other lesser penalties were given, such as fines, being put under special surveillance, or doing church penance.[47]

III

The increase in the judicial and police powers of the serf-owners had as its corollary an increase in their control over the private lives of their peasants. The marriages of their serfs were a matter of especial concern to the seigniors. They preferred to have their peasants wed one another and produce more serfs for the master, rather than have their female serfs marry a man who did not belong to them. If one of their women did want to marry someone outside her master's property, the law re-

[47] *Ibid.*, pp. 119-120, 212-213.

quired her to get his consent. He could refuse to give it except in the event the girl wanted to marry a soldier (Peter I had ordered this exception). Some proprietors demanded a fee for their permission. Often the amount they asked varied with the wealth of the applicant, and on occasion it amounted to hundreds and even thousands of rubles. Thus, two rich serfs of Ivanovo had to pay Count Sheremetev 7,000 and 9,000 rubles each for his consent.[48]

The law did not require serfs of the same master to get his permission if they wanted to marry. But this was a universal custom, and some lords charged a small fee for their consent. Often, too, serfowners who felt that their peasants' obligations to them included producing children and thereby adding to their master's assets, ordered two of his serfs to wed one another without regard to the couple's own wishes. Peter I had forbidden this practice in 1724, but serfowners paid no heed to the ban. Serfs tried to defend themselves against these unwelcome matches by standing together as sponsors at a christening, for church law prohibited a marriage between godparents. This stratagem had its obvious limitation; infants in need of baptism were not always available to a man and woman who had just been told to get married. But farsighted peasants who had always felt distaste for one another could use it, and so foil their master's wish if he should later decide to pair them off.

Another matter that interested seigniors was the real and personal property held by their peasants. This had long been considered as belonging ultimately to the master. Usually serfowners allowed their peasants to keep their property, and to take it with them when they were sold to another master. The law did not allow serfs to buy real property until a few years before the emancipation, but, as was pointed out earlier, many lords permitted their peasants to buy land and even serfs in the lord's name. But the lord always had the right to take anything he wanted from his serf's property without paying for it. Sometimes that happened. A group of serfs who belonged to Count Panin pooled their savings and bought a piece of land near Riga to raise vegetables. They made the purchase, of course, in

48 *Ibid.*, p. 78; Berlin, *Russkaia burzhuaziia*, p. 87.

Panin's name. A little while later Panin, inspired no doubt by patriotic ardor, gave the land to the state for a new railroad line. The serfs who had paid for the land received nothing. A wealthy serf owned by Count Sheremetev left 150,000 rubles in bank deposits when he died. His children, who had bought their freedom from the Count, tried to get the money as the heirs of their father, but the court awarded it to Sheremetev on the ground that he had owned the dead man and therefore owned his property.[49]

IV

In return for its grant to the serfowners of nearly complete powers, the government did charge them with certain responsibilities for the well-being of their serfs. But the nature and extent of these obligations were far from commensurate with the privileges allowed the seigniors, while the ease with which they were avoided gives testimony to the government's lack of interest in the lot of the common people.

The only provisions in the Code of 1649 concerned with welfare dealt with slaves and not serfs. The slaveowner was ordered to feed his thralls in time of famine. If he failed to do this, and his slaves had to seek alms, they were to be taken from him. When a captured runaway slave was returned, his owner had to pledge that he would not punish the fugitive by maiming or killing him, or starving him to death.[50] These pitifully inadequate ordinances provided the foundation for the legislation of the next two hundred years on the duties the proprietor owed his serfs.

In 1719 Peter ordered that if a serfowner's conduct worked undue hardships upon his peasants his land and serfs were to be placed under the guardianship of his kinsmen until he mended his ways. If he failed to reform he was to be sent to a monastery and put under ecclesiastical censure. Peter justified this law not by any reference to the need to protect peasants from cruelties and injustices they might suffer from their masters. Instead he pointed out that mistreated serfs were likely

---

[49] Kulischer, "Die kapitalistischen Unternehmer," p. 352n.; Turgenev, *La Russie*, II, 129.

[50] *Ulozhenie*, Chapter XX, sect. 41, 42, 92.

to run away, thereby depopulating properties and so reducing the government's tax revenues.[51] Empress Anna in 1734 enjoined private proprietors, and also the managers of lands owned by the crown, to care for their peasants during famines and see to it that they did not become beggars. This command was repeated a number of times in succeeding years, and seigniors were threatened with punishment for non-compliance. In 1775 Catherine II instructed provincial officials to be on the watch for lords who cruelly mistreated their serfs, or who lived so lavishly that they brought ruin to themselves and their peasants. She also tried to make it more difficult for nobles to free serfs when they became too old to work. These unfortunates were turned out of their holdings to fend for themselves. Catherine did not abolish nor even question the right of the seignior to do this, but she ordered that the serfs had to give their consent to be emancipated, and she made the lord responsible for the taxes of the freed peasants until the next revision was made. Her successor, Paul, issued a series of decrees ordering the construction of bins in every village to store food for emergencies, and instructed the serfowners to see to it that their peasants kept these granaries stocked.[52]

In the nineteenth century neither Alexander I nor Nicholas I introduced any substantive changes in the legislation dealing with the welfare of the serfs. Yet there was some improvement in the attitude of seigniors as the century wore on. The publication in 1832 of the *Svod Zakonov*, the first codification of the laws since 1649, may have provided stimulus for this melioration.[53] The laws that dealt with the lord-peasant relation, including the seignior's duties to his peasants, was brought together in volume nine of the code. This unified presentation not only acquainted the serfowners with their responsibilities, but also made it more difficult for them to overlook the provisions of the law. In fact, the appearance of the *Svod Zakonov*, and then of the Penal Code in 1845, may have made them overly-conscious of the law, for they sometimes believed that

[51] Semevskii, *Krest'iane*, I, 316; Miller, *Essai*, pp. 268n.
[52] Engelmann, *Die Leibeigenschaft*, p. 141; Dodge, *Abolitionist sentiment*, p. 127.
[53] Engelmann, *Die Leibeigenschaft*, pp. 211-212.

things were prohibited to them that really were allowed, such as the sale of serfs without land.

The inadequacies of the legislation and the government's lack of interest in protecting the serfs did not mean, of course, that every serfowner mistreated his peasants. Many, and probably most of them, moved by economic considerations and by fellow-feeling, looked after their people. They did not need the goad of law and the threat of punishment to feed their serfs when crops failed, or to take care of their aged and incapacitated serfs at their own expense.[54] Nonetheless, the nearly unlimited control the seignior had over his people, the fact that the serfs had no legal way to protect themselves against his excesses, and perhaps most important, the absence of social disapproval among the serfowner's peers if he did mistreat his peasants, opened the door to callousness, and often to brutality. Foreigners were shocked when they listened to people of fashion and prominence chat about whippings they had meted out to their serfs, or heard a noble at his club preen himself before an appreciative audience, because he had sentenced three of his serfs to nearly triple the legally allowed number of strokes with the cane.[55]

The serf lived always at the mercy of the whims, appetites, and temper of his owner. Women, and especially those who served in the master's house, could not defend themselves against a lustful seignior. Some proprietors kept harems of slave girls, and there were even seigniors (and in some cases stewards) who practiced *ius primae noctis*, though this had never been an established principal of Russian seignorial law. Captious or finical seigniors had a serf whipped because he upset a saltcellar—a serious offense because it was believed to foretell the coming of some misfortune—or because he made the soup too salty, or had not roasted the chicken to his master's taste. General Kropotkin lost his temper because he thought his serfs were stealing from him, became still angrier when he discovered he was mistaken, and vented his rage by having a serf beaten

---

[54] Cf. Le Play, *Les ouvriers*, II, 58; Haxthausen, *Die ländliche Verfassung*, pp. 121-122; Semevskii, *Krest'iane*, I, 238-240; Grekov, "Tambovskoe imenie," pp. 513-514.

[55] Passenans, *La Russie*, II, 124-130; Bernhardi, *Aus dem Leben*, II, 69.

with 100 blows of a birch rod. Ivan Turgenev's mother sent two of her serfs to Siberia because they neglected to bow to her when she passed by while they were working.[56]

The helplessness of the serfs proved too great a temptation for those proprietors in whose natures sadism lay close to the surface. These people inflicted frightful cruelties upon their peasants.[57] One of the most infamous cases was that of Dar'ia Saltykov who in 1756 inherited 600 serfs from her husband. In seven years she tortured scores of them to death for petty or imagined offenses. Her conduct became so notorious that the authorities decided they had to do something. So in 1762 they began an investigation. It lasted for six years. Finally, she was stripped of her noble rank, pilloried for one hour in Moscow, and then sentenced to spend the rest of her life in confinement in a convent. In contrast to her mild punishment, the serfs who at her command had aided in the torturing of her victims were beaten with the knout and then condemned for life to hard labor in Siberia.

Dar'ia Saltykov and the people like her were psychopaths. But thoughtless and unconscious cruelty was omnipresent. A story told by Peter Kropotkin about his father is a revealing, and at the same time wryly amusing, illustration of the inhumanity inherent in a society where men owned their fellow humans. The elder Kropotkin, as he emerges from his son's memoirs, is a familiar figure to readers of the great nineteenth century Russian novels—the bumbling, pompous, bigoted, self-indulgent landlord. He had been decorated for gallantry in 1828 during the war with the Turks and was inordinately proud of this honor. When his children asked him to tell them about it, he explained that he had been billeted in a Turkish village when fire broke out. His bodyserf, Frol, rushed into the flames to save a child trapped in a burning house. Kropotkin's commanding officer saw this and was so impressed that he awarded the Cross of St. Anne for bravery on the spot—to Kropotkin. The children, of course, pointed out that Frol had saved the

---

[56] Kulischer, "Die Leibeigenschaft," p. 9; Passenans, *La Russie*, II, 120-123; Kropotkin, *Memoirs*, pp. 49-51; Yarmolinsky, *Turgenev*, p. 13.

[57] Cf. Semevskii, *Krest'iane*, I, ch. VII.

child and so deserved the decoration, whereupon their father, nettled by their obtuseness, exclaimed, "What of that? Was he not my man? It is all the same."[58]

Seignioral injustices occurred with particular frequency in connection with the payments they required their serfs to make. Often they made excessive demands or failed to credit peasants with payments they had already made. Such offenses were reported to have been common among small proprietors, but there were great lords, too, who ordered their stewards to resort to these practices.[59] Some proprietors, not satisfied with what they received, stooped to low cunning to extort still more. When D. M. Wallace was in Russia soon after the emancipation he heard about a serfowner who had made it his business to find out about every detail in the lives of his serfs, and then used this knowledge to extract money from them. Thus, if he learned that one of his peasants had managed to save a few rubles he would tell the serf that he intended to send one of his sons into the army as a recruit, or propose that his daughter marry someone of whom the father was certain to disapprove. The peasant was pretty sure to use his savings to ransom his child from these threatened dangers.[60]

The government rarely acted against seigniors who mistreated their serfs, and then only when the matter had become notorious, as in the Saltykov case. In fact, Peter's ukase in which he ordered guardianships for the property of lords who caused their serfs undue hardships seems to have been entirely disregarded for decades after its promulgation. Catherine II in her instructions to the Legislative Commission of 1767 called attention to its neglect, saying that "the reason why it is not put into force. . . . is unknown."[61] Despite her wonderment, during the thirty-four years of her reign only six serfowners are known to have been punished for cruelty to their peasants.[62] In the next century, however, and especially during Nicholas's reign, when the government became much concerned about the lord-peasant

---

58 Kropotkin, *Memoirs*, pp. 10-11.
59 Turgenev, *La Russie*, II, 135-136; Semevskii, *Krest'iane*, I, 177-178.
60 Wallace, *Russia*, p. 109.
61 Reddaway, *Documents*, p. 256.
62 Semevskii, *Krest'iane*, I, 191-205.

relation, new provisions were elaborated,[63] and prosecutions became more frequent. In 1838, 140 properties, by 1852, 193 properties, and by 1859, 215 properties were in guardianship because of their owners' mistreatment of their peasants.[64]

The peasants themselves had no legal way of calling official attention to injustices inflicted upon them by their masters. The code of 1649 had not outlawed the right of serfs to present petitions of complaint against their lords, but had declared that no credence was to be placed in them unless they contained proof of treason by the person against whom the complaint was lodged.[65] Despite this rule it had been customary for serfs to send petitions to their sovereigns, and especially to tsaritsas, presumably because women were thought to be more tender-hearted (a serious error in judgment so far as Russian empresses were concerned). Then Catherine II, after a tour in which she had been besieged with petitions, decided that this nuisance must cease. In a ukase of 22 August 1767 she decreed that henceforth it would be a criminal act for serfs to present petitions against their masters. Those who violated this law were to be beaten with the knout and sent to forced labor in Siberia.[66] Serfs could still denounce their owner if they presented evidence that he was treasonous, or plotting an attempt on the life of the tsar, or evading taxes by not having serfs entered on the assessment lists.[67] These exceptions were of small moment. Catherine's decree had stripped the serfs of the only legal weapon they had to protect themselves against the wilfulness of their masters.

Early in the nineteenth century a Frenchman who had lived in Russia for many years, wrote that the serfowner's domination over his peasants was greater than that of any sovereign in the world. He pointed out that the authority of a crowned despot was limited by law, custom, and public opinion, but in Russia these forces supported and furthered the prerogatives of the

---

[63] *SZ*, 1857, IX, sect. 1109-1113.

[64] Semevskii, *Krest'ianskii vopros*, II, 573, 575; Wallace, *Russia*, I, 484n.

[65] *Ulozhenie*, Chapter II, sect. 13.

[66] *PSZ*, XXVIII, no. 12966, pp. 334-336. Later legislation mildened these penalties.

[67] *SZ*, 1857, IX, sect. 1036.

seigniors.[68] He was scarcely exaggerating. For, as Empress Catherine II herself explained in a letter to her friend Denis Diderot, Russian serfowners were "free to do in their estates whatever seemed best to them, except to give the death penalty which is prohibited to them."[69] She could have added that the death penalty, too, was meted out by serfowners under the guise of ordering a serf to be whipped. If enough blows were given the victim died, but that of course was not the master's fault.

[68] Passenans, *La Russie*, I, 86-87.
[69] Quoted in Schkaff, *La question*, p. 58.

22

SILENT OBEDIENCE

IN THE EARLY DAYS of serfdom in Eastern Europe the seigniors had the right to exact as much as they wanted in goods and services from their serfs. But as time went by, the central power in all of the Eastern lands, save one, had ultimately intervened in the relation between lord and peasant, and had established norms beyond which the serfowners could not go. Russia was the one exception. The only restrictions the tsars placed upon the seigniors were that the peasants "must not suffer ruin" because of the demands of their lords, and that they be allowed enough time to get their own work done. The serfs, for their part, were instructed to give "silent obedience" to their masters in everything that was not contrary to the laws of the land.[1] That represented the total of the government's regulation of the obligations of the Russian serf to his master.[2]

In actual practice local custom served as the regulator, so that the serf usually knew how much his lord was going to ask of him. But custom did not protect him if his master decided to increase the amount of goods or services he had to pay, or take him from his holding and convert him into a landless field hand or factory worker or domestic. If any of these things happened he had to obey, for he had no law to appeal to, no court to defend him.

Since each proprietor could impose whatever dues and services he wished, the nature and the quantity of the obligations that peasants had to pay varied widely. A few illustrations drawn from different times and places give an idea both of their size and the diversity. The village of Boshchazhnikovo in Iaroslav guberniia, owned by B. P. Sheremetev, had 601 homesteads in 1708, a male population of 1,868, 2,275 desiatins of arable, and meadows that produced 9,095 stacks of hay. The villagers had to pay Sheremetev an obrok of 899 rubles, farm 645 desiatins

---

[1] SZ, 1857, IX, sect. 1029, 1045.

[2] With the exception of the provinces annexed from Poland. v. pp. 460-463.

of demesne, and cut 262 stacks of hay for him. Another Sheremetev village, this one near Moscow, had just 68 homesteads,
259 males, 132 desiatins of arable, 19 desiatins of woods, and
produced 668 stacks of hay in its own meadows. These people
paid a cash obrok of only 8 rubles, but also had to give the
seignior annually 56 sheep, 42 *pudy* 15 *funty* of pork, 56 geese,
96 ducks, 56 hens, 2 *pudy* 33 *funty* of butter, 565 eggs, 7 chetverts (dry measure) of nuts, and 4 chetverts of mushrooms. In
addition to all this they worked 120 desiatins of demesne for
Sheremetev, cut 3,000 stacks of hay, and wove 150 *arshiny* of
linen for him.[3] In the 1750's the 1,214 souls who belonged to the
Pokrovskii Monastery in Kaluga tilled 93 desiatins of demesne,
cut 943 stacks of hay, paid a cash obrok of 112 rubles, an obrok
in kind of 23 chetverts of hemp seeds (for oil), 47 chetverts of
honey, 47 chetverts of rye, 6,016 hens' eggs, and 188 *sazheni* of
lumber, furnished six men to work full-time in the monastery,
and another six to serve as watchmen. On properties owned by
the Iusupovs in Tula and Riazan each serf *tiaglo* (assessment
unit) tilled 4 desiatins of land for the seignior and paid him 2½
assignat rubles (later 58 kopecks silver). This cash obligation
replaced dues in kind of 1 *pud* of pork, 1 sheep, 2 hens, 20 eggs,
and 1 *funt* of butter, that each *tiaglo* had hitherto paid. The
tiaglo had also to cart produce three times a year to the Iusupov
palace in Moscow, or commute this service by paying 8, and
later 10, rubles per trip.[4]

Commonly in the history of European serfdom the dues the
peasant owed his lord depended upon the size of the peasant's
holding. In the provinces of Great Russia this correlation was
usually not present. The seignior in setting the obligations of
his serfs either named a global figure for the village and gave
the peasant commune the task of dividing the total obligation
among its member households, or else he prescribed the specific
amount each *dvor* or *tiaglo* had to pay. But whatever method
he employed, he rarely decided how much land each household
or *tiaglo* was to have. He usually left it to the commune to

[3] Shchepetov, *Krepostnoe pravo*, table 1, pp. 286-287.
[4] Sivkov, *Ocherki*, pp. 157-158; Semevskii, *Krest'iane*, II, 202. Cf. *ibid.*, pp. 201-206 for other examples.

partition the fields among the peasants, and to see to it that each family had enough land to meet its needs. As a consequence, a family with a small holding might be required to pay as much or more to the seignior, as one that had a larger amount of land. For example, on a property in Tambov owned by M. S. Lunin one household with eight people in it had 7½ desiatins of arable. This family was counted as two assessment units. Another household with 16 people in it had 24½ desiatins of arable. Yet it, too, was counted as two units, and so had to pay the same amount of obligations to Lunin that the first household did. A third household with 10 people in it, and with 7½ desiatins of arable, was counted only as one *tiaglo*, and therefore had half the obligations of the first household. Clearly, neither family size nor amount of arable by themselves determined the number of assessment units for a given household and, therefore, the amount of obligations it owed the proprietor. Instead, an overall appraisal must have been made of each family's economic resources, including not only the land it held but all other sources of income, such as handicraft production, that it might have. Nor can the possibility of favoritism shown, say, by the steward to a friend or kinsman be excluded.[5]

Though there was much variation between villages, and even between the homesteads in a single community, in the total amount of dues and services and in the ways in which the obligations were combined, the nature of each individual obligation was much the same throughout the empire. Barshchina was demanded usually for farm work, including such wintertime occupations as threshing, or cutting and hauling timber. On some properties the peasants had to work in the lord's factory, or make cloth and other goods in their cottages from materials he supplied them. On occasion carting was included as part of the barshchina, though commonly it was in a category of its own. Since the law put no limit on the amount of labor services the lord could demand, it was not unknown for serfs to do five, six, and even seven days of barshchina a week. Sometimes this happened only during haying and harvesting, but there were lords

[5] Grekov, "Tambovskoe imenie," pp. 490-491.

who demanded this much throughout the year. The unfortunate serfs who belonged to these seigniors had to till their own holdings at night or on Sundays and holidays—if the lord did not make them work on those days. Still other proprietors required their serfs to give up their holdings and spend all their time working for their masters.[6]

By far the majority of seigniors, however, demanded just three days of barshchina a week. Data from the second half of the eighteenth century and the first half of the nineteenth show that this had become the accepted standard.[7] As a report in 1780 of a group of St. Petersburg landlords put it, the custom was for "the peasant and his wife to work the year through half for his master and half for himself."[8] In Little Russia the usual barshchina obligation in the eighteenth century had been two days a week, but by the 1850's three days had become the rule.[9]

In a manifesto of 5 April 1797 Emperor Paul ordered that proprietors should not make their serfs perform barshchina on Sunday. He pointed out that the other six days of the week were "as a rule split into equal parts and divided" between work for the lord and work on the serf's own account, and that this gave time enough to meet the needs of agriculture.[10] He did not command that barshchina was to be limited to three days a week, nor did he even recommend this. He merely recognized the fact that most proprietors demanded that amount. The only substantive change he introduced was to forbid barshchina on Sunday. Nonetheless, his manifesto was widely interpreted in later years as a prohibition of more than three days of barshchina a week.[11]

[6] Red. Kom., *Pervoe izdanie*, I, ch. 6; Radishchev, *A Journey*, p. 47, Ivan Pososhkov quoted in Schkaff, *La question*, p. 49; Semevskii, *Krest'iane*, I, 60-63.

[7] Red. Kom., *Pervoe izdanie*, III, Doklad no. 17, app. pp. 1-19; Turgenev, *La Russie*, II, 132; Köppen, *Statistische Reise*, p. 58; Krzhivoblotskii, *Materialy*, p. 284; Mikhalevich, *Materialy*, p. 177; Baranovich, *Materialy*, p. 242; Domontovich, *Materialy*, table following p. 148; Merkel, *Die Letten*, p. 87.

[8] Semevskii, *Krest'iane*, I, 58-59; cf. *idem*, *Krest'ianskii vopros*, I, 186.

[9] Semevskii, *Krest'iane*, I, 87-88; Red. Kom., *Pervoe izdanie*, III, Doklad no. 17, app., pp. 8-9, 12-13.

[10] *PSZ*, XXIV, no. 17909, p. 577.

[11] Cf. Haxthausen, *Studien*, I, 126; Wallace, *Russia*, pp. 475-476; Simkhovitch, *Die Feldgemeinschaft*, p. 196; Engelmann, *Die Leibeigenschaft*, pp. 150-151. But see Kornilov, *Modern Russian History*, I, 53 and Kulischer, "Die Leibeigenschaft," pp. 40-41.

Probably the most influential person among those who viewed the manifesto in this light was Michael Speranskii, compiler of the first edition of the *Svod Zakonov*, the law code of 1832.[12] One of the sections of volume nine began with the words, "The peasants are obligated to work three days a week for their seigniors." Paul's manifesto was cited as the authority for this statement. The section then ordered that serfowners must not demand barshchina on Sundays and on fourteen specified church holidays, and concluded with the injunction that "the strictest supervision of this is laid upon the chiefs of provincial governments through the agency of the local police." A law of 30 September 1818 was given as the authorization for these latter parts of the section.[13] Actually this decree only forbad barshchina on church holidays, and instructed local officials to use police for the enforcement of this ban and of Paul's prohibition of barshchina on Sunday.[14] Neither this law of 1818 nor any other decree prior to the publication of the *Svod Zakonov* said anything about the enforcement by local or provincial authorities of a maximum of three days for the barshchina. Obviously, Spernaskii's reformulation of Paul's manifesto and of the law of 1818 went beyond the wording and the intent of the earlier legislation. And in any event, regardless of what Paul meant or what the *Svod* ordered, some proprietors continued to demand barshchina as they pleased. When a serfowner of Tula gave up his practice of requiring barshchina on Sunday, his fellow proprietors protested that he was damaging them as well as himself, and that he was coddling the peasantry.[15]

In demanding labor services the serfowners made distinctions between the work of men and women, between barshchina in summer and winter, between working with animals and without, and so on.[16] Data from the 1850's for a number of provinces show that able-bodied serfs were expected to perform the full labor service from the age of 17 or 18 until 55 for men, and 15 or

[12] Speranskii, "Istoricheskoe obozrenie," p. 41.

[13] *SZ*, 1832, IX, sect. 590.   [14] *PSZ*, XXXV, no. 27549, pp. 582-583.

[15] Kulischer, "Die Leibeigenschaft," p. 41.

[16] Cf. Red. Kom., *Pervoe izdanie*, V, Dopolnitelnyi Doklad . . . k no. 12, pp. 1-6, 29-39.

16 until 45 or 50 for women. The peasants had to provide their own draught animals and implements. Light work, or a reduced amount of regular barshchina, was often required of children when they reached 14 or so. Frequently women were excused from their barshchina for six weeks after childbirth. The work day usually lasted twelve hours from March or April until September or October, and nine hours the rest of the year, though sometimes it ran from sunrise to sundown, with rest periods during the day. In many provinces time spent going to and coming from work counted as part of the work day if the site was a certain number of versts away (usually 4, though sometimes 5, 6, and even 10 versts). Each verst counted as a half hour of working time in most guberniias, but in Saratov each verst counted as one hour, and in Vladimir one quarter of an hour. In a number of provinces custom dictated that the proprietors could not send their serfs beyond a certain distance from their homes (10 to 25 versts depending upon the province) to do barshchina without the peasant's consent.[17]

The serfs often had to perform their labor services throughout the year, though in some places they were excused from them during the winter months. In Kostroma, for example, the men usually worked from March until December, and the women from around the end of April until the end of threshing around mid-November. Proprietors who required their peasants to work three or four days throughout the year compensated them by paying their taxes for them. Some of the lords in Little Russia called upon their female serfs for labor only during the growing season.[18]

In addition to the regular barshchina services serfowners commonly demanded additional days at certain times when they needed more labor, as at haying or harvesting. The conditions regulating this boon work and the number of days required varied widely. Custom often dictated the amount demanded. Some lords credited the extra days to the serf's annual barshchina

[17] *Ibid.*, I, ch. 6, pp. 75-95; III, Doklad no. 16, pp. 5-10.
[18] Krzhivoblotskii, *Materialy*, p. 284; Domontovich, *Materialy*, table following p. 148.

obligation, or even paid their peasants wages for these days, while others demanded as many days as they wanted and gave their serfs nothing in return.[19]

Many proprietors used the task system rather than straight day work, and allowed the peasants to leave when he completed the job assigned him for the day.[20] The set task in plowing often was one-half desiatin a day, in sowing it was around four desiatins, and at harvest time it was reaping and binding 100 to 150 sheaves. Another method used at harvest was to assign a team of serfs—usually around eight men—to reap one desiatin in a day.[21] Sometimes the task system worked to the benefit of the serf. Baron Haxthausen visited a property in which the barshchina was set at three days a week, but where the day was measured by work done, and not by the sun. Plowing half a desiatin (about $1\frac{1}{3}$ acres), or mowing a certain amount of hay, counted as a full day's work. According to Haxthausen the serfs usually had their tasks completed by noon, so that they actually did less that two days of barshchina a week.[22]

Obrok, the other chief payment demanded by the serfowners, continued to be much the easier obligation for the peasants to meet. As was pointed out on an earlier page, the serf who was responsible only for obrok, unlike the man who did barshchina, was not under the direct supervision of the lord or his steward. He was, therefore, much less likely to suffer from the whims of his master, and he was apt to have much more freedom in running his own life. Often he was allowed to leave his village to follow his chosen calling, or to take a job in which he could earn more than he could if he stayed at home. The peasants, of course, recognized these advantages, and when they could, tried to be put on obrok. In fact, serfowners sometimes

19 Red. Kom., *Pervoe izdanie,* I, ch. 6, pp. 38-41; Haxthausen, *Die ländliche Verfassung,* p. 118n.

20 Red. Kom., *Pervoe izdanie,* I, ch. 6, pp. 75-95, III, Doklad . . . 16, pp. 10-42.

21 *Ibid.,* Dopolnitelnyi Doklad . . . k no. 16, pp. 14-22.

22 Haxthausen, *Studien,* II, 86.

Haxthausen indicated that the peasants performed these tasks satisfactorily. If he was right this was a remarkable accomplishment, at least so far as plowing was concerned. Contemporary data for the United States, and for the Habsburg Monarchy, for free hired workers paid by the day, show that the average rate of plowing in both these lands was slightly over one acre in a full work day. (Blum, *Noble Landowners,* p. 190).

punished villagers who had incurred their disfavor by shifting them from obrok to barshchina.[23]

Originally the obrok had been paid predominantly in kind, but with the increase in the use of money in the sixteenth and seventeenth centuries, cash quitrents became more frequent. In the eighteenth and particularly in the nineteenth century, as the market economy continued to grow, the shift to money dues took on new momentum. The trend had already become so pronounced by the third quarter of the eighteenth century that Catherine II commented on it in her instructions for the Legislative Commission. She regarded it as a harmful development.

"It seems [wrote the empress] that the new method of collecting their incomes introduced by landowners, diminishes both the people and agriculture. Almost all villages are on obrok. The landlords, who are seldom or never on their manors, tax each soul at the rate of one, two, or even five rubles, taking no consideration of how the peasant is going to be able to get this money."[24]

The tsaritsa seems to have had her facts wrong, for as the preceding chapter showed, barshchina was in wide use at the time that she wrote these words. In any event, her misgivings notwithstanding, the proprietors who did use obrok continued to change it into a money obligation. By the middle of the nineteenth century the serfowners who continued to demand payments in kind usually considered them as supplements to the money dues they collected from their peasants.[25]

The practice of commuting dues in kind into cash, combined with the increased need of the seigniors for money and the decrease in the value of the ruble, produced a rise in the nominal amount the peasants had to pay. In 1708, on five properties owned by the Sheremetevs where the peasants paid only obrok, the average annual cash payment per male had amounted to 63 kopecks. By 1765 the average had gone up over three times to 2 rubles 7 kopecks. By the late 1790's it was around 5 rubles.

---

23 Cf. Le Play, *Les ouvriers*, II, 50; Sivkov, *Ocherki*, pp. 134-135.

24 *Nakaz*, par. 269, pp. 92-93.

25 Red. Kom., *Pervoe izdanie*, III, Doklad . . . no. 17, app., pp. 2-19; Haxthausen, *Die ländliche Verfassung*, pp. 115-116.

These averages were for all five properties together; in individual villages the average rose five to eight times between 1765 and 1798, and in one village it went up 14.4 times between these two dates.[26] These increases were typical of what was happening generally. Semevskii, on the basis of data from a number of provinces, estimated that the annual average cash obrok per revision soul rose from 2 rubles in the 1760's, to 3 rubles in the seventies, 4 rubles in the eighties, and 5 rubles in the nineties.[27]

Much of the rise in the last third of the century, however, and perhaps all of it, turned out to be only nominal because of currency deflation and price increases. By the late 1790's the paper ruble (first issued in 1769) was worth only around five-eighths of a silver ruble.[28] The 5 ruble obrok of the nineties was therefore equal to 3.12 silver rubles, and so in terms of silver was only 56 percent more than the two ruble obrok of the sixties. Meanwhile, inflation and war had pushed up prices. Though the inadequate information on prices disallows firm conclusions, it is entirely possible that in terms of real buying power the value of the money obrok may have fallen between the sixties and the end of the century. In the 1760's a chetvert of rye cost an estimated one ruble in the non-black earth region, so that the average cash obrok of that decade (2 rubles) could buy two chetverts of this basic commodity. In the seventies and early eighties the estimated average price of a chetvert of rye went up to 2 rubles. The average money obrok (3 rubles in the seventies and 4 rubles in the eighties) was now equal to 1½ to 2 chetverts of rye. In the first half of the nineties the estimated price had gone up to over 4 rubles, so that the obrok of that decade (5 rubles) could purchase only 1¼ chetverts. Assuming the accuracy of these price estimates, the landowner actually received less real revenue from the cash obrok of his serf in the nineties than he had in the sixties, despite the increase in its size. But not all the advantage lay with the peasants. Many of them paid their obrok from wages they earned in nonagri-

26 Shchepetov, *Krepostnoe pravo*, pp. 27-29, 68-71, 286-287, 348-352.
27 Semevskii, *Krest'iane*, I, 54.
28 Voznesenskii, *Ekonomika Rossii*, p. 174.

cultural occupations, and wages, characteristically, lagged behind price increases.[29]

The cash obrok continued to mount in the nineteenth century, but the exiguity of the price data for this era makes it
extremely difficult to determine whether this represented a real
increase in the payment the serf made. Two of mid-century
Russia's most competent statisticians, Platon Storch and Peter
von Köppen, estimated the average cash obrok in the forties at
15 silver rubles per *tiaglo*, or about 7½ silver rubles per male
soul.[30] If they were right the real value in the forties of the cash
obrok may have been only slightly greater than it had been half
a century before. The average grain price in the early forties
was estimated at a little over 5 rubles per chetvert,[31] so that an
obrok of 7½ rubles per soul could buy about 1½ chetverts.
In the early 1790's the average obrok was equal to the price of
1¼ chetverts. Data collected at the end of the fifties in 21
provinces show that the obrok had risen to between 20 and 30
silver rubles per *tiaglo*—or 10 to 15 rubles per male soul.[32] But
prices had gone up, too, so that the usual payment just before
the emancipation was possibly no heavier a burden on the serf
than it had been in the forties.

Obviously, this evidence is much too fragmentary to allow
any confident statements about changes in the real value of the
obrok. But regardless of whether it increased or not, the obligation could become an excessively heavy burden if it did not
correspond with the economic capacities of those upon whom
it was levied, or if the lord made no adjustments in it during
times of famine or other disasters. The huge arrearages that
sometimes piled up give witness to this. In one district 181
families owned by Count Sheremetev accumulated arrearages
between 1812 and 1824 that totalled 43,100 rubles, an average

29 Semevskii, *Krest'iane*, I, 54-55. Kliuchevskii, however, estimated that the real
value of the ruble declined by only about 25 percent between the 1760's and
1790's, *History*, v, 79. If this estimate is accepted the value of the cash obrok
in the nineties was nearly double that of the sixties.
30 Storch, "Der Bauernstand," 1848, p. 81; Köppen, *Statistische Reise*, pp. 29-30.
31 Liashchenko, *Istoriia*, I, 571.
32 Red. Kom., *Pervoe izdanie*, III, Doklad . . . no. 17, app., pp. 1-19; Baranovich,
Materialy, p. 244; Mikhalevich, *Materialy*, p. 177; Krzhivoblotskii, *Materialy*,
p. 285.

of almost 240 rubles per family. On another Sheremetev property the unpaid back obrok amounted to 57,941 rubles in 1861.[33]

Many of the serfs who paid only obrok were able to leave their villages to seek work elsewhere. These peasants took jobs as hired workers in factories, in transportation, in service occupations, or busied themselves in trade or as travelling artisans. Legislation introduced in 1724, and elaborated in later years, required the serf who wanted to leave his village to have a permit from his lord, or his lord's agent, or the local priest. Should he want to go more than 30 versts from his home, or stay away longer than six months, he also had to have a passport from the government, for which he paid a fee that varied with the length of time he planned to be absent. Serfs found away from their homes without passports were held as fugitives.[34]

Most of the peasants who applied for government passports lived in the Central Industrial and Lake provinces. Infertile soil, harsh climate, competition from the farms of the chernozem, employment opportunities in nearby cities, and the expansion of trade and industry, all served to spur the outward movement from the villages of these regions. Scattered information about the number of passports issued these migrants indicate the large proportions of the exodus. In the last years of the eighteenth century, as many as 20 percent of the men of Iaroslav guberniia, and 10 percent of those in Moscow guberniia, received passports. In 1826 a total of 574,000 passports were issued to serfs and state peasants; in 1857 the number had increased to 1,084,000.[35] Sometimes villages were almost emptied by these periodic migrations. In the 1780's in a property in Kaluga that belonged to Prince Golitsin, two out of three workers in a family often had jobs away from the village. The third stayed at home to till the family's holding. In the 1850's in villages owned by Count Sheremetev in the non-black earth over half the adults left home to find employment.[36]

---

[33] Shchepetov, *Krepostnoe pravo*, pp. 170-175.

[34] *PSZ*, VII, no. 4533, 26 June 1724, pp. 310-318; 11 Jan. 1728, 7 June 1737, 21 June 1743, etc.; *SZ*, 1842, XIV, sect. 99-162.

[35] Tugan-Baranovskii, *Russkaia fabrika*, I, 44-45; Druzhinin, *Gosudarstvennye krest'iane*, I, 74; Jourdier, *Des forces*, p. 190.

[36] Drakokhrust, "Rassloenie," p. 133; Shchepetov, *Krepostnoe pravo*, pp. 180-182.

Often the migrants from a certain district or province followed the same line of work. Gardening, for instance, was the
specialty of those who came from the Rostov district of Iaroslav,
many of the workers in the inns and taverns of Moscow and
St. Petersburg came from Kostroma, and most of the masons and
carpenters in the two capitals were natives of Iaroslav and
Vladimir. Many of the peddlers who travelled the roads of the
empire also hailed from these two last-named provinces.[37]

Some of the migrants spent the winter months away from
home, others—particularly those in the building trades—were
away during the summer. Still others went off for most of the
year, and even for years at a time, and some never returned.
But whether they came back periodically, or never saw their
homes again, these émigrés had to pay a regular obrok to their
masters. The size of the obrok depended upon the wages the
serf earned, or if he started a business, upon the amount of his
capital or his annual volume of trade. Some serfowners even
capitalized each of their serfs at a certain value according to the
individual serf's age and skill. Then they ordered the serf to pay
them an obrok that provided them with what they considered an
adequate return on this capitalized sum. This practice was said
to have been especially common among lesser officials, who
adopted it as a way of supplementing their inadequate salaries.[38]

Barshchina and obrok, of course, did not complete the list of
the serf's obligations to their seigniors. They almost always
were responsible for a number of other dues and services. The
carting duty was the most common of these obligations, and also
one of the most detested of all the payments the serfs had to
make. This particular service (which, as mentioned earlier,
sometimes counted as part of the barshchina) obliged the peasant to spend days and weeks, usually in winter, transporting
goods for his master. An economist of the 1840's estimated that
in summer 800,000 serfs, and in winter nearly 3,000,000 (almost
one-third of the total adult male serf population), were en-

37 Turgenev, *La Russie*, II, 123; Krzhivoblotskii, *Materialy*, p. 199; Jourdier,
Des forces, p. 120.
38 Haxthausen, *Studien*, I, 118; III, 60-61.

gaged in fulfilling this obligation. He set the value of their work at 50 million rubles.[39]

The peasant had to use his own horse and cart or sled and maintain himself and his animal during these trips. The service was measured by distance covered rather than by elapsed time, that is, a certain number of versts was considered the equivalent of a day's work. This distance varied from 15 to 30 versts loaded and as many as 60 versts empty. The goods the peasant carted went either to market or to the master's home in the city. Some serfs had to make two and even three trips each winter of 200 to 400 versts, and peasants in more remote provinces who were unlucky enough to belong to a master who had a home in one of the two capitals, made journeys of as much as 600 versts.[40]

Some of the other—and lesser—dues and services were fixed in amount, some fluctuated, some recurred regularly, and some were levied at irregular intervals. Many, and on occasion all of them, were commuted in the course of the eighteenth and nineteenth centuries into a single cash payment. Building and maintenance work, service as watchmen, and, for women, spinning and weaving in the winter months, were frequently demanded, though in some places these services counted as part of the barshchina. It was fairly common, also, to require each serf household to furnish barnyard products at stated times for the lord's table. The value of this particular obligation varied widely between villages. For example, on the Iusupov properties in the Central Agricultural zone it was commuted at the end of the 1840's into a cash payment of 58 silver kopecks, while data collected from other serfowners of this region in the late 1850's showed that some of them valued it at from 2 to 5 silver rubles.[41] Irregular payments included charges for milling, fines levied under certain conditions when a serf sold or inherited personal property, and the fee that had to be paid on marriage. Seigniors made special assessments to pay for the expenses incurred by some unusual event, such as a visit of the tsar to the region.

[39] A. P. Zablotskii-Desiatovskii cited in Liashchenko, *Ocherki*, I, 127.

[40] Baranovich, *Materialy*, p. 242; Haxthausen, *Die ländliche Verfassung*, p. 33n.; Semevskii, *Krest'iane*, I, 68.

[41] Sivkov, *Ocherki*, p. 54; Baranovich, *Materialy*, p. 242.

Count Sheremetev even levied assessments to pay for elaborate balls that he gave.[42]

In addition to these dues and services the peasants paid directly to their seigniors, they also bore a number of other manorial charges. Sometimes they had to contribute to the salaries of the stewards and other administrative employees who ran the property on which they lived, pay salaries to their communal officials, support their priest, and build and maintain the village church. The serfs owned by lords who obeyed Paul's law about the construction of emergency granaries had to build these storage bins, and contribute grain or cash, or both, to keep them stocked.[43]

II

All these obligations added up to a formidable burden. Still, the peasants who had to meet them at least lived with their own families in their own homes, had their own property such as animals and tools, and above all had some time they could call their own. There were others who had nothing of their own— neither property nor time. These were the serfs called the *dvorovye liudi*, the household people, who lived in the household (*dvor*) of a serfowner, or in nearby huts, and spent their lives serving him and his family.

These serfs had once been like other peasants, living on the land and paying dues and services to their lord. Then their lord had taken them from their holdings and their families and converted them into his personal servants. There was nothing the peasants could do about this. In other countries the central power had placed limitations upon the serfowner's right to make domestics out of his peasants.[44] In Russia the law put no limitations on the lord's power to make his serfs do any work that he wanted them to do.

The seigniors used *dvorovye liudi* for every imaginable kind of service. Most of them did domestic work as butlers, cooks, maids, seamstresses, and nurses. Others were gardeners, car-

42 Drakokhrust, "Rassloenie," p. 125; Shchepetov, *Krepostnoe pravo*, pp. 80-85.

43 Drakokhrust, "Rassloenie," p. 125; Indova, *Krepostnoe khoziaistvo*, pp. 95-96; Haxthausen, *Die ländliche Verfassung*, pp. 120-121. For Paul's law v. p. 436.

44 Cf. Knapp, *Die Bauern-Befreiung*, I, 23-24; Blum, *Noble landowners*, pp. 78-79.

penters, tailors, stable hands, and the like. Wealthy proprietors had serf orchestras and singers and actors and teachers and dwarfs and giants and jesters, and even serf authors and composers, all existing and performing for the pleasure and convenience of their master.[45] Eccentrics among the proprietors assigned their domestics unusual duties. An English visitor told about a countess who had several of her women read to her each night until she fell asleep. They had to continue reading or talking all the while she slept, for if they stopped the countess immediately awakened.[46]

The number of servants kept by Russian lords amazed foreign visitors. William Tooke, in Russia in the last part of the eighteenth century, found that some of the great establishments of St. Petersburg had as many as 150 to 200 menials.[47] Another British visitor who was invited to the houses of the greatest nobles of St. Petersburg and Moscow during his stay in Russia from 1805 to 1807, found them ". . . filled with vassals, or servants, both male and female, who line the halls, passages, and entrances of the rooms in splendid liveries. In almost every antichamber some of these domestics are placed, ready to obey the commands of their lord or his guest; and continually your ears are saluted with the theatrical call of 'Who waits?' when two or three run in at the same instant, as promptly as I ever saw the gentleman-in-waiting answer the like summons from the boards of Drury-Lane or Covent-Garden."[48]

Men of lesser wealth had smaller staffs, but still kept more servants than seemed reasonable by other than Russian standards. Foreigners claimed that the Russian lord kept three and even five to six times as many domestics as the noble of equal rank and income in other European lands.[49] Prince Alexander Kropotkin, for example, as the owner of 1,200 male serfs was rich but was far from being a magnate. His son, Peter, recalled

---

[45] Robert Ker Porter quoted in Putnam, *Seven Britons*, pp. 325-326; Esterhazy, *Nouvelles lettres*, p. 297.

[46] William Richardson quoted in Putnam, *Seven Britons*, p. 166. Richardson was in Russia from 1768 to 1772.

[47] Tooke, *View*, III, 307; cf. Esterhazy, *Nouvelles lettres*, p. 297.

[48] Robert Ker Porter quoted in Putnam, *Seven Britons*, pp. 326-327.

[49] Cf. Tooke, *View*, III, 307; Passenans, *La Russie*, I, 91; Ford, *Writings of J. Q. Adams*, III, 395.

that his father maintained fifty domestics in his house in Moscow, and seventy-five in his country retreat, and considered this not one too many. At dinner a dozen men waited on the family of eight Kropotkins, with one man standing behind each person at the table. Three chefs prepared the family's food, and two others cooked for the servants.[50]

It was a matter of pride to a serfowner to have unusual skills among his household serfs, so that when a guest complimented him, say, on the pastries served at his table and surmised that they came from the most fashionable *pâtisserie* in town, he could casually answer that they had been made by his own serf confectioner. Prince Kropotkin preened himself especially on his orchestra, though his son's account of that ensemble plants doubt in the reader's mind about the quality of its music. Kropotkin's servants literally doubled in brass. The second butler was also piano tuner and flautist, the tailor played the french horn, one of the footmen played trombone one day, bassoon the next, and occasionally second violin. The confectioner was first put on the drum, but, wrote the younger Kropotkin, "he misused his instrument to such a deafening degree that a tremendous trumpet was bought for him, in the hope that his lungs would not have the power to make the same noise as his hands; when, however, this last hope had to be abandoned, he was sent to be a soldier." Only the first two violins were "violins" and nothing else. The Prince had purchased them and their families for a large sum of money from his sister.[51]

Life as a house serf was often the harshest and the most demoralizing of all peasant experiences. Living as they did in constant contact with their lords who had complete control over them, they were much more liable than other serfs to frequent—and sometimes frightful—punishments from captious lords and mistresses, while the women among them were often misused by lecherous masters. Since they spent all their time working for their owners they had to rely for their support upon his bounty. Some proprietors set up regular schedules for periodic distribution of clothing, food, and small amounts of cash.

[50] Kropotkin, *Memoirs*, p. 28.
[51] *Ibid.*, pp. 28-30.

The domestics of less prosperous or less thoughtful masters were not so fortunate, and went about in rags and frequently had not enough to eat.[52]

Their complete dependence, and their helplessness, seemed to have sapped many of the *dvorovye liudi* of vitality and self-respect. The redundancy of menials in many households made matters still worse, for there was not enough work to keep them occupied, and the empty hours of idleness demoralized them still more. They quarreled with one another, they filched from their master's larder and barns, and they were reputed to be generally unhappy.[53]

Some among the serfowners recognized the economic waste and human costs of large domestic staffs. E. S. Karnovich, one of the empire's outstanding agriculturists (v. pp. 411-412), wrote in the 1830's that the maintenance of each family of household serfs cost the proprietor over 500 rubles a year. "And of what use are these sponges?" he asked. "None at all except for constant losses. . . . In a word, when a property has a lot of household serfs things always go badly there."[54] Prince Iusupov during the first half of the nineteenth century converted a number of his servants into regular agricultural peasants living on their own holdings. M. S. Lunin employed *dvorovye liudi* in shops he established on his property in Tambov, and paid them wages in cash and kind. He sent some of their children to St. Petersburg to learn trades needed in the operation of his holdings. Those whose skills he could not use were allowed to take employment elsewhere, and paid Lunin an annual obrok out of their earnings.[55] Other landlords, too, permitted some of their *dvorovye liudi* to live and work elsewhere in return for a cash obrok. Sometimes the obrok they demanded was surprisingly small; Princes M. B. and A. A. Golitsin asked only 3 rubles a year from each of 27 families of their domestic serfs who

---

[52] Red. Kom., *Pervoe izdanie*, I, ch. VII, 29-42; III, Doklad . . . no. 29, July 1859, app.; Semevskii, *Krest'iane*, I, 142-143; Grekov, "Tambovskoe imenie," p. 511; Buschen, "Die Freibauern," p. 241.

[53] Cf. Passenans, *La Russie*, I, 91; Le Play, *Les ouvriers*, II, 53; Tooke, *View*, III, 307-308.

[54] Quoted in Grekov, "Tambovskoe imenie," p. 510.

[55] *Ibid.*, pp. 511-513, 515-517; Sivkov, *Ocherki*, pp. 124, 140-141.

worked elsewhere, four other families paid 5 rubles, and two 10 rubles. Savva Tekeli, the Serbian statesman who visited Russia as a young man in the 1780's, asserted that some proprietors let pretty daughters of their domestics go to the city to become prostitutes, on condition that they pay their seignior 100 to 200 rubles a year. That, at least, is what one of these women told him.[56]

The highest government circles, too, showed concern about the problems raised by the *dvorovye liudi*. Michael Speranskii, who as one of Tsar Nicholas's chief aides had much influence, pointed out in a memorandum in 1826 that the conversion of peasants into domestics reduced productive peasants to idleness and dissoluteness, and led to ruinous luxury for their lords. He noted, too, that the serfowners' reliance upon the output of their household artisans for manufactured goods held back the growth of urban industry and trade, and thereby hindered the development of a prosperous burgher class.[57] In the 1840's the need to improve the lot of the household serfs became the main topic of discussion in two of the special secret committees established by Nicholas to consider the peasant problem. The tsar himself, always on guard against the threats of subversion and revolt, warned the serfowners of perils that lurked within their own dining rooms and parlors. In his speech to the representatives of the St. Petersburg nobility on 21 March 1848 Nicholas (whose hackles must have stood on end throughout that revolutionary year) said:[58] "These people generally are demoralized and are threats to society and their own masters. I ask you to be extremely cautious with respect to them. Frequently, at table or in an evening conversation, you discuss political or governmental or similar matters, forgetting that these people listen to you, and from their ignorance and stupidity construe your conversation in their own way, that is, incorrectly. Moreover, these conversations, harmless among educated people, often suggest to your servants ideas that they never would have thought of themselves. That is very dangerous!"

[56] Semevskii, *Krest'iane*, I, 144-145.
[57] Semevskii, *Krest'ianskii vopros*, II, 6.
[58] *Russkaia Starina*, Sept. 1883, p. 595.

Finally, the large numbers of the *dvorovye liudi* made the rest of the serfs unhappy. More menials in the master's house meant heavier burdens for the other peasants. In the end they were the ones who supported the household staff, since the domestics were maintained out of the payments the rest of the serfs made to the seignior. Often, too, they had to pay the government tax for these people, though it was not uncommon for the lord to take care of this charge himself.[59]

Statistics on the total number of household serfs were not assembled until the last three decades of serfdom. These revealed a striking increase in their number, especially in the fifties. The returns of the Eighth Revision, carried out in the mid-thirties, showed 914,524 of these people, including both men and women. This equalled 4.14 percent of the total serf population of that time. According to the returns of the Ninth Revision there were 1,035,924 domestic serfs in 1851, or 4.79 percent of all serfs, and by the Tenth Revision, in 1858, their number had grown to 1,467,378, amounting to 6.8 percent of the empire's serf population.

Analysis of the returns of the revisions show that nearly all of the increase in the number of the *dvorovye liudi* occurred in black earth provinces, and especially in Little Russia and New Russia. Between 1851 and 1858 the population of male domestics in Kharkov, Poltava, and Chernigov grew nearly three and one-half times over, going from 32,271 to 110,678. In the New Russian provinces of Kherson and Ekaterinoslav there was a fourfold increase, from 15,013 in the Ninth Revision to 59,574 in the Tenth. In nearly all of the non-chernozem provinces the number of household serfs either declined or remained unchanged during these years.[60]

III

The freedom of the serfowner to demand as much as he wanted from his peasants did not extend to the western provinces that had been annexed from Poland in the eighteenth

---

[59] Red. Kom., *Pervoe izdanie*, I, ch. 7, pp. 81-96; Baranovich, *Materialy*, p. 242.

[60] Troinitskii, *Krepostnoe naselenie*, pp. 57-58, 59-60. For an explanation of some of the increase v. p. 586.

century. In White Russia, Lithuania, and the Southwest, the obligations the serf owed to his master had been subjected to regulation while these regions had been under Polish rule. On each estate the lord, together with his peasants, had been required to draw up an "inventory," as it was called, that defined the size of the holdings of the peasants, and fixed the amount of dues that had to be paid for them.

The provisions of the inventories varied, of course, from estate to estate, but all of them bore one common feature: the proportionality of each peasant family's obligations to the size of its holding. The basic unit, called a *uvolka*, consisted of 19½ desiatins divided between plowland, meadow, house lot, and garden. This was considered a full holding. A small number of peasant families had a full holding, but most of them had from one quarter to three quarters of a *uvolka*, some had only a house lot and garden, and others were landless and lived as boarders in the homes of fellow peasants. The amount of dues and services the serf owed depended upon the size of his holding. For example, on a property in Podolia owned by the crown the peasant with a full holding had to do 158 days of barshchina a year, two thirds of it with a team and one third without. Those who held three quarters of a *uvolka* did 128 days of barshchina, half with a team and half without. The holders of a half of a *uvolka* were responsible for 106 days, all of it hand labor. On this particular property the next stratum were the cotters, who had just a house lot and garden. They had to work 24 days, all without a team. Finally, the landless laborers had no barshchina obligation.[61]

At first, the Russian government viewed the retention of the inventories in the newly-won provinces as undesirable. The Senate declared that the nobility there should have the same plenitude of powers that serfowners enjoyed in the rest of the empire. This equalization had to wait, however, upon the completion of the codification of the Russian law. In 1840 the new *Svod Zakonov* was introduced into the Western prov-

[61] Red. Kom., *Pervoe izdanie*, IV, "Inventarnyia polozheniia zapadnykh gubernii," pp. 1-3; Haxthausen, *Studien*, II, 471-472, 487-488; Semevskii, *Krest'ianskii vopros*, II, 489-491.

inces, supplanting the Polish law and thereby extinguishing the legal authorization for the inventory system. Now, the serfs there, like their fellows in the rest of the empire, were subject in law as well as in fact to the will of their seigniors.

But soon thereafter a surprising thing happened. The government decided to reintroduce the inventory system, and thus restore the legal restrictions upon seignioral power that it had only just abolished. The primary motive behind this contradictory action seems to have been to check the powers of the Polish Catholic nobles who had revolted against Russian rule in 1831, and to win the support of the peasantry, who were Russian or Ukrainian in nationality and Orthodox in religion. The government's efforts to reintroduce the inventories met with the determined opposition of the serfowners. In the White Russian and Lithuanian provinces (Vitebsk, Mogilev, Minsk, Vilna, Grodno, and Kovno) they were able to postpone establishment of the system. In the Southwestern guberniias (Kiev, Volynia, and Padolia), however, firm government policy succeeded by 1848 in setting up norms applicable to all properties.

The obligations of the peasants in these Southwestern provinces had, in general, been lighter than those of serfs elsewhere. Under the new regulations they continued to be less burdensome. A peasant household with a full holding had to furnish the proprietor one male worker with a team for three days a week and a woman worker one day a week. The *dvor* with a half holding had to provide one man without a team for two days a week, and one woman for one day. Cotters had to do 24 days of barshchina a year, but paid an annual obrok. Landless peasants paid only an annual obrok of 1½ to 2½ rubles for men and half that for women, or if they wished they could work out this obligation. The lord had the right to demand twelve additional days of barshchina a year from all his serfs, but had to pay them a wage fixed by the provincial government for this work, and could not ask for more than two extra days in any one week. Each household could be called upon for eight days a year for building and maintenance work, and had to provide a watchman once a month. All other payments were abolished, save for the carting service for which precise norms were fixed.

Finally, the seigniors were forbidden to take serfs from the land and convert them into *dvorovye liudi*.[62]

On top of all his responsibilities to his seignior the serf had also to satisfy the demands made of him by the state. Of these, by far the most important were the soul tax and military service. Both were innovations of Peter I.

The tax system that had developed during the seventeenth century had just about broken down by the time Peter took over the rule of the empire (v. pp. 232-234). Peter's military expenditures worsened the government's long-standing financial predicament. He tried all manner of expedients, including such oddities as his famous tax on beards and adding oaken coffins— "the final luxury of old-time wealthy Russians"—to the list of state monopolies,[63] but none of them overcame the crisis. Finally, he decided that a clean break had to be made with the past. He scrapped the existing system in which the household, or *dvor*, was the unit of assessment, and ordered that henceforth taxes would be levied upon each individual adult male, or "soul." At one stroke he swept into oblivion the old Muscovite concept that taxes should be based upon ability to pay. The government was no longer interested in finding out the economic capacities of each household. The tax was the same for rich and poor alike. The only people who did not have to pay it were the nobles, the clergy, and certain numerically unimportant groups.

The new system did away with the complications that had bedevilled the tax assessors. It also corrected the chief failing— from the fiscal point of view—in the use of the *dvor* as the unit of assessment. That method, introduced as an *ad hoc* device in the latter part of the seventeenth century, had enabled grown sons with their own families to escape taxation by living in their father's household. Now every adult male paid the same tax no matter where he lived or what he did. All the treasury

---

[62] Ignatovich, "Pomeshchich'i krest'iane," x, 68-70; Haxthausen, *Die ländliche Verfassung*, p. 117.

[63] Kliuchevskii, *Kurs*, IV, 169. The government took over the stock of all coffin makers, forbade their further manufacture, and sold the coffins at four times their original price.

needed to know was how many adult males there were in the empire.

To get this information the government on 22 January 1719 ordered a census of the male population "not excluding the oldest men to the very latest infants."[64] Every adult male listed in the census registers had to pay the tax, or have it paid for him, until the next revision of the registers was made. That included the people who died in the interim—the "dead souls." On privately owned properties the serfowner had the responsibility for the collection and forwarding of the tax. Among state peasants the officials of the commune were charged with this duty.

The revenues from the new levy had been earmarked for military expenditures, so it was easy for the authorities to decide how much the tax should be. They merely divided the number of taxpayers into the estimated military disbursements. In 1724 the rate was set at 74 kopecks per soul. The next year it was reduced to 70 kopecks. It stayed at that figure until the 1790's, except for a few years around the middle of the century when it was slightly lower. In 1794 the government increased it to 1 ruble, and in 1797 to 1 ruble 26 kopecks. Tsar Paul prevented a further rise by imposing a tax on the hitherto untaxed dvorianstvo that brought in 1,640,000 rubles a year. But Alexander repealed this new levy and increased the soul tax. By 1812, under the pressures of war and financial difficulties, it had climbed to 3 assignat rubles. No further changes were made until 1839. It was then converted, at the official exchange rate set that year of 3½ assignat rubles to 1 silver ruble, into 86 silver kopecks. It remained at this amount until after the emancipation, when a sliding scale adjusted to local economic conditions was introduced. Finally, on 1 January 1887 the tax was abolished in European Russia.

Arrears began to pile up from the outset and soon became an important fiscal problem. Efforts to compel payment met with only limited success. By the accession of Elizabeth in 1741 unpaid taxes amounted to 5 million rubles (this was the total for all soul tax payers and not just serfs alone). The figures con-

---

[64] *PSZ*, v, no. 3287, pp. 618-620.

tinued to mount until, in 1752, Elizabeth issued a manifesto wiping out all arrears. Yet, ten years later when Catherine II took over rule, back taxes totaled 800,000 rubles. They kept piling up during the following years. In 1787 Catherine, on the twenty-fifth anniversary of her reign, remitted unpaid back taxes up to 1 January 1776, gave delinquents twenty years to pay the taxes they owed for the years between 1776 and 1787, and allowed them to make their payments in grain valued at local prices. This did not prevent the accumulation of new arrearages, and each tsar from Paul on to Alexander III (1881-1894) followed the practice of forgiving unpaid back soul taxes, usually issuing this order soon after ascending the throne.[65]

The accumulation of unpaid taxes points to the conclusion that for many peasants the soul tax must have been too heavy a burden. Yet, despite the large increase in the size of the levy in the last sixty years of serfdom, the real value of the tax fell precipitously—fell, that is, if the available price information can be accepted as a trustworthy guide. In terms of rye prices the tax equalled about .75 chetverts in the 1760's, about .3 chetverts in the 1790's, and about .17 chetverts in the 1840's.

Military service, the other chief obligation the state demanded of the peasant, owed its origin to Peter's determination to build up his army after its crushing defeat by the Swedes at Narva in 1700. The tsars of the seventeenth century had required serf-owners to furnish recruits in time of need, or pay a cash quittance, according to the number of peasant dvors they owned. But Peter needed more cannon fodder than such a system could provide him. So he began to conscript peasants and townsmen, taking a certain number of men from each settlement. When he first started, he drafted peasants and slaves without bothering to get the permission of their owners. In a ukase of 1700 he even invited voluntary enlistments from all bound people. He freed the recruits from their servitude, gave them the right to take their wives and children from their owners, welcomed runaways and promised them pardons from the punishments usually meted out to captured fugitives, and ordered that all

---

[65] *Entsiklopedicheskii slovar*, XXIV, 123-138; Rukovskii, "Istoriko-statisticheskiia svedeniia," pp. 1-17, 183-203.

physically fit serfs and slaves who had been emancipated by their masters were to be drafted.[66]

The system that Peter introduced under the pressure of war became a permanent part of Russian life. Periodic conscriptions were made in peace as well as in war. Initially Peter had set the draft quota for each settlement according to the number of homesteads it contained, but after the First Revision the quota was apportioned according to the number of souls. The draft was made on the settlement rather than on the individual. It was left to the village commune, or to the seignior, to select and send forward the number of recruits demanded. For over a century the calls came at frequent but irregular intervals; between 1724 and 1830 there were 94 of them. Then in 1831 conscription in peacetime was placed on a regularly recurring basis. The empire was divided into an eastern and western half and each half alternated in supplying conscripts, so that normally the draft came to a village every other year.

The number of men taken at each call fluctuated with the military needs of the hour. In the 1720's and 1730's it ran from one recruit for every 100 or so males to one for every 300. In the second half of the century it was around one to two for every 500, except in wartime, when it was stepped up to one to five out of every 100 males. After the reform in 1831 the usual call was for less than seven conscripts per 1,000 males, augmented calls were for from seven to ten per thousand, and at extraordinary calls ten or more men were taken out of every thousand. The recruits—the term was first used in 1705—were supposed to be between the ages of 20 and 35, and not less than 63 inches tall. In the 1850's the upper age limit was dropped to 30. The term of service for most of the eighteenth century was for life. In 1793 it was reduced to 25 years, in 1834 to 20 years plus 5 years of ready reserve in the militia, and in 1855 to 12 years on active service and 3 years in the militia.

The peasant village not only had to provide the recruits, but also had to outfit them and pay their transportation to their military post. This amounted to considerable sums of money, especially in years of heavy conscriptions. On a property in

[66] Engelmann, *Die Leibeigenschaft*, pp. 81-83.

Kaluga the cost to the peasants in the late eighteenth century for each recruit averaged 27 rubles 40 kopecks, and in the first quarter of the nineteenth century state peasant communes laid out an estimated 50 to 80 rubles for every man they sent into the army.[67]

Since the government did not summon individuals by name to the colors, but instead called upon each village to supply the requisite number of conscripts, communes and individuals who could afford it bought substitutes. The army was unconcerned about this evasion. All it wanted was men. Some proprietors, reluctant to lose serfs to the military, encouraged and even compelled their peasants to avoid service by this device. A few seigniors aided their serfs in making these purchases by giving them subsidies or exempting them for a time from dues and services.

Masters and serfs also resorted to illegal methods to evade service. One trick used by seigniors when they learned that the recruiting officer was on his way to one of their villages, was to send eligible men from that village to another of their properties. When the officer arrived they told him that the village had no one in it who was fit for military duty. Some lords took advantage of a provision in the draft law that permitted owners of less than 20 male serfs to pay a cash indemnity in lieu of a recruit. These men divided their peasants into units of less than 20 souls, and made a fictitious transfer of ownership of each unit to obliging kinsmen and friends. Those who did not practice these deceits made the conscriptions less burdensome for themselves by turning over village trouble makers and idlers to the recruiting officers, rather than adhering to the usual procedure of drawing lots, or following some previously agreed-upon list of eligibles. Serfs sometimes deliberately maimed themselves, or while still infants were crippled by their parents. The government meted out barbaric punishments when such deliberate mutilations were detected. The mutilated man was made to run three times through a gantlet of 500 soldiers armed with whips. If he survived he then went into the army as a line soldier, or

[67] Storch, "Der Bauernstand," 1848, p. 98; 1849, pp. 99, 103; Druzhinin, *Gosudarstvennye krest'iane*, I, 52; *Entsiklopedicheskii slovar*, xxvia, 530-532; Drakokhrust, "Rassloenie," p. 124.

as a driver if his mutilation prevented him from bearing arms. Those who had made themselves entirely unfit for any military service, if caught, were whipped mercilessly, and then sentenced to hard labor for life. Their seigniors received recruit credit for them.[68]

The state also called upon the peasants for a number of other lesser dues and services. They had to build and maintain many roads and bridges, billet soldiers in their homes or in barracks they constructed themselves, supply carts and horses upon demand for government use or for persons on official business, furnish postal service where the state did not provide it, build, maintain, and supply fuel and illumination for government buildings in their locality, provide campsites, pasture, food, and forage for military units, pay a small annual cash levy for the support of provincial officials, and pay extra imposts when the local government needed additional money for some special occasion or celebration. Decrees of 1810 and 1811 ordered peasants in the Western provinces to pay an annual tax of 2 assignat rubles (later converted into 58 silver kopecks) because they had the right to distill their own beverages. This tax was abolished in 1851 except in the Baltic provinces, where it was retained until 1863. In 1816 a special tax on every male soul was introduced everywhere except Siberia to pay for building and maintaining roads and waterways. At first this levy was 25 kopecks, in 1818 it went up to 30 kopecks, and in 1839 it was set at 9 silver kopecks.[69]

v

As the preceding chapter showed, the personal status of the serf deteriorated in the eighteenth century, and the most that can be said for the nineteenth century is that this deterioration was arrested. Reduced to a chattel who was bought and sold in the market place, the serf was scarcely distinguishable from a slave. The only essential differences between the Russian serf and the American Negro slave that a contemporary apologist

---

[68] Semevskii, *Krest'iane*, I, 303-306; Drakokhrust, "Rassloenie," 124-125; Shchepetov, *Krepostnoe pravo*, pp. 142-143.

[69] Storch, "Der Bauernstand," 1848, pp. 89-92, 114-117.

for serfdom could think of were that the serf had the privilege of taking the oath of allegiance to the· tsar, paying a personal tax, and serving in the army.[70] The throne itself recognized the true status of the serf. Catherine II in her instructions to the Legislative Commission of 1767 referred to the seignioral peasantry not as serfs but as slaves (*raby*).[71] Several decades later Alexander I in a private letter wrote that "For the largest part the peasants of Russia are slaves; I do not need to dilate on the degradation and the misfortunes of such a position."[72]

Possibly the only people who saw a clear distinction between serfdom and slavery were the serfs. They did not think of themselves as slaves of their masters, but rather as the true owners of the land they tilled. Such at least is the meaning that has been put upon the phrase that reportedly was often on their lips: "We are yours," they told their owners, "but the land is ours."

It might be assumed that the economic welfare of the serfs paralleled their abysmally low social and legal status, so that they were harshly exploited and kept on the bare margin of subsistence. The decline in the rate of increase of the serf population seems to lend support to such an assumption. Actually, the available information on the serfs' standard of living is so scanty that this view can neither be proved nor disproved. Opinions of contemporaries are inconclusive and contradictory, and are colored by personal bias. To cite just a few, William Tooke, who spent the last quarter of the eighteenth century in Russia, spoke of the general economic wellbeing of the peasantry,[73] while A. N. Radishchev in the same period and same region saw only suffering and poverty.[74] In the early 1840's the Prussian ambassador to St. Petersburg reported that the peasants had been reduced to the last extremes of misery.[75] But Baron Haxthausen, in Russia in these same years and who was a much better judge of such matters than his diplomatic compatriot,

---

[70] A. Boutowski quoted in *Journal des economistes*, XXVI (1850), 249.

[71] *Nakaz*, ch. XI, par. 261. In 1786 the use of the word slave (*rab*) was forbidden. Speranskii, "Istoricheskoe obozrenie," p. 41.

[72] Quoted in Schnitzler, *Histoire intime*, I, 49-50.

[73] Tooke, *View*, II, 348-349.

[74] Radishchev, *A Journey*, pp. 46-48, 151-152, 158-159, 219-221.

[75] Quoted in Stupperich, *Die Anfänge*, p. 84.

presented a different picture.[76] Ferdinand Le Play in his studies of budgets of "typical" European worker and peasant households in the 1840's, found that the living standards of the Russian families he investigated compared very favorably with those of peasants and proletarians in supposedly more fortunate Western lands.[77] Even Paul Ducret, in his ringing denunciation of the cruelties of serfdom, allowed that serfs on obrok (and state peasants) were better off economically than the proletarians of Western Europe.[78]

The difficulties in assigning a cash value to the non-monetary payments the serf made, the wide variation in the amount of obligations demanded, and the inadequate price data, make estimates of the total cash value of the serf's dues and payments highly tentative. Nonetheless, within the limits set by these handicaps, they permit a comparison of the burdens of the peasants at different times during the last century of serfdom. Semevskii figured that the cash value of the obligations of the adult male serf to his seignior amounted to 3 rubles in the 1760's, 4 rubles in the seventies, 6 rubles in the eighties, and 7½ rubles in the nineties. But he pointed out that this monetary increase was more than compensated for by the price rise during these decades. In the sixties the estimated cash value of the serf's obligations to his master equalled 3 chetverts of rye, in the seventies and first half of the eighties 2½ chetverts, and in the nineties slightly less than 2 chetverts.[79] Around the middle of the nineteenth century Platon Storch estimated the average value of the serf's total obligation to lord, state, and commune at 12.80 rubles, 10 rubles of this going to the seignior, 1.85 rubles to the state, and 95 kopecks for communal charges.[80] In terms of prices then current this equalled about 2⅓ chetverts of grain. The payments to the lord alone were equivalent to a little less than 2 chetverts.

These estimates indicate that the real value of the serf's dues and services diminished in the last part of the eighteenth cen-

[76] Haxthausen, *Studien, passim.*
[77] Le Play, *Les ouvriers*, II, 47 ff., 179 ff.
[78] Passenans, *La Russie*, I, 84.   [79] Semevskii, *Krest'iane*, I, 54-55.
[80] Storch, "Der Bauernstand," 1848, pp. 107-124.

tury, and remained at this lower level during the first half of the nineteenth century. Data presented in the preceding pages on specific obligations lend support to this judgement, and point to the possibility that the burdens of the peasantry may actually have decreased in the last decades of serfdom. Thus, the real value of the obrok apparently did not increase, while the real value of the soul tax dropped sharply. The period of military service was much reduced, though the number of men drafted per thousand peasants rose in the nineteenth century. There does not seem to have been an overall increase in the proportion of serfs on barshchina, and the norm for those who performed this service remained unchanged at three days per week (save for Little Russia where it went up from two to three days). The increasing number of peasants who were taken from their holdings to become *dvorovye liudi,* or factory workers, or landless field hands, often must have been worse off than they had been before, but these people formed a minority of the total serf population.

Though firm conclusions about the economic welfare of the peasantry as a whole cannot be drawn, it is possible to make some generalizations about the relative position of different groups among the seigniorial peasantry. The serf on obrok was better off than the barshchina peasant, in that he had more time to work for himself and he usually had a larger holding. Those who were able to earn part or all of their income by some non-agricultural employment were likely to be more prosperous than the peasants who spent all their time on the land. The *dvorovye liudi,* who had nothing they could call their own and were entirely dependent upon the bounty of their masters, were the worst off of all.

Within each of these groups, of course, some peasants were much better off than their fellows. The serfs who lived on fertile land, or who had larger holdings, or who had markets nearby, or who were more enterprising than their fellows, were likely to be more prosperous. The few studies of individual peasant settlements that have been made indicate a high degree of economic stratification within the village. For example, the

78 homesteads on a property in Kaluga were divided in the 1780's by their seignior into four classes according to their economic status. Sixteen were in the top bracket, 17 in the second, 29 in the third, and 16 in the lowest rank. Each of the top 16 owned on the average 8 horses, 4 cows, 18.8 sheep, and 4.4 swine. The average size of their holding was 5.4 desiatins, and each rented on the average an additional 14 desiatins. The 16 poorest homesteads had on the average only 2 horses, 1.4 cows, 7.5 sheep, 1.5 swine, had holdings of 2.5 desiatins, and rented no additional land. The wealthiest peasants occupied themselves in trade and in handicraft production as well as farming. The poorest, for the most part, spent all their time in agricultural work.[81]

A few among the millions of serfs managed to become remarkably wealthy through trade and industry. This phenomenon inevitably attracts interest, but it was of little importance in the overall structure of peasant life. The serf Croesuses represented only one of the most peculiar aberrations of the servile Russian society. Many of them were eager to buy their freedom from their masters and become members of the merchant class. But often seigniors were reluctant to part with such valuable pieces of property. The obrok these men paid was scaled to their incomes, so that their owners collected hundreds and thousands of rubles from them each year. Large sums could also be extracted from them as the price for special favors, such as permission to marry or to obtain a recruit quittance. They were useful, too, as sources for loans. Count Sheremetev in 1793 borrowed 10,000 rubles for four months from E. Grachev, richest of the Ivanovo textile manufacturers, and in 1794 borrowed 5,000 for two months. Another advantage of holding on to rich serfs was that the principle of mutual responsibility in the peasant village required them to pay the obligations of their impoverished fellows. Sometimes, too, human perversity explained why seigniors kept these men in bondage. A proprietor named Ogarev was said to have refused big offers from his

---

[81] Drakokhrust, "Rassloenie," pp. 127-130; cf. also Bibikov, "Rassloenie," pp. 108-111; Sivkov, "K voprosu," pp. 283-285; Kovalchenko, "Khoziaistvo," app. tables 1-4.

wealthy serfs for their freedom because he was proud that he owned people who were all but millionaires.[82]

When seigniors did agree to allow their wealthy peasants to redeem themselves they often set fantastically high terms. In 1795 Count Sheremetev charged Grachev, the Ivanovo manufacturer, 135,000 rubles in cash, plus the factory, land, and serfs owned by Grachev. Thus, in exchange for his freedom Grachev had to give up some of the fruits of a half century of work by two generations of his family.[83] But not all—for Grachev reportedly had large assets concealed in the name of merchants who acted for him. Instead of being ruined by Sheremetev's exorbitant price, he not only continued as one of the biggest textile operators in Russia after his emancipation, but soon began to expand.[84] Savva Morozov, another serf industrialist, paid his owner 17,000 rubles for his freedom. A proprietor in Kostroma in 1822 sold eight people their freedom for a total of 320,000 rubles. By 1861 about 50 of the serf entrepreneurs of Ivanovo had redeemed themselves and their families at an average price of 20,000 rubles.[85]

Setting the redemption price was sometimes the occasion for much haggling and for sharp practices. It was in the lord's interest to know exactly how much his serf was worth so that he could charge the maximum price he knew he could get. The serf, for his part, did his best to conceal his assets. The device Grachev is supposed to have used, of having property in the name of a merchant, was apparently employed by other serfs, too.[86] One proprietor ruefully told how, after much bargaining, he charged one of his peasants 16,000 rubles for his freedom, only to learn later that the man was worth 200,000 rubles. He admitted that his sister was much shrewder than he, for she got 30,000 rubles from one of her serfs whose total worth was 45,000.[87]

[82] Shchepetov, *Krepostnoe pravo*, pp. 107-108; Berlin, *Russkaia burzhuaziia*, p. 88.

[83] Shchepetov, *Krepostnoe pravo*, p. 109.

[84] Meshalin, *Tekstil'naia promyshlennost*, pp. 122, 176-177.

[85] Berlin, *Russkaia burzhuaziia*, pp. 87-88.

[86] Cf. Meshalin, *Tekstil'naia promyshlennost*, p. 122.

[87] Kulischer, "Die kapitalistischen Unternehmer," p. 353.

Not all the bondsmen who redeemed themselves were men of great wealth, nor did they all pay huge prices for their freedom. Data for 28,944 serfs who bought themselves out of serfdom during Alexander I's reign, show that 900 of them paid between 139 and 199 rubles, 8,839 paid between 200 and 400, 14,968 paid around 500 rubles, 4,149 paid between 500 and 1,000, 78 paid between 1,000 and 2,000, 8 paid 4,000, and 2 paid 5,000 rubles.[88]

One of the best known stories about the purchase of freedom by a rich serf involved Count Sheremetev and a serf named Shelyshin. Shelyshin traded in Riga and had made a lot of money. But he was an unhappy millionaire because his sons could not find wives that befitted their wealth. None of the Riga families that were suitable would allow their daughters to marry a Shelyshin, for the wives of serfs had to take their husbands' status. In desperation the father had offered Sheremetev 200,000 rubles for his freedom, but the Count had turned him down. Once, while on a business trip to St. Petersburg, Shelyshin decided to call on his master and plead his case again. It was his last day in town, and he bought a barrel of oysters on his way to the Sheremetev palace. He found the Count, at lunch with some guests, listening to his agitated maître d'hôtel explain that he had not been able to buy oysters anywhere in the city. The Count looked at Shelyshin and said, "Ah, Shelyshin, you are offering me 200,000 rubles for your freedom in vain, for I don't know what to do with it. But get me some oysters for lunch and you will have your liberty." Shelyshin bowed deeply, thanked the Count for his kindness, and announced that the oysters were waiting in the antechamber. The cask was brought into the dining room, and Sheremetev, using the barrelhead as a desk, wrote out a statement of emancipation, handed it to his ex-serf, and said, "Now then, Mr. Shelyshin, won't you join us for lunch?"[89]

Unfortunately, this pleasant tale somehow does not ring true. No Sheremetev would ever have said he did not know what to do with 200,000 rubles.

[88] Berlin, *Russkaia burzhuaziia*, p. 89.   [89] Iatsevich, *Krepostnye*, p. 26.

23

THE NON-SEIGNIORAL
PEASANTRY

RUSSIA before 1861 is usually, and accurately, styled a serf society. But often this has served to obscure the fact that by the mid-nineteenth century over half of the peasants in the empire were not serfs. This is not to say they were free men, but only that they were not the property of private seigniors. Instead, they were under the superintendence of the state. The degree of their subjection to the government differed according to the category or subclass of the non-seignioral peasantry to which they belonged, and some were much closer to freedom than were others. But all of them had more control over their own lives and activities than did the seignioral peasantry.

By far the largest group among the non-seignioral peasantry was made up of the people who were called "state peasants" or "treasury peasants." Like so much else in eighteenth- and nine-teenth-century Russia, the state peasantry owed its origins as a legal and social category to Peter I's determination that none among his subjects should escape performing duties for the state, and to his efforts to simplify the collection of taxes and other obligations. Peter formed the core of the state peasantry out of peasants who had managed to avoid enserfment. Among these were the remnants of the once-numerous black people, the descendants of the minor servitors who had settled in earlier centuries on the then southern frontiers, migrants to Siberia, and the Tatar and other non-Slavic peoples who lived in the Volga basin and beyond. Beginning in 1719 Peter in a series of ordinances imposed taxes, quitrents, and conscription upon one after another of these groups. In 1724 he referred to them collectively for the first time as "state peasants."[1]

1 Druzhinin, *Gosudarstvennye krest'iane*, I, 23-24.

The tsars after Peter, as part of a continuing program of administrative simplification, shifted other non-seignioral peasants into the state peasant class. Nearly always these people had certain privileges that they had gained during their historical development, and that had served to distinguish them from other groups. Once incorporated into the state peasantry they tended to lose their special rights, and a single homogeneous class tended to emerge. Some of them, however, succeeded in preserving their identity and even part of their old privileges, so that the state peasantry was split into a host of subclasses. An official listing in 1838 named thirty-three special categories, some with hundreds of thousands and even millions of people in them, and others with just a few hundred.[2] Meanwhile, the name "state peasant," or its synonym "treasury peasant," was employed in various and confusing ways by bureaucrats and lawmakers. In its strictest use it meant only the black people, or the black plowing people as they were called officially. More loosely, it referred to all peasants living on property owned by the state and administered by the treasury. In its widest sense it covered all peasants who were not serfs of private seigniors.[3] I have adopted the second of these three meanings for these pages.

The government's policy of putting more and more people into the state peasantry, and natural increase, made this class grow far more swiftly than the serf population. At the time of the First Revision there were about 1.04 million male state peasants, comprising almost one fifth (19 percent) of the empire's total male peasant population. By the Fifth Revision in 1796 they had increased to 6.03 millions, or 39 percent of the male peasant population. After 1800 the number of non-seignioral peasants transferred by government fiat to the state peasantry was much less than it had been in the preceding century, so that the rate of growth slowed down. Still, between the Fifth and Tenth Revisions the male state peasant population more than doubled. The 1858 census showed that there were 13.4 million of them. Meanwhile, the serf population had grown at a much slower rate. As a result, the state peasants now formed

[2] *Entsiklopedicheskii slovar*, xvia, 693.
[3] Druzhinin, *Gosudarstvennye krest'iane*, I, 44.

52 percent of all male peasants. In other words, at the time of the emancipation there were more state peasants than there were serfs. A contemporary estimate based on the returns of the Tenth Revision listed 27,397,289 state peasants of both sexes, and 22,846,054 serfs of both sexes.[4]

As with the serfs, the accidents of history and geography produced an uneven distribution of the state peasants among the different parts of the empire. In the 1850's they made up 51 to 82 percent of the entire population of eleven provinces of European Russia, 25 to 50 percent in sixteen others, 10 to 24 percent in still another sixteen, and less than 10 percent in four. In general, they were concentrated most heavily in the guberniias that rimmed European Russia on the north, east, and southwest, while the provinces with the least numbers lay along the western borders. In Siberia nearly all of the population belonged to the state peasantry.[5] Through conquest, annexation, and confiscation, the area of state-owned land remained vast, despite the huge amounts the tsars gave away to private proprietors. By the middle of the nineteenth century almost half of the surface of European Russia belonged to the government (940,000 out of 1.9 million square miles). This was three and one half times larger than the area of the entire Austrian Monarchy, the second largest European state of that day. Fifty-seven percent of the government's land lay in just seven northern provinces, and almost 25 percent more was in the tier of eight eastern provinces that stretched along the Urals and the Volga.

[4] *Ibid.*, p. 45; Tsentral'nyi statisticheskii komitet, *Statisticheskiia tablitsy* . . . *za 1858 god*, p. 306.

[5] MGI, *Statisticheskii obzor*, pp. 750-753.

Over 50 percent population state peasants: Viatka 81.7, Kazan 73.19, Poltava 70.80, Tauride 70.80, Olonets 66.98, Voronezh 65.95, Archangel 64.85, Samara 57.26, Vologda 57.24, Kursk 52.15, and Astrakhan 51.08, percent.

Between 25 and 50 percent: Ekaterinoslav 49.65, Perm 49.56, Tambov 46.72, Chernigov 45.70, Kharkov 45.46, Penza 41.77, Saratov 41.57, Pskov 33.93, Tver 32.31, Riazan 31.96, Orel 31.23, Grodno 28.61, Iaroslav 27.73, Courland 27.07, Vladimir 25.68, and Vilna 25.57, percent.

Between 10 and 24 percent: Nizhnii Novgorod 24.16, Novgorod 24, Kovno 23.10 Moscow 22.73, Orenburg 22.62, Kaluga 19.43, Kostroma 18.12, Smolensk 17.93, Vitebsk 17.81, Tula 16.59, Kherson 16.51, Bessarabia 14.91, Lifland 13.81, Volynia 12.64, Kiev 11.79, and Minsk 11.24, percent.

Less than 10 percent: Podolia 9.73, Mogilev 8.70, St. Petersburg 7.26, and Estland 1.74, percent.

The rest was scattered through the other parts of European Russia, with the smallest amounts found in the western guberniias. About 55 percent of this huge domain was in the hands of state peasants. Most of the rest was in forest.[6]

The largest of the many groups who lived on the state land[7] were the black plowing people. Once most of Russia's rural population had been in this category, but by the latter part of the seventeenth century the black people had been reduced to a small fraction of the peasantry, and were concentrated in the north and east of European Russia, and in Siberia. In the eighteenth century their number began to increase, at first slowly, and then with mounting speed. In the 1740's 550,000 males had been included in this rubric: in 1838 there were five million male black plowing peasants. Natural increase was responsible for part of this growth, but most of it was due to the government's inclusion of other non-seigniorial peasants in this category.[8]

The second largest category among the state peasantry were the people called the *odnodvortsy*, or the "one-homesteaders." They were the descendants of the minor servitors of the sixteenth and seventeenth centuries who had been sent by the tsars to guard the eastern and southern frontiers. Instead of the 200 or more chetverts of arable that pomeshchiks were supposed to receive, they had been given much less land. Many of them held fewer than twenty chetverts, and some had as little as five (v. pp. 208-209). Still, it was their land, and like other pomeshchiks they had been able to hand it on to their descendants.

The way of life of these miniature proprietors often differed scarcely at all from that of peasants. Yet, so long as they retained their military role they were distinct from, and superior to, the ordinary rustic. But when the frontiers were pushed out beyond the lines on which they had been settled, their status began to decline. In the later seventeenth century when the tax base had been shifted to the *dvor*, they alone among the landowning class had been required to pay the government's levy.

---

[6] *Ibid.*, pp. 716-722, 729-733, 742-746, 750, 755-757.
[7] For complete list of the groups v. *SZ*, 1857, IX, sect. 614.
[8] Semevskii, *Krest'iane*, II, 850.

They were still called upon for military service when they reached fifteen, but many of them secured exemptions from this duty. Finally, during Peter's reign, the government decided to regularize their position in the social hierarchy. A few of them managed to gain acceptance into the dvorianstvo, but all the rest were made members of the state peasantry. *Odnodvortsy,* the name given to them, was an appropriate one, for nearly all of them were, in truth, one-homesteaders. Only a small minority among them had serfs, so that the only *dvor* they owned was the one in which they themselves lived. In deference to their quasi-noble origins, the government until late in the eighteenth century made somewhat lighter demands of them than it did of the rest of the state peasantry. Then Catherine II ordered that their obligations should be the same as those of the rest of the state peasants, except for a fifteen year term of military duty, instead of the life service then required of other recruits.

In the 1740's there were 453,000 male *odnodvortsy*. By the 1850's their number had grown to 1.9 million. Most of them lived in the Central Agricultural provinces of Kursk, Tambov, Orel, and Voronezh, where the frontiers had been in the early days of the conquest of the steppe.[9]

Several smaller groups in other parts of the empire closely resembled the *odnodvortsy* in origin and status. The "military residents" (*voiskovye obyvateli*) were the descendants of men who had served in the regiments that once guarded the frontier between Great and Little Russia. Most of these people lived in Kharkov guberniia. The Little Russian cossacks traced their origins to the days when they had been a semi-autonomous military force under Polish rule. Lesser gentry of the annexed Polish provinces who could not furnish documentary evidence of their noble origin were incorporated into the state peasantry as "*odnodvortsy* of the Western provinces."[10] Another and much smaller group in these provinces who were called the "*panzer* boyars," were descendants of lesser military servitors of the Grand Dukes of Lithuania. If they could prove their noble

<hr />

[9] *Ibid.*, pp. 721-733, 761; *Entsiklopedicheskii slovar*, xxxviiia, 726-729.
[10] *SZ*, 1857, ix, sect. 677.
Lesser gentry of the towns who could not prove their noble origin were made burghers. Köppen, "Russlands Gesammt-Bevölkerung," p. 410.

descent they were taken into the dvorianstvo; if not they became state peasants.[11]

The people who once had belonged to religious institutions formed another major group within the state peasantry. The church had owned nearly a million male serfs when its lands were secularized in 1764. These peasants had been allowed certain privileges that set them apart from the serfs of lay proprietors. They could not be sold, they could enter complaints with government officials against their owners, and their masters could not exile them without the approval of their fellow villagers. But they had heavy obligations put upon them, their holdings could be taken from them at will, members of their households were compelled to become domestics in monasteries and episcopal residences, and they were subjected to detailed supervision and interference in their personal lives. Above all, churchmen seemed to have been cruel and oppressive masters. Unrest became endemic among these peasants; indeed, Catherine used this as the excuse to take the church's properties from it. Most of the secularized land was turned over to the people who lived on it. They were made state peasants, but were put under the supervision of the newly revived Economic College for Church Property, and so were called Economic peasants. In 1786 the Economic College was abolished, and the Economic peasants were fused with the other state peasants. It is of interest to note that after secularization, the outbreaks that had been so common among these people when they had belonged to the clergy, were conspicuous by their absence.[12]

Well over a million state peasants (1.6 millions of both sexes in 1858) lived in the nine provinces that had been annexed from Poland—or reunited with Russia as the tsarist regime preferred to put it. The land on which they dwelled had belonged to Polish seigniors who had been dispossessed after the annexations. The government kept a minority of the confiscated properties under its own direct control, so that the peasants who

---

[11] SZ, 1857, IX, sect. 872-875.

In 1838 there were 373,833 male "military residents," 553,691 Little Russian cossacks, 121,074 male *odnodvortsy* of the Western provinces, and 6,007 male *panzer* boyars. *Entsiklopedicheskii slovar*, XVIA, 693.

[12] Semevskii, *Krest'iane*, II, 194ff.

lived on these lands were like state peasants elsewhere in the empire. All the other properties were leased to the highest bidder at public auctions. The peasants on the leased estates had to pay dues in cash and kind to the lessee, or arrendator as he was called. The form and amount of these obligations were usually defined in the inventories that had been drawn up for each property. But there was little or no supervision of these arrangements by the authorities, so that the arrendators demanded more dues than the inventories specified, handed out illegal and inhuman punishments, compelled the peasants to work on other properties they owned, and even had peasants entered as their own serfs when revision lists were drawn up, thereby actually stealing peasants from the state. The complaints of the leased peasants went unheard until the 1830's. Then, the change in the government's attitude toward the state peasantry, symbolized by the creation of the Ministry of State Domain, brought on investigations of the activities of the arrendators. The findings persuaded the government, in 1853, to declare that it would no longer lease out populated state land.[13]

Others enrolled in the state peasantry were people who for one reason or other were no longer eligible to remain in their old class, or who were entirely classless. Among these were freed serfs, burghers who had settled on the land and whose sole occupation was farming, children of non-hereditary nobles and of bureaucrats who had not reached officer rank in the government service, clerics who had forsaken their calling, certain discharged soldiers and their children, and foundlings. In some cases the law allowed these people to choose between becoming state peasants or burghers, while others were placed automatically in one or the other of these classes.[14]

Freed serfs formed the most numerous contingent in this heterogeneous group. There were many ways in which the bondsman could win liberty. The most common was through military service. The conscript, his wife, and those of his children who were born after he entered the army, were liber-

---

[13] MGI, *Statisticheskii obzor*, pp. 721-722, 751; Druzhinin, *Gosudarstvennye krest'iane*, I, 343-345; Semevskii, *Krest'ianskii vopros*, II, 493-494, 508.

[14] *SZ*, 1842, IX, sect. 496, 633-635, 644-651.

ated from serfdom. Some of the other means included emancipation by serfowners, serfs buying their freedom, banishment to Siberia, return from war imprisonment, conversion to Christianity of non-Christian serfs who belonged to non-Christian proprietors, and purchase by the government at the petition of a serfowner. Wealthy peasants, who had amassed their riches in trade and industry, entered the burgher class after they redeemed themselves from bondage. But many of those who were freed had always made their livings from agriculture. They remained on the land as state peasants.[15]

Some non-seignioral peasants who in a strict sense were not members of the state peasantry were often counted in that class. The foreign colonists were one of the largest of these groups.[16] The government had inaugurated the organized settlement of immigrants in the 1750's, but the project had not been successful. Then in 1762 Catherine II issued an invitation to all foreigners to settle as farmers in the unpeopled parts of her realm, and Russian diplomats, and agents working on commission, began an active recruiting campaign. The government held out generous inducements to newcomers, including payment of transportation from their homelands, tax exemptions for five to ten and in some cases thirty years, freedom from military service, subsidies, loans that were partially or entirely free of interest, freedom of worship, and a large measure of autonomy within their settlements. The amount of land that each immigrant family was supposed to receive was set in 1764 at thirty desiatins. In practice, special arrangements were made for each new large group of colonists, so that there was much variation in the size of the holdings the immigrants actually had. Each family's land became its hereditary possession. The govern-

---

15 Semevskii, *Krest'iane*, I, 323-325, 326, 328.

Peasants who were purchased by the state at the petition of serfowners had to pay back the money the government had laid out to buy them and their land. Full data are not available on the number of peasants the government bought, but between 1838 and 1855 it purchased 178 properties with 54,349 male peasants on them just in the Great Russian provinces alone, at a total cost of 8,735,872 rubles. Semevskii, *Krest'ianskii vopros*, II, 566-568. Cf. also Mikhalevich, *Materialy*, p. 170; Köppen, *Statistische Reise*, Beilage 16, pp. 69-70.

16 The information presented here on the colonists is drawn, except where otherwise noted, from *Entsiklopedicheskii slovar*, XXIVa, 672-675; *Entsiklopedicheskii slovar* (Granat), XXIV, 526-530.

ment also set aside a reserve of empty land to take care of the anticipated natural increase of the settlers.

During Catherine's reign about 75,000 colonists came into the empire. They received a total of 1½ million desiatins of land, and cash advances that totalled 5,682,307 rubles, of which 2,026,454 rubles did not have to be repaid. Nearly all of them settled in New Russia, or along the Volga in Saratov and Samara. Though they came from a number of lands, most of them were Germans (who remained German in language, religion, and customs, until their dispersal by the Soviet regime in World War II). At first, they were reported to have had difficulties in adjusting to their new lives, possibly because many of them had followed trades other than farming in their homelands.[17] With time, and the generous aid given by the government, they became well established and reasonably prosperous.

Early in the nineteenth century the government began to depart from Catherine's open door policy. The number of colonists was restricted to 200 families a year, only skilled artisans and farmers were admitted, the immigrants had to have at least 300 gulden, and the amount of state assistance was reduced. Finally, in 1819 the recruiting of foreign settlers was ended. The few cases of group immigration in the years that followed came at the instance of the would-be colonists themselves, and special permission had to be given for each group to come into the empire. Despite these barriers the number of colonists grew, chiefly by natural increase. In the 1850's there were 449,553 of them (229,542 males), holding over 2.3 million desiatins of land.[18]

A very small group of people in the North, known as the "taxfree proprietors" (*obel'nye votchinniki*), were the most unusual among those sometimes included in the state peasantry. They were by all odds the freest commoners in the entire empire. They owned their own land, they paid no taxes, and they were not called upon for military service nor for any other state obligation. They owed their unique position to some

---

[17] Falk, *Beyträge*, I, 110-111.
[18] MGI, *Statisticheskii obzor*, pp. 646-649, 660-663; Tsentral'nyi statisticheskii komitet, *Statisticheskiia tablitsy . . . za 1858 god*, p. 272.

special service to royalty performed by their ancestors. Thus, a community on an island in Lake Onega, that had 133 male residents in the 1840's, was descended from a priest named Grigorii Merkur'ev who had cured Boris Godunov of an injured foot. According to the story told on the island, Grigorii had employed an unorthodox and unattractive therapy; he licked Boris's foot until it healed. Another settlement, with 150 people in it in 1845, were tax-free proprietors because their forebears had taken care of Martha Ivanova Romanova, mother of the later Tsar Michael, when she was exiled to their lonely village. A priest named Ermolai Gerasimov had also helped Martha in her banishment, and his descendants, numbering 28 males in 1835, were among the tax-free proprietors. So, too, were the descendants of Ivan Susanin, a peasant of Olonets, who in 1612 had sacrificed his life to save Michael from capture by Polish troops, and of Ivan Riaboev, who in 1714 had found a mineral spring in whose waters malady-ridden Tsar Peter had found some relief.[19]

The sharecroppers (*polovniki*) were another special group who lived in the North, mainly in Vologda guberniia. Originally black plowing peasants who had lost their holdings, they rented from other peasants, or from nobles or merchants. They paid their landlords from two fifths to one half of their crops, and in some instances even more, made a number of other payments in kind, labor, and sometimes in cash. They were in the process of becoming the serfs of the men from whom they rented, until the tsar in 1725, ordered that they were to be free to go from one property to another within the same district, although they had to get permission from local governmental officials for their move. A century later, in 1827, the Ministry of Interior issued regulations designed to limit the amount of the sharecropper's payments, and protect him from undue exploitation by his landlord. The government also settled *polovniki* on state land, and gave them temporary tax exemptions and subsidies to help them get started. These people became state peasants, and after their exemptions ran out paid the same obligations as the rest of the state peasantry. Yet they continued to be identified as *polovniki*.

[19] Bergstrasser, "Beschreibung," pp. 320-322.

Their numbers declined steadily during the eighteenth and nineteenth centuries, from around 15,000 males in the 1740's, to less than 3,000 in the late 1850's.[20]

II

Like all other non-nobles in the empire, the state peasants had to pay the soul tax. Except for certain designated groups, the tax was the same for them as it was for the serfs.[21] They also had to pay a quitrent to the state. This obligation was not a tax or rental fee, but was the analogue of the obrok that serfs had to pay to their masters. By demanding this quitrent the state was asserting its claim to ownership of all land not privately owned, and its seignorial authority over the peasants who lived on that land.

The obrok of the state peasants, however, was considerably smaller than that paid by most serfs. Peter set it at 40 kopecks and it stayed at this low figure (except from 1746 when it went up to 65 kopecks) until 1761. In that year it was increased to 1 ruble, in 1769 it went up to 2 rubles, and in 1783 to 3 rubles. Though part of this rise was cancelled out by the fall in the buying power of money, the real increase was still large.

In 1798 the obrok went up once more, but this time the treasury made a rudimentary effort to scale it to ability to pay. The provinces of the empire were divided into four classes, according to their general economic development and wealth. The peasants who lived in the most prosperous guberniias (most of these provinces were in the Central Industrial and Central Agricultural districts) paid a quitrent of 5 rubles per revision soul, those who lived in the provinces of the second class paid 4½ rubles, in the third 4 rubles, and in the poorest guberniias 3½ rubles. These rates were pushed up in 1810 and again in 1812, when they were set at 10, 9, 8, and 7½ assignat rubles,

20 Semevskii, *Krest'iane*, II, xxxv-xxxvi; *SZ*, 1857, IX, sect. 703-740; Haxthausen, *Studien*, I, 286-294.

21 The exceptions in the 1850's (when the soul tax was 86 silver kopecks) were the Little Russian cossacks who paid 2 rubles if they lived in Chernigov or Poltava guberniias, and 1 ruble 36 kopecks if they lived elsewhere; *panzer* boyars who rented from private landlords (i.e., did not live on state land) paid 2 rubles; Jewish farmers paid 2 rubles; and certain assigned peasants paid 58 kopecks. *SZ*, 1857, V, suppl. to sect. 17, pp. 199-200.

respectively, for each of the four zones. The increases, however, were only nominal because of the monetary depreciation. By 1812 the assignat ruble was worth about one fourth of a silver ruble. In terms of silver money, then, the obrok rates of that year ran from 2 rubles 50 kopecks to 1 ruble 87 kopecks, or considerably less than the flat 3 ruble fee the peasants paid in 1783.[22] In 1839, when taxes were converted from assignat to silver rubles at 3½ to 1, the obrok became 2 rubles 86 kopecks in the 20 provinces in the first class, 2 rubles 58 kopecks in the 10 provinces of the second class, 2 rubles 29 kopecks in the 18 that were in the third class, and 2 rubles 15 kopecks for the 3 provinces in the fourth class.[23]

Though these rates were much less than the obrok paid by contemporary seigniorial peasants, they apparently represented a large increase over the quitrent of the last quarter of the eighteenth century. The available price data (v. p. 450) indicate that in the 1770's the 2 ruble obrok equalled the price of one chetvert of rye; in the first half of the nineties the then current obrok of 3 rubles could buy three quarters of a chetvert; the obrok rates of the early forties were the equivalents of from 1.8 to 2.4 chetverts.

Early in the nineteenth century some of the people in the top levels of government expressed the belief that the obrok should be related to the ability of the individual peasant to pay it, and not to the general economic condition of the provinces in which he lived. In 1824 the Minister of Finance offered a plan to accomplish this reform, but his proposal and others like it made in succeeding years came to nothing. In 1837 Tsar Nicholas transferred the supervision of the state lands and peasants to the

[22] Rukovskii, "Istoriko-statisticheskiia svedeniia," pp. 20-31, and app. no. 6. For list of the guberniias in each class v. *ibid.*, pp. 30-31. In 1823 the government decided that 16 provinces had made enough economic progress to warrant their transfer to a higher classification for obrok payments. Four provinces were shifted to the first class, seven to the second, and five to the third. *Ibid.*, pp. 33-34.

[23] *SZ*, 1842, v, pt. 1, pp. 163-164.

Certain specified groups were exempted from paying the obrok. The Little Russian cossacks paid a special tax, the foreign colonists paid a rental fee per desiatin. Storch, "Der Bauernstand," 1848, pp. 83-84; *SZ*, IX, sect. 832. The "free farmers," the *panzer* boyars who rented from private landlords, and the "tax-free proprietors" paid no quitrent. Druzhinin, *Gosudarstvennye krest'iane*, I, 343; Storch, "Der Bauernstand," 1848, p. 80; *SZ*, 1857, IX, sect. 885.

just-created Ministry of State Domain. The head of this new ministry, Count P. D. Kiselev, was unique among the men of his class and station; he was as much interested—and perhaps even more interested—in raising the standard of living of the millions of state peasants, as he was in increasing the revenues the state received from them. One of the many projects he initiated was a study of the relation between the income of these people and the obrok they had to pay. The results of this survey revealed the injustices of the existing system. In Eka-terinoslav, Voronezh, and Tver, for example, in 1853 the quitrent amounted to 9 percent of the peasants' net income, in Novgorod 14 percent, in Kharkov 16 percent, and in Kursk 20 percent. Adjustments were obviously needed, but bureau-cratic inefficiency and delays held up the adoption of a more equi-table method of assessment. Then, in 1857 Count N. M. Murav-iev succeeded Kiselev as head of the Ministry. Unlike his prede-cessor, Muraviev's primary concern was to increase the revenues the state received from its peasants. He was uninterested in the niceties of just assessments, and in 1859 ordered an overall increase in obrok rates.[24]

Besides the soul tax and the obrok, the state peasants had a number of other obligations. Like the serfs they paid a road tax of 9 silver kopecks, had to build and maintain highways, provide horses, carts, and postal services when called on, and so on. In many cases these lesser services were commuted into a cash payment. Like the serfs, too, they paid a small levy to the provincial government that ranged (in the 1830's) from 26 assignat kopecks to 1½ assignat rubles, special local taxes, and a communal tax. They made no payments in kind (except for those made by the leased state peasants in the western prov-inces). They had to provide recruits on the same basis as the serfs. Those who lived in settlements with less than 200 males, or on the frontiers, or in Archangel guberniia, could commute this obligation into a money payment. Foreign colonists, tax-free proprietors, and holders of elective communal offices, were exempt from military duty.[25]

[24] Khodskii, "Ocherk," no. 11, pp. 29-32, 41-46.
[25] Druzhinin, *Gosudarstvennye krest'iane*, I, 46-48, 50-52, 328-331, 338-342.

Platon Storch, using data for the years 1842-1846, estimated the cash value of the state peasant's obligations at 5 rubles 43 kopecks per revision soul.[26] This figure was undoubtedly more precise than Storch's estimate of the cash value of the serf's obligations (v. p. 470), for the state peasant commonly paid all his obligations in cash, and there was far less variation in the type and amount of payments demanded of him. At the estimated current grain price of 5.05 rubles per chetvert, the state peasant's obligations was the equivalent of slightly more than 1 chetvert. Storch's estimate of the cash value of the contemporary serf's obligations (12 rubles 80 kopecks) equalled about 2⅓ chetverts.

III

The smaller burden of obligations borne by the state peasants was not the only advantage they enjoyed over the serfs. They also were allowed rights that made them a privileged class in comparison with the seignioral peasantry. In fact, the new law codification of 1832 referred to them as the "free rural inhabitants" (*svobodnye sel'skie obyvatelii*). That was a big overstatement, but it is revealing of the official view of the status of these peasants.

During the eighteenth century the government felt it necessary, in the interests of administrative and fiscal efficiency, to deprive the people it put into the state peasantry of many of the freedoms they had previously enjoyed. Like the serfs they had to get passports before they could leave home for a journey. These permits were granted only for a limited period and then had to be renewed. On occasion, for one reason or other, permission to travel to or from a certain area would be denied all applicants. A fee had to be paid before a girl could leave her village to marry and live elsewhere. The peasants were not allowed to operate factories and workshops, to be parties to leases and contracts, or to draw or accept bills of exchange. They were split into different administrative units, one for the payment of their monetary obligations to the state, another for conscription, a third for road work. Each unit was made collectively respons-

---

[26] Storch, "Der Bauernstand," 1848, p. 123.

ible for all its members. Government officials were set over them to supervise their activities, and to make sure they met their obligations to the state. Because of the power these bureaucrats had, the corrupt among them found it easy to extort money, and sometimes even land, from the peasants in their charge.[27]

Then, in the late eighteenth and first part of the nineteenth centuries, some of these restrictions began to be weakened or entirely withdrawn. The legal restraints on peasant activity in commerce and industry—which had been widely disregarded anyway—were gradually removed. The prohibitions on making contracts and leases, and drawing and accepting bills, were eased and then, in the 1820's, abolished. In 1782 the exit fee for the girl who married outside her village was done away with. Restrictions on personal freedom of movement were loosened for members of certain groups, and in the 1820's and 1830's it was made somewhat easier for all state peasants to move into a town, or to become members of urban classes.[28]

The state peasants also won the right to own land in their own name. In 1858 they owned around 3.7 million desiatins in all of European Russia[29]—an area about twice the size of New Jersey. That was an insignificant part of the vast Russian land mass. Nonetheless, it was the property of these peasants. The *odno-dvortsy*, Little Russian cossacks, *panzer* boyars, tax-free proprietors, and Crimean Tatars, had the right to own land before they were put into the state peasantry. Legislation of the eighteenth and nineteenth centuries allowed them to continue in their ownership, but placed restrictions on their freedom to alienate their land as they pleased. In 1801 all state peasants were given this privilege, when Alexander decreed that any of his subjects, except serfs, could buy uninhabited land and have full property rights over it. Data collected in 1835 for 25 provinces of European Russia showed that 130,607 state peasants had taken advantage of this law, and had purchased a total of 772,570 desiatins.[30]

27 Druzhinin, *Gosudarstvennye krest'iane*, I, 25-26, 66; Khodskii, "Ocherk," no. 11, p. 32.

28 *SZ*, 1857, IX, sect. 439-450, 683n., 826, 907, 910.

29 MGI, *Statisticheskii obzor*, pp. 740-741.

30 *SZ*, 1857, IX, sect. 861-864, 922, 927, 931; Veshniakov, *Krest'iane-sobstvenniki*, pp. 4-5, 7-8.

The *odnodvortsy*, the military residents, and the mirzas (Tatar nobles not recognized by the Russian law as members of the dvorianstvo), also had the legal right to own serfs. The total number they owned, however, was small, and decreased sharply in the last century of serfdom. Most of the serfs belonged to *odnodvortsy*, who in 1788 owned 21,531 male peasants. In 1858 they had just slightly more than a thousand.

The anomaly of state peasants legally owning serfs, when this was supposed to be a prerogative of the dvorianstvo alone, troubled the government for a long time. The difficulty rose from the fact that these peasants had once been members of the seignioral class. Though the government was willing to derogate their personal status, it did not want to confiscate their personal property. The unnatural situation that ensued created peculiar problems. Often there was little difference between master and serf, and sometimes they lived together in the same hut. So far as the tsar's recruiting officers were concerned they were indistinguishable, for if they found the serf unfit for military service they took the master in his stead. The *odnodvortsy*, who thought they should have the same rights that other serfowners had, wanted to be able to sell their serfs to whomever they wanted. The government disagreed, and in 1754 ordered that they could sell peasants only to other *odnodvortsy* who lived in the same county, and had to sell them with land. Two years later this law was amended to permit sales without land.

There were fiscal difficulties, too. The serfs of the *odnodvortsy*, like all peasants, had to pay the soul tax. Their owners, who had to pay both soul tax and quitrent, protested that their serfs were better off than they were so far as obligations to the state were concerned. The government decided that this complaint was justified, and in 1768 solved the problem in typical bureaucratic fashion—the serfs were ordered to pay the same quitrent to the state that their masters paid.

Unfortunately, the logic of this solution did not guarantee its success. The serfs, already responsible for obligations to their owners, were unable to carry this additional burden. Confronted with this dilemma, the government allowed *odnodvortsy* to free their serfs, and in 1827 decided not to demand the obrok of those serfs who still belonged to the one-homesteaders. Meanwhile, discussions had been going on for some time in governmental circles about freeing all these serfs and making state peasants out of them. These plans did not get beyond the talking stage until 1841. In that year Tsar Nicholas empowered the Treasury to buy serfs from the *odnodvortsy* at 75 to 100 rubles per soul, and settle them as state peasants on government land. Between 1842 and 1858 the Treasury purchased 7,886 males under this program.[31]

The smaller obligations of the state peasants, and the greater freedom allowed them, should have enabled them to live at a higher economic level than the mass of the seignioral peasants. Unfortunately, information that would permit a direct comparison of living standards between the two classes is lacking. Data on unpaid taxes, however, throw some light on their relative economic positions, and on differences within the state peasantry itself. According to information compiled by the Ministry of State Domain for the years 1821-1846 inclusive, the average annual assessment on the state peasantry amounted to 29,890,802 rubles. The average annual arrears during these years were 1,272,937 rubles, or somewhat more than 4 percent of the average annual assessment. The delinquency rate for the seignioral peasants was close to 5 percent, and for city dwellers almost 13 percent. A more detailed analysis for state peasants only, for the years 1843-1856 inclusive, showed that their average annual arrears during this period equalled 7.4 percent of the average annual assessment. In the nine Western provinces annexed from Poland, where the peasants suffered under the arrendator system, the delinquency rate averaged out at 22 percent. In two of these provinces, Minsk and Vitebsk, it was around 32 percent. The delinquency rate was also remarkably high in the Central Agricultural zone. In seven of these eight provinces it was well above the national average for the state peasantry, going from 7.8 percent in Kursk to 21.19 percent in Penza. In contrast, in seven of the nine provinces of the Central Industrial area the rate was below the national average, running from a mere .6 per-

31 Semevskii, *Krest'iane*, II, 770-775; Druzhinin, *Gosudarstvennye krest'iane*, I, 31-32.

cent in Kostroma to 5.46 percent in Vladimir. Only Nizhnii Novgorod with 8.26 percent and Smolensk with 12.72 percent were above the average for all state peasants.[32] Data on the delinquency rates during these years for serfs and city dwellers were not available to me.

The striking difference between the abilities of the state peasants of the Central Industrial and the Central Agricultural provinces to meet their taxes, points to a greater economic well-being for those who lived in the less fertile provinces. The peasants of the chernozem were handicapped by the lack of opportunity to supplement their incomes from non-agricultural work, by low prices of farm goods, by crop failures, and by the retardation of transportation and market development in their region.

In the 1840's the entire state peasantry began to benefit from the program of agricultural education instituted by the new Ministry of State Domain. Under the aggressive leadership of Count P. D. Kiselev, the Ministry promoted the cultivation of new crops, not hesitating to use compulsion if that was necessary to get peasant cooperation, tried to improve the quality of the peasant's livestock, published agricultural journals and manuals, and held prize contests. The Ministry was particularly interested in popular education, and by 1858 had established 2,905 village schools with nearly 220,000 students, a third of them girls. Besides the usual subjects these children were taught farming and handicrafts. Advanced agricultural instruction was given in six model farms owned by the Ministry, and in 28 special schools that gave training in branches of farming and forestry. There were also six schools to train village clerks. All together, in 1857 these special institutions had 1,146 students. The Ministry also arranged for courses in agriculture to be given in seminaries, so that when the students there became village priests they could spread the gospel of better farming to their parishioners.[33]

---

[32] Rukovskii, "Istoriko-statisticheskiia svedeniia," app. no. 24, 28. Druzhinin, *Gosudarstvennye krest'iane*, I, 99-100, cites the large cumulative arrears as evidence of widespread impoverishment among the state peasants. But he does not mention the total amount that was collected nor the delinquency rate, and thus gives a misleading impression.

[33] "Obozrenie upravleniia," pp. 489-493; MGI, *Statisticheskii obzor*, p. 698; Storch, "Der Bauernstand," 1850, pp. 187-190; Tegoborskii, *Etudes*, II, 183-184.

But no matter how many privileges were allowed the state peasantry, nor how much interest was shown by officialdom in improving their condition, the one great flaw in their status went uncorrected. They had no guarantee that they would remain state peasants. For the tsars, up to the time of the emancipation, continued to view the state land together with the people who lived on it, as their property to be disposed of as they wished. They could give state peasants to private proprietors, or could assign them as laborers in an industrial enterprise. If the former happened the state peasants became serfs; in the latter case their legal status was little better than that of serfs, and the conditions under which they lived were often worse. During the nineteenth century the danger of either of these things happening was greatly reduced. But it never disappeared entirely.

IV

In addition to the millions of state peasants, there were many hundreds of thousands of non-seignioral peasants who belonged to other categories. The people who lived on the properties that belonged to the imperial court formed the largest of these groups. In the 1720's the court peasants (*dvortsovye krest'iane*), as they were called, numbered about 350,000 male peasants.[34] Until 1711 they had been under the supervision of the *Bol'shoi Dvorets*, the special bureau that had been created by Ivan IV to administer the court lands. Peter abolished this agency, but neither he nor his successors for the rest of the eighteenth century were able to settle on a satisfactory replacement for it. Finally, Tsar Paul, in the Organic Act of the Imperial Family of 5 April 1797, set up an arrangement that lasted until the emancipation. The Organic Act had as its primary purpose the establishment of a fixed order of succession to the throne through primogeniture. Among the many collateral subjects discussed in this long ordinance (it had 208 articles in it), was that of the financial support of the members of the imperial family. Paul decreed that those who stood in the line of succession to the throne were to be maintained out of regular state

---

[34] Semevskii, *Krest'iane*, II, 1-2, 12-13.

revenues. The others who by the provisions of the act could not succeed, were to be supported by the revenues from the court lands. He put these lands and the peasants who lived on them under the supervision of a new agency, the Department of the Appanage (*Udel*).[35] From that time on, the court peasants were known as appanage peasants.

When Paul introduced this reform there were around 470,000 court peasants, and about 4.2 million desiatins of court land scattered through 36 provinces. Slightly over half of this area was in forest. In the succeeding decades both population and area grew steadily. By 1860 there were over 800,000 male appanage peasants, and nine million desiatins of appanage land, five millions of it in forest. Meanwhile, the number of imperial kinsmen who drew their livings from these properties increased, too. In 1805 only five had to be supported. They received a total of 385,000 rubles. In 1860 23 imperial personages drew 3,324,000 rubles from the appanage.[36]

During the eighteenth century the tsars had taken over some of the court properties as their own personal possessions, and had given others of them to members of their immediate family. The peasants on these properties were transferred from the court peasantry into a new category called the "sovereign's peasants" (*gosudarevy krest'iane*). By 1762, when Catherine II ascended the throne, there were 62,000 males in this class. When the holder of one of these properties died, his land sometimes reverted to its former status of court land, whereupon the peasants became court peasants again. But often the estate went to another member of the imperial family, either through the will of the deceased or as a gift of the tsar. In the Organic Act of 1797 Paul did not include these properties in the appanage, but he did change their nomenclature. The ones that belonged to the tsar himself—such as the famed rural seats of Tsarskoe Selo and Peterhof—were now called "Imperial estates," while those held by members of his family were referred to as "Court

[35] Glavnoe upravlenie udelov, *Stoletie udelov*, pp. 5-9; *PSZ*, xxiv, no. 17906, sect. 1-4, pp. 526-527.

[36] Glavnoe upravlenie udelov, *Stoletie udelov*, pp. 20-21, 28, 29, 43, app. Diagram 2.

estates." To add one last note to all this confusion, the peasants who lived on these properties, that is, the people who had been known as "sovereign's peasants" in the eighteenth century, now were called "Court peasants."[37]

In earlier centuries, and on into the eighteenth century, the peasants on court lands had been required to do barshchina, and to pay obrok and other dues in cash and kind. They had closely resembled serfs, though their total obligations were probably lighter than those demanded of the peasants of private seigniors. Then, in 1732 their quitrent was commuted into a cash payment of 40 kopecks, the same amount levied on the state peasants. In the following years the obrok was increased, until by 1783 (like the obrok of the state peasants) it had gone up to 3 rubles. Meanwhile, the area of the demesne on court properties steadily diminished, so that the court peasants had to do less and less barshchina. Finally, by 1780 all the demesne had vanished, and the barshchina with it. Now, the only obligations the court peasants had were their obrok, and the soul tax, military duty, and other levies that the state made on all peasants.

As a result of these changes, the court peasants at the end of the eighteenth century were much closer to the state peasants than they were to the serfs. Like the state peasants, however, they were always in danger of becoming serfs through the tsar's gifts of court land and people to private persons, and like state peasants, too, they could be assigned to work in industrial undertakings. In addition, and unlike state peasants, they could be made to serve as menials at the Court. Only a relatively small number were taken from their villages for this work, however, and usually they took turns in doing it, so that individuals were not removed permanently from their homes. They were exposed, also, to the danger of becoming "sovereign's peasants," through imperial action that converted court lands into the private possessions of the tsar or of members of his family. When that happened they became serfs for all practical purposes. Their dues and services varied according to the wishes of their master,

[37] SZ, 1857, IX, sect. 613n.

or more accurately of his stewards, and sometimes they were cruelly exploited and mistreated.[38]

In the nineteenth century, in contrast to the eighteenth, the condition of the court peasants, or the appanage peasants as they now were called, deteriorated. When Paul created the appanage in 1797, he visualized that the appanage peasants would pay a rental based upon the value of their holdings, rather than a uniform obrok. But the absence of data on the revenue each peasant family drew from its land made it impossible to introduce this equitable system, so that the uniform quitrent continued to be levied. Then, in 1829, the Department of the Appanage decided to abandon the obrok in favor of a method of assessment it called the "land fee" (*pozemelnyi sbor*). The Department maintained that this new system would enable charges to be adjusted to ability to pay, would increase appanage revenues without increasing the burdens of the peasants, and at the same time would make the peasants realize that they were the renters and not the owners of the land they tilled.[39]

The realities of the new system belied the official reasons given for its adoption. Actually, it was a tax on the peasant's gross income rather than a rental payment, and the charges were based on arbitrary norms and not on ability to pay. The Appanage Department ordered that the tax assessment unit, or *tiaglo*, in each appanage village was to be equal to half the number of male revision souls in the village. Each *tiaglo* was to have a holding that yielded it a gross income of 21 rubles 50 kopecks. The *tiaglo* had to pay two fifths of this income, or 8 rubles 60 kopecks, to the Appanage Department. This payment included taxes as well as rent. Land left over after the property had been divided into holdings that each yielded 21½ rubles could be farmed by the peasants of the village, but they had to pay the Department of the Appanage two fifths of the gross income they drew from it. If the holding was too small, or too infertile, to produce a gross income of 21½ rubles, the *tiaglo* paid an obrok, rather than two fifths of the income from the

---

[38] Semevskii, *Krest'iane*, II, 3-4, 10-11, 14-22, 35-53, 130-140, 151-160.
[39] *Svod udel'nykh postanovlenii*, II, sect. 111, 112.

land. The obrok was the same as that demanded of the state peasants who lived in their guberniia.[40]

In actual practice, of course, the appanage land was not split into neat holdings each yielding precisely 21½ rubles. Instead, the gross income of a village was determined by averaging the yield of its land during the ten preceding years, and multiplying this by the average grain prices of the decade. Officials then divided the average gross income by half the number of male revision souls in the village. If the quotient was exactly 21 rubles 50 kopecks, each *tiaglo* paid a land fee of 8 rubles 60 kopecks. If it was more, they paid an additional levy of two fifths of whatever the additional sum was. If the quotient was less than 21½ rubles, the peasants paid the obrok.[41]

The new system not only failed to introduce equitable assessments, but it increased rather than decreased the payments of nearly all the appanage peasants. The land fee was often larger than the sum of the obrok and taxes they had hitherto paid. Besides, they now were charged an additional fee for land they used over the arbitrary norm established by the Appanage Department. The obrok paid by those who lived on the less fertile or overcrowded properties also increased. When the appanage was first formed the obrok had been set at 3 assignat rubles, but was soon made the same as that of the state peasants—3½ to 5 rubles—depending upon the province in which the peasant lived. In the following years it was increased, though by slightly smaller amounts than the increases in the obrok of the state peasants. In 1842 it was again made the same as the obrok of the state peasants, that is, 2 ruble 58 kopecks (silver) depending upon the province.

To give the Appanage Department its due, it did make efforts to improve the economic welfare of the peasants in its charge. Starting in the 1820's plans for reforms and innovations poured from its offices, most of them inspired by L. A. Perovskii, assistant head and later chief of the Department. In the 1830's an arrangement with the treasury allowed the Department to exchange overcrowded properties in eighteen guberniias for state land and state peasants in the emptier and more fertile regions

---

[40] *Ibid.*, sect. 64, 115, 116, 131-134.   [41] *Ibid.*, app. no. 12.

along the middle Volga. By 1860 nearly 40 percent of all appanage peasants lived in the black earth provinces of Simbirsk, Saratov, and Samara.[42] The Department tried to promote the cultivation of new crops, and the use of better methods of tillage and improved farm implements. In 1832 it established a model farm and training school near St. Petersburg, at a cost of 261,000 silver rubles. In the latter forties the institution had 250 pupils, all in their late teens. The course of study lasted four years, and combined classroom instruction in winter and farm work in summer. Some of the graduates took jobs as officials in appanage villages, or in the offices of the Department. Others were sent back to their homes to establish model farms. The Department supplied them with all the necessary equipment, and in addition gave them a small library of books on agriculture. They were expected to use the methods they had learned at the school, and so serve as models for their neighbors to imitate.[43]

Early in the forties Baron Haxthausen visited the farm of a graduate of the training school, and was much impressed by his efficiency and progressiveness.[44] But the scheme proved unsuccessful. According to the official history of the appanage, it foundered on the problem of labor supply. The techniques used by the model farmers required more labor than did the old methods. The farmers, however, were young married men who usually were the only workers in their families. They could not afford to hire the additional hands they needed, and so they were unable to operate their farms with the improved methods. Enrollment at the training school dwindled, its graduates were no longer set up as model farmers, and the institution atrophied, though it did not shut its doors until 1867. Another school, established in the 1840's to train appanage peasants in handicraft production, proved unsuccessful, too. Attempts made by the Appanage Department to organize cloth and paper factories in the villages also failed.

[42] Tsentral'nyi statisticheskii komitet, *Statisticheskiia tablitsy . . . za 1858 god,* p. 272.

[43] Glavnoe upravlenie udelov, *Stoletie udelov,* pp. 39-45; Storch, "Der Bauernstand," 1850, pp. 190-191.

[44] Haxthausen, *Studien,* I, 238-240.

Much of the costs of these and other plans for improvement were paid for out of funds that belonged to the appanage peasant communes. They had accumulated the money by selling surplus grain from special communal fields introduced at the order of the Appanage Department in 1827 to raise food for storage against an emergency. The compulsory communal field system was unpopular with the villagers. The arbitrary disposition by the bureaucrats of the income from their communal efforts to introduce other innovations made them all the more resentful of the Department's program. This frame of mind, added to the inborn conservatism and suspicion of change of the peasants, goes far in explaining why most of the projects had only small successes at best, and often did not work out at all. Much of the blame, too, lay with the bureaucrats. They planned on too wide a scale, failed to take local and regional conditions into account, were excessively paternalistic, and entrusted the implementation of their plans to officials who all too frequently lacked the necessary knowledge and ability to carry them out.[45]

V

Still other groups among the non-seignioral peasantry had been assigned special tasks by the government. Among these were the people who had been ordered to work in industrial enterprises owned by the state or by private persons. Others included the stable peasants, falconers, ship forest peasants, postal peasants, and military colonists.

The stable peasants had appeared as a special group already in the sixteenth century. In 1760 they numbered about 40,000 males. Over 30,000 of these men worked in the imperial stables, and the rest were employed in cavalry regiments. Around this time their obligation began to be commuted into a cash obrok. In 1786 the Stable Chancellery, the bureau that supervised these people, was abolished and the stable peasants were transferred to the state peasantry.[46]

---

[45] Glavnoe upravlenie udelov, *Stoletie udelov,* pp. 41, 47-48, 75-79; *Entsiklopedicheskii slovar,* xxxiva, 596.
[46] Semevskii, *Krest'iane,* II, 161-171.

The origins of the falconers reached far back into medieval times, for hawking had long been a sport of Russian princes. In the 1780's there were about 1,000 male falconers. They were an especially favored group, and had been excused from many of the obligations that other peasants had to pay. But, apparently, the monarchs of the nineteenth century were not as fond of this pastime as their predecessors had been. In 1800 all but a handful of the falconers lost their special status and were fused with the state peasantry. In 1827 the few who had not been included in the earlier transfer—a total of 102 men—joined their fellows in the state peasantry.[47]

The ship forest peasants were organized when Peter decided to build up the Russian navy. He had to have a labor force to provide the timber he needed for his ambitious program. So in 1718 he commanded the Muslims of Mordvinian and Tatar stock who lived along the middle Volga to cut and transport timber in the Admiralty forests of that region. They worked at their assigned task only at certain periods of the year, and some, particularly those who lived at a distance, were allowed to commute their obligation into cash. They were called *lashmany*, from the Low German *laschen*, to chop. The Sixth Revision in 1811 listed 943,000 males in this category, but only a fraction of that number actually worked in the forests. In 1817 the government shifted all except 120,000 of these men into the state peasantry. The 120,000 who remained *lashmany* had to provide 8,000 workers between the ages of 18 and 55 each year. In addition, 300 families were settled in the forests as wardens. In 1859 the ship forests were transferred from the Admiralty to the Ministry of State Domain, and the *lashmany* were amalgamated with the state peasantry.[48]

The postal peasants (*iamshchiki*) had to carry the mails, and provide transportation for both official and private travellers. In the 1760's they numbered about 45,000 males. They were divided into units, usually of either 7 homesteads or 28 males, with each unit required to furnish a driver, wagon, and three horses for relay services. In 1846 the obligation of those

[47] *Ibid.*, pp. 183-193.
[48] *PSZ*, CXXXIV, no. 27023, 21 Aug. 1817, pp. 522-525; Köppen, "Über die Vertheilung," pp. 412-413.

iamshchiki who lived along the busy highway between St. Petersburg and Moscow was reduced to one horse for every eighteen males. They received a moderate fee for their work, and were exempted from most of the obligations that other peasants had to pay the state. Despite these compensations, many of them asked to be relieved of their special duties and were transferred into the state peasantry. As a result, their numbers diminished steadily in the last part of the eighteenth and first half of the nineteenth century.[49]

The military colonies were an innovation of the reign of Alexander I. In the latter seventeenth and eighteenth centuries peasants had been settled along the frontiers as guards against invasion, and in the eighteenth century communities of soldiers retired for age or disability had been set up in the interior. These establishments had not been part of an integrated project, and late in the eighteenth century they were liquidated. Soon thereafter, the military needs brought on by the Napoleonic wars made the government think about ways of strengthening its armed forces. Alexander was reputedly impressed by von Scharnhorst's plan to create a Prussian national army, and decided to organize military colonies as the Russian version of this idea. Possibly, too, the peasant garrisons in the Military Frontier of the Austrian Monarchy served him as a model.

Alexander proposed to settle regiments on state owned land. The soldiers would support themselves by farm work on holdings turned over to them, and would continue their military training so that they would always be ready for action. Alexander reasoned that this scheme would allow Russia to have a large and well-trained army at comparatively low cost. The system would benefit the soldiers, too, for they would live with their families, continue in the agricultural life to which they were accustomed, and have a home and a source of livelihood when they became too old for active duty.

The tsar's counsellors advised against the project because of its initial expense, and because of the unreliability of part-time soldiers. But Alexander persisted. He turned over the planning

---

[49] Coxe, *Travels*, II, 13-14, 13n.; Köppen, "Über die Vertheilung," pp. 411-412. Köppen, *Statistische Reise*, p. 4; Tegoborskii, *Etudes*, I, 328-329.

and direction of the operation to Count A. A. Arakcheev. Arakcheev, who is often erroneously considered the author of the scheme, had opposed it originally, and became its supporter only because he feared losing his influence with Alexander. Once in charge he showed much zeal—events were to prove it was overmuch—in developing and carrying out the tsar's idea.

The first colony was established in 1810 in the White Russian province of Mogilev. The outbreak of war in 1812 interrupted the program, but it was resumed and expanded when hostilities ended. Now, besides settling regular army units in certain designated areas, the government converted all the state peasants in these zones into military colonists. These people had to provide supplies and quarters for the regulars and their families. In addition, until they were 45 they had to undergo military training, and were considered members of the armed forces. Their sons were put in the same category as the sons of the regulars (who were called cantonists), received military training from an early age, and became regulars when they reached 18.

The government did much to improve the economic welfare of these peasants, providing them with sizable holdings, giving them cattle and even building model villages for them. But the colonists soon learned that with this solicitude went constant surveillance by army officers of all the details of their daily lives, and harsh, merciless, military discipline. Furthermore, the demands of army training cut deeply into the time they had for farming. Their discontent erupted into open resistance and violence, culminating in a mass rising in Novgorod guberniia in the summer of 1831. This revolt, rendered more bitter by a cholera epidemic and famine, was put down by the government only with the use of much force. Barbaric punishments were meted out to over 3,000 men. Many died from the whippings they received.

Yet the rebels won. In October 1831 Tsar Nicholas put the military colonists of Novgorod into a new class called "farming soldiers" (*pakhatnye soldaty*). Despite the name these people were no longer part of the military. All their special army duties and the military control of their lives were ended, and the only difference between them and state peasants was that they had to pay a much larger obrok to the state.

Nicholas's decree marked the beginning of the end for the entire system of military colonies. In 1836 the colonists in Mogilev and Vitebsk were made "farming soldiers," and in 1857 all the remaining military colonies were abolished. The people in these colonies, along with those who had earlier been made "farming soldiers," were transferred to the state peasantry. The changeover came while the Tenth Revision was in progress and the census takers made a separate count of the colonists. Their returns showed that there were 1,119,302 of them (571,989 males), scattered through nine provinces.[50]

[50] *Entsiklopedicheskii slovar*, XXIVa, 663-672; *Entsiklopedicheskii slovar* (Granat), XXIII, 106-111; Tsentral'nyi statisticheskii komitet, *Statisticheskiia tablitsy . . . za 1858 god*, p. 274; cf. Pipes, "Russian Military Colonies," pp. 205-219.

24

THE VILLAGE COMMUNITY

IN THE EARLY CENTURIES of Russia's history the peasants, whether black people or renters on privately owned land, lived usually in isolated farmsteads or in tiny hamlets. Each family ran its own holding as an independent unit, though often it shared common rights in forests, pastures, and streams with neighboring families. This pattern of settlement persisted well into the sixteenth century. Then it started to change into a new and totally different form. Peasants began to give up living in isolated farmsteads and came together into villages.[1] The transition was long and drawn out, and the available information does not allow the successive stages in it to be traced. But data collected in provinces of European Russia in the late 1850's on the number of homesteads and the population of rural settlements, show how far it had progressed by that time.

Twenty-two of these provincial surveys, representing most of the regions, and including nearly half (47 percent) of the total population, of European Russia, were available to me.[2] In 1859 these 22 provinces had 100,348 rural settlements in them. Of this number:

6 percent	(5,995)	had only 1 homestead
16 "	(15,885)	had 2 to 5 homesteads
18 "	(18,549)	had 6 to 10 homesteads
29 "	(29,417)	had 11 to 25 homesteads
24 "	(24,214)	had 26 to 100 homesteads
6 "	(6,002)	had 101 to 500 homesteads
.3 "	(299)	had more than 500 homesteads

[1] Sergeevich, *Drevnosti*, III, 76.

[2] Tsentral'nyi statisticheskii komitet, *Spiski naselennykh mest*, I (Archangel), VI (Vladimir), VII (Vologda), IX (Voronezh), XII (Don Cossack Land), XIV (Kazan), XV (Kaluga), XXIII (Ekaterinoslav), XXIV (Moscow), XXV (Nizhnii Novgorod), XXVII (St. Petersburg), XXIX (Orel), XXXIII (Poltava), XXXV (Riazan), XXXVI (Samara), XXXVIII (Saratov), XXXIX (Simbirsk), XLI (Tauride), XLIII (Tver), XLIV (Tula), XLVIII (Chernigov), L (Iaroslav).

Of the 299 settlements with over 500 homesteads, 265 had between 500 and 1,000 homesteads, and the remaining 34 had between 1,000 and 3,000.

These figures show that the village had become by far the predominant form of rural settlement in these provinces. If the line between hamlet and village is drawn, say, at 5 homesteads, 78 percent of the settlements fall in the latter category.

A comparison of the data for the 22 provinces discloses a regional variation in the patterns of settlement. The infertile northern provinces had the largest proportion of isolated farmsteads and hamlets; in Vologda 33.6 percent, in Archangel 31.6 percent, in St. Petersburg 38 percent, and in Iaroslav 24 percent of the settlements had five or fewer homesteads. The fertile provinces of the Lower Volga stood at the other end of the scale; only 2.4 percent of the settlements in Simbirsk, 4.7 percent in Kazan, 7 percent in Saratov, and 12.5 percent in Samara had five homesteads or fewer. In the Central Agricultural provinces, too, the ratio of isolated farmsteads and hamlets was small, with 9.1 percent in Riazan, 18 percent in Voronezh, 15 percent in Orel, and 11 percent in Tula. The apparent correlation between soil fertility and size of settlement, however, did not always hold true. In the agriculturally productive provinces of Poltava and Chernigov in Little Russia, 34 percent and 40 percent, respectively, of all settlements had five or less homesteads in them.

Villages with over 100 homesteads in them were much more frequent in the black earth than they were in the northern guberniias. 29 percent of the settlements in Samara, 26 percent in Saratov, 25.6 percent in Simbirsk, and 21.5 percent in Voronezh, were in this range. In six other chernozem provinces the proportion of these large villages ran between 10 and 17 percent. In contrast, in five (Iaroslav, Vologda, Tver, St. Petersburg, Archangel) of the nine northern provinces for which information is available, less than 1 percent of the settlements had over 100 homesteads, in three (Moscow, Kaluga, Vladimir) only 2 percent, and in one (Nizhnii Novgorod) 10.8 percent, were of this size.

In terms of population rather than number of homesteads, the most common settlement size was between 51 and 300 people. Out of 100,299 settlements:

5.2 percent	(5,238)	had fewer than 10 inhabitants
22.5 "	(22,456)	had between 11 and 50
53.0 "	(53,077)	had between 51 and 300
8.5 "	(8,593)	had between 301 and 500
6.6 "	(6,651)	had between 501 and 1,000
3.0 "	(3,030)	had between 1,001 and 2,000
1.2 "	(1,254)	had between 2,001 and 25,000

The largest settlements were nearly all in the black earth. Of the 1,254 villages with over 2,000 people, 1,183 were in chernozem provinces. The remaining 71, located in the non-chernozem, were frequently commercial and industrial centers rather than farming communities, even though their inhabitants were peasants.

The lack of information about the stages in the shift to the village form permits only surmises to be made about the reasons for it. Perhaps it was associated with the augmentation of seignioral demands upon their peasants, particularly the expansion in the barshchina obligation, and the simultaneous increase in seignioral powers. To achieve more effective control over their peasants, seigniors presumably compelled them to move from their isolated farmsteads into villages. It was simpler to supervise the peasants and exact obligations from them when they lived together as a community.[3] It seems possible, too, that the spread of a new kind of communal organization (to be discussed shortly) afforded a major stimulus in advancing the transition. The emphasis in these new-model communes upon equality, their practice of periodic redistribution of holdings and of seignioral and fiscal obligations, and their broad economic and social powers over their members, must have produced strong pressures from the peasants themselves to move into villages in order to facilitate the operations of the commune. It would obviously be far easier to exercise the central control and cooperation that this sort of joint effort demanded,

[3] Sergeevich, *Drevnosti*, III, 76.

if all the people involved in it lived close to one another. Thus, the fact that the peasants of Poltava and Chernigov did not organize land-equalizing communes may explain why so many of them continued to live in settlements of fewer than five homesteads. On the other hand, it is possible that the new communes could have been results rather than causes of the changes in the form of settlement. Once the peasants had moved into villages, and had their holdings scattered through the surrounding fields, they could have adopted the new communal form as the most efficient and equitable method of operation under the changed circumstances in which they now lived.

In the southern and eastern steppe provinces still other factors may well have played a part in dictating the choice of the village as the dominant mode of settlement. From the beginnings of the colonization of these regions down into the eighteenth century, there was constant danger of raids by the nomadic people who roamed the great Eurasian plain. To gain protection from these forays the settlers grouped themselves into villages.[4] The scarcity of water sources in the steppe must have also persuaded colonists to cluster in villages around places where a plentiful water supply was available.

Population growth probably had a role, too, in the move into villages. The increased pressure on the land often called forth a demand from the peasants for land-equalizing communes, and as was just pointed out, these organizations perhaps stimulated the establishment of villages. But the importance of the rise in population should not be overestimated. It did not begin until the second quarter of the eighteenth century, long after the village form of settlement had begun to supplant the isolated farmstead and hamlet. Furthermore, the data from the mid-nineteenth century for the 22 provinces show that sometimes there was no correlation between population density and the incidence of villages. Poltava and Chernigov were among the most heavily populated guberniias of the empire, while the Lower Volga provinces were much less densely peopled. Yet the latter had a far higher proportion of large settlements, and a

---

[4] Cf. Tsentral'nyi statisticheskii komitet, *Spiski naselennykh mest*, IX, xxi-xxii.

much lower proportion of small ones, than did the two Little Russian provinces.[5]

II

Whether they lived in a large village or a small one, in a hamlet or an isolated farmstead, most countrymen, whether non-seignioral peasants or serfs, by the middle of the nineteenth century were members of a new kind of commune. The most distinctive characteristic of this new organization was it periodic redistribution and equalization of the land held by its members. Its official name was the *sel'skoe obshchestvo*, the rural commune, but it is known best as the mir.

The problem of the origin of this institution became one of the most hotly disputed issues of Russian historiography, despite —or perhaps more accurately, because of—the sparseness of information about the earlier centuries of Russian communal development. The lack of evidence tempted some historians, and the publicists who joined in the controversy, to present generalizations that supported their political and philosophical views. It became a key issue in the famed battle of the books between the Slavophils and the Westernizers, each camp using its interpretation of the origins of the mir as a launching pad for its pet theories about the history, "spirit," and "destiny" of the Russian people.

Although there had been some slight interest in the origin of the mir as early as the era of Catherine II, it became a subject of major intellectual interest only after the appearance in 1847 of Baron Haxthausen's account of his travels through Russia in 1843-1844. Haxthausen, proud aristocrat and defender of traditional values, abhorred the changes brought on in Western Europe by the progress of individualism and of industrialization. He thought that he saw in the land-equalizing commune the bulwark that would save Russia from the fate of the West. He assumed that it was an ancient institution borne out of the deeply religious *Volksgeist* of the Russians. Its egalitarianism reflected the peasants' knowledge that God had given them

[5] For population densities v. Tsentral'nyi statisticheskii komitet, *Statisticheskiia tablitsy . . . za 1858 god*, pp. 188-189.

their land as a common heritage in which each was to share according to his need. The Russian people felt themselves to be members of one great family with the tsar as their father. Each commune was this great family in microcosm, with the mir elders as the wise parents whom every one in the commune heeded. To Haxthausen this was a refreshingly hopeful contrast to what he termed the "deep-seated illness" of Western European culture, and was far superior to the essentially anti-Christian panaceas that were being offered by social reformers of the West. With romantic disregard for historical fact and remarkably clouded vision of the future, the Baron concluded that Russia, unlike the nations of the West "has naught to fear from the revolutionary tides that at this very moment threaten Europe, naught to fear from pauperism, the proletariat, and the doctrines of communism and socialism. . . ."[6]

Haxthausen's book appeared at a time when Russian intellectuals were turning their attentions to the history of the peasantry, partly because of the growing interest in the abolition of serfdom, partly because of the eruption in the 1840's of the Slavophil-Westernizer controversy. His views, echoed by Tegoborskii, the author of the next important study of the Russian economy to appear,[7] attracted much attention and won many supporters among the Slavophils. The debate on the origins of the land-equalizing commune began in 1856 when B. N. Chicherin, renowned Westernizer, published an article in which he denied that the mir was of ancient origin, claimed that it was a modern institution created as a consequence of the government's fiscal policies and the enserfment of the peasantry, and argued that it had assumed its final shape only in the last quarter of the eighteenth century. The challenge was taken up immediately by I. D. Beliaev, Slavophil, who, in the pages of his party's journal asserted that the mir's origins went back in a direct line to pre-Varangian times. Chicherin quickly replied, Beliaev answered, and then other writers joined in on one side or the other.[8]

---

[6] Haxthausen, *Studien*, I, 134-157.

[7] Cf. Tegoborskii, *Etudes*, I, 340-342. Tegoborskii's first volume appeared in 1852.

[8] There are a number of surveys of the historiography of this debate. One of the

The argument continued for quite a while along the line laid down by Chicherin and Beliaev—the mir as a recent phenomenon created from above by the government for its own purposes, versus the mir as an ancient institution created by the people themselves as the natural expression of the Russian soul. Then, as so often happens, some scholars began to seek out a middle ground, while others struck out in entirely new directions and proposed other theories. By the first part of the twentieth century there was general agreement that the land-equalizing commune was not of ancient origin. This was just about the only aspect of the problem on which there was a meeting of minds, but the researches of the historians uncovered snatches of evidence that make possible a sketch of the mir's history up to the nineteenth century.

To begin with, the antiquity of the communal form of organization cannot be questioned. To this extent the Slavophils were right. As earlier pages have shown, little is known about the communes of the pre-Kievan and Kievan periods. The territorial commune, or *volost*, of the post-Kievan centuries had a number of functions that were much like the activities of the later commune. It managed the common forests, fisheries, and pastures, controlled the use and distribution of unused land, divided the tax burden among its members, and served as a tax collector. But it had not periodically redistributed and equalized the holdings of its members. Instead, each communer had nearly complete control over his holding, increasing or decreasing its size as he chose through sale, exchange, gift, or legacy.

Starting probably in the latter part of the fifteenth and early sixteenth centuries, and continuing on into the seventeenth century, the autonomy of the volost and of the individual peasant weakened and finally crumbled under the pressure of expanding seignioral powers and demands. The commune with its officials became agents of the proprietor, and the peasant's erstwhile rights over his holding were subjected to increasing restrictions. The distribution of holdings came more and more

best is Kizevetter, "Krest'ianstvo v russkoi nauchno-istoricheskoi literature," pp. 23-43. For surveys in Western tongues *v.* Kulischer, *Russische Wirtschaftsgeschichte*, I, 238-244; Miller, *Essai*, pp. 159-170.

under the control of the seignior, or of commune officials acting
as his agent. Data from the sixteenth century show that practices
were introduced on some properties that foreshadowed the
activities of the land-equalizing commune of the future. According to the Novgorod land register of 1500-1501, each of the 90
homesteads of the Uzhinsk commune tilled exactly the same
amount of land. These people, whose primary occupation was
fishing, rented their holdings from the Grand Duke of Moscow.[9]
Around the same time, Metropolitan Simon ordered the abbot
of St. Constantine's Monastery in Vladimir to divide the monastery's land into peasant holdings of equal size. In 1511 Simon
instructed his agents to measure the arable on church properties,
and then provide each peasant renter with the same amount of
plowland.[10] A register for 1580 of property in Tver owned by
Prince Simeon Bekbulatovich stated that the peasants had
divided their fields, meadows, and forests equally among themselves to remove the source of quarrels and strife. A source for
1588 shows that the same thing happened on a property owned
by the crown.[11]

Available data from the seventeenth century is equally meagre
and discontinuous. Thus, a village priest complains that the
peasants in the court-owned village in which he lives practice
frequent repartition of holdings, but that he never receives
enough, and what he does get is poor soil to boot.[12] A steward of
one of B. I. Morozov's properties reports that the village commune of Ignashka has failed to obey the master's order to divide
the land equally among all the residents.[13] In the second half of
the century, peasants on properties owned by N. I. Odoevskii in
Galits asked to have their holdings reduced, because the obligations demanded for the amount of land they now hold is beyond
their capacity to pay. Odoevskii's stewards and commune officials
investigated these requests, and if they found them justified took
some land away from an overburdened homestead, and trans-

9 Efimenko, *Izsledovaniia*, pp. 374-375.
10 Miliukov, *Spornye voprosy*, p. 32n.
11 Semevskii, *Krest'iane*, II, 5-6; Efimenko, *Izsledovaniia*, p. 377.
12 Semevskii, *Krest'iane*, II, 6.
13 Zabelin, "Bol'shoi boiarin," pt. 2, pp. 472-473.

ferred it to one they believed was able to carry the additional obligations.[14]

The very scant amount of evidence of the use of these practices points to the conclusion that communal repartition and equalization were highly exceptional procedures in the sixteenth and seventeenth centuries. Then, in the eighteenth century these practices became increasingly common. By the end of that century they were standard methods of operation on much privately owned land, on properties that belonged to the court and to the imperial family, and in many communities of state peasants. By the middle of the next century they had become nearly universal among both serfs and non-seignorial peasants in most of the empire.

Though the organization and activities of the new kind of commune were much the same among all categories of Russia's peasants, the reasons for its adoption varied with the legal and social position of the different groups. The major cause for its spread among the seignorial peasantry seems to have been the introduction of the soul tax in 1724. The tax was the same for every adult male serf, but it bore more heavily on the poorer peasants in the village than it did on those that were better off. The serfowners, saddled with the responsibility for collecting the tax, realized that it was in their own interest to see to it that each of their peasants had the economic capacity to pay the levy.[15]

The method many proprietors adopted to reach this goal involved the use of a new kind of assessment unit that bore an old name, the *tiaglo*. In earlier centuries the word *tiaglo* had been used as a collective noun for all the taxes imposed by the government, as the generic name for each individual tax, and also for the capacity of the individual taxpayer to meet his fiscal obligations. Now it meant the peasant labor unit, the land allotted this unit, and the obligations the unit had to pay to its seignior.[16]

Usually the labor unit consisted of a man and a woman, normally a married couple. But not infrequently a larger number were included. For example, in 1725 A. Volynskii ordered that

[14] Pushkarev, *Proiskhozhdenie*, pt. 1, pp. 150-153.
[15] *Ibid.*, pp. 188-191.   [16] Cf. *Svod udel'nykh postanovlenii*, II, sect. 131.

the *tiaglo* unit on his properties was to have two men and two women in it.[17] Similarly, on the votchinas owned by the Iusupovs in the black earth provinces, the *tiaglo* had two men and two women until 1780, when it was reduced to a man and wife.[18] On property in Tula owned by Prince Golitsin each unit had four couples until the end of the eighteenth century, when it was cut to one couple.[19] Data collected by the government at the end of the 1850's for privately-owned properties in eleven black earth and ten non-black earth provinces showed that in the chernozem guberniias the average number of adults per *tiaglo* was somewhat over 2½, while in the non-black earth the average was just about 2 per *tiaglo*.[20]

The age at which the individual member of a household was considered able to carry his full share of obligations, and so be counted as part of a *tiaglo*, depended upon local custom and seignioral wishes. Generally, it ran from 15-18 to 50-60 years of age for men, and from marriage to 50 for women.[21] Sometimes the work capacity of minors, and of the aged and infirm, was expressed as a fraction of the work an able bodied adult could perform and was included in the assessment unit, so that it was possible to have, say, 1¾ *tiagla* in a homestead. On some properties the number of animals the homestead owned and its farming equipment, or its overall income or general economic condition, was used as the basis for determining into how many *tiagla* it should be divided.[22]

Each *tiaglo* normally had to pay the same amount of dues and services. But the number of assessment units varied from one homestead to another according to the number of workers in the homestead, or its overall potential. Thus, the total sum of obligations each homestead paid varied. In this way the amount the serfowner demanded of each peasant family was adjusted to its capacity to pay.

17 Pushkarev, *Proiskhozhdenie*, pt. 1, p. 191.
18 Sivkov, *Ocherki*, p. 157.   19 Bibikov, "Rassloenie," p. 81n.
20 Skrebitskii, *Krest'ianskoe dielo*, III, 1278-1293.
21 Semevskii, *Krest'iane*, I, 98-99; Le Play, *Les ouvriers*, II, 181; Liashchenko, *Istoriia*, I, 503.
22 Semevskii, *Krest'iane*, I, 99-100; Haxthausen, *Die ländliche Verfassung*, p. 150; Grekov, "Tambovskoe imenie," pp. 490-491; Miller, *Essai*, p. 323.

This in turn led to the equalization and redistribution of holdings. Since each *tiaglo* had the same amount to pay, and since it usually derived all or most of its income from the land, the proprietor deemed it equitable to furnish each *tiaglo* with that amount of land that would provide each of them with equal quantities of produce. To maintain this equality in holdings and obligations periodic redistributions of land were necessary, for the number of *tiagla* in the individual homesteads changed with time. In actual practice the proprietor did not himself carry out these equalizing and redistributing operations. He turned these tasks over to the serf commune. The people of the commune were intimately acquainted with the quality of the soil and with the economic circumstances of their fellows, and so could distribute the land more equitably than could the seignior.[23]

Among the non-seignorial peasantry the land-equalizing commune appeared later than it did among the serfs. As with the serfs, fiscal considerations played a large part in its introduction and spread. The state wanted to make sure that the individual peasant had enough land to meet the obligations it demanded of him. The peasant, for his part, was equally interested in getting enough land to pay his taxes and obrok and support his family. In addition, political considerations may well have been an important factor in persuading the government to throw its weight behind land equalization. Those in high places perhaps feared that the discontent of those non-seignorial peasants who had little or no land, if allowed to go unappeased, might break out into violence. Count Kiselev, for instance, recognized the economic drawbacks of equalization and redistribution, yet, in a report to the tsar in 1859 he explained that "the division of the land according to souls, which is so harmful to any basic improvements in agriculture, has its advantages in that it eliminates the (rural) proletariat, and so this is a problem whose solution lies beyond purely economic considerations."[24]

The state's role in the adoption by non-seignorial peasants of the new kind of commune, however, did not always have the same importance. The government took direct action to intro-

[23] Cf. Pushkarev, *Proiskhozhdenie*, pt. 1, pp. 191-195.
[24] Quoted in Zablotskii-Desiatovskii, *Graf P. D. Kiselev*, ii, 199.

duce land equalization among the black plowing peasants of the North and the appanage peasantry, played a less important part in its introduction among the *odnodvortsy*, while in Siberia and among the cossacks of the Don the initiative came from the peasants themselves.

When the black plowing peasants first settled in the basin of the Northern Dvina they are believed to have organized themselves into patriarchal communes, much like the zadrugas among the Southern Slavs.[25] In time, members withdrew from these great family communes to set up their own homesteads. But it was difficult to divide the commune's land among the kinsmen who were withdrawing, for the nature of the infertile terrain was such that the arable was scattered and in irregular shapes. So instead of trying to split the land into separate holdings, an abstract division was made of it. That is, each homesteader was given an abstract share of the whole, corresponding to his mathematical share of the family's patrimony. This mathematical share depended upon the degree of his kinship to the founder of the commune. The abstract share gave its holder the right to use an amount of communal land equal to his abstract share. Periodically, redistributions were made to adjust to changed conditions, as when a peasant's mathematical share of the family patrimony increased through inheritance, or when new arable was cleared, or exhausted fields were withdrawn from cultivation.

This system inevitably produced inequalities with each successive generation. The line of descent from the original patriarch of the commune that had the fewest members in it had the largest abstract share of the communal patrimony, and therefore tilled the most land. Furthermore, the holder of an abstract share exercised just about complete property rights over the land that the abstract share represented. Actually, the land was owned by the state, and the black plowing peasants were only its users. But they acted as if they were its proprietors, selling, exchanging, mortgaging, or bequeathing it to anyone they wanted. That meant that the wealthier or more enterprising

[25] The following account of the evolution of the land-equalizing commune among the black-plowing peasants is drawn from Efimenko, *Izsledovanie*, pp. 204-228, 298-346, and Semevskii, *Krest'iane*, II, 604-659.

peasants could acquire much larger abstract shares, and therefore larger portions of land, than warranted by their places in the line of descent from the founder. It also allowed outsiders to buy their way into the commune and claim a share of its land. The acceptance of outsiders destroyed the familial character of the organization, and ultimately the blood ties that had originally held the commune together were forgotten. Yet the system of distribution according to abstract shares persisted in some places for a long time.[26] Finally, in the seventeenth century the individual homesteads began to be acknowledged as the permanent holders of definite pieces of arable, and in the eighteenth century communal title to the arable and control over its distribution disappeared. Communal ownership and management of meadows, pastures, and fisheries continued.

The inequalities in the size of holdings stirred up discontent among those peasants who had little or no land of their own. In cahiers they sent to the Legislative Commission of 1767 they asked for more land, and urged that they be allowed to divide it equally among themselves. Their demands found official support, for ever since the mid-seventeenth century the government had made unsuccessful efforts to forbid land alienations by the black plowing peasants on the ground that their land belonged to the state. Now the growing unrest among the peasants, and the fact that many of them were too poor to pay their taxes, impelled the regime to adopt far sterner methods than it had hitherto employed.

In 1785 officials in Archangel and Olonets ordered that land purchased by peasants was to be confiscated and divided among those commune members who needed more. If there still was not enough to provide an adequate holding for each household, the commune was ordered to clear new land. The wealthier peasants protested. Their outcries convinced the government that it should limit itself to persuading the peasants to hold enough land in common to meet everyone's need. But the attitude of bureaucrats, at least at the provincial level, was clearly expressed by the head of the state peasant administration in Archangel. He wrote that "justice demands that peasants

26 Cf. Ustiugov, "K voprosu," pp. 41-49.

who pay equal taxes should have equal shares in the land from which comes the wherewithal to pay the taxes," and therefore "equalization of holdings, especially in districts where tillage is the most important occupation, is considered an inevitable necessity, as much for providing the means for the peasants to pay their taxes, as for pacifying those who have not enough land."

In 1785 in Olonets, and 1790 in Archangel, peasant land owned by townspeople was confiscated and turned over to peasant communes for distribution among their poorer members. In Vologda repartition and equalization began in 1795. In 1797 the government set the norm for a black plowing peasant holding at 15 desiatins. Those with less were to be brought up to this standard through communal land repartitions.

By the end of the eighteenth century, then, communal repartition and equalization had become the rule among the black plowing people of the North. But the new order had not triumphed completely. For only that part of the peasant's holding that he had received through distribution of confiscated or newly cleared land was subject to communal control. The rest of his holding was unaffected. So there was still much inequality. This persisted until 1829, when the Ministry of Finance ordered that all black plowing peasant land was to be divided among the homesteads in proportion to the number of souls in each homestead. This equalization operation began in 1830-1831, and was carried through despite the bitter protests of the wealthier peasants, and the difficulties of deciding how much land should be included within each commune.

Communal repartition became standard practice on court-owned property in Central Russia during the eighteenth century. The peasants on the court lands in the eastern frontier provinces and in the North had not adopted it. Like the black plowing peasants, these people acted as if they were the owners of their land, selling it as they pleased to one another, and to outsiders. Inequalities in holdings appeared, and the poorer peasants demanded equalization. This was not carried out until after the creation in 1797 of the Department of the Appanage. One of the duties assigned the new bureau was to provide each appanage household with enough land to meet its needs. The

Department introduced repartition on appanage properties in Vologda in 1797, but proceeded much more slowly in other provinces. In Archangel communal repartition did not begin on appanage properties until 1812, in Perm in the thirties, and in Ufim and Orenburg only in the fifties.[27]

In appanage properties in other guberniias where repartition was already in use, but where the supply of land did not provide adequately for all the peasants, the Department arranged for exchanges among neighboring villages. Peasants with under-sized holdings could ask for land that belonged to another village that had a surplus. These demands for additional land dropped sharply after the introduction in the thirties of the new assessment system, for now more land meant heavier payments to the appanage administration.[28] Peasants in overcrowded villages could, at their request, have some of their number resettled on empty appanage land elsewhere and thereby relieve the pressure for land in the village.[29]

The *odnodvortsy*, the one-homesteaders of the old steppe frontier, also acted as if the state land on which they lived belonged to them. They bought, sold and exchanged it freely, despite specific governmental prohibitions of these transactions. Inequalities, of course, arose, and many *odnodvortsy* became landless or nearly so. In Kursk, for example, one out of every four *odnodvortsy* families had only the land on which their dwelling stood. Whenever they had the opportunity, these impoverished people complained about their condition, and urged that the government give them more land, or that all *odnodvortsy* land be divided equally. In the 1780's local officials took up this last proposal and recommended repartition. But higher authorities refused their approval unless all the *odnodvortsy* in a district consented to it. The government's reluctance stemmed in large part from the fact that many of the one-homesteaders still had the original charters awarded by earlier tsars to their ancestors for the land they held. It would have been both

[27] Semevskii, *Krest'iane*, II, 31-78.

[28] *Entsiklopedicheskii slovar*, xxxIVa, pp. 594-595. For the new assessment system v. pp. 496-497.

[29] *Svod udel'nykh postanovlenii*, II, sect. 161.

difficult and embarrassing for the regime to repudiate these grants. The many legislative acts of the eighteenth and nineteenth centuries that dealt with the *odnodvortsy*, however, revealed the official concern about the land problem among these people, primarily because of its adverse effect upon their ability to meet their tax and obrok payments.

As things turned out, direct state intervention proved unnecessary. The demands of the poorer *odnodvortsy* for equalization became so insistent in the last years of the eighteenth century that communities began to introduce it on their own initiative. Usually the wealthier peasants tried to head off repartition, but the tide—and the government—was against them. In some instances government representatives descended upon a community to propagandize for equalization and to organize a majority in its favor. But that assistance was not often needed. In district after district the poorer elements gained control, harassed opponents with all manner of inconveniences, warned them that they would receive poor land when redistribution was carried through, and threatened them with physical violence, and on occasion actually resorted to it. In a number of communities, however, the wealthier *odnodvortsy* supported equalization because their taxes had become disproportionate to the yield of their land, or because the principle of mutual guarantee which made them responsible for the taxes of poorer neighbors placed an intolerable burden upon them.

During the first half of the nineteenth century equalization spread rapidly; by the 1850's nearly half of the 1.9 million *odnodvortsy* had adopted some form of communal landholding and repartition. In some provinces the transition went faster than it did in others. In Tambov, for example, over four fifths of the one-homesteaders had made the shift by the end of the 1830's. The arrangements that were agreed upon varied. In certain districts the communes took over all the land and distributed it to each member homestead. In others only part was held communally, usually meadows and forests, and the rest continued as the permanent holdings of the individual families. In still other settlements some of the villagers pooled their land for communal distribution, while the others kept their holdings permanently.[30]

Even the small amount of government prompting in the adoption of the land equalizing commune among the *odno-dvortsy*, proved unnecessary among cossacks of the Don and colonists in Siberia. The peasants in those regions adopted the new system without official urgings, though the pressure of governmental obligations undoubtedly helped to persuade them in its favor. In both areas the changeover came later than it did elsewhere in the empire. In some places it was not carried through until the last part of the nineteenth century.

Cossacks first appeared on the broad, empty steppes of the Don in the sixteenth century. Initially they lived as pastoral nomads, dependent upon their flocks and upon hunting to fill their wants. They forbad settled tillage on pain of death, because they feared it would lead to the hated serfdom from which they had fled. (A nineteenth century British traveler suggested that the true reason for the ban was that most cossacks were "averse to all regular, laborious occupations.")[31] In time, however, they abandoned their old ways and became plowmen. In the beginning all their land had been common property. Each man used as much as he wanted. Then settlements formed and the land was divided between them, each *stanitsa*—as the settlement was called—laying claim to large stretches. Each homestead within a *stanitsa* was still able to till as much as it wanted, for the land was as yet thinly peopled. Then population increased, the amount of unoccupied land decreased, and inequalities in the size of holdings appeared. This gave rise to disputes, and sometimes to serious disorders. The state, meanwhile, demanded the same military obligation from each cossack, irrespective of the amount of land he had. The feeling grew among the poorer peasants that equality in responsibility should be reflected in equality in holdings. The pressure of their demands compelled the *stanitsa* to assume increasingly larger control over the distribution and alienation of holdings, until

---

[30] Simkhovitch, *Die Feldgemeinschaft*, pp. 74-81; Semevskii, *Krest'iane*, II, 729-762; Baranovich, *Materialy*, pp. 239-240; cf. Haxthausen, *Studien*, II, 74.
[31] Wallace, *Russia*, p. 361.

by the late nineteenth century communal repartition and equalization had become the accepted procedure in most cossack settlements.[32]

The pioneers in Siberia had settled in communal groups, but each family claimed as much land as it wanted and could do with it as it chose. The commune limited its functions to fiscal and administrative matters, settling disputes between its members, and keeping outsiders from settling in the area the commune members had staked out as their own. There was land enough for everyone. Then the increase in poulation created a greater demand for land, and inequalities in holding became a serious problem. The poorer peasants demanded restrictions on their wealthier fellows, and because the poor were in the majority their program was gradually adopted in commune after commune. The right of a homestead to have as much land as it wanted was amended to provide that, if it did not use the land for a certain period, it could be taken over by another homestead of the commune. At first, the period beyond which the land was lost if it lay untilled was as much as fifteen years, then it was reduced to three to five years, and finally land left unworked was declared forfeit immediately. Since wealthy peasants could afford to farm large areas, even if only superficially, it was still possible for one homestead to retain much land for itself. To prevent this the commune placed restrictions on the number of plows a homestead could use, or forbad the use of plows with more than one share, or put a limit on the total amount of arable one peasant could till. The alienation of holdings, hitherto entirely free, was allowed only if the commune gave its consent. Land that fell vacant through death or departure was distributed by the commune.

These and similar measures still did not satisfy the land hunger of the poor, and so communes began to take land from the wealthier peasants and give it to those who had less. This ultimately produced near-equality in the size of holdings within the individual communes. From this it was only a short step to general repartition of all the land in the commune's territory,

[32] *Ibid.*, pp. 361-363; Köppen, *Statistische Reise*, pp. 173-174; Kovalevskii, *Modern customs*, pp. 80-81.

[521]

although this was not accomplished without strong protests from the wealthier peasants.[33]

Although the land-equalizing commune spread through most of the empire in the eighteenth and nineteenth centuries, it did not prevail everywhere. It was conspicuously absent in the Little Russian provinces of Chernigov, Poltava, and part of Kharkov, despite the similarities between the peasants there and in other parts of the realm in communal background, and in pressures from state, seignior, and land-hungry villagers.[34] The people who had recolonized the region in the sixteenth and seventeenth centuries had settled as family communes. These organizations had persisted in certain places until the second half of the eighteenth century. By that time the communes had as many as seven or more conjugal families, who lived together as one household and operated one economy.[35] But usually the original patriarchal commune had broken down after a few generations into a number of individual homesteads, held together in a communal organization by their ties of common descent. The land continued to be held communally, and, as with the black plowing peasants of the North, each homestead's share depended upon its abstract share of the family patrimony. Repartitions were made periodically to adjust for changes in the size of the abstract shares held by the members, so that no homestead retained a piece of land permanently. In time, as in the North and for the same reasons, inequalities appeared. Then the practice of repartition was gradually abandoned (again as in the North), and by the last part of the eighteenth century most peasant households were the permanent possessors of their holdings. At this point the Little Russian experience diverged from that of the North. Instead of going back to communal control and equalization as happened with the black plowing peasants, in-

[33] Tschuprow, *Die Feldgemeinschaft*, pp. 115-133, Kulischer, *Russische Wirtschaftsgeschichte*, I, 244-249.

[34] The standard work on the commune in Little Russia was done by I. V. Luchitskii. He summarized his findings in French in "Etudes sur la propriété communale dans la Petite Russie," *Revue internationale de sociologie*, III (1895), and in German in "Zur Geschichte der Grundeigentumsformen in Kleinrussland," *Jahrbuch für Gesetzgebung, Verwaltung, und Volkswirtschaft*, XX (1896), XXI (1897).

[35] Cf. Keussler, *Zur Geschichte*, III, 105-122.

dividual landholding persisted. Each homestead continued in the possession of its specific holding, and no communal efforts were made to achieve equality in the amount of land held, or to provide landless peasants with holdings.

III

In the decades after the emancipation the land equalizing communes were often heralded as models of popular democracy in action. Donald Mackenzie Wallace, in Russia in the seventies, described them as "capital specimens of representative Constitutional government of the extreme democratic type." He went on to explain that he meant constitutional in the English sense, for, said he, the communes operated under "a body of unwritten, traditional conceptions, which have grown up and modified themselves under the influence of ever-changing practical necessity. . . . The Commune is, in fact, a living institution, whose spontaneous vitality enables it to dispense with the assistance and guidance of the written law."[36] Sir Donald's high praise echoed a view widely held among Russians—particularly intellectuals—of many political shadings.

The picture these men cherished of the mir as efficient and even-handed peasant self-government at work seems, however, to have been an idealized one. Certainly it does not square with the findings of a survey of state peasant villages made in the late 1830's by government inspectors. They reported that commune meetings often degenerated into drinking bouts. At elections of mir officials the successful candidate frequently turned out to be the man who bought the most drinks for the voters. The rich peasants in the commune generally did not run for office themselves. Instead, they backed others who, when elected, repaid their wealthy supporters by special favors, such as reductions in the payments they had to make. The clerk of the mir enjoyed much power and prestige, for often he was the only person in the commune who could read and write. Unfortunately, his learning was usually small and his palm easily crossed. As a result, in many communes the account books were in a state of confusion. That made it easier for dishonest officials to conceal

[36] Wallace, *Russia*, pp. 126-127.

their misuse or appropriation of the mir's assets. Sometimes these embezzlers stole just small amounts, but on occasion they gave full rein to their acquisitive instincts; the government inspectors discovered that in two communes in Vologda peculations amounted to 32,091 rubles.[37] Several decades earlier the vice-governor of Viatka, in a report, lamented the dishonesty of the clerks and elected officials in the communes of state and appanage peasants in that guberniia. He charged that they worked hand in hand with unscrupulous government officials, and that if a commune member complained about their dishonesty he was sent into the army as a recruit or was exiled to Siberia.[38]

In short, these communes, and since there is no reason to believe they were exceptional, probably many others, were not free of ills that, regrettably, have plagued popular democratic institutions in other times and in other lands.

Because there were so many village communes and so much variation in the functions and duties assigned them, only the broadest generalizations can be made about their internal organization and activities. The commune meetings seem to have been informal gatherings at which any villager could speak, but the right to vote was limited to the male heads of households. If a head of a household could not attend he could give his vote to a proxy, who could be a woman. Usually a simple majority was enough to carry a motion, but on important questions a majority of two thirds was considered necessary. The entire commune participated in arriving at most decisions. Certain matters such as the redistribution of holdings, arrangements of marriages, and provisions of guardians for orphans and the feeble-minded, were left to the discretion of the officials elected by the commune.

On privately owned land every act of the mir was subject to the review of the proprietor. He could cancel any of its decisions, could replace elected officials with men of his own choosing, could command repartition of holdings or forbid it, and, indeed, could disband the commune itself. But such actions

[37] Druzhinin, *Gosudarstvennye krest'iane*, I, 346-353.
[38] Schiemann, *Geschichte*, I, 393.

were exceptional. Normally the lord, even when he lived on his property and personally supervised its operation, allowed the mir much autonomy, conferred with its leaders before he introduced changes, and turned over to it much of the internal administration of the property. The mir officials apportioned the obligations the seignior demanded among its members in proportion to the amount and quality of land they had, or to their other sources of income. Since the fields were split into many strips worked by different households, communal tillage had to be practiced. That is, everyone had to perform the same operations in the fields at the same time. The mir decided what work was to be done in a field and when to do it. It had its own treasury, built up by levies on its members or by sale of communally produced goods, and used the money to care for its indigent, sick and aged members, and to rent and even buy land so that it would have more to parcel out. It usually determined the order in which its young men went into the army as recruits. Its officials assisted the proprietor in punishing minor infractions, and often he imposed severe penalties such as exile at their suggestion.[39]

On state land the government, in the first part of the nineteenth century, laid down a number of rules for the operation of communes. To begin with, it ordered the creation of mirs in every village of state peasants, though small settlements could choose to join the communes of neighboring larger places. The law ordered the land of the village to be held communally, and gave the mir the responsibility of dividing it among its members. The commune could rent additional state-owned land for its own uses, and with official permission could buy and exchange land with private persons, or rent part of its own land to outsiders.[40]

The periodic redistribution of communal land was the mir's most important function. The frequency of these repartitions fluctuated widely. Often they were carried out after each general revision. Some communes, however, made general redistribu-

[39] Wallace, *Russia*, pp. 127-133; Tschuprow, *Die Feldgemeinschaft*, p. 8; Semevskii, *Krest'iane*, I, 110-112, 255-256, 259-263; Miller, *Essai*, pp. 217-218.
[40] SZ, IX, sect. 664, 665, 668-671, 674-676.

tions at shorter intervals such as every six years, and even annual repartitions were not unknown.[41] Partial redistributions were made continuously to take care of minor changes, such as the establishment of a homestead by a newly married couple, or a change in the number of persons in one of the existing homesteads. Meadows were often redistributed more frequently than plowland, sometimes being divided anew each year.[42]

Repartitions seem to have been more common on properties where the peasants had to do barshchina, than on those where only obrok was demanded. A serfowner was likelier to change the nature and quantity of his demands when he was directly involved in the operation of his property. His decision to increase or decrease the area of land used for demesne production, or to introduce a new crop on the demesne, or to establish an industrial enterprise, affected the amount and nature of the dues the serfs had to pay, or the amount of land available for their use, and so occasioned a partial or general redistribution of holdings. When the peasants had only obrok to pay, the levy normally remained unchanged over relatively long periods, so that redistributions of land were likely to be less frequent.[43]

Most communes distributed the land to their members either according to the number of *tiaglo* units, or of adult male souls in each household. Serf villages, and particularly those on barshchina, often employed the former method, while serfs on obrok and state peasants preferred to divide their land according to the number of adult male souls in each homestead. Some communes employed a combination of the two methods.[44]

The actual division of the land was a difficult and complicated task. The commune officials had to split up the fields into pieces that were of approximately equal size and, more important, of equal productivity. To accomplish this they had to know the fertility, topography, accessibility, drainage, and every other pertinent fact about all of the commune's land. Then

[41] Buschen, "Die Freibauern," pp. 233-234.

[42] Baranovich, *Materialy*, p. 238; Köppen, *Statistische Reise*, p. 122; Wallace, *Russia*, p. 136.

[43] Baranovich, *Materialy*, pp. 237-238; Semevskii, *Krest'iane*, I, 115; Miller, *Essai*, pp. 328-330.

[44] Semevskii, *Krest'iane*, I, 95, 101-102.

they broke the communal acreage into a number of fields of equal quality, subdivided each of these fields into units of equal quality, and split each unit into strips of approximately the same size and shape. They distributed these strips to the households of the commune, each getting the number of strips appropriate to the number of souls or *tiaglo* units in the homestead. Thus, each *dvor* had its holding broken into separate parcels scattered through a number of fields.

In carrying through these complicated operations the peasants, who were ignorant of professional land measuring techniques, showed much skill and ingenuity. Trained surveyors and assessors checked the work of some of the mirs in Voronezh guberniia, and found it to be remarkably accurate.[45]

There were many variations in the techniques used by the communes to distribute holdings to their members. A description of the method used in Riazan in the 1850's, however, provides an illustration of the general line of procedure. In communes of state peasants in that province, after the mir officials had classified and divided the land, the males were split into groups of equal size. In a village of say 200 souls, four groups of 50 men each were formed. The groups drew lots to determine which fields it would get. Each group then divided the fields that it received into as many parts of equal value as there were souls in the group. Then the group's members drew lots to decide which of these pieces would be theirs. If the commune had an odd number of souls—say 203—the extra three had their land distributed to them individually. Serf communes in Riazan followed the same procedure, except that they made their divisions per *tiaglo* rather than per soul.[46]

IV

Communal repartition provided an equal amount of land for each soul or *tiaglo* in the commune. But each homestead did not necessarily have the same number of workers, so that the individual homesteads had holdings of different sizes. Similarly, in the villages that did not practice equalization the amount of

---

[45] Haxthausen, *Studien*, I, 125n., II, 124-126; Wallace, *Russia*, p. 136.
[46] Baranovich, *Materialy*, pp. 237-238.

land held by each homestead varied. There was, then, a considerable amount of disparity within each village, as well as
between villages, in the actual size of peasant holdings.

Data collected by the government, however, allow estimates
to be made of the average amount of land held by the individual
male peasant. V. I. Semevskii, using information gathered in
the last quarter of the eighteenth century for 20 provinces (13
in the non-black earth and 7 in the chernozem), concluded that
each male peasant on obrok had an average of 13½ desiatins,
including 4 desiatins of arable, and that each male peasant on
barshchina had 10.6 desiatins, including 3 desiatins of arable.
The average was smaller for barshchina peasants because seignioral demesne took up part of the land. Lords who demanded
only obrok had no demesnes so that all the land was available
for use by the peasants. Semevskii also found that the average
size of the holding per individual peasant in the thirteen non-
black earth provinces was larger than it was in the seven
chernozem guberniias, but that the amount of arable land per
peasant was less. He estimated the average size of the obrok
peasant's holding in the thirteen non-black earth provinces at
15.4 desiatins, including 3.8 desiatins of arable, and the average
per barshchina peasant at 11.2 desiatins, including 2.5 desiatins
of arable. In the seven chernozem provinces he set the average
holding per obrok peasant at 10.2 desiatins, including 4.4 desiatins of arable, and at 10 desiatins, including 3.5 desiatins of
arable, per barshchina peasant.[47]

Semevskii's estimates, however, have a strong upward bias.
His sources gave the area and peasant population of properties
and the nature of the obligations they had to pay. They did
not contain information on the actual amount of land each
homestead or peasant held. He arrived at his estimates by dividing the area of the properties on which there was obrok by
the number of peasants in these properties, and called the
quotient the average holding of the obrok peasant. He followed
the same procedure for properties that used barshchina, except
that he subtracted 1½ desiatins from the quotient to allow for
seignioral demesne. By following this method he included

[47] Semevskii, *Krest'iane*, I, 25-29, 32.

pastures, forests, and wastes in his estimates. But the peasants used the pastures in common, landlords normally retained forests, and the wastes went untilled and undivided.

More reliable, though still far from perfect, information was collected in the late 1850's by the Editing Commissions, who were charged with preparing the emancipation statutes. According to these data, which did not distinguish between the holdings of obrok and barshchina peasants, the average holding in the 43 provinces covered in the Commissions' study amounted to 3.2 desiatins per soul. The average tended to be slightly larger in the non-black earth provinces than in the chernozem; in most of the former guberniias the averages ran between 2½ and 3½ desiatins, while in the black earth they were between 2 and 3 desiatins.[48]

The mid-nineteenth century figures have sometimes been compared with Semevskii's estimates to show that there was a remarkably large decline during the last half century of serfdom in the average amount of land held by the individual peasant. The two sets of figures are, however, actually not comparable. The later averages, unlike those of Semevskii, are only for the land held by the peasant—his arable, meadow, and farmyard. Semevskii's inclusion of pastures, forests, and wastelands inevitably made his averages larger.

A partial comparison can be made, however, if it is limited just to the average amount of arable per soul in the two periods. Semevskii estimated the average arable at 4 desiatins for obrok peasants, and 3 desiatins for those on barshchina, in the 20 provinces for which he had information. In the mid-nineteenth century the average amount of arable per soul in 17 of the 19 provinces for which the data on arable is available, ranged from 1.6 to 2.5 desiatins (in the two others, Orenburg and Samara, the averages were 2.9 and 3.1 desiatins, respectively).[49]

[48] Red. Kom., *Pervoe izdanie*, VI, app. no. 3, Dopolnitel'nyi doklad . . . k no. 15. Another tabulation of the average size of holdings just before the emancipation, in which somewhat larger figures are given for most provinces than the ones contained in the Editing Commissions study, was presented in a government report of 1908. This report is condensed in Simkhovitch, "Russian Peasant," p. 585.

[49] Skrebitskii, *Krest'ianskoe dielo*, II, pt. 2, 1541-1551, III, 1278-1293. I computed the averages in the text, since the source gives only the average arable per *tiaglo* and the average number of persons per *tiaglo* in each province.

Of the 19 provinces for which I have computed the average arable per soul in the mid-nineteenth century, five are not among the 20 provinces for which Semevskii made estimates, so that the comparison is incomplete. Nonetheless, it indicates a decline in the average amount of arable per soul during the first half of the nineteenth century. It seems reasonable to assume from this that the average size of the entire peasant holding declined during these years. This probable but sometimes overestimated decrease has been attributed to a supposed increase in demesne, particularly in the chernozem, that lessened the amount of land available for distribution to the peasants, and to the increase in population. The assumed rise in seignioral production, however, is not supported by the available information (v. pp. 392-400); indeed, serfs were often shifted from barshchina to obrok, thereby making more land available for their own use.

Population growth, on the other hand, must have been chiefly responsible for the decline. In 20 provinces of the Central Industrial, Lake, and Central Agricultural regions for which comparable figures are available, the male serf population went up by 29 percent between the Fourth Revision in 1782-1783 and the Tenth in 1858.[50] By 1800 much of the land suitable for cultivation had been taken under the plow. Meanwhile communal repartition and equalization had become general among the serfs in these regions. Faced with the growing pressure of population, the only way the mirs could provide holdings for their increased memberships was to cut down on the size of allotments per soul or *tiaglo*. For example, the male serf population of the black earth province of Penza rose by 51 percent between the 4th Revision in 1782 and the 10th in 1858. During this same period the average amount of arable held by the individual male soul fell from 4.6 desiatins for obrok peasants, and 3.4 desiatins for barshchina peasants, to 2.3 desiatins. In Voronezh, another guberniia of the chernozem, serf population went up by 85 percent, while average arable per soul went down from around 5.5 to 2.5 desiatins.

[50] From 4.5 to 5.8 million.

The diminution in the average amount of land held by each soul did not necessarily mean that the peasantry's standard of living declined. The progress of regional specialization in the first half of the nineteenth century enabled the peasants north of the Oka to spend more time in non-agricultural activities, and so freed many of them from complete dependence upon the land. They occupied themselves in cottage industry and trade, and apparently often were better off than those who drew their livings entirely from agriculture. In fact, in some of these provinces land was apparently withdrawn from cultivation. The number of serfs in Smolensk in 1850 was only 8 percent greater than it had been in 1782. The average amount of arable per soul, however, dropped from 5.3 desiatins for obrok peasants and 3.3 desiatins for those on barshchina, to 2 desiatins. In Pskov serf population fell by 8 percent between these two dates. Yet the average amount of arable per soul, instead of going up, dropped from 4.8 and 3.5 desiatins for obrok and barshchina peasants, respectively, to 1.9 desiatins.[51]

In the black earth provinces there were fewer opportunities for non-agricultural employment, so that most serfs there could not use this way of making up losses in income that resulted from the reduction in the size of their holdings.

In addition to his land the peasant also had common rights in the use of pastures, forests, and streams. The pastures were run by the commune, while the rights to use woods and streams depended upon the wishes of the seignior. In many provinces the customary practice was for the lord to allow his serfs to take as much wood as they needed, or at least enough for fuel, and to catch as many fish as they could. In general, the serfs whose masters demanded only obrok had more freedom in the use of seignorial forests and streams than did those who had to perform barshchina.[52]

---

[51] Semevskii, *Krest'iane*, I, 492; Tsentral'nyi statisticheskii komitet, *Statisticheskiia tablitsy . . . za 1858 god*, pp. 272-273, for population figures. Semevskii, *Krest'iane*, I, 492-493, Skrebitskii, *Krest'ianskoe delo*, II, pt. 2, 1541-1551, III, 1278-1293, for averages of arable land.

[52] Skrebitskii, *Krest'ianskoe delo*, II, pt. 2, 1542-1551; Haxthausen, *Die ländliche Verfassung*, pp. 145-146, 149, 149-150n.; Le Play, *Les ouvriers*, II, 57-58.

In decrees of 1814 and 1827 the government ordered that a proprietor who wanted to borrow against his land but not against the serfs who lived on it, or wanted to sell the land but not the serfs, could not mortgage or sell all of it. He had to keep enough to provide at least 4½ desiatins for each peasant soul. If the mortgage or sale left the serfs with less, the seignior had to bring their holdings up to this minimum within a year. If he failed to do this the law ordered his serfs to be taken from him, converted into state peasants, and resettled on government property.[53] This legislation was provoked by instances such as that of a landlord in Tula who mortgaged 200 desiatins. His creditor foreclosed, and the 28 male souls and their families who lived on this property were left with just 10 desiatins.[54] These decrees seemed to carry the implication that the government considered 4½ desiatins per soul as the minimal size for a serf holding. But the state did not issue any laws that ordered all serfowners to provide their peasants with at least this amount of land.

The growth in the use of communal repartition and equalization brought about the near disappearance of the landless agricultural serf in most of the empire, for the mir's main purpose was to provide holdings for all of its members. A number of proprietors, however, who used all or much of their land for their own production, converted their peasants into field hands who worked full-time for their master. The master furnished these people with food, clothing, and a small money wage. Because they received these payments once a month they were known as *mesiachnye liudi*, monthly people. Soviet historians have sometimes indicated that there were many of these rural proletarians in the eighteenth century, and that their number rose during the first half of the nineteenth century.[55] Information from the latter part of the eighteenth century, and for the 1830's and 1850's, does not support this view, and shows further that in most places the serf field hands had small holdings of their own.[56] Only in Little Russia were there large numbers of

---

[53] *SZ*, 1857, IX, sect. 1107.   [54] Semevskii, *Krest'ianskii vopros*, II, 547.
[55] Liashchenko, *History*, pp. 314-315; Akademiia Nauk, *Istoriia*, II, 31.
[56] A. Bolotov in Vol'noe Ekonomicheskoe Obshchestvo, *Trudy*, 1766, pt. 2, 208;

landless farm serfs. On the eve of the emancipation they made up between 15 percent and 24 percent of the serf population there.[57] The explanation for this phenomenon is easy to find; the peasants of Little Russia did not practice communal repartition and equalization.

Inequalities in holdings, and landless peasants and cotters, seem to have been much more common among the non-seignioral peasantry than among the serfs. The total number of cotters and landless peasants in the latter part of the eighteenth century is unknown, but scattered data for the black plowing peasants indicate that it was large. In one district that had 602 souls in it 116 (19 percent) were landless, in another district with 504 souls 60 (12 percent) were cotters or landless, in a third district 54 (21 percent) out of 261 were in this category, in a fourth 79 (20 percent) out of 395, and so on.[58] In the mid-1830's, according to a report of the Ministry of State Domain, 63,000 state peasants (male souls) had no land, 56,740 had less than one desiatin, 212,000 had between 1 and 2 desiatins, and 275,000 had 2 desiatins or a bit more.[59] All together, these people made up over 7 percent of the total number of state peasants of that time.

By the middle of the nineteenth century, however, governmental action, and the spread of communal equalization among many non-seignioral peasants, had done much to correct this situation. Between 1839 and 1850 the Ministry of State Domain distributed 619,852 desiatins to peasants with small holdings and moved 131,657 male peasants from overcrowded state properties to less populous ones, so that they could be provided with larger allotments.[60]

Though comparative data are not available, the increase in the number of state peasants, and their adoption of communal equalization, undoubtedly produced a decline in the average size of their holdings during the first half of the nineteenth cen-

---

Skrebitskii, *Krest'ianskoe dielo*, ii, pt. 2, 1072; Povalishin, *Riazanskie pomeshchiki*, p. 43.

[57] Liashchenko, *Istoriia*, i, 574; cf. Domontovich, *Materialy*, table following p. 148.

[58] Semevskii, *Krest'iane*, ii, 665.

[59] "Obozrenie upravleniia," p. 473.

[60] *Ibid.*, p. 487.

tury. Yet, information collected in the last years of the 1850's by the Ministry of State Domain and by the Editing Commissions, reveal that the average holding of the state peasant in European Russia was over twice as large as the average holding of the serf. According to the data gathered in 43 provinces by the Ministry of State Domain, the average holding per soul was 6.6 desiatins. The Editing Commissions' average for 35 provinces was 6.1 desiatins. These averages were much inflated by the large size of state peasant holdings in the infertile provinces of the North where the peasants gained most of their income from forest industry, and in the fertile but still relatively sparsely settled border provinces. In Olonets, for example, the average was 18.5 desiatins per soul, and in Tauride, Orenburg, and Samara it was 12.7, 14.6, and 11.4 desiatins, respectively. The averages were much smaller in other provinces. But they were still larger than the averages for serf holdings. In most of the non-chernozem provinces the average amount of land per state peasant soul ran between 5 and 7 desiatins, compared with $2\frac{1}{2}$ to $3\frac{1}{2}$ for the serfs; in the chernozem the state peasant average was between 3 and 5 desiatins, and 2 to 3 desiatins for the serf.[61]

In some places, however, the average for the serfs exceeded that for the state peasants. A survey made in 1839-1840 found this to be the case in eight districts of Ekaterinoslav and in nine districts of Kharkov, and the Editing Commissions' data showed that the averages for serf holdings in Pskov and Iaroslav were slightly larger than the averages for state peasants.[62] These instances were very much the exceptions.

Illegal seizures of state peasant land by seigniors, mine owners, bureaucrats who used their office to enrich themselves, and even by merchants and townsmen, were sometimes responsible for decreases in the size of the holdings of the state peasants. Deputies of the black plowing peasants at the Legislative Commission of 1767 complained about these seizures, and later reports continued to tell of them. A community of state peasants in Kaluga lost 5,000 desiatins to neighboring private landowners, a village in Riazan had over 1,300 desiatins taken from it in 1821, another

---

[61] Skrebitskii, *Krest'ianskoe dielo*, II, pt. 2, 1541-1551.
[62] *Ibid.*, pp. 1548-1549, 1550-1551; Druzhinin, *Gosudarstvennye krest'iane*, I, 323.

community in Kiev lost 5,295 desiatins through land grabs by six proprietors, and so on. Legal actions brought by the injured peasants were costly, sometimes dragged on for decades through the bureaucratic maze, and then were usually settled in favor of the expropriators.[63] It also took more fortitude than most peasants possessed to go to law against a member of the ruling class, for the noble defendant might view such an action as insultingly presumptuous, and take direct action to teach the peasant "his place." Ivan Turgenev in one of his *Sportsman's Sketches* told of an incident of this sort that doubtless had many counterparts in real life. Ovsianikov, a prosperous *odnodvorets* of Orel, in conversation with a neighboring landlord speaks of a field that is part of this man's property: "It belongs to us—all of it, as it now stands, is ours. Your grandfather took it away from us; he rode out, pointed to it, said 'My property'—and took it. My father . . . wouldn't stand for this. . . . and entered a plea in court. He did it by himself for the others wouldn't join him. Your grandfather was told that 'Peter Ovsianikov is entering a complaint against you. . . .' Whereupon your grandfather immediately sent his huntsman, Bausch, with a gang. . . . And they grabbed my father and took him . . . to your home and flogged him right outside the windows. And your granddad stands on the balcony and watches; and your grandma sits beside the window and she watches, too. . . . Then they made my father promise to renounce the land and even made him say thanks for being let off with his life. And so the land remained yours. Go ahead and ask your peasants what that piece of land is called. It's called 'cudgel field' because it was taken with a cudgel. . . ."

63 Druzhinin, *Gosudarstvennye krest'iane*, I, 85, 86, 323-325.

25

REFORMERS, REBELS, AND
ABOLITIONISTS

AS PRECEDING CHAPTERS have shown, a paradoxical situation—paradoxical at least to our Western liberal ways of thinking—had developed in Russia in the era from Peter I to Alexander II. On the one hand, commerce made important advances, the factory form of production became increasingly common, and an industrial proletariat was called into being. On the other hand, during these same years the social structure of the empire retrogressed. The nobility emerged as a self-conscious class and established itself as the dominant group in society, while the mass of the people were either reduced to an unfree status, or if already in a servile condition had their positions worsened.

This mixture of modernity and medievalism seemed to provide a workable social organization. The empire expanded enormously in area and population; it became one of the major powers of the world; and it successfully withstood challenges from within and without. But as time went on, some people detected serious faults in the system that made them doubt its continued ability to survive. Above all else, they were concerned about serfdom, the central feature of the entire social order. Sooner or later, all of these people came to the conclusion that unless serfdom was reformed or abolished Russia faced certain disaster.

These critics of the existing order can be divided into three separate groups; the tsars and members of the topmost levels of the bureaucracy, the peasantry, and the intellectuals. Though they were all united in a common cause, each of these groups was motivated by different considerations, each employed different tactics in working for change, and each played a separate and distinctive part in bringing about the final abolition of serfdom.[1]

[1] Semevskii, *Krest'ianskii vopros*, is the standard work on the activities and

Beginning in the second half of the eighteenth century and continuing on in the next century, men who held high offices and who sat in the councils of the tsars, warned that serfdom held great dangers for the state. Some of them drew up specific proposals to remedy the evils that they saw and feared. But the implementation of these schemes, or their abandonment, depended upon the tsar. So great was the power and prestige of the emperor that his character and personal convictions were the decisive factors in every major decision of the government. If he was interested in reform, changes were made. If his interest flagged, the efforts at reform collapsed.

Until the reign of Catherine II the sovereigns of Russia had not evidenced any serious or sustained concern about improving the lot of the peasantry. The youthful Catherine, influenced by the Enlightenment, while still a grand duchess had written that it was "contrary to the Christian religion and to justice to make slaves of men (who are all free by birth)," and hailed Liberty as "the soul of everything; without Thee everything is dead."[2] When she became empress she talked and wrote about the pressing need to better the condition of the serfs. Nor did she miss the opportunity to advertise her enlightenment in imperishable stone for the benefit of posterity; the epitaph she chose for her tomb stated that "When she had ascended the throne of Russia, she wished to do good, and tried to bring happiness, freedom, and prosperity to her subjects."[3]

Princes have long been notorious for the gap between their words and their deeds, but surely few among the mighty have matched Catherine's hypocrisy. During her reign, and at her command, serfdom became more oppressive than it had ever been, and was introduced into parts of her realm where it had hitherto been unknown. Henry Shirley, secretary of the British legation at Catherine's court, described her well in a dispatch to London when he wrote that ". . . the Empress's intentions, at

---

ideologies of these critics. Surveys in English can be found in Mavor, *Economic History*, I, 311-417; Dodge, *Abolitionist Sentiment, passim*; Venturi, *Roots*, pp. 1-204. Since these are available I have not attempted an exhaustive summary in the following pages.

2 *SIRO*, VII (1871), p. 84.

3 Reddaway, *Documents*, p. xxvi.

first, were to show what pains She took to render Her subjects happy, but as these intentions did not proceed from principles of the purest nature, Her actions like false pearls have more éclat but less value than the genuine one."[4]

It has sometimes been argued that Catherine could not introduce reforms in the first part of her reign for fear of alienating the nobility to whom she owed her throne and upon whom she depended for support. Later, when she felt more secure, she was supposedly frightened by the excesses of the Pugachev rising and then by the outbreak of the French Revolution, and decided that change would lead only to disorder and unrest. This would make it appear that Catherine personally inclined to reform but was restrained by circumstances beyond her control. In actual fact, members of the nobility, among them men of the highest rank and office and ardent supporters of the empress, pressed reforms upon her. None of their proposals asked for the abolition of serfdom. Rather, they wanted only to put some limits on the authority of the landowners over their serfs in order to help the peasants, and thereby raise the welfare and strength of the state.[5] To all of these suggestions Catherine turned a deaf ear, even when they involved such relatively minor changes as forbidding the breakup of a serf family through sale.

To give the empress her due, she did permit, and indeed encouraged, discussions of the need for changes, even if she took no positive action. To this extent her reign represented progress over what had gone before. But Tsar Paul, her far less renowned successor, actually accomplished much more than she did. During his brief and troubled tenure on the throne he evinced no interest in any basic reforms in serfdom,[6] the censorship forbad the publication of any discussion of the peasant problem, and Paul commanded all serfs under threat of heavy punishment to give complete obedience to their masters in all things.[7] Yet this

---

[4] Shirley to Viscount Weymouth, St. Petersburg, 28 Feb. (10 Mar.) 1768, *SIRO*, XII (329). Shirley, in this dispatch, was reporting on the Legislative Commission convened by Catherine.

[5] For these proposals v. Semevskii, *Krest'ianskii vopros*, I, 22 ff.

[6] While heir apparent Paul had tried to introduce reforms at Gatchina, his personal estate, including converting the peasants there into leaseholders. Semevskii, *Krest'iane*, II, 146-147.

[7] *PSZ*, XXIV, no. 17769, 29 Jan. 1797, pp. 305-306.

capricious and unhappy tyrant was responsible for the first positive restrictions upon the serfowners. He outlawed barshchina on Sunday, and he prohibited the sale of serfs without land in Little Russia. Both decrees were often disobeyed, but they proved to be the turning point in the history of the lord-peasant relation. Up to Paul's reign the status of the peasantry had steadily deteriorated as a consequence of imperial legislation. From his time on the current ran the other way.

Paul's son Alexander while still heir to the throne had won a reputation as a person of liberal tendencies, and emancipation of the serfs was believed to be one of his most cherished ambitions. When he was crowned emperor in 1801 great things were expected of him. A number of his closest friends and advisers held liberal views, too, and urged agrarian reforms on him. In their discussions, and in the plans they drew up for his approval, they argued that serfdom had become an anachronism that damaged the best interests of the country, that it destroyed the creative energies of the people, held back economic growth, and that it stirred up popular unrest that could endanger the very existence of the state. They pointed out that the peasants looked to the tsar as their protector against their masters, and that he must act in their behalf if only to show them that he was indeed thinking of them. They warned, too, that the infiltration of Western ideas of civil liberties fed the springs of discontent and made for a potentially explosive situation.[8]

Yet, despite his own good intentions and the counsels of his intimates and of high officials, Alexander did little to help the Russian peasantry. His liberalism, like that of his grandmother Catherine, turned out to be a fashionable outer garment that he could easily doff. He was undoubtedly troubled by some of the crueller aspects of serfdom, and perhaps even by its very existence. But he lacked either the determination, or else the genuine desire, to institute reforms. He could be weak and indecisive, so that it was not difficult for men of firmer convictions to persuade him that changes were impractical, and that the serfowners, who were the truest servants of the autocracy, would be vastly disturbed by innovations that reduced their

[8] Dodge, *Abolitionist Sentiment*, pp. 134-136, 175-196.

powers over their peasants. Nor did Alexander seem at all disinclined to allow the peasant question to be shunted aside, while he busied himself with administrative reorganization of institutions of the central government and with the problems of international war and diplomacy.

His reign was not without its achievements, however. Soon after his accession he formed an "unofficial committee" of himself and four of his liberal friends to draw up plans for reform in the political and social order. The committee, which met from June 1801 to the end of 1803, discussed the peasantry, and agreed that its condition had to be improved. But it made no positive recommendations. Its single accomplishment in the area of agrarian legislation was the law of 12 December 1801 that permitted merchants, townsmen, and state peasants to buy unoccupied land.

This decree obviously gave no aid to serfs, but Count S. P. Rumiantsev, one of Alexander's close advisers, saw a way to employ it that he believed would promote emancipation. In a memorandum to the tsar he pointed out that now that the law allowed commoners to own land, the government should encourage serfs to buy their freedom and their holdings from their masters. The price and terms of payment would be fixed by voluntary agreement between buyer and seller. Rumiantsev claimed his plan would prove so advantageous to all concerned that it would be widely used, and so would lead to the eventual disappearance of serfdom. "This law," he wrote, "will be for us the initial reform, surpassing the accomplishments of Peter the Great. Now, without anxiety and without any fear, it is possible to begin the gradual destruction of serfdom, which is nothing other than actual and dreadful misery."[9]

Alexander was attracted by the voluntary character of the scheme, and made it the basis for a decree he issued on 20 February 1803. The new law allowed serfs who wanted to buy their freedom and land to deal directly with their masters, as individuals or as a commune. Once the transaction was completed the enfranchised peasants were to be enrolled in a new class called the "free farmers," and become members of the state

[9] Korf, "Imperator Nikolai," p. 105.

peasantry. They could do as they liked with their holdings, except split them into parcels smaller than eight desiatins. Those peasants who failed to carry out the terms of their agreements with their former masters were to revert to their previous condition of servitude.[10]

When the decree was promulgated Minister of Interior V. P. Kochubei informed the governors of the provinces that the new law was in no wise intended to undermine the existing state of affairs.[11] Kochubei's statement wanted in candor. Men in high places hoped that the free farmer act would indeed alter existing conditions by promoting a gradual emancipation. But as things turned out Kochubei proved entirely accurate. There was neither willingness on the part of the landowners to part with their land, nor money in the purses of the peasants to pay for it. During Alexander's reign the law was used only 160 times, and in Nicholas's reign about 250 times. At the Tenth Revision in 1858 the free farmers numbered just 151,895 males, or less than 1.5 percent of the total male serf population.[12] That was the answer time gave to Rumiantsev's naive prophecy.

The average cost of redemption paid by free farmers during Alexander's reign was around 127 rubles, and 115 rubles when Nicholas was tsar. Twenty-six landowners freed a total of 7,631 serfs without charging them anything, and a few others arranged for their former serfs to make their payments to charitable institutions. Data on the amount of land redeemed by about 65,000 of the free farmers show they purchased an average of around six desiatins per male soul.[13] The very scanty information indicates that they continued to operate their lands communally. In some of their villages the size of a family's holding was scaled to the amount of money the family had contributed in purchasing the village's freedom and land. In others the land continued to be divided according to the number of souls or of *tiagla* in each household.[14]

---

[10] *PSZ*, XXVII, no. 20620, pp. 462-463.   [11] Dodge, *Abolitionist Sentiment*, p. 166.

[12] Engelmann, *Die Leibeigenschaft*, pp. 182-183; Veshniakov, *Krest'iane-sobstven-niki*, pp. 61-65.

[13] Semevskii, *Krest'ianskii vopros*, I, 265-267, II, 207, 210-213; Mikhalevich, *Materialy*, pp. 169-170; Engelmann, *Die Leibeigenschaft*, p. 182.

[14] Semevskii, *Krest'ianskii vopros*, II, 220-221; Haxthausen, *Studien*, I, 104-105.

The "free farmer" law obviously fell far short of the hopes held for it. But Alexander had a much more successful accomplishment to his credit. Through his decrees over 400,000 male serfs and their families in the Baltic provinces won their freedom.

In the 1680's the Swedish government had carried out a "reduction" of the rights and property of nobles throughout the Swedish empire.[15] When Peter I took Lifland and Estland from the Swedes in the Great Northern War, he immediately set about restoring these privileges to the landlords there. Encouraged by the attitude of Peter and his successors, the Balt proprietors made increasingly heavy demands of their serfs. Then, in the last decades of the eighteenth century a large sector of the seignioral class became advocates of reform. Some had become infected with the new liberal ideas of the West, and, perhaps more important, the increase in rural unrest persuaded many of them that time was running out for the old system. In 1795 the Livonian diet accepted a reform plan advanced by Count F. W. Sievers, marshal of the provincial nobility and liberal leader. The proposal was sent forward to Paul for his approval, but he pigeonholed it. When Alexander became tsar Sievers resubmitted the plan, and after some amendment it became law by the imperial ukase of 20 February 1804. For the first time in history a Russian tsar had issued a decree designed to make general improvements in the condition of serfs.

The law did not free the peasants. Instead, it allowed them certain privileges such as the hereditary right to the use of their holdings, and it provided for the careful regulation of their obligations according to the quantity and quality of land they held. The decree satisfied neither lords nor peasants. Liberal nobles felt that it had not gone far enough, for serfdom had not been abolished. They objected, too, because they considered the grant of hereditary use of seignioral land to the peasants to be a violation of the property rights of the landlords. Serfowners complained also about the expense and difficulty involved in making the surveys needed to establish accurate norms for the

[15] Cf. Heckscher, *Economic History*, pp. 117-128.

obligations of the peasants. Finally, the serfs were disappointed because they had not received their long-hoped-for freedom.

Meanwhile, the Estonian diet in 1802 and 1803 had accepted much the same plan of reform, and Alexander had given it his formal approval on 27 August 1804. When, however, the Estonians saw how much trouble and expense their Livonian neighbors were put to in carrying out the reform, and how unpopular it was, they thought it would be better to go all the way. They decided to free their serfs, but without providing them with any land. Alexander gave his approval to this action in 1811, but did not proclaim it as law until 23 March 1816.

The seigniors of Courland, unlike their fellows in the two other Baltic provinces, did not initiate any reform plans. Alexander took the initiative in August 1814 when he instructed the governor-general of that province to appoint a commission of nobles who would draw up proposals for changes. The commission presented the tsar with a plan modelled after the Livonian law of 1804. Alexander then ordered the diet of the province to choose between this proposal and landless emancipation. By an overwhelming majority of 236 to 9 the diet voted for the latter alternative, and on 25 August 1817 an imperial ukase freed the serfs of Courland without land.

The emancipations in Estland and Courland persuaded the Livonian serfowners to replace the unsatisfactory law of 1804 with a landless emancipation. In 1818 the diet there set up a commission to work this out, and on 26 March 1819 Alexander gave his official consent to the plan presented to him.[16]

The liberty given the Baltic peasants was not complete. In Lifland, for example, the freedman had to wait fourteen years before he gained full civil rights, and even then could not travel or settle wherever he wished. Still, serfdom was gone, and many benefits were expected to follow from its abolition. The liberal Balt proprietors saw no harm in emancipating the serfs without land, for now the freed peasants had the right of contract, and so could lease land from a noble or take employment as a hired hand, as they wished. The tsar was especially pleased. He viewed

16 Transehe-Roseneck, *Gutsherr*, pp. 203-225; Tobien, "Zur Geschichte," XXVII, 276-301; Seraphim, *Baltische Geschichte*, pp. 338-339, 359-363.

the reform as a model for the rest of the empire and as a beginning of a nationwide abolition of serfdom. When the Livonians submitted their proposal to him in 1819 he told them, "I am indeed glad to see that the nobles of Lifland have come up to my expectations. You have provided an example that deserves to be imitated; you have acted in the spirit of our century, and you have felt deeply that the welfare of the people can be established only upon liberal principles."[17]

The sanguine expectations of sovereign and seigniors were destined to quick disappointment. The freeing of the Baltic peasants naturally provoked some interest and comment in other parts of the empire, but on the whole it made very little impression.[18] The three provinces were in a geographically isolated, small corner of the realm, with their own institutions and their own histories, languages, and cultures. Events there were of scant interest to Russians; to them the Baltic provinces were a foreign land. But most important, the reform itself turned out to be a failure. The vaunted advantages of freedom of contract proved illusory, and the peasants, deprived of their lands, could not make ends meet. Fresh waves of rural unrest swept the provinces, and the economy and social structure of the region tottered. Instead of serving as a model for the rest of the empire the Baltic emancipations became the example of what should not be done. In 1842 Tsar Nicholas in a talk to his Council of State declared that freed peasants must be allowed to keep their land "in order to avoid the unsatisfactory situation that now exists in the Baltic provinces—a situation which has brought the peasants there to a most pitiable condition."[19]

Nicholas, who succeeded his brother in December 1825, was supposed to have been a man of implacable will who knew what he wanted and how to get it. "Strong in force of mind and firm in resolve" was the way the Prussian ambassador to St. Petersburg characterized him.[20] He seems to have been reasonably normal in his personal behavior and appetites, and he was

[17] Schnitzler, *Les institutions,* I, 363.
[18] Engelmann, *Die Leibeigenschaft,* pp. 192-193.
[19] Korf, "Imperator Nikolai," p. 116.
[20] Stupperich, *Die Anfänge,* p. 82.

certainly devoted to the welfare of his country. Unfortunately, he was infatuated with military life of the spit-and-polish garrison variety. He once explained that his greatest pleasure was "to talk to my beloved soldiers, to know their needs, to assure myself of their schooling and progress—nothing interests me so much."[21] His idea of military schooling, however, was to produce soldiers so perfectly drilled that they resembled automatons. (Even then some of his highest officers were not satisfied. "Very good," Grand Duke Michael, younger brother of the tsar, once said of a regiment after having kept it for one hour at present arms, "only *they breathe!*")[22]

The tsar's preoccupation with his troops was harmless enough, though he did waste a great deal of his time in petty details of military administration. The trouble was that he wanted to run the empire as if it were an army command. Since many people, and especially men of spirit and intellect, resent living out their lives under the rule of a martinet, Nicholas wound up as one of Russia's most hated sovereigns.

From the very outset of his reign Nicholas made it clear that he believed that serfdom had to be reformed.[23] It is just possible that he could have acquired this conviction as part of his early education. Heinrich Storch, economist and one of the first popularizers of Adam Smith in Russia, had been selected to tutor young Nicholas and his brother Michael in political economy. Storch considered serfdom an insuperable barrier to national economic development,[24] and since he felt he would betray the trust put in him if, as he said, he presented "the delicate questions with which political economy is sometimes concerned. . . . in any light other than that of truth and of reason,"[25] he doubtless taught his opinions to his royal pupils. But whether Nicholas learned his lessons is another question—the future emperor did not distinguish himself as a student.

It is perfectly clear, however, that once on the throne Nicholas firmly believed that reform was essential to preserve the security

21 Grunwald, *Tsar Nicholas*, pp. 79, 81.   22 Kropotkin, *Memoirs*, p. 10.

23 Cf. Zablotskii-Desiatovskii, *Graf P. D. Kiselev*, II, 2; Korf, "Imperator Nikolai," p. 115; Engelmann, *Die Leibeigenschaft*, p. 209.

24 Cf. e.g., Storch, *Cours*, IV, 262 ff.

25 *Ibid.*, I, ix.

of the realm. At the time of his accession rural disturbances had broken out, and peasant unrest remained endemic throughout his reign. And though it had happened well before his time, Nicholas could not forget the peasant revolt led by Pugachev. The tsar feared, with much justification, that unless something was done to head it off, another great jacquerie was certain to sweep across the land.

He put the blame for the unrest squarely upon the serfowners who, he claimed, mistreated their peasants. Twice within the first ten months of his reign he denounced seigniors who handled their serfs harshly as un-Christian, and as disloyal subjects. He warned them that he was going to keep an eye on their behavior toward their peasants and would punish wrongdoers.[26] He returned to this theme on a number of occasions in the years that followed. His ordinances protecting the peasant against specific abuses by their lords,[27] and the increase in the number of properties placed under guardianship, give evidence that he meant what he said. He also accused serfowners of engendering peasant discontent by giving their serfs what he termed "higher education unsuited for their station, thereby developing in them a new level of understanding that made their status still more burdensome."[28]

Despite these and other statements, despite his commitment, and despite his reputation for resolution, Nicholas showed as much vacillation on the peasant problem as had his brother Alexander. He could not bring himself to take decisive action. He apparently had a built-in repugnance for any kind of change. He would have liked best of all for time to stand still. His reverence for tradition explains in large part his determination not to curtail the prerogatives of the dvorianstvo by agrarian reform. He recoiled even from minor limitations, such as fixing a maximum for the obligations that could be asked of household serfs. "That would be a violation of the rights of the proprietor," said Nicholas.[29] In an address to the delegates of the nobility of St. Petersburg he explained that he was already on record as

26 Engelmann, *Die Leibeigenschaft*, p. 209.
27 Leontovitsch, *Geschichte*, pp. 105-106.
28 Korf, "Imperator Nikolai," p. 115.
29 Miliukov, *Histoire*, II, 768.

having said that all of the land belonged to the nobility. "That," he continued, "is a holy thing and no one can encroach upon it."[30] In part, too, his concern about the rights of the dvorianstvo may well have stemmed from his fear that any effort to decrease these privileges could react against the throne itself. A discontented nobility might decide to seek new powers for itself at the expense of the autocrat, as compensation for the powers it had lost.

The problem of how to make reforms without clipping the privileges of the nobility was just one horn of Nicholas's dilemma. The other was his conviction that new waves of peasant discontent would be set off by public discussions of reform proposals. Such discussions, he thought, would raise the hopes of the peasants unduly, make them more impatient than they already were, and lead them to expect greater changes than the tsar thought could be made. Nicholas was by nature a worrier; as his Foreign Minister, Count Nesselrode, once said, he inclined "always to see black."[31] His anxieties were fed by the unbroken chain of rural disturbances, and by reports such as the one submitted in 1839 by his trusted Chief of Police, Count Benckendorff, who informed him that "the common people are not as they were twenty-five years ago. . . . The entire soul of the people turns to one goal, to liberation. . . . Serfdom is a powder barrel under the state, and is all the more to be feared because the army is made up of peasants, and now is officered by a huge mass of landless nobles who are driven by ambition and, since they have nothing to lose, rejoice over every disorder."[32]

The tsar revealed his frustration and perplexity in an address to the Council of State on 30 March 1842 when he said:[33] "There is no question that serfdom, as it now exists among us, is an evil, palpable and evident to everyone, but to touch it now would be even more disastrous. The late Emperor Alexander, at the beginning of his reign, had intentions to give freedom to the serfs, but later he gave up this idea entirely as

[30] *Russkaia Starina*, XXXIX, Sept. 1883, p. 595.
[31] Stupperich, *Die Anfänge*, p. 81.
[32] Shchepetov, *Krepostnoe pravo*, p. 236; Nifontov, *Rossiia*, p. 13.
[33] Korf, "Imperator Nikolai," pp. 114-115.

premature and impossible of execution. I, too, will never do it. reckoning that if the time when it will be possible to take this measure is still far distant, then all talk about it at present is nothing other than a criminal attempt upon the general peace and on the welfare of the state. The Pugachev rising shows how far peasant violence is able to go. . . . But if the present situation is such that it cannot continue, and if at the same time, decisive measures to end it are not possible without general commotion, then it is necessary at least to prepare the way for a gradual transition to another order of things, and without being afraid of change, calmly consider its usefulness and its consequences. It is not necessary to give freedom, but it is necessary to work out a way to a transitional stage. . . ."

The eruption of revolutions in 1848 created still more apprehensions in Nicholas's mind. He bristled and fumed at the thought of men who dared to challenge established authority. He could not even abide their lingo: on a report from one of his ministers that ended with the word "progress," he furiously scrawled "Progress? What progress? This word must be deleted from official terminology!"[34] The revolutions undoubtedly took some of the edge from his interest in reform, but the implication sometimes made that they dissuaded him from all plans for change is not accurate, as his actions after 1848 showed.

Nicholas liked to deal with major problems by creating secret *ad hoc* committees of his counselors to study a specific problem and make recommendations to him. During the thirty years of his reign he appointed ten such committees to work on the peasant problem, the first one in 1826 and the tenth in 1854. Some of them met regularly over a period of years, and others held only a few sessions. Though several laws intended to aid the peasantry resulted from their deliberations, the work of all of the committees proved ineffective. This is scarcely surprising in view of the emperor's conviction—shared by nearly all of the committeemen—that the rights of the serfowners should not be damaged, and that sweeping reforms must be avoided.

The third of the ten committees produced a scheme that was embodied in the decree of 2 April 1842. This allowed serfs to

[34] Masaryk, *Spirit*, I, 113.

make agreements with their proprietors by which they received their freedom and the right to till a piece of seignioral land, in return for dues and services they continued to pay the landowner. The payments were to be set in the agreement between lord and peasant and could be in money, kind or labor. The landowner would continue to have a considerable amount of administrative and police powers over his former serfs. The peasants who gained their freedom by these arrangements were to be put in a new category called "obligated (*obiazannye*) peasants."[35]

Nicholas and his advisers considered this law an improvement over the Free Farmer act of 1803, in that the earlier legislation had allowed peasants to get title to land that had belonged to their seigniors. The tsar felt he had made a real contribution, and anticipated that much use would be made of the decree. But only three proprietors took advantage of its terms. Together they freed a total of 24,708 male souls.[36]

The fourth and fifth secret committees discussed the problem of domestic serfs, and from their deliberations came two decrees in 1844 that permitted these people to purchase their freedom without land. Neither of these laws had any perceptible effect. The seventh committee, set up in 1847, studied the possibility of allowing serfs to buy their freedom if their village was sold at auction. Alexander I in 1824 had given this privilege to the peasants of Georgia, then not yet fully conquered by Russia, and Baron Korf, one of Nicholas's closest advisers, had suggested to the tsar that it might be extended to all peasants. After due consideration the committee recommended this, and Nicholas issued the appropriate decree on 6 November 1847. The new law required the peasants to buy the entire property; if the price they paid did not cover the entire debt for which the property was sold they had to assume responsibility for the unpaid part; and they were to receive no government assistance in financing the purchase. Under these circumstances it seemed highly unlikely that many serfs would be able to take advantage

35 *SZ*, 1857, IX, sect. 951-962.
36 Korf, "Imperator Nikolai," pp. 115-116; Semevskii, *Krest'ianskii vopros*, I, xliii.

of the law. Yet the decree aroused such a clamor of opposition from members of the nobility that the government felt it had to amend it. In 1849 it was changed to read that peasants could buy their freedom at these auctions only if their masters approved. This, of course, made it even more difficult for serfs to take advantage of the decree. Altogether, a total of only 964 male souls freed themselves by its terms.[37]

Nicholas's efforts, though, were not all unsuccessful. Under his aegis conditions among the state peasantry were much improved. Interest in raising the welfare of these people had been expressed in the eighteenth century as a way of increasing state revenues, but little had been accomplished then or later.[38] Some of Nicholas's advisers pointed out to him that a reorganization of the state lands and peasantry offered the best place to embark upon agrarian reform. Following their advice he established the Ministry of State Domain to carry out a program of improvement, and put the new bureau in charge of Count P. D. Kiselev. The agency began its operations on 1 January 1838. Kiselev had long been interested in the agrarian problem and in 1834 had presented Nicholas with a comprehensive plan for bettering the condition of the state peasantry. He conceived his mission as head of the Ministry to be the creation of a prosperous and responsible class of landed, free peasants, and to show the serf-owners of the empire the benefits to be gained from an enlightened peasant policy. He inaugurated an ambitious program aimed at bettering just about every aspect of state peasant life. Some of his plans never got beyond the paper stage, and others foundered on bureaucratic inefficiency and corruption, the suspicion of the peasants, and their resentment at the element of compulsion involved in many of the Ministry's schemes. But Kiselev managed to accomplish much in the eighteen years he headed the bureau. To him, and to Nicholas who trusted and supported him, belong the credit for a genuine and successful effort to better the lot of the Russian peasant.

Nicholas's government was responsible, too, for the reintro-

---

[37] Semevskii, *Krest'ianskii vopros*, II, 109-134, 154-161, 195-207.
[38] Druzhinin, "Gosudarstvennye krest'iane v . . . proektakh 1800-1833 gg.," pp. 149 ff.

duction of inventories in the provinces annexed from Poland, though, as was pointed out on an earlier page, this policy was not inspired primarily by an interest in helping the peasants. Instead, it was motivated chiefly by the government's desire to weaken the Polish Catholic lords who had lost favor in St. Petersburg after the Polish insurrection of 1831, and to win for the crown the loyalty of the peasant masses. Nicholas also issued decrees that forbad serfdom in Bessarabia, acquired by Russia in 1812, and in the land of the Black Sea Cossacks, and gave his approval to changes recommended by Baltic landowners designed to improve the condition of the peasantry in that region.

Finally—and this was his greatest achievement—Nicholas's never-ceasing preoccupation with the agrarian question readied the empire for ultimate emancipation. By the time he died in 1855 it was clear that reform was inevitable. For that realization Nicholas, more than any other man, was responsible. In his speech to the Council of State on 30 March 1842 he said that though reform was not then possible it was essential "to prepare the way . . . to another order of things." He accomplished precisely that, despite his fears, his hatred of change, and his despotism. His laws did precious little to help the peasant, but they established the principle that the serf was the subject of the tsar as well as the property of an individual. His unshakeable conviction that the continued existence of serfdom menaced the power and well-being of the state profoundly influenced the people about him, including some—among them his son and heir—who had originally opposed changes. The constant discussions he initiated among his top advisers about reform gave them valuable training and experience in the problems of serfdom, and among other things convinced them that when the time for emancipation came the peasants had to be freed with land.

II

The peasants were the second of the three groups arrayed against serfdom. Their record of opposition, of course, was far older than that of the tsars and the bureaucracy and the intellectuals. They had always been against it. But their servile

status, their dispersion, and their lack of leadership, had prevented them from mounting an effective campaign to destroy it.
The only way they could manifest their discontent was by flight
and by sporadic outbursts of disobedience and violence. Into the
nineteenth century these tactics had given the government much
trouble, but had not succeeded in persuading the rulers of the
empire that reform was necessary. Then, in the reigns of
Nicholas and Alexander II rural unrest reached proportions
that thoroughly frightened the tsars and their counselors, and
convinced them that changes designed to still peasant discontent
had to be made.

The peasants themselves never presented a work-out program
of reform. Their protests were essentially negative. They fled
from or revolted against specific injustices, such as increases in
the obligations demanded by their seigniors, cruel treatment,
the sale of their fellows for recruit substitutes, seizures by their
masters of their personal property, or reductions in the size of
their holdings. Nor was their discontent directed against the
tsar and the autocracy. On the contrary, they cherished the
sovereign and thought him their protector. Their enemies were
the seigniors who, they believed, gave the tsar evil counsels, kept
a knowledge of the true state of affairs from him, and circum-
vented the orders he gave to raise the peasantry from their
lowly condition.

Flight continued to be the most common form of protest. Just
between 1719 and 1727 the far from complete official sources
showed around 200,000 fugitives.[39] Not only individuals or
families but entire villages took off. Some of the runaways did
not go very far, while others travelled great distances to start new
lives in the Urals, Siberia, along the lower reaches of the Volga,
or in New Russia. Many in the western provinces crossed the
border into Poland, then still independent. According to complaints voiced by nobles at the Legislative Commission in 1767,
50,000 serfs of both sexes had fled to Poland from Smolensk
guberniia alone. The serfowners of these western provinces

[39] Pavlenko, "O nekotorykh storonakh," p. 398.

rejoiced when the partitions of Poland moved the frontiers much farther to the west.[40]

Flight did not always bring freedom. Often the fugitives settled on the land of some other seignior and so gained nothing, except that perhaps the new master demanded less from them. Sometimes they found themselves serfs of their old master from whom they had fled, as did runaways from the Spaso-Evfimev Monastery who settled on empty land in Penza and Simbirsk. The monastery discovered their whereabouts, and instead of bringing back the fugitives preempted the land on which they had settled. Others who went to the Urals and took employment in the industries there, found themselves assigned to the plant in which they worked. Those who got as far as Siberia, however, became state peasants and never reverted to serfdom. Local officials there were supposed to return the runaways to their owners, but the need for colonists outweighed the property rights of the serf-owners. In fact, the authorities in Siberia did everything they could to help the fugitives get settled, and even went so far as to hide them when they were in danger of being apprehended and returned to their old homes.[41] Similarly, officials in New Russia, eager to populate that newly won region, protected runaways from the efforts of their masters to recover them. By far the majority of the fugitives followed agricultural pursuits in their new homes, but some took employment in industry and transportation, others became professional vagabonds, and some turned to brigandage.[42]

Nothing the government or the serfowners did seemed able to check the stream of runaways. Scores of decrees, and harsh punishment of captured fugitives and of those who sheltered them, had no effect. There were more laws about runaways and their recovery than any other subject—a fact that in itself bears witness to the proportions of peasant flight. Periodically, hunts

[40] Semevskii, *Krest'iane*, I, 337-340.
[41] Pavlenko, "O nekotorykh storonakh," pp. 398-399; Treadgold, *The Great Siberian Migration*, p. 25.
[42] Sacke, "Adel und Bürgertum," pp. 843-844; Pavlenko, "O nekotorykh storonakh," pp. 399-400; Nolde, *La Formation*, I, 96.

were organized to track down all the fugitives in a district or town, and return them to their owners.[43]

Peasants did not always leave their old homes at their own volition. Large proprietors continued on into the eighteenth century to abduct serfs from the lands of less powerful seigniors. Peter I tried to end this practice by imposing heavy fines on the abductors, but his efforts proved unsuccessful.[44]

Flight was a passive mode of protest. Occasionally the peasants' discontent took the more direct form of revolt against their masters. Usually these were restricted to a single property or village, and could be handled by local authorities. But every once in a while whole districts took fire as if by some spontaneous combustion, and then the central government had to use its power to crush the rising. In 1707 a revolt against the government of Peter I broke out among some of the cossacks of the Don under the leadership of Kondratii Bulavin, their hetman or chieftain. In proclamations reminiscent of that earlier Don Cossack rebel, Stenka Razin, Bulavin promised freedom and a better life to all the oppressed. Word of his promises spread to the serfs of neighboring regions of the black earth, and violence directed against seigniors broke out in a number of places. The movement subsided in 1708 when regulars defeated Bulavin's forces and followed up their victory with a cruel repression. During Elizabeth's reign troops had to be used against the peasants on a number of occasions. Unrest seemed endemic on church properties, and in the factories of the Urals. Then Peter III's manifesto of 18 February 1762 that freed the nobles of their service obligation started rumors among the peasants of impending emancipation. They connected the requirement of the dvorianstvo to serve the state with their own enserfment, and reasoned that if the former was abolished then serfdom, too, must end. When their hopes were not realized some of them turned to violence. Official accounts recorded around 40 outbreaks between 1762 and 1772 in the great Russian provinces, and it is certain there were many more. Between 1764 and 1769 in Moscow guberniia alone thirty proprietors—nine of them

[43] Pavlenko, "O nekotorykh storonakh," p. 398.
[44] Kliuchevskii, *History*, IV, 333-334.

women—were slain by their peasants, and five others had attempts made on their lives.[45]

These risings gained the serfs nothing beyond the momentary exhilaration their acts of violence must have brought them. The seigniors continued to oppress them and the government did nothing on their behalf. The peasants seemed to realize the hopelessness of their position, and the first few years of the seventies were apparently free of open revolt. But the calm proved deceptive. Only a spark was needed to set off a new jacquerie. In 1773 it was provided by Emelian Pugachev, and for a few unbelievable months it seemed possible that rebelling peasants might overthrow the established order.[46]

Pugachev, who was born in 1726, was a Don cossack. In 1773, after many fantastic adventures, he appeared among the cossacks of the River Iaik as a fugitive from justice. He found these frontiersmen, who roamed the southeast corner of the empire, and their neighbors, who included many Old Believers, full of grievances against the government's efforts to impose new restrictions on them. Pugachev saw a ready-made opportunity to make himself the leader of a mass movement. So he adopted a ruse that was not new to Russian history. He declared himself to be the tsar, namely, Peter III, husband of Catherine and rightful sovereign of Russia. The circumstances of Peter's deposition and murder in 1762 were unknown to the people. Rumors had spread among them that he had been driven from the throne because he had wanted to help the peasants, and that he had miraculously escaped death and was in hiding, waiting the time when he could win back what was rightfully his and carry through the reforms he had originally planned. Several adventurers found it easy to convince ignorant peasants that they were indeed the tsar, but none of the other false Peters enjoyed Pugachev's success, nor, apparently, possessed his qualities of leadership.

The Iaik cossacks took him at his word and put themselves under his command. On 17 September 1773 he issued the first of the proclamations that made his rebellion a genuine social revo-

---

[45] Semevskii, *Krest'iane*, I, 347, 356-357.
[46] There is a large literature on this rising. The best work in a Western tongue that I have come across is Portal, "Pugačev: une révolution manquée."

lution. He promised his followers freedom and the ownership of all the land. The news that "Peter III" had declared a war for liberty spread quickly to the Bashkirs, the nomadic indigenes of the borderland, who had long harbored a hatred of Moscow's domination, and to the harshly exploited workers in the factories of the Urals. These people joined Pugachev. In an incredibly short time nearly all the Eurasian frontier was in revolt.

In October 1773 the central government realized it had a full-scale war on its hands, and launched a major campaign against the rebels. Pugachev suffered reverses and retreated northward. Here he began a new stage in his rising. For the first time he raised his standard in a farming area where the peasants were serfs of private landlords. He arrived outside Kazan and took the city. The road to Moscow lay before him. But once again government forces defeated him and he ordered a withdrawal to the south. On 31 July 1774 he addressed a manifesto to the serfs of the region through which he was passing, emancipating them from their bondage and from all obligations to lord and state, and giving them possession of "the fields, forests, meadows, fisheries, and saltpans without cost and without obrok." He commanded them to seize, punish, and hang the nobles whom he called "the foes of Our rule and the disturbers of the empire and the despoilers of the peasants," and proclaimed that "after the extermination of these enemies, these criminal nobles, everyone will be able to enjoy tranquility and a peaceful life that will endure till the end of time."[47] The serfs responded with wild enthusiasm to this trumpet call. Just at the rumor of his approach thousands of them left their villages to join his columns, and to plunder, burn, and kill.

But Pugachev's odyssey was nearing its end. His rag, tag, and bobtail army of peasants could not stand up against regulars. On 24 August 1774 in a battle not far from Tsaritsyn, where a century before Stenka Razin had first proclaimed his revolt, the army of Pugachev melted away. Pugachev himself fled into the steppe, was betrayed by his entourage, and executed in Moscow on 10 January 1775.

[47] *Russkaia Starina*, XIII (1875), 441.

Official casualty lists revealed that 796 men, 474 women, and 304 children of the dvorianstvo were murdered by the rebels.[48] No records were kept of peasants who were executed in the terrible retribution visited upon the rebellious districts. The gallows put up in the villages did not come down until January 1775, and not until the end of that year was a general amnesty declared. Nor did the rising suggest to the rulers of the empire the need to improve the condition of the peasantry. In fact, in the remaining years of Catherine's reign the government followed an exactly opposite policy.

Catherine tried to stamp out every memory of the *Pugachevshchina*—as the revolt is known in Russian history. She forbad it to be mentioned publicly, and ordered that henceforth the Iaik River and the town of Iaisk should bear the names of the Ural River and Uralsk. Her efforts, of course, were in vain. The government and the nobility never forgot the threat Pugachev had presented to them, and resolved that such a crisis must never rise again. The people remembered him, too, as their only defender against oppression.

After the *Pugachevshchina* official records tell of only twenty risings between 1774 and Catherine's death in 1796, though studies based on local archives and estate records indicate the number was much larger.[49] At Paul's accession a new rash of outbreaks swept across the land. In three years of his reign there were a reported 278 disturbances in 32 different provinces.

In the quarter century of Alexander's rule official sources show a total of 281 risings. During the three decades of Nicholas's reign the frequency of disturbances steadily increased. According to data of the Ministry of Interior there were 556 risings between 1826 and 1854, but this figure included only the most serious outbreaks. A later survey that included data from other official sources showed 712 disturbances in those years and reveals, too, the unbroken upward trend in the number of risings as the years went by. Between 1826 and 1834 there were 148 outbreaks, between 1835 and 1844, 216, and between 1845 and 1854, 348. Then, from 1855, when Alexander II became tsar

[48] Semevskii, *Krest'iane*, I, 381.
[49] Rubinshtein, "K kharakteristike votchinnogo rezhima," pp. 140-141.

to 5 March 1861, the day on which the emancipation decree was published, there were another 474 disturbances. Between 1801 and 1861, then, there were a total of 1,467 peasant risings.[50]

Many of these outbreaks were purely local affairs that were put down by whippings, arrest of ringleaders, and sometimes by soothing words and promises. But some of them took on the character of mass revolts. Out of 261 risings between 1836 and 1854 for which the details of pacification are known, troops were used to quell 132. Sometimes tens, and even hundreds, of thousands of peasants were involved and whole districts affected. Frequently the disturbances were only concerted refusals to obey seignioral commands or render certain obligations—in short, strikes or collective disobedience. On occasion the serfs beat their lords and estate officials, and burned, looted, and murdered. Between 1835 and 1854 Ministry of Interior reports show that rioting peasants killed 144 seigniors (among them the father of the novelist Dostoevskii) and 29 stewards, and made unsuccessful attempts on the lives of 75 other lords and stewards.[51]

Official studies of the causes of disturbances of 423 properties indicated that rumors of emancipation were as important as the harsh treatment and inordinate demands of seigniors in inciting peasant disturbances. This bore out Tsar Nicholas's conviction that all discussions of reforms should be secret, lest the peasant become impatient and resort to violence. The belief that the tsar had abolished serfdom was found to have been the cause of outbreaks on 210 of the 423 estates. The peasants, understandably excited by the false news, rose when their owners refused to free them. On 95 properties excessive barshchina was responsible for the disturbances, on 26 burdensome obrok, on 9 it was the exacting of arrears, on 30 famine was responsible, on 17 the resettlement of peasants, and on 13 reduction in the size of holdings started troubles.[52]

Peasant unrest was not confined to serfs alone. Non-seignioral peasants, too, expressed their discontent by open clashes with

[50] Liashchenko, *History*, pp. 280, 370; Ignatovich, "Krest'ianskie volneniia," p. 48.
[51] Semevskii, *Krest'ianskii vopros*, II, 583-584, 596; Linkov, *Ocherki*, p. 271.
[52] Liashchenko, *History*, p. 372; cf. Semevskii, *Krest'ianskii vopros*, II, 596.

the authorities. State and appanage peasants protested against demands made of them, and against corrupt and oppressive local officials; the military colonists rebelled against the regimentation of their lives; and peasants assigned to industrial enterprises rose against their compulsory employment and the conditions under which they had to work.[53]

The increase in the number of peasant risings in the first half of the nineteenth century did not mean that peasants no longer ran away. Fugitives left their old homes in a never ending stream that sometimes swelled to huge proportions, especially in the second quarter of the century. A rumor of freedom and land to be had for the asking in some frontier would sweep through a district and suddenly scores and hundreds of peasants would take off. So many runaways arrived in Astrakhan, New Russia, and Bessarabia that the government, interested in colonizing these regions, ordered that if the fugitives had lived in these places for a certain time they did not have to be returned to their owners if apprehended. The owners were to be compensated with a recruit quittance, or by a payment from the person on whose land the runaway had settled. Nor, apparently, were some officials in these colonial areas above issuing false papers to fugitives to protect them from being captured and returned to their old homes.[54]

Peasants also expressed their discontent with their masters by complaints to the government. The law specifically forbad this, and provided for heavy punishments of those who dared to go over the head of their owners. Yet some serfs were willing to take the chance, and a small but steady stream of petitions for protection and relief came to the throne and to the Ministry of Interior. In 1840, for example, the Ministry received three complaints, in 1842 it received seven and the tsar eight. The Ministry also reported in 1842 that local authorities received a large number of complaints from peasants about seignorial excesses, but "strict investigation" showed these charges to be unfounded. In 1844 the Ministry received 51 complaints, in 1845, 44 and the em-

[53] Linkov, *Ocherki*, pp. 42-72; Tugan-Baranovskii, *Russkaia fabrika*, I, ch. IV.
[54] Engelmann, *Die Leibeigenschaft*, p. 206; cf. Kohl, *Reisen in Südrussland*, II, 24-25.

peror 3, and so on.[55] Finally, some peasants found the only way of escape from the intolerable condition of their lives was through suicide. These were officially reported as "sudden deaths." After the emancipation a notable decline was reported in the suicide rate.[56]

The increase in rural unrest in the nineteenth century, and especially after 1825, was fearfully watched by the tsars. As earlier pages of this chapter have shown, Nicholas was certain that unless reforms were inaugurated social revolution was inevitable, even though he himself was incapable of introducing them. His successor, Alexander II, equally convinced of the dangers that peasant discontent portended, and possessed of the resolution to command emancipation, justified his act by warning that if serfdom was not abolished by legal methods the peasants would take matters into their own hands.

III

In an autocratic society the views of the autocrat, by definition, have much to do with shaping the course of events, so that the opinions of the tsars and of the men whose advice they sought were of obvious importance in bringing about agrarian reform. Similarly, the significance of peasant unrest in persuading the rulers of the empire that changes had to be made seems evident. But the contribution made by the third of the three reform groups, the intellectuals, is much more difficult to evaluate. It is always hard to measure the cumulative impact of the ideas of political and economic thinkers and of literary men upon their society. It is an especially perplexing problem in Russia, for the writers of that land had a very small reading public, and the rigorous censorship not only kept them from presenting a full exposition of their ideas but sometimes prevented them from expressing themselves at all. Yet these men unquestionably played a large part in preparing the minds of the thoughtful among their audience to recognize the need for emancipation.

Though a few isolated figures spoke out against the excesses of serfdom during the first six decades of the eighteenth century,

[55] Semevskii, *Krest'ianskii vopros*, II, 571-573.
[56] Masaryk, *Spirit*, I, 131 and note.

the intellectual attack on bondage got under way in earnest in the reign of Catherine II. In the 1760's the liberal and humanitarian ideas of the Enlightenment began to circulate among the leaders of society—Catherine by her interest and example deserves much of the credit for this—and some of these people developed a critical attitude toward conditions in Russia. A few who were close to the empress let her know that they believed that reforms were needed that would protect serfs from the abuses of their masters. Catherine herself in 1766 asked the newly established Free Economic Society to hold an international essay contest on the advantages of peasant land ownership, and offered a large cash sum for prizes. 162 entries were received, 129 of them in German, 21 in French, 7 in Russian, 3 in Latin, and one each in Dutch and Swedish. First prize went to a Frenchman and the second to a Russian. Both favored land and freedom for the peasants. Catherine read a number of the best essays and persuaded the directors of the Society, who thought that publication of some of the entries would stir up trouble, that their fears were groundless.

The essay contest had no practical results so far as the peasants were concerned. But it did have an important social and educational influence upon contemporaries. It made the peasant question a subject of frequent discussion in the highest circles, and when deputies came from the provinces to the Legislative Commission in 1767 they heard the problem talked about, and carried word of it with them when they returned home.[57]

The literary criticism of serfdom made its debut in Catherine's reign, too. The empress for a few years encouraged the publication of satirical journals modeled after the periodicals that were the rage in contemporary England. The editors, who wrote most of their pamphlets themselves, poked fun at old-fashioned prejudices, and some of them incidentally called attention to seignioral excesses. But one among them, N. I. Novikov, aimed earnest and hard blows at serfdom, portraying it as a demoralizing influence in Russian society. His attacks made Catherine decide in 1774 to put a stop to all of the satirical journals. Novikov then went into publishing, built up a large

[57] Semevskii, *Krest'ianskii vopros*, I, xi, 22-37, 47 ff.

enterprise, put out a number of works that dealt with moral regeneration, and exerted a considerable influence on the educated public. Catherine, suspicious of the man and of his social and philanthropic activities, had him arrested on trumped-up charges of political conspiracy. In 1792 he was sentenced to fifteen years of imprisonment. Paul ordered him released four years later. He came out of confinement a broken man, and spent the rest of his life wrapped up in mysticism.[58]

The most famous and outspoken attack on serfdom in the eighteenth century appeared in 1790 when A. N. Radishchev published his *Journey from St. Petersburg to Moscow*. Radishchev, scion of a wealthy noble family, had been one of twelve Russians sent by the government in 1766 to study at Leipzig. He became a disciple of the Enlightenment. His book, modeled after Laurence Sterne's *Sentimental Journey*, told of his experiences and observations in the countryside that lay between the two metropolises. In earlier writings he had expressed his hatred of serfdom and now, in heavily ornate language, he recounted specific experiences of its cruelties, and of the misdeeds of local bureaucrats and the injustices of the central government. He portrayed the peasants as long-suffering and noble children of nature, and their masters as brutal ignoramuses. In his dedication he explained that his conscience was tormented by the sufferings of mankind, and on his title page he placed a line from a Russian translation of Fenelon's *Telemaque* that read "A monster, gross, savage, hundred-mouthed, and bellowing."

Radishchev submitted his manuscript to the censors, who dutifully blue-penciled sections of it. He then proceeded to print the work, censored parts and all, on his own press. He sent a copy of the book to the censors for their approval. Being typical bureaucrats they assumed that the sections they had excised from the manuscript had been left out, and gave the book their imprimatur without bothering to check it. A copy soon found its way to Catherine. She read it with an indignation that mounted with each page, as her marginal comments showed. She described Radishchev as worse than Pugachev, claimed he was poisoned by the French venom, had a melancholy tempera-

---

[58] Mirsky, *History*, pp. 75-76.

ment, was haughty, and so on, and had him arrested forthwith. His penalty was a foregone conclusion—execution. After he begged for mercy and disclaimed any intent for his book other than to win literary acclaim for himself, the gracious empress commuted his sentence to ten years in Siberia. Paul allowed him to return to European Russia in 1796, and in 1801 Alexander gave him a complete pardon. He thereupon reentered government service, but the next year committed suicide at the age of 53.[59]

Already in Catherine's reign some critics had argued that serfdom was economically unprofitable. During the first decades of the nineteenth century this thesis received much development at the hands of scholarly writers. The censors, more lenient with learned publications than with belles-lettres, allowed a number of treatises that favored emancipation to appear. In 1806 A. N. Kaiserov, a Russian student at Göttingen, published his doctoral dissertation. Kaiserov, who dedicated his work to Tsar Alexander, claimed that national economic progress depended upon the peasants having their freedom and owning their holdings. In 1809 a Russian translation of a book by Count V. S. Stroinovskii, a Polish landowner, was published in Vilna. Stroinovskii, too, urged that reforms had to be made to increase the productivity of peasant labor, and suggested a landless emancipation with the peasants allowed to rent their holdings. In 1812 the Free Economic Society held an essay contest on the relative merits of free and serf labor. Fourteen entries were submitted, eleven of them in Russian. L. N. Jakob, formerly professor at the University of Halle and then holder of the chair of political economy at the University of Kharkov, won first prize. He claimed that serf labor was much less profitable to the landowner than was free hired labor because the forced workers, lacking initiative, were less efficient and less interested in their jobs. Second prize went to Garlieb Merkel, a German-educated Latvian, who already in *Die Letten*, a book published in Leipzig in 1797, had demanded emancipation for the peasants of his homeland. Merkel, too, argued that hired day labor actually cost the landowner much less in the long run than did serf workers.

[59] Radishchev, *Journey*, introd., pp. 10-19.

H. F. Storch, the one-time tutor to Grand Dukes Nicholas and Michael, published in French a six volume work on political economy, based on the lectures he had given his exalted pupils. At various points in his lengthy treatise Storch also asserted that serf labor was less efficient than free labor. Other economists advanced similar opinions.[60]

Many of these reform-minded economists wrote under the influence of Adam Smith. The *Wealth of Nations* had been translated into Russian in 1802-1803 at the order of the Minister of Finance, and the Scotsman's views quickly became the favored economic philosophy of many of the educated class. But adherence to the principles of laissez-faire and of individualism proved not always synonymous with the advocacy of agrarian reform. The magazine of the free traders, *Spirit of the Journals* (*Dukh Zhurnalov*), published from 1815 to 1820, argued that the Russian serf was better off than the Western European peasant or proletarian because his master took care of him. Like slaveowners in the southern United States, the Russian serf-owners who adopted Smith's doctrines saw no anomaly in accepting the philosophical arguments of economic liberalism, and at the same time defending human servitude.[61]

Up to the end of Alexander's reign the intellectual critics of serfdom had confined their strictures to words, written and spoken. Then in the last weeks of 1825, in the famed revolt of the Decembrists, some of them resorted to force to gain their ends. A group of young army officers seized upon the opportunity offered by the interregnum after Alexander's death to try to overthrow the autocracy. They had been hatching their program for several years in meetings of the secret political societies into which they had organized themselves. All of them were nobles, some from the greatest families of the realm. All of them were indoctrinated with western political theories they had picked up in travels abroad, and from their education, reading, and talks and correspondence with their fellows. A few extremists aimed at revolutionary dictatorship, but most of the conspirators wanted

[60] Semevskii, *Krest'ianskii vopros*, I, 295-301, 316 ff., 387-392; Storch, *Cours*, III, 152-154, 173-174; IV, 292-300.

[61] Tugan-Baranovskii, *Russkaia fabrika*, I, 274-277.

to transform the autocracy into a limited monarchy. Their primary interest was in political matters; so that the serf problem was not paramount in their thinking. But almost to a man they wanted to abolish serfdom—some favoring emancipation with land and some without—as part of their program of reform.[62]

The plotters turned out to be amazingly inept when they finally decided to act. Their rising was easily put down and the conspirators quickly rounded up. Once jailed the bold insurrectionists, with a handful of honorable exceptions, nearly fell over one another to beg the tsar's forgiveness, and to tell everything they knew. They even invented facts to win leniency for themselves, and they incriminated everyone they could think of, including enlisted men whom they had cajoled into supporting the movement. No tortures or beatings were needed. The goad of their consciences or, perhaps, just plain fright was enough. Even Paul Pestel, fire-eating radical leader who had cast himself as the Robespierre of the revolution, now announced that he despised himself for sharing in the conspiracy and vowed that henceforth "Every moment of my life will be filled with gratitude and boundless attachment to the sacred person of the tsar and of his most august family."[63] His mea culpa's did not save him; he was one of the five leaders executed for their part in the revolt.

Judged by the number of people involved—probably not more than a few hundred at most—or by its failure, the Decembrist rising was an unimportant affair. But it stands as a landmark in Russian history because for the first time men of the serfowning class had taken to arms in the name of freedom, not only for themselves but for their serfs as well.

The Decembrist conspiracy inevitably led to even greater watchfulness by the government for any signs or overt expressions of discontent. Yet, far from being stilled, the voice of intellectual criticism grew ever louder as the decades wore on. For Nicholas's accession marked the opening of what is justly called the Golden Age of Russian culture. The empire of the

---

[62] Bliumin, "Ekonomicheskie vozzreniia," pp. 214-218; Mazour, *First Russian Revolution*, pp. 7-11.
[63] Yarmolinsky, *Road*, pp. 51-52.

tsars became the scene of a spectacular intellectual outburst. Men of superior talent, and some who were endowed with the transcendent ability and vastly original creative power of genius, seemed to spring up everywhere. Naturally enough, the small, educated Russian public listened intently to what men of this stamp had to say. Nearly every one of them spoke out sharply and bitterly against many aspects of the existing order, and they attacked serfdom especially. The censorship forced them to resort to inference or indirection in their printed works, or to pass handwritten copies of their manuscripts from person to person, or to spread their ideas by word of mouth through discussion groups and salons, or even to leave their homeland and have their writings smuggled back into Russia. But in one way or another they made themselves heard.

These men, most of them of the nobility and some of them serfowners, were repelled by the immorality and inhumanity of the institution. They harbored a burning hatred of it, and from youth on they fought to wipe it out. N. I. Turgenev was speaking not for himself alone, but for many of his fellows, when in 1860 he wrote the following words:[64]

"There are some ideas which seize a man from the beginning of his life, which never leave him and which end by absorbing, in one way or other, his entire existence.

"That is what happened with the idea of the emancipation of the serfs in Russia. From my childhood I felt a pronounced repulsion for serfdom; I instinctively sensed all the injustices in it. . . .

"The sympathies of my youth became convictions when I was able to examine the question, when I was able to estimate the enormous evil that serfdom produced, first for the serfs, then and above all for the serfowners whom it degraded even more than the serfs, and finally for the state and for humanity, whom it dishonored.

"At that time I dedicated all my strength and intelligence to the struggle against this evil, this supreme evil. . . . When something revolts me or makes my heart bleed, if I think about it ever so little I find the principal, the first cause of the evil,

[64] Turgenev, *Un dernier mot*, pp. 1-2.

over and over again in this dreadful servitude. Thus all my thoughts end by concentrating themselves on the thought of emancipation."

In the 1820's young intellectuals, many of them university students, began to meet together to discuss the new philosophies that were appearing in Western Europe, and to express their desires to change the society in which they lived. These "circles," as they were called, for the next three decades were the foci of Russian intellectual life. The censorship made other channels of communication difficult and dangerous, so that conversation afforded the easiest way to exchange views. Even this method was not without its perils; police spies sometimes penetrated into the circles and arrests often followed. Most of the members of the circles came from the nobility, but as time went on men of the middle strata of society, sons of merchants and priests, joined the groups and had a large influence in them. Up to this era Russia's intellectuals had been almost exclusively from the landowning class. Now a new class, the intelligentsia, that transcended old class lines and that was to have enormous importance in Russian history, made its appearance.

Some of the circles turned for guidance to the liberal philosophies of the West, others became partisans of socialist theories, and still others believed that Russia need not look abroad but contained within herself the seeds of her own regeneration. But whether Westernizers or Slavophils, liberals or socialists, all shared a common determination to rid their country of serfdom, and talked at length about the ways to do it.[65]

The crowning glory of Russia's Golden Age proved to be belles-lettres. In the course of a few decades a constellation of geniuses—men such as Pushkin, Lermontov, Gogol, Nekrassov, Grigorovich, Turgenev, Dostoevskii, Goncharov, and Tolstoi— created one of the world's great literatures. Their writings proved to be the most overt, and perhaps the most effective, vehicle by which intellectuals could make known their critical attitude toward much of the existing order. Some of the greatest among them used their talents to attack serfdom. The censorship

[65] Cf. Semevskii, *Krest'ianskii vopros*, II, 296-324, 386-428; Riasanovsky, *Russia*, pp. 136-140.

made this hard, but they knew how to make a story convey its message without explicit statements of sympathy for the oppressed, or condemnation of the oppressor. They took chances, but their consciences would not let them do otherwise, for, as Ivan Turgenev, one of the greatest among them, said in after years, "Well nigh everything that I saw around me provoked in me a feeling of resentment, and finally of horror." The thing he hated above all else, he continued "had a definite form, bore a well known name: the enemy was ... serfdom. Under that name I gathered and I concentrated everything against which I had decided to struggle to the finish—with which I vowed never to be reconciled. This was my Hannibal's oath; and I was not the only one to take it in those days."[66]

They did not seek to romanticize the peasants when they wrote about them. They hated serfdom because they knew it was wrong for one man to own another, and because they knew that master and serf were equally sullied by it. That was the story they told. It was a shattering kind of realism. Even today's reader shudders at the conscious and unconscious cruelties, grieves for the wronged, and is overwhelmed by the stupidity and crudeness and viciousness they told about in their books and stories. It is easy to imagine the impact this literature made on the people who read it when it first appeared, above all, on those who for other reasons had already begun to have doubts about the value of serfdom.

Unlike the social and political thinkers of their day the novelists offered no plans on how to free the serfs. They left that to others. They took it as their task to tell their readers what an evil thing serfdom was.

I V

In contrast to the intellectuals, the mass of the serfowners rarely had the opportunity to express their views about serfdom publicly. They did not write books or articles, they had no forum in which they could hold forth, and the government was not in the habit of consulting them. As a result, there is relatively little information about their attitude toward serfdom.

---

[66] Turgenev, *Literaturnye i zhiteiskie vospominaniia*, pp. 58-59.

But the information that is available points to the conclusion that most serfowners saw no reason to get rid of it, and that only a minority, and this the most "enlightened" among them, thought some reform was needed.

The Legislative Commission summoned by Catherine in 1767 to draw up a new law code offered the first opportunity to the dvorianstvo as a class to express an opinion about serfdom. In none of the 151 cahiers they submitted did the nobles talk of serfdom as a "problem." So far as they were concerned the matter had been settled for all time, and they wanted the new law code to ratify the powers they had over their peasants. A very few of the cahiers allowed that some limitations might be desirable, such as forbidding the break-up of serf families on the division of a property between heirs, or the sale of peasants outside the district in which the rest of their family lived, or the sale of peasants as recruit substitutes. At the sessions of the Commission nearly all the deputies of the nobility defended the status quo, and some even argued that its inadequacies rose not from the system itself but from failings on the part of the peasants, such as drunkenness and sloth. A few among the delegates of the dvorianstvo did suggest that some reforms were necessary, but they were bitterly attacked by their fellow noble delegates.[67]

From Catherine's reign on, some of the leaders of aristocratic society, as was pointed out earlier, levelled criticisms at serfdom. But men of equal prominence vehemently opposed all proposals for change, and were much upset by the interest shown by Alexander and then by Nicholas in the peasant problem. To mention just a few examples, Gabriel Derzhavin, Procurator-General of the Senate and well known literary figure, believed that the Free Farmer act of 1803 would endanger society, provoke disturbances, produce no good for lord or peasant, and called the men who drew it up a "band of Jacobins."[68] The historian Nicholas Karamzin thought that without the guiding hand of their seigniors the peasants would turn to drink and idleness and crime, and endanger the safety of the realm. He considered serf-

---

67 *Velikaia reforma*, I, 199-200; Bak, "Ia. P. Kozel'skii," pp. 92-95; Semevskii, *Krest'ianskii vopros*, I, 95-120.
68 Engelmann, *Die Leibeigenschaft*, pp. 168-175.

dom the natural order of things.[69] "Serfs can be liberated," he wrote, "as soon as it is possible for wolves to be fully fed while sheep remain uninjured."[70] In 1820 the State Council warned that the prohibition of the sale of individual serfs apart from their families was a dangerous innovation, and argued that any change was superfluous since Russia alone of all states was peaceful and happy. Count S. S. Uvarov, Nicholas's Minister of Education— and coiner of the phrase "Orthodoxy, Autocracy, Nationality" that became the watchword of the regime—prophesied that to tamper with serfdom would bring disaster to the state. For the serfowners would demand compensations for their losses at the expense of the autocratic power of the tsar.[71] Count P. D. Kiselev's activities on behalf of the state peasants evoked scathing criticisms from important aristocrats. Baron Korf, high state official and courtier, in 1841 reported that Kiselev was hated because "rumor pointed to him as the instigator of the idea of the abolition of serfdom." Count Nesselrode, the Minister of Foreign Affairs, wrote in 1843 that "all the plans of emancipation with which Kiselev threatens us, at present can only lead to peasant riots and the ruin of the nobility," and warned that if the peasants were given their liberty they would use it badly.[72]

The opposition of these men and their fellows among the aristocracy and high bureaucracy reflected the attitude of most serfowners. They looked upon any move to reform serfdom as a direct threat to their property rights over land and peasants. In 1835 an official of the Ministry of Interior reported that the majority of the nobility were not even able to adjust themselves to thinking of the possibility of running their economies without serfs. They earnestly believed that emancipation would ruin the moral fibre of the peasantry, and lead to the violent destruction of the dvorianstvo as a class.[73] In their minds serfdom was a necessary condition for their own welfare, and for the welfare of the peasants and the state.

---

[69] Karamzin, *Memoir*, pp. 165-166.
[70] Quoted in Masaryk, *Spirit*, I, 90.
[71] *Ibid.*, p. 129; Engelmann, *Die Leibeigenschaft*, pp. 195-196.
[72] Grunwald, *Tsar Nicholas*, pp. 169-170.
[73] *Velikaia reforma*, III, 157.

There was a minority, however, that increased as time went by, who did not share these views. Influenced by humanitarianism, by the interest shown by the tsar and by high officials in reform, and by considerations of self-interest, these other-minded seigniors advanced proposals for freeing the serfs. Nearly all of their schemes involved emancipation without land, or with very small holdings for the peasants, and indemnification for the proprietors. In this way they hoped to keep their erstwhile serfs as hired laborers, spare themselves the troubles and expenses and responsibilities involved in owning serfs, and use the indemnification money to pay off their debts.[74] In short, they were looking out for themselves.

The first proposal of this sort came in 1819 from a group of proprietors of the Dinaburg district in Vitebsk guberniia. Of the sixty-three serfowners there, thirty-nine favored a landless emancipation. They forwarded their plan to St. Petersburg where the Imperial Council disapproved it.[75] Provincial lords elsewhere did not take such joint action until the latter thirties. By then the peasant problem had become a frequent and much debated topic of discussion in serfowning society. In 1837-1838 some proprietors of Tula sponsored a plan of emancipation, and in the 1840's groups of seigniors in Riazan, in Tula, in Simbirsk, in Smolensk, in Tver, in Vitebsk, and in St. Petersburg advanced proposals of one sort or other. None of their schemes had the support of the majority of the serfowners in their respective provinces, and none of them were permitted by the government to go beyond the paper stage.[76] Nonetheless, they gave important evidence of the appearance among some of the provincial nobility of a new attitude toward serfdom.

Self-interest seems to have played the premier role in persuading these men of the need for emancipation. They apparently had become convinced that they could make more money by using hired labor than they were presently making with unpaid but inefficient serf workers. Already in the eighteenth century

---

[74] Kornilov, "Gubernskie komitety," pp. 128-131, 136; Semevskii, *Krest'ianskii vopros,* I, 467-468, II, 615-617.
[75] Kornilov, "Gubernskie komitety," p. 129.
[76] *Velikaia reforma,* III, 170-172; Semevskii, *Krest'ianskii vopros,* pp. 135-136, 254.

critics had commented upon the poor performance of serfs doing barshchina, and had noted how much harder these same peasants worked on their own holdings. Seignioral complaints about this became common in the next century. As one serfowner put it in an article in the *Agricultural Gazette* in 1847:[77] "The peasant on barshchina arrives on the job as late as possible, looks around and gazes off at frequent and long intervals, and works as little as possible—to him it isn't a job to do, but a day to kill. He works three days for the lord and three days for himself. On his own days he works the land better, performs all his household chores, and still has plenty of free time. On the master's work, especially on tasks that can not be measured, he reduces zealous overseers either to despair or to anger. One disciplines unwillingly, but one comes to this solution as the only way possible to get the work moving."

Some proprietors maintained they could escape these drawbacks of barshchina by demanding only obrok from their peasants. Judging from the contemporary literature and reports, however, most of those who studied the problem believed that even with its shortcomings barshchina was preferable to obrok, from the viewpoint of seignioral income. They claimed that without the direct supervision of the owner a property tended to deteriorate in value, that obrok peasants used every possible dodge to get out of their payments or to reduce them, that arrearages piled up and efforts to collect them stirred up unrest, and that peasants on obrok preferred to earn their livings from non-agricultural work and tended to leave farming to their women who did it badly. Some writers presented data drawn from actual experience to show that seigniors in chernozem and Central-Industrial provinces alike received more than three times as much revenue from serfs on barshchina than they got from those on obrok.[78]

In other words, these men maintained that, despite the inefficiency of forced labor, a proprietor made more money when

[77] Quoted in Khromov, *Ekonomicheskoe razvitie*, p. 23. Cf. Baranovich, *Materialy*, p. 178; Storch, "Der Bauernstand," 1849, pp. 414-416; Haxthausen, *Studien*, II, 511; Tegoborskii, *Etudes*, I, 325.

[78] *Velikaia reforma*, III, 117-119; Struve, *Krepostnoe khoziaistvo*, pp. 91-93; Kulischer, "Die Leibeigenschaft," pp. 36-38.

he engaged in production on his own than he did when he only drew quitrents from his serfs. The problem, as they saw it, was to find a way to improve the quality of peasant labor so that seignioral incomes would increase. Some of them thought that more efficient management and closer supervision of the barshchina provided the answer. But as time went on, more and more of these proprietors came around to the opinion that the best solution was to employ hired labor. They based their belief on comparisons made between the performance of hired hands and barshchina workers. These studies showed that the hired hands worked harder, produced more, and cost less. To give just one illustration, an analysis of the experience of a proprietor in Tula revealed that each serf *tiaglo* cost him 288 rubles a year, including the costs at current prices of the land he furnished the *tiaglo* for its own use. A hired couple cost him just 170 rubles a year— 60 rubles for wages, 40 for board, and 70 rubles for the cost and maintenance of animals and equipment (barshchina workers supplied their own implements and animals). Similar findings were reported by serfowners in other provinces.[79]

Initially, when seigniors spoke of hired labor they meant serfs who had permission from their masters to work elsewhere, and state peasants who hired themselves out. It was a relatively easy step, however, for men who were convinced of the superiority of hired workers over serfs to begin to think of the abolition of serfdom, so that all workers would be on the open labor market. For if it could be shown that a landowner made more money when he used hired labor than he did when he used serfs, then obviously serfdom had outlived its economic usefulness for the seigniors. The sensible thing would be to emancipate the serfs without land, and thereby convert them into workers who had to hire themselves out to earn their livings.

Not everyone agreed that hired labor was preferable to barshchina. Opponents of this thesis pointed out that proprietors often lacked the capital needed to pay wages and buy needed farm equipment. They claimed that in many areas the crop produced by hired workers would not bring enough to cover

[79] Zablotskii-Desiatovskii, *Graf P. D. Kiselev*, IV, 281, 283-284; Kornilov, "Krest'-ianskaia reforma," p. 305; Kulischer, "Die Leibeigenschaft," pp. 54-55.

[573]

production costs. Hired labor justified itself economically only in fertile regions where relatively small numbers of workers could be used to produce crops such as wheat that commanded high prices, or where land values were so high that it was too expensive to use any of it for serf holdings. As for the low cost of hired labor, they noted that it was cheap only where serf population was so large that there was little demand for hired workers. In regions that had few serfs, hired labor was dear, and was regarded by the proprietors who had to use it as an unavoidable evil.[80]

Still others accepted the argument that serfdom was inefficient economically, yet defended the institution. These men had no confidence in the intelligence and judgement of the peasantry. They believed that the serfs were incapable of running their own lives, and foresaw only trouble for Russian society if ever the peasants were freed from the supervision of their masters. I. Ia. Vil'kins, one of the foremost agricultural experts of the thirties and forties, prophesied in 1832 that if the serf was emancipated he would "obey neither the village elder nor the landlord, he would work or not as he felt, drink and be idle as much as he wanted, and not be accountable to anyone for his behavior."[81] In November 1845 Minister of Interior Perovskii reported to Tsar Nicholas that the conviction was widespread among the dvorianstvo that hired labor was more profitable to them than barshchina, and this explained why so many of them "no longer fear that the abolition of serfdom will ruin them. But they dread the resulting changes which every sensible person, knowing the common people and the mind of the common people and their inclinations, ought to dread."[82]

That dread became the theme of the nobility's opposition to emancipation.

[80] Tegoborskii, *Etudes*, I, 325; Kornilov, "Gubernskie komitety," p. 137; Struve, *Krepostnoe khoziaistvo*, pp. 103-109; Kulischer, "Die Leibeigenschaft," pp. 53, 55.
[81] Quoted in *Velikaia reforma*, III, 158.
[82] Quoted in Semevskii, *Krest'ianskii vopros*, II, 138.

26

THE END OF AN AGE

THE attitude of the mass of the serfowners was a formidable barrier to change. The wishes and guidance of the tsar and his advisers, the menace of serf revolt, and the writings and teachings of the intellectuals, might ultimately have persuaded them to abandon their opposition. But it is possible that this might not have happened. It would have needed only a tsar who shared the views of the serfowners for the reform movement to have lost much—perhaps most—of its force. A general rising of the serfs might have had as its aftermath further repression rather than freedom. That happened after the Pugachev revolt, and after other great peasant risings in other lands. As for the intellectuals, if a count could be made it might well turn out that noble ideas have failed more often than they have succeeded in influencing men. Time alone could have told what course events in Russia would have followed. But the men who ruled Russia decided they could not wait to find out what the years might bring. For a new and entirely unanticipated circumstance had made an unwelcome appearance—the loss of the Crimean War. That defeat revealed weaknesses in the structure of the state that they had barely sensed or had not suspected at all, and that they feared would destroy the empire unless remedied immediately.

The Crimean War was an episode in the history of what the diplomatists of the nineteenth century called the Eastern Question: would the Ottoman Empire survive, and if it did not how was it to be divided among the Great Powers? The war's immediate origin, however, lay in a grotesque squabble between the Roman and Orthodox churches over the use and custody of places in Palestine associated with the life and death of Jesus. Each side marched into battle with the perfervid blessings of ministers who preached the gospel of the Prince of Peace.

The war cost 600,000 lives.

The Russian government had entered the conflict with full confidence of victory. In an unbelievably short time that assurance vanished. Russian materiel proved no match for the weapons and ships of the enemy. Russian generals turned out to be less capable even than the men who commanded the opposing forces—no mean feat. Russian soldiers lost battles in which they far outnumbered the enemy. Inefficiency, corruption, and above all, lack of adequate communications prevented the commissariat from providing the troops with the supplies and transport they needed. On the home front, too, troubles piled up. The state's finances, long in difficulties, buckled under the strain of the war effort and deficits soared to record heights. Far more serious, a great new wave of peasant unrest swept across much of the empire.

The failure of his diplomatic schemes, and the collapse of the army of which he had been so proud, was more than Tsar Nicholas could bear. His spirit and health broke and on 2 March 1855 he died—there was even talk that he had committed suicide.[1] Stronger men realized that Russia could never reach the greatness and power that nature and history seemed to promise her unless basic reforms were carried out. It was not the first time, nor the last, that a violent shock from outside served as the stimulus to great internal changes. And the first reform they wanted to make was to free the serfs. They welcomed the ending of the war, even though it meant the acceptance of defeat because, as one of them put it, "Peace gives us the opportunity to take care of domestic matters, and we ought to take advantage of it. The first business—we must free the serfs because there is the center of all evils."[2]

Above all others, the new tsar, Alexander II, came to the conclusion that serfdom had to go. As heir to the throne he had defended the rights of the serfowners.[3] On his accession men close to him were certain that a real "era of the gentry" had

[1] Schiemann, *Geschichte*, IV, 338-352.

[2] Prince M. D. Gagarin to Alexander II, quoted in Voznesenskii, *Razlozhenie*, p. 228.

[3] Kornilov, *Modern Russian History*, II, 3-5. According to reports of the Prussian ambassador to St. Petersburg in 1845, however, Alexander was then of the opinion that reforms were necessary and inevitable. Stupperich, *Die Anfänge*, pp. 127-128.

dawned, while abolitionists despaired of progress. The first, and one of the few, of his father's ministers that he dismissed was D. G. Bibikov, Minister of Interior, because he considered Bibikov's program of inventories for the Western provinces unfair to the serfowners there.[4] Count Lanskoi, the new Minister of Interior, on taking office sent out a circular to the marshals of the provincial nobility in which he explained that the emperor had commanded him to uphold as inviolable the rights that previous tsars had given the nobility. Serfdom was not mentioned in the circular, but everyone understood that Lanskoi's statement about inviolable rights referred to it, and the serfowners took it as a pledge from the throne to retain the institution.[5]

In person the new sovereign was nervous, indecisive, and given to spells of depression and violent fits of weeping. In a conversation in September, 1856 a member of his Senate described him to the Prussian ambassador as lacking in all initiative.[6] Yet this conservative, unsure man initiated and carried through a revolutionary change, because the shortcomings revealed by the Crimean War convinced him that this was the only way to guarantee the internal order and external power of his empire.

The story goes that long ago a visitor in a peasant's hut might see a picture cut from a newspaper or magazine of Napoleon III, Emperor of the French, hanging in a place of honor alongside a picture of Alexander II. For many rustics believed that when the Russians sued for peace in 1856 Napoleon said he would grant it on one condition; that Alexander free the serfs. The Emperor of the French made no such demand, but the people were close to the truth when they connected the defeat in the Crimea with the abolition of serfdom.[7]

Alexander gave the first public indication of his intentions in his manifesto of 19 March 1856 announcing the end of the war. He explained that the losses suffered by the terms of the peace treaty would be far outweighed by the benefits that his people

[4] Kornilov, *Modern Russian History*, II, 5.
[5] Engelmann, *Die Leibeigenschaft*, p. 236.
[6] Bernhardi, *Aus dem Leben*, II, 321.
[7] Simkhovitch, "The Russian Peasant," p. 569.

would enjoy in the new era of peace, in which everyone would be "under the protection of the law, with equal justice and equal protection for everyone, so that each can enjoy in peace the fruits of his own righteous labors."[8] These words excited the serfowners. They wanted to believe that they were only the unctuous pronouncements expected of sovereigns in such circumstances. But they could not be certain. So Count Zakrevskii, governor-general of Moscow and an opponent of reform, asked the tsar, who was then in Moscow, to reassure the dvorianstvo. Alexander agreed, and on 30 March 1856 he spoke to the representatives of the Moscow nobility. His talk proved to be the most famous speech that any tsar ever made. For Alexander, far from allaying the fears of the serfowners, told them flatly that their peasants had to be freed.

"I know, gentlemen, [he said] that rumors have circulated among you about my plans to destroy serfdom. To prevent various unfounded comments on such an important subject, I consider it necessary to let all of you know that I do not plan to do this immediately, but, of course, all of you understand that the existing conditions of owning souls cannot remain unchanged. It is better to begin to destroy serfdom from above, than to wait until that time when it begins to destroy itself from below. I ask you, gentlemen, to figure out how all this can best be carried out to completion. Convey my words to the nobility for their consideration."[9]

The secret was out. Alexander had made up his mind. Serfdom must go, not just for humanitarian reasons or for economic ones, but because the tsar feared peasant revolution.

The speech was not published but news of it spread like wildfire through the provinces. Nearly everyone, including men close to the tsar, were dismayed. They could not convince themselves that he meant what he said, and so, though they remained loyal to the throne, they disregarded the tsar's plea that they submit plans for emancipation. After months had passed Alexander realized they were not going to meet his request. He

8 *PSZ*, 2nd ser., XXXI, no. 30273, p. 132.
9 *Materialy*, I, 114.

decided to act without them, and in January 1857 he appointed a secret committee of high bureaucrats to lay down the basic principles for the emancipation. The committee, dominated by enemies of reform, dragged its feet until Alexander made his brother Constantine (who favored abolition) its chairman. Finally, on 18 August 1857 it presented a report recommending that the emancipation be carried out in three stages, beginning with the collection of information, then a period of transition, and ending with the liquidation of serfdom.[10] No time period was set for the completion of each of these operations, and no publicity was to be given to them. It seemed clear that the committee hoped to delay abolition, and perhaps even postpone it indefinitely.[11]

But Alexander thwarted these obstructionist tactics by seizing the initiative once again. Late in October 1857, V. A. Nazimov, governor-general of the Lithuanian provinces of Vilna, Grodno, and Kovno, arrived in St. Petersburg with a request from the nobles of these provinces for permission to free their serfs without land. The explanation for this startling action was easy to find. The Lithuanian serfowners were threatened with the imposition of inventories which would require them to furnish land to their peasants. Influenced by the example of the neighboring Baltic provinces, they preferred to keep all their land for themselves, even at the price of freeing their serfs. The secret committee on emancipation favored the proposal, but Alexander ruled against it. He instructed the committee to draw up an answer to the Lithuanian petition that would explain under what conditions they could liberate their peasants. The document the committee produced at Alexander's direction, known to history as the Imperial Rescript (answer) to Nazimov, was signed by the tsar on 20 November 1857. It turned out to be the point of departure for the working out of the mechanics of the emancipation.

The Rescript ordered the nobility of each of the three Lithuanian guberniias to form a committee to draw up plans for emancipation, and established the principles these bodies were

10 *Ibid.*, pp. 130-131.
11 Engelmann, *Die Leibeigenschaft*, pp. 247-256.

to follow. The lords were to retain ownership of all their land, but had to permit their peasants to occupy their homesteads, and had to arrange for the peasants to purchase them within a set time. The peasants also had to be furnished enough farm land to meet their needs, for which they were to pay rent in cash or labor; they were to be organized into communes; the lords were to retain their police powers; and provisions had to be made for the collection of taxes from the peasants.

The Rescript itself spoke only of "improving the existence of the serfs." But Minister of Interior Lanskoi in a memorandum to Nazimov on 21 November in which he elaborated on the Rescript, explained that this was intended to mean the abolition of serfdom. He stated also that the government expected the three provincial committees not to take more than six months to work out their proposals, which they were then to forward to St. Petersburg.[12]

At first the Rescript and Lanskoi's memorandum were kept secret, but Alexander quickly decided to publicize them. On 24 November, at the tsar's instructions, Lanskoi sent the two documents as a circular to the governors and marshals of the nobility of every province. Lanskoi's covering letter informed each recipient that the circular was "for your information and guidance in the event that the dvorianstvo of the province entrusted to you express similar wishes."[13] On 5 December a rescript akin to the one to Nazimov went to the governor-general of St. Petersburg guberniia in answer to a petition from nobles of that province. A few days later this rescript was published in the newspapers. The tsar's plans became public knowledge. Now there could be no turning back.

The circular sent out by Lanskoi on 24 November made the provincial nobility realize that the game was up. Though the covering letter came from Lanskoi they knew he spoke for the tsar, and though the letter explained that the material was being made available just in case some nobles might be interested in emancipation, no one was misled. As one writer put it a few years later, "Such vague words, when spoken by an autocrat,

12 *Materialy*, I, 137-153.
13 *Ibid.*, pp. 153-156.

have a very definite and unmistakable meaning, which prudent loyal subjects have no difficulty in understanding."[14] Moreover, the public release of the tsar's proposals meant that the peasants learned of them, and the serfowners faced the certainty of unprecedented peasant violence if they failed to accept them.

So they accepted them, but unwillingly and with bad grace. Protests came from aristocrats in the highest court circles, including men whom the emperor had chosen to carry out his plans, down to the least of the rural gentry. Statements from provincial governors and marshals on the reaction to the circular reported that in almost every province the serfowners were opposed to the government's plans. They all pointed out the difficulty and even the impossibility of carrying them out. They claimed that the public announcement had evoked general incredulity, for, as the governor of Kaluga put it in his report, "despite long-existing rumors the proprietors did not believe or did not want to believe that a question this serious occupied the government and that it had decided to enter upon its solution." With near unanimity they prophesied that emancipation would cause the landowners to lose their labor force, for the peasants, being naturally indolent, would not work. The production of the empire would, therefore, decline, prices would go up, and the nation would face hunger, disease, and poverty, while the lack of discipline among the peasants would lead to a new and greater *Pugachevshchina*. The only favorable reports came from the Little Russian provinces of Chernigov and Poltava, whose serfowners warned that the reform would be enormously difficult but, with an almost audible sigh of resignation, conceded that they understood the need for it.

There was, of course, a minority among the proprietors who favored emancipation. Some of these men felt that the government's plan did not go far enough. The more radical proposals they put forward were regarded as revolutionary, but ultimately some of their ideas were adopted by the government, and incorporated into the terms of the emancipation.[15]

The bitter protests of the majority of the serfowners proved to

14 Wallace, *Russia*, p. 488.
15 Solov'ev, "Zapiski," XXX, 745-750, 754.

be their only active opposition to the tsar's wishes. As a contemporary foreign observer pointed out, their custom of unquestioning obedience to the autocrat restrained them from going further.[16] They spoke their pieces, and then with heavy hearts and fears for the future, they elected their provincial committees. The first one was organized in St. Petersburg on 14 January 1858 and the last one, in Orenburg, on 11 December 1858. All told there were 48 of these committees, with a total of 1,377 members.[17]

To guarantee that these bodies would all discuss the same problems and follow the same general procedure, the government provided them with a flow of material for their information and guidance. While they were deliberating, Alexander decided to visit some of them to dispel doubts they might still have about his convictions, and to counteract the reactionary influence of some high aristocrats. Between 10 August and 20 September 1858 he traveled in six provinces in the Central Industrial region (Tver, Moscow, Vladimir, Kostroma, Iaroslav, and Nizhnii Novgorod) and four western guberniias (Smolensk, Minsk, Vilna, and Kovno). He met with the marshals of the nobility and with the committee members in these guberniias and made his wishes clear to them. The journey proved of decisive influence in convincing the provincial nobility that further efforts to postpone action would be fruitless.[18]

The Rescript to Nazimov had instructed the nobles that the holdings they were to provide the peasants should be large enough "to guarantee the existence of the peasants and meet their obligations to the government and the proprietors." The provincial committees were to recommend how much land was necessary to meet these conditions. There seems to be wide agreement among many historians that the position taken by the individual committees in this matter varied according to the geographical position and relative fertility of the province. In general terms, this view, which originated apparently with

[16] Henoumont, "Die Bauernfrage," p. 135.

[17] *Materialy*, I, 312-315, 316n.; Engelmann, *Die Leibeigenschaft*, pp. 294-295.

[18] Solov'ev, "Zapiski," XXXIV, 411; Engelmann, *Die Leibeigenschaft*, pp. 297, 298.

A. Kornilov around the turn of the century, holds that the lords in the black earth guberniias, and notably though not exclusively those in the Central Agricultural zone, wanted to free their peasants with as little land as possible, or even without any land. These lords were willing to emancipate the serfs without any indemnification, or only a small one, provided they kept all or most of the land themselves. The reason for this is said to have been that the proprietors of the chernozem drew their income predominantly or exclusively from their own agricultural operations. In contrast, the landowners in the less fertile non-black earth provinces, and notably those in the Central Industrial region, who according to this view drew their incomes predominantly from obrok, were willing to free their peasants with sizable allotments of land. But they wanted high redemption payments to cover their loss of income from the abolition of the obrok.[19] Kornilov allowed for exceptions to this general picture,[20] but as frequently happens, some who adopted his interpretation have been more dogmatic and inclusive.

Examination of the actual proposals made by individual committees on the size of peasant holdings and on redemption payments reveals that these generalizations go beyond the limits of the evidence. The clear cut geographical-economic division between provinces and regions that Kornilov, and those who followed him, have described does not emerge from the data, and in fact, some of the generalizations usually made are inaccurate. Geographical and economic considerations played a part, but they seemed to have operated with much less force than has often been assumed.

Eleven committees were willing to allow the peasant to retain holdings of the same size that he now had. Seven of these eleven were non-black earth provinces, three of them Lithuanian (Vilna, Grodno, Kovno), two White Russian (Minsk, Smolensk), one Northern (Vologda), and only one in the Central Industrial region (Tver). The other four were in the black earth, three

---

[19] Kornilov, *Modern Russian History*, ii, 20-22; *idem*, "Gubernskie komitety," pp. 249-251; *idem*, "Krest'ianskaia reforma," pp. 302-304.
[20] E.g., Kornilov, "Gubernskie komitety," pp. 250, 250n.

being in the Southwest (Volynia, Kiev, Podolia), and one in the trans-Volgan region (Samara).[21]

The committees of the other provinces, chernozem and non-chernozem alike, wanted to cut down on the existing size of the holdings per peasant. In general, the percentage of decrease suggested by the committees of the black earth provinces was larger than that recommended by the non-black earth committees. But some of the latter wanted to make reductions as severe as those proposed by the chernozem committees. In fact, the committees of Iaroslav, Kostroma, and Moscow urged cuts as deep as those recommended by the most grasping of the chernozem committees. Yet these three guberniias were in the heart of the Central Industrial region, and had among the highest ratios in the empire of peasants on obrok (87.4 percent in Iaroslav, 87.5 percent in Kostroma, 68 percent in Moscow).[22]

Finally, there were not only sharp variations between the recommendations of committees of provinces with the same general geographic and economic characteristics, as say between Tver and its neighbors Moscow and Iaroslav, but wide differences appeared within individual committees themselves. In Simbirsk, for example, the majority of the committee proposed holdings of $1\frac{1}{2}$ desiatins per soul, 5 members wanted 2 to 3 desiatins, and two wanted to keep the existing size; in Nizhnii Novgorod the majority voted for 5 desiatins per *tiaglo*, the minority for $3\frac{1}{8}$; and so on.[23]

Similarly, the proposals of the committees on the amount of the obligations the peasants should pay do not fit into a regional-economic pattern. The tsar had ordered in the Rescript to Nazimov that the peasants should pay the lords obrok or barshchina for their holdings as long as the lords retained ownership

[21] Committee recommendations summarized in tabular form in Skrebitskii, *Krest'ianskoe dielo*, II, pt. 2, 1542-1551.

Despite this evidence Liashchenko wrote (*History*, p. 380) that in the Southwest "the landowners were interested in retaining control over the largest possible area of land and . . . in releasing to the peasantry, whenever possible merely the homestead plot . . . ," and claimed that in the trans-Volgan provinces the landowners "were universally in favor of emancipation without land."

[22] Ignatovich, "Pomeshchich'i krest'iane," IX, 47.

[23] Red. Kom., *Pervoe izdanie*, I, ch. 5; Skrebitskii, *Krest'ianskoe dielo*, II, pt. 1, 11-12.

of the land. The committees could recommend the form of the obligation, that is whether it was to be obrok or barshchina or both, and its size. Subsequently, instructions from St. Petersburg explained that the amount of the obligation should depend upon the value of the land turned over to the peasants and the "industrial advantages" of the locality, that is, the opportunities present for deriving income from non-agricultural occupations.[24] Nearly all of the committees who wanted to decrease the size of the peasant holding voted in favor of reducing the obligations the peasants currently paid. But only two committees, both in the non-chernozem, wanted to abolish the barshchina entirely. All the others, in non-black earth and black earth alike, voted to retain it, but most of them wanted to reduce it to one to two days a week. The suggested decrease was no larger in the non-chernozem than in the chernozem provinces. Indeed, the committees of two of the Central Industrial provinces (Kostroma and Nizhnii Novgorod) recommended its retention at the old level of three days a week, while the committees of some of the Central Agricultural proposed that it be reduced, two of them (Voronezh and Tambov) voting in favor of just one day per week. The size of the obrok payments recommended by the various committees were in general a few rubles less than the average obrok that the peasants in the industrial provinces had been paying. Once again it is not possible to make any clear cut distinction between chernozem and non-chernozem; in both regions committees proposed decreases of the same size. As with the recommendations on the size of holdings, neighboring and geographically similar provinces forwarded disparate suggestions about the amount of obligations, and minorities within individual committees expressed views at variance with the majority opinion.[25]

Ruses employed by lords to forestall loss of land to peasants provide additional evidence of the similarity of their reactions irrespective of region. Reports from both black earth and non-black earth provinces told of seigniors taking holdings from their serfs in order to keep the best fields for themselves, moving

[24] Ivaniukov, *Padenie*, p. 283.
[25] Red. Kom., *Pervoe izdanie*, III, Doklad . . . k. no. 17; Kornilov, "Gubernskie komitety," pp. 269-274.

the peasants to inferior soil or resettling them elsewhere, and even sending them to Siberia or selling them as recruits, or freeing them without land.[26] Rumors that household serfs would be redeemed by the government, and would not have to be supplied with holdings, persuaded many proprietors to convert agricultural peasants into domestics.[27] Most of these conversions took place in the black earth provinces, especially in the southwestern provinces (v. p. 460), but the number of *dvorovye liudi* went up in some of the non-chernozem guberniias, too. In Kostroma the absolute increase of over 14,000 domestic serfs (from 108 to 14,771) between the Ninth and Tenth Revisions was larger than the increase in all but six of the black earth provinces, and the relative increase in Kostroma was far greater than that in other provinces of the empire.[28]

In contrast to the fears and forebodings of the mass of the dvorianstvo, the intellectuals greeted the news of the tsar's intentions with almost hysterical joy. Alexander Herzen opened and closed an account he wrote for his expatriate journal, *The Bell (Kolokol)* with the supposed last words of Emperor Julian the Apostate, "Thou hast conquered, Galilean!"[29] The censorship on the discussion of serfdom was relaxed, and the entire press, with the single exception of the *Landowners' Journal*, enthusiastically supported abolition, and through articles and discussions contributed importantly to the plan that ultimately was adopted.[30] Of the journals published within Russia *The Contemporary (Sovremmenik)* was probably the most influential. But *The Bell*, printed in London, was the most important publication of all. Herzen, who had gone into selfimposed exile so that he could speak out freely against the autocracy, began publishing *The Bell* on 1 July 1857 as a biweekly. Though it was officially banned from Russia copies poured in, it was sold almost openly, and was reproduced clandestinely to meet the demand for it. Nearly all literate people read it, from the tsar and his wife on down. Herzen published current information

[26] Zaionchkovskii, *Otmena*, pp. 92-93.
[27] Domontovich, *Materialy*, p. 165; Troinitskii, *Krepostnoe naselenie*, p. 61.
[28] Troinitskii, *Krepostnoe naselenie*, pp. 59-60.
[29] *Kolokol*, no. 9, 15 Feb. 1858, pp. 67-68.
[30] Ivaniukov, *Padenie*, pp. 88-103.

and memorandums that were sent him by correspondents within the empire, revealed facts that could not be mentioned by the press in Russia, and wrote lead articles that served to guide opinion within the government and outside it.

The news of the tsar's plans to free the peasants did not produce a decrease in rural disorders. According to the incomplete official data there had been 86 cases of peasant disturbances during 1858. In 1859, 90 were reported and in 1860, 108. Twenty-seven landlords and stewards were killed by peasants and thirty unsuccessful attempts at murder were made. The imperial chief of police in his report for 1858 explained the continued restlessness of the serfs in these words:[31] "The peasantry . . . while awaiting the change in its fate is in a tense state and can easily become aroused at any external reason. . . . The disorders now occurring most frequently consist in this, that the serfs either stop paying obrok and other obligations, or show disobedience to the village elder or even to the proprietor himself. Risings of entire villages, requiring action from high provincial authorities or the assistance of the army command. . . . took place in 25 provinces in the course of the year. . . ."

I I

Early in January 1858 the committee that Alexander had appointed a year before to work out the basic principles for the emancipation, gave up its secret classification and became the Main Committee for Peasant Affairs. It took as its function the supervision of the work of the provincial committees, and received and studied the proposals they made. In the summer of 1858 General Ia. I. Rostovtsev, one of the members of the Main Committee, went to Germany to study the way peasant emancipation had been carried out there.[32] He became convinced that

[31] Zaionchkovskii, *Otmena*, pp. 93-94.

[32] Rostovtsev first won attention for himself when, as a young officer, he informed Tsar Nicholas of the Decembrist conspiracy, and thereby betrayed intimate friends. For this act historians have sometimes censured him. It should, however, be pointed out that before he went to the tsar he tried to persuade his two brother officers, Obolenskii and Ryleev, who had told him about the plot, to give up their plans, and he finally warned them that it was his duty as an officer (as indeed it was) to inform the tsar unless they abandoned the conspiracy. Moreover, he did not mention names when he spoke to the tsar, he immediately

the lord should not be allowed to retain his police powers over his former serfs, as the Rescript to Nazimov had suggested. He also urged that the period of transition from serfdom to freedom, during which the peasant was to continue to pay his seignior barshchina and obrok, should be as short as possible. Alexander saw the wisdom of these suggestions and ordered the Main Committee to adopt them as guiding principles. Meanwhile, N. A. Miliutin and Ia. A. Solov'ev, high officials in the Ministry of Interior, were winning support for their view that the peasants should become owners of their holdings by redeeming them from the seigniors.

At Rostovtsev's suggestion the Main Committee suggested the establishment of two special boards to edit the recommendations of the provincial committees, and draft the emancipation statute. The tsar gave his approval and made Rostovtsev president of these two new bodies. They were called the Editing Commissions. They had a total of 36 members, half of them landowners (who were known officially as "experts") and half bureaucrats. As things worked out, the two bodies functioned as one organization, but the plural name was retained. Rostovtsev selected, or was able to influence the selection, of a number of members, and aided by Miliutin, chose men who were strong advocates of reform. There was, however, a minority of seven to nine members who were either outright foes of emancipation, or proponents of less liberal schemes of emancipation than that favored by the majority.

The Editing Commissions became operative on 4 March 1859. At their meeting the next day Rostovtsev presented the fundamental propositions that the tsar and his advisers now believed had to be included in the emancipation legislation. They represented a far advance beyond the directions the government had given in the Rescript to Nazimov, and bear witness to the influence of the liberal bureaucrats. Rostovtsev told the commissioners that the law they were going to draft should free the peasants with land; arrange for them to become the owners of

---

told Obolenskii and Ryleev of his action, and neither of these two men, at the time or later, held what he had done against him. (Kornilov, *Modern Russian History*, II, 16-17.)

that land through redemption payments to the landlords; provide for financial and administrative participation by the government in the redemption procedure; avoid if possible a transition period during which the peasants continued to pay obligations to their seigniors; if such a transition period was unavoidable make it as short as possible; abolish barshchina within three years except where the peasants wanted to retain it; and give the peasants communal autonomy.[33]

The Commissions made these precepts the basis of their work. Since the new government program differed sharply from the recommendations of the provincial committees, who had followed the line laid down in prior governmental proposals, the commissioners decided not to use these provincial recommendations except as material for their own conclusions. The tsar had promised that representatives of the provincial committees would participate in the final decisions on the reform. The bureaucrats of the Commissions, however, managed to have the promise amended to allow representatives of provincial committees to give their opinions, but not to vote on proposals. This naturally angered the provincial nobility, and much intriguing and political infighting went on between their representatives and the bureaucrats to win the tsar's support. The nobles lost out, partly because the bureaucrats were able to persuade the tsar that the overwhelming majority of the provincial committees were opposed to emancipation, and partly because the tsar took umbrage at the audacity of nobles who dared to question his will.[34]

The Editing Commissions worked at top speed for a year and seven months, holding 409 meetings, and turning out volumes of reports and memorandums. To save time in working through the vast pile of information that poured in on them they decided to use only data collected for properties with 100 or more souls. Conditions on properties with fewer souls were simply disregarded. On 10 October 1860 they completed the draft of the law and forwarded it to the Main Committee. That body discussed it until 14 January 1861 but made virtually no substan-

---

[33] *Ibid.*, pp. 28-31; Engelmann, *Die Leibeigenschaft*, pp. 318-321.
[34] *Materialy*, I, 3-17; Kornilov, *Modern Russian History*, II, 34-38.

tive changes. The draft went next to the Imperial Council where the tsar and his advisers studied it until mid-February. Here a provision was added that was to prove of much consequence in later years. It permitted the landowner to give the peasant, by mutual agreement, one fourth of the holding required by the law, whereupon all their obligations to one another were cancelled out. This amendment was proposed by Prince Gagarin, advocate of a landless emancipation, as a way to reduce the amount of land the freed peasants would have as their own.[35]

The Editing Commissions had carried on the last stages of their work in complete secrecy. When the completed legislation went to the government's printing office the workers there were threatened with exile to Siberia if they allowed any information to get out. Even high officials did not know what it contained.[36] People who thought they understood about matters of protocol expected the tsar to publish the law on 19 February, the sixth anniversary of his coronation. Alexander did sign the decree that day. But the pre-Lenten carnival was to begin a week later, on the 26th, and the government feared that the news of the emancipation, combined with the drinking and rollicking that went on during Carnival Week, could lead to serious disturbances. So publication was delayed until the day before Lent began, Sunday the fifth of March, in hope that the sombreness of the penitential season would dampen excitable spirits. On that day the tsar's manifesto, announcing the new law and summarizing its major provisions, was read in churches and distributed and posted. It took more time for the official word to get to outlying regions; some villages did not receive the manifesto and the text of the law until May.[37]

The manifesto was written in stilted and sometimes obscure language. But its meaning was clear to those who read it or had it read to them. Prince Kropotkin, writing forty years later, recalled that Sunday in St. Petersburg as a day of wild enthusiasm. Throngs gathered before the Winter Palace shouting hurrahs, at

[35] Engelmann, *Die Leibeigenschaft*, pp. 327-342; Kornilov, *Modern Russian History*, II, 42-44.

[36] Stupperich, *Die Anfänge*, p. 202.

[37] Gitermann, *Geschichte*, III, 163.

the opera the audience sang the Imperial Hymn over and over again, and delighted crowds ran after the tsar's carriage when he rode through the streets.[38] But all the excitement that Kropotkin remembered seemed to have escaped the eyes of the American minister at St. Petersburg. In a dispatch to Washington written just three days after the announcement of the emancipation he reported:[39] "St. Petersburg has been very quiet. . . . since the publication of the Serf-Manifesto. On Sunday I drove through the city, in order to observe the effect of the publication upon the people. It was received very tranquilly and there was no appearance of excitement any where. I met the Emperor several times, but his passage through the streets seemed to create no special enthusiasm. On Monday and Tuesday, I understand, there was some demonstration, and the crowd in one instance stopped his carriage and cheered him. A similar demonstration was made, I am told, for the Grand Duke Constantine. But, on the whole, it is marvelous to see how quietly so great a measure has been inaugurated."

There is some question, then, about the way the people of the capital greeted the news. But there is none about the reaction of most of the peasants. They were grievously disappointed. They could not believe that their beloved tsar had not given them land along with freedom, that they would have to pay for the holdings they had used so long, that some of them would have less land than they had as serfs, and that they would not be freed immediately. Some among them firmly believed that the proprietors, aided by corrupt officials and by priests, had suppressed the true manifesto and substituted for it one of their own devising. To make matters worse, the length and intricacy of the law itself led to endless confusion and sometimes fantastic misunderstandings. The authorities made no effort to explain its provisions in simple, straightforward language, and the peasants, who rarely could read, had to depend upon some half-literate priest or clerk to explain it to them.[40]

---

[38] Kropotkin, *Memoirs*, pp. 133-135.

[39] John Appleton to Sec. of State W. H. Seward, St. Petersburg, 8/20 Mar. 1861, U.S. State Dept. Records (U.S. Archives).

[40] Stupperich, *Die Anfänge*, pp. 203-204; Yarmolinsky, *Road*, pp. 101-102.

The mutterings of discontent quickly translated themselves into open and active resistance. Within a few days of the publication of the law reports of unrest and of risings began to come into St. Petersburg, and as the weeks and months passed by the number of outbreaks mounted alarmingly. In 1861 acts of insubordination were reported in 1,176 properties, in 1862 in 400, and in 1863 in 386.

The violent reaction of the peasants took some among the liberal reformers by surprise. They knew the law would not satisfy all the hopes that the people had for it, but they never expected them to rise against it. The government, and especially Tsar Alexander, proved more knowledgeable of the temper of the peasants. Already in 1858 the tsar had called attention to the probability of rural disturbances when the law was published, and careful plans and instructions had been worked out for police and military action against them. When the expected happened, the regime was ready. Peasants were shot down in their village streets, and many were flogged or exiled to Siberia. By these tyrannical repressions peace and order were gradually restored. In 1864 outbreaks were reported in just 75 estates.[41]

III

The law itself was an enormously long document of nearly 400 printed pages, divided into seventeen separate statutes and two annexes, and replete with complex and sometimes contradictory provisions.[42] To begin with, the law said the peasants were now free. But it ordered them to continue for the next two years to pay their former masters the same obedience and the same obligations they had paid as serfs. During this transition period necessary surveys and arrangements for emancipation were to be made for each property. At the end of these two years the peasants still did not become free, nor did they become land-

[41] Florinsky, *Russia*, II, 922; Simkhovitch, "The Russian Peasant," p. 572; Naidenov, *Klassovaia bor'ba*, pp. 23-27; Venturi, *Roots*, pp. 208-219.

[42] For the manifesto and full text of the law v. *Krest'ianskaia reforma*, pp. 39-497. For a semi-official French translation of the manifesto and a résumé of major sections of the law v. *Affranchissement des serfs*. For discussions of the contents of the law v. Haxthausen *Die ländliche Verfassung*, and "Die Aufhebung der Leibeigenschaft in Russland."

owners. Instead, they were to go into a status called "temporarily-obligated" (*vremenno-obiazannye*). The proprietor was to continue to exercise police jurisdiction over them, and to have powers over the village communes. He had to allow the peasants the use of their holdings, but he retained full ownership of the land. The peasants were to pay him a rent in cash, or if they chose, in labor. They left the "temporarily-obligated" status and became entirely free of seignioral authority, only when they had redeemed their holdings from the proprietor. Since the law ordered that redemption was to be optional, and could only be done with the consent of the landowner, many peasants seemed destined to long and even permanent "temporary obligation."

For the first nine years after the promulgation of the emancipation law every peasant who was qualified had to take a holding, and therefore had to enter the "temporarily-obligated" condition. Household serfs, however, were to become entirely free at the end of the two year transition period. But they were not to receive any land unless they had holdings on 2 March 1858, the date of a ukase that forbad further conversions of agricultural peasants into domestics. If they had holdings on that date they were to be treated like other peasants.

This seems a remarkably complicated way to go about giving people freedom, but it seems almost straightforward when compared with the provisions laid down for furnishing land to the peasants. In justice to the legislators, the matter of holdings offered many difficulties because of dissimilarities in existing forms of peasant tenure, and in economic conditions, among the several parts of the empire. They tried to deal with the problem by splitting the realm into four major divisions, and issuing a special statute for each sector. In addition, they drew up statutes for the Don Cossack Land, Stavropol, Siberia, Bessarabia, and for factory and possessional peasants. All of these special statutes were incorporated in the emancipation law.

The first of the four major special statutes was for twenty-nine provinces of Great Russia, the three provinces of New Russia, and Mogilev and part of Vitebsk in White Russia. Most of the peasants in these provinces were organized into land-equalizing communes. The statute retained the commune, turning the land over to it rather than to the individual peasant. The commune was given the responsibility of distributing the land among its members. It was to use the same method of distribution that it had employed before emancipation, that is, either according to family size or to need. The commune was also made responsible for obligations to the proprietor and to the state. The principle of mutual guarantee that made all members of the commune liable for one another's obligations was to be retained.

The area covered by this first special statute, including as it did the largest part of European Russia and by far the majority of the serfs, had, of course, many geographical and economic variations within it. To adjust for these differences the law-makers divided the entire region into three zones: the non-chernozem, the chernozem, and the steppe. They then split each of the three zones into nine, eight, and twelve subdivisions, respectively. The subdivisions were called "localities." The holding size and rental fee set by the law differed with zone and locality. In the first, or non-chernozem zone, the maximums for holdings for each locality varied between 3 and 7 desiatins per male serf. In most of the localities, however, they were between 3 and 5 desiatins. In the second, or chernozem zone, the maximums were from 2¾ to 6 desiatins, but for most of these localities they were set at between 3 and 4 desiatins. The minimum in all localities in both zones was one-third of the maximum. In the third, or steppe zone, a single figure was given for each locality, instead of maximums and minimums. This figure ran between 3 and 12 desiatins, but for the majority of steppe localities it was between 6 and 8 desiatins per male.

The proprietor had to turn over at least the minimum amount of land to the commune. The minimum amount was determined by multiplying the minimum individual holding for the locality, as set by the statute, by the number of male peasants in the commune. The proprietors in the first and second zone did not have to give the commune more than one third of their property, and in the third zone not more than one half. Forests were not included in the land that the peasants were to get, except for certain special instances, nor was the proprietor obliged to allow the peasants to gather free fire wood.

The statute fixed the rent for a holding of maximum size during the period of temporary obligation at 8, 9, 10, or 12 rubles a year, depending upon the zone and locality. The rental fee could not be changed for twenty years, and after that could not be increased or decreased by more than 20 percent. One of the most unfair provisions of the entire emancipation law required peasants who received holdings smaller than the maximum to pay more rent per desiatin than those who had holdings of maximum size. This was done by setting a higher rent for the first desiatin, and in certain localities also for the second desiatin, than for the remaining desiatins of the holding. For example, in the non-chernozem zone the rent for the first desiatin was equal to one-half, and for the second desiatin one quarter, of the rent for a holding of maximum size. Thus, the smaller the holding the higher the rent per desiatin.

The second of the four major special statutes applied to the Little Russian provinces of Chernigov, Poltava, and part of Kharkov. For purposes of determining size of holdings and rents, the statute divided these guberniias into two, three, and four localities, respectively. Unlike Great Russia, the communes in the Little Russian guberniias did not hold land collectively, nor did they practice repartition. Instead, each household retained hereditary possession of the same holding. The statute ordered this type of tenure to be retained. Some land, however, was to be turned over to the commune for distribution to landless peasants. The law established norms for the holdings carved out of the communal land, the maximum size ranging from 2¾ to 3½ desiatins per male serf, depending upon the locality. The minimums were fixed at one half the maximums. Peasant families who owned work animals were to have larger holdings than those who did not, so that the size of the holding was directly related to the economic resources of the household. The rental fee during temporary obligation was to be from 1.40 rubles to 2.50 rubles a year. The individual household bore the responsibility for all charges on its holding. The proprietor did not have to give up more than two-thirds of his land to the peasants.

The third major statute was for the southwestern provinces of Kiev, Podolia, and Volynia. Inventories had been introduced into these guberniias in the late 1840's. The statute decreed that the holdings and obligations of the peasants should be those called for in the inventories. The peasant households held their land individually. Some land, however, was held communally, and the law ordered that it was to remain in communal possession.

The last of the major special statutes applied to the Lithuanian provinces of Vilna, Grodno, and Kovno, and to Minsk and parts of Vitebsk in White Russia. Communal landholding was almost unknown in these areas, so the statute decreed that all peasant land was to be held by the individual household. The size of the holdings was to be based upon the inventories that had been drawn up for these provinces, but the landowner did not have to give up more than two-thirds of his property. The peasants' rent during their temporary obligation was to be the same as that called for in the inventories, but was not to exceed three rubles a year except in special circumstances.

To return to provisions of the law that applied to all parts of the empire, it will be recalled that after the two year transition period the peasants were to enter the "temporarily-obligated" status. The law established two methods by which they could leave this status, and become owners of their holdings and free of seignorial control. One method enabled the peasants to get land at no cost. The other involved long-term indebtedness. The first way allowed the proprietor to give the peasants, if they consented, holdings equal in size to one-fourth of the maximum size fixed by the law for holdings in the particular locality. In return for this sacrifice in land the peasants became the full owners of these "gratuitous holdings," as they were called, and paid nothing for them. Peasants, especially in regions where land was still plentiful and could be rented cheaply, were attracted by this opportunity to get holdings at no cost, and some proprietors were willing to cooperate because they could thereby keep more land for their own use. By 1 January 1864, 405,112 had chosen to take these reduced allotments, and by 1 January 1878 the total had risen to 640,380.[43]

The other way by which the peasants became the owners of their holdings was through redemption. The 1861 law allowed them to do this only if the proprietor consented to the peasants' request, or if he himself wanted it, regardless of whether the peasants agreed or not. A decree of 28 December 1881, however, made redemption compulsory. The cost of redemption of a holding was determined by capitalizing its annual rent at 6 percent. The government advanced most of the cost, paying the proprietors the requisite amount in 5 percent government bonds. It paid 80 percent of the redemption price if the peasants received holdings of maximum size, and 75 percent if they were less than the maximum. If the redemption was at the proprietor's request, this payment became the full settlement for the land. If it was done by mutual agreement between proprietor and peasant, the peasant paid the remaining 20 to 25 percent directly to the proprietor, the method of payment to be determined by agreement between the two parties. The law ordered the peasant to repay the state at the annual rate of 6 percent of the amount the state had advanced (5 percent to reimburse the government, 1/2 percent for costs, 1/2 percent for amortization). The operation was to last 49 years, at the expiration of which time the peasant would be the full owner of his holding. The government did not aid in the purchase of the homestead; the peasant had to pay for this entirely on his own.

The cost of redemption and the annual payment the peasant had to make to the state, then, were based upon the rent the peasant paid as a "temporarily-obligated" peasant. The law, however, set this rent in most provinces at a higher figure than the value of the land warranted. The proprietors thereby received inflated prices for their land, and the annual redemption installments paid by the peasants were much greater than they should have been. A study made in the latter part of the 1870's of redemption charges showed that they often exceeded the cash income of the holding, in some cases by as much as 200 percent

43 Preyer, *Die russische Agrarreform*, p. 7n.

and even 565 percent. Obviously, these peasants had to find employment outside their holdings to earn the money they needed to redeem their land. This contravened one of the principles of the emancipation avowed by the government, to wit, that the peasant must be provided with enough land to support himself and meet all his obligations to lord and state. It has been suggested that the men who drafted the law deliberately subverted this principle because the government had decided that the peasants would pay the serfowners for the land they received, but not for their personal freedom. The serf had a cash value to the seignior, and so the seignior suffered a financial loss when he surrendered his right of ownership of the peasant. By setting rents at a level higher than the value of the land justified, the lawmakers provided for a concealed indemnification to the former serfowners for this loss.[44] Another, and possibly much more important reason for the high rents, as well as the small size of the holdings, was to make sure that the peasants would have to seek outside employment to make ends meet, and thereby supply a cheap labor force for the proprietors.

The drafters of the law feared that when the serfs were freed of seignorial supervision their supposed lack of self-discipline, or their ignorance or incapacity, would cause social dislocation, and make it difficult for the proprietors and the state to collect rents and redemption payments. They decided, therefore, to replace the seignior with the commune as the supervisor of the peasants' activities. These communes could be, but were not necessarily, the same ones the peasants had before the emancipation. For instance, the law ordered that the peasants on each property were to form a separate commune unless they were fewer than twenty revision souls, in which event they were to join with peasants on neighboring properties to form a commune.[45]

The commune's function was to provide local government for its members. In regions where land was held communally it also was responsible for the periodic redistribution of holdings. It was run by an assembly of peasant householders and elders. The

44 Cf. Simkhovitsch, *Die Feldgemeinschaft*, p. 244.
45 Cf. Robinson, *Rural Russia*, pp. 67-80, for a discussion of some of the legal confusion that surrounded the post-emancipation commune.

assembly was given a certain amount of police power, and sat as a court of first instance. A new territorial unit created by the emancipation law, and called by the old name of *volost*, formed the next level of government. The *volost* was a sort of township, made up of adjoining communes with a total membership of not less than 300, and not more than 2,000, revision souls. It had its own elders and officials and its own assembly, composed of representatives from the member communes, and its own courts whose judges were elected by the assembly. It had extensive rights of self-government, and broad powers over its members.

The emancipation law of 19 February 1861 applied only to the peasants of private seigniors. The other unfree rural classes, however, were not forgotten. In 1858 the government established a commission to work up plans for the emancipation of the appanage peasants. Imperial decrees of 20 June 1858 and 26 August 1859 gave these people their personal freedom, and laws issued on 5 March 1861 and 26 June 1863 provided them with holdings and regulated the conditions of their tenure. All the land they had hitherto used was turned over to them, and its redemption made obligatory. They were to continue for the next 49 years to make the same payments they had hitherto been paying, to reimburse the government for their use of the land and to amortize its cost. At the end of this period they would be the owners of their holdings.[46]

Plans began to be made in 1859 for the eventual emancipation of the state peasants. On 5 March 1861 the Ministry of State Domain received instructions to work out a statute that applied the principles of the law of 21 February 1861 to these peasants. Early in 1863 the emperor gave his approval to the basic provisions of the suggested legislation, but the law was not issued until 24 November 1866. It gave the state peasants permanent use of the land they had been occupying in return for a rental payment, permitted them to redeem their holdings and become proprietors, allowed them communal autonomy, and ordered that they were to hold their land communally or individually, depending upon the existing situation. Although the law in-

[46] Simkhovitsch, *Die Feldgemeinschaft*, pp. 260-261; Glavnoe upravlenie udelov, *Stoletie udelov*, pp. 32-38.

creased rents in a number of places over what they had been, the outcome of the emancipation operation proved much more favorable to the state peasants than to the serfs. The former received holdings that almost everywhere were larger than those given the former serfs, and their rental payments were much less, so that their annual redemption charges were as much as 50 to 60 percent smaller than the payments made by former serfs.[47]

[47] Simkhovitsch, *Die Feldgemeinschaft*, pp. 265-272.

27

SOME CONCLUSIONS AND
GENERALIZATIONS

IF THE THOUSAND-YEAR HISTORY of the relationship between Russian lords and peasants that has been told
here had to be characterized in a few words it could be
said to have been a function of the political and economic evolution of that land. The institutional arrangements in rural life
reflected the needs and the demands of the state and the long-
term trends of economic growth and contraction. These two
controlling forces did not exert equal influence at every stage.
Sometimes one was paramount, sometimes the other. If the
record is balanced, the political considerations seem more often
to have predominated, but this nowise diminishes the critical
influence of the economic factor. Indeed, the two sometimes
were so closely interrelated that to disentangle them, and to
assess their relative importance, involves the risk of oversimplification. At the same time, the lord-peasant relationship itself
was not a dependent variable; the conditions out on the land had
much to do with shaping political and economic life.

The sparse sources of early Russian history show that these
interactions evidenced themselves from the very outset. In the
eighth and ninth centuries a new ruling elite, made up of
warrior princes and their retinues, had established its hegemony
over the Eastern Slavs. At first, the princes and their followers
had supported themselves through tribute, war booty, brigandage, and trade. Then, in the tenth and eleventh centuries, they
decided to establish themselves as the proprietors of large
landed complexes. They built up their possessions by expropri-
ating land that belonged to peasant communes, and by internal
colonization and frontier settlement.

Several explanations suggest themselves for this shift to landowning. One is that the increase in the size of the retinues made
it too expensive for the princes to maintain them out of their

own incomes. It is possible, too, that the members of the new elite did not care to settle down as landowners until they had gained a feeling of permanence in the land they had conquered. Finally, new opportunities for profitable agricultural production may well have served to stimulate large-scale private landownership. For the Kievan era was a period of economic expansion (as were these same centuries in Western Europe), characterized by active local and interregional trade, improvements in the techniques of farming, a rise in industrial production, the increased use of money, the growth of cities, colonization of new territories, and a large increase in population. These developments offered an expanding market for farm products. Presumably, the new landowners realized this, for the slender and indirect evidence about the internal organization of their properties indicates that they engaged in direct production. They probably used much of the goods they raised to maintain their own establishments. But in view of their experience as traders, and the fact that they could have provided for their own needs by renting out land in return for payments in kind, it seems likely that some of their production, and possibly much of it, was intended for the market.

The introduction of large-scale private landowning by men of the ruling class marked the starting point in the history of the subjugation of the Russian peasantry. The available evidence points to the conclusion that into the eleventh century all free men enjoyed a certain amount of equality. But when land that belonged to peasant communes was converted into the private property of a large landowner, the peasants found themselves changed into the renters of fields that had been theirs, and some of them were apparently pushed off their holdings and became the hired hands, indentured workers, or contract laborers of the proprietors. They remained free, but their economic dependence upon the proprietors brought about a deterioration in their legal and social status, in comparison with those peasants who still lived in the independent communes.

In contrast, the establishment of large-scale private landownership served to enhance the political and economic position of the princely retainers. As a landed proprietor the retainer no longer had to depend entirely for his support upon the continued bounty of the ruler. Moreover, though he received his land as a reward for his services to the prince, he did not hold it on condition of continued service. Instead, he became its full proprietor. If he left the prince's service he kept the land as his own, even if he entered the service of another ruler. Inevitably, this allowed the retainer to become far more independent of his principal than he had hitherto been. Now his income and his prestige became increasingly dependent upon his ownership of land.

In the twelfth century Kievan society began to disintegrate under the impact of the ceaseless feuds among the princes, and of invasions by nomads of the steppe. It collapsed completely in the next century when the Mongols invaded in force. Many of the people of the Dnieper valley had already migrated into the forested land of the Oka-Volga triangle, and after the Tatar onslaught that area became the center of Russian life. The region was under the suzerainty of the Mongols, but they allowed the descendants of the Kievan dynasts to rule in the many princedoms into which it was divided. The continued feuds of these princes, and further invasions by the Mongols and by others, brought about political chaos. Matters were worsened by the severe economic contraction that began in the thirteenth century and lasted until well into the fifteenth century. Population declined, much land lay untilled, trade and industry languished, and most cities became little more than administrative and military centers.

The changes in political and economic life worked initially to the benefit of the peasants, and against the interests of the lords. The princes and the private landowners, confronted with the phenomenon of declining population, held out many inducements to attract settlers to their lands. They no longer engaged in market production, but turned over their properties to the peasants in return for rental payments. They allowed the renter virtually all the rights of ownership over his holding, so long as he worked it and met whatever obligations were required of him.

The princes and landowners made these concessions because their political power and their economic well-being depended upon their having peasants on their lands. Had they held out less favorable terms they would not have been able to attract the renters they needed, and their fields would have yielded them no income. They sought a remedy for their predicament by trying to limit the peasant's freedom of movement. But the competition for renters worked against the success of their efforts. They were able, however, to restrict the time the renter could leave his holding to settle elsewhere to certain periods of the year, and to levy an exit fee.

The unsettled political and economic conditions, however, did not operate in favor of the peasants in the long run. Princes, seeking to win support for themselves, gave much black land to nobles and churchmen, thereby converting the independent peasant communers on this land into renters. Other peasant communes, seeking protection in those troubled times, voluntarily became renters of powerful lords and monasteries. The inability of the weak princes to control their realms effectively, their need to win the support of the nobles and churchmen, and the need of the latter for the ability to make fiscal concesssions that would attract settlers to their lands, persuaded the rulers to give jurisdictional and administrative privileges to landowners. There is evidence that princes had sometimes conferred these powers upon landowners in the Kievan period, but during the era of the Mongol domination the practice became general. As a result, the peasant who rented from a private landowner became the subject of his landlord.

By the latter part of the fifteenth century the status of the peasant renter had deteriorated in comparison with what it had been early in the period of Mongol hegemony. In the succeeding era, when the Grand Dukes of Moscow established themselves as the absolute rulers of the Russian land, the retrogression in peasant status continued, until finally the renter became the serf of his landlord.

To achieve their goal of absolute supremacy the Muscovite princes had to overcome the opposition of the great aristocracy, and had to win the loyalty of the lesser nobility. Through confiscations and, ultimately, extermination, they destroyed the power of the great lords. They gained and held the support of the lesser ones by giving them land and peasants—to be held on condition of continued service to the crown—and by raising them to positions of eminence in the administration of the state.

Meanwhile, the fluctuations in economic life introduced conditions that, in the context of the changed political milieu, made it advantageous for the lords to have ever greater authority over the peasants who lived on their lands. The rise in prices, the greater use of money, the opportunities for profitable production for market offered by the economic expansion of the era, combined with the increased demands made by the tsar's service on the income of the nobles, persuaded them to demand more in money dues and labor services from their peasants. These heightened demands reduced the peasants to still greater economic dependence upon their lords. Then the economic crisis and depopulation of the last decades of the sixteenth century, and the continued hard times in the next century, convinced the seigniors that it was essential to their own economic well-being to deprive their peasants of the right of free movement.

The state, for its part, cooperated to the full with the nobility. For it identified its own interests with the interests of the lords, reasoning that if the seigniors could not support themselves for their lands they would not be able to meet their service obligation to the state. Above all, the lesser lords, who were the chief supporters of the regime, faced economic ruin as a class unless they could keep their peasants from leaving them. The government's fiscal interests were involved, too, for the peasants' ability to move about made it difficult to collect the steadily mounting tax levies. And so in decrees and ordinances issued from the last years of the fifteenth century on through the first half of the seventeenth century, and especially from the 1580's on, the tsars gradually destroyed the freedom of the peasants, and bound them to the will of their seigniors.

But the lords had to pay a price for the favors they received. That price was service to the state for all lay landlords, whether they owned their land or held it as a pomestye. The right to have land and peasants depended upon the performance of that obligation. In the unique Service State that the Muscovite rulers created, each of their subjects, from the greatest to the least, was assigned a role that was determined by the interests of the state. The lord was bound to state service, and the peasant was bound to the lord, in order to provide him with the means to perform his service to the state.

To this extent the story of the relationship between lord and peasant and of the enserfment, is the story of the subjection of both lord and peasant to the will of the state. But there is far more to it than that. The institutions and practices that evolved in the centuries before the establishment of the unified and absolute state, and the adjustments of landlords to the long-term fluctuations in economic life before and during the era of absolutism, were the decisive elements in shaping the nature and form of the relationship between lord and peasant. The new absolutism only channeled and intensified already existing tendencies. That was its contribution. To ascribe more to it is to take much too narrow a view of what actually happened.

In fact, it seems to me that the history of agrarian institutions in Russia would have taken much the same course without the creation of the absolute state. For the Russian experience was not unique. Instead, it was part of a broad movement that transcended national frontiers to involve all the lands of Eastern Europe. During precisely the same centuries in which the Russian peasant was forced into bondage, the peasants of Eastern Germany, Livonia, Poland, Lithuania, Bohemia, Silesia, and Hungary, also lost their freedom. By the end of the fifteenth century most of the peasants from the Elbe River to the Volga were well on their way to serfdom. During the next century the obligations and restrictions that pressed upon them continued to grow, so that by the end of the sixteenth century the process of enserfment was just about complete, even though the laws that spelled this out were not issued in some lands until the seventeenth century, and even though there were groups of peasants who managed to escape the lot of their fellows.

Though the particulars of this development varied within each of these countries, when their histories during these centuries are compared certain phenomena that were common to all of them manifest themselves. These common traits, I believe, provide the explanation for the origins and growth of serfdom in each of these lands. Absolutism is not among them; it appeared only in Russia.

The phenomena that were common to these lands were the increase in the political power of the nobility, and especially of the lesser nobility; the grants by princes to seigniors of jurisdictional authority over the peasants who lived on their properties; the adjustments of the seigniors to the secular trends of economic life; and the failure of the urban middle class to establish itself as an economic and political force. I have discussed these matters at length in another place,[1] so that it will suffice here to outline the part these factors played in bringing on serfdom.

The political ascendancy of the Eastern nobility was at the expense of the sovereign. The rulers, weakened by dynastic rivalries, wars, rebellions, and financial difficulties, had constantly to make concessions to win and hold the support of their nobility. This had been true in Russia, too, until the Muscovite rulers unified the country. But they owed their triumph over their rivals to the support of the lesser nobles, and, as we have seen, they rewarded these men with land, peasants, and influential offices.

The growth in the political influence of the nobility gave them the power to make successful demands on their sovereigns for a freer hand in dealing with their peasants. As a result, the state in each of the Eastern lands, during the course of the fifteenth to. seventeenth centuries, withdrew from the relationship between lords and peasants. That left the way open to the seigniors to solve their labor problems by converting their free tenants into serfs.

The grant by rulers of jurisdictional and administrative privileges to seigniors reflected the political dependence of the prince upon the support of the nobility. For in giving these powers to the seigniors the rulers were yielding many of their own sovereign rights over their subjects. Although the extent to which this transfer of sovereignty from prince to seignior varied among the different lands, the peasant in all of them became more the subjects of their lords than of the crown. The lords,

1 Blum, "Rise," pp. 807-835.

armed with these public powers, levied for their own use obligations originally imposed for the benefit of the prince, tightened the restrictions on the freedom of movement of their peasants, demanded increased amounts of goods and services from them, changed the terms of peasant tenures, and evicted peasants from their holdings to build up their own demesnes. Thus, through entirely legal means, the lords were able to set themselves up as despots of their villages, and to press their peasants into a condition of subjection and dependence upon them.

The kind of adjustments that the seigniors made to the secular trends of economic contraction and growth is the third of the developments that I believe explain the enserfment of the European peasantry. The very slim data indicate that Eastern Europe, like Western Europe, suffered a severe economic contraction during the fourteenth and fifteenth centuries, marked by a decline in agricultural production, many empty holdings, and a large fall in population. The nobles, dependent for their incomes upon the work and payments of their peasants, found themselves seriously affected by the drop in population. They tried many avenues of escape from their deteriorating economic position, some of them even turning to brigandage. But their most common reaction was to place restrictions upon the right of the peasant to come and go as he pleased. In every one of these Eastern European states from the mid-fourteenth century on, and especially during the course of the fifteenth century, steady infringements were made upon the peasant renter's freedom of movement.

Then, at the end of the fifteenth century the Eastern lands, along with the rest of Europe, entered on a new era of economic growth. The Eastern lords saw the opportunity to profit from the changed conditions by producing for market on their own account. They expanded their demesnes, often at the expense of peasant-held land; they increased the obligations of their peasants, notably the labor service; and with the aid of their governments, they imposed still further restrictions upon peasant freedom of movement. The acquisition by the nobles of seignorial privileges over their peasants, and the political influence they enjoyed with their sovereigns, enabled them to carry through these encroachments upon the land, labor, and freedom of the peasants. The latter were powerless to resist, save by such illegal —and almost always unsuccessful—acts as flight or revolt.

Finally, an urban bourgeoisie strong enough to act as a countervailing force to the nobility did not emerge in Eastern Europe. From the thirteenth on into the fifteenth century the cities of Eastern Germany, Bohemia, Livonia, and Poland, acting often in cooperation with the central power, had been able to hold their own against the nobility. Then in the fifteenth century they began to lose ground. Their retrogression seems to have been attributable in large part to the decline of the Hanseatic League (to which a number of the Baltic cities belonged), the competition of the English and the Dutch in the Baltic, the weakening of the Teutonic Order whose members had controlled much of the Eastern trade, the market contraction resulting from the depopulation, wars, invasions, and domestic strife of the era, and, finally, the anti-urban policies adopted by the East German, Livonian, Polish, and Bohemian nobility. The seigniors of these lands exerted pressures on their governments from the early fifteenth century on for restrictions on the cities, and for concessions that would further their own economic interests at the expense of the townsmen. By virtue of their political power they succeeded in carrying through much of their program, to the grave detriment of the urban centers.

Hard hit by these reverses, most cities of Eastern Europe, instead of benefiting from the economic revival of the sixteenth century, stagnated into sleepy provincial centers, and lesser towns declined into villages. In Russia, on the other hand, urban settlements grew in number and importance. Indeed, they apparently provided the chief markets for expanding seignorial production, for, unlike the other Eastern lands, Russia was not at this time a grain exporter. Nonetheless, a politically privileged and economically important Russian bourgeois class did not develop. Instead, events took a completely contrary course. The government deprived the city people of their right to come and go as they pleased from their towns, and bound them to their settlements. Peasants whose lords permitted them to come to the towns carried on much of the local trade. These people

remained in the legal status of peasants, and had to pay obligations to their seigniors, no matter how long they lived in the
town. Interregional trade was in the hands of seigniors, a special
class of travelling merchants, and the tsar, who, through his
agents, was the chief trader of the realm.

The absence of a strong bourgeois class in the Eastern European lands meant that the claims of the nobility to social,
political, and economic predominance went uncontested. Try
as they might, the peasants alone lacked the leadership and
the strength to overthrow the supremacy of the seigniors, as the
many peasant risings of these and later centuries showed all too
clearly. The impotence of the urban middle class, then, is of
fundamental importance in explaining the evolution of the
relationship between lord and peasant in Eastern Europe.

Meanwhile, in Western Europe during these same centuries
the status of the peasantry improved steadily. At the beginning
of the twelfth century most peasants in the lands that lay west of
the Elbe River had been serfs. By the end of the sixteenth
century serfdom had disappeared in many of these lands, and
where it still lived on was far less onerous than it had formerly
been.

The collapse of the old seignorial order in the West has sometimes been attributed to the growth of a money economy, or to
the increase in commerce, or to the development of capitalism.[2]
But in the East money economy, trade, and capitalism (as
evidenced in the direct production for market by the seigniors)
also grew, and yet serfdom was established. It seems to me that
the fundamental reason for this difference between East and
West lay in the contrast in their political development. In the
struggle for domination in the state the nobility of the East won
out over the princes and the towns, or in Russia became the
class upon which the throne depended for its support, while in
the West the bourgeoisie emerged as an important political
force. The nobility of the Eastern lands, because of their un-
challenged political preeminence, were able to gain concessions

---

[2] Cf. Grekov, *Krest'iane*, pp. 375-376; Gras, *Evolution*, pp. 24-31; Pirenne,
Economic and Social History, p. 84; Nabholz, "Medieval Agrarian Society,"
pp. 503-504.

and privileges from their sovereigns that enabled them to establish economic and social control over the peasantry, and to dominate the townsmen.

The divergence between East and West in the nature of the relationship between lord and peasant turned out to be the decisive watershed in the history of freedom in the modern world. For it meant that Russia and the other lands of Eastern Europe remained backward agrarian societies that accepted coercion as the premise of social organization. A tradition of compulsion and servility, and acquiescence in the right of a few men to hold millions of their fellows in bondage, became the heritage of the peoples of Eastern Europe. The West moved forward into an era where the idea of freedom to live as one wished, and the conviction that individual liberty was a natural and inalienable right, could take root and flourish. Not that these beliefs won acceptance and implementation immediately upon the disappearance of serfdom. Far from it. But as R. H. Tawney observed in writing of sixteenth-century England, though liberty long remained more in shadow than in substance, "yet the shadow is itself an earnest of greater things."[3] The modern concept of individual freedom is often traced back to the Renaissance and the Reformation. It seems to me that the emancipation of the peasantry of Western Europe is of equal importance to the history of this great Western contribution to the progress of man.

II

The long process of enserfment of the Russian peasant came to its end in 1649 with the publication of the *Sobornoe Ulozhenie*. This codification of the laws and customs that regulated the relationship between lord and peasant gave notice, as it were, that serfdom had become a mature institution. During the next two hundred years, down to the emancipation in 1861, though some changes were introduced, the fundamentals of the lord-peasant relationship in Russia remained unaltered.

In the course of these two centuries the pattern of interaction between political and economic evolution and agrarian institu-

[3] Tawney, *Agrarian Problem*, pp. 43-44.

tions continued to manifest itself, as it had since Kievan times. The demands of the state and its conception of its own best interests, the creation of a noble caste, the economic growth that began in the second quarter of the eighteenth century, the increase in population and area, all molded and conditioned the relationship between lords and peasants, and were themselves influenced by this relationship.

In my discussion of these and other matters I had two purposes in mind. One was to analyze and describe these developments as parts of the history of Russian agrarian life. The other was to explain the coming of the emancipation. The causes of that event—like the causes of that other great happening of 1861, the American Civil War—have been much debated and disputed by historians. Most of the writers who have dealt with the problem have recognized a multiplicity of causes, but usually have stressed one as the most significant. In the preceding chapters I have presented the materials upon which these interpretations are based, and have indicated my own views. It seems to me that by marshalling major findings of these chapters within the framework provided by the explanations for the abolition of serfdom, I can, in these last pages, simultaneously review these findings and restate my own opinions about the causes of the emancipation.

The explanations for the abolition can be divided into five general causal categories. The first of these themes associates the emancipation with the process of economic development. Those who have emphasized this interpretation claim that the growth of an exchange economy, marked by the expansion of the market and an increase in the use of money, made serfdom obsolete. The old system, because of its inefficiency, low productivity, and restrictions on free movement, was an obstacle to the growth of towns, commerce, and industry, and so it was abolished.[4] Modern Soviet historians have adopted this line of reasoning, but have put it into a dialectical setting.[5] Following

[4] E.g., Schulze-Gaevernitz, "Der Nationalismus," pp. 340-341; Kizevetter, "Krest'-ianstvo v istorii Rossii," p. 12; Pokrovskii, Brief History, I, pp. 110-112.
[5] E.g., Liashchenko, History, pp. 358-374; Khromov, Ekonomicheskoe razvitie, pp. 7-25; Druzhinin, "Konflikt," pp. 73-76; Tsagalov, Ocherki, pp. 7-56.

standard Soviet practice they usually begin with texts from the classics of Marxism-Leninism that declare that serfdom could exist only so long as a "natural economy" persisted. The "feudal" estate formed a self-sufficient closed entity, with only the weakest sort of connection with the rest of the world. When it began to produce for the market it doomed itself, for the "feudal" producers could not by their very nature adjust themselves to the market and become commercial producing units.[6] Lack of capital, the low productivity of serf labor, and the nature of the structure of the entire "feudal" economy, blocked the introduction of technical improvements and efficient organization. For these reasons a crisis developed in agriculture in the last decades of serfdom that evidenced itself by violently fluctuating prices, an absolute decline in the number of serfs, increasing seignioral indebtedness, and a quickening in the tempo of peasant unrest. The agricultural crisis, in turn, was responsible for the political crisis of the mid-fifties. "The Sevastopol defeat and the oppressive peace terms that followed were a clear symptom of the collapse of the entire political and economic system of the old feudal order in Russia."[7]

Another economic interpretation that is much less sweeping attributes the emancipation to the self-interest of the serfowners. According to this view, the interest of seigniors in production for market increased during the first half of the nineteenth century. They became convinced that serf labor was an insuperable barrier to the increased productivity of their properties. They believed that free hired labor would prove more profitable to them, and therefore they supported emancipation. They wanted to liberate the serfs without land so that they would become a rural proletariat whose only means of livelihood would be to work for their former masters. But these seigniors had to give up this part of their program because serfowners of the non-chernozem provinces, who drew their incomes from obrok payments, had no desire to keep all their land for themselves. The proprietors in the less fertile regions wanted to free their peasants with sizable allotments, and with

6 Lenin in *Sochineniia*, III, pp. 140-141.
7 Liashchenko, *History*, p. 370.

a correspondingly high cost of redemption. The fear that a land-less emancipation would bring on a storm of peasant violence also dissuaded serfowners from insisting on it.

The economic explanations of the emancipation won much acceptance among Russian historians before 1917, as well as after that time. The materialistic interpretation, as Lazar Volin pointed out, "had become intellectually fashionable long before it gained the monopolistic exclusiveness of a political orthodoxy after the Revolution."[8] Attractive as these interpretations may have been, or still are, they ignore or glide over too many facts. Their most glaring deficiency is that they disregard the indisputable evidence that the overwhelming majority of the serfowners did not want to give up serfdom. Far from regarding it as wasteful and inefficient, most proprietors had a very high regard for serfdom as both a social and an economic institution. They tried to extend it to other parts of the empire, they resisted the attempts the government made to limit the system or to improve the status of the serf, they protested bitterly when the tsar told them to draw up plans for emancipation, and they procrastinated for as long as they could. There can be no question that most serfowners felt strongly that the emancipation was very much against their economic interests.

Moreover, it seems very likely that they knew what they were talking about. The available evidence does not support the arguments of the minority among the proprietors that free labor was more profitable to the landowner than the barshchina of serfs. In the Central Agriculture provinces, with their heavy concentration of serfs, hired farm labor was cheap because there was little demand for it. Peasants there who wanted to hire out as farmhands had to migrate southward. The proprietors of the Central Agricultural region were well satisfied with these conditions, as is evidenced by their great reluctance to have them changed. In the provinces of the Lower Volga and in New Russia, where the density of the serf population was much less, labor was in short supply, and so hired hands were more expensive than they were in the Central Agricultural guberniias.

---

[8] Volin, "The Russian Peasant," p. 59.

To reduce their labor costs the proprietors transferred or bought serfs from the Center. So they wanted to keep serfdom, too. Nor were the serfowners who drew their incomes from payments in cash and kind any less desirous of retaining the system. Indeed, data on the prices paid for land and serfs in the mid-nineteenth century indicate that these proprietors found serf ownership more profitable than did those who demanded labor services from their peasants.

The argument that serfdom had become anachronistic within the context of the growing Russian economy also has serious weaknesses. Factory industry was able to find the labor it needed among the serfs and state peasants who left their villages to find work elsewhere, and plants owned by nobles and manned by serfs continued to thrive up to the emancipation. Commerce, much of it conducted by serfs and state peasants, also expanded. The shortcomings of the transportation system, and the inadequacies and poor distribution of natural resources, and not serfdom, offered the greatest obstacles to Russian economic growth.

The belief that agriculture itself was engulfed in a crisis in the last decades of serfdom also seems ill-founded. The producers of the Central Agricultural provinces certainly felt some competitive pressure from the southern steppes. Possibly this may help in explaining why the proprietors in the Central Agricultural regions did not increase their production for market sale during the first half of the nineteenth century. The high cost of shipping grain from the south, however, served to protect a large share of the domestic market for them.[9] The claim that the grain supply normally exceeded demand, and that this had much to do with creating a crisis situation, is also open to serious question.

P. B. Struve, in his critique of the argument that the internal development of serfdom led to its liquidation, presented an entirely original explanation for the emancipation. He insisted that serfdom was not obsolescent in the mid-nineteenth century. Instead, it reached the peak of its productivity in the

9 Cf. Gerschenkron, "An Economic History," p. 155.

decade of the fifties. Nonetheless, economic necessity demanded the liberation of the serfs. For, said Struve, the economic future in the form of the railroad had thrown its shadow across serfdom and had condemned it, despite its flourishing condition. The introduction of the railroad effected a revolution in economic relationships, and Russia would not have been able to endure the chains of an unfree labor system.[10] It is difficult (to understate the matter) to do much with an historical interpretation that places the cause after the effect, except to observe that the evidence does not support the assumption that the men who urged abolition, or who drew up the emancipation legislation, were discounting the railroad.

The other major explanations that have been developed to explain the coming of the emancipation seem to me to have more validity than those that base themselves primarily upon supposed economic phenomena or motivations. One of these themes emphasizes the importance of humanitarian and liberal ideas.[11] According to this view, liberal Russian intellectuals from Radishchev on had laid the foundations for the abolition of serfdom. The scholars among them had worked out the theoretical bases for liberation, and the publicists and novelists acted as apostles of freedom. Their work convinced enlightened people of the era, who were almost exclusively members of the nobility, that even though emancipation seemed against their self-interest they would benefit from it morally and spiritually. A conversation in *Anna Karenina* between the Levin brothers can serve to illustrate this attitude. Tolstoi has one brother say:

"Excuse me, self-interest did not induce us to work for the emancipation of the serfs, but we did work for it."

"No!" Constantine Levin broke in with still greater heat, "the emancipation of the serfs was a different matter. There self-interest did come in. One longed to throw off that yoke that crushed us, all devout people among us. . . ."

The fear of peasant revolt is another theme that is emphasized by nearly all historians. They point out that the never-ending current of unrest served to convince the rulers of the

[10] Struve, *Krepostnoe khoziaistvo*, pp. 151-156, 159.
[11] Cf., e.g., Ivanukov, *Padenie, passim.*

empire that emancipation was absolutely essential to preserve public order. Alexander II gave the classic formulation of this conviction when he said that serfdom had to be abolished from above before it destroyed itself from below. There were also serfowners who supported abolition because they feared peasant violence. But to judge from the reaction when Alexander announced his intention to free the serfs, a far larger number were certain that emancipation would engender still greater dangers to the social order. They warned that the freed peasants, lacking self-discipline and responsibility, would turn to idleness, drink, and trouble-making.

The Crimean War, too, nearly always is counted as one of the major factors in bringing on the emancipation. Some have assigned it primary importance, arguing that sweeping reforms are only possible after some great disaster from without reveals the weaknesses within a society. For even though people may have lost their faith in their old institutions, the *vis inertiae* of custom is so strong that radical change can only be made under the stern compulsion of military collapse. Most historians, however, consider the defeat in the war as a catalyst that speeded up the adoption of reforms certain to have been introduced in any event.

The final major interpretation sees the emancipation as the outcome of Alexander's decision that abolition was necessary for *raisons d'état*. The great authority of the sovereign allowed him to carry through social revolutions whenever he saw fit. Alexander II imposed his wishes upon the nobles without regard for their vested interests, and without heed to their outraged protests. Tsar Nicholas had already recognized the need for reform, but his repugnance for change made him temporize. The shock of the Crimean defeat compelled Alexander to take positive action.

There is much to be said, I think, for this last view. The arguments and writings of the humanitarians and liberals provided intellectual and technical preparation for the emancipation among educated men, and especially among some of the bureaucrats who played a key role in drafting the emancipation legislation. Similarly, the discontent of the peasantry made it clear that rural unrest jeopardized the security of the realm.

Given the autocratic structure of the Russian state, however, emancipation or any other great change was impossible without the approval of the tsar. Alexander, convinced by the defeat in the Crimea that his state teetered on the edge of political collapse, had the will to introduce reforms, and the determination to carry them out.

III

The emancipation law wiped out the powers and privileges that the lord had for so long held over his peasants. He could no longer sell his peasants, or compel them to move from one place to another, or have them shipped off to Siberia, or to the army, and so on through the list of powers the seignior once had over his serfs. The age of "silent obedience" was forever abolished. With its disappearance Alexander's government was able to introduce a series of laws designed to reform the legal and administrative structure of his empire. These reforms had as their most significant result the replacement of class privileges and distinctions by legal equality.

Legal equality, that is, for everyone except the peasants. In his proclamation of emancipation the Tsar-Liberator (for so Alexander was called) had promised the peasants that "within the period fixed by the law" they would be allowed all the privileges of free men. There is every reason to believe that this was a sincere pledge. Alexander looked forward hopefully to the day when the freed peasants would enjoy the same civil rights as the rest of his subjects. But he and his counselors believed that the peasants were not ready for the privileges and the responsibilities of full citizenship. Besides, the state had advanced the freedmen money to buy their holdings from the lords, and the drafters of the emancipation statutes wanted to make sure that the peasants would pay back their debt. So they decided that the peasants must go through a transitional stage. The former serfs and state peasants were placed in a peculiar legal category in which they were recognized as free persons, yet were deprived of many of the civil rights that adhered to personal freedom. In most of the empire the individual peasant was not given the right of private landownership. Instead, the commune held title to all the land of a village and distributed it to its member households. Every peasant had to belong to a commune and to a household whether he wanted to or not, and every household had to accept a land allotment regardless of its own wishes. The peasant did not have the right to renounce his membership in his household and commune, and he retained his membership even if he left the village and spent his life elsewhere. All commune members were mutually responsible for taxes and other obligations. To make sure that no one would escape his share of these burdens, the commune and the head of the household concerned had to give their approval before a peasant could leave the village for a lengthy absence. The freed peasant did not have the right of free movement any more than he had it in the days before the emancipation.

All these limitations on personal liberty were supposed to fall away when the peasant completed his redemption payments to the state. That, at least, was the intention of the men who framed the emancipation law. But this intention was soon forgotten. Instead of being thought of as candidates for full citizenship, the peasantry came to be regarded as a unique class whose communal life contributed irreplaceable moral values to Russian society. It therefore had to be accorded special attention and protection. Peasant land was considered to be fundamentally different from other kinds of land, for its purpose was to guarantee the continued existence of the peasantry as a class, and therefore it could not become the private property of those who tilled it. Nor could the members of the peasantry be permitted to leave that class and become workers, for the proletarianization of the rustic would lead to the moral decay of the Russian people. To implement these concepts a special body of law was created for the peasants that dealt not only with their property relationships, but with their other legal relationships as well. There were even separate provisions of the criminal law that applied only to peasants.[12]

The change in attitude toward the peasantry evidenced itself within a few brief years of the emancipation, and became firmly

[12] Leontovitsch, *Geschichte*, pp. 144-163.

entrenched in the reign of Alexander III (1881-1894). These views were not restricted to the ruling circles alone. They were shared by men from one end of the political spectrum to the other, from the blackest reactionaries to the wildest radicals. The leftist agrarian program that, in its broadest sense, was called Populism, was as Zaitsev pointed out "nothing other than a fined version of the attitude toward the rights of the peasants that had to a certain extent been brought to maturity by measures taken by the government, and that were firmly fixed in the text of the laws."[13]

Then, after the revolutionary storm of 1905, the government instituted a dramatic reversal of its policy. A series of decrees abolished most of the restrictions upon the personal liberty of the peasant, allowed him to free himself from his subjugation to the commune and become the owner of his holding, replaced the joint family ownership of the peasant household with in-dividual ownership, wiped out the remaining redemption pay-ments, and set up credit facilities for the purchase of land by peasants. Still further measures were planned to close the gap between the status of the peasantry and that of the other classes of Russian society.

The freedom that had been promised in 1861 seemed at hand at long last. But the hopes for full civil equality for the peasantry were doomed by war and revolution. The new order that came to power in 1917 offered pledges of freedom, too, but its realities turned out to be worlds removed from the utopia promised by its leaders. Instead, "bullying and fawning, arrogant command and servile obedience," for so many centuries the lot of the Russian peasantry, became its fate once more.

[13] Zaitsev, "Die Rechtsideologie," p. 58.

GLOSSARY

altyn. Old monetary unit, equal to 6 *den'gi,* or 3 kopecks.

arshin. Measure of length equal to 28 inches, or 71 cm.

barshchina. Labor obligation of peasants.

berkovets. Weight, varying in amount at different times and places.

bobyl. Old term for cotter or landless peasant.

bochka. Old dry measure equal to 4 chetverts, or about 24 bushels.

chernozem. Black soil.

chetvert. Dry measure equal to 5.95 bushels, or 2.099 hectolitres.

chetvert. Land measure, one half of a desiatin.

chin. Grade in the Table of Ranks.

den'ga. Silver coin equal to one half of a kopeck.

desiatina. Desiatin, a land measure equal to 2.7 acres, or 1.092 hectares.

deti boiarskie. Lesser gentry, minor servitors of the princes.

dikoe pole. Steppe frontier.

druzhina. Military retinue of early princes and great lords.

dvor. Peasant homestead; also the court of the prince.

dvorianstvo. The nobility.

dvorovye liudi. Household serfs.

funt. Measure of weight equal to .9 lbs.

grivna. Old monetary unit, varying in value at different times.

guberniia. Province.

kabala. Debt servitude in the 15th and 16th centuries arising from a promissory note; also the promissory note itself.

kniazhata. Collective name for the serving princes of Muscovite Russia.

kormlenie. An administrative post in the 14th-16th centuries whose occupant retained for his own use part or all of the revenues that accrued to the post.

kormlenshchik. Holder of a *kormlenie.*

korob'ia (pl. *korobei*). Old dry measure equal to about 12 bushels.

kustar. Peasant engaged in cottage industry.

mestnichestvo. System that correlated rank of nobles in government service with the genealogical rank of their families.

mir. Peasant commune.

nogata. Old monetary unit.

obrok. Quitrent paid by peasants in cash or kind.

obzha. Old unit of tax assessment; old measure of tillable land.

odnodvorets (pl. *odnodvortsy*). "One-homesteader." State peasant descended from the small servitors settled on the southern frontiers in the 16th and 17th centuries.

Oprichnina. Special royal domain created by Ivan IV.

oprichniki. Servitors of the *Oprichnina.*

piatok. Old dry measure equal to 5 *gorsti,* literally, 5 handfuls.

podseka. Slash-burn tillage used in forested areas.

podzol. Light gray soil of the forest zone.

polovnik. Share cropper.

pomeshchik. Until the early 18th century the holder of land on service tenure; later, the general name for noble landowners.

pomest'e. Pomestye. Until the early 18th century land held on service tenure; later, the general name for estates owned by nobles.

Pravda Russkaia. The Russian Law, the law codes of the Kievan era.

pud. Weight equal to 40 *funty,* or 36 lbs.

Pugachevshchina. Peasant rising led by Emelian Pugachev in 1773-1774.

sazhen. Measure of length, equal to 7 ft., or 2.13 meters.

serebrennik. Peasant debtor of a landlord in the 14th-16th centuries.

smerd. Free peasant of the Kievan era.

sokha. Old unit of tax assessment; old measure of tillable land.

sokha. Primitive plow.

starozhilets (pl. *starozhil'tsy*). In the 14th-16th centuries a longtime peasant tenant of the same lord.

Sudebnik. Muscovite law code.

svoezemets (pl. *svoezemtsy*). Small landowner.

tiaglo (pl. *tiagla*). Total of the fiscal obligations owed by the peasant; also the capacity of the peasant to meet these obligations; also the unit of assessment for the levying of these and other obligations.

udel. Independent and semi-independent domains of princes in the era of the Mongol domination; in the 19th century the land that belonged to the Imperial family.

uezd. District or county.

Ulozhenie. Law code of 1649.

vedro. Liquid measure equal to 3.25 gallons, or 12.30 litres.

versta. Verst. Measure of length equal to .66 miles or 1.067 km.

volost. Territorial commune; administrative unit.

votchina. Hereditary landed property of a noble; also the landed patrimony of early princes.

votchinnik. The owner of a *votchina.*

vyt. Old unit of tax assessment; old measure of tillable land.

vyvoz. "Exportation" of peasants by landlords.

zakup. Indentured peasants of the Kievan era.

LIST OF WORKS CITED

THE PURPOSE of the following list is to provide the full titles of works cited in the foregoing pages. It is limited, therefore, to works that are actually cited in the footnotes. It is not a complete bibliography of the subjects covered in this book, nor does it include works that were consulted but not cited.

Abel, W., *Agrarkrisen und Agrarkonjunktur in Mitteleuropa vom 13. bis zum 19. Jahrhundert* (Berlin, 1935).

Adams, C., "The Newe Navigation and Discoverie of Moscovia, by the Northeast, in the Yeere 1553," Hakluyt, *Principal Navigations*, II.

Adelung, F. von, *Kritisch-literärische Übersicht der Reisenden in Russland bis 1700, deren Berichte bekannt sind* (St. Petersburg, 1846).

Affranchissement des serfs. Traductions de documents officiels. Résumés explicatifs et annotations [Extrait du Journal de St.-Pétersbourg] (St. Petersburg, 1861).

Akademiia Nauk, Institut Istorii, *Akty feodal'nogo zemlevladeniia i khoziaistva XIV-XVI veka* (Moscow, 1951-1956).

———, *Akty sotsial'no-ekonomicheskoi istorii severo-vostochnoi Rusi kontsa XIV-nachala XVI veka*, I (Moscow, 1952).

———, *Istoriia SSSR* (2 vol., Moscow, 1947-1949).

———, *Khoziaistvo krupnogo feodala-krepostnika XVII v.* [*Materialy po istorii feodal'no-krepostnogo khoziaistva*, Vol. VIII] (Leningrad, 1933).

———, *Materialy po istorii krest'ianskoi promyshlennosti XVIII i pervoi poloviny XIX v.* [*Trudy* Istoriko-Arkheograficheskogo Instituta, Vol. XV] (2 vol. Moscow, Leningrad, 1935-1950).

———, *Sudebniki XV-XVI vekov* (Moscow, Leningrad, 1952).

Aksakov, S., *Semeinaia khronika i vospominaniia* (Moscow, 1856).

Akty tsarstvovaniia Ekateriny II, Uchrezhdeniia dlia upravleniia gubernii i zhalovannyia gramoty dvorianstvu i gorodam (Moscow, 1907).

Alef, G., *A History of the Muscovite Civil War: the Reign of Vasili II (1425-1462)*, (dissert., Princeton Univ., 1956).

Alefirenko, P. K., "Russkaia obshchestvennaia mysl pervoi poloviny XVIII stoletiia o sel'skom khoziaistve," Akademiia Nauk, Institut Istorii, *Materialy po istorii zemledeliia SSSR*, I (Moscow, 1952).

Amburger, E., *Die Familie Marselis: Studien zur russischen Wirtschaftsgeschichte* (Giessen, 1957).

Andreev, A. I., "Nakaz votchinnika krest'ianam 1709 g.," *Istoricheskii Arkhiv*, VIII (1953).

Aristov, N. Ia., *Promyshlennost drevnei Rusi* (St. Petersburg, 1866).

Arkheograficheskaia Ekspeditsiia. *Akty sobrannye v bibliotekakh i arkhivakh Rossiiskoi Imperii* (4 vol., St. Petersburg, 1836-1838).

Arkheograficheskaia Komissiia, *Akty istoricheskie* (4 vol., St. Petersburg, 1841-1842).

———, *Akty iuridicheskie* (St. Petersburg, 1838).

———, *Akty otnosiashchiesia do iuridicheskago byta drevnei Rossii* (3 vol., St. Petersburg, 1857-1884).

———, *Dopolneniia k aktam istoricheskim* (12 vol., St. Petersburg, 1846-1872).

Arsen'ev, K. I., *Statisticheskie ocherki Rossii* (St. Petersburg, 1848).

Artsikhovskii, A. V. "K istorii Novgoroda," *Istoricheskie zapiski*, no. 2, 1938.

Bak, I, "Ia. P. Kozel'skii (filosofskie, obshchestvenno-politicheskie i ekonomicheskie vozzreniia)," *Voprosy istorii*, 1947, no. 1.

———, "K voprosu o genezise kapitalisticheskogo uklada v krepostnom khoziaistve Rossii," *Voprosy istorii*, 1948, no. 4.

———, "Vozniknovenie russkoi sel'skokhoziaistvennoi ekonomii," *Sotsialisticheskoe sel'skoe khoziaistvo*, 1945, no. 9.

Bakanov, P. F., "Tovarnoe proizvodstvo v feodal'noi votchine XVII veka," *Voprosy istorii*, 1953, no. 5.

Bakhrushin, S. V., *Ivan Groznyi* (Moscow, 1945).

———, "Kniazheskoe khoziaistvo XV i pervoi poloviny XVI v.," *Nauchnye Trudy* (3 vol., Moscow, 1952-1954), II.

———, "Moskva kak remeslennyi i torgovyi tsentr XVI v.," *ibid.*, I.

———, "O territorial'nom razdelenii truda v XVI- nachale XVII v.," *ibid.*, I.

———, "Predposylki 'vserossiiskogo rynka' v XVI v.," *Uchenye zapiski*, Moskovskii Gosudarstvennyi Universitet, no. 87, 1946.

———, "Russkii gorod XVI v.," *Nauchnye trudy*, I.

———, "Sel'skie torzhki i iarmarki," *ibid.*, I.

———, "Vozniknovenie gorodskikh poselenii v XVI v.," *ibid.*, I.

"Bankovye dolgi i polozhenie gubernii v 1856 godu," *Zhurnal Ministerstva Vnutrennikh Del*, Feb. 1860.

Baranovich, M., *Materialy dlia geografii i statistiki Rossii sobrannye ofitserami General'nago Shtaba. Riazanskaia guberniia* (St. Petersburg, 1860).

Barbaro, G., "Travels of Josafa Barbaro," in *Works issued by the Hakluyt Society*, XLIX, 1873.

Baster, N., "Some Early Family Budget Studies of Russian Workers," *American Slavic and East European Review*, XVII (1958).

Baykov, A., "The Economic Development of Russia," *Economic History Review*, 2nd ser., VII (1954).

Bazilevich, K. V., *Denezhnaia reforma Alekseia Mikhailovicha i vosstanie v Moskve v 1662g.* (Moscow, Leningrad, 1936).

———, "Novgorodskie pomeshchiki iz posluzhil'tsev v kontse XV veka," *Istoricheskie zapiski*, no. 14, 1945.

———, "Opyt periodizatsii istorii SSSR feodal'nogo perioda," *Voprosy istorii*, 1949, no. 11.

Berg, L. S., *Natural Regions of the U.S.S.R.*, transl. by O. A. Titelbaum (New York, 1950).

Bergson, A., *The Structure of Soviet Wages* (Cambridge, Mass., 1946).

Bergstrasser, C., "Beschreibung des Olonetz'schen Gouvernements im Allgemeine und in landwirtschaftlicher Hinsicht ins besondere," *Mittheilungen der kaiserlichen freien ökonomischen Gesellschaft zu St. Petersburg*, 1845.

Berlin, P. A., *Russkaia burzhuaziia v staroe i novoe vremia* (Moscow, 1922).

Bernhardi, T. von, *Aus dem Leben Theodor von Bernhardis* (9 vol., Leipzig, 1893-1906).

Bibikov, G. N., "Rassloenie krepostnogo krest'ianstva v barshchinnoi votchine v kontse XVII i nachale XIX v.," *Istoricheskie zapiski*, no. 4, 1938.

Bilmanis, A., *A History of Latvia* (Princeton, 1951).

Bliumin, I., "Ekonomicheskie vozzreniia dekabristov," *Problemy ekonomiki*, 1940, no. 5-6.

Bloch, M., *La société féodale; les classes et le gouvernement des hommes* (Paris, 1940).

———, "The Rise of Dependent Cultivation and Seignioral Institutions," *Cambridge Economic History*, I.

Blum, J., *Noble Landowners and Agriculture in Austria, 1815-1848* (Baltimore, 1948).

———, "Prices in Russia in the Sixteenth Century," *Journal of Economic History*, XVI (1956).

———, "The Rise of Serfdom in Eastern Europe," *American Historical Review*. LXII (1957).

———, "Transportation and Industry in Austria, 1815-1848," *Journal of Modern History*, XV (1943).

Bol'shaia sovetskaia entsiklopediia, 1st and 2nd editions.

Borovoi, S., "K voprosu o skladyvanii kapitalisticheskogo uklada v Rossii XVIII v.," *Voprosy istorii*, 1948, no. 5.

———, "Vspomogatel'nyi Bank," *Istoricheskie zapiski*, no. 44, 1953.

Brinkmann, C., "Die ältesten Grundbücher von Novgorod in ihrer Bedeutung für die vergleichende Wirtschafts- und Rechtsgeschichte," *Vierteljahrschrift für Sozial- und Wirtschaftsgeschichte*, IX (1911).

Brutzkus, B., "Die historischen Eigentümlichkeiten der wirtschaft-lichen und sozialen Entwicklung Russlands," *Jahrbücher für die Kultur und Geschichte der Slaven*, N.F., x (1934).

Budovnits, I. U., *Russkaia publitsistika XVI veka* (Moscow, 1947).

Buschen, A. von, *Bevölkerung des russischen Kaiserreichs in den wichtigsten statistischen Verhältnissen dargestellt* (Gotha, 1862).

———, "Die Freibauern Russlands," *Zeitschrift für die gesammte Staatswissenschaft*, xv (1859).

Campense, A., "Lettera d'Alberto Campense intorno le cose di Moscovia al Beatissimo Padre Clemente VII. Ponefice Massimo," *Biblioteka inostrannykh pisatelei o Rossii* (St. Petersburg, 1836), i.

Chadwick, N. K., *The Beginnings of Russian History* (Cambridge, 1946).

Chanceller, R., "The Booke of the great and mighty Emperor of Russia, and Duke of Muscovia," Hakluyt, *Principal Navigations*, ii.

Chechulin, N. D., *Goroda moskovskogo gosudarstva v XVI veke* (St. Petersburg, 1889).

Cherepnin, L. V., "Iz istorii drevnerusskikh feodal'nykh otnoshenii XIV-XVI vv.," *Istoricheskie zapiski*, no. 9, 1940.

———, "Iz istorii formirovaniia klassa feodal'no-zavisimogo krest'-ianstva na Rusi," *Istoricheskie zapiski*, no. 56, 1956.

———, *Russkie feodal'nye arkhivy XIV-XV vekov* (2 vol., Moscow, 1948-1951).

Chicherin, B., *Opyty po istorii russkago prava* (Moscow, 1858).

Chuprov, A. See Tschuprow.

Constantine Porphyrogenitus, *De administrando imperio*, ed. by G. Moravcsik transl. by R. J. H. Jenkins (Budapest, 1949).

Contarini, A., "The Travels of Magnificent M. Ambrosio Contarini," *Works issued by the Hakluyt Soc.*, xlix (1873).

Coulbourn, R., ed., *Feudalism in History* (Princeton, 1956).

Coxe, W., *Travels into Poland, Russia, Sweden and Denmark* (6th ed., 3 vol., London, 1803).

Crisp, O. in *Slavonic and East European Review*, XXX (1951).

Cross, S. H. and Sherbowitz-Wetzor, O.P., tr. and ed., *The Russian Primary Chronicle* (Cambridge, 1953).

Danilova, L. V., *Ocherki po istorii zemlevladeniia i khoziaistva v Novgorodskoi zemle v XIV-XV vv.* (Moscow, 1955).

Danilova, L. V. and Pashuto, V. T., "Tovarnoe proizvodstvo na Rusi (do XVII v.)," *Voprosy istorii*, 1954, no. 1.

DeBow, J. D. B., *Statistical View of the United States* (Wash., 1854).

D'iakonov, M. A., *Ocherki iz istorii sel'skago naseleniia v moskovskom gosudarstve XVI-XVII vv.* (St. Petersburg, 1898).

———, *Ocherki obshchestvennago i gosudarstvennago stroia drevnei Rusi* (4th ed., St. Petersburg, 1912).

"Die Aufhebung der Leibeigenschaft in Russland," *Mittheilungen der Kaiserlichen Freien Ökonomischen Gesellschaft,* 1861.

Dodge, W. R., *Abolitionist Sentiment in Russia 1762-1855* (dissert., U. of Wisconsin, 1950).

Dolgorukii, P., *Notice sur les principales familles de la Russie* (Berlin, 1858).

Dollinger, P., "Le chiffre de population de Paris au XIVe siècle, 210,000 ou 80,000 habitants," *Revue historique,* CCXVI (1956).

Domontovich, M., *Materialy dlia geografii i statistiki Rossii sobrannye ofitserami General'nago Shtaba. Chernigovskaia guberniia* (St. Petersburg, 1865).

Dovzhenok, V. I., "K istorii zemledeliia u vostochnykh slavian v I tysiacheletii n.e. i v epokhy Kievskoi Rusi," Akademiia Nauk, Inst. Istorii, *Materialy po istorii zemledeliia SSSR,* I (Moscow, 1952).

Drakokhrust, E. I., "Rassloenie krepostnogo krest'ianstva v obrochnoi votchine XVIII v.," *Istoricheskie zapiski,* no. 4, 1938.

Druzhinin, N. M., *Gosudarstvennye krest'iane* (2 vol., Moscow, Leningrad, 1946-1958).

———, "Gosudarstvennye krest'iane v dvorianskikh i pravitel'stvennykh proektakh 1800-1833 gg.," *Istoricheskie zapiski,* no. 7, 1940.

———, "Konflikt mezhdu proizvoditel'nymi silami i feodal'nymi otnosheniiami nakanune reformy 1861 goda," *Voprosy istorii,* 1954, no. 7.

Duchesne, E., transl., *Le Stoglav; ou les cent chapitres* (Paris, 1920).

Ducret, P. See Passenans.

Dukhovnye i dogovornye gramoty velikikh i udel'nykh kniazei XIV-XVI vv., S. V. Bakhrushin and L. V. Cherepnin, eds. (Moscow, Leningrad, 1950).

Eck, A., "Le grand domain dans la Russie du moyen âge," *Revue historique du sud-est européen,* XXI (1944).

———, *Le moyen âge russe* (Paris, 1933).

———, "Les non-libres dans la Russie du moyen âge," *Revue historique de droit français et étranger,* 4th series, IX (1930).

Efimenko, A., *Izsledovaniia narodnoi zhizni* (Moscow, 1884).

El'iashevich, V. B., *Istoriia prava pozemel'noi sobstvennosti v Rossii* (2 vol., Paris, 1948-1951).

Engelmann, J., "Die Entstehung und Aufhebung der Leibeigenschaft in Russland," *Baltische Monatschrift,* XXVII (1880).

———, *Die Leibeigenschaft in Russland* (Leipzig, 1884).

Entsiklopedicheskii slovar, edited by F. A. Brockhaus and I. A. Efron (41 vol. in 82, St. Petersburg, 1890-1904).

Entsiklopedicheskii slovar (Granat) (52 vol., Moscow, 1910-1934).

Esterhazy, V., *Nouvelles lettres à sa femme, 1792-1795* (Paris, 1909).

Falk, J. P., *Beyträge zur topographischen Kenntniss des Russischen Reichs* (3 vol., St. Petersburg, 1785-1786).

Fedotov, G. P., *A Treasury of Russian Spirituality* (New York, 1948).

Fekhner, M., *Torgovlia russkogo gosudarstva so stranami vostoka v XVI veke* (Moscow, 1956).

Fennell, J. I., ed. and transl., *The Correspondence between Prince A. M. Kurbsky and Tsar Ivan IV of Russia, 1564-1579* (Cambridge, 1955).

Fletcher, G., *Of the Russe Common Wealth*, in *Works Issued by the Hakluyt Society*, xx (1856).

Florinsky, M. T., *Russia: a History and an Interpretation* (2 vol., New York, 1953).

Ford, W. C., ed., *Writings of John Quincy Adams* (7 vol. New York, 1913-1917).

Ganshof, F. L., *Feudalism*, transl. from French (London, 1952).

Georgi, J. G., *Geographisch-physikalische und Naturhistorische Beschreibung des Russischen Reiches* (10 vol., Königsberg, 1797-1802).

Gerschenkron, A., "An Economic History of Russia," *Journal of Economic History*, xii (1952).

Gille, B., *Histoire économique et sociale de la Russie du moyen âge au XXᵉ siècle* (Paris, 1949).

Gitermann, V., *Geschichte Russlands* (3 vol., Zurich, 1944-1949).

Glavnoe upravlenie udelov, *Stoletie udelov 1797-1897* (St. Petersburg, 1897).

Glavnyi General'nyi Shtab, *Materialy dlia geografi i statistiki Rossii sobrannye ofitserami General'nago Shtaba* (29 vol. in 26, St. Petersburg, 1860-1866).

Goetz, L. K., *Das russische Recht* (3 vol. in 2, Stuttgart, 1910-1912).

———, *Das Kiever Höhlenkloster als Kulturzentrum des vormongolischen Russlands* (Passau, 1904).

———, *Staat und Kirche in Altrussland. Kiever Periode 988-1240* (Berlin, 1908).

Golubinskii, E. E. *Istoriia russkoi tserkvi* (2 vol. in 4, Moscow, 1901-1904).

Gorchakov, M., *O zemel'nykh vladeniiakh vserossiiskikh mitropolitov, patriarkhov i Sv. Sinoda, 988-1738 gg.* (St. Petersburg, 1871).

Got'e, Iu., *Zamoskovnyi krai v XVII veke* (Moscow, 1906).

Gras, N. S. B., The Evolution of the English Corn Market from the Twelfth to the Eighteenth Century (Cambridge, 1926).

Gregoire, H., Jakobson, R., Szeftel, M., *La geste du Prince Igor* [Annuaire de l'Institut de Philologie et d'Histoire Orientales, viii, 1945-1947].

Grekov, B. D., "Dvizhenie Pskovskikh smerdov 1483-1486 gg. i 'smerd'i gramoty,' " *Istoricheskie zapiski*, no. 20, 1946.

——, *Feodal'nye otnosheniia v kievskom gosudarstve* (Moscow, Leningrad, 1937).

——, *Glavneishie etapy v istorii krepostnogo prava v Rossii* (Moscow, Leningrad, 1940)

——, "Khoziaistvennyi krizis v moskovskom gosudarstve v 70-80kh godakh XVI v.," *Voprosy istorii*, 1945, no. 1.

——, "Khoziaistvo krupnoi russkoi votchiny XVI-XVII vv.," *Izvestiia Rossiiskoi Akademii Nauk*, VI series, 1925, no. 6-8.

——, *Kievskaia Rus'* (Moscow, Leningrad, 1944).

——, *Krest'iane na Rusi s drevneishikh vremen do XVII veka* (Moscow, Leningrad, 1946).

——, "Tambovskoe imenie M. S. Lunina v pervoi chetverti XIX v.," *Izvestiia*, Akademiia Nauk SSSR, *Otdelenie obshchestvennykh nauk*, VII series, 1933, no. 6-7.

Grunwald, C. de, *Tsar Nicholas I*, transl. from French (New York, 1955).

Hakluyt, R., *The Principal Navigations Voyages Traffiques & Discoveries of the English Nation* (12 vol., Glasgow, 1903-1905).

Hakluyt Society, *Works Issued by the Hakluyt Society* (216 vol., London, 1847-1959).

Hammer-Purgstall, J. von, *Geschichte der Goldenen Horde in Kiptschak* (Pesth, 1840).

Haumant, E., *La culture française en Russie 1700-1900* (Paris, 1910).

Haxthausen, A. von, *Die ländliche Verfassung Russlands. Ihre Entwickelungen und ihre Feststellung in der Gesetzgebung von 1861* (Leipzig, 1866).

——, *Studien über die innern Zustände, das Volksleben und insbesondere die ländlichen Einrichtungen Russlands* (3 vol., Hannover and Berlin, 1847-1852).

Heckscher, E. F., *An Economic History of Sweden*, transl. by G. Ohlin (Cambridge, Mass., 1954).

Heimskringla, see Snorri Sturluson.

Henoumont, E., "Die Bauernfrage zur Zeit Kaiser Alexander II," *Preussische Jahrbücher*, XV (1865).

Herberstein, S. von, *Notes upon Russia*, transl. from Latin by R. H. Major, *Works Issued by the Hakluyt Society*, X, XII (1852).

——, *Rerum moscoviticarum* (Basil[?], 1606).

Hill, C., *Economic Problems of the Church from Archbishop Whitgift to the Long Parliament* (Oxford, 1956).

Hintze, O., "Wesen und Verbreitung des Feudalismus," *Die Welt als Geschichte*, IV (1938).

Hobsbawm, E. J., "The General Crisis of the European Economy in the 17th Century," *Past and Present*, 1954, no. 5-6.

Holdsworth, W. S., *A History of English Law* (13 vol., London, 1922-1952).

Hommaire de Hell, X., *Les steppes de la Mer Caspienne, le Caucase, la Crimée et la Russie mériodionale* (3 vol., Paris and Strasbourg, 1843-1845).

Hötzsch, O., "Adel und Lehnswesen in Russland und Polen und die Verhältnis zur deutschen Entwicklung," *Historische Zeitschrift*, cviii (1912).

Hrushevsky, M. S., *Geschichte des ukrainischen (ruthenischen) Volkes*, transl. from Ukrainian (Leipzig, 1906), i.

Hupel, A. W., "Ueber den Nationalkarakter der Russen," *Der Nordischen Miszellen*, i (1781).

Iakovlev, A. F., *Ekonomicheskie krizisy v Rossii* (Moscow, 1955).

Iakovlev, A. I., ed., *Akty khoziaistva boiarina B. I. Morozova* (2 pts., Moscow, Leningrad, 1940-1945).

———, *Kholopstvo i kholopy v moskovskom gosudarstve XVII v.* (Moscow, Leningrad, 1943).

Iakovlev, B., "Vozniknovenie i etapy razvitiia kapitalisticheskogo uklada v Rossii," *Voprosy istorii*, 1950, no. 9.

Iatsevich, A. G., *Krepostnye v Peterburge* (Leningrad, 1933).

Iatsunskii, V. K., "Promyshlennyi perevorot v Rossii," *Voprosy istorii*, 1952, no. 12.

Ignatovich, I., "Krest'ianskie volneniia pervoi chetverti XIX veka," *Voprosy istorii*, 1950, no. 9.

———, "Pomeshchich'i krest'iane nakanune osvobozhdeniia," *Russkoe bogatstvo*, 1900, no. 9-10.

Indova, E. I., *Krepostnoe khoziaistvo v nachale XIX veka po materialam votchinnogo arkhiva Vorontsovykh* (Moscow, 1955).

———, "Krest'ianstvo tsentral'no-promyshlennykh votchin Vorontsovykh v pervoi polovine XIX v.," *Istoricheskie zapiski*, no. 38, 1951.

Iushkov, S. V., *Istoriia gosudarstva i prava SSSR* (Moscow, 1950).

———, *Ocherki po istorii feodalizma v Kievskoi Rusi* (Moscow, Leningrad, 1939).

Ivaniukov, I., *Padenie krepostnogo prava v Rossii* (St. Petersburg, 1882).

Jordanes, *Romana et Gettica, Monumenta Germaniae Historica, auctores antiquissimi, v* (Berlin, 1882).

Jourdier, A., *Des forces productives, destructives et unproductives de la Russie* (Paris, 1860).

Kafengauz, B. B., "Khlebnyi rynok v 20-30kh godakh XVIII sto-letiia," Akademia Nauk, Institut istorii, *Materialy po istorii zem-ledeliia SSSR* (Moscow, 1952), I.

Kalachov, N. V., *Materialy dlia istorii russkago dvorianstva* (3 vol., St. Petersburg, 1885).

Karamzin, N. M., *Istoriia gosudarstva rossiiskago* (12 vol., St. Peters-burg, 1816-1829).

———, *Memoir on Ancient and Modern Russia*, transl. and edited by R. Pipes (Cambridge, Mass., 1959).

Keussler, J. von, *Zur Geschichte und Kritik des bäuerlichen Gemein-debesitzes in Russland* (3 vol., Dorpat, St. Petersburg, 1876-1887).

Khlebnikov, N. I., *Obshchestvo i gosudarstvo v do-mongolskii period russkoi istorii* (St. Petersburg, 1872).

———, *O vliianii obshchestva na organizatsiiu gosudarstva v tsarskii period russkoi istorii* (St. Petersburg, 1869).

Khodskii, L. V., "Ocherk razvitiia pozemel'nykh otnoshenii byvshikh gosudarstvennykh krest'ian," *Russkaia mysl*, 1889, no. 11-12.

Khromov, P. A., *Ekonomicheskoe razvitie Rossii v XIX-XX vekakh 1800-1917* (Moscow, 1950).

Kilburger, J. P., "Kurzer Unterricht von dem Russischen Handel, wie selbiger mit aus- und eingehenden Waaren 1674 durch ganz Russland getrieben worden," *Magazin für die neue Historie und Geographie*, III (1769).

Kirsten, E., Buchholz, E. W., Köllmann, W., *Raum und Bevölkerung in der Weltgeschichte* (Würzburg, 1955).

Kizevetter, A., "Krest'ianstvo v istorii Rossii," *Krest'ianskaia Rossiia*, II, III (1923).

———, "Krest'ianstvo v russkoi nauchno-istoricheskoi literature," *Krest'ianskaia Rossiia*, V, VI (1923).

Kliuchevskii, V. O., *A History of Russia* transl. by C. J. Hogarth (5 vol., London, 1911-1931).

———, *Kurs russkoi istorii* (5 vol., Moscow, 1904-1921).

———, "Podushnaia podat i otmena kholopstva v Rossii," *Opyty i issledovanniia* (Petrograd, 1918), I.

———, "Proiskhozhdenie krepostnogo prava v Rossii," *ibid.*, I.

———, "Russkii rubl XVI-XVIII v.," *ibid*, I.

Knapp, G. F., *Die Bauern-Befreiung und der Ursprung der Landar-beiter in den älteren Theilen Preussens* (2 vol., Leipzig, 1887).

Kogan, E. S., "Volneniia krest'ian Penzenskoi votchiny A. B. Kura-kina vo vremia dvizheniia Pugacheva," *Istoricheskie zapiski*, no. 37, 1951.

Kohl, J. G., *Reisen in Südrussland* (2 vol., Dresden and Leipzig, 1841).

Kolokol, London, 1857-1867.

Konovalov, S., "Thomas Chamberlayne's Description of Russia, 1631," *Oxford Slavonic Papers*, v (1954).

Kopanev, A. I., *Istoriia zemlevladeniia Belozerskogo kraia XV-XVI v.* (Moscow, 1951).

———, "Naselenie russkogo gosudarstva v XVI v.," *Istoricheskie zapiski*, no. 64, 1959.

Köppen, P. V., "Russland's Gesammt-Bevölkerung im Jahre 1838," *Mémoires de l'Academie Impériale des Sciences de St.-Pétersbourg*, VIme série, Sciences politiques, histoire, philologie, VI (1844).

———, *Statistische Reise in's Land der donischen Kosaken, durch die Gouvernments Tula, Orel. und Woronesh im Jahre 1850* (St. Petersburg, 1852).

———, "Über den Kornbedarf Russlands," *Mémoires de l'Academie Impériale des Sciences de St.-Pétersbourg*, VIme série, Sciences politiques, histoire, philologie, v (1845).

———, "Über die Vertheilung der Bewohner Russlands nach Ständen, in den verschiedenen Provinzen," *loc.cit.*, VII (1848).

Korf, M., "Imperator Nikolai v soveshchatel'nykh sobraniiakh (iz sovremennykh zapisok stats-sekretaria barona Korfa)," *Sbornik Imperatorskago Russkago Istoricheskago Obshchestva*, XCVIII (1896).

Kornilov, A. A., "Gubernskie komitety po krest'ianskomu delu v 1858-1859 gg.," in A. A. Kornilov, *Ocherki po istorii obshchestvennago dvizheniia krest'ianskago dela v Rossii* (St. Petersburg, 1905).

———, "Krest'ianskaia reforma 19 fevralia 1861 goda," *Krest'ianskii stroi* (St. Petersburg, 1905), I.

———, *Modern Russian History*, tr. from Russian by A. S. Kaun (2 vol., New York, 1943).

Kosminsky, E. A., "Services and Money Rents in the Thirteenth Century," *Economic History Review*, v (1935).

Kotoshikhin, G. K., *O Rossii v tsarstvovanie Alekseia Mikhailovicha* (St. Petersburg, 1884).

Koval'chenko, I. D., "Khoziaistvo barshchinnykh krest'ian v Riazanskoi i Tambovskoi guberniiakh v pervoi polovine XIX v.," *Istoricheskie zapiski*, no. 56, 1956.

Kovalevskii, M., *Die ökonomische Entwicklung Europas bis zum Beginn der kapitalistischen Wirtschaftsform*, transl. from Russian by A. Stein (7 vol., Berlin, 1901-1914).

———, *Modern Customs and Ancient Laws of Russia* (London, 1891).

Krest'ianskaia reforma v Rossii 1861 goda; sbornik zakonodatel'nykh aktov (Moscow, 1954).

Kritzmann, L., Popov, P., Iakovlev, Ia., *Sel'skoe khoziaistvo na putiakh vosstanovleniia* (Moscow, 1925).

Kropotkin, P., *Memoirs of a Revolutionist* (Boston, New York, 1899).

Krzhivoblotskii, Ia., *Materialy dlia geografii i statistiki Rossii sobrannye ofitserami General'nago Shtaba. Kostromskaia guberniia* (St. Petersburg, 1861).

Kuczynskii, R. R., "Population," *Encyclopaedia of the Social Sciences*, XII.

Kukiel, M., *Czartoryski and European Unity, 1770-1861* (Princeton, 1955).

Kulischer, J., "Die kapitalistischen Unternehmer in Russland (insbesondere die Bauern als Unternehmer) in den Anfangsstadien des Kapitalismus," *Archiv für Sozialwissenschaft und Sozialpolitik*, LXV (1931).

———, "Die Leibeigenschaft in Russland und die Agrarverfassung Preussens im 18ten Jahrhundert," *Jahrbücher für Nationalökonomie und Statistik*, CXXXVII (1932).

———, *Ocherk istorii russkoi torgovli* (Petrograd, 1923).

———, *Russische Wirtschaftsgeschichte*, I (Jena, 1925).

Kusheva, E. N., "Khoziaistvo saratovskikh dvorian Shakhmatovykh v XVIII veke," *Izvestiia Akademii Nauk SSSR, Otdelenie gumanitarnykh nauk*, VII series, 1929, no. 7-8.

———, "Proekt uchrezhdeniia aktsionernogo 'Obshchestva uluchsheniia chastnogo sel'skogo khoziaistva' 30-kh godov XIX v.," *Istoricheskii arkhiv*, VII (1951).

Laehr, G., *Die Anfänge des russischen Reiches* (Berlin, 1930).

Lane, F. C., "Economic Consequences of Organized Violence," *Journal of Economic History*, XVIII (1958).

Lappo-Danilevskii, A. S., ed., *Zapisnaia kniga krepostnym aktam XV-XVI vv.* (St. Petersburg, 1898).

Lebedev, V. I., *Krest'ianskaia voina pod predvoditel'stvom Stepana Razina* (Moscow, 1955).

Lebedev, V. I., ed., *Reformy Petra I. Sbornik dokumentov* (Moscow, 1937).

Lenin, V. I., *Razvitie kapitalizma v Rossii*, in V. I. Lenin, *Sochineniia*, III.

Leontovich, V., *Die Rechtsumwälzung unter Iwan dem Schrecklichen und die Ideologie der russischen Selbstherrschaft* (Stuttgart, 1949).

———, *Geschichte der Liberalismus in Russland* (Frankfurt a. M., 1957).

Le Play, F., *Les ouvriers européens* (6 vol., Tours, 1877-1879).

Leroy-Beaulieu, A., *L'empire des tsars et les russes* (2 vol., Paris, 1883).

Letopis po Ipat'evskomu spisku, Arkheograficheskaia Komissiia (St. Petersburg, 1871).

Letopis po lavrentievskomu spisku, Arkheograficheskaia Komissiia (St. Petersburg, 1872).

Liashchenko, P. I., *History of the National Economy of Russia to the 1917 Revolution,* transl. by L. M. Herman (New York, 1949).

———, *Istoriia narodnogo khoziaistva SSSR* (2 vol., Moscow, 1947-1948).

———, "Krepostnoe sel'skoe khoziaistvo Rossii v XVIII veke," *Istoricheskie zapiski,* no. 15, 1945.

———, *Ocherki agrarnoi evoliutsii Rossii* (2 vols., St. Petersburg, Leningrad, 1913-1926).

Linkov, Ia. I., *Ocherki istorii krest'ianskogo dvizheniia v Rossii v 1825-1861 gg.* (Moscow, 1952).

Liubavskii, M. K., *Obrazovanie osnovnoi gosudarstvennoi territorii velikorusskoi narodnosti; zaselenie i ob'edinenie tsentra* (Leningrad, 1929).

Liubomirov, P. G., *Ocherki po istorii promyshlennosti, XVII, XVIII i nachalo XIX veka* (Moscow, 1947).

Luchitskii, I. V., "Etudes sur la propriété communale dans la Petite-Russie," *Revue internationale de sociologie,* III (1895).

———, "Zur Geschichte der Grundeigentumsformen in Kleinrussland," *Jahrbüch für Gesetzgebung, Verwaltung, und Volkswirtschaft,* XX (1896), XXI (1897).

Man'kov, A. G., "Dvizhenie i geografiia khlebnykh tsen v russkom gosudarstve XVI v.," *Istoricheskie zapiski,* no. 28, 1949.

———, *Tseny i ikh dvizhenie v russkom gosudarstve XVI veka* (Moscow, Leningrad, 1951).

Margaret, J., *Estat de l'empire de Russie et Grand Duché de Moscovie* (Paris, 1860).

Masaryk, T. G., *The Spirit of Russia,* transl. from German by E. and C. Paul (2 vol., London, New York, 1919).

Maslov, P. P., *Agrarnyi vopros v Rossii* (2 vol., Moscow, 1905).

Materialy dlia istorii uprazdneniia krepostnogo sostoianiia pomeshchich'ikh krest'ian v Rossii v tsartsvovanie imperatora Aleksandra II (3 vol., Berlin, 1860-1862).

Mavor, J., *An Economic History of Russia* (2 vol., London, New York, 1925).

Mayerberg, A. von, *Relation d'un voyage en Moscovie,* transl. from Latin (2 vol., Paris, 1858).

Mazour, A. G., *The First Russian Revolution, 1825* (Berkeley, 1937).

Medieval Russian Laws, transl. and edited by G. Vernadsky (New York, 1947).

Menander, *Fragmenta,* L. Dindorf, ed., *Historici Graeci minores,* II.

Merkel, G., *Die Letten* (Riga, 1924).

Meshalin, I. V., *Tekstil'naia promyshlennost krest'ian moskovskoi gubernii v XVIII i pervoi polovine XIX veka* (Moscow, Leningrad, 1950).

Mikhalevich, V., *Materialy dlia geografii i statistiki Rossii sobrannye ofitserami General'nago Shtaba. Voronezhskaia guberniia* (St. Petersburg, 1862).

Miliukov, P. N., *Ocherki po istorii russkoi kultury* (3 vol. in 2, St. Petersburg, 1896-1903).

――――, "Russkaia agrarnaia politika proshlago stoletiia," *Russkaia mysl*, XI, May, 1890.

――――, *Spornye voprosy finansovoi istorii moskovskago gosudarstva* (St. Petersburg, 1892).

――――, "Zur Geschichte des russischen Adels," *Archiv für Sozialwissenschaft und Sozialpolitik*, XLI (1916).

Miliukov, P. N., et al., *Histoire de Russie* (3 vol., Paris, 1932-1933).

Miller, A., "Considérations sur les institutions financières de l'etat muscovite au XVIᵉ et au XVIIᵉ siècles," *Revue internationale de sociologie*, XL (1932).

――――, *Essai sur l'histoire des institutions agraires de la Russie Centrale du XVIᵉ au XVIIIᵉ siècles* (Paris, 1926).

Ministerstvo Gosudarstvennykh Imushchestv, *Ob'iasneniia k khoziaistvenno-statisticheskomu atlasu evropeiskoi Rossii*, I. Vil'son, ed., (4th ed., St. Petersburg, 1869).

――――, *Statisticheskii obzor gosudarstvennykh imushchestv za 1858 god* (St. Petersburg, 1861).

Mirsky, D. S., *A History of Russian Literature* (New York, 1927).

Mittheilungen der Kaiserlichen Freien Ökonomischen Gesellschaft.

Mulhall, M. G., *The Dictionary of Statistics* (4th ed., London, 1899).

Muliukin, A. S. *Ocherki po istorii iuridicheskogo polozheniia inostrannykh kuptsov v moskovskom gosudarstve* (Odessa, 1912).

Nabholz, H., "Medieval Agrarian Society in Transition," *Cambridge Economic History* (Cambridge, England, 1941), I.

Naidenov, M., *Klassovaia bor'ba v poreformennoi derevne 1861-1863 gg.* (Moscow, 1955).

Nakaz eia imperatorskago velichestva Ekateriny vtoryia samoderzhitsy vserossiiskiia dannye Kommissii o sochinenii proekta novago ulozheniia (St. Petersburg, 1893).

Nazarevskii, V. V., *Iz istorii Moskvy 1147-1913* (Moscow, 1914).

Nifontov, A. S., *Rossiia v 1848 godu* (Moscow, 1949).

Nikishin, I. I., "Nekotorye voprosy ekonomiki krepostnogo khoziaistva pervoi poloviny XIX veka," *Istoricheskie zapiski*, no. 44, 1953.

Nolde, B., *La formation de l'empire Russe* (2 vol., Paris, 1952-1953).

Novgorodskaia pervaia letopis, Akademiia Nauk, Institut Istorii (Moscow, Leningrad, 1950).

Novgorodskiia pistsovyia knigi, Arkheograficheskaia Kommissiia (6 vol., St. Petersburg, 1859-1910).

Novosel'skii, A. A., "K voprosu ob ekonomicheskom sostoianii beglykh krest'ian na iuge moskovskogo gosudarstva v pervoi polovine XVII veka," *Istoricheskie zapiski*, no. 16, 1945.

———, *Votchinnik i ego khoziaistvo v XVII v.* (Moscow, Leningrad, 1929).

Ob'iasneniia. See Ministerstvo Gosudarstvennykh Imushchestv, *Ob'-iasneniia* . . .

"Obozrenie upravleniia Gosudarstvennykh Imushchestv za posledniia 25 let c 20 noiabria 1825 do 20 noiabria 1850 g.," *Sbornik Imperatorskago Russkago Istoricheskago Obshchestva*, xcviii (1896).

Obshchestvo rasprostraneniia tekhnicheskikh znanii. Uchebnyi otdel. Istoricheskaia komissiia, *Velikaia reforma* (6 vol., Moscow, 1911).

Odinetz, D., "Les origines du servage en Russie," *Revue historique de droit français et étranger*, 4th series, x (1931).

———, "Poteria prava perekhoda vladel'cheskimi krest'ianami moskovskogo gosudarstva," *Sbornik statei, posviashchennykh Pavlu Nikolaevichu Miliukovu 1858-1929* (Prague, 1929).

———, *Vozniknovenie gosudarstvennago stroia u vostochnykh slavian* (Paris, 1935).

Pallas, P. S., *Voyages du Professeur Pallas dans plusieurs provinces de l'empire de Russie et dans l'Asie septentrionale*, transl. from German (8 vol., Paris, 1794).

Pamiatniki russkogo prava.

Passenans, M. P. D. de, *La Russie et l'esclavage dans leurs rapports avec la civilisation européene* (2 vol., Paris, 1822).

Paul of Aleppo, *The Travels of Macarius, Patriarch of Antioch*, transl. from Arabic (2 vol., London, 1829-1836).

Pavlenko, N. I., "O nekotorykh storonakh pervonachal'nogo nakopleniia v Rossii (po materialam XVII-XVIII vv.)," *Istoricheskie zapiski*, no. 54, 1955.

Pavlov-Sil'vanskii, N., *Feodalizm v drevnei Rusi* (St. Petersburg, 1907).

Pavlovsky, G. A., *Agricultural Russia on the Eve of the Revolution* (London, 1930).

Pazhitnov, K. A., "K voprosu o roli krepostnogo truda v doreformennoi promyshlennosti," *Istoricheskie zapiski*, no. 7, 1940.

Perel'man, I. L., "Novgorodskaia derevnia v XV-XVI vv.," *Istoricheskie zapiski*, no. 26, 1948.

Petrikeev, D. I., "Zemel'nye vladeniia B. I. Morozova," *Istoricheskie zapiski*, no. 21, 1947.

Petrovskaia, I. F., "Nakazy votchinnym prikazchikam pervoi chetverti XVIII v.," *Istoricheskii arkhiv*, VIII (1953).

Pipes, R. E., "The Russian Military Colonies," *Journal of Modern History*, XXII (1950).

Pirenne, H., *Economic and Social History of Medieval Europe* (New York, 1936).

Pistsovyia knigi moskovskago gosudarstva, K. N. Kalachov, ed. (3 vol., Moscow, 1872-1895).

Plano-Carpini, John of, *History of the Mongols*, in C. H. Dawson, ed., *The Mongol Missions* (New York, 1955).

Platonov, S. F., *Boris Godunov* (Prague, 1924).

———, *Ivan Groznyi* (Berlin, 1924).

———, *La Russie moscovite* (Paris, 1932) [M. A. Cavaignac, ed., *Histoire du monde*, VIII, pt. 4].

———, *Ocherki po istorii smuty v moskovskom gosudarstve XVI-XVII vv.* (Moscow, 1937).

———, *Smutnoe vremia* (Prague, 1924).

Pokrovskii, M. N., *Brief History of Russia*, transl. by D. S. Mirsky (2 vol., New York, 1933).

———, *Russkaia istoriia v samom szhatom ocherke ot drevneishikh vremen do kontsa XIX stoletiia* (Moscow, Petrograd, 1923).

Pokrovskii, V., "Naselenie," *Entsiklopedicheskii slovar*, XL.

Polianskii, F. Ia., "Naemnyi trud v manufaktornoi promyshlennosti Rossii XVIII veka," Akademiia Nauk, Institut Ekonomiki, *Voprosy istorii narodnogo khoziaistva SSSR* (Moscow, 1957).

Pollock, F. and Maitland, F. W., *The History of English Law* (2 vol., Cambridge, 1952).

Polnoe sobranie russkikh letopisei (25 vol., St. Petersburg, Leningrad, 1841-1949).

Polnoe sobranie zakonov Rossiiskoi Imperii s 1649 goda (45 vol. in 48, St. Petersburg, 1839-1843); 2nd series, 1825 to 1881 (55 vol., St. Petersburg, 1830-1884).

Polosin, I., "Le servage russe et son origine," *Revue internationale de sociologie*, XXXVI (1928).

Popov, P. I., "Khlebofurazhnyi balans," in Kritzmann et al.

Poprotskii, M., *Materialy dlia geografi i statistiki Rossii sobrannye ofitserami General'nago Shtaba. Kaluzhskaia guberniia* (2 vol., St. Petersburg, 1864).

Portal, R., "Das Problem einer industriellen Revolution in Russland im 19. Jahrhundert," *Forschungen zur osteuropäischen Geschichte*, I (1954).

———, "La Russie industrielle à la veille de l'émancipation des serfs," *Etudes d'histoire moderne et contemporaine*, V (1953).

———, *L'Oural au XVIIIᵉ siècle* (Paris, 1950).

Portal, R., "Manufactures et classes sociales en Russie au XVIIIᵉ siècle," *Revue historique,* CCI (1949).

———, "Pugačev: une révolution manquée," *Etudes d'histoire moderne et contemporaine,* I (1947).

Possevino, A., *Moscovia* (Antwerp, 1587).

Povalishin, A., *Riazanskie pomeshchiki i ikh krepostnye* (Riazan, 1903).

Pravda Russkaia, ed. by B. D. Grekov (2 vol., Moscow, Leningrad, 1940-1947).

Presniakov, A. E., *Obrazovanie velikorusskago gosudarstva* (Petrograd, 1918).

Preyer, W., *Die russische Agrarreform* (Jena, 1914).

Pushkarev, S. G., *Proiskhozhdenie krest'ianskoi pozemel'no-peredel'noi obshchiny v Rossii* (2 pts., Prague, 1939-1941).

Putnam, P., *Seven Britons in Imperial Russia 1698-1812* (Princeton, 1952).

Radishchev, A. N., *A Journey from St. Petersburg to Moscow,* L. P. Wiener transl., R. P. Thaler, ed. (Cambridge, Mass., 1958).

Raeff, M., *Siberia and the Reforms of 1822* (Seattle, 1956).

Rashin, A. G., *Formirovanie promyshlennogo proletariata v Rossii* (Moscow, 1940).

———, *Naselenie Rossii za 100 let, 1811-1913* (Moscow, 1956).

Red. kom. See Redaktsionnye komissii.

Redaktsionnye komissii dlia sostavlenniia polozhenniia o krest'ianakh vykhodiashchikh iz krepostnoi zavisimosti, *Pervoe izdanie materialov* (18 vol. St. Petersburg, 1859-1860).

Reddaway, W. F., ed., *Documents of Catherine the Great* (Cambridge, 1931).

Riasanovsky, N. V. *Russia and the West in the Teaching of the Slavophils* (Cambridge, Mass., 1952).

———, "The Norman Theory of the Origin of the Russian State," *Russian Review,* VII (1947) no. 1.

Rikhter, D. I., "Zabytyi material po statistike prodazhnykh tsen na zemliiu," *Trudy Imperatorskago Vol'nago Ekonomicheskago Obshchestva,* 1897, no. 4.

Robinson, G. T., *Rural Russia under the Old Regime* (New York, 1932).

Romanovich-Slavatinskii, A., *Dvorianstvo v Rossii ot nachala XVIII veka do otmeny krepostnago prava* (St. Petersburg, 1870).

Rostovtzeff, M., "Les origines de la Russie kiévienne," *Revue des études slaves,* II (1922).

Rozhdestvenskii, S. V., *Sluzhiloe zemlevladenie v moskovskom gosudarstve XVI veka* (St. Petersburg, 1897).

Rozhkov, N., *Russkaia istoriia v sravnitel'no-istoricheskom osve-shchenii* (12 vol., Leningrad, 1930).

———, *Sel'skoe khoziaistvo moskovskoi Rusi v XVI veke* (Moscow, 1899).

Rozhkova, M. K., "K voprosu o znachenii iarmarok vo vnytrennei torgovle doreformennoi Rossii (pervaia polovina XIX v.)," *Istoricheskie zapiski*, no. 54, 1955.

———, "Promyshlennost Moskvy v pervoi chetverti XIX veka," *Voprosy istorii*, 1946, no. 11-12.

Rubinshtein, N. L., "K kharakteristike votchinnogo rezhima i krest'-ianskogo dvizheniia v kontse 70-x gg.," *Istoricheskie zapiski*, no. 40, 1952.

———, "Nekotorye voprosy formirovaniia rynka rabochei sily v Rossii XVIII veka," *Voprosy istorii*, 1952, no. 2.

Rukovskii, I. P., "Istoriko-statisticheskiia svedeniia o podushnykh podatiakh," Kommissiia vysochaishaia uchrezdennaia dlia peresmotra sistemy podatei i sborov, *Trudy*, I (1866).

Russell, J. C., *British Medieval Population* (Albuquerque, 1948).

Russian Primary Chronicle, transl. and ed., S. H. Cross and O. P. Sherbowitz-Wetzor (Cambridge, Mass., 1954).

Russkii biograficheskii slovar (25 vol., Moscow, 1896-1918).

Rybakov, B. A., "Obrazovanie drevnerusskogo gosudarstva," Akademiia Nauk, Institut Istorii, *Desiatyi mezhdunarodnyi kongress istorikov v Rime sentiabr 1955g.* (Moscow, 1956).

———, *Remeslo drevnei Rusi* (Moscow, 1948).

———, "Znaki sobstvennosti v kniazheskom khoziaistve Kievskoi Rusi X-XII vv.," *Sovetskaia arkheologiia*, VI (1940).

Sacke, G., "Adel und Bürgertum in der Regierungszeit Katharinas II. von Russland," *Revue belge de philologie et d'histoire*, XVII (1938).

Samarin, Iu. F., *Sochineniia* (Moscow, 1877-1911).

Samokvasov, D. Ia., *Arkhivnyi material* (2 vol., Moscow, 1905-1909).

Savich, A., "Die Agrarwirtschaft der Klostergüter des russischen Nordens im 14.-17. Jahrhundert," *Zeitschrift für osteuropäische Geschichte*, V (1931), VI (1932).

Sbornik Imperatorskago Russkago Istoricheskago Obshchestva (148 vol., St. Petersburg, 1867-1916).

Schiemann, T., *Geschichte Russlands unter Kaiser Nikolaus I* (4 vol., Berlin, Leipzig, 1904-1919).

Schkaff, E., *La question agraire en Russie* (Paris, 1922).

Schnitzler, J. H., *Histoire intime de la Russie* (2 vol., Paris, 1847).

———, *L'empire des tsars: au point actuel de la science* (3 vol., Paris, 1862-1864).

———, *Les institutions de la Russie depuis les réformes de l'empereur Alexandre II* (2 vol., Paris, 1866).

Schultz, L., *Russische Rechtsgeschichte* (Lahr, 1951).

Schulze-Gaevernitz, G. von, "Der Nationalismus in Russland und seine wirtschaftlichen Träger," *Preussische Jahrbücher*, LXXV (1894).

———, "Die Moskau-Wladimirsche Baumwollindustrie," *Jahrbuch für Gesetzgebung, Verwaltung und Volkswirtschaft*, XX (1896).

———, *Volkswirtschaftliche Studien aus Russland* (Leipzig, 1899).

Semevskii, V. I., *Krest'iane v tsarstvovanie imperatritsy Ekateriny II* (2 vol., St. Petersburg, 1881-1901).

———, *Krest'ianskii vopros v Rossii v XVIII i pervoi polovine XIX veka* (2 vol., St. Petersburg, 1888).

———, "Po povodu stat'i G. Rozhkova 'K voprosu ob ekonomicheskikh prichinakh padeniia krepostnogo prava v Rossii," *Russkaia mysl*, XXIII (April, 1902).

Seraphim, E., *Baltische Geschichte im Grundriss* (Riga, 1908).

Seredonin, S. M., *Sochinenie Dzhil'sa Fletchera "Of the Russe Common Wealth" kak istoricheskii istochnik* (St. Petersburg, 1891).

Sergeevich, V. I., *Drevnosti russkago prava* (3 vol., St. Petersburg, 1909-1911).

———, *Lektsii i izsledovaniia po drevnei istorii russkago prava* (St. Petersburg, 1903).

Shapiro, A. L., "K istorii krest'ianskikh promyslov i krest'ianskoi manufaktury v Rossii XVIII v.," *Istoricheskie zapiski*, no. 31, 1950.

Shchepetov, K. N., *Krepostnoe pravo v votchinakh Sheremetevykh* (Moscow, 1947).

———, "Sel'skoe khoziaistvo v votchinakh Iosifo-Volokolamskogo monastyria v kontse XVI veka," *Istoricheskie zapiski*, no. 18, 1946.

Simkhovitsch, V. G., *Die Feldgemeinschaft in Russland* (Jena, 1898).

———, "The Russian Peasant and Autocracy," *Political Science Quarterly*, XXI (1906).

Sivkov, K. V., "Biudzhet krupnogo sobstvennika-krepostnika pervoi treti XIX v.," *Istoricheskie zapiski*, no. 9, 1940.

———, "K voprosy ob imushchestvennom rassloenii krest'ianstva v XVIII v.," *Istoricheskie zapiski*, No. 11, 1941.

———, *Ocherki po istorii krepostnogo khoziaistva i krest'ianskogo dvizheniia v Rossii v pervoi polovine XIX veka* (Moscow, 1951).

———, "Voprosy sel'skogo khoziaistva v russkikh zhurnalakh poslednei treti XVIII v.," Akademiia Nauk, Institut Istorii, *Materialy po istorii zemledeliia SSSR*, I.

Skrebitskii, A., *Krest'ianskoe dielo v tsarstvovanie imperatora Aleksandra II* (4 vol. in 5, St. Petersburg, 1862-1868).

Smirnov, I. I., "Klassovye protivorechiia v feodal'noi derevne v Rossii v Kontse XVI v.," *Problemy istorii material'noi kul'tury*, 1933, no. 5-6.

————, *Vosstanie Bolotnikova 1606-1607* (Leningrad, 1951).

Smirnov, P., "Obrazovanie russkogo tsentralizovannogo gosudarstva v XIV-XV vv.," *Voprosy istorii*, 1946, no. 2-3.

————, *Posadskie liudi i ikh klassovaia bor'ba do serediny XVII veka* (2 vol., Moscow, Leningrad, 1947-1948).

Smith, R. E. F., *The Origins of Farming in Russia* (Paris, 1959).

Snorri Sturluson, *Heimskringla, or the Lives of the Norse Kings*, transl. and edited by E. Monsen and A. H. Smith (Cambridge, 1932).

Sobornoe ulozhenie tsaria Alekseia Mikhailovicha 1649g., Pamiatniki russkogo prava, VI (Moscow, 1947).

Sobranie gosudarstvennykh gramot i dogorov (4 vol., 1813-1828).

Solov'ev, Ia. A., "Zapiski Senatora Ia. A. Solov'eva o krest'ianskom dele," *Russkaia starina*, XXVII (1880), XXX-XXXI (1881), XXIII-XXXIV, XXXVI (1882), XXXVII (1883), 1884, no. 2.

Solov'ev, S. M., *Istoriia Rossii s drevneishikh vremen* (6 vol., St. Petersburg, 1896).

Speranskii, M. M., "Istoricheskoe obozrenie izmenenii v prave pozemel'noi sobstvennosti i v sostoianii krest'ian," *Arkhiv istoricheskikh i prakticheskikh svedenii otnosiashchikhsia do Rossii*, II (1859).

Spiridonova, E. V., *Ekonomicheskaia politika i ekonomicheskie vzgliady Petra I* (Moscow, 1952).

Spuler, B., *Die goldene Horde* (Leipzig, 1943).

Staden, H. von, *Aufzeichnungen über den Moskauer Staat*, ed. by F. Epstein (Hamburg, 1930).

Stählin, K., *Geschichte Russlands von den Anfängen bis zur Gegenwart* (4 vol. in 5, Berlin, 1923-1929).

Stashevskii, E., *Narodnyia volneniia v moskovskom gosudarstve* (Kiev, 1912).

Statesman's Handbook for Russia (2 vol., St. Petersburg, 1896).

"Statistische Übersicht über die Ausdehnung der Eisenbahnanlagen," *Jahrbücher für Nationalökonomie und Statistik*, XLIX (1887).

Stender-Petersen, A., *Die Varägersage als Quelle der altrussischen Chronik* (Aarhus, 1934).

Stepanov, I. V., "Guliashchie-rabotnye liudi v Povolzh'e v XVII v.," *Istoricheskie zapiski*, no. 36, 1951.

Stephenson, C., *Mediaeval Feudalism* (Ithaca, 1942).

Stoglav. See Duchesne, E.

Storch, H. F., *Cours d'economie politique* (6 vol., St. Petersburg, 1815).

Storch, P., "Der Bauernstand in Russland in geschichtlicher, statistischer, staatsrechtlicher und landwirtschaftlicher Hinsicht," *Mittheilungen der kais. freien ökon. Gesellschaft zu St. Petersburg*, 1848-1850.

Strumilin, S. G., *Istoriia chernoi metallurgii v SSSR* (Moscow, 1954).
———, "O merakh feodal'noi Rossii," Akademiia Nauk, Inst. Ekon., *Voprosy istorii narodnogo khoziaistva SSSR* (Moscow, 1957).
———, *Promyshlennyi perevorot v Rossii* (Moscow, 1944).
Struve, P. B., *Krepostnoe khoziaistvo. Izsledovaniia po ekonomicheskoi istorii Rossii v XVIII i XIX vv.* (Moscow, 1913).
———, "Medieval Agrarian Society in its Prime," *Cambridge Economic History*, I.
———, *Sotsial'naia i ekonomicheskaia istoriia Rossii* (Paris, 1952).
Stupperich, R., *Die Anfänge der Bauernbefreiung in Russland* (Berlin, 1939).
Sudebnik of 1497 in *Pamiatniki russkogo prava*, III (Moscow, 1955).
Svod udel'nykh postanovlenii (4 vol., St. Petersburg, 1843).
Svod zakonov Rossiiskoi Imperii, 1st edit., 1832; 2nd edit., 1842; 3rd edit., 1857.
Svodnyi tekst krest'ianskikh poriadnykh XVI v. (St. Petersburg, 1910).
Swinton, A., *Travels into Norway, Denmark, and Russia in the years 1788, 1789, 1790 and 1791* (London, 1792).
Szeftel, M., "La condition juridique des declassés dans la Russie ancienne," *Archives d'histoire du droit oriental*, II (1938).

Tarakanova-Belkina, S. A., *Boiarskoe i monastyrskoe zemlevladenie v Novgorodskikh piatinakh v domoskovskoe vremia* (Moscow, 1939).
Tawney, R. H., *The Agrarian Problem in the Sixteenth Century* (New York, 1912).
Tegoborskii, L. de, *Etudes sur les forces productives de la Russie* (4 vol., Paris, 1852-1855).
Tesnière, L., "Les antécédents du nom russe de la gare," *Revue des études slaves*, XXVII (1951).
Tikhomirov, M. N., *Drevnerusskie goroda* (Moscow, 1956).
Timoshenko, V. P., *Agricultural Russia and the Wheat Problem* (Stanford Univ., 1932).
Tobien, A., "Zur Geschichte der Bauernemancipation in Livland," *Baltische Monatschrift*, XXVII (1880), XXVIII (1881), XXIX (1882).
Tomsinskii, S. G., *Ocherki istorii feodal'no-krepostnoi Rossii* (Moscow, Leningrad, 1934).
Tooke, W., *View of the Russian Empire during the Reign of Catherine the Second to the Close of the Present Century* (3 vol., London, 1799).
Transehe-Roseneck, A. von, *Gutsherr und Bauer in Livland im 17. und 18. Jahrhundert* (Strassburg, 1890).
Treadgold, D. W., *The Great Siberian Migration* (Princeton, 1957).

Troinitskii, A. G., *Krepostnoe naselenie v Rossii po 10-ii narodnoi perepisi* (St. Petersburg, 1861).

Tsagolov, N. A., *Ocherki russkoi ekonomicheskoi mysli perioda padeniia krepostnogo prava* (Moscow, 1956).

Tschuprow, A., *Die Feldgemeinschaft* (Strassburg, 1902).

————, "Eisenbahnen in Russland," *Jahrbücher für Nationalökonomie und Statistik*, LXXIII (1899).

Tsentral'nyi statisticheskii komitet, Ministerstva Vnutrennikh Del, *Spiski naselennykh mest Rossiiskoi Imperii* (40 vol., St. Petersburg, 1861-1885).

————, *Statisticheskiia tablitsy Rossiiskoi Imperii. Nalichnoe naselenie imperii za 1858 god*, A. Buschen, ed. (St. Petersburg, 1863).

————, *Statisticheskiia tablitsy Rossiiskoi Imperii za 1856-i god* (St. Petersburg, 1858).

————, *Statistika Rossiiskoi Imperii* (St. Petersburg, 1890).

Tugan-Baranovskii, M.. *Geschichte der russischen Fabrik*. transl. by B. Minzès (Berlin, 1900).

————, *Russkaia fabrika v proshlom i nastoiashchem*, I (St. Petersburg, 1898).

Turgenev, I., *Literaturnye i zhiteiskie vospominaniia* (Leningrad, 1934).

Turgenev, N. I., *La Russie et les russes* (3 vol., Paris, 1847).

————, *Un dernier mot sur l'émancipation des serfs en Russie* (Paris, 1860).

Tymieniecki, K., "Le servage en Pologne et dans les pays limitrophes au moyen âge," *La Pologne au Xe Congrès International des Science Historiques à Rome* (Warsaw, 1955).

Tysiachnaia kniga 1550g. i dvorovaia tetrad 50-kh godov XVI v., A. A. Zimin, ed. (Moscow, Leningrad, 1950).

Ulozhenie. See *Sobornoe ulozhenie, etc.*

United States Dept. of Agriculture, *Climate and Man, Yearbook of Agriculture* (Washington, 1941).

United States State Dept. Records, U.S. Archives, Washington, D.C.

Ustiugov, N. V., "Instruktsiia votchinnomy prikazchiku pervoi chetverti XVIII v.," *Istoricheskii arkhiv*, IV (1949).

————, "K voprosu o zemel'nykh peredelakh na russkom severe v seredine XVII v.," *Istoricheskii arkhiv*, V (1950).

Vasiliev, A., "Economic Relations between Byzantium and old Russia," *Journal of Economic and Business History*, IV (1932).

Velikaia reforma. See Obshchestvo rasprostraneniia tekhnicheskikh znanii.

Venturi, F., *Roots of Revolution*, transl. from Italian (London, 1960).

Verlinden, C., *L'esclavage dans l'Europe médiévale* (Bruges, 1955), I.

Vernadsky, G. "Feudalism in Russia," *Speculum*, XIV (1939).

————, *Kievan Russia* (New Haven, 1948).

————, *Medieval Russian Laws* (New York, 1947).

————, *Russia at the Dawn of the Modern Age* (New Haven, 1959).

————, "Serfdom in Russia," X Congresso Internazionale di Scienze Storiche, *Relazione*, III (Florence, 1955).

————, "The Death of the Tsarevich Dimitry: a Reconsideration of the Case," *Oxford Slavonic Papers*, V (1954).

————, *The Mongols and Russia* (New Haven, 1953).

————, "The Status of the Russian Church During the First Half-Century Following Vladimir's Conversion," *Slavonic and East European Review*, XX (1941).

————, *Zven'ia russkoi kul'tury* (Berlin, 1938).

Veselovskii, S. V., *Feodal'noe zemlevladenie v severo-vostochnoi Rusi*, I (Moscow, Leningrad, 1947).

————, "Iz istorii drevnerusskogo zemlevladeniia," *Istoricheskie zapiski*, no. 18, 1946.

————, "Monastyrskoe zemlevladenie v Moskovskoi Rusi vo vtoroi polovine XVI v.," *Istoricheskie zapiski*, no. 10, 1941.

Veshniakov, V., *Krest'iane-sobstvenniki v Rossii* (St. Petersburg, 1858).

Virginskii, V. S., *Nachalo zheleznodorozhnogo dela v Rossii, do 40-kh godov XIX veka* (Moscow, 1949).

Vladimirskii-Budanov, M., ed., *Khristomatiia po istorii russkogo prava* (6th ed., 3 vol., Kiev, 1901-1908).

————, *Obzor istorii russkogo prava* (3rd. ed., Kiev, St. Petersburg, 1900).

Volin, L., *A Survey of Soviet Russian Agriculture*, Agricultural Monograph 5, U.S. Dept. of Agriculture (Washington, 1951).

————, "The Russian Peasant and Serfdom," *Agricultural History*, XVII (1943).

Volkov, S. V., "Instruktsiia upraviteliam dvortsovykh volostei 1731g.," *Istoricheskii arkhiv*, VI (1951).

Vol'noe Ekonomicheskoe Obshchestvo, *Trudy* (139 vol., 1765-1914).

Voronin, N. N. "K itogam i zadacham arkheologicheskogo izucheniia drevnerusskogo goroda," Institut Istorii Material'noi Kul'tury, *Kratkie soobshcheniia*, XLI (1951).

Voznesenskii, S. V., *Ekonomika Rossii XIX-XX vv. v tsifrakh*, I (Leningrad, 1924).

————, *Razlozhenie krepostnogo khoziaistva i klassovaia bor'ba v Rossii 1800-1860 gg.* (Moscow, 1932).

Wallace, D. M., *Russia* (New York, 1877).

Weber, F. C., *Das veränderte Russland* (3 pts., Frankfurt, Leipzig, 1738-1740).

Willan, T. S., *The Early History of the Russia Company 1553-1603* (Manchester, 1956).

———, "Trade between England and Russia in the Second Half of the Sixteenth Century," *English Historical Review*, LXIII (1948).

Wührer, K., *Beiträge zur ältesten Agrargeschichte des germanischen Nordens* (Jena, 1935).

Yarmolinsky, A., *Road to Revolution* (London, 1957).

———, *Turgenev* (New York, 1959.

Yver, J., "Les caractères originaux de la coutume de Normandie," *Memoires de l'Academie des Sciences, Arts et Belle-Lettres de Caen*, N.S., XII (1952).

Zabelin, I. E., "Bol'shoi boiarin v svoem votchinnom khoziaistve (XVII-yi vek)," *Vestnik Evropy*, 1871, no. 1-2.

Zablotskii-Desiatovskii, A. P., *Graf P. D. Kiselev i ego vremia* (4 vol., St. Petersburg, 1882).

Zaionchkovskii, P. A., *Otmena krepostnogo prava v Rossii* (Moscow, 1954).

Zaitsev, K., "Die Rechtsideologie des russischen Agrarwesens und die russische Agrarrevolution," *Archiv für Rechts- und Wirtshafts- philosophie*, XIX (1925).

Zaozerskaia, E. I., "K voprosu o razvitii krupnoi promyshlennosti v Rossii v XVIII veke," *Voprosy istorii*, 1947, no. 12.

———, *Manufaktura pri Petre I* (Moscow, Leningrad, 1947).

Zaozerskii, A. I., *Tsarskaia votchina XVII v.* (Moscow, 1937).

Zimin, A. A., "Sostav russkikh gorodov XVI vv.," *Istoricheskie za- piski*, no. 52, 1955.

Zlotnikov, M., "K voprosu ob izuchenii istorii rabochego klassa i promyshlennosti," *Katorga i ssylka*, I (1935).

———, "Ot manufaktury k fabrike," *Voprosy istorii*, 1946, no. 11-12.

Other Titles in European History
and International Affairs
Available in Princeton Paperback